REPUBLICANS
on the THRONE

NEW HORIZONS IN ETHIOPIAN STUDIES

The New Horizons series aims to bring to the general and scholarly public original studies and critical reflections on Ethiopian history, society, politics, arts, and philosophy. Because Ethiopia has yet to engage in a full-fledged critique of the traditional and modern social practices, beliefs and institutions that inform private and public life, and because without a thoroughgoing critique of these practices, beliefs and institutions Ethiopia will not be able to bring to fruition the aspirations for emancipation that gestate in her history, the series will publish, in Amharic and English, manuscripts that explore and reflect upon the conditions of possibility and impossibility of freedom, equality, justice, and prosperity.

Dr. Maimire Mennasemay
Series Editor
Dawson College, Montreal, Canada

A Political History of the Tigray People's Liberation Front (1975-1991)
AREGAWI BERHE

Republicans on the Throne:
A Personal Account of Ethiopia's Painful Quest for Democracy
TEKALIGN GEDAMU

Society and State in Ethiopian History – Selected Essays*
BAHRU ZEWDE

* forthcoming

REPUBLICANS

on the THRONE

a PERSONAL ACCOUNT *of* ETHIOPIA'S MODERNIZATION *and* PAINFUL QUEST *for* DEMOCRACY

TEKALIGN GEDAMU

TSEHAI
Publishers & Distributors

TSEHAI
Publishers & Distributors

Tsehai books may be purchased for educational, business, or sales promotional use. For more information, please contact our special sales department.

Tsehai Publishers
Loyola Marymount University
1 LMU Drive, UH 3012, Los Angeles, CA 90045

www.tsehaipublishers.com
info@tsehaipublishers.com

ISBN: 978-1-59907-047-6

First Printing: Summer 2011 | Second Printing: Fall 2011

Publisher: Elias Wondimu
Series Editor: Maimire Mennasemay, Ph.D.
Typesetting and Layout: Tessa Smith (www.tessasmithdesign.com)
Cover Design: Jana Vukovic (www.janavukovic.com)

A catalog record for this book is available from:
Institute of Ethiopian Studies Library at Addis Ababa University
U.S. Library of Congress Catalog Card Number, Washington, DC
British Library Cataloguing in Publication Data

10 9 8 7 6 5 4 3 2 1

Printed in the United States of America

LOS ANGELES | NEW YORK | ADDIS ABABA | JOHANNESBURG

In enduring memory of my family:
grandparents Emahoy Itagegnehou Lemma and Aleqa Biressaw Yimer,
uncle Endale Biressaw,
my father Gedamu Gizzaw
and my paternal uncle Tadesse Gizzaw,
from all of whom I learned enormously about our country's values and traditions.

Contents

Preface

It was after several years of hesitation that I finally decided to put together the story of my life. This is not exactly an autobiography. Rather it is a selective memoir of a life that attempts to highlight some of the more underlying historical forces at play. Though I had put together material for a possible monograph on the 1974 revolution, the idea of writing a full length memoir had not entered my mind. The fact that I had not kept a systematic diary for the greater part of my life was one reason. Another was that the bulk of my career had been with international organizations: eight years with the United Nations and almost seventeen years with the African Development Bank. I did not think that there was much in it that would be of interest to the general public.

As the years went by, friends occasionally posed questions about an autobiography. To most, I casually responded that I had little of interest to say. To those who had an interest in Ethiopia's history and have written on it, I posed my own question: of what possible interest would a career like mine be for my countrymen, the core of the book's readership? Their view was that personal records or memoirs are essential building blocks for historians, much as bricks are to a builder. I was also reminded that I should not underestimate the interest that the present generation of Ethiopians and possibly others might have in my recollections, especially of the earlier part of my life. What finally liberated me from the inhibition to write was the notion of offering a brick, albeit a modest one, to those professionally interested in the Ethiopia of my time. And to bring to the present generation of Ethiopians a measure of awareness about their immediate past.

It was on the 9th of February 2006 that I typed a few pages and filed them in my computer under "Memoirs." By then the dust had settled on the principal event I had initially set out to write on. I had also retired and needed to occupy myself with some purposeful routine. As I had to rely on memory for the unrecorded portion of my life, I was initially not sure how much, or how accurately, I might be able to remember. Much to my surprise, my recollections turned out to be clearer and more extensive than I had first imagined. There was a good reason for this. I had frequently shared the more interesting anecdotes of my life and those of my family with close friends, often recounting them multiple times. Although a nuisance to my interlocutors, that habit kept the stories fresh at the back of my mind. Indeed, such was the extent of my recollections that I had to be selective.

In one way or another, the bulk of the book deals with the 1974 revolution: its antecedents, its immediate impact, and its aftermath. While I am aware that much has been written on the subject, I am also of the view that I should tell the story from the perspective of an eyewitness and member of a group of early players outside the tight circle of the military who advised, unsuccessfully as it turned out, against extremist measures. Whether it adds materially to what is already known is a question I leave to the reader.

The effects of the revolution are still reverberating. In Part Five of the book, I try to take up the question which is uppermost in the minds of most Ethiopians today: where do we go from here? As can be imagined, writing this part of the book has not been easy. At one point I even considered giving it up altogether, leaving the intractable subject to the care of those better qualified than I. But I was not sure this was the right thing to do and increasingly felt that I should not forego the opportunity of joining many of my compatriots in saying something about the future of our country.

We Ethiopians are excessively passionate about our politics. Many of us take great pride in our history and culture and celebrate the accomplishments of our forebears. But an equal number are more preoccupied with past injustices. There is inevitable tension between the two outlooks. Although we have a heritage of constructive dialogue, we are still trying to find our feet in the adversarial politics of modern democracy. We tend to be needlessly confrontational, and are often inclined to overstate our views. An added reason for our excessive passion is the fact that our politics is still in a state of flux; a factor driving many to throw out ideas in the hope of making an impact. The process leaves precious little room for tempered dialogue.

It is plain that we cannot make much headway in our efforts to work towards a genuinely democratic political order unless we have the will to restrain our passions, the wisdom to recognize that there is much that unites than separates us, and the determination to reject narrow minded leaders who thrive on the politics of division and acrimony. The thrust of this book is driven by the belief that we as a people are capable of rising to the challenge. But on a more practical level, I am buoyed by an optimism that emanates from a general assessment of our human and natural resources potential. And in no small measure by our long history as a nation state. That is what I attempt to convey in the last three chapters of the book.

In a country like ours, crystal ball gazing is not an altogether prudent exercise. Nor is it always rewarding. Yet it is unavoidable, given the predicament in which we currently find ourselves. I hope the ideas in the concluding chapters will be of some relevance to the dialogue on where our country is headed or, more accurately, where it should be headed.

Philadelphia
April 29, 2011

Acknowledgments

Many friends have been generous with their time and advice in helping me put this book together. Richard and Rita Pankhurst were among the first to suggest that I write a full-length memoir and kindly went through much of the early material. My friend Zaude Retta is a mine of information on our recent history, of which I have freely availed myself. Ato Haddis Alemyehou, another friend who regrettably passed away a few years ago, was an inspiration and a valuable source for several historical anecdotes; as were of course close members of my family. Belatchew Asrat, Mulugeta Wodajo and Semret Medhane read several chapters critically and counseled on a number of key points. The late Ato Menassie Lemma was the principal source for the early history of Ethiopian Airlines. Semret helped additionally in the drafting of the story of how, over the years, the carrier grew to become one of the more notable landmarks in the history of third-world aviation.

Paul Henze made helpful comments on an early draft of the first four chapters. Professor Jemal Abdulkadir and Engineer Bekelle Gebre-Mariam, both childhood friends, read the first chapter and filled in critical gaps. The late Professor Merid Wolde-Aregay and Professor Shiferaw Bekele of Addis Ababa University (the former a high school and college friend) reviewed and made suggestions on some of the material on Ethiopian history. Afenegus Tashoma Haile-Mariam provided information on Colonel Workineh's reform efforts and precious insights into our history and culture. Berhanu Asres supplemented information on the Colonel's role as imperial confidant as well as on his belated part in the failed coup. Dejazmatch Wolde-Semait Gebre-Wold was instrumental in helping refine the narrative on the attempted coup d'état of 1960 and sections on Emperor Haile-Selassie's profile. Fantaye Wolde-Yohannes shared his impressions of Germame Neway, the principal force behind the coup. Ian Campbell went through Chapter 7 with a fine toothcomb and made several editorial improvements. Colonel Fikru Wolde-Tensai of the Ethiopian Army shared his thoughts on General Aman and the Negelle mutiny. Assefa Wolde-Giorgis Wolde-Yohannes was helpful in providing comments on an early draft of the section on his father and kindly offered valuable material in his possession.

Petros Aklilu went through a number of chapters in Part One and provided copious comments. Getachew Tessema, Yayehrad Fikre, Mengiste Desta, Mersie Ijigu, Tefera Wolde-Semait, Tesfaye Mekasha, Demeke Metaferia, Argaw Kabtamu, and Eleni Makonnen offered helpful ideas on various chapters. Zemedu Worku and Fana

Wolde-Giorgis went over the section on land and agriculture in Chapter 20. Dereje of Access Capital and two consultants working for the firm kindly provided economic data and commentary on Chapter 20. Yemane I. Demissie gave editorial comments which improved the narrative quality of Chapter 1. Alitash Kebede has maintained a keen interest from the beginning and frequently came up with a range of ideas on publishing. Henock Kifle, Bisrat Aklilu, Aklilu Habte, Dr. Fisseha Tekle-Wold, Abiy Fesseha, and many more friends than I could mention here have offered support and encouragement. Elias Wondimu of Tsehai Publishers who was introduced to me by my daughter Beshowamyellesh has maintained an interest in the book from the outset and has been helpful in many ways. It was thanks to him that Germame Neway's picture was secured after a long search. He also supplied the pictures of Mengistu Haile-Mariam and Meles Zenawi. Maimire Mennasemay, Tsehai's erudite series editor, provided indispensable assistance. I am grateful to Tsehai's design team, especially, Tessa Smith, who was exceptionally assiduous with her typesetting skills, and Jana Vukovic for her cover design. Fiammetta Kaypaghian, a family friend for a good part of the period covered by the book, drew my attention to a number of orthographical corrections. These have been incorporated in the fall edition of the book.

The Institute of Ethiopian Studies provided Emperor Haile-Selassie's picture on a foreign visit and the one of Ras Abebe Aregai. Amde Akalework supplied electroninc copies of the pictures in which Prime Minister Aklilu Habte-Wold, his uncle, figures. Lij Endalkatchew Makonnen's photograph was made available by Tessema Makonnen and Abeselom Zikie and Ras Nadew's by Nadew Assefa, his grandson. Mulugeta Wodajo turned to Girma Abebe for photographs of Haddis Alemayehu, who kindly obtained two copies from the picture archives of the United Nations Headquarters. Alemante Gebre-Selassie located Colonel Workineh's picture and sent me an electronic copy. And Michael Ketema offered the photograph in which his father Ketema Yifru, our Ambassador in Beijing, Makonnen Kibret, and I appear during a courtesy call on Prime Minister Chou En Lai. The photograph of General Mulugeta Buli was kindly offered by his sister-in-law, Princess Mahezent Hapte-Mariam.

To all the above and to many others who helped in other ways but whom I am constrained from mentioning, I express my sincere thanks. I naturally take responsibility for any errors of fact or judgment that might have defied my best intentions to offer a narrative that is accurate, balanced, and not altogether unfair.

Lastly, my wife Roman and our three children have had to endure the periodic frustrations and irritations of an undertaking that has taken four years, not to mention the stressful three months they had to put up with on account of the unpleasant political encounter I describe in Chapter 18. I hope the result goes some way to make up for their troubles.

PART I

The Twilight Years of Monarchy

CHAPTER 1

A Glimpse of Feudal Life

Growing Up with Grandparents

I was always curious to find out. Yet no one could tell me. The date of my birth was not recorded in the flyleaf of the family book of Psalms, as was often the practice in those distant days. That of my father had been. I wondered how my father. Gedamu Gizzaw, had not observed this custom while his own father had. As I found out later, my grandfather was an older man when Gedamu was born and was more likely to observe the practice. My father was only seventeen when he married my mother Zauditu Biressaw, who was younger still at about eleven. Although I was born five years later, I reasoned that my parents were still too young to bother about the inconsequential detail of recording the birth of their second son. Whether they had noted down that of my elder brother Mulatu who died at the age of four a few months after I was born, I never asked. It too was probably not.

Upon my brother's death I was named Tekalign ('the Lord's replacement'), as the family believed that the good Lord had given them a new son in place of the one taken away. What was my name during my first few months when Mulatu was still alive; I asked my father years later one day? Surely, my parents did not yet know that I had come as his replacement, for Mulatu was apparently in good health and showed no sign of imminent death. My father only said that I had posed an interesting question.

As with my elder brother who had been given over to his paternal grandparents soon after his birth, I was placed under the care of my maternal grandparents: Aleqa Biressaw Yimer and his wife Woizero Itagegnehu Lemma, both well past their sixties. I, too, was only a few months old at the time. My parents were perhaps considered not old enough to look after their children.

Aleqa Biressaw was the head of St. Mary's Church in Gore. He lived in what would then be regarded as a fairly comfortable home a couple of hundred yards in the vicinity of St. Mary's. Like most traditional houses, Aleqa's had a thatched roof supported by sturdy wooden poles held together by plaster made of mud mixed with dried grass. There was a smaller building a few yards away which served as a kitchen and home for relatives and domestic staff. The premises were not large but adequate for most purposes: for laundry lines, for drying grain, spices, and other food items in the sun. Surrounding the grounds was a sparsely constructed wooden fence reinforced with the ubiquitous *sensel,* a local hedge that was allowed to grow profusely to ward off the eyes of curious passersby.

For the first few years of my youth, I grew up in the belief that Aleqa Biressaw and Itagegnehu were my biological parents. I was encouraged to take my mother Zauditu for an older sister and would address her in that manner (*Iteitei*) whenever she came to visit us. I grew fond of her as I gradually realized that she was my mother. Occasionally, she expressed dismay about the way I was being brought up and reminded her mother that I needed to be reined in. As with most children brought up by grandparents, I was spoiled. But only within narrow limits, as I shall explain later in this story.

When I was in my late teens, I took up the question of my date of birth with my uncle Endale Biressaw, who spent some time discussing it with an old family friend. The two first established that I was born about two years before the Fascist invasion of Ethiopia in 1935. They then determined the month and the date after recalling that my mother had delivered some five days following St Mary's day in the month of Hedar; which is to say that I was born on 26 Hedar 1926 in the Ethiopian (Julian) calendar, or 5 December 1933 in the Gregorian. When I needed a birth certificate in 1967 for some purpose I no longer recall, I went to the Municipality of Addis Ababa, explained my situation and obtained one. I do not know how many people can claim to have been awarded a birth certificate thirty-four long years after the event.

Gore, the small town of my birth located some 340 miles southwest of Addis Ababa, was the capital of Illubabor province. The town, including its long and narrow airstrip at the eastern end, occupies the length and breadth of an uneven plateau. From houses perched on its edge, one got an arresting view of a vast expanse of forest land and rolling hills interspersed with scattered homesteads. The thatch roofed peasant homes were better constructed and more spacious than those I would see years later in the villages around Addis Ababa. Illubabor villagers were also generally better dressed, especially on market days when many came out in their traditional white *shammas.* Gore had an average rainfall of 72 inches a year, among the highest in the land. Little wonder that the countryside was lush green all year round. Located at an altitude of about 6,000 feet and a latitude eight degrees north of the Equator, the temperature was warm but comfortable: mostly in the low to the mid- eighties Fahrenheit for the greater part of the year as I would guess now; and with little humidity.

The town was once among the three or four most important urban centres in the country. About 90 miles to the west was the small settlement of Gambela that served as Gore's gateway to the outside word. Gambela was located on 1000 acres

An early family picture showing (seated from left to right) the author's mother Zauditu Biressaw, her sister Belainesh and her brother Endale

of land along the Baro River and was leased by Emperor Menelik to Great Britain in 1902. Britain was then administering the Sudan (and Egypt) and was engaged in a demarcation of the border between the two countries. The purpose of the lease was to develop the area as commercial station and inland port. I would also hazard the guess that this was part of an overall plan by Britain to keep an eye on the flow of the Nile into the Sudan and Egypt. Baro was a principal tributary of the Nile and when it flooded during the rainy season, boats brought merchandise of British make from Khartoum (textiles, footwear, spirits, soap, matches, kitchen ware etc.) to exchange for the province's agricultural products.

Illubabor province produced considerable quantities of coffee for export. Other products were also exported, though on a modest scale: beeswax, civet, onions, spices, hides and skins. As a young boy in the early forties, I also recall rubber being brought to the Saturday market. It was circular, flat and thin like *injera*, the pancake-like Ethiopian bread. I was later told that liquid rubber sapped from trees was baked, just like the *injera*, on flat clay pans; an imaginative adaptation of traditional cooking ware to the needs of modern commerce. The peasants would perforate these in the middle, drive a stick through a dozen or so, and carry them to the market on their shoulders.

This happened during the Second World War when Japan's occupation of Malaya, a rubber producing British dependency, led to a sudden drop in supply causing Britain to scurry around in search of new suppliers. My speculation is that the British sent their agents to the province to collect as much rubber as they could. They knew of the area's potential for rubber production, for a British firm had been given a concession by Emperor Menelik to grow rubber trees in the Gambela region at the beginning of the twentieth century.[1] With the end of the War, the rubber *injeras* dropped from view.

A wide variety of agricultural products figured in domestic trade: maize, *teff*, wheat, barley, pulses, oilseeds, spices (coriander, garlic, pepper, ginger), livestock products (meat, dairy, hides and skins, tumblers made from cattle horns), honey, cotton, timber, and a variety of fruits and vegetables (bananas, pineapples, papayas, citrus fruits, onions and hops). A small community of expatriate merchants (Greeks, Armenians, Coptic Egyptians, Christian Syrians) dominated domestic and export trade and gave Gore a whiff of cosmopolitanism.

A number of fairly large buildings bestowed on Gore a degree of urban respectability which was a source of pride for the townspeople. These included the Governor General's Palace perched on a hill, the residences of the Archbishop and those of the expatriate traders, the customs house, the municipality, the courthouses, and private homes of a few well to do persons; all built of stone which was plentiful. There were three fairly large churches: the principal church of St Mary built by Ras Nadew (the Governor General we shall soon encounter in this story), St George's and St Michael's. There was also a busy branch of the government owned Bank of Ethiopia and an elementary school, one of a handful established by the young and progressive Emperor, Haile-Selassie. A hotel run by one of the expatriate residents added to the town's claim as a leading urban centre in Ethiopia. In his memoires which I shall have occasion to cite in a moment, Ras Imru was impressed by Gore's buildings and network of roads during his wartime visit and judged it to be the third most advanced town in the nation, Addis Ababa and Dire Dawa presumably taking first and second place.

A telephone line connected the town to Addis Ababa and the smaller towns in the province. On their way to Addis or elsewhere in the province, governors carried along telephone receivers with long cables that they would hook to the suspended lines and communicate with government officials. District governors assumed the responsibility for guarding the lines. Damage caused by storms or vandals would be repaired in reasonable time.

Gore also hosted a resident diplomat, the British Consul. The Consulate was perched on the northwestern edge of the town with a commanding view of the road to Gambela. It occupied spacious grounds which accommodated the Consul's residence, office, stable, and living quarters for the domestic staff. Every so often, Consulate staff would ride their handsome Arabian horses in the direction of the airstrip located some six miles at the eastern end of town, with curious children running behind in amazement at the sheer beauty of the well-groomed animals. I was one of these children.

All in all, Gore was a bustling centre of commerce and an agreeable place to live in. Little wonder that the names of provincial governors read like a Who's Who of the prominent officials of Emperor Menelik, Empress Zawditu, and Emperor Haile-Selassie. Perhaps the most prominent of these was Ras Gobena Datche, one of two or three preeminent *rases* in the earlier part of Menelik's reign (about 1878). Although not a resident governor, Ras Gobena surveyed the province and re-asserted Ethiopia's sovereignty over the Western territories.[2] The first resident Governor

Ras Nadew Aba Wollo, Governor of Illubabor province from 1918-1928 and signatory of Ethiopia's instrument of accession to membership in the League of Nations

and founder of Gore (in the latter half of the 1880s I believe) was Ras Tessema. Subsequently the Ras became guardian to Lij Iyassu, the young Prince Regent (1913-16). In 1918 Ras Nadew Abba Wollo was appointed Governor and administered the province for ten years. Nadew was principal envoy and signatory to the instrument of Ethiopia's accession to membership in the League of Nations in 1921. Around 1929 Ras Mulugeta Yegezu became Governor. His tenure lasted four years. He was appointed Defence Minister on the eve of the Fascist invasion. After him came Dejazmatch Makonnen Endalkatchew who later led the province's men against the invading Fascist army in the Ogaden. After the war, he was promoted Bitwoded and became the first post-war Prime Minister.

Memorable anecdotes about these governors peppered the conversations of the townspeople during my youth. Ras Nadew Aba Wollo was by far the most talked about. Having traveled to Europe on a number of occasions and to the U.S. once, the Ras would frequently meet with the expatriate residents of the town to exchange stories of the wider world. Nadew was reputed to be a man of some taste. He would ask an Armenian merchant to prepare his national dish, or a Greek to do some handiwork on a decorative or functional object, as in the case of a flywhisk given him by a friend.

The gift did not quite come up to his aesthetic standards and was a matter of concern to the fastidious Ras. The ivory handle was somewhat out of proportion to the short, shimmering white horsehair.

Nadew wondered whether the handle could be shortened without causing damage. He called upon the Greek Monsieur Vayonakis to see what he could do. A few days later, the handle came back shorter with a beautifully decorated finish where it had been sawn off. The Ras was favourably impressed and said to the people gathered around him. "You see this beautiful finish. I'd rather have one Greek servant like Vayonakis than thirty of you milling around me all day." Monsieur Vayonakis bowed deep, with his forehead almost touching the ground in appreciation of the kindness showed him by the Ras. In those days, being the servant of someone of the standing of Ras Nadew was a mark of no mean social distinction.

A major project for which Ras Nadew would be long remembered was the construction of Gore's major streets. In the course of his visits to Europe, he had been impressed by the cobbled streets of cities and soon embarked on a project to transform his town's network of footpaths into proper roads. There were no cobbles of the kind used in Europe. And, of course, there were no granite quarries. The Ras was not to be discouraged, however. Black basaltic stone was plentiful in Gore. He would use this for his project. To maintain a steady supply of stones, he introduced a penal measure for minor felonies which consisted of imposing fines of five or ten pieces of stone on offenders. The graver the offence, the higher the number of stones supplied. In time, Ras Nadew had enough stones to complete his project. Basaltic stone is difficult to dress properly and the new roads were rough to walk on. But they were preferable to the mud in the rainy season and the dust in the dry.

Gore has the distinction of having been selected as the capital city of the nation three quarters of a century ago. When Italy's Fascist invaders were approaching Addis Ababa in the early months of 1936, it was decided to move the seat of the central government to Gore from where the Emperor was expected to coordinate a country-wide guerilla movement. But advisors prevailed upon the Emperor to go to Geneva instead and present Ethiopia's case to the League of Nations. He was consequently not able to travel to Gore. Instead, Bitwoded Wolde-Tsadik was designated acting head of state and proceeded to the temporary capital. The town was chosen for its convenient location; being a short distance from British administered Sudan from where arms and ammunition could be secured to fight the Fascists; or so it was thought.

Ras Imru was at the time in command of one of the armies in the Northern Front. After putting up a stiff resistance there, he and his men retreated in the face of overwhelming arms and the indiscriminate use of poison gas by the Fascist military. He was eager to regroup and continue the fight, but by the time he reached central Ethiopia his forces had dwindled from forty thousand at the beginning of the war to no more than five hundred. Following a war council with his remaining men, he decided to go to Gore and see whether he and his men could put up a resistance there from where he could cross the border to the Sudan if his plan to fight the enemy ran into trouble. He had heard that the government had been transferred there with Bitwoded Wolde-Tsadik at its head and that the Emperor had gone to Geneva to plead with the League of Nations, which "made us all happy," he says.[3]

On his way there, the Ras sent an advance letter to the Bitwoded in which he did not mention the idea of regrouping in Gore, saying only that he was going abroad to consult with the Emperor and others in exile as to how the war effort could be conducted. Bitwoded replied that he should come to Gore and that they should discuss the matter there. Ras Imru agreed and upon arrival in Gore, the Bitwoded asked him to remain behind and join them in resisting the enemy. A letter also arrived from the Emperor in London instructing that Bitwoded Wolde-Tsadik should act as head of government and that Ras Imru should assume responsibility for the military campaign. It soon transpired, however, that Bitwoded Wolde-Tsadik was reluctant to confront the Italians. Ras Imru and his men, later joined by young officers and civilian members of the Black Lion resistance movement which had been briefly active in Wollega, were on the move once again; this time in the direction of Kurmuk, a town on the Sudan boarder. But Fascist forces (largely consisting of Eritrean conscripts) stood in the way. In a brief but fierce battle, Ras Imru's men beat off enemy forces, but it was clear that they could not proceed to Kurmuk. They then headed in the direction of Jimma, believing that the area was still under government control. A few days later the Ras found himself battling a large and well-armed Italian army contingent on the Gojjeb River near Jimma. The Ras's under-equipped and undersupplied men were overwhelmed by enemy forces. The Ras surrendered after arranging for a few of his followers to cross over to Kenya to resume the resistance at a more suitable time. Not long afterwards Gore itself fell; bringing to a close its short-lived status as the new capital of the nation. Bitwoded Wolde-Tsadik returned to Addis and reportedly died during the massacres of Addis residents following an attempt on the life of Marshall Grazziani, the Fascist Viceroy.

This small historic town is today a dim shadow of its past. Decades of deforestation, social turmoil, and economic stagnation have turned the garden town into a dusty collection of decaying buildings with rusted corrugated roofs. The population has declined as other nearby towns have grown in importance, including Mettu which has overtaken Gore as the seat of a new administrative zone. Gambela itself has been transformed into the capital of a new ethnic region.

In addition to being the head of St Mary's Church, Aleqa Biressaw (my grandfather) was also responsible for the administration of the provincial clergy. Several years later I would read in *Zikre-Negger* by Balambaras Mahteme Selassie Wolde-Meskel that Aleqa acted for Archbishop Markos of Illubabor six months out of the year when the Archbishop was in Wollega, the other half of his diocese. Gradually, I came to understand that Aleqa was a distinguished scholar in the teachings of the

Ethiopian Orthodox Church. He was originally from the parish of Gabitcha Michael in Gozzamen district of Gojjam province.

In adult life Aleqa had ventured into Bale in southeastern Ethiopia with his cousin, Memhir Abozen Derseh. After some time there, the two found the weather a little too cold and traveled back to Addis Ababa en route back to their home province, Gojjam. As it happened, Ras Tessema was at the time looking for a man well versed in the teachings of the Ethiopian Church to head a new church he planned to build in Gore. While in transit in Addis Ababa, Aleqa was introduced to Ras Tessema and accepted the Ras's offer to serve as the leader of the proposed church. Instead of going back to Gojjam, both he and Memhir Abozen now proceeded to Gore.[4]

My early recollection of Aleqa goes back to the time I used to help out as an errand boy. This occasionally consisted of fetching Ge'ez books from his collection in a large trunk beside his bed. The domestic staff would often fumble and flounder trying to locate the particular book he wished to read from the unhelpful description he gave (the size of the book or the colour of its binding, for the staff were unable to read). Even someone like me who could read had difficulty; as the books were all covered in leather or wood binding, showing no titles and therefore difficult to identify. Looking at the inside pages was no help either as they were all in Ge'ez, a language I did not (and do not today) understand. In comparison with the hapless domestic staff, however, I was considered a phenomenon, only because I took far less time and almost always succeeded in fishing out what my old man was looking for. The secret was simply that I enjoyed the task and performed it more frequently than the domestic staff and became quite adept at it. The staff had more demanding chores to occupy their time and must have regarded chasing the Ge'ez books as insufferable nuisance.

Aleqa spent a good part of each week sitting at the porch of his house going through these books. He was much respected for his erudition by members of the clergy, the laity, and by provincial officials. Often, priests and *debteras* from Saint Mary's would come to consult with him in preparation for a forthcoming church holiday, or to exchange views on theological subjects. Ras Nadew, the longest serving governor of the province, would speak of him as a fine example of clerical scholarship and a role model for the clergy. There were times, however, when the governor was not too pleased with Aleqa's advice on matters temporal, as the following story demonstrates.

In the course of a banquet given at his residence on one occasion, Ras Nadew got annoyed over a trifling matter and ordered a servant to be flogged. Aleqa Biressaw, who was at the banquet, intervened to say that the punishment was uncalled for and pleaded with the governor to drop the matter. The latter, usually deferential to the Aleqa but somewhat tipsy on the occasion, persisted in his decision. As the man was being readied for the flogging, Aleqa slipped out in protest and subsequently stopped visiting the Ras. Noticing his absence one day and totally oblivious of the reason, Ras Nadew sent someone to Aleqa to find out why he had been missing. "Tell the Ras that I will no longer be able to visit him," said Aleqa to the messenger. "I appreciate his many favours. But that is not why I am by his side so often. Rather, it is because of his commitment to our Church. More importantly it is to advise him to desist from committing acts of injustice or sin that harm citizens and bring dismay to the Lord. If he does not pay attention to my advice, I have little reason to be with him."

The standoff soon became the talk of the town and a number of people felt obliged to intercede. Aleqa gave in to the pressure but after being fairly certain that no one would thenceforth be unjustly penalized. In his confrontation with the Ras, Aleqa was only following the guidelines of the *Kibre Negest,* the great Ethiopian epic described in

Emahoy Itagegegnehou Lemma (the author's grandmother) with her son Endale Biressaw

the opening pages of Chapter 10. Clergy are required to admonish anyone, be he king or commoner, whenever he deviates from the word of God. "Behold you priests," says one provision of the *Kibre Negist.* "Be not afraid to reprimand men when they commit sin. Be not afraid of either sword or banishment.... Remember that [the prophet] Samuel reprimanded Saul the king. You too should not be afraid to reprimand and to teach [the king] whenever he wrongs [his subjects] ..."[5]

I should in fairness hasten to interpose here an example of Ras Nadew's judicious administration of the province. Some peasants in a village not too far from the provincial capital killed a young man, the son of a prominent local judge, and immediately came to the governor to explain their case and plead for justice. Ras Nadew presided over the case in an open court in which, as always, he listened to the *tichit* (i.e. the views expressed by those attending the proceedings), and determined that the peasants had killed the young man in self-defence. They were therefore not guilty of murder and should feel free to go back to their village. The parents, relatives, and friends of the young man, all influential personalities in his court, protested.

A group of concerned citizens later armed themselves and surrounded the telephone house (a pretty grave act of defiance of authority) and placed a call to the office of Crown Prince Tafari Makonnen in Addis Ababa. The protestors explained their case and appealed to the Crown Prince (later Emperor Haile-Selassie). Ras Tafari had Ras Nadew summoned to the telephone to hear his side of the story. Nadew explained that the case had been adjudicated in accordance with the relevant provisions of the *Fit-ha Negest* (the Imperial code). He would, of course, have no objection if his verdict were to be reviewed by higher authorities in Addis Ababa, but he himself could not go back on his judgment. Ras Tafari accepted the explanation and Ras Nadew's verdict stood.

My grandmother, Woizero Itagegnehu Lemma, was from the parish of Beyyeda Iyesus in Semien (today's North Gondar). Itagegnehu was strict in the management of the household, and particularly in the way children were brought up. She was fond of me and I of her, but she made it quite clear that I would never be spared the cane (or, more accurately, the *archumie,* a sturdy twig) if I did not behave properly. Naturally, there were the usual norms of discipline to observe. As with her religious practice, however, Itagegnehu's were more demanding.

No matter how cold or wet the evening hours were, young boys should not warm themselves in front of the kitchen fire. They should never use warm water to wash. For boys would grow up to be men, and men would go on long journeys or be called to war. Who would then make a fire for them or warm water for their bath? And a young boy should never say he is hungry and ask for something to eat. He should learn to control his craving for food and always decline politely if offered food outside the home. Children shouldn't drop in at their relatives' homes (announced or unannounced), especially at mealtime. When guests are served food at home, children should be out of sight, to avoid bothering guests with the customary offer of small morsels from their *messob.* And children should never presume to take part in conversations among adults, and never raise their voices when speaking. Boys should never enter the kitchen, especially when the women are busy. What would they do there? And if perchance the smell of the *injera* or *wat* beckons them, they should resist giving in to the temptation. And so on and so forth.

Inevitably, I would be caught in breach of one or another of my grandmother's interdictions and be punished for it. My mother Zauditu would complain, however, that I was not getting enough of the *archumie*. Woizeo Itagegnehu often replied that she was doing her best, but was faced with an unusually troublesome kid. It all seemed that I was impossible to handle, even after being whipped by a nettle's twig. I recall an incident which exasperated her patience. Itagegnehu was sensitive to noise and always pleaded with us, and particularly with the incorrigible Tekalign, to show some understanding. The incident involved my drumming a dry log out in the yard with two sticks, in imitation of my school's accomplished drummers. Itagegnehu was predictably irritated and told me to stop. I did, only to go a little further to a sheep skin being dried in the sun and start all over again. She descended upon me in fury and was about to administer the *archumie* when I meekly put in my case. "Mama! I obeyed you and left the old log in peace. I am only beating on something else now.

What did I do wrong?" In desperation, she laughed and asked me not to linger too long on the sheep skin.

On another desperate occasion, she said that I must surely have been sent by the good Lord as a punishment for her past sins. For she, not appreciating that it was He who ultimately had the power to make children behave themselves, had wrongly prided herself in raising her children to the highest standards. She knew better now and beseeched "the good Lord to bring you, Tekalign, to your senses".

Itagegnehu was a devout Orthodox Christian. Though only modestly tutored, she took the church's teachings seriously, and often literally. On special church holidays, she would get up in the wee hours of the morning, say her prayers, first at St. Michael's, then at St George's, and finally attend Mass at St. Mary's. She would cover all three churches in the town, located at considerable distances from one another, in the depth of darkness, walking barefoot on rough roads with hyenas roaming around freely.

Humility was one of the church's teachings that Itagegnehu took literally and, to her loved ones, unwisely. Coffee was being served one day at home. There was often a short supply of coffee cups, imported luxuries which were difficult to replace when broken. The young maid who wanted to begin the second round with Woizero Itagegnehu took a cup used by an old clergyman living with the family and was about to go to the kitchen to wash it when Itagegnehu intervened. "Don't you wash that cup," she said, "He and I are equal in the eyes of God, and what he has used I, too, shall". The girl had reason to wash the coffee cup. The old clergyman was in poor health, couldn't look after himself, never washed, never changed, never shaved, was a veritable filth from head to toe, and filled any room he entered with bowel-turning bad odour. If it were not for Itagegnehu, he would not be living with us. The maid dutifully poured coffee into the unwashed cup. And Itagegnehu drank the contents.

When the old man left after coffee, the more prudent Aleqa turned to her and said that she was wrong if she thought she would get some religious credit for courting trouble. He was similarly dismissive of her going to the three churches in the dead of night, needlessly risking life and limb. He would often say "Don't think that going to three churches instead of one in the pitch of darkness would strengthen your case for inheriting the kingdom of God. One church is good enough." Itagegnehu ignored her husband's counsel, and continued in her ways.

People facing hard times were Itagegnehu's constant preoccupation. On Easter Sundays she would think of persons who could not afford to break the long fasting period with meat or dairy and discretely send them food from the house. I often delivered the food and was told to be sure no one was looking as I did so. Years later one day (in the early sixties I believe), she asked if I could buy her a blanket. Vahak Karribean's shop in Addis Ababa carried quality blankets, carpets, drapes, textiles, and other merchandise as it does today. As always eager to get the best for her and be showered with her blessings, I proceeded to the shop and purchased a Scottish made, red woolen blanket for $15.00, a goodly amount in those days. I handed it to her and was duly blessed. When I returned the following day for lunch, the blanket was missing from her bed. I could not resist asking her what had happened. But she got annoyed with what she thought was an unseemly nosiness.

As I was leaving the house after lunch, I took the maid aside and asked what had become of the blanket. "Well", she said, "the old nun living down the road came yesterday and said that this year's cold was unbearable and that she wasn't sure she would survive it." "And so?" I asked. "And so," replied the maid. "Your grandmother pulled the new blanket off the bed and gave it to her." I immediately went back to my grandmother and said. "I bought the blanket especially for you. It is of good quality. Had you asked me, I would have been more than glad to get the old woman a less expensive blanket." She looked at me sternly and said, "If you were truly a man of God my son, you wouldn't be talking that way. In the eyes of the Lord, that woman and I are equal. It is vanity that makes you talk that way. You should mend your ways." There was nothing to do but get another Scottish wool blanket from Vahak's shop.

As Itagegnehu advanced in age, going to St. Mary's on Sundays increasingly became a major effort, though she was living no more than six hundred yards from the church. She would not accept the advice of her family that she should go to church only on special occasions, and even then only when she had the strength to do so. She should in any event begin to wear shoes to walk more comfortably on the rough stretch of the road to church. Throughout her life, Itagegnehu considered footwear as something of a luxury and not in keeping with her modest Christian ways. When walking to church barefoot became increasingly uncomfortable in her nineties, she reluctantly agreed to wear inexpensive rubber slippers. But she would remove them when off the road!

Even advice offered by church authorities was firmly resisted. During Mass one Sunday morning, the provincial Archbishop sent a message through a deacon that she must be tired standing for so long and that she should feel free to sit down for the remainder of the Mass. "Go away and leave me in peace," said she peremptorily to the messenger. "Is the man proposing to stand as my attorney on Judgment Day?"

Aleqa Biressaw was, of course, more moderate in matters religious as well as mundane. Knowing this, Itagegnuhu not only did not pay attention to his advice regarding her religious practice but also kept him at bay on questions of disciplining the young. Whenever he intervened, and he did whenever I was about to be caned, she would urge him to leave this 'impossible child' to her care, apprehensive that his more liberal disposition might undo her work. She always had her way, and there was really little the old cleric could do.

In any event, Aleqa had his own preoccupations and did not spare much time on the management of the household. Matters of Church administration kept him fairly busy. Besides, he was widely consulted on various questions of doctrine or practice.

People would often talk admiringly of his erudition and his mastery of the double entendre in Amharic and of *quine*. When in 1936 the Italians captured and were about to execute the Archbishop of Western Ethiopia, Abune Michael, they ordered the residents of the town (especially Aleqa and the clergy) to assemble at the scene of the execution. The Archbishop had opposed the Fascists and had fled with a few followers when the invaders were approaching the town. After his capture, he was sentenced to death in a hasty trial.

At the scene of the execution, his crime was read out to the assembled townspeople. Immediately afterwards, he and his followers were shot. Aleqa was then asked by the Fascist officer who had given the order to shoot if the execution had not been the appropriate punishment for the Archbishop's defiance of Italian rule. A moment of suspense followed before Aleqa, a good friend of the Archbishop and a man who doubtless harboured patriotic sentiments, responded ponderously. When he spoke, the Ethiopian interpreter, a man uninitiated in the ways of the double entendre, could only grasp the superficial meaning of the Amharic which was that the execution had been justified. But the hidden meaning was that the Italians had killed a good man.[6]

Getting Started in School

I started my traditional schooling in 1942 under *debtera* Zeru in the precincts of St. Mary's Church with a handful of pupils. There were no girls in our midst. Such girls as were schooled (and these were the privileged few) were tutored at a safe distance from the boys; i.e. in the privacy of their homes. Proficiency with the Ge'ez syllabic alphabet took time. One had to master the 231 basic letters (which represent syllables), some 25 auxiliary ones, and the Ge'ez system of numerals. This was followed by *abugida*, a display of the 231 letters arranged in seven columns and thirty-three rows which at first sight appeared haphazard but which was in fact a diagonal placement of the letters in which the pupil (unaware of the arrangement) was expected to quickly identify each letter as he went through line after line of seven characters each. The next stage consisted of a short piece from the gospel of St. John that the pupil read and re-read until he almost committed it to memory. Writing lessons were given after the pupils were adept at identifying the letters. One was first asked to write one's name, followed by copying exercises from Amharic or Ge'ez texts. Then came months of reading of the book of Psalms in *Ge'ez* until the pupil was able to whip through each page of the text with ease. An appropriate award from the pupil's family would crown the reading achievement.

Primary School

I continued with my church education for about a year or so. One afternoon in late 1943 Gerawork, a family friend who was passing by the house, casually took me to the government school that had re-opened after the Fascist occupation. I was presented to the headmaster and was enrolled. When I returned and told my grandmother about it, she asked how my name had been inscribed in the school register, for up to that point I had gone under the name of Tekalign Biressaw. I said that Gerawork had suggested to the headmaster that he follow the normal practice of registering a pupil with the first name of his father, not his grandfather's, as his second. So I was registered as Tekalign Gedamu. My grandmother was unhappy about this, and unhappier still that I had been taken by the irresponsible Gerawork to a secular school. She had wanted me to remain with the Church, eventually becoming a priest or a *debtera*. Her own son, Endale Biressaw, had been admitted to the government school before the Italian occupation. A number of people were unhappy that the son of Aleqa Biressaw, leader of the local Orthodox Church, should be allowed to attend a school where the risk of conversion to the Protestant faith was on everyone's mind.

There was, of course, no such risk at the government school. Yet the general perception at the time was that boys who went to these new fangled schools mostly run by foreigners or by Ethiopians who had adopted foreign ways would be made to abandon their Orthodox faith. And my uncle had been pulled out of the school for precisely that reason. He did not, however, object to my enlistment, for he had gradually come to regret his own involuntary withdrawal. A number of his schoolmates (among whom was his cousin Kebede Abozen) had stayed on and had later become high government officials, while he had remained a modest church official ultimately earning the honorific but inconsequential title of *Like-Tebebt*. He was in favour of my modern public school education, as he did not want me to share his fate. I on the other hand was not too fond of school at the time. His insistence that I attend the government school often translated into a seemingly unending series of reminders, threats and, on occasion, the inevitable cane. Ultimately, it all worked out as I started to enjoy school at the secondary level. The enjoyment was long in coming, however, since Haile-Selassie Elementary School in Gore had to be negotiated first. And what a negotiation!

The headmaster of the school was the formidable Ato Lentcho Ejetta: taciturn, workaholic, and a man of intense discipline. In the eyes of his pupils and their parents he was among the most educated of the country's citizens. His voice had a nasal ring to it. The town's people admiringly said that Lentcho was the only one among the men of high learning who 'spoke English through the nose.' Lentcho abhorred absenteeism, good cause or no. There was, for instance, the case of young Muzzeyen Hussein whose father had a stall in the town's market place. On Tuesdays and Saturdays (the designated market days), Muzzeyen's assisted his father in selling merchandise. The roll call would be read out every morning and Muzzeyen's absence, recorded each Tuesday, would be the first order of business to be executed every Wednesday morning before the beginning of class. The teacher would summon the boy to his desk after the roll call and administer five strokes of the ruler on each palm for his absence the previous day: week in week out, month in month out, for as long as I can remember. Or so it seems to me now.

Being an incurable truant, I was spared none of the punishments. One depressing morning, I struck upon an idea that I believed would put Lenctcho's terrors behind me for good. Immediately after breakfast, I set foot on the usual route to school but veered left and descended to the beautiful valley of Meshi half a mile later. The lush meadow of Meshi was where the town's cattle grazed. The wood surrounding it offered wild fruits; and the pristine creek quenched one's thirst. I spent a blissful four hours or so with the shepherd boys; frolicking, competing in make believe lance fights, exploring the length and breadth of the wood and otherwise engaging in any activity that caught my fancy.

The school bell, perched as it was on the western edge of the town's plateau, could be heard far and wide. I waited for it to ring, signaling lunchtime. As soon as it did, I made my ascent, reached the road leading back from school, and surreptitiously joined the noisy procession of students just out of class, scrupulously avoiding my classmates lest I be confronted with the embarrassing question about my whereabouts. When I arrived home, I showed every sign of fatigue that follows a strenuous day at school. I was given lunch, waited for students in my neighbourhood to begin making their way to school, joined them, once again studiously avoiding my classmates, and later dropped out of sight to repeat my morning adventure.

This went on for a few days, and I was beginning to believe that my plan had gotten the better of the wily Lentcho when my grandmother asked one day, "Are you going to school these days?" I could only answer in the affirmative. "The headmaster wants to see you first thing tomorrow morning," she said. I wasn't too eager to accept the invitation. Instead, I rejoined my newly acquired friends, the shepherd boys. As I climbed the hill back home for lunch that day, a stranger suddenly grabbed me from behind. I shrieked in fright, only to be shouted down. The stranger was none other than Endale, my uncle, who had been informed about me by a neighbour who had apparently taken notice of my secret ploy. Endale had hidden himself along the footpath leading up to the town, awaiting my emergence from the valley below. He made his catch when I got near enough, remarking that he was not aware a new school had opened in the valley below. "But Ato Lentcho's school would be a little better, wouldn't you agree?" he asked mockingly. He took me home, waited until I had finished lunch and accompanied me to the dreaded headmaster. As can be imagined, I wasn't exactly treated like a prodigal son who falls into the loving arms of family and friends.

On another occasion, I was detained for the day for some minor offence I no longer recall. Everyone except me went home for lunch. I had to stay behind in an empty classroom, watched by the school guard. The teacher of the class, Ato Fisseha, had given me some work to do during the lunch-less lunch break. All of a sudden Ato Lenctcho appeared as if from nowhere, and asked what I was doing. I replied that I had been told by Ato Fisseha to stay behind and study.

On one page of my notebook was a nice little wax drop from a homemade candle I had been using to go over my lessons the previous evening. Lentcho came across it as he was inspecting the pages and asked "What is this?" I was overjoyed. "I was studying by candle light yesterday evening at home, sir. I was so focused on my studies that the candle I was holding with my left hand tilted slightly and the liquid around the wick started to drip. Only one drop got on the page, however," I said confidently. He took me to his office, scribbled a few English sentences in red ink on the margin of the page which carried the precious evidence of my diligence and instructed me to show it to Fisseha after lunch.

Partly because of my limited knowledge of English and partly because of the headmaster's illegible handwriting, I was unable to make head or tail of Lentcho's marginal remarks. I was relieved, however, that he had finally seen incontrovertible proof of how committed I was to my studies, contrary to what he had probably been told. I eagerly awaited the return of Fisseha and handed him the notebook as soon as he arrived, proudly showing off the headmaster's note. And the wax stain next to it! Fisseha read the note, looked at me and said: "The headmaster says that you are to be detained for one more day for not keeping your notebook clean!"

My recollection of the range of subjects taught and the textbooks used is hazy. English was initially taught by Ato Fesseha, as I now recall. Mrs. Henry, the wife a Presbyterian Missionary, was brought in later on. My first encounter with her was after I had come back from the long holidays. As usual, I had arrived late from an enjoyable three-month break with my father in Bure. I was astonished that there was no one in class to translate what Mrs. Henry was saying. Ato Fesseha used to do it himself when teaching English. I could not follow Mrs. Henry, could not ask questions, and was at a loss.

One day I turned to a bright classmate and friend. Could he be my interpreter for a question I wished to pose? That would not be possible, he replied, for he had once heard the American lady say to a pupil who needed an interpreter, "Is he deaf or dumb?" I had to learn the language quickly to be able to raise questions. It took time but I was eventually able to ask my first question in English. Mrs. Henry had succeeded in her method. She turned out to be a friendly teacher and would often invite us to her Mission where we practiced our English in the course of playing different games: an obvious attraction. No one was obliged to attend Sunday Service, however, although some did. I, the grandson of the local head of the Orthodox Church, did not dare although much attracted by the hymns.

Ato Haile Selassie Ayele, the teacher of arithmetic and the man who had spent some time at a Coptic college in Asuit, Upper Egypt, was a peppery man. Haile Selassie also taught what sounded like general science. The only teaching aid he had was a plastic model of the human torso showing the inside of the chest and stomach. I forget who taught Amharic but do remember the textbook used which was the widely admired poetry and prose writings of Ato Kebede Michael: *Tarikina Missale* (Historical Notes and Proverbs). The exquisite rhyme and rhythm of some of the author's poems were a delight and have remained so down the years. Only recently, I purchased all four volumes of his work and re-read poems like, *Azmarinna Yewuha Mulat* (The Minstrel and The River in Flood), *Eroro* (Grief) and *Aytina Dimet* (Ethiopia's version of Tom and Jerry which came out long before the two characters became cartoon celebrities on U.S. television). Kebede Michael, like Mengistu Lemma a generation after him, was a great craftsman of the Amharic language, and the works of both provide immense enjoyment.

Ato Ashagari Abozen (brother of Kebede Abozen), was the carefree teacher of geography and was the least inclined to pick up the cane. Unsurprisingly, he was popular with the students, as was the amiable clergyman and teacher of morals, Aleqa Issa-iyas of St. George's Church. Aba Tsega Eshetie, another clergyman from the Church of Abune Gebre-Menfes Kidus located outside town, was a teacher of the two R's: reading and writing, as he was blissfully unaware of the third R. To most students he was a terror. Not showing up in school was for him a sin against the Holy Spirit. An absent pupil would occasion a visit to his home. Aba Tsega would look for him in all the dark corners of the house: under the bed, under a pile of old blankets, behind the open door, at the back of the house; everywhere. And when he made his catch, the boy would be given a *kurkum* (the painful knock of the knuckles on the head).

And there was Beyene Gemeda, the teacher of physical education who had invented his own sequence of physical exercises. He would bark and bluster if these were not properly executed. "Gymnastics number 10," he would shout during the physical education period. If someone stretched his hands parallel to the ground instead of at right angles, or turned his head to the left rather than to the right, he would be reminded of all his previous errors (real or imagined) and humiliated in front of everyone. As I recall now, the sequence went up to 40! Who could possibly remember the correct sequence of all 40 exercises arranged with little rhyme or reason, one differing from the other ever so slightly? The inventor of the system himself was probably not infallible in this regard. But who was to take the master to task?

When I gave an account of my experience of early school to a friend many years later, he remarked that I did not really have teachers in grade school; only sadists. I do not believe that the handful of my surviving friends would agree. Bringing up children in Ethiopia in those days involved physical punishment. "Spare the rod and spoil the child" was as wise a saying in England as in Ethiopia. My own grandmother, as I have said, often followed up her admonishments with a liberal use of the twig. Knowing the strong bond between us, I would find it ludicrous to see her labeled a sadist. My recollection of the headmaster and the teachers under him is that of a group of zealous promoters of education in a country that was backward and had succumbed to Fascist might for precisely that reason. Educating the young was the surest way to guard against a possible recurrence.

There were, of course, also moments of fun that were eagerly awaited. Gizzaw Eshete, a man of letters, produced plays. The girls' school would put up similar plays independently. The older boys would eagerly await a call from the girls' school to perform roles for males. The calls would never come, since the girls were dressed up as boys for the purpose. The notional wall between the two groups was more real and far more daunting to scale than any physical barrier the school authorities could have put up; such was the control they exercised on the minds of the young. Even if segregated, plays did provide moments of gaiety in an otherwise austere world.

Soccer games were another recreation. There was hardly any organization or coaching. A few students, the more sturdy among us, would bring out a soccer ball, select two teams, throw in one or two pleading, less sturdy pupils and have a game without an umpire. Much more entertaining was the handkerchief game. A white handkerchief was attached to a stick planted in the middle of the football pitch. Beyene would line up boys facing each other on opposite sides of the stick. Once satisfied that everyone was standing straight in line and ready for the game, he would blow his whistle with a bronchial energy that would put many a bugler to shame.

At the sound of the whistle, the first in line from each competing side dashed to the handkerchief and began moving around it making sure that he was as far from his contender as the game allowed, but not so far as to prevent him from snatching the handkerchief and running away with it before being caught. If not caught, the snatcher ran to his mates waving the handkerchief victoriously. If caught, he surrendered and dropped out of the game. This must be the simplest of games ever contrived by the mind of man. But it brought fun and laughter in an environment of crushing discipline.

As I said earlier, the girls' school was forbidden territory. The only time boys had a chance of getting within sight of the girls was when coming to or going out of school. Male and female pupils walked separately in groups. If a girl caught a boy's fancy, he would fall behind, try to catch her attention and communicate with her by exchanging fleeting glances. Never would he go and talk to her in full view of onlookers. That would ignite rumours instantaneously, making him an object of derision among the boys for manifesting conduct unbecoming of a well brought up young man. Worse, he might face disciplinary measures.

If the boy's discreet approach drew a friendly glance from the girl and this was sustained for a few days, he would drop her short, unsigned, handwritten note expressing (in the mildest manner possible) his admiration. Delivery of the note would be executed with the utmost of discretion: through the boy's sister or a female relative. If the boy was not lucky enough to have a trusted female intermediary, he would wait for the girl on the footpath leading to her home. He would then discretely drop the note fifty yards or so in front of her, making sure she had got a glimpse of him and, more importantly, of the valued note making a safe landing.

Having accomplished the mission, the young man would disappear from sight instantaneously. Anxious moments of suspense would follow. The girl would take her time before manifesting her interest in a manner and place judged prudent. No matter how many fleeting glances might be exchanged, amorous notes (especially initial ones) were always viewed with awe. For someone who had luck on his side, a positive response would take the form of a renewed friendly glance, followed perhaps with a friendly smile, or even perhaps a good morning or a good afternoon, the sweetest music to the young man's ears. These would mark the beginnings of a blissful but short-lived relationship, filled with juvenile fantasies that would perhaps reach their crescendo in stolen kisses. If the boy were not lucky enough to get an encouraging response, he would suffer days and weeks in anguish. Severe punishment and humiliation would follow if the girl complained of harassment. No wonder such high-risk adventures were only attempted by the foolhardy or the dauntless few.

As for me, fun and adventure took place largely outside the school environment. My father visited me at my grandparents' home and would often be allowed to take me during school breaks to the small district where he was an administrator. These getaways developed into thoroughly enjoyable escapades which extended far beyond the end of the Easter and Christmas breaks, or the long vacation period during the big rains. After my plan with the shepherd boys was foiled, going out on holidays 30 miles to where my father lived looked like a god-sent plan to ditch school altogether. When reminded to go back to school, I would always respond that the time for my return was not yet due. I fell easy prey to horse riding in open country, shooting, and having great fun with the village boys.

When my father was transferred as a judge to the town of Bure, I eagerly awaited going to the new place. My first vacation after the transfer found me there in no time. One night I was taken to a most exciting event. It was the merrymaking of Oromo boys and girls in the pitch of darkness. The boys lined up in front of the girls (each boy facing a girl), leaning against long thin wooden sticks held with the right hand, feverishly shaking their bodies from head to toe, and singing away until it was time for the girls. These brought out their own song and dance. Each boy approached the girl in front of him singing, shaking his body, and finally delivering a kiss. The end came when they all disappeared into the nearby bush to resume in blissful privacy the kisses they had been exchanging only gingerly during the dance and song session.

Unhappily for me, I could do nothing but watch and (after their disappearance into the bush) wildly imagine the goings on in utter frustration. I was perhaps too young to take part, or wasn't expected to as a visitor. Nor did I possess the requisite skills even if I were invited to join. The person who took me to the event, noticing my jaws drop at the sight of the boys and girls slipping into the bush, told me to rein in my fantasies; for it was a matter of the strictest traditional protocol for the boys not to go beyond passionate kisses. How else would parents be expected to give their daughters a green light to this traditional get together under the cover of darkness?[7] After being dragged back to school, I would inevitably daydream about these salacious village events, often in class. The end of term results would confirm that I had not been paying attention to my teachers.

A Memorable Political Event

On Sundays and church holidays, I usually accompanied my grandfather to St. Mary's. I had traveled to Addis Ababa with him in 1943 and had taken the rites to be a deacon from Abuna Kerillos, the last Egyptian metropolitan of the Ethiopian Orthodox Church. I began serving as an auxiliary deacon, following the initiation ceremony for novices. At about this time, a political event occurred that captured the attention of young and old alike.

Immediately following Mass one Sunday morning in 1947, I saw someone reading aloud a copy of the government daily, *Addis Zemen*, to a handful of clergymen huddled around him. The paper carried an article on the execution of Belai Zelleke, the celebrated resistance leader who had fought the Fascists during the entire five-year period of occupation. People were stunned; such was the reputation of this legendary man. And so were the young who referred to him as *Atse Begulbettu* (Emperor Mighty Man). As I was researching for this book one day at the National Library Archives in Addis Ababa, I accidentally stumbled upon a manuscript regarding Belai Zelleke's trial.[8]

Belai Zelleke was the son of a "common man," in the words of the manuscript. He was born in the district of Bichena (Gojjam) in 1908. Following a quarrel and murder of an adversary, he became an outlaw. As most outlaws, he lived on extortion and plunder, and was reputed to be ruthless in his ways. Over time, he also built a reputation for bravery. When Fascist Italy invaded Ethiopia, all outlaws were pardoned and urged to take up arms against the enemy. Overnight Belai, aged 28 years, became a patriot resisting the Fascists. Several men were attracted to him, some voluntarily others less so. His success as a resistance leader was such that he was popularly referred to as *Le'ul* (Prince), a royal title for a man of modest origin.

Early in 1941, Emperor Haile-Selassie crossed the Sudan border with a band of followers to join an advance force made up of 1700 strong Ethiopian, Sudanese, and British soldiers under the command of Colonel Orde Wingate. Belai was one of the resistance leaders with whom contact was established. On their way to Gojjam province, the royal party instructed Belai to block the advance of an Italian contingent marching towards Gondar with a plan to join forces with the army of Italian General Nasi. In a grave act of insubordination, Belai pointedly ignored this wartime order. He repeated it a second time when asked to block the road against yet another Fascist contingent in retreat.[9]

Colonel Orde Wingate was incensed. Unconfirmed stories said that he wanted Belai to be court marshalled.[10] This would have been an impolitic thing to do for the Emperor, given the unsettled political situation in the country as well as Belai's standing in the region. Belai's two cases of ill-advised defiance of imperial authority were passed over quietly. But there was resentment in the Emperor's party regarding Belai's insolence. Some advised that he and his men should not be allowed to take part in the parade being organized at Debre Markos to honour the Emperor's homecoming.

Getahun Tessema, a resistance fighter who had accompanied the Emperor during the long journey from the Sudan border to Debre Markos and a Gojjame like Belai, advised otherwise. Belai was permitted to pay his respects to the monarch and his men took part in the parade.

The Emperor was eager to proceed quickly to Addis Ababa but was advised by the British to delay his departure. General Cunningham had already arrived in Addis Ababa at the head of a large British force. He did not want the monarch to set foot in the capital before the 30,000 Italian citizens had been evacuated. There was fear in British circles that the Emperor's arrival might provoke the population into acts of uncontrolled revenge against Italians. Emperor Haile-Selassie was therefore kept in Debre Markos while arrangements were made for the evacuation. Having stayed in Debre Markos for a whole month, he and his group felt that they had stayed long enough and left for Addis against the wishes of the British.

Together with his party, the Emperor arrived in the capital on 5 May 1941 and was received by residents with an outpouring of wild jubilation. His radio address to the nation contained a section on the issue that had caused much concern to British officials. It went as follows: "Today is the beginning of a new era in the history of Ethiopia...Do not pay evil for evil. Do not commit acts of cruelty like those committed against us by the enemy. Do not give the enemy any excuse to smear the good name of Ethiopia. We shall take his weapons and put him on the road back to where he came from." No retaliation took place.

Emperor Haile-Selassie commenced his rule with a number of appointments at both the central government level and in the provinces. Belai was given the title of Dejazmatch and was appointed governor of his native district of Bichena. He was more than a little unhappy, as he had raised some of his own subordinates to that rank during the resistance. While he might have understood the imperial message that his initiatives in that regard had now been nullified, he could not be expected to be entirely satisfied with an honorific title which he felt did not take full account of his wartime stature and service to the nation. Lij Hailu Belew, another resistance leader and member of the royal house of Gojjam, was appointed to the more elevated rank of Ras and made Governor General of Gojjam province. Belai might have coveted the post for himself. The Emperor of Ethiopia had measures of eligibility other than ambition or wartime fame for that important position. First, there were a number of contenders for the post who belonged to the ruling family of the province. And it would not be unreasonable to speculate that the people of Gojjam expected the post to go to one of these, not to a plebian like Belai. Secondly and more importantly from the Emperor's vantage point, Ras Hailu was a less assertive personality.

Another resistance leader, Dejazmatch Mengesha Jembere, was appointed second in command to Ras Hailu Belew. This was a further disappointment to district governor Belai who reportedly told the Emperor that he would find it difficult to work under Mengesha. The Emperor advised him not to be unduly concerned and that he was available to thrash out problems if things took the wrong turn. All appointees, including Belai, subsequently left for their posts. Before long, petitioners from Belai's district made the long journey to Addis Ababa to protest acts of injustice committed by their new district governor. Facing a specially organized tribunal, Belai pleaded innocent to the charges saying that it was his followers, not he, who had committed the alleged acts. His followers were found guilty and given heavy sentences. He himself got away with a light sentence and was allowed to go back to his district.

Reports later arrived in Addis that Belai was not cooperating with the Governor General. The Emperor called a meeting of all senior government officials of the province to discuss administrative matters. Ras Hailu, the Governor, his immediate collaborators and district governors (including Belai) were instructed to present themselves in Addis Ababa by a certain date. On that date, all except Belai were present. The meeting was postponed to another date. Surprisingly, Belai chose not to show up yet one more time. Insubordination had gone beyond tolerable limits. A military contingent was dispatched from Addis to capture and bring him to the capital.

Before engaging him militarily, however, it was decided to resolve the problem by negotiation. Peace envoys (members of the clergy and elders of the local community) were dispatched to persuade Belai to settle his differences with the authorities amicably. He refused. A detachment of soldiers under Dejazmatch Temesgin Fenta, a local grandee, was ordered to Bichena, with the central government troops under Yilma Beshe staying behind as a reserve force. A day-long battle took place in which 38 persons were killed and 92 were wounded. The following day, Belai surrendered. He and 19 of his accomplices were brought to Addis and put on trial. All except one were found guilty of sedition and the killing of government troops. They, including Belai, were sentenced to death, but the Emperor commuted the sentence to life imprisonment.

Belai started to serve his sentence, not in a regular government prison, but in the home of the resistance leader Dejazmatch Bekelle Woya. Before long he got busy with a plan to escape back to his province. Correspondence to this effect was uncovered and Belai was handed over to the Imperial Guard troops for a more secure custody. No charges were brought against the planned escape. While under the custody of the Imperial Guard, Belai met with someone whose death sentence had, like his own, been commuted to life. Again like him, the detainee had plotted to escape and had been brought to Imperial Guard premises. This was Mamo Haile-Michael, the grandson of Ras Hailu Tekle-Haimanont who, like his grandfather, was a notorious collaborator with the Fascists.

The restless Mamo soon embarked upon yet another escape plan to which he brought Belai. On December 28, 1946 the two managed to slip away in the dead of night, thanks to night guards who had been bribed. A huge manhunt was mounted by the mayor of Addis Ababa. Colonel Mulugeta Buli, the commander of the Imperial Guard, also sent out search units across the city. Belai, Mamo and a couple of followers straggled for the remainder of the night in the direction of Sululta, an area some 20 miles northwest of Addis Ababa. They were apparently on their way to their province, Gojjam. A few hours later Belai, Mammo and their followers were taken by surprise, were detained and brought to Addis Ababa. Belai and his friends were now back in jail, some forty-two hours after their attempted escape. They were put on trial. All were found guilty of the murder of a policeman during their attempted escape and were sentenced to death. Even if he had been so inclined, the Emperor might not have been in a position to commute Belai's death sentence for a second time.[11] Belai, Mamo, and the others were hanged on January 13, 1947 in Addis Ababa.

My Father's Side of the Family

There is not much more that I can write about my early life with my father. My mother had died when I was only ten, and my father had re-married. As I said earlier, my recollection of her is that of an elder sister who occasionally came to visit me and her parents. My relationship with my father was formal. I never addressed him as *ababa* (dad), only as *Getoch* (Sir). And this continued into adult life. His elder brother, Tadesse Gizzaw, got to know me (and I him) fairly well later in life; and I must say we enjoyed each other's company enormously. It was he, not my father, who would tell me stories about life in traditional Ethiopia. I found these stories fascinating and vividly illustrative of the lifestyle of the day.

Fitawrari Gizzaw Deresso, my paternal grandfather, was from Sekota in Wollo province. When only twelve years old, he had been given to the care of Dejazmatch Nadew Ashebir of Shoa. This was in keeping with the tradition of asking an acquaintance in the King's court to take custody of one's son in order that the boy might be exposed to the art of governance for a possible career in public service. Dejazmatch Nadew was an influential personality in Emperor Menelik's court. While on some political mission to the north, he met Gizzaw's father Deresso, who requested him if he could take his twelve-year old son to Shoa to be groomed in the King's court. Nadew obliged and took Gizzaw with him.

Upon the death of Dejazmatch Nadew and in accordance with his will, Gizzaw was moved to the household of his son, Dejazmatch Tessema. Tessema was later appointed governor of Illubabor province with the rank of Ras and took young Gizzaw with him. One day, the Ras told Gizzaw that he was thinking of marrying him to Beshowamyellesh Bellettte, the daughter of his cousin, Woizero Sakamyellesh who, like him, was from the parish of Adisge Kidane-Mehret in Tuglet, Shoa. Like Gizzaw, Beshowamyellesh had also been brought up in Tessema's household. Gizzaw was taken aback and said he and the girl had grown up together under the same roof, that she was like a sister to him, and that he could not bring himself to entertain the thought of becoming her husband. "Don't be silly," came the reply, "she is no sister to you, nor you a brother to her". And that was that. Ras Tessema took care of the wedding arrangements and Gizzaw was duly married to the girl.

Brothers Balambaras Tadesse Gizzaw (left) and Balambaras
Gedamu Gizzaw, the author's father

Sometime later, Tessema elevated his son, Kebede, to the rank of Grazmatch and Gizzaw to Balambaras, a rank that was a notch lower. Gizzaw took offence. Was he not the husband of Beshowamyellish, the Ras's close relative? And had he not been brought up in the same household with Kebedde who was like a brother? Why this slight? Ras Tessema got wind of this, had Gizzaw summoned and said: "I understand you are not entirely happy with your new title and are asking why you were ranked below my son Kebede." Gizzaw had to deny this outright, for he knew that trouble would follow if he admitted. Tessema did not, of course, accept Gizzaw's denial. He believed what his informants told him. "Go bring back the wife I gave you," he ordered. And that was that. Gizzaw went home, collected his wife, and returned her to the Ras's residence.

Young Gizzaw pondered over the double humiliation. He had been slighted by the inferior rank. And now, he was robbed of his wife. There was no point in staying with his mentor. He had to leave. And leave he did. It appears that Ras Tessema was only expressing a momentary displeasure and, after things had cooled down, asked for Gizzaw. No one could say where the man was. Months passed and there was no news of Gizzaw. The Ras instructed one of his officials to marry Beshowamyellesh whom he said had been abandoned by her husband. The official complied unhesitatingly. Two daughters were born to the new couple in quick succession.

Three years later, Ras Tessema was in Addis on official business. At Menelik's palace one morning, an aid spotted the prodigal Gizzaw in a far corner of the palace and promptly informed his master. The Ras gave instructions that Gizzaw should be forcibly taken away. His men approached Gizzaw from behind, overpowered him, took him to where they were staying in Addis, and ultimately to Gore. The second husband of Beshowamyellesh was summoned and instructed to promptly hand her back, for her first and true husband had been found! And that was also that. Beshowamyellesh returned to her former husband. Gizzaw was now given the more elevated title of Fitawrari.

After listening to all this, I couldn't help asking the narrator of the story, my uncle Tadesse, what a bizarre drama all this was. To the best of my knowledge nothing remotely similar had ever happened to anyone on my mother's side. Couldn't someone say no, or find a way of getting the Ras to change his mind? Why didn't Gizzaw try to appeal to the Ras when first asked to surrender his wife? Did Beshowamyellesh's new husband have a wife at home? If so, could he not ask to be excused? And even if there were no wife at home, how could he allow as important a decision as marriage to be imposed on him? And poor Beshowyellesh! Couldn't she have pleaded with the Ras (who after all was a close relative) to be left in peace?

"You obviously do not understand the times," replied my uncle. "In his province, the Ras was like a king, and could pretty much do what he fancied. Besides, he wasn't doing anybody any harm. He was just expressing his displeasure for what he thought was an ungrateful remark by my father, a young man whom he had brought up as a son and to whom he had given the hand of his relative. But my father had a keen sense of personal honour", continued Tadesse, "and did the right thing to run away from his mentor. And as for young Beshowamyellesh? Who other than a politically powerful close relative could find her a suitable husband? Young boys and girls in those days were not expected to know what was in their best interests. Regarding her second husband, he would have been an idiot if he had considered wriggling out of the great opportunity to be the Ras's in-law, wife or no wife at home. For in those days one's station in life very much depended on how close one was to men of power and influence. Being selected by the Ras to marry into the family was an irresistible offer."

The first child to be born after the re-marriage of Gizzaw and Beshowamyellesh was a boy. A suitable name was searched; and he was named Tadesse (the narrator of this story), a not uncommon name in Ethiopia but one whose meaning ('it is renewed') was particularly apt, as it signified the resumption of the previous marriage. A couple of years later, another son was born. The search for an appropriate name was once again under way. Ras Tessema, the initiator of the marriage, the cause of its temporary break up, and now of its resumption, had been recalled to Addis Ababa and been replaced by another governor. The recently rejoined husband and wife were now at a safe distance from the Ras, and named their second son, my father, Gedamu. Gedam is 'monastery' in Amharic. Monasteries are places of reverence, entirely free of disturbance by outsiders. In giving this name to my father, his parents obviously felt that they were now as free from Ras Tessema's disturbances as any monastery in the land.

Tadesse's own marriage turned out to be an altogether different affair: a truly audacious defiance of the culture of the day. Following tradition, Gizzaw had made arrangements for the marriage of his two sons. He called Tadesse and Gedamu one day and told them that they would soon be married and should hold themselves in readiness for the double wedding. The two were not told who they would be married to. Although curious, they could not pose the obvious question to their father and were left totally in the dark.

An excited young man approached Gedamu one day and told him how lucky he was to be married soon to the daughter of Aleqa Biressaw. She was a lovely girl, was admirable in her manners, had superb culinary skills, and was from a respectable family. Tadesse waited anxiously for some fragment of information about his own would-be wife. There was not a word about her. The story of his brother's fiancée gathered momentum and soon everyone in town was talking about her. Tadesse's curiosity about the identity of his own fiancée increased as the story of his brother's fiancée continued to spread. Was she from another town? Was she perhaps not from the right kind of family? Surely, his father would take great care in choosing the bride's parents, if not the bride herself. Maybe that was the problem. Anxious days and nights passed. Tadesse was determined to find who the girl was, the girl about whom no one would speak.

He searched desperately and his efforts finally paid off. She was not from another town, and was the daughter of one of the local judges. But how could one get a precious glance? He ran into the judge's servant one day and invited him for drinks. The offer was accepted. Tadesse had to prepare the ground with great care. The subject was not raised at the first meeting, nor at the second. On the third encounter, Tadesse sensed that the fellow had taken a liking to him. He held back as the waitress poured more and more *tej*. After a while, Tadesse pulled himself together and said: "It is very unusual; we have become friends in a short time." "Yes indeed, and you are a nice fellow. I like you." "I like you, too," continued Tadesse. "Say, could you do me a favour?" he asked. "Sure, I would be more than happy to oblige. What is it?" replied the man. "Well, it is a small matter. It is just that I wanted to see, from a safe distance I want to assure you, someone I am expected to marry," said Tadesse. "That is perfectly understandable. Who is she?" replied the invitee. "They tell me that she is your master's daughter." The unsuspecting servant was stunned into silence as if struck by a bolt from the blue.

"WHHAAT!" he roared back. "You must be out of your mind. My old man would chop my head off with his sword if I get involved in any such thing. Imagine me parading his daughter in front of a young man! I had better get out of here. Good bye, Sir." The man rushed out, leaving Tadesse crestfallen. But Tadesse pulled himself together and resolved not give up. He looked for the man after a decent interval and ran into him in the bustling small town.

The fellow was reticent, but the indefatigable Tadesse persisted and finally got him to agree to spend a few minutes over a glass of *tej*. This time, Tadesse did not spend time getting to the point. "I have an idea of how this thing could work without putting you, or me, in harm's way", started Tadesse persuasively. "And what is that?" asked the man. Tadesse said that it is the custom for girls to go to church every day for Holy Communion during the fifteen-day period of our Lady's Assumption. The period was approaching. "If we can hide in the bush adjacent to St. George's, which is where I presume the girl would be going, you can point her out to me as she approaches the gate of the Church," said Tadesse. The man dropped his head for a minute, raised it and said "That is not a bad idea, but do keep it to yourself. Let's have another round."

On the appointed day, the two crawled into the undergrowth of the bush near St. George's Church and lay flat on their stomachs, with their heads pointing in the direction of the footpath leading to the gate of the Church. Suspense followed heightened suspense until finally the girls started to march by in groups of two or three, giggling and frolicking. Tadesse would ask, "Is this the one?" every time a pretty girl passed their gaze. After several "No's" from the man, Tadesse got a little tired and turned on his back to be more comfortable. All of a sudden his friend said "Taddey (the diminutive for Tadesse), there she comes". Taddey turned over and took a glance, and another, and yet another. His worst fears had come true. She was a split image of her father. He said good bye and jumped out of the bush and headed home.

The next day, he went to another *tej* house he had been frequenting. He talked earnestly to the owner, a middle-aged lady he knew well. "Who was the beautiful girl I saw here a few months ago," he asked. He took time to describe her good looks, her demeanour, the circumstances and time of the girl's sighting, for it was no more than that. The lady said, "Oh, she is an adorable soul. She is my Godchild. Why do you ask?" "My parents are planning to marry me off," said Tadesse. Before he could finish his sentence, the lady interjected. "Lucky you, when is the big day?" "There isn't going to be a big day for me. I am not interested in the girl my parents have in mind for me. I want to marry your girl. Tell her to come over in a couple of days or so. I will propose to her and take her home." Astonished, the lady informed Tadesse that the girl was already married. "Who too?" asked Tadesse. The Greek merchant on the other side of town, replied the lady. "Forget the old Greek merchant. What business has he marrying one of our girls. In any event, I would make a far better husband."

And that was how the story would end. The beautiful girl came, heard a perfunctory proposal, was whisked away by young Tadesse and became his wife. To go into a full account of the aftermath of this audacious marriage: the vociferous but futile objections of Tadesse's parents, their loss of face in regard to an event which had been carefully planned but had been unceremoniously blown away (or half blown away to be accurate, for his brother's marriage went ahead as planned), the embarrassing disclosure of the bad news to the fiancée's father and the protocol required to undo the whole thing, the suspicions about the family background of Tadesse's new wife; going into all this would needlessly prolong the story. Suffice it to conclude that when confronted by his father about his scandalous marriage, and told to get rid of that *galemotta* (whore), Tadeese's irreverent response was, "My dear father, it is not you but me who is marrying the girl you have in mind for me. You have a beautiful wife in the shape of my dear mother. Why should I spend my days (and nights) with a hideous creature? You haven't seen her. She is a split image of your respectable old friend, the monstrously ugly judge, if I may say so. I shall never marry her."

There was nothing to do but annul the wedding arrangement and allow time to heal the rupture between father and son. Gedamu's marriage to Zewditu went ahead as planned. Tadesse's wife gave birth to a daughter, Mintiwab, at about the same time as my mother gave birth to her first son, Mulatu. Mintiwab's first daughter Kelemework would be adopted by my father several years later, becoming a virtual sister to me. She is today happily married to Dr. Bona Hora and is blessed with a son and daughter, Jocky and Mimi.

Tadesse's actions were clearly not that of an elder son whose conduct set the standard for those coming after him. He was unusually independent and on occasion irreverent, as the following anecdote demonstrates. Tadesse was once confronted with an instance of paternal indiscretion that he felt needed to be stopped before it went too far. He acted accordingly and paid a painful price immediately afterwards.

One afternoon in 1929 following a banquet given by the new Governor of Illubabor, Ras Mulugeta Yigezu, Tadesse's father and a friend were gossiping about the Ras, and drawing unflattering comparisons with his predecessor, Ras Nadew Aba Wollo. Tadesse was concerned that the two elderly gentlemen were airing their views within earshot of the governor's servants. He noticed that his father and the friend were a little high and consequently not fully conscious of the risk that their conversation might find its way to the governor's ears before long. After a moment's reflection, Tadesse decided to caution his father. He stepped forward and whispered in his ear: "Would it not be more prudent if you were to hold this conversation at home?" What impertinence! "I have been told by my son that I should go home. Good bye, sir" said his father to his friend, and told Tadesse to follow him.

Gizzaw spurred his mule and reached home in half the time it normally took. Immediately upon arrival, he called the sturdiest of his servants, and instructed him to beat up the uppity young man. Blow after blow landed on Tadesse's back, which he took without resistance. He had the physical strength to fend off the blows and even subdue the attacker, but was deterred by the thought of his none-too-sober father coming to the assistance of the servant. Better to bear the pains of the blows than to witness the painful sight of his father joining the fight to assist his servant. Tadesse's restraint brought the punishment to a quick end. The servant was instructed to stop and Tadesse to hand back his handgun and rifle (presents from his father) and wait outside the house until called.

It was time for dinner. Mother and father were served while Tadesse waited outside. Fitawrari Gizzaw, more sober now, gave orders that Tadesse should come inside for dinner. Tadesse entered, turned away from the dinner, and made a dramatic

*Balambaras Gedamu Gizzaw at centre, his wife Woizero Debritu Jembere at right,
and daughter Kelemework Gedamu at left*

announcement of a rupture in relations. "I have been reflecting over this afternoon's incident to find out why I have been subjected to such beating and humiliation? The answer is plain. I was concerned to protect my father from a possible falling out with the new Governor. And I have been made to pay a price. In our tradition, it is a father who takes the decision to disown a son. The reverse is never done. But I, Tadesse, am deciding now to no longer consider you, Fitawrari Gizzaw, as my father; and would not henceforth want you to regard me as your son. I have nothing to add. Good bye, sir." And he walked straight out of the house.

Tadesse vowed never to talk to his parents again. The rupture in relations was painful, especially for his mother. After a few months he was approached by the father confessor of his parents, was told that the old man had regretted the incident, that his mother missed him much, and that both mother and father badly wanted him to come back. Other intermediaries also got involved. Happily, relations were eventually restored. Tadesse was reconciled and given back the handgun and rifle. The event turned Tadesse into a wise man of the family often asked for his views on knotty problems.

I shall wind up these anecdotes with Tadesse's brief account of the war years. Both Tadesse and my father had fought against the Fascists on the Ogaden Front. With victory going to the Italians, the Ethiopian army disbanded; a few men going into guerilla warfare, but the bulk simply going home. Together with his brother and some friends, Tadesse trekked back home to Gore.

Home bore little resemblance to the place they left behind when they went to war. As they had lost their parents, the house was left in the custody of servants. One bright day, the servants were surprised by the sight of two disheveled young men approaching the house. The two identified themselves and asked to be allowed in. Areru, the more senior of the servants, came out to talk to them. He said that times had changed. The house was no longer their parent's but his, thanks to the Italian Government which had liberated all former vassals and given them the property of their masters. And he would now report them to the Italian police. Tadessse and Gedamu said that they were unaware of what had happened and were prepared to give up their claim to the house. Could Areru please desist from reporting them to the police? And could he please give them temporary shelter? Areru turned down both requests, and took off to the district governor's office, shouting *Gizzaw yimut alekatchihum* as he did so (a form of swearing widely used at the time which could roughly be rendered thus : "In the name of Gizzaw, my old master, I shall not leave you in peace").

Areru had them summoned to the office of the District Commissioner who asked him: "Why are you reporting these men?" "Because they are *shiftas* (bandits), sir" "Why are you *shiftas?*" asked the Commissioner. "We are not, sir. There was a general mobilization for war and we were ordered to join the Ogaden Front. We have only recently returned." The Commissioner turned to Areru and said, "They are not *shiftas*; they were only carrying out the orders of the government of the day." Areru, visibly taken aback, said "Okay, sir, but I have been liberated by the great Italian Government and am going to stay in the house." Tadesse, noticing that things were tilting his way, said; "He was living with us as a regular servant and a free man, not as someone rendering service against his will as he would like you to believe. He had been told to leave at anytime he wanted, but had on several occasions responded that he had no place to go, and had been allowed to stay. Besides, the house was built by our father."

"Who owns the house?" the official asked Areru. "Thanks to the good and great Italian government, I now own the house". "That is rubbish. The Italian Government does not rob the private property of an individual to give it to another. You hand over their father's house and all other assets promptly and quit!" Tadesse and Gedamu were delighted. As they walked back to the house, they told Areru that he would now have to account for all the property attached to the residence at the time of their departure for the Front: cattle, horses, mules, sheep, even chickens. Areru started to plead in the name of Gizzaw (*begizzaw mot*). The sons of Gizzaw were amused at the barefaced use of their father's name for the purpose of pleading only hours after it had been used to intimidate.

The two veterans moved to their father's home. Areru stayed and relations were restored. But the brothers soon discovered that they could not find employment with the kind of military service record they had, and were obliged to move out of Gore to the countryside. They managed to be employed as roving tax collectors for a group of market towns working under someone they had known before the war. That is how they spent the remaining years of occupation. When news spread that resistance forces were approaching Gore, the promptly joined them and fought Italian forces one more time. This time the enemy was defeated.

Times were hard during the Occupation. "One good thing the Occupation did for us, however, was to make us understand what it really meant to be a free people," Tadesse would often say. And in this, the role of Emperor Haile-Selassie as the liberator of the nation was indelibly etched in the minds of Tadesse and his generation. The Emperor was revered in a way not easily understood by the present generation of Ethiopians. He was perceived not simply as their deliverer from unaccustomed bondage but as some quasi-divine being whose miraculous leadership had driven away a formidable foreign foe that gave no sign of ever leaving the country.

During occasional visits to Addis, Tadesse would always ask about the health of the Emperor. He would talk about his chance encounters with him with great excitement. One day, he said he had seen the Emperor coming out after visiting a patient in a hospital. "And so? Did you execute your skills of the deep bow?" I asked him. "What do you mean 'deep bow'. I almost touched the ground with my forehead. Let us go to a more serious subject" he continued. "When the Emperor came out of the Hospital he stood on the porch for a few moments and gently pulled up the collar of his cape with both hands. Not once, not twice, but three times. Exactly three times! What does this mean?"

My response was that the Emperor did that all too often, as the cape tends to slide back from his shoulders whenever he walks or gestures with his arms. "If you were wearing a cape, you too would do the same," I said to him casually. "My good Tekalign, I do not think you understand. I am inclined to think that it is some special body language of His Majesty. Maybe it was to signal his Aide-de-Camp that the visit is over and that he should order the limousine to come forward. Or perhaps he had something else in mind. Whatever it was, there definitely was some message behind the three tugs on the cape's collar." It was plain that I did not succeed with my none-too-insightful explanation. "You may be right," I conceded.

Tadesse would often ask: "Do you know why we lost the war?' And would go on provide his own answer: "Because our people were not educated." And when the Emperor embarked upon an extensive programme of public education after the war, Tadesse was an ardent supporter. As administrator of a district he would speak at market towns about the benefits of modern education and strongly urge farmers not to keep children from school to do chores on the farm. In the case of a somewhat carefree farmer, he reminded him that he was in breach of the Emperor's orders and that appropriate action would be taken if he did not mend his ways. The threat was sufficient to coerce the farmer into sending his eldest son to class regularly. The young man completed his elementary, secondary, and college education and became, years later, the General Manager of an oil company in Addis Ababa.

Tadesse was extremely happy to see the Emperor at close quarters in the course of his only royal visit to Illubabor in the early fifties. He told me of an interesting incident that took place during the visit. The Governor General of the province, Dejazmatch Tassew Wallellu, asked for a special audience to introduce a small group of the province's traditional chiefs. Among these was Kegnazmatch Gudetta Jawei, a man reputed for his quips. Kegnazmatch Gudetta's turn came to step forward to be introduced to the Emperor. After the introduction, the Governor General asked the Kegnazmatch if he could say a few words to the Emperor.

My lord," started Gudetta, "I am an old man who has had the good fortune of learning about our country's past from knowledgeable elders when young. I can say with confidence that never in the past has a leader of your wisdom and generosity occupied your exalted position. I am inclined to say that no one like you is likely to come in the future either; but the young man standing next to you is listening and looking at me, and I had better shut my mouth." The young man was the Emperor's son, Prince Makonnen Haile-Selassie, who was often talked about as a potential successor.

CHAPTER 2

Being Groomed for a Post Feudal World

Guinea Pigs for a New Secondary School

After completing my elementary education in 1947, I and three of my classmates were informed by the headmaster that we would be going to the nation's capital for secondary school. Four years earlier, I had accompanied my grandfather to Addis on a Church related visit which had lasted for a month or so. But I was now going there for a much longer stay. The idea was heady. Besides, this was no trip by a battered truck as was the previous one, which took the better part of a week. I was to fly. It would be my first experience and I would be in Addis in less than two hours. My neighbourhood friends eagerly succumbed to my infectious excitement and showered me with questions about how I felt deep inside, how I was preparing for the flight, whether I would ever come back, if I would occasionally think of them in the new place, etc, etc.

Ethiopian Airlines had started regular services to Gore the year before. What was it like to fly? How did it feel on takeoff? Did anyone have the courage to look down through the window? How did passengers manage to stay in their seats as the aircraft banked to the left and to the right? And as it landed? In an attempt to find answers, my friends and I combed our respective neighbourhoods in search of persons who had flown before.

Air sickness was much talked about in those days. But I could not find a single person who had flown and admitted having been air sick. "I had no problem at all, but a lot of others did," was the standard response to my query. "It is only the faint-hearted who get into this kind of trouble. Just pluck up some courage, board the aircraft, clench your teeth for a few minutes after take off, then close your eyes and doze off," one man told me. Doze off! How could anyone sleep in that thing? After putting questions to a few airworthy folks, I was no wiser than when I started, except being advised that I should abstain from all food the day before the flight.

When I informed my grandmother that I was to go to school in Addis, she asked how long it would take to finish and get back home. I of course had no idea. Did I really want to go? she continued. I did not wish to disappoint her with an affirmative response and equivocated. She fell silent. It was disheartening to us both. I do not recall exactly how my grandfather reacted to the idea, but I don't remember him raising objections.

So, I and three other young country bumpkins (Makonnen Kibret, Assefa Tokon and Aleffe Milidos) left Gore for Addis one November afternoon in 1947. The flight in a C47 former military transport aircraft was surprisingly uneventful, except for the continuous noise and the occasional bumpy ride. We all said that we had needlessly worried. Abstaining from food for a day earlier was, however, a good precaution. Travel culture in those days prescribed a hearty meal before a long journey. A number of passengers inevitably experienced air sickness as a result, throwing up the generous meals they had earlier taken to fortify themselves for the trip. The gang of four were unaffected by the unpleasant experience.

The first leg of the journey took us to Jimma and lasted about fifty minutes. An image that has lingered in my mind these past six decades is the long stretch of forests that the aircraft frequently flew over in the course of the trip. In some cases it took as long as ten minutes to cover a stretch. At an estimated ground speed of 155 miles per hour, ten minutes would translate to slightly more than 25 miles in length, or breadth. I could see no such stretch of forest on my flight to Gore in 1988, my last air trip to the town.

It took us another thirty-five minutes from Jimma to reach Addis. Upon arrival, the headmaster of our school who had preceded us there met us at the airport and arranged for our stay at Menelik School until a place was found for us in one of the three secondary schools of the city (and the country): the Haile-Selassie I School, the General Wingate School, or the Tafari Makonnen School. The latter had formerly been an elementary school, but had started admitting students for secondary education in the previous two years or so. At Menelik, we were joined by eight students from Harrar and Tigrai provinces.

Menelik (part boarding part day school) had many students from a number of provinces. Some communicated with one another in their mother tongue, but learned Amharic quickly to make friends with other groups and to follow their studies. Ogadeni students were the most rambunctious and did things their own way. I once saw a young Ogadeni tied to an electric pole in the school yard for a good part of the day for some infringement deemed punishable by his pals. They also tended to be short tempered and belligerent. Every time they went home for the long holidays, fewer and fewer returned until, in the end, only a handful remained.

The Ministry of Education building was near Menelik and we soon started to frequent its offices to ask where we were going to be placed. Ato Belette Gebre-Tsadik, the influential and ever smiling Director of the Ministry, invariably responded that we would be informed in due course. The smile and the promise continued without much else happening. One day, the headmaster of Menelik told us that the Ministry of Education had authorized him to start a secondary school within its premises. And he was happy to inform us that we were the first batch to be accepted. But to us, the thought of being used as guinea pigs was hardly exciting. We trooped to Ato Belette's office to express our dismay. He received us with his customary smile and said he would look into the matter. Before long, we saw masons, carpenters and painters busy renovating a vacant room. The door was labeled Grade 7 and new desks were brought in. Teachers were assembled and a timetable posted on the door.

And so, the fourth secondary school in the land started with twelve students from three provinces: the gang of four from Illubabor, five from Harrar, and three from Tigrai. We all believed we had fallen prey to a hurried initiative of overzealous officials, reasoning that it was our very presence that had given them the idea of opening a new secondary school. Why hadn't they thought of it before? We were unhappy and started showering questions on our provincial mates in the other three secondary schools. We asked them what subjects were taught in their schools, the textbooks used, the quality of teachers, of labs, etc.

Soon we embarked on a remedial plan to shore up our inadequate education at Menelik. Following the advice of our frends, we purchased textbooks from Giannopoulos, the Greek bookseller, and assiduously applied ourselves to mastering the concepts, theories, and formulae contained in them. It was far from easygoing. When we ran into problems, we got back to our friends and, on occasion, we approached our own teachers. The former provided considerable help. The latter less so. But for the most part, we relied on our own efforts. In the process, we discovered that necessity was not only the mother of invention but of self-reliance as well.

Teaching oneself was sometimes carried to extremes. There was a schoolmate of ours (Amberbir from Debre Birhan) who had bought a small English dictionary. During the morning break one day, he asked if I could accompany him to the school backyard to avoid the noise. A relative had recently given him money to buy a small dictionary (*The New Method English Dictionary*, as I think it was called) on which he was spending a good chunck of his free time. "Please open the first page," he said when we were well away from the noise. I leafed through the first few sheets and came across the preface. "No, no, no. I mean the first real page." He took the dictionary from me, opened the page where 'A' was boldly printed, handed it back and said, "Follow me line by line as I go down the first column. .... *a*: the first letter of the English alphabet; *a*: (adj.) one, any; *ab-*: a prefix signifying *from, away, off,* as in *ab*duct, *ab*scond..."

"Wait a minute!" I said to Amberbir. But he was not listening. With eyes firmly closed, he was swooping down the first column. I followed the text as he recited each word and its meaning exactly as it was written in the dictionary. "I am amazed, Amberbir. How far into 'A' have you gone?" I asked when he came to the bottom of the page. "I am done with 'A' and 'B' and will pass on to 'C' this evening" he said calmly as the bell rang signaling the end of the morning break.

I was envious that someone a class below me had gone far ahead in what looked like an exciting new venture. Should I not follow suit, I asked myself? Much as I tried, I could not bring myself to get started. Neither was I inclined to ask how Amberbir was doing. Given his zeal, I had little doubt that he would go on to the end of the small dictionary. The young man had many admirers, but I do not recall if anyone had the audacity to follow in his footsteps.

Two uninterrupted years after my boarding school life at Menelik, I left Addis for Gore to visit my grandparents during the long summer break. My grandparents were both delighted to see me, as of course I too was. Aleqa Biressaw asked if I had met 'his king' and whether he was in good health. I had obviously seen Emperor Haile Selassie several times and told him that he appeared to be in very good health but slimmer and shorter than I had initially imagined. The conversation went in circles for a few minutes as my description of the monarch was very much at variance with the image of his king. I soon realized that we were talking of two entirely different persons when he asked who I was describing. "Emperor Haile-Selassie, of course" I replied. "No, no my son, I was asking you about *my King*, Ras Hailu of Gojjam, not the Emperor of Ethiopia" he said in his fragile voice.

Aleqa was 82 years old and had been in poor health while I was away. He died a month after I arrived. I was told that sometime before his death he had a premonition of the impending event and composed a *quine* chanted for him by one of his *debteras*. Unfortunately, I never was able to get the full length of the *quine*, but was told that it involved a metaphor about a shepherd (himself) who was about to depart from his flock and who was asking the owner of the flock (St. Mary) to find a replacement to keep the wolves at bay. Who he had in mind when he spoke of the wolves, we never shall know. He may have been concerned about unsavory characters among the clergy vying to take his place. Or perhaps he was apprehensive of the deleterious effects on religion that the country's modernizers might leave in their train.

At Menelik the quality of teachers improved over time. This was in part due to the efforts of the school officials. But it was in no small measure also due to our frequent strikes for better teachers. We once had a friendly Canadian teacher named Nelson who taught an easy subject. As there was no teacher for the more demanding physics course, he was asked by the headmaster to take over. We were apprehensive, but decided to wait and see. Soon, our fear was confirmed. Nelson's performance was poor. Just before class one day, we all agreed that after getting up to greet him with the customary "Good morning, sir" we would remain standing after his "Sit down, boys" response. He came into class, greeted us and told us to sit down. When no one did, he said: "What is going on here? Is this a strike?" "We want to talk to our headmaster," said someone from behind. Nelson left the class and Captain Smith, a tall broad-shouldered Canadian ex-army officer, walked in shortly afterwards.

"What is your problem?" he asked menacingly. "Mr. Nelson is not a good physics teacher and we are worried that we might not pass our school leaving certificate exam if we do not get a better teacher." He went back to his office, returned a few minutes later and informed us that he had found a solution to our problem. He, Captain Smith, would be the new physics teacher. We had to acquiesce in the face of the husky and intimidating World War II veteran. Before long we found out that Captain Smith's command of the subject was at about the same level as Nelson's. We could do nothing, except feel guilty at what we had done to the amiable Nelson. Mercifully, a more qualified teacher was brought in subsequently.

Ge'ez and Amharic were taught by Aleqa Likyelleh Kibret, a very pleasant, antiseptically clean cleric who once or twice got into a meditative mood and disappeared from view. It was said that he had abandoned the world and had entered a monastery. We never confirmed whether his short disappearances were caused by his sojourn at monasteries, but we could tell that he was a man of deep faith. His Ge'ez teaching was perfunctory and the class in Amharic grammar was conducted at a leisurely pace over a good portion of the duration of our secondary school.

Food was very bad at Menelik and was naturally a subject of much conversation and grievance. Emperor Haile Selassie and Empress Menen once visited our newly built spacious dining room while we were having lunch. Amidst the din of clanking knives and forks, Menen was seen taking out a handkerchief from her purse to swipe her imperial nose. Rumour spread rapidly that she couldn't stand the smell of the bad food. Of course, no one could say for sure whether the Empress used her handkerchief for that reason or simply to keep her nose dry.

Strikes in protest against the quality of food were not infrequent. The headmaster would come occasionally and see for himself what we were being fed. Finley Barnes, Captain Smith's predecessor, came once or twice, as did Smith himself, but to no avail. On occasions like Easter and Christmas, the food would improve, but would get back to its usual dreariness immediately afterwards. Boys from Addis went home on weekends, made up for the ordeal of the previous five days and fortified themselves for the next. Those of us coming from the provinces could only await the long holidays to get a respite.

Extracurricular activities often eased our preoccupation with the dismal food. Among these were after dinner films put on by the British Council. Charlie Chaplin's silent movies and Walt Disney cartoons were the obvious highlights. Second World War documentaries were also shown. Just before the screening, the man from the British Council would make a few introductory remarks during which he would be listened to with rapt attention. A prolonged and tumultuous applause would follow if Charlie Chaplin was announced and a somewhat less pronounced one if it was a Walt Disney cartoon. War films were welcomed with nods of approval. Any other film was met with murmurs of disappointment.

Soccer was a major leisure activity. This included organized class matches and games for the school's first and second teams with those of other schools. Recreational games played outside class hours took the bulk of our time for soccer. For the most part tennis balls were used. The tiny rubber balls were obviously much more challenging to manage, especially for goalkeepers. The sole football pitch often accommodated two matches simultaneously. One can imagine the resulting confusion caused by some twenty odd non-uniformed players chasing one or the other ball and occasionally mistaking the other team's ball for theirs. The confusion would be greatly enhanced if the material covering the tiny rubber balls was about the same colour, which was often the case. Further confusion was caused if there was a shortage of players. A player in defence might be asked to play for both teams and would find it difficult which way to go if approached by two attacking players of the opposing team simultaneously. The same with a poor goalie who would run hither and thither to fend off the fast flying balls. A raging argument would be provoked by a ball found lying in the grass behind the goal posts. Did it go through, or off to the right, the left, or perhaps over the cross bar? Nets hung on the goal posts to restrain the balls were a luxury in those days, even for major matches between schools.

Matches of the Ethiopian Football Federation were a major diversion for the Addis Ababa school population, as they of course were for the city's residents. Most fans were for the St. George team. Few missed watching the star player of the day. Yidnekatchew Tessema (affectionately called 'Yidne'). He was the team's centre forward and principal scorer. Spectators were never more uproarious than when Yidne deftly negotiated his way through the Army team's defences and finished with a dramatic kick of the ball into the net. Or when he dribbled the ball with aplomb forwards, backwards, sideways, and forwards again towards his target, as the hapless Army players desperately tried to tackle him. In this they often failed, drawing howls of derision from St. George fans. Army players were less known for their brain than for their brawn and were consequently regarded with considerable scorn.

Yidnekatchew Tessema would later become President of the Ethiopian Football Federation (of which he was the founder and foremost leader), co-founder (and probably the principal advocate) of the African Football Confederation (AFC), and a member of FIFA's governing board. He was a greatly respected figure in the world of soccer and in the Olympic movement as well. His leadership qualities were such that AFC delegates attending football conferences in Addis Ababa expressed their pride in this distinguished son of Africa. In the euphoric early days of the Organization of African Unity, a French speaking West African delegate was once heard saying: "The day Africa decides to have a single government, we shall make Tessema our President!"

Much as I and my friends whined about the bad food and education at Menelik, something happened which cured my loathing for learning. I do not recall why, how, or at precisely what point this major transformation in my life occurred. All I remember is how blissfully liberated I was of all symptoms of distress with school. Indeed, I began to enjoy subjects like mathematics, physics, chemistry, and English. Writing English composition was a special pleasure, as was solving mathematical problems. There were only two subjects I disliked: biology and geography. I still believe (no doubt erroneously) geography to be a hodgepodge of material lifted from other disciplines. I found the two subjects to be insufferable. Place names and a list of a country's exports and imports (the stuff of much geography lessons in those days) did not exactly make one sit up on the edge of the school chair. Biology was taught by an Egyptian Copt in the dreariest of fashions. The absence of a lab and the fun of experimenting with plants and animals was the other reason for my aversion to biology.

Among the teachers I remember most vividly is Finley Barnes, the much admired headmaster and physics teacher. Barnes was a disciplinarian and a perfectionist. His classes were methodical and his explanations crisp. As headmaster, he took pains to keep the school compound clean. He was often seen picking up pieces of paper thrown on the ground and putting them in his pocket saying, "Boys, I want you all to do that and get rid of the paper at a convenient spot." Patton and Young (Canadians as well) were great teachers of English. Johnson from India was a hard driving instructor and a superb imparter of mathematical logic.

Our class was blessed with a strong *esprit de corps*. I remember one particular incident where this came out robustly. We were about to be promoted to Grade 12 in preparation for the matriculation exam, a long awaited first-time event at Menelik. When the final year's exam results for grade 11 were announced, it was discovered that one boy had not scored the minimum required for promotion to grade 12. The decision was taken by the school authorities that the boy should repeat Grade 11. Immediately, the class took the position that unless the boy was promoted along with everyone else, we would all boycott our promotion. The headmaster was in a quandary. What was he to do? Stick to the decision and face the possibility of not having a graduating class the following year? Or let the boy go through and see Menelik join the exclusive club of the three secondary schools in the Empire. He did not agonize over the decision. The boy who did not make the grade was promoted along with his friends.

I believe it was early during the first term of grade 12 that someone brought a copy of the brochure of the Ethiopian Students Association in North America. In it were pictures of college graduates who were coming back home. A few of us huddled around the publication and pored excitedly over the proud pictures of the graduates. To this day, I remember one picture, that of Fantaye Wolde-Yohannes, wearing a black bow tie and his trademark broad smile. The caption at the bottom of the picture said that he had obtained his Bachelor of Commerce degree from the University of Toronto. We wondered what position the government would offer him when he arrived. The post of Prime Minister? That did not look likely, we concluded, given that it was occupied by a leading aristocrat, although we had little doubt that Fantaye was more than qualified for the post. An ordinary ministerial post? No. Fantaye we thought was overqualified for that. We couldn't think of a suitable post and left the question unresolved.

Years later, I met Fantaye and told him the story. He broke into a hearty laugh and said to me, "You know what my first job was? Sacks of grain destined for export had been piling up at the harbour in Djibouti. Foreign buyers had complained that the contents showed an unusually high percentage of impurities and would not take them. I was given the responsibility to ensure that all necessary measures were taken to prevent another pile-up at the harbor." Had we Menelik boys been aware of this act of feudal insolence, we would probably have marched to the Emperor's palace in protest.

Undergraduate Days

June 1952 witnessed the first graduates of Menelik Secondary School. A year and half earlier, the government had established the University College of Addis Ababa. In September, practically all of Menelik's graduates were admitted to the College, joining the influx of freshmen from the three other secondary schools to make up some twenty per cent of the college population of ninety odd for that year. One or two of our classmates from Menelik were enrolled at the College of Technology which had opened a year earlier.

Getting into college is a high watershed in a young's man's career. At Menelik, my friends and I had looked up to the students of University College which was located adjacent to our school. We envied everything about them, especially their uniform: a navy blue blazer jacket (with matching grey pants) displaying the colourful coat of arms of the College affixed to the left breast pocket. On Saturdays and Sundays, the students strolled in the streets of the capital admired by passersby, especially by girls. Occasionally, friends at the College invited us to lunch, where the menu was incomparably superior to Menelik's. We longed to set foot on the campus.

Within a week of our admission in September 1952, we were issued with the distinctive uniforms and lost no time in showing them off on the first weekend. The College had a student recreation room with music, chess and checkerboards, and plenty of reading material. In a week or two, we heard talk of elections for the student union. Soon, campaigning started and the freshman class was surprised to be the focus of attention. How could we, so green and awestruck by the whole environment, be of any interest to our more experienced seniors? We soon realized that our importance lay in our numbers, our first object lesson in democracy. In high school, our prefects were appointees of the Director. Here we were going to elect our own leaders.

Candidates started lobbying, but very discretely. They talked to us as if we had been old pals. How were we adjusting to the college environment, the food, the classes, the dormitories? Every kind of question except their intentions to run for office was raised. Of course, the bulletin boards carried little else. Campaign slogans and candidates' exceptional suitability for this or that post were writ large. It was an unreal world far from the curious eyes of the government's intelligence agents who were aware that the College was one of the Emperor's prized projects. They could not afford to be too intrusive even if they were so inclined.

With an enrollment of some ninety students, life at University College was much more comfortable than at Menelik. The food was excellent and the physical facilities commodious. Initially accommodated in a large refurbished old building which provided space for classes, dormitories, dining room, labs, offices for faculty, as well as an auditorium, we soon moved to fresh new quarters where each student had his own private room furnished with a bed (including linen, pillows, and blankets), a desk, a cupboard, a bookshelf, a chair and reading lamp. Our rooms and toilets were cleaned every day by hired staff. Linens and clothes were washed and ironed weekly. The dining room, kitchen, and laundry were in a large brick building. A football field, a tennis court, an old cinema house converted into a basketball court which also served as a theatre were made ready in short order. A good variety of extracurricular activities was also available: a debating society, a drama club, a glee club, a photography club with dark room facilities, regular music appreciation sessions, and an ethnological society headed by the late Stanislaw Chojnacki, who was the Librarian and would later become curator of the University Museum and a leading authority on the history of Ethiopian art.

The College curriculum was a novel experience. After initial hesitations, I settled on a liberal arts education and was enrolled at the Faculty of Arts. Philosophy, English literature, sociology, education, economics, civil law, bookkeeping and statistics formed the backbone of the curriculum. We were largely new to most of these subjects. Three subjects were taught from the first to the fourth year in this Jesuit-run college: philosophy, English literature and bookkeeping. The first year of philosophy consisted of logic, the second of epistemology, the third ethics and the fourth of metaphysics. Marxism came in for a hard knock in the ethics course, while Christian doctrine was given a non-theological, rational underpinning, based on the teachings of St Thomas Aquinas, St Augustine and others. Philosophy was not exactly the most popular of subjects, but had to be endured. It wasn't a waste of time, however, as we acquired analytical skills in handling abstract ideas and in marshalling arguments during debates.

Hard going at first, English literature under the British lecturer Thomas Downs was to leave us with a lasting interest in the language. A freewheeling course labeled Survey of Europe given by Czeslaw Jessman, an exile from communist Poland, was a haphazard mélange of contemporary cultural, intellectual, and political trends. But it was at once an entertaining and highly educational exposé of issues. Jessman had a streak of the artist in him and managed to open our eyes to the beauty emanating from shapes and colours. Our campus was once visited by Ethiopian girls who had just returned from school in England. Who, he asked, was the most beautiful among them? None, we replied. Our traditional notion of beauty was obviously at variance with his. Another girl we drew his attention to as a fine specimen of beauty was brusquely dismissed by him. We for our part turned down the "beautiful" girl he chose for her singular lack of the waxen complexion and chiseled features of an Ethiopian belle.

The first group of girl students at the University College, Addis Ababa (1954), Woudnesh Amsalu (left) and Fiammetta Protta (right) are in front row, at back (left to right) are Almaz Eshete, Genet Awalom, and Azenegash

The famous Semitist Wolf Leslau conducted a short course in Ge'ez, enough to raise an awareness of this important heritage of ours, but otherwise unmemorable. A course in public administration and civil law was no more memorable. Economics was interesting, but not easy to grasp at that stage, partly because of the professor's difficulty with the English language (another stateless person from Poland) and in part because there was precious little in our lives that seemed to relate to what was being taught. A course in jurisprudence given by an amiable professor and former judge in pre-Communist Poland was equally uninteresting. There was a short course on public speaking which some of us enjoyed. The American textbook was easy to follow, was generously illustrated with photographs, and contained excerpts of famous speeches (Abraham Lincoln's Gettysburg address being one such). Above all there was no final exam.

A major event in the college social calendar was the twice yearly ball organized by the student body. Dancing lessons were given by the *avant guard* among the students. These were assiduously pursued and mastered in preparation for the event to which girls from the various schools were invited. One ball was given at Christmas and another at graduation in June. Relations between boys and girls in those days were very restrained; an obvious enough nuisance but a subject of intense preoccupation for that very reason. The dance events were much talked about both before and long after they took place. For many a student they provided an opportunity to translate or, more accurately, attempt to translate, youthful fantasies into ephemeral fragments of reality.

Graduation balls were more elaborately prepared than those for Christmas, and it quickly became a tradition for the junior class to take charge of all the arrangements for a roaring sendoff party for the graduating class. The Jesuit faculty members were uneasy about the growing importance of these events, but could hardly do anything, as the events were held off campus and as all expenses were met by the students themselves. But they soon found a pretext to poke their fingers.

After the spacious dining room was built on campus, the student union struck upon a brilliant idea. Why not hold the annual ball in this brand new hall? We would proudly show it off to the girls. More importantly we would save money, for we paid high fees to the hotels in town. The savings would go towards making the occasion more sumptuous. A formal letter was therefore prepared requesting use of the hall and addressed to the Dean of students, Guillaume Beland. A delegation was selected to hand deliver the letter.

Members of the Ethnological Society of University College, 1953, front row (from left) the author, Habte M. Markos, Hailu K., Mengesha G.H., Aklilu H., in the back Abraham D., Bekelle., Tashoma H.M., Kifle W., Yohannes W.G.

After studying it, the Dean summoned the delegation to his office and said that dances were "a Western, not an Ethiopian custom, and we believe that the Ethiopian Orthodox Church would not look kindly at such an event held within the precincts of the College." The students replied that this was his assumption and did not appear plausible to them, the followers of the Church. "I am not in a position to take chances with your Church and need to be authorized to allow you the use of the hall for your party." Authorization for such a small matter? "This is no small matter," he replied. There was no alternative but to get the consent of a Church authority.

The College had an Ethiopian Orthodox chaplain assigned by Archbishop Tewoflos, the Assistant to the Patriarch. The chaplain was asked to arrange an appointment with the Archbishop. Four officers of the student's union (including myself) subsequently proceeded to the Archbishop's residence in the premises of Trinity Cathedral. The prelate was somewhat surprised to see us, this being our first time to pay him a visit. Pleasantries were exchanged and tea was served. In about half an hour the subject was broached.

There was a moment of silence after one of us introduced the subject in the most general of terms, the Archbishop seemingly agreeing with the idea of a party. But how should the delicate subject of *dancing* with girls be mentioned? Soon someone said, "Your Holiness, but our *Catholic* professors do not seem to understand." He asked

Following the author's graduation from University College Addis Ababa in the summer of 1956, Balambaras Gedamu is on left and Ato Kebede Abozen at right

what the reason was. Another moment of silence ensued. "It is just that they say boys and girls should not be seen celebrating the event together in the College campus." "What girls are these?" asked the Archbishop. The slightest sign of nervousness or delay in responding to the question would put our project at risk. Someone had to be quick on his feet and provide a reassuring response with calm confidence. "Your Holiness," said one of us, "these are students from the various schools. We have done this several times before. We call it a dinner/ dance but it is all very innocuous. There are strong lights, our professors take part, and we occasionally move around to Western music, something akin to our own traditional dance at weddings."

His Holiness paused for a few unbearable moments and said: "If you clap your hands and the girls do the same at a distance, as in our weddings, that is fine." We had carried the conversation to its tolerable limits, keeping a firm lid on the mildly romantic details occurring during and after the dances. The Archbishop's response was good enough for our purpose. We thanked him for his understanding and took leave.

The Dean was duly informed that permission had been secured. "Where is the paper authorizing the College?" he asked. We told him that it would have been exceedingly discourteous to have asked His Holiness to give evidence of his consent in writing. He said he understood, but suggested that the remarks of His Holiness be put down in writing at the bottom of which all those who attended the Archbishop's meeting should affix their signatures. We had gone a long way and were not about to retreat. We agreed and subsequently handed him the signed note. He said he would get back to us in due course.

After a few days we were called to the Dean's office. "I have discussed the matter with the President and we are both of the view that this note falls short of what we require." We were astonished, murmured a few words and finally said, "In that event, we would like to get back the note we signed." "I understand your concern," he replied, took a folded piece of paper from his pocket and said it was the signed note. He told us he would dispose of it.

As we left we all asked the obvious question: was the folded note really the one we had signed? If so, why did he not show it to us? In any event, its disposal was our business, not his. Our suspicions grew as we looked at different aspects of the problem. Mischievous Jesuit, we all thought. What was he going to do with the signed note? Send it to the Archbishop for confirmation? What would happen then? We could be in trouble if the Archbishop were to say that the full details of the ball had not been revealed to him.

We had wasted a precious two weeks on a fruitless mission and had to hurry to find a hotel. A contentious issue in our time, this would be a routine matter years later, as many alumni (including the veterans of the skirmish with Dean Beland) would regularly be invited to graduation balls in that beautiful hall on campus. Apart from minor incidents of this nature, College life was generally agreeable. And it was at College that some of the most enduring personal friendships were forged.

Graduation was a happy event. Indeed four years in college had given us the curious feeling that the world of knowledge was at our feet, possibly because practically all of us were first degree earners in our respective families and additionally because we were graduating from the premier educational institution in the land. Though we were not aware at the time, our liberal arts education was neither liberal nor sufficiently educative. It was perhaps partly for this reason that everyone was sent overseas for further study. And soon, members of our graduating class started to make preparations for the travel. I recall someone asking me what I was looking for in my graduate studies overseas. I was unhesitating in my response: "Just the experience of being abroad, for I don't believe that there is all that more knowledge to acquire in my chosen field." And, of course, we all wanted to get back home at the earliest opportunity, and commence serving the nation.

Sipping rich café latte at the Trianon in the Piazza with my uncle Endale Biressaw, I told him that I was about to go abroad to pursue my graduate studies. Endale had single-mindedly seen to it that I would get the secular education he himself had been unfortunate to forego. The man to whom my education meant so much was now a little perplexed. "Isn't there an end to this education of yours?" he asked. And I, who in my youth and with equal single-mindedness, had done everything to show him that I was not meant for school nor school for me, was now calmly explaining that I only needed a short stay in the West to round off my long years of schooling.

Endale was not persuaded and, rather than going further into the question, leaned back and withdrew into a momentary introspection. I, in turn, was struck by this reversal of roles and likewise sank into my own inner thoughts. What a nice little puzzle life is, I thought to myself. After a few silent minutes, I repeated that I was more or less at the end of the road and my overseas stay would be short. He smiled and said "We should leave the question in the good hands of the Lord." We did our farewells, he back to Gore and I to the premises of the University College where the graduating class was lodged pending travel.

Preparations for the journey were completed and it was time to take leave of the Emperor. We were accompanied to the Palace by the Vice Minister of Education. The Emperor said a few words in which he underlined the need to complete our studies and come back to serve the country. He also said that it had been his wish that we would go overseas in 'better shape' but things had not worked out that way. He finally wished us a safe journey. This was the first time that I had the opportunity to spend any length of time with the Emperor. We were all impressed by his proverbial dignity. Everything about him was measured: his words, his unhurried gestures, the movements of his head and his eyes. In later years when I saw him often, I would see more of this: the way he walked, the subtle expression of incredulity on his face when he was doubtful of a minister's report, his guarded sentiments, and his utter imperturbability.

All who came into contact with him were struck by his distinctive royal bearing. Captain C. E. Morgan of H.M.S Entreprise was one of these. In 1936 the Emperor was on board a ship from Djibouti to Haifa on his way to the League of Nations in Geneva. "I have seldom been so impressed with any man, black or white," wrote Captain Morgan in a short note on the voyage. "His consideration, courtesy, and above all his dignity has left a very deep impression on every officer and man in my ship."[1] His appearance before the League would leave a much more powerful impression of serenity and dignity when heckled by Mussolini's hooligan journalists as he was about to make his historic plea for assistance to his country.

After a brief twenty minutes or so of our farewell audience with the Emperor, we took leave. We wondered what the Emperor meant when he said that he would have liked to see us depart in 'better shape.' We were not an impressive looking lot physically; being thin, short, and appearing younger than our years. That probably was what the Emperor had in mind. We would confirm this to ourselves later.

Graduate Studies in the United States

The professor of economics at the University College of Addis Ababa had instilled in us a degree of interest in the dismal science, notwithstanding the difficulties we had in coming to grips with some of the basic concepts. He believed that economics, and particularly agricultural economics, was of particular relevance to a country like Ethiopia and advised that we pursue our graduate studies in one of the land grant universities of the U.S. Following his advice, two of his students from the graduating class, the late Mezmur Yiheyis and I, applied and were accepted by the University of Illinois.

We left Addis in August 1956. Our first exposure to the great cities of the West was not as mesmerizing as we had imagined. The streets were covered with tarmac, just as in Addis. Buses looked more or less the same, though cleaner and in larger numbers. London's double-decker buses naturally caught our fancy, but we remarked that these were an unnecessary exception to the norm. There were many bars and restaurants, but we had a few of our own too back home. The Paris Metro was the first thing we wanted to see when we arrived in the city. We quickly spotted a station, climbed downstairs, paid our fares and saw a train pull out of a dark tunnel. We boarded it, took a short ride and resurfaced after a few minutes. There was nothing extraordinary to talk about or send postcards to our friends. Nothing we saw matched the improbable expectations we had conjured up in our minds.

It would take some pretty mundane things for the differences between Ethiopia and the West to sink in. After arrival in Washington D.C. on a weekend, a friend of ours proceeded to the hotel gift shop and asked the salesperson for a newspaper. "Go pick it up from there," said she, pointing to a three-foot high pile of newspapers. The young man carefully removed the outer sheet from the fat Sunday issue of the paper at the top of the pile, and came to the desk to pay. "What are you doing, take the whole stuff," said the girl. It took our friend a while to realize that all the inside pages formed part of the day's issue. "Newspapers are dirt cheap in this country, aren't they" he remarked with amazement. Addis newspapers usually did not go beyond one sheet (four-pages), Sunday issues or not.

On a different occasion, another friend approached a milk machine in a cafeteria and asked the man behind the counter what he should do to get a glass of milk. "Take this glass, press that red button and you'll get your milk" was the laconic reply. Our friend did precisely as he was told: he took the glass, pressed the red button, and saw the milk poosh-sh-sh-ing down the drain. It took him a few seconds to realize that he should have first placed his glass under the milk fountain. (The man behind the counter had not said anything about precisely where the glass should be placed or how and when the machine should be operated). Our bemused friend quickly placed his glass under the fountain as the milk was pouring out. But he only managed to get it one third filled. He wasn't going to be shortchanged, and so pressed the red button once again. Poosh-sh-sh came down the milk, overfilled the glass, and was again going down the drain. The man behind the counter shook his head in amazement. The machine, once its red button was pressed, would of course pour out exactly one glass of milk, no more, no less. An empty glass, not one which was a third full, had to be placed below the faucet prior to pressing the red button.[2]

Over the next few days, incidents of this kind multiplied. Someone would see an escalator moving downwards and, improbably thinking that it might somehow reverse course and take him upstairs, would try to climb only to be thrown back, suitcase and all. Another would get into an elevator and in a moment of confusion be attracted by an eye-catching red button. He would press it and get everyone rushing down the fire escape. It was thanks to these and similarly amusing incidents that we began to understand that things were really different in the West, and disabuse ourselves of the notion buried deep in our minds that we hailed from a country with few peers in God's universe; a sentiment in full consonance with the image of Ethiopia depicted in the *Kebre Negest.*

Prior to leaving Addis, we had all been forewarned of racial discrimination in the West. During our trip, we were particularly on the lookout for this novel challenge, wondering how it might surface and how we might react. My friend Mezmur and I went to a crowded restaurant one evening during our stopover in Rome. We were seated and ordered dinner. A while later, we looked at our watches and noted that ten long minutes had passed. We called the waiter and asked what had happened to our order. He said the food would be coming soon. A few more minutes passed, and both Mezmur and I solemnly concluded that we were experiencing our first case of racial discrimination, got up and started to walk towards the door. The maitre d'hôtel rushed towards us and asked if something was amiss. "We know exactly what is going on in this restaurant, and will never come back again," we said. And out we walked, leaving the bewildered soul to figure out for himself what was amiss. In the U.S. we would find out that one didn't have to strain one's imagination to see the disagreeable face of Jim Crow.

After touching base with the educational attaché at the Ethiopian Embassy in Washington D.C. and being registered as new arrivals on government fellowship, Mezmur and I flew to the University of Illinois at Urbana-Champaign. The University Y.M.C.A. had sent us a letter prior to our departure that they would offer temporary accommodation and that we should contact them upon arrival. We had responded and informed them of our flight particulars. The first person to meet us at the airport was a young YMCA volunteer. He picked up my suitcase and that of my friend as if they were stuffed with feathers and briskly walked to the waiting bus. I asked him how far he was in his university education. He said he was only fourteen and was still in high school. What the Emperor said to us at our farewell now made sense. No Ethiopian fourteen-year old who walked the face of the land could scarcely look so husky and self assured.

The University of Illinois was a huge institution with an enrollment of some 30,000 students. We felt as lonely as a Gambela stranger in the midst of a busy day in Addis's bustling Merkato, the largest open air market in Africa. After a few days at the YMCA, we found our bearings, rented a basement room and moved out. We completed registration formalities and started classes. Our advisors indicated which courses were mandatory, what our majors and minors might be, and the normal load for a semester. A couple of courses in economic theory were mandatory and would soon become a major headache.

We had, of course, taken economics at University College and done some work on economic theory. Apart from the appellation, however, there was little resemblance between the courses we took at the College and those that confronted us at the University of Illinois. We worked hard, often staying up until well past midnight. We absorbed the essential reading materials and most of the optional ones. But we weren't making much headway. Mid-term exams came and our worst fears crashed upon our heads like a ton of bricks.

Our generation of students was secretive about grades, especially if they were bad. With some trepidation, my friend Mezmur and I had left pre-paid self-addressed post cards at the offices of our professors to be sent back with our grades. Mezmur and I opened our common mailbox a few days after the end of mid-term exams and found the anxiously awaited cards. There was no way of keeping our respective results away from each other's eyes. They were there for the whole world to see. Our grades on economic theory left both Mezmur and I feeling as if we were hanging to dear life on the edge of a precipice.

My thoughts went back to the time when I was preparing to leave Addis for Illinois and to the response I gave a friend when asked about my expectation of graduate studies in the U.S. The words of my response rang in my ears. "I am going abroad just for the experience, for I don't believe that there is all that more knowledge to acquire in my chosen field." I don't know what was going on in my friend Mezmur's mind as he pored over his card, but I felt that we should move fast. I told him that we should waste no time in seeing the professor of the course, Flanders, and say that we had never been bad students, that we were graduates of the University College of Addis Ababa where economic theory was taught, and that we just could not understand the terrible results. He owed us an explanation as to how he had arrived at the absurd grades!

We presented ourselves at Professor Flanders's office and told him the reason why we had wanted to see him. A salvo of questions was launched by the intimidating professor: a graduate of Yale wearing his scholastic honour key dangling from a golden chain across the vest of his three-piece suit. What was our country of origin, the college we had graduated from, and the courses we had taken in economics? What kind of professors had been teaching us, what textbooks had we used, how many hours a day were we putting into our studies now, etc.? We had poor grades because, and he took a pause here, "because your answers to the questions were wrong for the most part. Work harder, that is all I can say to you for now," he said unhelpfully.

I went straight back to my advisor and told him the problem I was having with Professor Flanders's course. He suggested that I take additional classes in economic theory and mathematics at the undergraduate level. I followed his advice in the next semester. That mercifully put an end to my misery. The University College of Addis Ababa was a fledgling institution and the students of the first decade or so were guinea pigs for an evolving curriculum. No wonder we were having difficulty in the first year of graduate school.

At our first Christmas break, I and half a dozen friends attending universities in neighbouring states organized a get together in Chicago. One thing that clearly came out when we exchanged notes about our academic experience was the initial shock of poor grades. Adjustment to a new environment was obviously one reason. But the inadequacy of our undergraduate education was the main one. After the initial shock, we adapted quickly and stopped worrying about grades any more.

Social life was an altogether different kettle of fish. The twin University towns, Urbana and Champaign, were not exactly the epicenters of America's cultural life. The townspeople were provincial in outlook, as were the students who were mostly from Illinois and the Midwest. Some would ask where we were from and when told, would wonder in which part of Europe or the U.S. Ethiopia was located. For the most part, they kept to themselves and were not particularly friendly. This brought students from the developing world closer together.

Accommodation was a principal preoccupation. Landlords discriminated against African and Asian students. Mezmur and I were looking for a place to stay at the beginning of our second year. We went to the University Y.M.C.A where information on rental accommodation was posted on the bulletin board and came across an advertisement for two rooms in a house close by. We asked Mr. Price, the genial Secretary of the 'Y', to telephone the landlady on our behalf. He telephoned and told her that two graduate students were interested in what she had advertised. "Where are they from," she asked? When told that we were from Ethiopia, she wondered where it was located and what we looked like. "Ethiopia is in East Africa and I would say that these guys look like Indians," he replied. "Send them over," she said.

Mr. Price gave us an escort and we arrived at the landlady's house in about five minutes. The escort, a Czech student, rang the doorbell. A bespectacled, grizzled, wiry, old creature answered the bell and when told that Mezmur and I were the two students about whom Price had called, she said, "I am so sorry but the rooms have been taken already." "How come? " asked Mezmur and I in unison, reminding her that she had said the rooms were available only five minutes earlier. "Yes, but they were rented out soon after Mr. Price called," she replied and slammed the door in our face. Quite a different kettle of fish from what had confronted us in that Rome restaurant, we both recalled. To the fading eyes of the gray old lady, we probably didn't look sufficiently Indian. Or perhaps she had never seen Indians from the Asian subcontinent and expected people that looked like native Americans.

There were frequent irritants of this nature. No barber could be found within walking distance, all the barbers (white) on campus saying they didn't have the skill to handle our type of hair. Rare were our classmates, male or female, who socialized with African or Asian students. Even among the professors, there were some who were visibly biased against our group. It must be remembered that this was a period of considerable racial tension in the United States, especially in the South where political resistance was being vigorously expressed against court rulings outlawing racial segregation in educational establishments and public facilities. In 1957 Arkansaw Governor Orville Faubus had called out the state National Guard to bar admission of African American students to the all white Little Rock High School, in flagrant defiance of the Supreme Court ruling banning school segregation three years earlier. To most foreign students with little understanding of U.S. history, the Governor's defiance appeared incomprehensible and detestable in equal measure. While President Eisenhower's robust decision to send 1000 soldiers to protect the African American students was obviously welcomed, it did leave a bitter after taste about a country which professed freedom and equality for its citizens but which was a long way from practicing what it preached. We detested life at Urbana-Champaign and eagerly looked towards the day when we would finally leave behind the disagreeable place and its no less disagreeable people.

Some students and nearby families went out of their way to make up for the bigotry of their compatriots. Families often invited us to their homes on Thanksgiving and Christmas. American students who had been on overseas trips joined us for lunch or dinner at the Union cafeteria and asked about our countries and cultures. We often felt sorry for these well-meaning folks, for we believed that their compatriots had placed too heavy a burden on their shoulders. None of the gestures of friendship could remove our strong and growing resentment of America and the hollow ring of the lofty phrases of the Declaration of Independence. Many of us vowed we would never ever step on the shores of the U.S., once we were through with our studies.

How distant these sentiments and how different the place looks half a century later. To be sure, the U. S. today is by no means a post racial society. Bigotry, especially by poorly educated blue collar whites, racial profiling, post 9/11 xenophobia and unequal employment opportunities still haunt minority communities. And ignorant white supremacists still dot the heartland of conservative America. But there is little doubt that the social, economic, and political situation of minorities has undergone remarkable change.

Corporate America has opened its doors to a good number of African-Americans, Asian Americans and Latinos. Ivy League universities have minority professors and officials. Massachusetts, the seat of the most prestigious of these, has an African-American as its Governor. An Asian American is Governor of Louisiana. Another Asian-American (a female) has just been elected Governor of South Carolina. The Supreme Court has an African American, and three women one of whom is a Latina. An African American has served as Chairman of the Joint Chiefs of Staff. For eight consecutive years, the U.S. was served by two African Americans as Secretaries of State. And the most improbable story of all: a non-white American now occupies the White House for the first time in the nation's history. The ringing words of the Declaration of Independence which sounded so hollow to our ears in the mid fifties now resonate with audible credibility.

Had these occurred during those grim days in Illinois, the lives of foreign students would have been far more lively and discussions about America as a democracy and as a land of opportunity far less scathing. Under the circumstances, we had to take refuge in the generous programme of extracurricular activities in our free time. One had to be selective, and students from the developing countries especially so, given our desire to get the most out of our stay in the country. We pored over bulletin boards for distinguished guest speakers on economics and public policy and listened to their talks with rapt attention: C. Wright Mills of Columbia University, Theodore Schultz of the University of Chicago, Robert Oppenheimer of Princeton, and E. Dubois, the civil rights leader. We attended performances by celebrities in the entertainment world like Marianne Anderson and Louis Armstrong, or frequented concerts, film shows, major debates, or anything of educational value organized by the university. These assuaged social and intelectual pains.

Many were also avid followers of the classic television interviews by Edward Morrow of CBS who later became President Kennedy's Director of the United States Information Agency. His guest list bristled with guiding lights like as Jawahalral Nehru, Clement Attlee, Aneurin Bevan, Edward Teller, Frank Lloyd Wright, Buckminster Fuller, Malcolm Muggeridge, Leonard Bernstein, Ludwig Erhard, post-war Germany's economics Minister and architect of its economic miracle, and many others. When such programmes were aired, foreign students were attracted in large numbers. There would be trouble if another channel showed a football or a basketball match, very low on our list of priorities but a must watch for American students. Being the majority, the Americans would often have their way.

Sports programmes were regarded as a waste of time by most foreign students who believed they had come to the U.S. to study and not to fritter away time. In any event there were not too many temptations on programmes offered on TV. Basketball was familiar but not baseball or American football, the most spectacular of all games. To the uninitiated fhe goal of football seemed to be a frequent pile up of husky individuals until an umpire would come to the rescue of the poor man with the ball at the bottom of the pile. Hardly a minute passed after the pile was dispersed for a resumption of the game when yet one more pile would take shape, the team trying to recover the ball savagely attacking all those on the other side, not just the man with the ball. In our eyes, there did not appear to be any rhyme or rhythm to the spectacle. Didn't the umpires (and there were more than half a dozen !) have nothing better to do than to wait for the interminable piles to form and suddenly scurry around to rescue the poor fellow with the ball from being smothered to death? To us foreign students, the blessed of the earth watched soccer, a game practically unknown then to most college students.

One Saturday evening, my friend Mezmur and I were coming back from the library when we met a group of intoxicated students zigzagging back to their dorms. We were about to pass them when the young man in the lead stopped us with the words "wasn't Abe just great today?" We did not know who he was talking about and said so. "Holy cow! You say you don't know Abe? Abe Woodson? And you go to school here?" Our bewildered look moved his friends to say that he should have pity on the poor creatures from outer space and leave them in peace. We went home wondering who Abe Woodson was. When we opened the morning papers the following day, we saw an extensive coverage of the previous day's football match against a rival team in which a six-foot 200 lb giant of a man playing for the fighting Illini (as the University football team was affectionately known) had been the principal scorer who helped his team win the game. It was he who was Abe Woodson.

There were other areas of interest outside extracurricular activities which we pursued. I followed a correspondence course on music appreciation, subscribed to two British journals, *The Economist* and *The New Statesman & Nation,* and managed to obtain a fellowship at Harvard one summer. Mezmur found a summer job at the U.N. as an intern. And we made it a habit to go through the major American papers: *The New York Times, The New York Herald Tribune, The St. Louis Post Dispatch, The Chicago Tribune*; and magazines: *The New Republic, The Nation, Time* and *Newsweek* as part of our effort to make the most of our education.

In the periodicals section of the library one day, I stumbled upon *Monthly Review,* the Marxist journal. Back in my University College days, Marxism had been portrayed as an egregious moral evil of our time. The articles in *Monthly Review* rehabilitated Marx's image in my mind and made his writings appear relevant to the problems of the developing world. After going through the current issue, I got interested and started reading the older ones. I could not stop until I reached volume 1 number 1, the initial issue which came out in 1947. Albert Einstein had contributed an article. Going back that far meant reading more than one hundred issues of at least 80-90 pages each. It was an exhilarating experience. Thenceforth, I was hooked to *MR.*

Two years into my three-year stay at Illinois, I obtained my Master's degree in agricultural economics and was awarded a fellowship from the University to work for a PhD. I had benefited from the courses on economics, had been to summer school at Harvard in 1957 where I had done more work on economics, had taken advantage of Illinois' extra-curricular activities, and had done a good bit of extra reading and study on my own. Despite the fellowship, I became skeptical of working towards a higher degree without the benefit of some real life experience. I preferred to spend some time as a practicing economist and come back to work for a higher degree, fortified with an exposure to the practical problems an economist faces working in a developing country environment. I consequently decided to discontinue the PhD programme a year into my fellowship.

A few months prior to that, one of my professors (Stewart) called me to his office and showed me a letter he had received from the United Nations Secretariat in New York. He had been asked to recommend African economics students at the University who might be interested in a U.N. career. Would I be interested, he asked? My knowledge of the U.N. was scant. Nothing that I knew suggested that it engaged in economics work. Though the professor corrected my impression, working for the organization appeared to be totally outside my calling.

From the very beginning of my education, serving my country had been an abiding goal. While young, I had often heard my father and his friends talk of the day when they would make way for educated people to take over the affairs of government. While at the University College of Addis Ababa, faculty members as well as the Emperor had spoken to us about our responsibilities to serve our people. A favourite question of the Emperor in the course of his frequent visits was: "In what area of study would you like to get your diploma and serve your country?" A student once replied that he wanted to get a degree in business administration. "Egoist" was the dismissive imperial remark. The Emperor preferred fields like medicine, engineering, law, or mathematics. I had no doubt that economics was among the Emperor's short list of key subjects for the country's development. I therefore told Professor Stewart that I wasn't interested in a U.N. job. My wish was to go back home at the earliest opportunity and serve my country.

Stewart said I should not dismiss what looked like an attractive opportunity and said he saw no harm in forwarding my name to the organization. I could always turn down a job offer if I was not interested. Besides, he said to me, working for the U.N. was in some ways like working for your country, although indirectly. I did not find that line of reasoning persuasive, but agreed that he could propose my name as there was no commitment involved. For me that put an end to the matter.

Late in the winter of 1958, I was surprised to receive a letter from the personnel department of the U.N. in New York signed by a certain Mrs. Muller, saying that Professor Stewart had recommended my name. Could I get in touch with her a couple of months before completing my studies? I wondered if I had half-committed myself, despite Stewart's assurances. Reflecting on the issue again, I came around to Professor Stewart's idea. I would in any event have to go through New York on the way back to Ethiopia and saw no great inconvenience in spending an additional couple of days to touch base with the organization. I replied saying I would complete my programme of studies in June and would pass through New York in the middle of the month.

I wrote a letter to the Ethiopian Educational Attaché in Washington D.C. informing him that I would be returning home in June and wanted him to arrange for the shipment of my books and personal effects, send me an air ticket to Addis Ababa, as well as the pocket money to cover the journey's expenses. The air ticket and a check for $100 for the travel expenses arrived duly. I shipped my belongings and left Urbana-Champaign for New York in the second week of June 1959. My friend of University College days, Mulugeta Wodajo, was at Columbia and lived in a nearby apartment in Morningside Heights. I planned to stay with him for a few days.

A day or two after arriving in New York, I took a bus to U.N. Headquarters on First Avenue and 42nd Street in Manhattan. When I got there, I saw a long queue of people and asked the security officer what special programme was on. He said people were lined up for the regular tour of the Headquarters building. He guided me to the staff entrance to contact Muller. An air of curiosity mixed with mild condescension was evident on the face of the security officer who met me at the staff entrance. I must have looked a little odd, as I was in brown sandals with orange socks attracting everyone's attention. I was short and slight, my oversized brown Dacron summer suit serving as a weather vane to all curious passersby. The officer picked up the phone, located Muller and said, "There is a young fella down here who is look'n for a jab. He says he wants ta see ya." A few minutes passed while the bewildered lady tried to figure out why a young job seeker would wish to go up to the 26th floor to see her personally. The officer interrupted the conversation to put a few questions to me. I told him about the exchange of letters and showed him a copy of Muller's letter. The lady remembered and told the security officer to let me in.

Madame Muller asked how long I could stay in New York and quickly put together a panel to interview me when I informed her I only had four or five days. I can only recall the last of the series of questions put to me by the panel. If you were to pass the interview, were to become an international civil servant, who would you designate as a beneficiary for your life insurance, asked a member of the panel. Never had the subject crossed my mind. I reflected for a few moments and said 'the Ethiopian government'. The panel was not sure that I had understood the question, and repeated it. I too repeated my response. Seeing their puzzled faces, I explained that the Ethiopian government had financed my education and that I wanted to give back something in return. Perhaps the money could finance the education of another Ethiopian. This left a distinctly favourable impression on the panel, and a correspondingly positive impression on me about the probabale outcome of the interview.

Three days went by before I heard from Muller. On the fourth day she called to say that I had passed the interview and would be employed at the P1, Step 1 level, the very first entry level for professionals. I was told to report for duty at U.N. Headquarters on the 24th of June 1959. With subdued excitement, I informed my friends that I had become an international civil servant.

CHAPTER 3

Early Career and a Surprise Coup D'État

New York: Learning the Ropes

The Industrial Development Branch of the Department of Social and Economic Affairs was where I was posted when I reported for duty at the U. N. on 24 June. Didn't the personnel office see from my file that I had obtained a degree in agricultural economics, I wondered. My first assignment in the department made me wonder even more: I was asked to write a paper not, as one might expect, on some aspect of industrial development but on the transport sector in the West African region.

My supervisor was an unusually cheerful Swedish economist who quickly understood my predicament. He advised how I could handle the unfamiliar subject and what publications to consult. I should feel free to talk to him at any time, he added thoughtfully. The paper was finished in due course, read by him, suggestions made for improvements, and a revised draft submitted. I was later assigned to write another paper, having been told nothing about what had become of the first. I sensed that I was on a trial run and refrained from asking about the fate of the first paper or the purpose of the second.

In those days it was the U.N., not the World Bank or the IMF, that was at the frontiers of development economics. Economists like Arthur Lewis (who was later awarded the Nobel Prize), Nicholas Kaldor, Hans Singer, to mention only those I saw and briefly came in contact with, were brought in as short-term consultants. They often gave talks or seminars on subjects they were asked to study. Young economists read their final reports eagerly. The level of professional motivation among U.N. staff was high and there were several other occasions to meet informally to discuss issues and improve one's analytical tools. Econometrics was one instance of this. An able and helpful Dutch economist named Martin Ekker was in charge of a staff initiative in which half-hour sessions were held during lunch breaks. There was a genuine intellectual ferment on development economics. In sharp contrast to today's Afro-pessimism, the mood was upbeat about development prospects for Africa; and, needless to say, for Asia and Latin America as well.

I had rented a new apartment with my friend Mulugeta Wodajo in Morningside Heights, upper Manhattan. Slowly, I got used to the incessant noise and frantic pace of New York City, although it quickly became clear that I would not enjoy living there. New York was America's cultural capital, and working at the U.N. made it easy to get access to various events. Opera and concert tickets were readily available at Headquarters. This was a welcome opportunity to resume the interest in Western music I had developed while in Illinois. I made it a point to see performances at the New York Philharmonic and the Metropolitan Opera Theatre.

Aida, the story of an Abyssinian Princes captured in a war between her country and Egypt of the Pharoes, was the first opera I saw on stage. I could only afford the less expensive tickets (in the $5.00 to $10.00 range) which meant sitting high up in the back gallery of the theatre hall. The richness of the costumes, the subtleties of colour, and the expressions on the faces of the performers did not come out in full at that distance, unless one used binoculars as few in the audience did. But the spectacle and the *arias* lifted one's spirits, even those of a relative novice like me. During the intermission, I descended to the reception area on the mezzanine floor and saw another spectacle: women in glittering jewelry and shimmering evening dresses and men in black ties sipping Champagne or wine from crystal glasses. It did not take me long to realize that a poorly clad, green international civil servant from the Third World was sorely out of place. I quickly climbed back upstairs to scrutinize the evening's printed programme a safe distance from the sumptuous commotion below.

New York's nightlife was fabulous. Apart from perhaps half a dozen sorties to nightclubs, I on the whole kept away from that side of the city's cultural life. I never took to the noise, the smoke, the drinks, and the congestion at the clubs and have more or less remained that way. There was no shortage of other distractions, however. New York and the U.N. in the late fifties and early sixties were magnets to the emerging political leaders of Africa. The drama of decolonization was unfolding and leaders of the various liberation movements made their world debuts at the U.N., at the Universities in the city, and in places like Carnegie Hall. For me and other young Africans, New York was a thrill.

In Carnegie Hall one evening I listened to the fiery Dr. Hastings Banda of Nyasaland (Malawi) rousing the crowd ("I am the extremist of all the extremists"). I also saw Guinea's Sekou Toure, who seemed to embody the then prevailing image of an Africa unbound, ready at last to release its long repressed energies as it entered a new era of political emancipation, equality, and prosperity.[1] Crown Prince Asfa Wossen of Ethiopia also came to the UN in the course of a low profile visit to the U.S. Haddis Alemayehu, Ethiopia's Ambassador to the U.N., hosted a cocktail in his honour at the delegates' lounge where we had a glimpse of an Emperor in waiting. Working

Haddis Alemayehu and UN Secretary General Dag Hammarskjold (obtained from UN Photo Library)

at the U.N. as staff members were a number of Africans who would subsequently rise to prominence in their respective countries. Among these was Edouardo Mondlaine of Mozambique who years later became the first leader of FRELIMO. He was assassinated by a parcel bomb during a visit to Dar es Salaam. J.H. Mensah of Ghana was another. When Busia became Prime Minister, Mensah joined his cabinet as Minister of Finance. And when Jerry Rawlings usurped power, Mensah found himself behind bars. He had apparently ruffled the feathers of the ruffian military leader with a scathing tract.

African staff at the U.N. closely followed the speeches of the more prominent Ambassadors of the Third World and of Eastern Europe. Krishna Menon of India was a veritable star. He had lived in England for years and had mastered the language. We took delight in his debating skills, his charm, and his cultivated irreverence. Speeches by the Soviet and East European Ambassadors were scrutinized for their vignettes on the weaknesses of capitalism and the glories of socialism. For many years, Saudi Arabia was represented not by her own citizen but by a Lebanese man who had connections with King Feisal. Educated at the American University in Beirut where he reportedly met members of the royal house of Saud, he was a resident of New York, his family was half Christian half Moslem, and he was married to an American. A colorful and acerbic critic of the West and occasionally of the East, he was popular among young Third World employees at the U.N. To Western diplomats he was an unpredictable clown. George Bush who served as U.S. representative to the U.N. once referred to him as an unguided missile. Haddis Alemayehu, a resistance fighter at the beginning of the Italo-Ethiopian war and prisoner of War for seven years in Italy, was in many ways a self-made man. His statements were ponderous, restrained, and balanced. They drew the admiration of young Ethiopians and their African friends.

Dag Hammarskjold of Sweden was Secretary General when I worked at the U.N. Staff in my position did not, of course, have the opportunity to see him at work in the Secretariat building. The first time I met him was on UN Day, October 24, 1959. Each year, a special programme was organized on that day to commemorate the establishment of the organization. This included a concert in the General Assembly Hall. At about four o'clock in the afternoon, a reception for staff was given in the gardens of the Headquarters building. On that day in 1959, I was with a group from my department sipping Coke and listening to the more senior staff talk about similar occasions in the past. All of a sudden someone appeared from behind. He extended his right hand and said, "Hello, I am Dag Hammarskjold." We quickly brought out our hands in response. I was surprised that he was not as tall as his photographs or as my own stereotype notion of a Swede suggested. Despite his outward courtesies, Hammarskjold was known as an autocrat in his management style and was regarded with considerable deference.

One morning, I was walking towards one of the dozen or so elevators to go to my office on the 26th floor when a security officer gently signaled that I take the next elevator that was about to arrive. I ignored him and walked to the elevator door that was open. As I was about to enter, I saw Hammarskjold approaching. It dawned on me then that the security officer was trying to reserve the elevator to take the Secretary General non-stop to his office on the 37th floor. I stepped back and allowed Mr. Hammarskjold to go in. He beckoned that I enter. I politely declined the invitation, bowed à l'Ethiopienne, and proceeded to the elevator suggested by the security officer.

New York overflowed with progressive periodicals. I scoured the bookshops and newsstands for coverage of political events of the developing countries. I eagerly went through every issue of Monthly Review. One Saturday morning, I decided to visit the offices of the journal in lower Manhattan with the view to meeting the editors, Leo Huberman and economist Paul Sweezy. I found Huberman in a dingy office and exchanged a few words with him. Afterwards, I became an even more avid reader of MR and the left wing books advertised in it. Incisive articles were written on Castro's victory, China's Cultural Revolution, the wondrous performance of the economies of East European countries, the iniquities and inefficiencies of the capitalist world, and the unrivalled supremacy of central planning over free market economies. The July/August 1960 issue of the magazine was entirely devoted to the Cuban revolution and predicted that great prospects awaited Cuba, indeed the world.

"It is almost impossible to imagine a revolution with better prospects of success than the Cuban Revolution," said the magazine in its concluding section of that special edition. " The Cuban Revolution marches on, gaining strength and self confidence as it proceeds, inspiring the young and the oppressed everywhere by its magnificent example, helping to blaze a new trail for humanity to a brighter socialist revolution."[2] Mao's Cultural Revolution was similarly treated in another issue. There were other like-minded publications, too many to recall now, which preached the Socialist gospel. Many Ethiopians of my background and generation (and doubtless many Africans as well) fell easy prey to this captivating vision of a new, more egalitarian, democratic, and just world. A truly new Jerusalem, especially for Ethiopians to whom that phrase struck a powerfully emotive chord. We were convinced that African countries badly needed a genuinely radical socialist transformation.

Antipathy to the West was common among the young of the developing world. In graduate school, I had a Venezuelan friend who was critical of the U. S. imposed two-party system in his country which, so he said, only resulted in like-minded conservative people conveniently grouped into two seemingly opposing parties, but which in reality promoted capitalism. Mexico was even worse. It had only one supposedly revolutionary party under the hegemony of a capitalist neighbour. He taught me two lines in Spanish about Mexico which he insisted I should commit to memory. Not until I had mastered the pronunciation of each word would he reveal their meaning. And the lines were:

Pobre Mexico, tan lejos de Dios,
Y tan cerca de los Estados Unidos.

When I had advanced to the stage where I was pronouncing the words to his satisfaction, he unveiled their meaning: *Poor Mexico, so far from God; And so close to the United States.* He said the poem was by a celebrated Mexican Communist poet, although Mexican President Profirio Diaz (1830-1915) is generally credited with the saying.

A year and a couple of months had passed since I started work at the U.N. The Personnel Section informed me one day that it was time for me to go to the Economic Commission for Africa in Addis Ababa. I tried to extend my stay a little longer as I was beginning to learn much from my work at the U.N. as well as my exposure to the cultural life of New York City. However, I was told that the Executive Secretary of the Commission, the Sudanese Mekki Abbas, was eager to have a full complement of staff for his new organization. Initially, I had been told that I would stay for six months. This had been extended once and there was no more justification for a further extension. Indeed, an effort was under way to persuade other African staff at Headquarters to join Abbas in Addis Ababa. It was clear that I had to leave early and did so after an extra month or two.

Addis Ababa: The First Few Months

I arrived in Addis Ababa in August 1960, four years almost to the day of my first trip to the U.S. A day or so later, I went to Abbas's office for a courtesy call. Abbas had served as the first Sudanese General Manager of the Gezzira cotton plantation in his country, mentioned in some circles as a model project of its kind in the developing world. He had been appointed Executive Secretary of the Economic Commission for Africa largely on that account. "It was difficult for you, wasn't it, to get away from the lights of New York City," he bantered. I wasn't sure if the remark was offered in jest or if it was meant as a mild reprimand by a boss I was seeing for the first time. His demeanour was a shade authoritarian, even feudal. I replied that I had always meant to come to Addis, but felt a few more months of experience at the U.N. would be helpful for my job at the ECA.

Next I went to the office of the Deputy Executive Secretary, R.K.A. Gardiner of Ghana. It was said that he had been the earliest African employee at the United Nations in New York (he had worked there in 1948), had gone back to his country at independence, and had finally been selected as Abbas's deputy. Gardiner was a soft-spoken, self-effacing, articulate father figure. "I know that people of your generation have strong republican sentiments, but I would suggest that you go and pay your respects to your Emperor," he advised. Indeed, the Minister of Education accompanied returning graduates to the Palace, with the Emperor usually posing questions about the diplomas earned and the potential postings. As I was already employed by the U.N., I did not wish to provoke awkward questions about why I had avoided government service.

Instead of seeking a Palace appointment, I started making preparations to visit my grandmother. While in the U.S., I had always worried that I might not find her alive upon my return; for when I left in 1956 she was already in her nineties. Upon my arrival, I was relieved to learn that she was alive and was in fairly good condition for her age. I took a week's leave of absence and flew to Gore to see her. She was happy to see me and happier still to find that my secular education she had initially deplored had finally done me some good. In her eyes, it had calmed me down and, contrary to the arrogance typical of most of our church-educated men (so she said), the Western system had turned me into a modest soul, thank God. So it wasn't all that bad after all. I was of course delighted to hear that and happy to see her. She was in good spirits and looked well.

Was I married? she asked. I replied in the affirmative, though I had seventeen years to go before finally settling down. But I could not resist the temptation of having a little fun with her. "Whose daughter is she?" she continued. "How could you possibly know the parents of all the eligible girls," I responded. "Don't you worry about that, just give me some details about her family and what part of the country they are from, and I shall tell you whether you have landed on the right girl". "You wouldn't be able to tell in any event, mama, because she is a white girl from America". "Well, well, well! There you go again with your old mischievous ways. You haven't changed after all, have you?"[3] Seeing that she was upset, I told her I was just joking, only to discover that I was making matters worse; for she collected herself and asked imperiously: "Since when have you and I started trading jokes?" She was, of course, right, as I had never ever had the temerity to trade pleasantries with her. A few years in America had dimmed my recollection of a deeply revered and awesome personality.

The question of my marriage resurfaced a couple of days later. My maternal uncle, Endale Biressaw, asked me for lunch one day and raised the subject. His wife was sitting with us, an unusual thing for her to do so soon after serving lunch. She would, like most wives of the day, occupy herself with providing lunch for others in the household and would re-appear only for coffee. With his wife beside him, my uncle asked if I should not now settle down with a suitable wife. He seemed to have something up his sleeve. I put on a serious air and said that it was the obvious thing to do, but that I needed time. "Time to do what?" he asked. I had just arrived, was still staying at a hotel, and should find accommodation. "But that should not take time," was Endale's swift remark. I went on to say that a few things went along with renting a house: furnishing it, getting the right kind of domestic help, and perhaps saving some money. He would not be persuaded. And then bang! "All that is secondary," he said. "The main thing is to find the right girl. And we have found you one! The father, the Governor General of the province whom you called upon yesterday, has been approached and he is delighted with the idea. We shall take care of the wedding expenses, and there is nothing to worry about on that score."

I was left speechless and did not know what to say for a few moments. It had been suggested that I visit the Governor General as a matter of courtesy only. I now saw that it went beyond that. I pulled my thoughts together and protested, "How could you do such a thing without talking to me? I do not even know what the girl looks like: be she yellow, blue, or green." My uncle said there was nothing to talk about. She came from a good family, had spent *eight long years* in school (as if to say 'what more education does a girl need?'), and was, of course, neither yellow nor blue; or green. His wife interjected at this point and said that she was a comely little soul and that I really needed to make up my mind pretty fast. She would not be available for long.

Of course, I was aware that things like this could happen, and had indeed happened within my own family. But four years in a different culture had rendered me oblivious of my own. I told Endale that I would think about it and get back to him shortly. "But we have already sent elders to the Governor General, as is our custom, and everything is now settled." Unsuccessful with an attempt to steer the conversation away to other subjects, I left for my father's home where I was staying. There I found my other uncle, Tadesse Gizzaw, who had rebelled against marrying the girl chosen for him by his parents several decades earlier and had successfully, if unconventionally, managed to marry a girl of his choice. I was delighted to see him, and immediately unburdened myself.

"You know what my uncle Endale tells me?" I started. "He says he has found me a wife, that everything has been arranged and that I have little to say on the matter. Can *you* believe that?" The reply was swift. "Of course I can. I am in it, too. And so is your father. We are all happy for you." I reminded him of his own personal experience: how he had protested and managed to get out of a similar predicament by going against the decision of his parents and marrying someone he had himself chosen. "Yes, but that is an altogether different story. I told you that the girl picked for me was an ugly creature. This one is beautiful and has, moreover, *eight long years of school* in her bag. What more could you ask for?" There was no way I could be persuaded. I put down my foot, said that they should get out of the mess as swiftly as they had dived into it; and returned to Addis. How they managed to disentangle themselves from their self-imposed predicament, I never found out.

Back in Addis at the ECA, I found out that I had been posted to the Research Department where there were a number of recently recruited staff. Bernard Chidzero who many years later would become Deputy Secretary General of UNCTAD and Zimbabwe's first and long-serving Minister of Finance was one. I was told that Ethiopia's Belai Abbai had been employed recently and was working for the U.N. mission in the Congo. There were other young staff from Kenya, Sierra Leone, and Egypt and non-Africans from the Netherlands, France, Norway, and Afghanistan. A good rapport prevailed among the staff of the organization, especially among us Africans. Much of our spare time was taken up with lively discussions on the impending challenges and prospects of the handful of countries which had become independent and those that were well on their way.

Among the non-Africans was an agreeable Dutch economist who was my supervisor; a not-so-agreeable diminutive French economist of Hungarian origin whose intellectual pretensions were at odds with his real capabilities; and an easy going Yugoslav economist who avoided controversy to keep his cushy job. There were also two Frenchmen, Philippe Berthet and Jacques Royer, who were proficient in statistics. It occurred to me that these two might lead a lunchtime session on mathematical economics of the kind I had attended in New York. This could benefit staff who wished to enhance their quantitative skills. Both were willing to conduct such a class. However, there was not much interest from the junior staff. The Hungarian-French economist who had little expertise in the field and whom I reckoned might benefit the most from the course, listened intently to my suggestion and gave me an amusing response. He said he was willing to give a class on general economics to such a group! It was obvious that he could not persist in his intellectual pretensions if he joined the proposed session.

Faced with this combination of vanity and lethargy by staff, there was no point in pursuing the idea and I gave it up. After my rewarding experience in New York, I wondered how much I could really learn from the senior non-African economists at the ECA who in general were mediocre. The Norwegian Director of Research looked able, but I wasn't working with him directly. I was assigned to work on the African Economic Bulletin, a yearly publication presenting current information on the economies of different African countries gathered from a wide variety of national and international publications. Though tedious, the work was an opportunity to learn about African economies and to hone my writing skills.

A Coup D'État

After an extended hotel stay of three months, I moved to a modest rented house with my childhood friend Dr. Jemal Abdulkadir. I drove him to work each day in my newly acquired Volkswagen beetle until he bought his own beetle a few months later. After lunch on Wednesday 15 December 1960, we got into the car and drove to the Princess Tsehai Hospital where he practiced. Soon after dropping him off, I ran into a crowd of people just outside the Hospital gate. They were listening to a small transistor radio placed on the window of a kiosk. I got curious, parked my car and joined the group. Someone was in the middle of an important political statement. It was delivered in ponderous Amharic and was extraordinary in content, coming as it did from the government's own broadcasting system.

The person making the statement talked of the oppressed people of Ethiopia, a proud country with a long history which was marking time while others, especially the recently liberated states of Africa, were making rapid progress. Martial music followed. I asked someone to tell me who the speaker was. He said it was Crown Prince Asfa Wossen Haile-Selassie. A repeat of the announcement came after the martial music. It was indeed the Crown Prince's voice. A coup d'état had been launched with him as the new monarch. Two important appointments were announced. The new Prime Minister was to be Ras Imru Haile Selassie (the progressive cousin of Emperor Haile-Selassie). General Mulugeta Buli, Minister of Community Development and Social Affairs, would go back to his old post of Chief of the General Staff.

Back at my U.N. office, I found everyone talking about the event. A large crowd of students was marching by the office building, carrying placards, singing, and shouting slogans. We came out of the balcony on the third floor to get a better view. While there, I was called by Executive Secretary Mekki Abbas who wished to know about the march, the placards, the songs and the coup. I explained what I saw and as much of its significance as I could make out.

At lunch break, I picked up Jemal from the Princess Tsehai. We had little information to exchange. In the evening, we went to the Itegue Hotel bar which was frequented by foreign educated young men and ran into a group discussing the day's events with great excitement. Names of the coup leaders, a few of them known to the crowd, were bandied about. The Commander of the Imperial Guard, General Mengistu Neway, was the front man. His brother, University of Columbia graduate Germame Neway who was widely known for his radical views, was the key figure behind the General. What kind of change would they introduce? Would it be peaceful? What would happen to the Emperor who was abroad? And to his ministers? The consensus in the smock-filled noisy bar was that whatever happened, things could only get better.

The following morning (Thursday, December 16), I picked up Jemal from the Princess Tsehai at 1:00 p.m. As we were driving back to the Hospital after lunch, we heard intense rifle, machine gun, and artillery fire a few hundred yards past Mexico Square. We could not tell exactly where it was coming from, although it seemed to be behind us in the general direction of the Ministry of Defence. My reaction was to pick up speed and get to the Hospital fast.

As we got closer to the Hospital, the shooting became less and less intense. It was plain that we were driving away from it. Jemal got off at the Hospital and I drove back in the direction of my office building which occupied one side of a three-sided structure shared with the Ministry of Defence. The shooting became progressively more pronounced on the way back. Three miles or so before I reached my office, the shooting got worse. I could drive no further and entered the premises of the Russian Red Cross Hospital where I parked my car and walked into the safety of the hospital building. Minutes and hours passed, but there was no end to the shooting.

In the corridor of the Hospital where I and a few other people were stranded, I met a middle-aged person whom I did not know at the time but who years later would become a friend: Ato Hagos Tewolde-Medhin. I asked him if he knew anything about the shootings. He said he did not. That put an end to a conversation I had hoped would help us while away the hours. A stocky Russian nurse passed by to whom I said: "This is like your great October Revolution." I could only get a poker face in response. Perhaps she did not wish to comment on a sensitive political subject. Or perhaps she did not understand English. She continued to walk with undiminished pace and was soon out of sight.

It was dusk when the fighting finally died down. I had told Jemal that I would pick him up if the situation improved. I now thought it would be more prudent to go home and find out how the situation was in my neighbourhood. On the way, I passed by the Ministry of Defence building, around which military personnel in battle dress kept watch. The building had been a target of the shooting and showed signs of damage. I got home and tried to call friends to find out about the day's event. The telephone lines had by now been disconnected. The following day, Friday, I did not venture into the city as there was more shooting. Bedraggled Imperial Guard troops whose leader had initiated the coup were passing by our neighborhood away from the city centre, as if they were retreating from the Army which had remained loyal to the Emperor. On Saturday afternoon, the Emperor arrived from Asmara and was welcomed rapturously by dignitaries and numerous government officials, civil as well as military. Surrounding his car shouting and gesticulating in triumph as he drove towards his Palace was a motley crowd of the city's poor. They too had improbably joined the welcoming party. Everything was now back to normal. The coup d'état had lasted three days (Wednesday the 15th, Thursday the 16th, and Friday the 17th of December), and the shooting approximately a day and a half (Thursday afternoon and Friday).

I went to the U.N. office the following Monday morning. People wondered where I had been over the previous few days, and especially on Thursday. After describing my brief experience, I asked for theirs. That Thursday, Mr. Abbas had ordered the office closed and, carrying a small U.N. flag, had led his staff to the Ras Hotel some six hundred yards across the street from his office. The location of ECA was not exactly the safest in town. As Imperial Guard troops fired at loyalist forces in the Ministry of Defence building, they could not avoid hitting the ECA offices which occupied one side of the building complex. Bullet marks were visible on the external walls and one person, the librarian, had been killed in the crossfire.

The attempted coup was a hurried affair staged while Emperor Haile Selassie was on a state visit to Brazil. The leaders of the coup had apparently been discussing the overthrow of the government over the previous few years, but had never got down to preparing a detailed plan. What triggered the coup was the knowledge by the Neway brothers that Makonnen Habte-Wold, Minister of Commerce and Industry and the Emperor's confidant with his own intelligence network, was following their every step.

Prior to his departure for Brazil the Emperor had instructed Germame, on the advice of Minister Makonnen Habte-Wold, to return to his post of District Governor of Jijiga without delay. Soon after the Emperor left Addis, Makonnen dispatched a telegramme to the Emperor that Germame was still in town. The Emperor sent a message to General Mengistu saying that his brother Germame should be told to return to his post immediately. It was now plain to the two brothers that their clandestine plan was an open book and that the Emperor would disband the plotters immediately after his return. Worse could follow. The two brothers decided to strike.

Colonel Workineh Gebeyehu, an Imperial Guard officer close to both General Mengistu and Germame, was unaware of this last minute decision when he received word to come to a meeting at the Guard's Headquarters. His associates believe that he was not only aware of their general plan in his capacity as the Emperor's head of special intelligence but that he was a reformer in his own right. His long-held view, however, was that those who desired reform could not initiate change without having the Emperor on their side. Germame often spent long hours in Workineh's office. Observers had little doubt of the subject they discussed. But the precipitate decision to launch a coup and preempt the punitive measures the Emperor might take upon his return was not Workineh's. It was Mengistu's and Germame's. Colonel Workineh, General Mulugeta Buli, and General Tsigie Dibbu, the Police Commissioner, were also unwittingly brought in at the very last minute.

The Army, the Police, and the Air Force did not take part in the plot. This would prove to be fatal, as their numbers were far larger than Imperial Guard troops. In

General Mulegeta Buli

the early hours of the coup, a messenger was dispatched to General Mulugeta to say that the Crown Prince wished to see him. He was driven to the headquarters of the Imperial Guard, of which he was the first post-war commander. When he arrived he was closeted in a room all by himself. A young government official sympathetic to the plotters, Getachew Bekelle, was curious about the movement of Imperial Guard soldiers near his home and asked his brother (an Imperial Guard officer) to drive him to the Guard's headquarters. There he found General Mulugeta lying on a camp bed in a room. Getachew informed him that the national radio had announced a change in government and that he had been appointed Chief of Staff.

General Mulugeta was saddened by what Getachew told him and said he was not aware of what was going on. He said that he had been under the impression that his detention was ordered by the Emperor, as he was always suspected of plots against the regime. He was now greatly disappointed that Mengistu (his former deputy at the Imperial Guard) had embarked on a futile venture. "Please try to find him and tell him to come and see me. If he refuses or is unable to come, tell him his actions would turn Ethiopia into another Congo and that he will not succeed in his plan. My advice is that he should find a way to escape." The message was delivered by Getachew, but it was too late for Mengistu to reverse course or make a safe exit.

Apart from the street march by college students which the coup leaders had instigated, there was no visible manifestation of support or sympathy from the general population. Even senior commanders of the Imperial Guard who were carrying out General Mengistu's directives were initially not told that they were participating in a plan to remove the Emperor. During the first few hours, they and their men were told that the Army had rebelled against the Emperor and that they had to discharge their responsibility of *defending* the Crown against usurpers. It was only when the coup was announced over the national radio that they understood they had been misled. When the Neway brothers realized that they had lost the game, they decided to shoot a number of ministers they had previously enticed to the Palace on different pretexts.

Those killed included Ras Abebe Aregai, the resistance leader, General Mulugeta Buli and Makonnen Habte-Wold, Germame Neway's nemesis. Germame believed that Minister Makonnen and others like him were obstacles to progress. Makonnen was perceived to be conservative. Like most Ethiopians, Makonnen was suspicious; which partly explains his tendency to micro manage departments under his watch as well as his tendency to procrastinate decisions. He was also excessively loyal to the Emperor. These were not appreciated by the young generation of public servants. But Makonnen was a passionate patriot working for the progress of his country in a manner he deemed durable. He believed that progress, to be sustainable, needed to go in measured steps and rest firmly on Ethiopian values. He was convinced that Germame was a threat to the country's orderly march towards modernization. Through his own intelligence network, he closely followed the young coup leader's movements until the very last moment. By acting fast, Germame foiled whatever preemptive measures Makonnen might have had in store for him.

After shooting the Ministers, the coup leaders made their escape. General Mengistu Neway, his brother Germame, and Captain Baye Telahun fled to the neighbouring countryside. But they had walked only a few kilometers southeast of Addis Ababa when security police confronted them. Shots were exchanged. Realizing that there was no escape, Germame first shot his brother Mengistu and subsequently turned the gun on himself. He died instantly but Mengistu was wounded and captured alive. Captain Baye Telahun was killed in the exchange of fire.

Colonel Workineh Gebeyehu had been contemplating an escape even while the coup was still in progress. After he joined Germame and Mengistu at the last minute, he was said to have expressed dismay over the inadequate measures taken, including the fact that the two most senior generals of the Army, Chief of Staff General Merid Mengesha and Ground Forces Commander General Kebede Gebre, were at large. His intention appears to have been to secretly foil the efforts of the Neway brothers.[4] When all seemed lost, he too left the Palace grounds, the last theatre of battle. On Saturday, he was discovered hiding not far from the Palace. After an exchange of fire he took his own life, purportedly citing the example of Emperor Tewodros of Gondar who shot himself when Lord Napier's soldiers were approaching his mountain fortress at Magdala. Workineh was from Gondar.

The victors (especially the top brass of the Army and certain highly placed civilian officials) were determined to meet out severe punishments to the leaders and supporters of the failed coup. But the Emperor spoke differently to senior justices and officials (among whom were the Chief Justice, Afenegus Kitaw Yitateku, Justice Blata Matias Hilete-Work, and future Chief Justice Tashoma Haile-Mariam who was then serving as legal advisor in the Emperor's Special Cabinet). The Emperor underlined the importance of ensuring that justice was observed. "The maxim of the fathers, 'May the Lord pass his judgment upon me if I have judged you, the defendant, wrongly', should guide your actions," he said. He was no doubt aware of the damage that a questionable trial might do to his standing domestically and internationally. Tashoma subsequently attended a meeting called by highly placed officials who had drawn up a list of the instigators and sympathizers of the coup. Seeing a tendency for a hasty retribution, Tashoma cited the Emperor's directive to the meeting. This and similar other interventions eventually restrained the officials from acts of vindictiveness.

General Mengistu and a few others were put on trial in an open court and in the presence of a representative of the international association of jurists, the Norwegian Dr. Hambro. In the course of his trial Mengistu caught sight of relatives of the executed officials who were watching the proceedings. He knew many of them personally. It was not he, he said to them, but 'gizzei' that had been responsible for the death of their loved ones.[5] He was found guilty of treason and sentenced to death. He did not wish to exercise his right of appeal and was hanged in a public square in Addis Ababa.

Although it failed in its aim to overthrow the government of Emperor Haile-Selassie, the 1960 coup d'état was a bellwether of the more cataclysmic events that would eventually rock the country. An attempt to bring to light the historical context in which the coup took place as well as a brief assessment of the personality of the leading protagonists is consequently crucial for a better understanding of an event that continues to be talked about. I shall take up this in the following chapter. In the meantime, I shall continue with the narrative of my professional work at the ECA.

Settling Down to Work

More and more staff were being recruited and we soon moved from the Ministry of Defence building to our new premises, Africa Hall. This was a donation by the Ethiopian Government which had been promised during the negotiations for the location of the organization's headquarters. Not only was it a brand new building but was also of a standard nonexistent at the time in much of Africa. The spacious conference room soon became the venue for many pan-African meetings, and would soon serve as the birthplace of the Organization of African Unity.

Missions to member countries were a major feature of the programme of work at the ECA. My first one was to Ghana. An incident I recall from my stay in Accra is a rally at which Kwame Nkrumah gave a major address. Coming from a feudal culture where political rallies were a rarity, I felt a bit out of place. Nkrumah mounted the podium, was cheered thunderously, and began his address. What the occasion was I have long ago forgotten. His talk was frequently interrupted by drum beats and loud applause. All of a sudden, I noticed that Nkrumah was being heckled when he said, "We should get rid of negative slogans like one man, one car."

The crowd did not agree. The slogan had been aimed at Ministers and highly placed public servants who were beginning to show signs of illicit affluence. One eye-catching manifestation was the sight of multiple cars in the garages of the home of high officials. The man in the street was airing his disapproval through the catchy slogan. In response to the heckling, Nkrumah said: "Wait, wait. You haven't heard what I said. What I said was..." and he repeated exactly what he had said minutes earlier. He then offered what sounded like an unpersuasive explanation of why he said the crowd should not mouth the negative slogan. To my surprise the crowd looked satisfied and resumed its cheering. Whether it was an instance of deference to a popular leader or expert mob control, I never could figure out.

I completed my mission and returned to Addis in ten days. Prior to my departure, some people had noticed a mild tension developing between African and non-African staff in the professional category. The Non-Africans had started to air criticism of the way Abbas managed the organization. A general staff meeting was called one day by Abbas in which he expressed dismay about rumors concerning the way the organization functioned. "If some of you feel that you are on a sinking ship, you can jump off into the sea like frightened rats!" he said at the meeting.

I was puzzled. My African colleagues told me what had actually taken place while I was in Ghana. Philippe de Seynes, the French Undersecretary General for Economic and Social Affairs, had come to Addis to attend a U.N. meeting. Some European staff had met with him clandestinely and had expressed misgivings about Abbas's management style. Abbas had got wind of this and had decided to confront the staff. Whether on account of this or for some other reason, it was Abbas himself who later abruptly resigned. It appeared that the European dominated U.N. bureaucracy was not willing to work under African leadership even in an organization created to serve Africa.

In time staff relations improved with the recruitment of abler and more experienced non-African staff. Among these was Dudley Seers, the respected English economist who had worked at ECA's sister institution, the Economic Commission for Latin America in Santiago, Chile. He was the new Director of Research. Arthur Ewing, another Englishman, became Director of the Industry Department. Something approaching the quality of staff which I had seen at the U.N. in New York was beginning to be available at the ECA.

Dudley Seers launched a new research programme which involved undertaking in-depth studies on the economies of individual African countries in which ECA staff had substantive input. I was asked to write a short economic profile on Southern Rhodesia (today's Zimbabwe) based on desk research. I showed it to Seers and was told to proceed to the country, together with a new Ugandan staff member, Joseph Mubiru, to prepare a fuller report.

Mubiru and I arrived in Salisbury (Harare) in April 1963, with Dudley Seers as leader of our mission. We were taken to the Ambassador Hotel, the only one in the city which was open to non-European guests. In the morning, we went to the Ministry of Commerce and Industry where we paid a courtesy call on the under-secretary. Seers introduced the two of us and explained the purpose of our mission. He soon left, having satisfied himself that we would be treated by the settler regime as regular employees of the United Nations.

A couple of days later, we saw the under-secretary for further discussions. He had apparently never come across African professionals and closely questioned us about our work and position in the U.N. He was surprised when I told him that I had worked at U.N. Headquarters in New York as an economist. The poor fellow tried to conceal his incredulity, but it came through. He complimented both me and Mubiru for our proficiency in the English language. We thanked him for his kindness, adding that we were condemned to be good in that language. We had to use it in conducting research, writing reports, as well as in taking part in meetings, seminars, lectures and missions.

For the first few days, we followed a routine that kept us out of trouble. We were international civil servants and were sensitive to incidents that our unwanted presence in hotels or restaurants reserved for whites might possibly provoke. We had to restrict our movement. After ten days or so, we were tired of the food at the restaurant of our hotel and wondered if there wasn't another we could try. Someone at the front desk said that there was an Indian restaurant in the vicinity if we didn't mind spicy food. Didn't mind spicy food? It was a godsend for an Ethiopian; I told the hotel attendant and made it a point to have dinner every night at the restaurant.

Mubiru found the Indian food somewhat of a challenge for his palate and stopped going. Without the Indian restaurant and without, I should add, my short-lived habit of smoking cigarettes which I picked up there, my month long stay in race conscious Salisbury would have been depressive. The fact that Southern Rhodesian cigarettes were inexpensive and attractively packaged provided the enticement to smoke. Fortunately, I stopped smoking four years later.

The Birth of the OAU

Mubiru and I returned to Addis Ababa in early May 1963; in good time for the anxiously awaited first all African Heads of State and Government meeting. Ethiopia's Emperor Haile-Selassie and Liberia's President Tubman had worked hard to reconcile countries that had previously adopted two competing political orientations: the Monrovia and the Casablanca groups. To the first belonged Liberia, Ethiopia, Nigeria and most of the French speaking West African countries. They were perceived to have a moderate political orientation in regard to both domestic and external affairs. All desired close cooperation among African states and were open to amicable relations with the western democracies. Ghana, Tanzania, Guinea, Morocco, Algeria, Egypt, and others belonged to the so called progressive Casablanca group. They favoured rapid political and economic integration among African states and close ties with socialist countries. Thanks to the diplomatic efforts of Emperor Haile-Selassie and President Tubman, all of Africa's leaders agreed to take part in a meeting scheduled to be held in Ethiopia's capital.

With the exception of the ailing King of Libya, all of the continent's leaders attended the meeting in Addis Ababa. The Emperor had asked Ketema Yifru, his Minister of Foreign Affairs, to prepare a draft agreement that would create a continent-wide organization. And it had been well prepared. A team of Ethiopian lawyers, both from within and outside the Ministry, was mobilized. A Charter establishing a continent-wide institution espousing the high ideals of economic and political integration was crafted and closely scrutinized. It was ready in time for a formal presentation to the leaders at a plenary session. As was to be expected, opinion was initially divided about the timing and nature of intra-African cooperation. Advised by his ministers, the Emperor was adamant that leaders should not leave Addis Ababa without signing the document. Following protracted negotiations and late night sessions, the Charter was unanimously endorsed and signed. And the Organization of African Unity came into being.

I attended the closing session together with a few friends. It was well past midnight. We sat in the press gallery, looking down at the conference hall as one Head of State after another made his statement. Kwame Nkrumah's turn came. He was slow going when he started, his baritone voice showing signs of fatigue after a long day's deliberation over a historic document. With each passing minute, however, he seemed to gather pace and energy. He spoke of the historic nature of the charter and of the unique significance of the venue. The references to Ethiopia (a country of enduring symbolism to black peoples) could not have been more seductively framed for the audience.

Nkrumah's eulogized Ethiopia as the land of the wise, the beacon of freedom for black peoples in the world, and the repository of Africa's culture. Ethiopians in the hall went berserk. The late Debebe Habte-Yohannes was a few seats away from me. He leaned towards the railing in front of his seat as Nkrumah started to talk about Ethiopia. When he heard the phrase "Ethiopia, the repository of Africa's culture" Debebe jumped up shouting, "Osageyfo, Osageyfo, Osageyfo," (the Ghanaian traditional title bestowed upon Nkrumah only a few years earlier) and went on in that manner for two or three minutes. Nkrumah had instantaneously transformed himself into the darling of the Ethiopian audience. He reveled in the adulation and seemed to fight back a broad smile. It was a scene that would be etched in our minds for as long as we lived.

The party was over. Mubiru and I completed the economic report on Southern Rhodesia and submitted it to Dudley Seers. Mubiru returned to his country soon afterwards to head one of the commercial banks there. In time he would become Governor of the Central Bank of Uganda. When Idi Amin assumed power, Mubiru sadly joined the large number of professionals who fell victim to the tyrant's sword.

At the ECA, more and more consultants began to visit the organization. The British economist of Hungarian origin, Thomas Balogh, was one. Years later I would read Thomas Balogh was also a romantic figure. Balogh was among several lovers of British novelist Iris Murdoch. He was someone, she said, whose perfect beauty was only marred by a receding hairline. I can bear witness to this description, save the receding hairline. By the time I met Balogh in the early sixties, the hair had almost all gone, but he was otherwise strikingly good looking. And he was a leading economist of his generation.

Hans Singer was another distinguished economist. I had first met Singer I New York. In later years he became a regular consultant at the ECA. His advice was sought on a range of subjects, including the idea of creating a development bank for Africa, on which he wrote a report. His proposal was accepted and the African Development Bank was duly established. The Bank's evolution is described in a chapter later in this book. I was fortunate to work with him on a number of assignments at the ECA. His clarity of thought, analytical skills, and lucid style inspired many a young economist.

In the course of writing this book on day, I casually turned to the obituary page of The Economist and read that Hans Singer had died on 26 February 2006, aged 95. Professor Singer's long and productive association with the U.N. was mentioned in the article, as was his life-long commitment to the cause of the developing world. He had pioneered the effort to mobilize grants and technical assistance, for which he was dubbed as "one of the wild men of the U.N." by the infamous Senator Joseph McCarthy of the U.S. and World Bank president Eugene Black, also of the U.S.

W. Arthur Lewis was yet another leading economist whom I had also met both when I was working at the U.N. in New York and subsequently at the ECA in Addis Ababa. These men gave extended talks to staff every time they came for consultations,. They were a source of considerable inspiration to the staff. As luck would have it, I would soon be presented with another opportunity to get further exposure to scholars whose names resonated among the economics fraternity.

The Harvard Interlude

I had attended summer school at Harvard in Cambridge, Massachusetts in 1957, although I had not met any of the world famous scholars gracing the University campus, save perhaps Henry Kissinger at one lecture who had not yet gained renown. I eagerly looked forward to going back again. The opportunity came when I joined some 15 mid-career professionals from different parts of the world, called Mason Fellows, after Harvard economist Edward Mason, We were enrolled at the Center for International Affairs, Harvard's CIA. The Center was later renamed the Harvard Institute for International Development (HIID) to avoid confusion, I would guess, with the intelligence outfit in Langley Park, Virginia.

The Mason programme was designed to enable the professionals to get advanced training in economics and subjects of relevance to their field of work. There was only one seminar in development economics which was mandatory and for which a major term paper had to be written. Otherwise, each Mason fellow took graduate courses of his choosing in any department at Harvard. With two exceptions, I took all my courses in the Department of Economics at Littauer.

Professors in the Department were guiding lights in the economics firmament. While at Illinois I had come across most of their names and had read their books and articles. What was exciting at Harvard was the opportunity to come face to face with them: Wassily Leontieff, Simon Kuznets, Hollis Chennery, John Kenneth Galbraith, John Dunlop, Albert Hirschman, James Duesenberry, to name but a few. Among the more luminous of the luminaries was Professor Paul Samuelson of MIT, also in Cambridge, who came over to Harvard for seminars. The intellectual atmosphere of Cambridge was truly stimulating. And, needless to add, intimidating as well.

One of my professors was Simon Kuznets under whom I took a semester's course on modern economic growth. He came to class with notes on a few sheets, glanced at them only occasionally, paced up and down the platform in front of the class, and rolled out a captivating analysis of the process of economic growth in the modern era. In my U.N. days I had sometimes witnessed intellectual virtuosity of Kuznets's class, but only fleetingly. Taking notes while he lectured turned out to be a challenge, however. I got around the problem by simply sitting still throughout the lecture, with my eyes and mind transfixed at the stooping, short professor as he shuffled up and down the room. I refrained from taking notes, for fear of missing a link in the beautifully crafted chain of ideas gushing out of his robust mind. At the end of class I rushed to a nearby coffee joint, took out my notebook, and tried to recapture as much as I could of what the professor had said over a forty-five minute period while it was still fresh in my mind. The method worked.

Professor Galbraith taught a course in economic development, sharply different in approach and content from that of Simon Kuznets: much less rigorous, more free flowing, and peppered with insightful remarks about the challenges of development facing the countries of Asia, Africa, and Latin America. His sharp tongue would be unsparing of whatever subject, personality, or country caught his fancy. A country had to have a minimum cultural base for sustained economic development, he said one day in class;[6] and named countries that had such a base, with China and India topping the list. He also named those that did not, among which was Guinea in West Africa. Knowing that there was an Ethiopian in class, he mentioned the country as a case of particular interest. "The Ethiopians do have the minimum cultural base required for economic development," he started. "But they have one handicap which they need to overcome if they are to succeed in their efforts to develop their country". He took a pause and brought down his axe swiftly. "And that handicap is their strongly held conviction that they were Christianized before the birth of Christ!"[7]

A course I took outside the Economics Department at Littauer was on the intellectual history of Europe in the 19th century. Stuart Hughes of the Department of Social Sciences gave the course. It was as exciting as Kuznet's course. Although done at the end of term for Kuznets, an appreciative round of applause was given at the end of several classes during the semester in the case of Professor Hughes. When he finished class, he would hurriedly gather his papers and rush out to escape the applause which was obviously overdone. For the last class of the semester, the applause was the most sustained, and Hughes's exit the swiftest.

Professor Hughes's coverage of existentialism would have a lasting impact on me. A book recommended for reading was Kaufmann's *Existentialism from Dostoevsky to Sartre*. The copy I bought in a Cambridge bookshop in the winter of 1966 (still with me today) had been through twenty-two printings. What attracted me most in the book was Kaufmann's analysis of Sartre's philosophy and the thoughts offered in a short story by the philosopher entitled *The Wall*, which was described as one of the classics of existentialism.

Briefly told, *The Wall* is a story narrated by a fictional character, Pablo Ibbieta, who represents an anarchist fighter for the Republican cause in the Spanish Civil War. Ibbieta is imprisoned by the Falangists along with two other fellow fighters. All three are sentenced to death by firing squad. They are put in death row with the certain knowledge of their imminent death and an overwhelming preoccupation with their predicament. The existentialist question of how each person faces the certainty of his death is given an answer in Sartre's minute-by-minute absorbing account of each person's reaction. Ibbeita's two companions are shot. When his turn comes, he is taken to two Falangist investigators who ask him for the whereabouts of a Republican colleague and close friend, Gris. Ibbieta says he does not know. "It is his life against yours. You can have yours if you can tell us where he is," say the investigators who give him fifteen minutes to make up his mind.

An account of the thoughts that go through his mind during the fifteen minutes is best rendered in Ibbieta's own words. "I would rather die than give up Gris. Why? I didn't like Ramon Gris any more. My friendship for him had died a little while before dawn at the same time as my love for Concha [a girl friend], at the same time as my desire to live. Undoubtedly, I thought highly of him: he was tough. But it was not for this reason that I consented to die in his place; his life had no more value than mine; no life had value. They were going to slap a man up against a wall and shoot at him till he died, whether it was I or Gris or somebody else made no difference. But I thought to hell with Spain and anarchy; nothing was important. Yet I was there, I could save my skin and give up Gris and I refused to do it. I found that somehow comic; it was *obstinacy*. I thought 'I must be *stubborn!'* And a droll sort of gaiety spread over me." (Italics added).

But Ibbieta wants a last laugh before his impending execution. He, of course, had knowledge of where Gris was hiding (with his cousins) but tells the two investigators that he is hiding in a cemetery. "It was a farce. I wanted to see them stand up, buckle their belts and give orders busily." And so they did. "I'll let you off if you're telling the truth," said one of the officers," but it'll cost you plenty if you are making monkeys out of us." As fate would have it, Gris had left his hiding place at his cousins' residence. He had gone to hide in the town cemetery! He was caught by the police. And Ibbieta was set free.

There is, of course, more to *The Wall* than this dramatic finale. It is Ibbieta's standing up to death. His *obstinacy* and *stubbornness* is Sartre's way of demonstrating the existentialist response of someone confronting death: with *integrity* which Sartre says is *utterly independent of social utility*. A person confronting death should seek no alibis: "no gods are responsible for his condition; no original sin; no heredity and no environment; no race, no caste, no father, and no mother; no wrong-headed education, no governess, no teacher; not even an impulse or disposition, a complex or a childhood trauma...Man is free...stands alone in the universe...responsible for his condition..." Man is, behaves, or acts in one way or another as a matter of *choice*.

My young mind was deeply impressed by all this. I persuaded myself that in my own modest way, I would try to live by the precept of this outlook on life. When the Dergue came to power in 1974, several of my colleagues in the Emperor's government were imprisoned and later shot. My own name subsequently appeared in a hit list of former officials. When two or three people in the list were subsequently shot, I realized the possibility of being killed and decided to face my end as calmly as I could; expressing my views without fear, and never allowing myself to sacrifice anyone "to save my skin." Thanks to *The Wall* I was able to weather the storm of the year and a half of my association with the Dergue with a modicum of integrity and inner calm; although I must say that I never came quite as close to death as many of my friends in those terrible days.

Studying economics at Harvard was an ordeal and took long hours each day. The most intellectually demanding courses were those involving mathematics and statistics. Some Mason Fellows had been exposed to mathematics in graduate school, but many years had passed. We consequently had to take an introductory course on mathematical economics. It was after this course that we took the more advanced econometrics classes. The going was rough and most of us often wondered why we had to rack our brains when we could take other less demanding subjects. I recall one incident in particular which, apart from illustrating the predicament in which we found ourselves, also provided an opportunity for one of our colleagues to drive home a political point. It was also an occasion for me to learn the virtue of not making clever remarks at other people's expense.

It involved a Nigerian, and a South African young man who was thin, blond, blue eyed and unusually friendly, especially to Africans and Asians. He too was uncomfortable with mathematics and would often ask for help. The Nigerian unkindly said one day that the South African was to be given no help by the Africans and Asians, as he thought he belonged to a class of people who felt intellectually superior. He should not stoop down to solicit assistance. The poor guy somehow sensed this and kept his distance. The dreaded end of term exam came in February. As we feared, the questions were difficult and far more numerous than we expected. It would obviously take more than the three-hour time limit to go through them all, but the idea was to provide a wide range of questions to choose from. At the head of the exam paper was the advice that students should try to answer as many of the questions as they could. Nervous students didn't take to this kindly, as the very sight of the long list of questions, all seemingly equally difficult, only raised the level of intimidation.

An hour into the exam, I saw the South African fellow handing in his papers and walking out of Memorial Hall where the exam was held. I was a little surprised that he should leave so early. When the supervisor announced after three hours that time was up, we reluctantly handed in our papers. The South African was waiting outside a short distance from the entrance of Memorial Hall. As soon as he caught sight of us exiting, he paced quickly in our direction. His face was ashen. The inevitable question soon followed: "How did you folks do?" he asked.

The Nigerian replied he had attempted about half of the questions. The rest of the group had similar responses. The South African said he had attempted no more than a quarter, and had decided to give up, as there was no point in prolonging the agony. "I have been completely destroyed" he murmured, said goodbye and disappeared, never to be seen again on campus. When the results came in, we found out that most of us had scraped through, except the South African and his none-too-friendly Nigerian classmate. The thought crossed my mind that the Nigerian might be consoled by the fact that he, a Nigerian and the blue eyed, blond South African had finally turned out to be of about the same intellectual aptitude; a not entirely welcome kind of equality, but something that would drive home a valuable lesson for many a racist bigot in South Africa. In an unguarded moment, I said so to my Nigerian classmate, who naturally did not take kindly to my remarks. I felt terrible over the folly I had committed. I would learn the bitter lesson that trying to make a point, however well taken, at someone's expense hardly earns a pat on the back.

My Cambridge stay enhanced my understanding of economics considerably. The price paid was high in terms of leisure time foregone. A few times, I was able to attend concerts by the Boston Philharmonic and the Boston Pops under Arthur Fiedler. Given my feeling of academic contentment as well as my sentiment that I now had enough practical experience to work for a higher degree, I started to explore possible funding. I talked to a few of the professors on the faculty. Regrettably, the search was undertaken rather late, and there was nothing available at the time. I was not unduly disappointed, however, as I had a secure job to return to.

CHAPTER 4

More on the 1960 Coup D'État

The Antecedents of the Coup

As I pointed out in the preceding chapter, it might be helpful to consider briefly the historical antecedents of the hurried attempt by the Neway brothers to remove Emperor Haile-Selassie and initiate what they believed to be a process of radical reform in the country's social and political life. The failed coup was not an isolated event. Rather, it was one which was preceded by years of criticism of the regime's inadequacies. In the absence of an open political space for the public airing of views, many post-war officials and concerned citizens had been expressing muted dissent against the Emperor's rule. The dissenters were by no means revolutionaries. They were mostly reformists whose ideas did not go beyond a system of government in which the Emperor's authority would be limited by a constitution, and where there would be a good measure of participatory government.

The dissenters could be conveniently grouped into two broad categories: (i) those who generally allied themselves with the Emperor's reforms before the 1936-41 Fascist occupation and (ii) the progressive intellectuals of the post-war era. In both groups, there were individuals trained overseas; much more in number in the second than in the first. Both were for the most part officials of the government and were on the whole sympathetic to the general direction of the Emperor's reform efforts initially. In time, however, their sympathies would wane. The pre-war generation became somewhat disillusioned by the Emperor's rule after the occupation years, although one or two had become dissenters by the time of the Fascist invasion. The post-occupation dissenters, all young civil servants with different educational backgrounds, found themselves immobilized by the deadweight of bureaucracy and by the lack of opportunity to express their views. Most simply adapted themselves to the environment, but a few continued to harbour resentment at the slow pace of change and the conspicuous indifference of those wielding power to the challenges facing the nation.

To the first category belonged Fitawrari Tekle-Hawariat Tekle-Mariam who completed his training in a school of artillery in Czarist Russia; Afenegus Takele Wolde-Hawariat and Afenegus Gebre-Medhin Haile-Mariam, both products of Ethiopia's traditional system of education; and Dr. Alemework Beyenne, a veterinarian from the University of St. Andrews (Scotland). There were others whose dissent arose from grievancs of a purely personal nature, like Bitwoded Negash Bezabih, resistance fighter and scion of the royal house of Gojjam; or who obviously wished reform but who were perhaps not adequately explicit about their intentions, such as Blatten-Getta Lorenzo Ta'ezaz, graduate of Montpelier University (France). Beyond these there were malcontents to whom it would not be entirely justified to accord the label of dissident, but whom many perceived as liberal in their outlook and hence not entirely sympathetic to the men in power. Examples would include Makonnen Desta, the U.S. trained anthropologist, and French trained painter Agegnehu Engida. Negadras Afework Gebre-Yesus, a pre-war senior official of the government who was trained in Italy and was married to an Italian, became a mouthpiece for the Italian administration during the occupation years and was bitterly critical of the Emperor's policies. But he was a man widely perceived to be unpatriotic and it would be wrong to consider him a dissident in the manner that we regard the others.

In the second category were Germame Neway and his overseas graduate friends (mostly from the United States); Colonel Workineh Gebeyehu of the Imperial Guard and his coterie of young officer colleagues like Colonel Imru Wonde (all graduates of the Swedish run cadet school); a growing body of young civilians murmuring progressive political views; and finally vocal lone wolves like the writer Abe Gubegnaw and Seyoum Sebhat. Haddis Alemayehu was in many ways different from the post-war dissenters but was perceived by traditionalists as a dissident who often expressed his non-conformist views to people in positions of authority, including the Emperor. There will be an occasion later in this book to come back to him. For the moment it might be relevant to mention his name *en passant* as a dissenter in residence, as he for the most part occupied senior government posts both at home and overseas. It is important to keep in mind in this context that there were many like him in government who kept the light of reform burning, if only dimly.

Tekle-Hawariat had spent eleven years studying in Tsarist Russia. Upon his return he was presented to Emperor Menelik who asked what he had studied. The young man replied that he had graduated from a school of artillery. The Emperor wished to know if he was familiar with the technique of manufacturing heavy artillery. Tekle Hawariat explained that he was trained as an artillery officer. Weapons were produced in a factory employing qualified engineers and thousands of workers. It would take a long time for Ethiopia to manufacture artillery pieces. Brushing aside what to him sounded like an unhelpful response, the Emperor asked how much it would cost to put up a plant for the manufacture of heavy artillery. About fifteen million birr was Tekle-Hawariat's reply. "My good man, our country cannot afford such a sum and I am afraid it will remain a remote dream," was the Emperor's despondent reaction.[1] Tekle-Hawariat was given the title of Kegnazmatch and assigned to be chief of artillery under Fitawrari Habte-Giorgis, the Minister of War. It soon dawned on him that he would not be taken seriously, partly because of his young age and partly also because he could make no contribution to the manufacture of the weapon. There was no shortage of good artillery men in Ethiopia, so thought the authorities. What the country needed were people who could make the stuff. Tekle-Hawariat therefore decided to pick up new skills in a more relevant area and proceeded to France to study agriculture.

After three years in Paris Tekle-Hawariat returned with a plan to establish his own farm. But when he met with Dejazmatch Tafari Makonnen, a childhood friend whose father had helped him to go to Russia, he was told that an educated man like him should serve in government. Tafari, who was then a young Governor General of Harrar Province, offered him an administrative post. Partly because of his somewhat inflexible ways and in part because of his progressive views, Tekle-Hawariat soon fell out with Tafari and was at one point put in chains for insubordination. When Tafari later became Emperor of Ethiopia, Tekle-Hawriat served in several posts, including the post of Minister of Finance. While in that post, he helped draft the first Ethiopian Constitution. Just prior to the outbreak of hostilities with Fascist Italy in October 1935, he was appointed as Ethiopia's representative to the League of Nations, where his efforts to secure support for his country's cause were frustrated by an organization more preoccupied with efforts to appease Mussolini than to listen to the plights of the victim of the dictator's aggression.

Returning to Ethiopia in the early months of 1936, Tekle-Hawariat advised the Emperor to adopt guerilla warfare to counter Fascist invasion. His idea had already been dropped in favour of the Emperor's travel to Geneva, as will be explained in a moment. From then on, his relations with the Emperor deteriorated to the point where he occasionally wrote letters to leaders in the resistance movement that the Emperor should not be allowed to return to the country. He himself spent two decades in exile. Intermediaries brought a degree of reconciliation between him and the Emperor and he was finally able to return home. But he never again engaged in politics, though he would be long regarded as the doyen of dissenters.

Among the handful of pre-war reformers who later became dissidents was Afenegus Takele Wolde-Hawariat. Prior to the occupation, Takele strongly supported Emperor Haile-Selassie's modernization programme. He fell out with the monarch when the latter decided to travel to Geneva to present Ethiopia's case in person before the League of Nations. The decision was made at a meeting in Addis soon after the Emperor's return from Maichew in the Northern Front. He had led his forces and fought valiantly like an ordinary soldier. Indeed when his men were retreating, Haile-Selassie had refused to budge from the battle field despite the odds and would have 'remained behind' had he not been beseeched by Etchegue Gebre-Giorgis, the head of the Ethiopian Orthodox Church, and other senior Church officials.[2]

At the meeting in Addis, Takele argued that it was essential to conduct guerrilla warfare against the enemy and that the Emperor had to remain in the country to lead the effort. He proposed Gore in the west from where the monarch could coordinate the guerilla movement. But others, including Foreign Minister Blatten Guetta Hiruy Wolde-Selassie and Makonnen Habte-Wold, argued that the Emperor should make the trip to Europe instead and try to secure assistance from the League. Haile-Selassie left and Takele stayed behind to pursue his plan. It would later be clear that the Italians would have spared no effort or expense to capture the Emperor, as indeed they quickly overwhelmed Ras Imru's force and captured him in Gojeb. Emperor Haile-Selassie would have been too big a fish to be left roaming the bush like other less well known resistance fighters.

Takele felt that the Emperor had abandoned his country. Together with Abebe Aregai (a resistance fighter who was then only a low ranking police commander) he worked on a plan to designate a rival member of the royal family to lead the resistance. Young Melake-Tsehai Iyassu, son of Lij Iyassu, was chosen for the purpose. Lij Iyassu had been Emperor Menelik's designated heir who had been pushed aside to make way for Emperes Zawditu Menelik when he turned out to be unsuitable. Melake-Tsehai Iyassu died soon afterwards, however, although the guerilla war continued without him. Later Takele reportedly toyed with another plan: to establish a republic after the war. The plan did not go far either. He accomplished little of significance in other ways. Indeed, some in the resistance accused him of disruptive conduct.[3] After the war, he persisted in his dogged opposition to the Emperor, despite being pardoned and given senior positions in the government. In the end he was implicated in a plot to assassinate the Emperor. When police approached his home to arrest him, he locked himself up and committed suicide.

Afenegus Gebre-Medhin was an undercover agent for resistance forces during the years of struggle. A man of probity and great character, he was chosen to be President of the Patriotic Association when rivalry among the heavyweights of the anti-Fascist resistance made it difficult for a military leader to emerge as head of the Association. His first major clash with the government occurred when, as Deputy Chief Justice, he rebuffed an attempt to influence a case over which he was presiding and in which the government was the defendant. His judgment was in favour of the plaintiff, a Greek merchant. Such was the contemptuous view of foreign merchants at the time that the verdict incensed the senior minister involved in the case. For Gebre-Medhin, it was a case of judicial independence.

The defiant judge was eased out of the job and exiled to Gore. The Governor General there kept him under close watch and in an unusually damp little room with a cement floor. Gebre-Medhin appealed for a transfer and was moved around to locations where conditions improved progressively. He was finally brought back to Addis Ababa and lived on a modest pension given him by the Emperor's government. When the military took over power in 1974, they announced that all political prisoners had been amnestied. This did not affect Gebre-Medhin as he had already been freed. But the Dergue got wind of his story. An agent was sent to his home with a proposal.

After he listened to his ordeal, the agent proposed that Gebre-Medhin share his story on Ethiopian television. The old dissident declined, saying that he did not see any useful purpose in dramatizing his lifetime of suffering in that manner. He was an old man awaiting the call of his Creator and was disinclined to recount his travails to the public. "You know what happened later" said Gebre-Medhin to me and a friend who had gone to visit him at his residence. "When someone went to the Treasury to pick up my monthly pension of Birr 200 granted me by the Emperor's governmet, he was told that it had been discontinued." The man lived without a pension until his death in 1996.[4]

It is uncertain what Dr. Alemework Beyene, the veterinarian, did prior to the Fascist invasion. When Italy launched her offensive against Ethiopia in the last quarter of 1935, Alemework set about establishing an anti-Fascist resistance organization (the Black Lions) whose membership consisted of young graduates from the country's only military school and other young educated people. He deployed his men in Wollega (Western Ethiopia) where they managed to destroy an enemy aircraft at a makeshift runway. The apprehensive local chieftain pleaded with them to quit and move elsewhere. Along with his men, Alemework travelled further west to Gore to join Ras Imru, a recent arrival from the Northern Front. A few months later, they fought against an Italian army detachment that had been pursuing them and surrendered near the River Gojjab south of Jimma.

Alemework spent the years of occupation in Addis Ababa and joined government service after liberation. The feisty and independent minded veterinarian soon got into trouble with his superiors and left his post. An unidentified person later hurled a hand grenade at him, severing his arm. Subsequently, he was kept under house arrest in Gore where I attended primary school. He was a stocky, defiant, friendly, and loquacious individual who was never treated by the townsfolk as anything other than a respected guest of the government sent for rest and recreation. I once accompanied a relative who visited him at his residence. When we arrived in the middle of the morning he was struggling with his remaining arm to place a belt around his waist. As he was not making much headway, my relative got up and offered to help. Alemework dismissed him brusquely with the remark: "Do I send for you each time I want to tie my belt?"

I saw Dr. Alemework once again when he came to visit my grandfather who had fallen ill. There was no doctor in town, and my relatives turned to him. He came, gave the old man some advice and told him not to worry, as he would soon recover. Recover my old man did and he was eternally grateful to the veterinarian whose cheerful encouragement had more to do with my grandfather's recovery than any medical advice he might have offered regarding a problem outside his expertise. Alemework was resourceful in other ways. Years later Haddis Alemayehu told me of an incident immediately after their surrender and arrest on the Gojjeb River. One night Alemework took off in the direction of the building where their Italian captors were lodging. Haddis and the other inmates, anxious about their fate, were stunned to see this man take off for the lion's den. A few minutes later, they were relieved to see him walking in their direction. When he arrived, relief turned into amazement as Alemework pulled out a few bottles of Chianti wine from a soiled bag offered him by the officers guarding them.

One cannot be certain about Alemework's political views. But two points can be safely made. Alemework was clearly at odds with the government and could be regarded as one of the dissidents of the day. Secondly, Alemework's stay in Britain must have left a mark on his impressionable mind about the future political evolution of his country. As with almost all students who had spent several years abroad, Alemework must have observed the way people lived and were governed in the West. It would not be unreasonable to assume that he favoured a constitutional monarchy along British lines.

Bitwoded Negash Bezabih, grandson of Tekle-Haimanot, King of Gojjam during the reign of Emperor Menelik, had been a resistance leader during the five-year occupation period. On the eve of the arrival in Gojjam of the Italian army, he had been briefly acting Governor of the province; temporarily occupying the throne of his grandfather, so to speak. After the war, another scion of the royal house of Gojjam and a resistance leader in his own right, Ras Hailu Belew, was appointed Governor-General of the province. Although Negash was given a number of high level posts, including that of Deputy Minister in the Prime Minister's office, he was apparently not entirely satisfied. It was while he was Deputy Minister that he was involved in a plot to assassinate the Emperor and, so it was claimed, establish a republican form of government. Given his background, it is unlikely that Negash was driven by republican ideals. His dissent probably rested on the sentiment that he was not awarded posts that were commensurate with his station in life and his services as a guerilla leader.

Lorenzo Ta'ezaz, a man who closely worked with Emperor Haile-Selassie for several years but who was eventually sidelined, was an Eritrean who had come to Ethiopia at an early age. By and large, Eritreans did not relish their status as Italy's colonial subjects living next door to a free and independent Ethiopia. A major grievance of the young was lack of higher education. A tiny number who expressed a desire to serve the Catholic Church and who made the grades were allowed to go beyond primary school and pursue their studies in Rome.

There were also the usual few who were not so good in school but who would strenuously ingratiate themselves with the Italian authorities for the privilege of being sent to Rome to perform odd administrative tasks. Among these was Zer'ay Deresse. This would doubtless astonish Ethiopians of my generation, brought up as we were with the perception of Zer' ay as an exemplary Ethiopian patriot. A courageous act for which he was widely admired was the declaration he made of his strong patriotic sentiments atop the statue of the Lion of Judah in a public square in Rome. Like the Axum obelisk, the statue had been taken to the city by the Fascist invaders. One Sunday morning in the late thirties, Zer'ay mounted the statue and, swashbuckling his Ethiopian sword, denounced the Italians and spoke glowingly of his indomitable country which had unjustly fallen to the Fascists. In the early forties when Emperor Haile-Selassie's government was making every effort in the United Nations to re-unite Eritrea with the motherland, the Ethiopian press found it convenient to play up this story over an extended period of time. Among Addis residents, Zer'ay's patriotic declaration was embellished to include anecdotes of a good number of Italian spectators who were mowed down by his sword on that fateful Sunday in Rome.

There is a fragment of truth to the story. Zer'ay did indeed mount the statue to make his declaration, but no one fell victim to his sword. Indeed he was shot in the legs and captured by the Italian police when he refused to climb down from the statue. But much more tellingly, he had entertained strong anti-Ethiopian sentiments until that celebrated event in a Rome public square. A person who was Zer'ay's grade school classmate in Eritrea spoke to me of the young man's slanderous remarks about Ethiopia and Emperor Haile-Selassie. Zer'ay, he said, was often at odds with him and other students who were aware of the preparations the Italians were making to invade Ethiopia and consequently harboured strong pro-Ethiopian sympathies. Their Italian teacher was a socialist and was similarly disposed to the country. It appears that Zer'ay was eager to please the Italians to realize his dream of one day finding himself in Italy. It was perhaps for this reason that he was openly anti-Ethiopian.

The substance of the story is corroborated by the account of an Ethiopian prisoner in Italy who said that Zer'ay often acted as an interpreter and was well known to the prisoners. An old person well past her nineties today, she informed me several years ago how well she remembered him greeting them routinely with the words "Haile-Selassie's slaves." Fed up with his taunts, she retorted one day that he himself was a worse slave: Benito Mussolini's. After he was shot and incapacitated by the police, Zer'ay was taken to a hospital where the narrator of my story was recuperating from an illness. Although she did not see him, an Ethiopian Catholic priest who visited him told her about his condition and state of mind. The priest informed the lady that in an attempt to shore up Zer'ay spirits, he had told him to put his trust in the hands of the Lord and simply follow His guidance. In a revealing response, Zer'ay said that that was precisely what he had done on that particular Sunday at the public square. After his wounds were treated, Zer'ay was taken back to Asmara and was never heard of again. The lady guessed that he might have been killed. The true reason why Zer'ay changed his mind and turned against his masters is not entirely clear. Talking with my sources, I was left with the impression that he might have had high expectations when he first came to Rome. When these did not materialize, he turned against them.

To get back to Lorenzo, he had apparently completed his primary education in Asmard. Not willing to curry favour with the Italians to be sent to Rome nor being inclined to join the Catholic clergy, he started exploring other avenues for higher education. His resentment of Italian rule led him to establish clandestine contact with Ethiopia's Consul in Asmara, Negadras Wodajo Ali, to whom he frequently provided valuable intelligence on Italy's designs about her imminent invasion of Ethiopia. Wodajo Ali later arranged for Lorenzo to travel to Addis and meet the Emperor. When asked what he wished to do upon arrival in Addis, Lorenzo requested government assistance for higher education. His request was granted and he was awarded a scholarship to study law in Montpellier, France. After securing his law degree, he returned home and served in various posts and ultimately became a public relations attaché to the Emperor, an important post on the eve of Fascist occupation. Lorenzo later accompanied Emperor Haile-Selassie to Geneva, assisted in the drafting of the Emperor's historic address to the League of Nations, and remained with him during the years of exile in England where he was one of three principal aides.

Upon the Emperor's return, Lorenzo was made Minister of Foreign Affairs with the honorific title of Blatten Getta. During exile, there had been some friction between him and the Emperor's other aide, Wolde-Giorgis Wolde-Yohannes, who was now elevated to the post of Tsehafe Te'ezaz, or Minister of the Pen. As head of the Emperor's secretariat, Wolde-Giorgis wielded enormous power. Lorenzo was ill at ease with someone who, an aide like him only a few years previously with equal access to the monarch, was now the officially designated channel of communication with the monarch. Inevitably, rivalry emerged between the two long time aides. Step by step, Lorenzo was distanced from the centre of power. He was first moved to the Ministry of Posts, Telephones, and Telegraphs. From there, he was made Chairman of the Upper Chamber of the Parliament. Finally, he was appointed Ambassador to the Soviet Union where he died.

There has been talk of Lorenzo's sympathy for a constitutional monarchy. It is said that he once intimated this to Ras Abebe Aregai, a veteran of the resistance, a powerful post figure, and in many ways a man of considerable political skill; but hardly a visionary. Lorenzo might have calculated that having Ras Abebe's sympathies was indispensable for any future movement in the direction he had in mind, but obviously misjudged the Ras's political orientation and great prudence. For, so the story goes, the Ras went to the Emperor and said he was not sure what the young Lorenzo was talking about. The Emperor was of course in a better position to figure out Lorenzo's intensions. It is difficult to substantiate this story but if true, it must have been one more reason for sidelining Lorenzo.

Makonnen Desta, a trained anthropologist from an American University, had returned home before the war. After the war, he was made Minster of Education. His liberal views and freewheeling life style did not sit well with the political establishment. He was first moved to be the Governor General of Wollega province. Later, he was appointed to the inconsequential post of General Manager of Ecclesiastical affairs in the Ethiopian Orthodox Church. He finally left government service altogether and died years later of leukemia.

Prior to the occupation, Agegnehu Engida had executed wall paintings for the Parliament building as well as some churches. He had also painted portraits of distinguished personalities, including that of young Emperor Haile-Selassie and Empress Menen. It is unclear how he spent his time during the years of occupation. In subsequent years, he continued with his art work, spasmodically as it appears. He was an appointed member of the Upper Chamber of Parliament where there was little to do. By most accounts, he took liberally to the bottle and was equally unrestrained in his remarks about the powers that be. An acquaintance has recently informed me that he would talk with obvious relish about Wolde-Girogis's failed attempt to be the Emperor's son-in-law, contrasting Wolde-Giorgis's modest origins with the exalted station of Princess Tenagne Work. He subsequently died in a mysterious car accident, widely presumed to have been engineered by his foes in government. This gave rise to stories that he was assassinated for his progressive political views. Although nothing credible has surfaced to support this view, the perception persists that he was among the small group of reform-minded post-war dissenters. And pereceptions can sometimes be strong motivations for social or political projects.

There were other dissenters expressing varying degrees of disaffection with imperial rule: Blata Kidane-Mariam Yemane-Birhan, Yohannes Remha, Bekele Anasimos, Gebre-Medhin Gossa and others; practically all of whom had been in government service at one time or another. They were disparate individuals and advocated no articulated reform programme. They resented the fact that corrupt officials were tolerated; they were intolerant of condescending members of the aristocracy; and they yearned for a more liberal political environment. All this was a good enough indication of trouble to come if the government failed to take remedial measures.

Dissenters of the second category were by and large products of the Emperor's reformist policies. After his return from exile, the Emperor proceeded with the modernization programme which had been interrupted by the Fascists. Elementary and secondary schools were built in Addis and the principal provincial centres. Military training schools were established for the Imperial Guard, the Police, and the Air Force and the old Army training centre at Guenet resuscitated. As there were no institutions of higher learning, graduates of secondary schools were sent overseas (principally to the U.K., U.S. and Canada) to pursue their college and university studies at government expense. By 1950/51 they started to trickle back and were posted in different government departments.

As expected, the returnees began to exchange notes on their respective experiences. The hotel where they stayed upon arrival soon turned into a beehive of intellectuals mouthing libertarian views. Ras Imru, a member of the aristocracy reputed for his progressive views, offered them a building where they could meet far from the glare of informers and exchange views on the country's problems. Germame Neway became the man in charge of the building. He soon began to organize meetings among the returnees. In a none-too-prudent move, he started inviting young Imperial Guard officers serving under his brother General Mengistu. One of these was Workineh Gebeyehu.

Workineh was born in the Debre Tabor region of Gondar around 1930. His father was an Orthodox priest and his early education religious. He was trained in *quine* (Ge'ez poetry) by a number of celebrated scholars in Gondar and Lasta. His yearning for learning was such that, at the age of fourteen or thereabouts, he decided to travel to Addis Ababa to further his education. Some suggest that his final destination was Jerusalem, the eternal dream of men with a clerical background. Having spent some time in the seminary of Addis Ababa's Trinity Cathedral, he secured the assistance of someone at the Ministry of Education to get a transfer to the Menelik II elementary school. After a few years there, he applied to the newly established Imperial Guard cadet school run by the Swedes. He was accepted and graduated three years later at the top of his class. Inevitably, he caught the eye of Emperor who was now following his progress through the ranks. The young officer did not disappoint, as he excelled in any assignment given him by his superiors. He became the favourite officer of both the Commander and Deputy Commander of the Imperial Guard.

Workineh joined the Ethiopian battalion which was sent to South Korea as part of the United Nations' military mission to defend the country from invasion by North Korea and China. This gave him the first opportunity to take part in modern warfare. More importantly, his association with military officers from the west opened his eyes to liberal democracy. His return to the Imperial Guard did not last long, for the Emperor had decided to bring him into the country's intelligence establishment. As a senior intelligence officer, he obtained training in Sweden and visited a number of other countries. He now started to work closely with the Emperor. His relationship grew closer when he was brought in to work in the monarch's private cabinet. Workineh was now in a position to express his views on issues of national importance: land reform, civil service reform, the transformation of the military establishment into a coherent and effective instrument of national defence and, more generally, how improvements could be made in the way the country was governed. On some of these issues he brought outside consultants and submitted proposals for reform. He made headway with some, but not with the more consequential issues like land reform and internal administration.

Germame Neway's story shall be presented in some detail in the section below, but his views on land reform merit a few words at this juncture. Germame did his graduate studies at Columbia University. His master's thesis was on the white settlement policy in the Kenyan highlands, a natural enough subject for a young Ethiopian who was preoccupied with his own country's land tenure system. When he returned to Ethiopia, Germame was assigned to the Ministry of Interior and became, along with like-minded young friends like Haile-Mariam Kebede and Wolde-Semait Gebre-Wold, a member of a committee created to distribute government land to landless peasants. These young men approached their work with gusto but with little else. They got together a thousand landless peasants from four districts neighbouring Addis Ababa (Ambo, Sululta, Merhabete, and Debre-Libanos). Papers indicating that each peasant had been awarded 20 hectares of government owned land in the Gibbe River valley were distributed and the peasants instructed to go there promptly.

Workneh Gebeyehu

When the army of a thousand peasants from highland Ethiopia arrived in the valley, they were confronted, perhaps for the first time in their lives, with intense heat and malaria. They immediately started to trek back to their more salubrious environments. Those familiar with the Dergue regime will recall a similar fiasco, but played out on a huge scale, with departing peasants being forcibly returned to their new settlements. As we shall see later, Germame would repeat the mistake as Governor of Wollamo a few years later.

Germame Neway: The Angry Young Man Behind the Coup

The attempted coup d'état of December 1960 took place in this general context. Colonel Workineh, the chief of intelligence, had full knowledge of the political orientation of the Neway brothers. But he was not privy to their plan and was enticed only at the very last moment. So was General Mulugeta Buli, the first post war commander of the Imperial Guard and by most accounts a man of outstanding leadership qualities. General Tsigie Dibu, the Police Commissioner, was also brought in unawares at the last minute. The hurried and poorly mounted coup was destined to fail.

Many persons would later speculate how lucky the country would have been had the attempt succeeded. A constitutional monarchy would have been established and the 1974 blood bath as well as the costly civil war avoided. A golden opportunity for peaceful change was sadly missed, argue these people. It is not all that evident that Germame Neway, the driving force behind the coup, would have presided over such a peaceful transformation, had he succeeded in his scheme. What we know of him does not suggest a man with the kind of leadership qualities required to skillfully steer the country towards a peaceful social and political transformation.

There is little doubt that Germame had his heart in the right place. He was selfless and championed the underdog. There is anecdotal evidence which confirms this. When a friend living overseas sent word that he was strapped for money, Germame, who had little cash to spare, sold his car and came to his rescue. Often, he went to the family church, St. George's in Arada, to distribute money to mendicants. Berating a friend who was awaiting change from a shoeshine boy one Sunday morning, Germame made him give up the change. The shoeshine boy, who was only expecting to receive the normal charge of ten cents, was jubilant with a windfall that was the equivalent of shining nine pairs of shoes. As Governor of Wollamo, Germame was openly sympathetic to landless peasants and equally openly hostile to landed chiefs. In his office, he unfailingly attended to cases brought up by people of modest means, but would walk past local grandees awaiting their turn. A friend recently informed me that Germame, noticing a poor peasant walking behind his mounted master, stopped both, told the latter to get off his horse and ordered the bemused peasant to mount the animal and proceed, with the humbled master in tow.

Germame was a revolutionary. Perhaps alone among his dissident friends, he made no secret of his convictions. He wore his revolution on his sleeve. He was often in a modest khaki suit and wore a red necktie. But one cannot say that he was always deliberate in his actions. Often, he was disinclined to weigh the different forces at play in a given situation. He seems to have believed that reasoned assessment would lead to inaction. He was decisive; perhaps impulsively so. His way was to take audacious steps that would somehow sweep aside all obstacles in his path. In this he fit the mold of the much admired social model, the *defar* (the dauntless macho). He was doubtless conscious of, perhaps even inspired by, the Amharic maxim *'defarina chis mewtcha ayatam'* (the smoke from the fire inside a hut and the brave always manage to find a way out).

A good instance of this was his decision when Governor of Wollamo to remove tenant farmers from a highland region and relocate them on government granted individual plots in a river valley. Germame won the hearts of the peasants. They were delighted to leave their rented holdings for the freehold he provided them. Their joy was short-lived, however, as they were soon driven away by the blaze and malaria of the Blatten valley. The unfortunate peasants swallowed their pride and asked their former landlords to allow them to return to their previous holdings. While in the Ministry of the Interior years before, Germame had been involved in a similar failed effort. This second initiative was hardly an act driven by careful judgment, or the memory of the previous incident.

Germame had done enough to infuriate the local chiefs in Wollamo. They were now plotting to get rid of him. The central government got wind of this and sent Imperial Guard troops to evacuate him to Addis Ababa.[5] Today's conventional view of the Emperor's Government might lead one to assume that Germame was perhaps disciplined or even thrown behind bars for his Wollamo debacle. On the contrary, he was appointed Governor of the district of Jijiga in Eastern Ethiopia. Jijiga was a much larger and politically more sensitive district than Wollamo.

Germame detested the officials who surrounded the Emperor. He believed that they stood in the way of progress and the only way to deal with them, so he said openly to friends, was to finish them off (*mefjet new*). When failure stared both him and his brother in the face on that fateful December day in 1960, Germame's oft repeated threat to finish off the old guard was given vent. Some fourteen ministers and senior officials of the Emperor were gunned down, with Germame initiating the shooting as some later alleged. Among the victims was a man under whom Germame had served and whom he was said to have admired enormously: the resistance leader Ras Abebe Aregai. Also killed was Ethiopia's leader in the making, General Mulugeta Buli.

Germame Neway as a student in the U.S.

The picture of Germame that emerges from all this is that of an impulsive young revolutionary who might have had his heart in the right place but who was violent (witness, for instance, the shooting of his own brother when they were about to be captured) and who seemed unable to calmly weigh forces arrayed against him in any given situation. His inclination was to sweep aside such forces through precipitate action and, when deemed necessary, through violence. Had he succeeded in his plan to overthrow the government in December 1960, he might have continued to use force to achieve his goals; much as Mengistu Haile-Mariam did later. And the end result would probably have been no less ruinous.

It might appear reasonable to speculate that Germame would have been restrained or even pushed aside by the more deliberative General Mulugeta and/or Colonel Workineh, had the attempted coup succeeded. And that these two might have joined hands in a peaceful political transformation of the country. But that would be to underestimate the differing visions and personal ambitions of the two strong willed officers; and the potential for an ultimate struggle between them. It would be idle to speculate precisely how that struggle might have ended. Given, however, the personalities of the principal protagonists involved, especially Germame's, one would be hard put to contend that an opportunity for peaceful change was missed.

CHAPTER 5

In the Service of the Imperial Ethiopian Government: The Initial Three Years

An Ethiopian U.N. Expert to Ethiopia

At the ECA, my work was becoming increasingly tedius. My learning curve appeared to have reached the point of diminishing returns and I began thinking of other opportunities. As luck would have it, I was called to the office of the Executive Secretary one day along with two other staff members. We were informed that the new Ethiopian Minister of Planning and Development, Haddis Alemayehu, had approached the ECA for support in preparing the country's Third Five-Year Development plan. We were to work on this important exercise.

After a courtesy call on Minister Haddis, James Pickett of the U. K. and I got down to preparing background papers for the Plan. The third member of the team was head of a Department at ECA and dropped out on account of his administrative duties. Jim and I were among a dozen or so professionals engaged in the exercise. It was curious that I, an Ethiopian, should be serving as a U.N. technical assistance expert in my own country. Was there a precedent? Would there be problems? The intellectual excitement of working on a major policy document left little room for these questions.

At the UN, I had always felt that the work did not expose me sufficiently to real world problems. Even in the case of Southern Rhodesia where I had spent some time gathering and analyzing data, the report was discussed only perfunctorily and there was no further interaction with the country's officials, to say little of its impact on their day-to-day management of the economy. The work in the Planning Ministry was intensely interactive and plainly aimed at formulating policy.

Working on my own country and with my own compatriots was also a welcome experience. To be sure, there were occasional problems. The Yugoslav economists at the Ministry saw Jim and I as unwelcome squatters on what had been their special turf for several years. They had been sent by their country to draft the First and second five-year plans. But they were now playing second fiddle to two U.N. experts. On the whole, they were unenthusiastic about the new task of preparing the third five-year plan. There was also an economist from Communist Poland who was in an economics universe entirely his own: uncomprehending of what was going on around him and in turn incomprehensible in his weird interventions at meetings. There were a few exceptions, of course; an agricultural economist from Yugoslavia being one. Having prepared the required background studies, Jim and I returned to the ECA after three months. Preparations would soon begin for the actual drafting of the plan.

A Curious Call From the Prime Minister

A few weeks later, I received an unusual telephone call. The man on the phone said I should come to the Prime Minister's office at four o'clock on a certain day. "You probably think that this is a government department," I responded. "This is the Economic Commission for Africa." "You are Ato Tekalign Gedamu who works at Africa Hall, are you not?" asked the man. To my affirmative response, he said an appointment had been made for me to see the Prime Minister and that I should present myself at his office on the appointed day and hour. I was puzzled and called a close friend in government to shed some light on this strange incident. "There is no puzzle, as far as I can make out," he said. "If the Prime Minister of Ethiopia wishes to see you, what are you going to say? That your have no business with him?" But what was the business, I asked. He replied that I was putting the question to the wrong party.

Perhaps the call had something to do with my recent work at the Ministry of Planning, I surmised. If so, why should it be raised at the level of the Prime Minister? Was there another reason? My speculation led nowhere. And so I presented myself at the Prime Minister's office as requested. His secretary, Abitew Gebreyes, didn't know me, or I him. "Ato Tekalign Gedamu?" he asked as I entered his office. Assured that I was indeed that person, he led me to the waiting room across his office. A short while later, he came back and escorted me to the Prime Minister, Tsehafe Te'ezaz Aklilu Habte-Wold. To my surprise the Tsehafe-Te'ezaz got up from his chair and extended his arm for a handshake. Should a Prime Minister take the trouble to greet a relatively unknown young man in that fashion, I wondered.

"You are Tekalign Gedamu?" I said yes with a voice purposely kept low: a sign of respect for a man of his station. "Why is it that I do not know you?" How am I supposed to answer that question, I asked myself, and responded with some hesitation: "But I know Your Excellency." Somewhat surprised, he asked where and how. I told him that when I was in secondary school in the late forties, I occasionally leafed through the pages of the local daily where his interventions at the U.N. regarding Eritrea's reunion with Ethiopia were extensively reported. I had also heard his response to Somalia's attack on Ethiopia at the inaugural meeting of the Organization of African Unity four

Emperor Haile-Selassie talking to Prime Minister Aklilu, c. late 1960s

years previously. "That is really not enough to make you say you really know me," he replied. Asked what I was doing at the ECA, I gave a brief description of my duties. "Very good," he said. "That is all. I just wanted to meet you."

The encounter could not have lasted for more than five minutes. What kind of meeting is this, I asked my friends in government. "Something is clearly brewing," said one. I myself could guess as much, but what precisely was brewing? Perhaps people in government were discussing a possible post. Belai Abbai who was at ECA had recently been offered a job. It looked likely that my name was being considered for some position. Sooner or later I would know.

In my office at the ECA a few days later, a headline on the first page of *The Ethiopian Herald* caught my eye. "His Imperial Majesty Makes Appointments," it read. I went down the list of appointees. At the bottom, my name appeared as the new General Manager of the Technical Agency, an autonomous project preparation body under the Minister of Planning and Development. The riddle was finally solved, but why did it happen this way? I was an international civil servant working for the UN and not for any government, as the personnel manual which I was given on recruitment indicated. Would the newspaper article raise doubts within the ECA about my loyalties to the U.N.? Would people suspect that I had all along been some low level agent of the host government? Though far-fetched, it was disconcerting. I decided to do two things: explain to Mr. Gardiner, the Executive Secretary, the circumstances of my appointment; then see the Prime Minister.

I told Gardiner I regretted that my name had appeared in the paper without my prior resignation from the services of the U.N. and that the initiative had been taken by the government soon after an enigmatic meeting with the Prime Minister. He told me that he understood my concern and that I should not worry. I told him I intended to resign retroactively. He agreed.

Next, I met with Tsehafe Te'ezaz Aklilu and explained that, being an international civil servant, I was concerned that the notice of my appointment might create the false perception that I had been working for the Ethiopian government in contravention of U.N. rules. Why had he not at least intimated my appointment even if only in general terms to enable me to hand in a letter of resignation? He smiled and said, "You young people do not know your country's traditions well enough. Imperial appointments are never revealed to the appointee prior to the formal act. As to the U.N., there is nothing to worry about. Don't forget that I was Foreign Minister for several years[1]. This is a small matter over which you should not lose sleep. You should now talk to the Minister of Planning about your new duties."

I had always wished to know who exactly in government had proposed my name to the Prime Minister. It would take almost a quarter of a century to unravel this small mystery. While I was working at the African Development Bank in the late eighties, my friend Zaude Retta had come to Abidjan on a short term assignment for the bank. Over dinner one evening, he asked if I recalled his visit to my ECA office in the sixties and his subsequent dinner invitation for me and a few friends. I could only remember vaguely. "I was on the lookout for young educated people on behalf of the Prime Minister," he said. "That invitation was to get to know you. From then on, I observed your work and life style and finally recommended a suitable posting to the Prime Minister." I had, of course, known Zaude over the years. He had been trained in France as a journalist and had returned to the Ministry of Information as a middle level civil servant. Later he had become Ethiopia's Ambassador to Italy. After the revolution, he had joined U.N.'s IFAD in Rome. We had kept in touch all along. However, I had no clue that he had ever acted as a talent scout for the Prime Minister.

After my meeting with the Prime Minister, I went back to my office and submitted a letter of resignation to the Executive Secretary, conveniently backdated to precede my appointment. Next, I met Haddis Alemayehu who explained the post I was to occupy. A meeting was arranged later with the incumbent General Manager of the Technical Agency, Habte-Ab Bairu. He took me through the work of the agency. The handing over formalities were completed in short order. It appeared he had been sidelined, and I was a bit concerned. Although he did not look troubled, I felt that my service to the Imperial Ethiopian Government had begun on a none-too-felicitous note. But I was relieved to learn later that he had been posted at another department of government.

The Technical Agency

The mission of the Technical Agency was to increase the flow of development projects for investment, both private and public. This was very much in line with the thinking in the development community in the sixties that underdeveloped countries were not generating enough bankable projects and that measures were required to address the problem. Every year, the agency was allocated money from the central government budget to fund feasibility studies. Bilateral aid agencies also supported the Agency's programme. USAID, for instance, provided a team of experts from the Stanford Research Institute.

I got down to work with Ethiopian, German, American and Yugoslav experts to formulate terms of references for overseas consulting firms to prepare feasibility studies. In the basement of the Agency, an old Englishman presided over maps, charts, and sheaves of paper in a hall labeled the Operations Room. There was hardly any operation to speak of. The bespectacled, stooping gentle old soul with a head sparsely covered with strands of long, gray hair had been a Brigadier in the British Army. The room's appellation was no more than an echo of his military past.

Sitting down with him a few days after I arrived, I asked what exactly he was doing. People who knew him had alerted me that his abstract and sweeping ideas were often difficult to decipher. I had to give him my undivided attention. Brigadier Rouse had also been an employee of Bolton and Hennessey, a British consulting firm working on water resources in Ethiopia. When the firm left the country, the Brigadier stayed behind with maps and data accumulated by the firm over a number of years.

As much of his thinking as I could make out focused on the need to develop water resources and increase food supply. Rouse was burdened with a profound concern over declining food supplies. He was worried about droughts not just in Ethiopia but in India as well. Famine would drive wave upon wave of starving Indians to swarm the East African shoreline and Ethiopia. A response to this titanic challenge had to be made. Rouse's thought process struck me as being more mystical than analytical; and his almost inaudible voice accentuated that impression. I found him more arcane than I was led to believe. No mundane terms of reference or feasibility study was ever likely to negotiate the short flight of stairs from the Brigadier's Operations Room in the basement of the Agency to my office on the first floor. I was left with a feeling of unease at the old soldier's arresting vision of a looming catastrophe and his none-too-specific plan to counter it.

The Brigadier rarely attended meetings of staff, hardly commented on the terms of references regularly prepared by the Agency, or on the feasibility studies that came in their train. Some people believed that he was on to something that would serve as a wakeup call for somnolent bureaucrats. For this and other reasons, he was left pretty much on his own. He himself was rarely inclined to make his office colleagues aware of his presence in the building, let alone share in his speculations.

One day, the Brigadier said he wanted to talk to me urgently. As always, he started ponderously. It soon transpired that he was having a problem with the Inland Revenue Department of the Ministry of Finance. He had been informed that he had to pay a substantial sum of money in back taxes. How could this happen? I asked. The consulting firm he worked for had left the country without paying their taxes, claimed the Department. Brigadier Rouse was the only man the staff of the Department could lay their hands on. I addressed a letter to the Minister of Finance, Yilma Deressa, indicating that it was rather odd to hold the Brigadier responsible for the firm's tax obligations. Rouse was not their agent. The Department should get in touch with the firm in the U.K. The Minister reviewed the letter and instructed his officials to let go of the old man: an instruction typical of the self-confidence and decisiveness with which this highly regarded official often resolved day to day problems.

It might be of interest to mention in passing that, upon my arrival at the Agency, I had arranged for a subscription to *Monthly Review*, the Marxist journal. It did cross my mind that if the government's security agents were to know, I might be required to explain the use of public funds to subscribe to a journal whose subversive mission figured prominently on its cover. Neither I nor the young Ethiopian staff working with me hardly lost sleep over this. We read the articles of each issue of the journal with youthful zeal and commitment.

A good portion of my time was taken up assisting with the preparation of the Third Five-Year Plan at the Ministry of Planning. As I previously mentioned, I had written some background papers for this when working as a U.N. expert. There were now more experts in the Ministry. The World Bank had sent a senior economist to advice the Minister and there was a contingent of multinational experts (the Harvard Group) funded by the UNDP. All worked on the preparation of the Plan. A policy committee chaired by Minister Haddis had been established to monitor their work and I became a member. The committee met twice a week and got busier as the work progressed.

Haddis Alemayehu's commitment to the Plan was extraordinary. He was attentive to every detail and was never in a hurry to wind up the twice weekly afternoon meetings which went into the late hours of the evening. He was a widower and had no family awaiting him for dinner. Those who had families complained, though never to the Minister himself. Had they done so, he would have probably shot back awkward reminders about the importance of the exercise. And that would have silenced everyone; such was the sense of abhorrence of anything that might suggest less than a total commitment to one's duties. The seemingly interminable evening sessions had to be endured. I myself was a bachelor and had no one waiting for me at home, although I did not suffer from any shortage of social commitments.

The draft of the Plan was duly completed. Prior to its submission to the Cabinet it was reviewed by a group of high-level visiting economists, among whom was the Nobel Laureate Jan Tinbergen of the Netherlands. (With Ragnar Frisch, Tinbergen was the co-winner of the first Nobel Prize for Economics in 1969, just after his visit to Addis Ababa). The economists had come to Addis for a U.N. meeting and it was thought that the opportunity should not be missed of getting their views on the document. To the best of my recollection, their comments did not lead to a major revision of the document's analyses or recommendations. In due course it was submitted to the Cabinet and was finally adopted by the Parliament as official government policy. Implementation would prove to be a more demanding challenge, however.

A few weeks after the Plan was adopted, I received a telephone call to present myself at the Grand Palace as soon as possible. I was in a meeting at the Technical Agency, but that was hardly a good reason to be excused. I got into my car and drove the five- minute journey from the Technical Agency at Arat Kilo to the grounds of the Grand Palace of Emperor Menelik. The guards let me in after the customary checking.

On the verandah of the old building which served as Emperor Haile- Selassie's office, a crowd of government officials was milling around. People talked about the impending appointments of the morning. I wondered where I was going to be moved. Presently, the name of the most senior official among us was called out. He was led to a small office which Prime Minister Aklilu kept in the building and came out a few minutes later with a broad smile on his face. He had been promoted to a post which elicited the smile. Everyone jostled towards him to offer their congratulations and the customary kiss on the cheeks.

My name was called towards the end. I entered the Prime Minister's office and found him standing behind his desk. As soon as I shut the door behind me, he proceeded to read a piece of paper in his hand: "I bring to your attention His Imperial Majesty's pleasure and gracious command that you have been appointed as the Managing Director of the Development Bank of Ethiopia." In making the formal announcement, Aklilu was acting in his capacity as Minister of the Pen, i.e. as the head of the Emperor's Secretariat, a post he held concurrently with that of Prime Minister. He congratulated me with a kiss on the cheeks. I said thank you and I left his office promptly for the next in line to come in. "What post have you been promoted to?" asked everyone standing outside. I explained my new post, was duly kissed by several people, and drove back to my office to resume my meeting.

No sooner had I arrived than another call from the Palace followed saying I should return instantaneously. Wondering whether they had made a mistake in posting me at the Bank, I quickly drove back to the Palace. As soon as I reached the verandah of the Emperor's office, someone shouted, "What happened to you? How could you leave without rendering the customary homage to His Majesty?" The procedure was for newly appointed officials to line up in order of seniority after their brief encounter with the Prime Minister, be presented to the Emperor, render a deep bow, wait a few minutes to hear the Emperor say a word or two, bow again and leave. I had missed this last step. As soon as I arrived, an official rushed me towards the Emperor who was already seated in his car. I bowed, was told to "show commitment to duty," and left for my office. I was a novice to Palace protocol and had gotten off unscathed. I wondered what would have happened had I been a long serving official accustomed to the ways of the Palace.

The Development Bank of Ethiopia: Chairman Haddis Alemayehu and a Contentious Board Meeting

The Development Bank of Ethiopia had been established in 1951. Years later, I learned that it was among the first institutions of its kind in the developing world. Its first Managing Director was Alfred Abel, an Austrian and long time resident of Ethiopia. Butkus, a German, succeeded Abel who was in turn succeeded by two Ethiopians: Araya Ekubagzi and Worku Habte-Wold. I was the last member of this quintet, for the Bank would be merged with another finance institution upon my departure two years later.

My immediate predecessor had been hobbled by a contentious relationship with the Board of Directors and his lending authority had been severely constrained as a result. When I started, I spent a couple of months familiarizing myself with the work and staff of the Bank. At my first working meeting with the Board, I requested that the original lending authority of the Managing Director be restored, for it would be difficult to run the Bank effectively under the new straightjacket. My predecessor had been the only one in the history of the Bank to work under a tight leash. I explained that a new manager should be given the benefit of the doubt. Nothing should prevent the Board from re-imposing the constraints subsequently if it so desired. I had no reason to believe that the Board would take this as anything other than a gesture intended to secure initial support and encouragement.

Haddis Alemayehu, the Chairman of the Board, was someone under whom I had worked at my previous post. Our relationship had been cordial. I respected his commitment and his single-minded effort to grasp enough of the fundamentals of economic policy to provide effective leadership to the Ministry of Planning. And in my view, if not in the view of others, he had done relatively well in this regard. I expected him to appreciate the justification behind my proposal and to lend his support. As it turned out, he was the only member of the Board to object and persist to the end.

His reasoning appeared cogent. We had grounds, he said, to withdraw the discretionary authority from the previous Managing Director after he had worked with us for some time. Tekalign is new to the Bank, though all of us know him from his previous work. He does not have a track record here. On what basis do we restore the previous lending authority? There was a pause in the room. A few persons spoke in support of my proposal. I took the floor again and said that the Board's recent decision to limit the authority of my predecessor had arisen from a specific set of circumstances. All previous managing directors had worked with a broad lending mandate. That was the norm. And I was only asking for the norm. All members of the Board except Haddis agreed.

At the end of the meeting, I stayed behind to talk to Haddis. "Your Excellency," I started. "I was a bit taken aback by what has just transpired. You know me. We have worked together for a number of years. And I was only saying that norms should be respected until some compelling situation dictated otherwise..." Haddis interrupted me and said that he was guided by principles, not personalities, that he had made his point to the Board, and that he is a person who did not like to be dictated to. He was visibly annoyed, which surprised me further. In deference to his age and position, I refrained from carrying on with the conversation.

Coming to Grips with the Bank's Business

Chairman Haddis's minority view was recorded in the minutes, and the discretionary lending authority of the Managing Director duly restored. A few months later, Haddis left the Board. For a long time, he had been expressing a desire to resign. He had been promised a very active role when he was persuaded to become Minister of Planning and Development. But he had been frustrated with bureaucratic wrangling and turf warfare and felt that his Ministry wasn't being given adequate support to carry out its important mandate of coordinating development policy. His request for resignation was accepted and he was appointed a member of the upper chamber of Parliament where many frustrated former public servants found shelter. Agriculture Minister Abebe Retta took his place as Chairman of the Bank board.

There were a number of management problems that I had to address. A few good staff were sprinkled in the various departments, but on the whole there was considerable deadwood. Moreover, the Bank's financial resources were modest. This had been noted when we were preparing the Third Five-Year Plan, and it had been recommended that the Bank should be merged with another finance agency, the Investment Corporation, with the view to pooling resources and to laying the foundations for a more vigorous lending institution. I decided to push for the merger and, in the meantime, try to improve the Bank's performance to the extent possible.

In the course of my visits to Bank funded projects I had been surprised that a few of our loans in Eritrea were granted to Italian settlers. But I was satisfied that they were among the bank's more performing clients. A large number of small loans were given in Tigrai, Shoa, and in the western and southern provinces. They were not doing well. There were loans in the Awash Valley to farms run by graduates from the College of Agriculture at Alemaya and there were a few coffee farms in Jimma. These performed better. A tea plantation in Wush Wush some 60 miles South-West of Jimma was a total failure, with an old lonely Swedish manager doing little beyond telling stories of the project's misfortunes and sharing his problems with hardly a friend outside the *araqui* bottle. On the whole, loan repayments were inadequate to finance a meaningful number of new projects.

One day, half a dozen persons representing sesame farmers in the Humera district in the province of Semien and Begemdir came to see me. They said that their region had been neglected. There was no bank they could go to for loans. Every year sesame traders descended upon them offering loans in cash which had to be repaid within months. Sesame commanded a high price in the world market. It was only the traders and exporters who reaped the benefits. "We the farmers are always deep in debt," they said. "This Bank was established by our government to assist farmers. We have come to ask you to provide us with credit and deliver us from the loan sharks."

I was not entirely comfortable with their story. Apart from being dismayed by their predicament, I was pained by the Bank's paucity of resources to meet their needs. But telling them my side of the story wasn't going to be of much help. Though I felt I had little to offer, I could at least listen sympathetically as they unburdened their frustrations with the loan sharks who would come when the crop was still in the field and when the farmers were most in need of cash. Any amount of money the farmers asked for would be given, with the undertaking that the repayment be made during the harvest months not in cash, but in kind. For instance, a farmer who borrowed Birr 2,000 from a merchant in August would be made to sign an undertaking that he would repay the loan at harvest time in December with 20 quintals of sesame seed; i.e. at a rate of Birr 100 per quintal (100 kilogrammes). In December a quintal of sesame seed would fetch Birr 200. In other words, the merchant would collect Birr 4,000 in December for a loan of Birr 2,000 advanced in August, charging an interest rate of 100% in four months, or 300% a year. I had been told about loan sharks before, but had never heard a graphic story like this.

The inevitable question came at the end of the story. "How can you help us?" I wasn't going to make a fool of myself saying that the Bank was strapped for resources and that their problem would be addressed in the context of the forthcoming merger of my bank with another financial institution. My reply was that I would be prepared to send a team from the Bank to visit their region and talk to them again after studying the team's report. What I said sounded positive enough and made them happy. I was a little concerned, however, that I might have raised false hopes.

The idea I had thrown out to avoid sounding negative increasingly appeared worth following in earnest. A few days later, I talked to Bisrat Jemaneh, one of the abler members of staff, to make a trip to the region, conduct a study and submit his findings. He did this in fairly short order. The conclusion was that something needed to be done. Farmers who produced a cash crop in high demand and who regularly repaid principal and interest charges of 300% per annum were unlikely to default on the Bank's low interest loans. Our lending rates were low at the time.

But where was the money to come from? It was estimated that the farmers needed a crop loan of some Eth $3 million; a staggering amount for the Bank. Our loans averaged about Birr 50-60,000 and the biggest loan we extended to a mill making toilet paper was no more than Birr 300,000. There was another problem. The farmers had no collateral. In other regions, there was land which we routinely accepted for this purpose. In Humera, there was no freehold land. Farmland had not been measured and parceled out. When I asked what the merchants took as collateral, I was told that they did not require any collateral. This appeared to be one reason for the confiscatory nature of their interest rate: they were covering their risk of extending loans without collateral.

Solutions had to be found to these two problems. Our Bank had an overdraft facility from the Commercial Bank of Ethiopia. It was of the order of Birr 500,000. I picked up the phone one day and explained the problem I faced to Tafarra Deguefe, the General Manager of the Commercial Bank of Ethiopia. I told him that a study had been undertaken which showed that Humera farmers were a good credit risk. Could he make available an overdraft facility of Birr 3, 000,000? It didn't take him long to say yes, but he added that we would have to pay 9% instead of 6% on our overdraft. I agreed.

For the collateral problem, I decided to extend the loan to a cooperative, not to individual farmers. When they next visited the Bank, the Humera farmers were advised to form a producers cooperative registered by the regulatory authority, the Ministry of Community Development and Social Affairs. The cooperative would borrow from the Bank, distribute the loan proceeds to individual farmers based on its own assessment of individual need and ability to repay, collect the repayments at the end on behalf of the Bank, and finally act as a guarantor of the loan. It all came to a surprisingly happy ending. A cooperative was duly formed, was registered, obtained a loan of Birr 3,000,000 at 12% interest (compared to the 300% for the money borrowed from the merchants). The loan was repaid in full and our Bank earned an income of Birr 90,000 from the 3% margin added to the interest of 9% paid on the overdraft facility from the Commercial Bank of Ethiopia. The farmers were delighted to get money at 12% interest, a far cry from the 300% they had been paying to sesame traders. Overnight, our Bank's reputation soared in Humera.

This was an exceptional case. The loan was for an export product of high demand extended to a farming community motivated by the desire to be liberated from the burden of loan sharks; and eager to be in the good books of the Bank. We could not repeat this example without further funds and without incurring risks which would sooner or later reach unacceptable levels. For the most part, we used the limited repayments on our loans to fund new projects. It was a frustrating experience, knowing that the opportunities were great but our resources paltry. Added to this frustration were occasional calls to the Palace which meant that the Managing Director had to be on his toes at all times. Borrowers experiencing difficulties with their repayments often took their cases to the Emperor directly, if they were fortunate enough to have contacts in the Palace. In the Ethiopia of those days, every citizen had the right of appeal to the Emperor, whatever the nature of his grievance against an official or department of government and whatever his station in life. The Development Bank of Ethiopia was a government owned institution perceived as the Emperor's initiative to encourage investment. If borrowers encountered difficulties in meeting their repayment obligations, or if they thought the Bank was not helpful, they took their case to the Emperor, and the Bank's Managing Director was summoned to the Palace to explain himself.

One morning, I was called to the Palace to respond to questions regarding one of the Bank's clients, Ato Sebhatu Gebreyesus. Years ago, Sebhatu had borrowed money to expand his large horticultural farm located (then) in the outskirts of Addis Ababa. The loan had not been serviced for a long time and the Bank had taken the client to court and obtained a judgment to foreclose. The collateral for the loan, his home, was to be sold at a public auction. When the auction notice appeared in the papers, Sebhatu went straight to the Palace.

He had me summoned to explain why the Bank was taking this drastic step. I explained to the Emperor that the borrower had defaulted and that the Bank had taken legal steps to recover its money. The Emperor, appreciative of Sebhatu's unusual entrepreneurial and innovative talents, posed an interesting question. "Sebhatu is using this money on a good project. If you were to force him to repay, what would you do with the money?" I replied that I would be making another loan with it. "So long as the money is put to good use, what difference does it make whether it is Sebhatu or some other borrower that is involved?" It was a question of offering the opportunity extended to Ato Sebhatu to other borrowers, I replied "Well, give him more time to pay" was the Emperor's unambiguous directive. Rescheduling was the inevitable outcome. The auction process was temporarily stopped in return for a good faith immediate repayment of a portion of the loan to work out a rescheduling. Little did I know at the time that Ato Sebhatu would one day become my father-in-law.

I was called to the Palace on several such cases, and was often obliged to find some compromise that would simultaneously satisfy the Bank, the client and, needless to say, His Imperial Majesty. There was one case that involved more than the usual quick fix. Woudassie Tesfaye had applied for a loan to expand her poultry farm in the eastern town of Dire Dawa. We had extended loans to a number of small poultry projects and were ready to consider her request favourably. But we were faced with a client who was asking for special treatment. She wanted to import an electric powered structure from Germany composed of a series of metal cages to accommodate her chickens. Feed and water were carried on conveyer belts to each fowl in its individual cage in the structure. Chicken droppings would be disposed of similarly.

The Bank's technical personnel took one good look at the loan request and said the project would not fly. Who is to run and maintain such a sophisticated equipment? What would happen to the birds if something went wrong and they were stranded in their cages? It was a high risk project and the loan committee rejected it outright. I endorsed their recommendation. The lady was told to forget the fancy metal structure and resubmit a request based on the time-tested methods many poultry farmers were

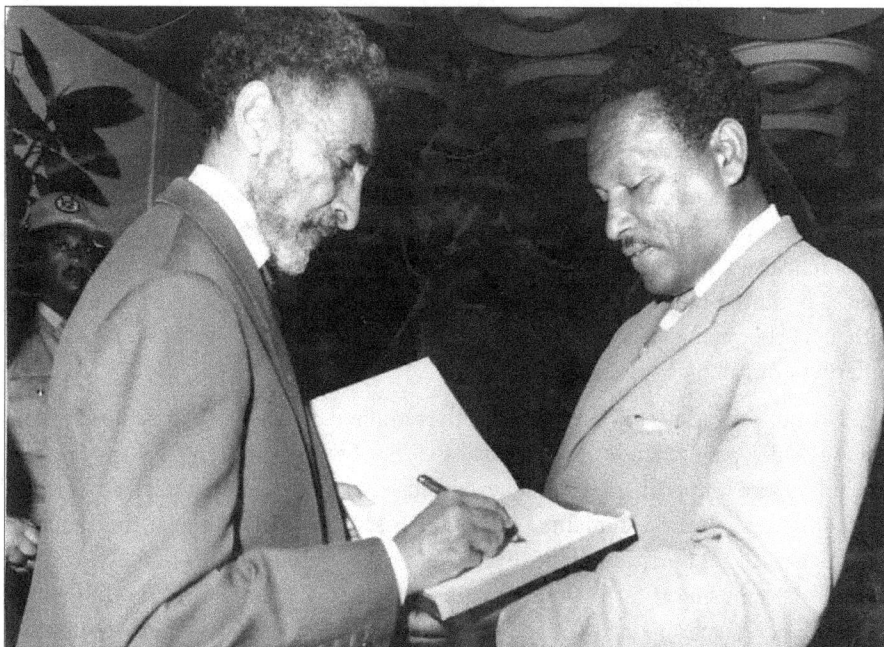

Emperor Haile-Selassie signing the guestbook during a visit to the horticultural farm belonging to Ato Sebhatu Gebre-Yesus, who is holding the book

using successfully. Having set her sights on the fancy gadget, Woudassie had no use for the backward methods of ordinary farmers. Hers would be a showcase poultry farm.

Woudassie had first caught the Emperor's eye during the ribbon cutting ceremony marking the reunion of Eritrea with Ethiopia in 1952. She was an attractive young girl who had been selected to offer a bouquet of flowers to the Emperor. He took a liking to her, brought her to Addis, and installed her at a boarding school. In time she became a protégé.

Woudassie pulled strings in the Palace and had me summoned. She was already there when I arrived. We entered the Emperor's office and she opened her remarks with the usual complaints of disgruntled borrowers: the bank had been established by the Emperor to help promote development, but all it did was to throw up hurdles in the way of borrowers who wished to toil and improve their station in life. And for good measure she added: "It is only you, Your Majesty, who is encouraging me to work. I am really tired, and should perhaps give up the whole thing." All her body language was summoned to put me in a bad light. By then, I had grown accustomed to theatrical presentations of unhappy clients. The best thing to do was simply to focus on the merits of the Bank's response.

The Emperor calmly turned to me and asked why she had been refused the loan. As I was quietly presenting the Bank's justifications, he was distracted by the commotion of a fairly large crowd on an open space in front of the Parliament building, about a quarter of a mile distant from his office. He had an unobstructed view of the milling crowd from his large window. He picked up his binoculars to have a better look. Imperial distraction was no excuse for discontinuing one's response. So I continued and soon finished. The Emperor kept watching the crowd through his binoculars. The lady reacted with annoyance to my explanation and said she was sick and tired and was ready to give up the whole venture. And she started to go down what appeared to be a well rehearsed list of chicken diseases which were making her life miserable. At that precise point the Emperor, who was only half listening, put down his binoculars and, with a face betraying intense curiosity at what the lady had just said, asked: "Are you suffering from all of these diseases?"

"No, no, Your Majesty" she replied with restrained amusement. "It is the chickens, not me, which are infected with these diseases, but I was saying...." When she finished explaining, the Emperor appeared relieved and said: "Good. I thought it was you who had contracted all these ailments," It was the first time for me to hear the Emperor refer to himself as "I" instead of the royal "We." In the presence of His Majesty, a hearty laugh at an amusing turn in a conversation was hardly permissible. The Emperor's personal secretary, Yohannes Kidane-Mariam, I and Woudassie struggled to suppress the gush of laughter trying to find its way out. Some of it inevitably sputtered in subdued chuckles. The Emperor took it all with a gracious smile.

He then turned to me and asked how the problem was to be resolved. I was quite sure that the advice of our technical personnel could stand the scrutiny of any expert, and suggested an independent technical review whose findings I would gladly accept. And I proposed that any one of the poultry science professors at the Agricultural College in Alemaya some 25 miles from the lady's farm be asked to undertake a review. "No Your Majesty" shot back Woudassie. "They will introduce their chicken diseases into my farm!" I was incredulous and said as much. But she said she had been at the College's poultry farm a number of times and would not accept a review by College staff. I suspected that she had probably approached them with the idea of the cage and had been advised against it. Indeed, this was precisely what had happened, as confirmed to me forty-two years later by Assefa Adefris in a chance encounter at a funeral in Washington D.C. only weeks before my book was sent to the press. Assefa told me he had examined Woudassie's proposal with a couple of colleagues at the College and had advised against it.

At the meeting in the Palace, a German poultry expert came to my mind and I suggested his name. The Emperor agreed and Woudassie accepted. I invited the German expert to my office and explained the problem. He said the technology proposed by the client was inappropriate for Ethiopia and that the Bank was right in its decision. I asked him to keep the thought to himself, go to Dire Dawa and prepare a written report on his findings. He thought it would be a waste of money and time, but he would make the trip if the Bank insisted. We sent him to the lady's farm to make an assessment.

A few days later he returned and came to the Bank to give an advance oral report. He walked into my office, sat down and dropped his bomb. The Bank's experts were wrong, his initial assessment was wrong, and the lady was right! She was exceptionally dynamic and capable of handling all the management problems pointed out by the Bank. She had, for instance, contacted the equipment supplier in Europe and had identified a local electrician who, with some training, could handle the maintenance problems. Our staff was wrong to turn down this and the other proposals of the lady which would render the project feasible.

The attractive lady had won over the young German expert. There was nothing to do for me but honour my word. When she came to see me a few days later, I asked what she had done to the good German to make him change his mind so drastically. He, unlike the Bank's experts, had seen the merit of the case, she replied with cheek. I could not avoid the thought that the young lady's formidable charms had been summoned to ease the German expert's pains of going back on his initial assessment.

My attention was soon taken up with a new assignment when I was appointed as the third member of a panel of experts to evaluate the agricultural research and extension programme run by the Ethiopian and Swedish governments at the Chilalo: the Chilalo Agricultural Development Unit (CADU). The second member of the panel was a Swedish professor of economics at Lund University and the third was the French agronomist, René Dumont. Dumont was a life-long socialist with considerable experience in agriculture. He had worked as a consultant in Castro's Cuba and Ho Chi Minh's Vietnam and in many other developing countries.

This was a period in my life when I was greatly attracted by Fidel Castro and his revolution. Dumont was much less enamoured than I with Fidel whom he described as a cigar chomping, wine drinking, and prime steak devouring dictator, looking down upon ordinary Cubans with disdain. What most incensed Dumont were the intellectual pretensions of Fidel: he was the great expert on everything. Cuban agronomists working with Dumont would express their viewpoints competently in their discussions. In Fidel's presence, they would be terrified to say anything likely to draw the ire of the all knowing dictator. I vividly recall my uninformed attempt at defending Castro which Dumont brushed aside effortlessly.

René Dumont was the author of a book on Africa: *L'Afrique Noire est Malpartie* (False Start in Black Africa). I invited him to give a lecture to Bank staff one evening and said in my introduction that his book must have created a lot of enemies among African readers. In those euphoric post-independence days, it was rare to see left-wing intellectuals criticizing African countries or their leaders. Dumont's reply was simple. "Don't worry about me. The book has also made me a good many new friends."

It was about this time that I was woken from my sleep early one morning to be told that my grandmother had passed away. I had been out of the country on official business for a month and was not present at her funeral. I flew to Gore the next day and bid farewell at her graveside. Emahoy Itagegnehu Lemma had died in September 1969. She was some five years past the century mark. Though not unexpected, her death was the first deeply felt personal loss for me. Such was the bond between us that I have a vague sense of her presence somewhere inside me even today, from where she occasionally surfaces in fantasies of happy days gone by.

The recommendation to merge the Development Bank of Ethiopia with the Investment Corporation was finally endorsed by the Cabinet. When I was informed of the news, I asked for an appointment with the Prime Minister and requested a year's leave of absence to do research at a University. I had already made arrangements with the University of Strathclyde in Glasgow where James Pickett, an old friend from my U.N. days, was now a Senior Lecturer. My request, initially suspected as the first step to leave government service altogether, was finally accepted when I assured the Prime Minister that I was not preparing the ground for an exit. I shall come back to this story after the following digression.

The Genesis of a Fateful Relationship

On Easter Sunday in April 1970, my friend Belatchew Asrat and I were leaving the Hilton Hotel after coffee. On the way out, we met an attractive girl in the reception area. She shook hands, led him to the flower shop her father had opened for her, and proudly showed off its display; I being studiously ignored in the manner of the times. Afterwards, I asked him who the beautiful girl was. "Do you find her beautiful?" he asked. "You, a happily married man may not be aware; but there is no question in my mind about her good looks. And manners," I responded. And then the inevitable question, "Whose daughter is she?" She is Ato Sebhatu Gebreyesus's daughter he replied. The name rang a bell.

Ato Sebhatu was, of course, the Bank client who was behind one of my many summonses to the Palace. Besides being a horticulturalist, he was a man with artistic inclinations and possessed an impressive collection of *objects d'art* from different parts of the world. I was a bachelor in my mid-thirties, ever reminded by relatives and friends alike of the virtues of matrimony. As I have said earlier, I had been confronted with an arranged marriage soon after returning from my studies in the U.S., but had managed to fend it off. Once or twice after that, I had seriously thought of abandoning my much-enjoyed status of being single, but had dropped the idea. This didn't prevent me from embarking upon what would turn out to be a routine of weekly visits to the flower shop at the Hilton. The pretext was to purchase copies of the British weekly (*The Observer*) on sale at the shop.

I attempted to strike up a conversation with the pretty girl on one or two occasions, but the response was restrained each time. I persisted as, unbeknown to me, a thorough background check was being conducted behind my back. An invitation for coffee at the hotel was turned down. The pretty girl said she did not accept such invitations, and that her father would in any case not allow it. It was the usual response.

I continued to remind her of my standing invitation at decent intervals. One blessed day she accepted an evening out for dinner, but said I must promise to get her back at the shop by 7:00 p.m.

I immediately accepted the impractical sounding condition, patted myself on the back about my way with girls, and took her to a Swiss restaurant called *Au Vieux Logis*, conveniently tucked into a wooded area in the northern outskirts of Addis Ababa. It wasn't anything I did or said that made her change her mind. The reason was the background check. She had directed queries about my marital status and character to couple of her friends who fortunately happened to be relatives of my own college friends. Contrary to what Roman thought initially, I was not married or divorced and was judged to be not a bad catch.

As her father was my Bank's client, I was concerned lest our casual but increasingly frequent meetings should develop into something more serious. Could a conflict of interest situation arise, I wondered, as her father's loan was still in arrears. Should the relationship be allowed to grow to the point where marriage might become a possibility? There was obviously no connection between the loan and my chance encounter with the borrower's daughter. But those were days when public officials were extra careful about their image and I, being relatively new to government, even more so. Once the background check was over, Roman had made up her mind that the relationship should be more serious than casual. Marriage was never raised explicitly, but it wasn't too far from her thoughts; or from mine. I hesitated, however. She was only 19, just fresh out of high school and I was in my early thirties.

When I obtained a year's leave of absence to go to Glasgow, I told her about it and said we could resume our relationship upon my return. But she too decided to leave the country to pursue her studies in the U.S. Much as I had wished for her to continue with her education, her precipitous decision to travel to the U.S. caught me by surprise. Couldn't she pursue her studies at the local university? She said she would not. So, both of us left; she for California and I for Glasgow.

The Glasgow Interlude

I arrived in Glasgow in September 1970. The obligations of a research fellow at the University of Strathclyde were minimal. I wrote a research paper on the relationship between economic growth and employment and gave a talk on development to graduate students. On the side, however, I managed to write a longish paper on the future of Ethiopia. Indeed this had been my main purpose for taking a year off. Ten years had passed since the attempted coup of 1960. The Emperor was not getting any younger, student demonstrations were occurring with increasing frequency and audacity, and everyone was worried about the future. I was still largely in my leftist mode, despite the creeping doubts that I was beginning to harbour on account of the passing years and the increasing challenge to my views from the real life experience of socialists and former socialists. The paper I wrote on Ethiopia was entitled *The Road Ahead*. In a moment of vanity, I felt that I was dealing with a subject no less weighty than what Lenin was addressing in his pamphlet *What is to be Done?*

Like many of my generation, and indeed of the one immediately following, I was struck by the outward resemblance between the history of Tsarist Russia and that of Imperial Ethiopia: the monarchy and its courtiers, the dominance of the Orthodox Church in social and political life, the landowning aristocracy, the peasantry; all holding back, I believed, the march towards modernization. It didn't take much intellectual effort to come to the conclusion that Ethiopia, too, needed to go through her own October Revolution to make the historic transformation from a medieval to a modern nation state. The Bolsheviks had been bloody, and had caused extensive suffering to their people. But was this not the inevitable pain that accompanies any such transformation? The remoteness of the Soviet experience, in time as well as in geography, the eagerness of the young naïve mind to give in to the utopian vision of the just society depicted by Marx and the tendency to overlook the specific conditions and practical difficulties of translating that vision into reality led to an inadequate appreciation of the 'inevitable pain.' Perhaps there were a few wise souls among us who had the inclination to pause and weigh things. I was not among them.

As I was putting together the 60-odd-page monograph, the idea of the 'inevitable pain' surfaced. My principal preoccupation at the time was how best to adapt the Russian experience to Ethiopia's conditions, cock sure of myself that it was the best way forward. And so, happily but simplistically, I came to the conclusion that we needed to have, not communism, not social democracy, (all copies of other lands), but something more appropriate to our specific situation; at once sufficiently socialist and authoritarian but one that would take account of Ethiopia's values and reality, and one that might possibly avoid bloodshed. I called this 'Radical Socialism'.

I had made an attempt at a structural analysis of Ethiopia's body politic, but entertained no illusion that *The Road Ahead* was a blue print for the future of the country, as the title seemed to suggest. After all, I did not have the time or the commitment of the professional politician to spell out in sufficient detail what the adaptation of the Soviet experience to Ethiopia's situation would require. A more serious study and collegial discussion was needed to come up with a coherent and original framework of ideas to respond to the historical, social and cultural conditions of Ethiopia. I was nevertheless satisfied that I had at least taken the first step in that direction. I took the liberty to show the draft to persons I knew would treat the seditious paper with prudence: Haddis Alemayehu and his close friend Abebe Retta whom I had come to know after he took over the Chairmanship of the Development Bank of Ethiopia. Haddis said that there were ideas he did not agree with, although he did not say which ones or why. Abebe commended the writing and gave me the impression that the exercise was generally on the right track. Michael Imru was the third person to read it four years later when I worked with him on new policy directions. If my memory serves me right, I also showed it to Henock Kifle.

Glasgow of the early seventies was a somewhat forbidding metropolis, which was the strong impression left on me as I drove past the long rows of soot-sheathed tenement houses on my day of arrival. Edinburgh was far more impressive. Outside these two, I visited places like Aberdeen, Gourock and Greenock and found the Scottish people to be very friendly to foreigners. Their view towards the English manifested a lively rivalry; as I occasionally observed during my short stay.

One Saturday afternoon, I was sitting in front of a large television set to watch a football game between the English and Scottish national teams. A Scottish student was seated to my left and an English one to my right. My Scottish neighbour was visibly nervous. I could not resist asking him who he thought might win the game. "The English, I am afraid, which is why I am so upset," he said. The English student overheard us and responded. "It is not only in football that we excel; it is in everything." If so, replied the Scot in annoyance, why did you come to a Scottish University? "For the very simple reason that I wasn't good enough to be admitted to an English University," shot back the young Englishman. The conversation froze.

I returned from Glasgow in the summer of 1971 and reported to the office of the Prime Minister. He had not seemed entirely convinced that I would return, thinking perhaps that I was looking for greener pastures. When I met him I said I would wait to be assigned to a government post, but could find an alternative job if a post could not be found. He told me to wait a little. A month later, Belai Abbai was moved from his sub-Cabinet post of Planning Commissioner and promoted to the post of Minister of Land Reform. I took his place.

Haddis Alemayehu and His Instructive Anecdotes

At this point, I should perhaps take the opportunity of reverting to my long association with Haddis Alemayehu and present some of the more instructive anecdotes I was fortunate to learn from him. My friendship with Ato Haddis continued right up to his death in 2003. He was a man who, like most public officials of his day, was largely self-taught. Haddis was also a man of principle and great integrity. He was perhaps the foremost modern novelist of his generation.[2] He had also seen action in the war against the Fascists and had spent seven years as a prisoner of war in Italy.

Haddis, it must be added, was opinionated, defiant, and inflexible to the point of being stubborn. Some of these traits come out in the following anecdotes, most of which relate to the strained relationship he frequently had with Emperor Haile-Selassie. The anecdotes (all narrated to me by him) also throw light on some important personalities of the period, on the way the Ethiopian government functioned, and on the attempts by the liberal-minded to introduce speedier reforms.

The first anecdote relates to his years as Minister of State in the Ministry of Education in the early sixties, during which the Emperor himself assumed the responsibilities of a Minister. Haddis was summoned to the Palace one day to discuss a student strike at the Technical Secondary School in Addis Ababa. The Director had apparently approached the Palace to request a temporary closure of the school in order to sort out problems. As I indicated previously, it was not unusual in those days for individuals with contacts in the Palace to take their cases to the Emperor directly, if these were deemed urgent, appeared to carry some political weight, or were unlikely to solicit a positive response from a supervisor. Haddis argued against the school's closure on the grounds that out-of-town students at the school, unlike those who were from Addis, had nowhere to go. After listening to both parties, the Emperor turned to Haddis and said something along the following lines: the Director is saying that he is not able to manage the school under the present circumstances. He, not you, is on the front line. You are looking at the problem from the sidelines. He has a persuasive case. Why don't you understand? Haddis did not budge, and stuck to his position.

The Emperor, somewhat vexed, said that it was Haddis's responsibility to grant the request of the school Director for a temporary closure. Haddis's reply was, "It does not seem to me that this is the best way of handling the problem, and I would only give instructions for closure if I, in turn, am instructed by Your Majesty." It was not altogether customary for a Minister to talk back to Emperor Haile-Selassie in this manner. The Emperor, knowing Haddis's inflexibility, finally said "You are so instructed." Haddis bowed and left. A couple of minutes later, the Emperor's *Aide-de-Camp* stepped outside and called back Haddis. "How long can one go on bickering like this every time an issue comes up for decision?" asked the Emperor. It was after the Emperor's death that Haddis narrated the anecdote to me. He did not say what his response was but only reminisced, "How tolerant he was with me."

The second anecdote is about a memo Haddis wrote to the Emperor soon after the 1960 attempted coup d'état. In the memo, Haddis offered his analysis of the incident: the reasons behind the attempt and the steps that needed to be taken to prevent the recurrence of a similar incident in the future.[3] It was a thirteen-page note in which Haddis aired strongly worded criticisms of the government he was serving. According to the Constitution, sovereignty emanated from the Emperor, not from the people of Ethiopia; Parliament had no power to legislate on its own; citizens did not have the right to participate in the political life of their country; there was no freedom of speech; Ministers and government officials were accountable to the Emperor, not to the people; public servants were corrupt and inefficient, etc. At the end of the note, Haddis proposed that the constitution be revised, that elections be held for the executive and the legislature branches, that a system of government in which Ministers were accountable to the people be introduced, that freedom of speech and assembly be observed, and so on and so forth.

Haddis Alemayehu recording a message at UN Radio in Lake Success, New York (1950), for a rebroadcast to Ethiopia; at the time, Haddis was Ethiopia's delegate to the General Assembly; he would later serve as UN Ambassador

Haddis appreciated perhaps more than anyone that these ideas would not necessarily please the Emperor. In his memo, he acknowledged that the Emperor had done a lot for his country but quickly added that far more needed to be done. "Sycophants are the sole beneficiaries of their sweet words. Those to whom such words are addressed continue to live with the bitter truth… Rather than covering up the harm from which the country suffers and flattering you with false praise" concluded the memo, "I have chosen to offer my candid views, which might have a bitter taste, but which might be of some help as well."

A few days after receiving the memo, the Emperor sent for Haddis. "The note was on the whole well thought out. It will be studied by a committee of senior Ministers. Before that, however, you need to change certain terms in your note, like the term 'false praise' which does not serve any useful purpose," said the Emperor. "Your Majesty," replied Haddis stubbornly, "every word in the note is mine. If I start making changes in response to comments, the note ceases to be entirely mine. I regret that I would find it difficult to make changes."

The Emperor had been very accommodating, had said nothing about the far more painful statements of the memo, asking only for a few changes in the wording of that part of the text which seemed to insinuate that the Emperor regarded "false praise" favourably. And here was this unreasonable man putting down his foot and saying no, not to some friend or official, but to the Emperor of Ethiopia! Haile-Selassie was annoyed and said to Haddis, "We have done a lot for this country and against great odds. You are not old enough to remember the serious obstacles we have faced to come this far. You don't know us!" "Your Majesty, you don't know me either," replied Haddis. Fireworks!

"What?" retorted the Emperor with unmistakable indignation. In the course of the discussion, Haddis had been so absorbed by the weighty issues he had raised that he had momentarily forgotten who he was conversing with, as he confessed to me. The Emperor's single-worded question jolted him back to reality. He was deep in trouble and had to extricate himself.

"Your Majesty," started Haddis in an attempt to make amends, "when I wrote these words, I was fully aware that they would cause offence but had made up my mind to face the consequences. I know that you have the power to discipline, to punish, and even to hang. I'd rather face all that than tinker with the note." The clever Haddis had exhibited dexterity of argument. "Of what relevance are thoughts like discipline and hanging to this conversation?" remarked the Emperor graciously, satisfied that Haddis had realized his *faux pas* and was beating a hasty retreat. Haddis's clever response had massaged the Imperial ego sufficiently for the conversation to proceed on an even keel. He was told that his memo would be passed on, unchanged, to Deputy Prime Minister Aklilu Habte-Wold and three senior ministers for their views.

Haddis was not the only one who drew the conclusion from the failed coup that things needed to change if worse was to be avoided. In an untitled and unpublished narrative of his service to his country, hurriedly put together in prison just before his murder by the Dergue in 1974, Aklilu Habte-Wold tells us that soon after he was appointed Prime Minister following the 1960 coup d'état, he had proposed reforms in many areas of public life.[4] After securing the Emperor's consent, he had consulted a number of senior Ministers about the urgent need for such reforms. He had later prepared a detailed written proposal indicating fourteen key areas requiring reform, among which were: the constitution, land tenure, the administration of justice, the civil service, pensions, provincial administration, industrial relations, and cabinet government. After the Emperor's endorsement, seven committees had been established to study each subject and submit recommendations.

Figuring in the list of areas for reform which Aklilu proposed in the month of July (six months after Haddis's memo was presented) are included practically all the key issues raised in the memo: reform of the constitution, of the government machinery, of cabinet government, as well as other questions that Haddis had not raised, specifically land reform, the administration of justice, the civil service, a new pensions law, and a labour law. Details on the revision of the constitution with the view to making it a more democratic law of the land were presented to the Emperor. Regrettably, Aklilu does not say how this proposal was discussed, or what decision was taken. He only says that the Emperor "did not suggest any revisions of a fundamental nature." At the end of this hurriedly drafted story, a series of topics are jotted down as areas where other reforms were proposed. The text was finished in the month of July and was submitted in September 1975. In November Aklilu was murdered along with some 59 other officials.

While Haddis's proposals were studied by the reform committees mentioned by Aklilu Habte-Wold, he himself does not appear to have taken part in their work. Why, it may be asked, was he not drafted as a member of any of the committees, for he had been working with Aklilu for many years in the Ministry of Foreign Affairs? The answer probably lies in the perception that Aklilu and others had of Haddis as an obstinate man not easy to work with. On his part, Haddis probably believed that few of his cabinet colleagues genuinely stood for fundamental change, and that it mattered little if he did not participate in their deliberations as long as he made his views known.

The third anecdote shows Haddis at his most defiant, leaving no room for Emperor Haile-Selassie's ego. In one of his meetings with the Emperor, Haddis talked at length about the crushing poverty under which the Ethiopian people lived. Hardly any leader of a developing country, least of all a monarch who firmly believed that he had taken his country out of the quagmire of the Middle Ages, would be expected to draw pleasure from reminders that abject poverty was the hallmark of his country and its folk. The Emperor had had enough of Haddis's talk on poverty and asked, "What do you know about poverty?" "I know quite a bit, Your Imperial Majesty", said Haddis. "My own father is a poor man." The man born with a silver spoon in his mouth probably knew in his heart that Haddis was better placed to appreciate the pains of poverty. But he was unaccustomed to be put on the spot in this manner. Very fortunately, nothing more serious happened to Haddis than a terse reprimand and a swift fling backwards of the Imperial cloak; a familiar gesture of displeasure at a subject's impertinence. The conversation did not go further.[5]

Another anecdote is on Ras Imru Haile-Selassie, the Emperor's cousin. Soon after their capture by the Fascists in Western Ethiopia, Imru, Haddis and others were taken to the island of Ponza. One of Mussolini's strategies prior to and immediately after the occupation had been to woo leading Ethiopian personalities to collaborate with Italy. He had used a variety of enticements in this regard (honorary feudal titles, government jobs, cash, property, pensions, etc.) and had made some notable gains. Among his prime targets was Ras Imru. One evening, Haddis heard a knock on his door in the prison house of Ponza. When he stepped outside, he saw the Governor of the island and someone he had not seen before but who had an air of gravitas about him. The Governor asked Haddis to inform Ras Imru that with him was a high official with a message from *Il Duce*. Haddis replied that once the Ras retired, he did not like to be disturbed, and wondered if the message could not be delivered in the morning.

The Governor was irritated with the impudent response of someone who after all was a prisoner, and told Haddis to do as he was instructed.

The three proceeded to the nearby building where the Ras was accommodated. Haddis knocked on the door, gingerly at first but more and more assertively with each knock. The Ras finally responded and inquired who it was. When Haddis identified himself and told him the reason for the persistent knock on the door, Ras Imru asked why the Governor could not come in the morning. The Governor was not about to be told by anyone on *his* island when he could or could not see *his* prisoners, least of all by one of the prisoners themselves, prince of Ethiopia or not. Haddis got closer to the unopened door and said that the Governor was with a guest who carried an important message from *Il Duce*. The man wished to deliver the message right away.

The Ras took his time dressing, opened the door slowly, got back inside and sat down on the solitary chair in the lounge of his modest prison house. Haddis stepped in ahead of the guests and, noticing that there were no chairs for the two officials, proceeded to the bedroom of the Ras where he knew a couple of chairs were kept. "Where are you going?" inquired the Ras with irritation. "To get chairs for the guests, your honour" replied Haddis. "Who ordered you to do that?" asked the Ras's tersely. Haddis's response to the rhetorical question was to turn back, step outside and request the two officials to come in and meet Ras Imru; they standing and the Ras seated! Seeing that no chairs were available, the Governor walked out with his guest after the briefest exchange of greetings, saying that they would return the following day.

Haddis was in no doubt what he had to do for the morning visit of the officials. Before the arrival of the Governor and his guest, he went over to the Ras and asked to be allowed to bring two additional chairs into the lounge. It was only after the Ras's fellow prisoner and relative, Dejazmatch Taye Gullilatte, intervened ('it is funny that you forget we are prisoners') that Ras Imru allowed two chairs to be brought in. The Governor and his guest duly arrived moments later, entered the room, now saw that there were chairs for them and sat down. Mussolini's envoy remarked that the Ras had sizeable assets in his country. The local administration was not sure they were being properly looked after. Could he designate someone in Ethiopia to act as his agent? The colonial administration would do everything to facilitate the proper management of his property. *Il Duce* wished to know, concluded the envoy, the name of the agent for instructions to be sent to Ethiopia.

Ras Imru asked Haddis to interpret his response carefully. "I am someone without a country," he said "and consequently without personal property. You are the ones who own the country today and everything in it. I have nothing more to add."

"What a patriot," said Haddis to me as he finished narrating the anecdote. "That day I was proud to be counted an Ethiopian," he added. Haddis had good reason for feeling that way; for, unlike Ras Imru, many former officials of Emperor Haile Selassie had given in to temptations easily, sometimes going out of their way to curry favour with the occupiers.

I shall end this series of anecdotes with two on the resistance leader, Ras Abebe Aregai. When young, I had heard several folk songs on the exploits of Abebe Aregai during the Fascist occupation. The names of Belai Zelleke, Amorraw Woubneh and others also resonated in these songs. But Ras Abebe was in a class by himself. Stories circulated about his clever escapes from enemy encirclements and of his ploys to deceive the enemy into sending him badly needed supplies for his troops on the assurance that he had made up his mind to abandon the armed struggle. He had a similar repu-

Ras Abebe Aregai, the war time leader, with an afro hair style reminiscent of his days in the resistance

tation as a peace time leader and the Emperor often entrusted him with complex and sensitive issues. Abebe had a sharp intellect, was endowed with a remarkable capacity to unravel knotty issues, possessed a keen sense of justice, an ability to delineate the seminal from the peripheral, and the knack to pull together the essential strands of complex issues into an intelligible summary which often led to solutions. Above all, he handled issues without fear or favour.

I was interested in Ras Abebe and often asked individuals who either knew him or worked with him for an assessment of his leadership qualities. Almost without exception, those I talked to (young progressive intellectuals, traditionalists, dissidents, professionals, disgruntled people from the centre of the country, from the north, etc) spoke admiringly of this man. I shall try to illustrate a few of these qualities through two anecdotes narrated to me by persons who themselves figure in the anecdotes. The first is Haddis and the second Hagos Tewolde-Medhin, a Deputy Chief Justice of the Supreme Court during the reign of Emperor Haile-Selassie.

I asked Haddis Alemayehu if he could say something about his personal experience with the Ras. Haddis recalled an incident in which he was called to the Council of Ministers chaired at the time by Ras Abebe. The Council was in the middle of a discussion involving Djibouti in which Foreign Minister Aklilu had taken part the previous week. As Aklilu was on mission, Haddis was asked to stand in for him. "It was my first time to come face to face with Ras Abebe" started Haddis. "He put to me a chain of tightly interconnected questions. I did my best to provide responses. The rigour and quality of the questions surprised me, as did his summary at the end. He then opened the floor to questions. A few were asked, but none as searching as his own interventions. One was from the Minister of Justice who said: ' Your honour, last week you summed up this case with your customary eloquence. What you say today stands in sharp contrast to that summary. How come, Sir?' "

"I was in for another surprise," continued Haddis. "The Ras's response was arresting, and it went something like this. 'Excellency, the Minister of Justice. I hope you will recall the series of questions we put to Foreign Minister Aklilu last week and his answers to the questions.' The Ras paused here and recalled the previous week's questions and answers in remarkable detail. He did the same with the questions of the day and my answers to the questions. 'I now leave it to you to judge, Excellency Minister of Justice. Give us your assessment of this complex issue, if you please.' The Minister of Justice was unpersuasive in his response. Ras Abebe had carefully weighed the totality of the evidence and had made his conclusion on the basis of the latest and more compelling set of explanations. A few wise words were addressed to the Minister of Justice. 'I would like you to know that when issues of grave national interest are at stake, there should be no room for one's ego. I am not bothered about contradicting myself. I go where the weight of evidence leads me, even if this involves a radical departure from a position I had previously taken. I am not given to vanity, and would not hesitate to go back on any position I have taken whenever the nation's interests dictate."

Both Haddis and I marveled at this. Ras Abebe Aregai had no formal education to speak of and no exposure to the works of political thinkers or military strategists. It was natural intelligence of a high order, coupled with years of following intricate political and juridical cases at the royal court which had given him such an ability to analyze, to probe, to get to the kernel of issues, to summarize and to persuade. He was a fine product of Ethiopia's heritage of jurisprudence and public service.

On another occasion, I asked Hagos Tewolde Medhin if he knew Ras Abebe. "Who does not know Ras Abebe?" he replied. Did he recall a personal incident involving the Ras which in his judgment gave an indication of what kind of man he was? Hagos quickly remembered a problem which had caused him considerable distress and which he had taken up with Ras Abebe.

While working in the Ministry of Finance before becoming judge, Hagos had been humiliated by his minister and was at a loss what to do. The Minister had asked him to train some young people under his supervision. Hagos had trained five young persons well and was awaiting the commendation of his minister. The reward came in the shape of one of the five being appointed to be Hagos's supervisor! "Every day I go to the office, I feel humiliated. What a Minister? What a country? Where can one go?" said Hagos to a friend one day. The friend listened intently and told him that there was one person who could do something about his problem: Ras Abebe Aregai.

The Ras was at the time Minister of Defence. Hagos was working in another department of government. But it was customary in those days to take up a personal grievance with a distinguished intermediary wherever he worked if the case was deemed grave enough. The aggrieved would ask the person to intercede with the Emperor on his behalf.

Hagos accepted the friend's advice and presented himself one early morning at the Ras's residence. After paying his respects to the Ras, Hagos said: "I have come this morning to Your Excellency to ask one simple question." To the Ras's query as to what the question was, Hagos said: "A senior official is asked to train his subordinates. He spends time and energy in their training. After the completion of the training programme, one of the trainees is appointed to be the direct boss of his trainer and supervisor. Tell me Excellency. Is this fair?" Ras Abebe looked Hagos in the eye and replied: "Am I to understand that the reason for your coming to my residence so early in the morning is your inability to figure out the answer to that straightforward question on your own?" Hagos was embarrassed and meekly replied: "Your Excellency, I am the victim in the story." "Why take cover behind a general question when you have a serious issue to raise? Explain to me how and why this has happened to you," asked Ras Abebe.

Hagos put his case to Ras Abebe in great detail, the Ras listening intently and with great patience, as was his habit. Hagos was so worked up with his own eloquent portrayal of his minister's mischief that he concluded his narrative with the words: "There is no point in my serving this government any longer. I must resign." Abebe calmly responded: "Now you are giving me a second reason for coming to my residence in the early hours of the morning: to declare your resignation. Say, why don't you make the declaration at a more leisurely time, in a more appropriate place, and in the presence of officials more involved with your work? Why chose me, my residence, and an ungodly hour?" Hagos apologized. He had been unfairly treated and hoped Ras Abebe would understand. The Ras advised that excitement and dramatization were not necessarily the most effective ways to present one's case. He should go back home now and give him time to work on his problem.

Eventually, Abebe took up the matter with the Emperor (as was conveyed to Hagos by a friend), explained that treating officials insensitively could only result in alienating the very people committed to serve it, and that Hagos should be more fairly treated. Thanks to Abebe's intervention, Hagos was later appointed to a respectable post in another ministry.

Anecdotes are no substitute for a balanced assessment of a person of Abebe's stature. There are doubtless less flattering sides to his persona. I hope historians would one day turn their attention to the life of someone who so distinguished himself on the battlefield and in peacetime that many would later say that he was among the finest public servants of his time.

CHAPTER 6

In the Service of the Imperial Ethiopian Government: The Succeeding Three Years

Trials and Tribulations at the Planning Commission

One of the earliest post-war initiatives of Emperor Haile-Selassie to promote economic development was the establishment of a government department for development planning. In the initial years, the experts were largely drawn from Yugoslavia, a non-aligned country with which Ethiopia had close diplomatic ties. A Planning Board was set up and the first five-year development plan was launched in 1959. This must have been among the earliest such initiatives in the non-communist world. India's Planning Commission brought out its first five-year plan in 1951.[1]

Notwithstanding the seniority of the two successive Ministers of Commerce and Industry (Yilma Deressa and Makonnen Habte-Wold) who were ex-officio Chairmen, the Planning Board did not immediately become an effective instrument of policy. The novelty of the initiative posed obvious difficulties, especially in regard to the coordination of economic policy. Another difficulty was the near total reliance on foreign experts for policy analysis and formulation. It would take two decades for development planning to benefit from the indispensible input of Ethiopian professionals.

In March 1965, Aklilu Habte-Wold was reappointed Prime Minister with more authority (so it was said at the time) than he had before: he could now pick his Cabinet Ministers, a prerogative previously reserved for the Emperor. In addition, the Cabinet was to be collectively responsible to the monarch, rather than individually as was the previous practice. Teamwork was expected to improve in the new scheme of things. From his diplomatic post in London, Haddis Alemayehu was brought in to head a newly created Ministry of Planning and Development. Aklilu told him that development planning was a priority of his new Cabinet.

The drafting of the Third Five-Year Development Plan (1969-73) was Haddis's first responsibility in which, as I mentioned earlier, I had taken part initially as a U.N. advisor and later as a staff member of the Ministry. The new ministry soon faced difficulties, however. Haddis did not think he was getting enough cooperation from his Cabinet colleagues, especially from the Minister of Finance. In theory, the Planning Minister was expected to coordinate economic policy. In practice, Haddis's colleagues were not too keen to accept the notion of an equal assuming the role of coordinator, which implied a certain degree of monitoring and guidance. The Minister of Finance had a similar authority on matters pertaining to revenue and expenditure. But people had long been accustomed to the authority wielded by someone who controlled the purse strings. Haddis could not accept this traditional source of fiscal clout at the expense of exercising his own statutory responsibility as a minister for development and economic policy coordination. After three years in the job, he concluded that he could not work effectively in this contentious environment and resigned.

It was principally with the view to resolve this conflict that a decision was taken to abolish the Ministry of Planning and Development and put in its place a Planning Commission chaired by the Prime Minister himself. Members of the Commission would consist of Ministers that in one way or another were involved in development activity. Under the new arrangement, the country's development programmes as well as matters relating to economic policy coordination came directly under the Prime Minister's authority who was assisted by a new junior Minister called Planning Commissioner. The new Commissioner and the staff of the former Ministry of Planning and Development were now under the umbrella of someone whose authority for coordinating the entire gamut of government policy could not be questioned. It was to this reorganized department of government that I was brought in as Planning Commissioner in 1971.

Aware of the tug-of-war between Finance and Planning, I was not sure that the problem would be solved as neatly as the new guidelines suggested. And so I called on the Minister of Finance to say that I would do whatever I could towards establishing smoother working relations between our two contending departments. What both of us should try to do was to narrow down issues of divergence that would inevitably arise and leave the more stubborn issues to the care of the Prime Minister. The message was well received and I left his office feeling cautiously optimistic.

The responsibility of the Ministry of Finance was to prepare the administrative budget and to estimate available funding (foreign and domestic) for the administrative as well as for the capital budgets. Preparing and monitoring the execution of the capital or development budget was the responsibility of the Planning Commission. When I started work at the Commission, the capital budget for the coming year had just been passed, which meant that this challenging exercise would come up only a year later. But there was plenty to do in the meantime.

Monitoring the implementation of the capital budget was a key concern and it kept Planning staff busy with officials of the development ministries. Often they received complaints that Finance personnel did not release approved allocations and that this was causing delays in project implementation. Planning staff did their best to work with their counterparts in Finance to minimize disruptions in project execution.

Finance bureaucrats often faulted their opposite numbers in individual ministries for such disruptions. Planning staff were not always persuaded, believing that revenue was slow in coming and that spending had to be put on hold on non-urgent expenditures like roads, school buildings, agricultural research activities, etc. But Finance would not admit this, as it implied deficiencies in their revenue collection efforts. It was also believed that Finance would occasionally delay funding to remind all concerned as to who was in charge of the purse strings (and hence where bureaucratic clout lay). Bureaucrats in Finance were, of course, no different from their counterparts in the ministries; i.e. that they were often not up to their jobs. I soon sensed that bureaucratic infighting was not a matter that would be blown away by the kind of amicable talk I had initiated with the Minister of Finance.

The Ministry of Finance could not, of course, be blamed for everything. The development ministries themselves had their fair share of problems. Not every budget allocation was executed effectively or accountably. Although corruption was generally not a serious problem at the time, financial indiscipline and inefficiency were, and Finance personnel occasionally had good grounds to withhold funds. Sometimes, certain departments frivolously challenged decisions by budget personnel, needlessly impairing relations and impacting negatively on budget management.

The Planning Commission was of course not immune from bureaucratic wrangling. It too had disputes with various departments. Most of these occurred during debates on which projects should be included in the capital expenditure budget and which should not. The Commission had a standing committee which reviewed project proposals by ministries. The committee posed standard questions to assess whether or how much of a proposed project should be included in the year's budget. If it is a new project, questions revolved around the project's relevance to the priorities of the five-year plan, its costs versus its benefits, its feasibility, and the source of funding; especially the extent of external assistance required. If it is an ongoing project, issues of implementation effectiveness, achievement of targets, cost overruns, etc. were raised. These provoked intense wrangle. Government departments fought tooth and nail for their pet projects as Commission staff tried to hold the line on costs, priorities, and planning guidelines.

Another vetting exercise was applied at a more senior level in which the Planning Commissioner himself reviewed complaints by staff of ministries that their submissions had not been properly handled by the standing committee. Some of the grievances would be resolved, and the rest deferred to another theatre of battle. A capital budget would be put together and sent to the Ministry of Finance for onward submission to the Cabinet. The Ministry of Finance sometimes appended its comments, creating further altercation.

The penultimate theatre of the budget drama (the final one being the Parliament) was the Budget Committee of the Council of Ministers where the skirmishes involved combinations and permutations of departmental personnel: Ministry of Finance staff versus their counterparts in the Planning Commission regarding overall revenue estimates or individual development projects, staff of other ministries confronting staff of Finance and Planning on their administrative and capital budgets, Finance staff improbably teaming up with their opposite numbers in the Planning Commission to fend off last minute efforts by different departments to reinstate their pet projects, etc.

How on earth, one might ask, did a budget proposal negotiate all these hurdles and end up bearing any resemblance to its initial draft? How did the machinery of government ever function in the face of these feuds? Mercifully, changes to budget proposals were not proportional to the fury and bluster (often contrived for tactical advantage) of protagonists. And so the budget would survive in some revised form. But departmental relations would be impaired in the process.

This was particularly true of Finance and Planning. No two departments of government were ever designed to cause so much friction between their staff. The foremost responsibility of the Minister of Finance was to make sure salaries were paid and the wheels of government were kept rolling. His focus was on the events of the day, the week, the month, or at most the year: in brief on the short term. No immediate problem would occur if some plan or project proposed by Planning was deferred. So why worry unduly?

The Minister responsible for planning would, on the other hand, be inclined to take the day-to-day problems of the administrative budget as an unending series of minor hiccups which would ultimately be resolved one way or the other. By their immediacy, these inevitably attracted attention and the resources to deal with them. Development issues did not always have that advantage and consequently tended to be pushed to some future, more suitable date, sometimes risking irretrievable relegation, compromising economic development in the process. It was the Planning Minister's duty, therefore, to keep development priorities at centre stage. In the long term they were far more important than the routine business of keeping the wheels of government clanking along.

Beyond these objective reasons of conflict, there were the usual tussles among individuals having different personal chemistries. And in my own case, I was relatively young and inexperienced in the art of turf warfare. I had been in the placid environment of report writing at the U.N. My youthful appearance also left the impression on many that I was not old enough to shoulder the responsibilities of my office. This was no ordinary matter in an age where gray hair lent gravitas to a corpulent body, to neither of which I could lay credible claim.

Out of the blue one fine afternoon, Prime Minister Aklilu Habte-Wold asked how old I was. A bit puzzled, I replied I was thirty-six. "You can't be," he shot back. A quick exercise in arithmetic was the simplest way to persuade him. I added the years of my primary, secondary, and university education to my services to the U.N. and the Ethiopian government, and came up with 29 years. I presented this compelling arithmetic to the Prime Minister and said that I must have been between six and nine when I started school. That would make me approximately 36 years old. He nodded in agreement, but I was still puzzled why he had brought up the subject in the first place; and so unexpectedly.

"You know what," he started answering my question before I could put it to him. "I can't tell you how many people have been critical of your appointment as Planning Commissioner. 'He is too young and has been with the government barely four years. Here we are with fifteen and twenty years of loyal service. Where are we today, compared to this youth who has been catapulted to the post of Minister of State?' they all say." I replied that I was ready to leave my post to anyone who was willing to assume the title along with its trials and tribulations. He smiled and replied that most people fancied the title, not the headache that came with it.

One of the responsibilities of the Planning Commissioner included bilateral and multilateral relations regarding grants and technical assistance. By and large, our rapport with the bilateral and multilateral agency representatives in Addis Ababa was cordial. They all supported the thrust of the five-year plan. Occasionally there was rivalry among some. While healthy, it sometimes went overboard. And this created difficulties for me.

Sweden had a fairly substantial aid programme focusing largely on agriculture, education and health. The one on agriculture revolved around the Chilalo Agricultural Development Unit (CADU). This was a comprehensive research and development effort (hence labeled 'comprehensive package programme') strongly supported by the Ethiopian and Swedish governments. A 'minimum package programme' was later developed focusing on the more critical inputs designed to replicate Chilalo's results in pre-selected areas of the country. Chilalo's research findings were made available to farmers through extension agents who monitored outcomes and reported back to the Unit. CADU seemed to hold considerable promise for agricultural productivity and soon became a conversation piece among donor agencies. The local Director of the United States Agency for International Development ran a fairly substantial assistance programme which got nowhere near Chilalo's level of visibility. He decided to do something about it.

He came to my office one day and said that he had agreed with the Minister of Agriculture to provide twenty-five man-years of expert service. I was a bit taken aback by the concentration of so much foreign expertise in one centre of decision making, as well as by the claim that the Minister's authorization had been already secured. The Director knew that it was the responsibility of the Planning Commissioner to ensure the consistency of every such new technical assistance offer with the guidelines of the five-year plan and that nothing could be done without the approval of the Commissioner. Setting this aside for the moment, I proceeded to ask him what such a relatively large influx of experts to a single government building was expected to accomplish. I was concerned that the high level advisors would exert excessive influence on the Minister and his senior officials.

When the Director said that the Minister needed additional support for the comprehensive package programme, I replied that this was a programme funded by the Swedish government and if more foreign assistance were required the Swedes would be the first to be approached. Only if they were not in a position to offer help would other donors be asked. The pushy viceroy of a great power was not prepared to accept anything standing in his way. He said he did not understand how a junior minister (i.e. me) could turn down a request from a respected senior minister? For good measure, he also said that he had the responsibility to ensure that the agreement between Emperor Haile-Selassie and President Nixon for a yearly grant of U.S. $20 million was carried out in full, but that this was proving difficult.

I had to respond to him formally and professionally. And my response was along the following lines. I reminded the Director that the duties of the Planning Commissioner and the Minister of Agriculture were spelt out in the official gazette. The language of the gazette made no reference to 'junior' or 'senior' officials. My responsibility was to ensure that all departmental requests of the kind the Director was talking about conformed to the guidelines of the Five-Year Plan. Regarding the yearly grant of $20 million, it would be easy enough for me to make a fairly speedy distribution of the amount among different ministries, if I chose not to be concerned with the way it was spent. But that would not be consonant with the letter and spirit of the gazette. My job was to ascertain to the extent practicable that every minister followed the guidelines of the five-year plan. "Incidentally," I asked, "where is this agreement between the Emperor and President Nixon?" I had been surprised when he first mentioned it, for agreements on all such grants came under the purview of my office. "Oh it was a gentleman's agreement, not a written one," he replied. He was clearly trying to bluff his way through. I wasn't too displeased that his bluff had been called.

Such incidents added to my problems; for rumours started to circulate among the expatriate community that I was 'anti-white' and inflexible. This was confirmed to me by none other than the Prime Minister himself when he said one day that I needed to be careful with the Americans, as they were saying that I was not a suitable person for the post of Planning Commissioner. I replied that I would not stay one more day in my post if he thought the problem was that serious. He said he was only bringing it to my attention to ensure that I was aware of what was being said. The question of quitting did not arise.

Before long, another problem surfaced from a different corner: the French Embassy. I had been working with the Ambassador on the details of a meeting in Paris of the Franco-Ethiopian Mixed Commission, a bilateral consultative group which met every two or three years to review France's assistance programme in Ethiopia. We had agreed on a date for the meeting (mid-August) and I had accordingly informed Ethiopian participants from various government departments. The Ambassador called one day to say that the date was not convenient for French officials, as most would be on summer vacation at that time. The meeting had to be brought forward by a month. I was puzzled. Did the Ambassador overlook the tradition of French civil servants to go on a summer break in mid-August? Had he not contacted Paris before giving his consent? Why was the Ethiopian side not consulted for an alternative date acceptable to both sides?

I informed the Ambassador that I needed to talk to the Ethiopian participants in the various ministries before I could give my response. This prompted the Ambassador to take up the case directly with the Prime Minister who called to say that I should make an effort to accommodate the Ambassador's request. It was better to suffer a minor inconvenience at my level than to allow an unnecessary misunderstanding to surface between the two governments. Djibouti, a vital seaport for Ethiopia under French colonial administration, was of strategic importance and we needed to be careful in our dealings with the French, he said. I agreed to inform all participants that we should change our travel plan.

Much relief was to come my way after the meeting in Paris with French officials and another one involving the World Bank and Ethiopia's major donors. The Prime Minister learned of our delegation's performance through the grapevine and was very happy when we returned home from the meetings. As a consequence, a major burden was lifted from my shoulders. I now moved forward more vigorously in my work, assured that I had the confidence of the Prime Minister.

There were also occasional skirmishes with the Governor of the National Bank of Ethiopia, the country's central bank. The national currency had been pegged to the U.S. dollar for the previous thirty years. Some of us in the Planning Commission were of the view that no one had given thought to managing the exchange rate in response to the demands of the economy. At a suitable moment one day, we took up this question and came to the view that there was a good case to be made for a moderate devaluation of the Ethiopian currency. A little concerned that this would ruffle feathers at the central bank, I thought that I should first broach the issue informally with the Governor, Ato Menassie Lemma. The fact that nothing had changed on the exchange rate front for such a long time appeared to be a case more of benign neglect than of deliberate policy. The time had come to address the issue, I said to the Governor. He was open to the idea and I volunteered to have a short note prepared for discussion. A proposal was quickly put together by Commission staff, discussed internally, and cleared for submission to the central bank.

I sent the note to the Governor a few days before a meeting scheduled in his office. In attendance at that meeting were senior officials of the Bank, the Ministry of Finance and the Ministry of Commerce and Industry. I was not accompanied by staff of the Commission and so took it upon myself to explain the case for a moderate devaluation. After going through the technical and policy features of the note, I paused for questions. The Governor took the floor and gave his reaction. He and I started to exchange views. I do not recall if the other officials took part. At the end the Governor said that he would set down his own position in a memo.

The memo was ready a few days later and was discussed at a follow up meeting at which the Governor single-handedly argued against devaluation. It did not seem to me that he had made a convincing case. The fear of the unknown proved to be too powerful a deterrent to begin using an instrument of economic policy widely employed by other countries but never by Ethiopia. Admittedly, the economy wasn't in dire straits, but there did seem to be a case for adjusting the exchange rate moderately. Apart from whatever economic benefits devaluation might have brought, it was a good opportunity for policymakers and technical staff to familiarize themselves with a potent tool for managing a nation's economy. It would be another twenty odd years before Ethiopia's authorities would be obliged to devalue the currency. For more than half a century, foreign exchange management remained foreign to managers of Ethiopia's monetary policy. But Ato Menassie persisted in his view until late in life. For when I reminded him of the incident some three years ago, he reiterated his view with undiminished self assurance.

There were moments, of course, when one felt progress was being made. One of the more gratifying developments taking place at the Planning Commission was the gradual transformation of the department into a relatively effective institution for the formulation of plans and policies. This was made possible thanks to a programme of institution building which was supported by international assistance. Over a period of five to six years, the number and calibre of qualified Ethiopian staff grew to a point where the previous dependence on expatriate staff was substantially reduced. The performance of the new staff became a subject of favourable comment by their peers in other government departments. Many of these young people would occupy senior government positions in subsequent years.[2]

There was forward movement on other fronts as well. A modest network of modern social and economic infrastructures had been put in place by the late sixties when I joined government. A network of secondary, post secondary, and higher educational institutions had also been established contributing to a steady flow of skilled manpower. Institutions to accelerate the nation's network of transport and communications had been created through bilateral and multilateral assistance. It would be tedious to go into a description of these, but it might enhance the understanding of the present generation of Ethiopians if I were to pause here and briefly narrate the story of how Ethiopian Airlines, perhaps among the few outstanding examples of successful parastatal bodies in the third world, was established and how it was gradually brought under full Ethiopian management. I should add that the airline's strength is such that it has been able to weather two powerful political storms: the 1974 soldiers' revolution and the 1991 takeover of the country by the northern guerillas. In Chapter 17, I shall give a brief account of the Addis Ababa Fistula Hospital, another inspiring success story in a country and continent which often evoke sentiments of misery and despair.

Highlights of Development: The Story of Ethiopian Airlines

In 1945, Emperor Haile-Selassie instructed members of the Ethiopian delegation going to San Francisco for the signing ceremony of the U.N. Charter to talk to the Americans about introducing commercial aviation to the country.[3] On the way back from San Francisco, Foreign Minister Aklilu Habte-Wold and Menassie Lemma (a senior Ministry of Finance official at the time) paid a visit to the State Department and expressed their country's need for an air link with the outside world. TWA had recently started services to Cairo. Couldn't the airline extend its route to Ethiopia? The State Department advised the Ethiopians to talk directly to the President of TWA. When they did, they were told that TWA was not interested.

It took President Truman's intervention to get TWA's president to change his mind. As it would not be commercially viable to extend TWA's route to Addis Ababa, the idea of establishing a national carrier managed by TWA seemed a better alternative. About half a million U.S. dollars would be required to start the venture. Was the country able to put up that much money in U.S. dollars, asked TWA's President. The Ethiopians replied that they could only make the payment in sterling, since that was the currency the country used for its foreign trade transactions. Reluctant at first, the company president later accepted the idea of a lien on half a million dollars worth of coffee (the major export commodity of the country) proposed by Menassie and a deal was struck. An agreement was duly signed in December 1945 and Ethiopian Air Lines (EAL) started operations in April 1946 under TWA management.

Senior personnel were recruited largely from within TWA but also from outside. From the outset, however, it had been decided to operate the airline with a full complement of Ethiopian managers, flyers and other senior staff at the earliest opportunity. The expatriate staff were initially not too keen to train their replacements. This inevitably slowed down the process of Ethiopianization.

Following EAL Board's directive, Ethiopian pilots were recruited from the Imperial Ethiopian Air Force in 1951, five years after the launch of the airline. The first Ethiopian to be checked out as captain, Alemayehou Abebe, took over the controls of a regular EAL flight in January 1957.[4] Technical personnel were employed from the secondary and vocational schools. But progress was slow at management level. At one point, the Board asked the American General Manager how long it would take to have an Ethiopian in his place. Twenty-five years came the reply. When asked what qualifications a future Ethiopian General Manager should have, he replied that the person should be an airline captain, have a university degree in aeronautical engineering, be a qualified lawyer, a graduate of a good business school, etc. "But you do not have all of these qualifications," remarked an Ethiopian Board member. "Ah, but an Ethiopian Manager has to be better qualified than I!" The response's discernible undertone of bigotry was probably not lost on the Board. It was obviously far from being reassuring.

The Board launched a search for a qualified Ethiopian to be groomed for the post. The guideline given was that the candidate must first and foremost be a pilot and have a degree in aeronautical engineering. The files of all engineering graduates were examined. Only one aeronautical engineer was found. He was Semret Medhane, graduate of Imperial College, London. At the time, Major Semret was serving as head of Technical Services of the Imperial Ethiopian Air Force. He had been a bright student in high school and had built a good record as a combat pilot. He had also undertaken special training in the U. S. and had been on extensive study tours to the Israeli, the Swedish, and the U.K. Air Forces. All agreed that he was the best available candidate. Semret himself was reluctant to leave his challenging job at the Air Force as head of all support activities and a close collaborator of the Commander of the Air Force, General Assefa Ayene. When instructions came from the Emperor's secretariat that he should report to Ethiopian Airlines, the good military man complied.

Semret was appointed Deputy General Manager in April 1964. One of his early initiatives was to open a pilot school. He followed this up with a technical school and different training programmes with the view to creating a steady flow of skilled manpower for the airline. The objective was not simply to replace expatriate staff but to ensure a healthy growth of the airline as well. Semret spent seven years as an understudy with three successive American General Managers before taking over as General Manager in 1971, an unhurried span of time but far shorter than the twenty-five years estimated by the American General Manager.

Under Semret the company made considerable strides. Staff numbers increased and revenue grew by more than fifty per cent at a time when most airline companies were reeling under the four-fold increase in oil prices. This was largely due to the airline's ability to lease aircraft and crew to Iran Air and Saudia. Two projects provide an illustration of the ability of Semret and his senior colleagues to manage the airline and contribute to the country's aviation development. The first involves the manufacture of a light aircraft and the second an attractive commercial agreement with an aircraft firm.

In 1972, the well known Swedish aviator, Count von Rosen spoke with Semret regarding the possibility of Ethiopian Airlines acquiring a light aircraft. Von Rosen had long known Ethiopia and had been the commander of the fledgling Imperial Ethiopian Air Force in the forties. He had also fought for Biafra's war of independence using the Swedish built SAAB MFI-15. He proposed to Semret that the airline purchase the later version of the aircraft, the SAAB MFI-17, for multi-purpose use. Their discussions soon turned to the viability of building and marketing the aircraft in Ethiopia.

Potential users would be the airline itself (for its pilot training programme and charters), the Air Force, the Army Aviation unit, and organizations engaged in spraying insecticides and dropping supplies. Following a thorough evaluation of the prototype, Semret travelled to Sweden to persuade SAAB to agree to install one production line in Ethiopia. The Technical Services Department of Ethiopian Airlines (headed by Captain Mohammed Ahmed, Semret's close collaborator and former Air Force colleague) was equipped to handle the task. Repair facilities at the department could easily handle the manufacture of the aircraft. SAAB did not appear to be too keen.

Several negotiations followed in Addis Ababa, Malmo and Linchoping. SAAB was eventually persuaded to offer the detailed design of the aircraft as well as a production line in return for a fee of $5,000 for every unit sold outside of Africa. One aircraft would cost approximately $60,000 to produce and would sell for $100,000; which meant that SAAB's fee for aircrafts sold outside the continent was 5% of the sale price. EAL mobilized in-country demand for the project. The retiring Swedish head of quality inspection at SAAB volunteered to work two to three months a year in Ethiopia as advisor. He would only ask for his transport and living expenses to be covered by the airline. EAL agreed. The objective was to initially establish a wholly owned subsidiary of EAL which would later stand on its own.

The project was presented to the Emperor who gave his endorsement. A committee of Ministers was established under the chairmanship of the Minister of Finance, Mammo Tadessee, with Foreign Minister Ketema Yifru, Defence Minister General Kebede Gebre, and Chief of General Staff and former Head of the Air Force, General Assefa Ayene, as members. After initial hesitations, the project was given the go ahead by the Committee, thanks largely to the strong support of the Committee Chairman and the Chief of Staff.[5] Some seventy of these aircraft were to be produced for multi-purpose use in the country and a similar number for export.

Regrettably, this coincided with the 1974 military takeover of the government. The soldiers had more important things on their mind. No one cared about the project. Years later the same aircraft was used by relief organizations in Ethiopia, but with a 'Made in Sweden' marking. By the time the military rulers were ready to go ahead with the project, the production rights had been sold to Pakistan. They now made one of their precipitous political decisions: to build a light aircraft at whatever cost. A license was obtained from a small American company to produce the AV-Cat, a spray aircraft. In due course production commenced, but the expenses turned out to be unsustainable and the prospects for marketing the aircraft severely limited. All in all, sixteen units were built, four of which were in operation at the time of writing. AV-Cat was a far cry from the commercially sound, multipurpose SAAB which was to serve a larger market. But AV-CAT did prove EAL's capability to manufacture light aircraft.

The second project involved a plan to replace the Airline's ageing DC-3 aircraft fleet. As Chairman of the airline's Board of Directors in the mid-seventies, I had the opportunity to see at close range Semret's understanding of management issues, his technical knowledge, his skills in negotiating contracts with third parties, and his impeccable integrity. And, I should add, the airline's strong management culture. The contract negotiated with the Canadian manufacturer regarding the purchase of a small passenger aircraft is a good illustration of all these.

As early as the 1960s, EAL had been on the lookout for an aircraft that would replace its World War II vintage C-47s and DC-3s. The airports for these consisted of 50-odd high altitude, short, unpaved landing strips. The aircrafts available in the market were largely built for low attitude, paved, and long runways. Besides, their undercarriages were not sufficiently sturdy for Ethiopia's rough landing strips. They also suffered from poor power-plant performance at high altitudes, especially at take-off under one engine failure conditions. In the early seventies, managers at EAL (now rechristened ETHIOPIAN) learned that De-Havilland of Canada (DH) was planning to build the four-engine Dash-7a for city-centre to city-centre service. The operating specifications of the aircraft responded to the country's low-air density and rough landing strips. They were interested.

Negotiations commenced and DH soon found out that they were dealing with an all-Ethiopia team which was not only up to scratch professionally but which was also prepared to drive a hard bargain. DH came to the conclusion that something needed to be done. They informed the Ethiopian team that a 'package' was available to grease the wheels of progress. The Ethiopians had already secured favourable price reductions for five aircraft. They gladly accepted the 'package' and decided to apply it to the purchase of a sixth aircraft which the company was using for demonstration purposes. It would be sent back to the assembly line for retrofitting to the latest production model.

With the benefit of the 'package', the sixth aircraft was obtained at the bargain price of $900, 000. ETHIOPIAN also obtained special concessions. As the sole launch carrier, the airline's maintenance facility would be designated as DH's approved maintenance centre for Africa and the Middle East. DH would in addition stock the centre, at its own cost, with DH 7a parts. Thirdly, a 2% commission would be paid by DH to ETHIOPIAN for each aircraft sold in these areas and for services rendered by the airline as DH's agent.

A presentation was made by DH at the airline's Board meeting which I chaired one afternoon. Explanation was given on different features of the new aircraft as well as the concessions obtained by ETHIOPIAN. Management had previously informed the Board of the final results of the negotiations only in general terms. The Board was unaware of the intricacies and the hard bargains driven. After completing his presentation, the leader of the DH team informed the Board of something Semret had been silent about: the company's engineers had picked Semret's brain in adapting the design of the aircraft's landing gear to Ethiopian conditions.

In the course of the technical discussions, Semret had noticed that the landing gear of the new aircraft was not sturdy enough and had suggested a suitable alloy for the purpose. And DH had accepted the proposal. Board members were pleasantly surprised (and proud) that a compatriot had made a contribution to the technical specifications of an aircraft which was still on the drawing board. And he had obviously received nothing in return. Semret would prove to be among the best managers in the airline's history. Unfortunately, he did not see eye to eye with the Dergue and was moved from the airline to a Cabinet post.

The sequel to the DH story needs to be told. After Semret's departure from ETHIOPIAN the attractive DH deal was suspended and eventually cancelled. Regrettably, it was the airline, not DH, which lost an advantageous business deal. DH breathed a sigh of relief that it had liberated itself from what it later realized had become a costly set of concessions. Moving forward, DH was able to penetrate African (Cameroon) and Middle Eastern (Yemen) markets with their new product.

Why, it may be asked, was an attractive deal thrown away so casually; a deal that had been bargained with so much resourcefulness and commitment? First, Semret was no longer at the helm of ETHIOPIAN and the new management environment was not particularly favourable to take the next steps. Second, it was not uncommon in the early days of the Dergue to be suspicious of projects initiated during the regime of Emperor Haile-Selassie. More specifically, some self promoting aircraft sales agents who had been shut out of the deal began to circulate rumours that the 2% commission on the sale of the new aircraft had been passed under the table to the previous management. ETHIOPIAN would become, they argued, a guinea pig for unproven equipment. When it dawned on Dergue officials that the rumour was self-serving, attempts were made to revive the agreement. DH's response was an unequivocal no. Prices had sky rocketed and the arrangements the airline had secured had become too costly for DH.

It might be of interest to the present generation of Ethiopians to add two elements to this brief narrative of Ethiopia's development during the decade of the fifties and sixties: namely Ethiopia's economic relations with the socialist world and a few ideas about the person at the helm: Emperor Haile-Selassie I.

Socialist Countries and Ethiopia's Development

Contrary to current thinking that Ethiopia's development programmes relied exclusively on the West during the reign of Emperor Halie-Selassie, considerable efforts were made to benefit from the expertise and resources of East European and other socialist countries.

Ethio-Yugoslav Economic Cooperation

As I indicated earlier, the preparation of the country's first and second five-year plans relied heavily on Yugoslav experts. Besides generating a flow of development projects, planning contributed to the quality and coherence of economic policies. Yugoslav experts were also active in different sectors of the economy. The extension of the Port of Assab was carried out by a Yugoslav engineering firm. There were engineers, architects, economists, agronomists, and other experts in various government departments. A sizeable number of medical doctors worked in the country's principal hospitals. Many Ethiopian doctors were trained in Yugoslavia. It was in development planning, however, that Ethio-Yugoslav economic cooperation had the most constructive and durable impact on the country's development efforts.

Ethio-Soviet Cooperation

In the summer of 1959, Emperor Haile-Selassie paid a state visit to countries in Eastern Europe and the Middle East. The visit to the Soviet Union was the high point of his itinerary. Nikita Khrushchev's new policy of raising the profile of the Soviet Union in the developing world enabled the Emperor to secure a loan of 400 million rubles (U.S. $400 million at the prevailing rate of exchange) for the various projects of the first five-year development plan (1959-64). Upon his return home, the Emperor made two long and uncharacteristically rousing addresses to the nation in which he announced the good news and urged the country's farmers to brace themselves for a concerted effort to develop Ethiopia's agriculture.[6]

The speeches were unusual for two reasons. First, the Emperor talked directly to farmers. Indeed, he underlined the point in his second address when he said: "although we have up to now worked through our officials, the present programme brings us into direct contact with our people." Secondly, the Emperor's language was more like a politician's exhorting his followers to seize a rare opportunity to move ahead in life than the ponderous and measured words he often used in his addresses.

In his first address, he told the country's farmers that a long- term low-interest loan had been secured to fund the different projects in the new five-year plan. "Stand up and compete.... Get up early in the morning....Brace up for work..... Look down from the mountain tops on the rich valleys below....The bare mountains you see are no less bountiful than these valleys..... With the new money, we shall send you experts who will advise you on how you should look after your health, live better, and use the money wisely..."

"We have been informed that you are pleased with our earlier address and are eagerly awaiting the launching of the programme," the Emperor said in his second address. "And that you stand ready to work closely with us. This has raised our hopes for the plan..." The Emperor promised money and land to those possessing neither, money to those who had land but no means to develop it, and cooperative farming to all. He told his listeners that preparations have been made to launch the programme: loans at 2.5% interest, work plans, and expert advisors.

"Get down to serious work...." he exhorted the farmers. "Do not falter from your goals....Be strong in spirit and determined in your struggle..... We consider the New Year an opportunity for you to learn the benefits of cooperative work. Help yourselves and in the process help us to develop the country....... And to those who wander around in search of work but end up begging, we say, go back to your places of origin. For there you shall find the work which you have long been seeking........ Understand the value of time. Do not allow even a second to slip by...... If you fail to follow the guidelines we have laid before you and spend the money frivolously, you shall put yourself and your country in debt...." For twenty-one consecutive days, the government daily carried extensive first-page commentaries on different aspects of the two speeches.

What was the outcome of this rousing and unprecedented peacetime effort by the Emperor to get Ethiopia's agriculture going? And what was the magnitude of resources deployed? The funds earmarked were Birr 5 million (roughly U.S. $2.5 million). Perhaps this was intended as the first of many installments. But nothing followed. And there was little advance planning. The government's capacity to implement a country-wide plan of the nature the Emperor had in mind was limited. Persons involved with the programme recall that the money which was distributed to the farmers was spent frivolously, as the Emperor had feared. Some of the money went to absentee landlords who did not invest on their land. The whole venture ended in regrettable failure.

Part of the unspent loan was used to put up the Assab Oil Refinery, an outdated plant dismantled from a Soviet region in central Asia and reassembled in Assab at a cost of $11 million. It is difficult to ascertain the use made of the remaining balance of the Soviet loan (about 96%). Sources familiar with the credit are of the view that it was only after the revolution in 1974 that the loan was consolidated with the huge military credit that was made available to the Mengistu regime. A sad finale, to be sure, of a venture much talked about by both borrower and creditor. But one which demonstrated that Emperor Haile-Selassie's government went to great lengths to work with East European countries to develop Ethiopia's economy.

Sino-Ethiopian Cooperation

Economic relations with China provide yet another instance of Emperor Haile-Selassie's attempts at developing economic ties with countries in the non-western world. The Emperor visited China in 1971 during which he met the ageing Mao Tse-tung. An economic and cultural cooperation agreement was signed, the economic part of which included China's offer of a $200,000,000 loan to support different development projects in Ethiopia. In those days China's foreign exchange coffers were not awash with hard currency, and the loan was not intended to be disbursed in dollars. The idea was that the Chinese would build projects, using Chinese labour and materials that would add up to $200 million.

Upon his return from China, the Emperor was keen to get started on the new agreement and frequently met with officials to monitor progress. I attended many of these meetings. The Ethiopian bureaucracy was accustomed to preparing projects for the World Bank and similar other agencies. The Chinese conception of assistance posed a number of technical and practical challenges that made it difficult to identify suitable projects. It was therefore decided to send a special mission to China to come up with answers.

The mission, of which I was a member and which was led by Commerce and Industry Minister Ketema Yifru, proceeded to China in 1973. Members of the mission immediately got down to the business of working out the practical problems faced in using Chinese labour and materials to get projects started in Ethiopia. And how, moreover, the Ethiopian government was to make repayments on goods in kind that were offered in the form of loans

Three days or so into our discussions, our Chinese counterparts informed us that we were scheduled to meet with an 'important person' in the Chinese hierarchy and that we should take a short break to pay our respects to him. We did not know for sure who the important person was, although some among us guessed it could be the Prime Minister or perhaps even Mao himself. Seeing a top official without coming to an agreement on the knotty problems we faced did not appear appropriate, however. We asked if the meeting could be deferred. Our hosts were troubled. We, on the other hand, felt that we would be hard put to respond to questions that the person might ask about the progress we were making. It would be better to take the discussions as far as we could and report that agreement had been reached if we were to come to that, or suggest issues to be resolved at a higher political level if we faced hurdles. The worried Chinese would not say whether they could reschedule the meeting. The following morning they looked relieved: the appointment had been pushed back.

A couple of days later, the discussions ended satisfactorily. Amidst a flurry of chauffeurs and official minders on the appointed day, we were driven to where the 'important person' was, the Great Hall facing Tiananmen Square. We entered the cavernous building and were led to a meeting room with easy chairs each of which displayed a round lace mat carefully placed in the geometric centre of the head rest of each sofa. Our host entered the room after a few minutes. He wore a restrained smile. It was someone whose pictures we had often seen but who nevertheless looked different. His right arm was bent at the elbow and rested across his abdomen; the result of an accident during the Long March, we were later told.

Prime Minister Chou En-Lai was genial. He asked about the health of the Crown Prince who had suffered a stroke a few months earlier. He spoke positively of the solidarity of the African countries. There was nothing in Asia that resembled

During a courtesy call on Prime Minister Chou En Lai; the Ethiopians are (from left to right)
Tekalign Gedamu, Makonnen Kibret, and Ketema Yifru

the Organization of African Unity. He also told us that our delegation had taught its Chinese counterparts an important lesson when we said that it was premature to meet with him prior to the conclusion of the negotiations. Work should always precede protocol. After asking Ketema's age he turned to Fung Yee, the Minister for Science and Technology and leader of the Chinese side, and said, "You are sixty-five or thereabouts, and yet here is a forty-five year old Minister teaching your staff about the priority of work over protocol." The Minister exhibited the obliging smile of a pupil being taken to task by a stern schoolmaster. We felt sorry for Fung Yee, but did not fail to take note of the Chou En-Lai's intent to flatter our delegation.[7]

The Premier then got into a discussion of world affairs. At one point he interrupted his nervous young female interpreter when she used a wrong expression in referring to some European organization he was talking about. When she said 'League of Nations' the Prime Minister said something to her in Mandarin. "I am sorry," said the young interpreter to us "I meant the opposite of the League of Nations," "No opposite!" shot back the man who was supposed not to speak English. Ketema guessed what the Prime Minister had in mind and said "Allied Powers," the precursor to the League. The Prime Minister concurred and went on talking sternly to the nervous girl for a couple of minutes.

The interpreter turned to us and said "The Prime Minister is asking me why I, a trained interpreter, could not get the right term while the Minister of Ethiopia could, and with such ease." Ketema quickly came to the defence of the pour little soul: "Your Excellency, I served as Foreign Minister of my country for ten years, but she is only a young lady and has many years of learning ahead of her." "Perhaps it is our fault. We have not educated her properly" replied the Prime Minister understandingly. The girl was relieved. As we were about to take leave, Ketema asked if the Chinese government might consider building a sports stadium in Addis Ababa as a symbol of Sino-Ethiopian friendship. Chou agreed.[8]

We wound up our work and signed a protocol on the mechanics of implementing the Chinese loan. As I said before, the Chinese did not make available any hard cash for financing projects. They only offered materials and Chinese labour. All local expenses (such as transporting men and equipment to and from project sites, local supplies, etc) had to be covered by Ethiopia. There was a shortage of domestic revenue to provide resources for this purpose, which is why donor funds from the West were preferred. Where would local currency for the Chinese loan come from? The problem was resolved in the following way.

Under Ethiopia's foreign trade protocol, importers of merchandise deposited the Birr equivalent of the cost of their imported goods at Ethiopia's central bank. These were converted into hard currency by the bank for onward payment to the exporter's bank. For the Chinese loan, we decided that the central bank should not convert the birr amount into hard currency but make it available for financing the local currency expenses of Chinese projects. Appropriate accounting arrangements should be made to ensure that these amounts were treated as a component part of the loan. When the loan was due, the birr amounts paid by the government would be converted into dollars for repayment to the Chinese.

While all this was going on, the Chinese kept telling us not to be unduly concerned, as they would ultimately cancel the loan in a gesture of third world solidarity. We could not, however, take them at their word in the absence of a signed agreement. It was for them to forgive the loan, if they were so inclined. For our part, we had to exercise prudence and maintain proper records.[9]

When we returned to Ethiopia, we were able to present a few projects for funding under the loan, thanks to the foregoing accounting device. Among the principal projects which the Chinese agreed to build was the 160 mile road from Woldiya to Worreta in Northern Ethiopia. This project had been presented for World Bank funding but had been rejected on economic grounds. The Chinese told us that they were aware of this, but that they were prepared to build it as a gesture of China's friendship. Construction started on the eve of the 1974 revolution and was completed a few years later, opening a vast hinterland that had been deprived of surface transport. Other projects implemented under the loan included the supply of water for provincial towns and technical assistance to train Ethiopians in bamboo handicrafts for which the Chinese are well known. The inexpensive small bamboo chairs offered by petty traders in Addis today date back to this project.

I should perhaps make a digression here and say a word or two about my frequent meetings with the Emperor around this time. The Emperor maintained his keen interest in the progress of the Chinese loan and often inquired why projects were not coming up in sufficient numbers. Whenever a minister responsible for a China-funded project was called to appear before the Emperor, I was summoned.

In one such meeting, Minister of Mines Emmanuel Abraham, I and a third official appeared before the Emperor. Emmanuel was asked why his Ministry had not proposed projects for funding under the Chinese credit. He responded that experts in his Ministry were working on proposals and would soon have them ready for submission. The Emperor asked what these projects were. "We have extensive potash deposits in the Danakil desert and will soon present some projects." The Emperor was not impressed and asked if the Minister truly believed that potash "which was like salt" could be packaged into a mining project worthy of the name.

"Your Majesty," replied Emmanuel, "it is the view of the experts, not mine, that anything which is retrieved from the bowels of the earth is classified as a mining activity." The Emperor's poker face betrayed a faint sign of annoyance. He then said: "You people have neglected your duties." Emmanuel, a forthright person who had been commended by the Emperor for his services at various times in the past, responded that he was not negligent, was working to the best of his abilities, and perhaps even beyond that.[10] The Emperor did not take kindly to the arguments advanced in an obvious spirit of defiance. "Where were you yesterday evening when we called your home" he asked? "I was out at a dinner invitation, Your Majesty." "Precisely," retorted the Emperor with satisfaction. "Dinner invitations, unlike work, are rarely neglected." That put an end to the argument.

How unfair, I thought as we walked out of the Emperor's office. To the third official who was at the meeting and whom I suspected of having misinformed the Emperor that the Minister of Mines was dragging his feet, I said that it was painful to see a Minster who had served his country loyally for many years to be taken to task in this manner on the basis of false information. Had he by any chance talked to the Emperor about the Chinese project before our meeting? I asked. Sensing that I suspected him as the culprit, he said he had not said anything to the Emperor. For me, however, his presence at the meeting was sufficient indication that he was playing some game behind the scene. He was suspected by many as a self promoting imperial informer on matters big and small.

In another incident unconnected with the Chinese loan but which was typical of the imperial practice of keeping officials guessing about their effectiveness on their jobs, I found myself the object of a similarly unflattering royal remark. One morning, the Palace telephone operator said that I was urgently needed and should present myself without delay, a standard enough expression that did not cause undue concern. Upon arrival, I was ushered to the Emperor's office. Three senior officials were huddled around him in what seemed like a confidential discussion, all in a standing position, including the Emperor. The three were the Minister of the Interior, the Minister of Defence, and the Governor General of Shoa province. I stood at some distance from the conversation, as I had to until signaled otherwise by the Emperor. A few minutes passed, but nothing happened. Why was I summoned? I wondered. In such situations, one of the Emperor's private secretaries usually reminded him. But there was no secretary present.

A few minutes passed, but the hushed consultation continued. After a while, the Emperor looked at me and said: "You have recently become negligent of your duties, have you not?" It was a busy time for me in the office. Often I started work at 7:30 a. m., a full hour and half before the start of regular office hours, took a short lunch break, and stayed late into the evening. I could not say so without sounding disrespectful. So I just smiled as I stood in front of him. It was evident I had to say something in reply. But I kept silent. "Do you not understand?" asked the monarch.

I kept quiet and let it be known that I did not have a response. At that precise moment the Minister of Finance, to whom the Emperor was said not to be too favourably disposed, entered the room. "Is your Ministry also in as bad a shape as his?" he was asked. The man was momentarily alarmed and said something inaudible. I now realized it was the Emperor's usual tactic to ensure that his officials were not indolent. I started walking backwards, initially gingerly and almost imperceptivity, one gentle step after another with my eyes fixed on the group as if to say 'I am still around if you need me.' Soon I reached the exit of the large office, kept my eyes firmly on the Emperor, took a deep bow and, ascertaining that there was no objection to my imminent departure, slipped away quietly.

I was walking downhill towards my car when, just before I opened the door, I heard the Minister of Finance calling my name. "Tell me, what is going on?" I told him what had happened (or more accurately what had not happened) before he arrived and said: "My guess is that you and I were called to a meeting where some budget matter was probably being discussed. The meeting must have ended swiftly, to be followed immediately by the present one to which our two departments have apparently little to contribute. Unfortunately, there were no Palace staff to tell us that we were no longer needed. The ageing Emperor had to say something. He resorted to the time-tested royal technique of putting everyone on their toes. The French educated Minister was reassured and said "*Ah Bon. C'est ça, alors!*"

More on Highlights of Development: The Man at the Centre

Education had been one area where the reforms of Emperor Haile-Selassie suffered a serious setback during the Fascist occupation. There was a severe shortage of qualified people in government afterwards. A not insignificant number of university graduates had been liquidated by the Italians. The Fascists had also completely arrested the Emperor's programme of training Ethiopians for the professions. It would take another ten years or so for university graduates to begin to join government service, with the result that practically all parastatal bodies and many senior civil service posts were initially headed by expatriate personnel: the State Bank of Ethiopia by a Canadian; the Telecommunications Board by a Swede; the High Court by an Englishman; the

Attorney-General's office by a British subject; the Development Bank of Ethiopia by an Austrian; Ethiopian Airlines by an American; the Highway Authority by another American; the training school for the Imperial Guard by a Swede; the Air Force also by a Swede; and most elementary and secondary schools by a wide variety of expatriates.

The result was a considerable pace of modernization and economic growth in the first twenty-five years or so after the return of the Emperor from exile. By the late sixties "major highways had been brought under construction, airstrips built, a new seaport (Assab) constructed, and a telecommunications network had begun to operate."[11] Large scale commercial farming (sugar cane, cotton, bananas, coffee, and tobacco) was making strides and the manufacturing sector was growing at 16% in the early sixties. And per capita income grew by about 3%.[12]

By the time of the Third Five-Year Plan (1969/70 to 1973/74), agriculture had become a major focus of development. It was in the course of this plan that an encouraging development started to emerge. For centuries, Ethiopian agriculture had been dominated by peasants employing antiquated methods. A new class of progressive educated young investors (a good number of whom were graduates in agricultural sciences) now began to make an entry.

Also joining their ranks were frustrated civil servants attracted by the rewards of high returns in commercial agriculture. People began to dream about a turnaround in the country's agriculture.

A wide range of donor programmes supported the thrust of the five-year development plans. By the time I was appointed Planning Commissioner many multilateral and bilateral development agencies (the World Bank, FAO, UNESCO, UNICEF, UNDP, SIDA, USAID to mention only a few) were running fairly sizeable credit and technical assistance programmes in the transport, telecommunications, energy, health, education, and agricultural sectors. As I have noted previously, Sweden's International Development Agency (SIDA) spearheaded a major agricultural research and development initiative. Research results were offered in deliverable packages to the farming population which, if sustained, promised to bring changes in farming practices and productivity. By the end of the third five-year plan, per capita income was grossing at 2.2% per annum, a fairly respectable achievement even when allowance is made for the usual weakness in national accounts data.

Along with these developments, the civil service was being revamped. A number of para-statal bodies began to function effectively under a generation of able Ethiopian managers: Ethiopian Airlines under Semret Medhane; Ethiopian Telecommunications led by the competent British trained engineer Betru Admassie; the Commercial Bank of Ethiopia run by Canadian trained Tafarra Deguefe; Ethiopian Electric by the knowledgeable and calm engineer Assefa Tilahun, another British educated engineer; the Agricultural Research Institute under the bright scientist and University of Purdue graduate Dr. Dagnatchew Yirgu; the Oil Refinery at Assab by Kebede Akale-Wold, yet another engineer trained in the U.K.; the Imperial Highway Authority headed successively by Dr. Haile-Giorgis Workineh, Abashawal Wolde-Mariam, and Hailu Shawul, all foreign trained engineers.

Over a relatively short span of time, Haile-Selassie University had evolved into a credible institution of higher learning under the leadership of its President, Dejazmatch Kassa Wolde-Mariam, and later under the quiet, able, and doggedly committed duos: Dr. Aklilu Habte and Dr. Mulugeta Wodajo. Scholars like Merid Wolde-Aregay, Tamrat Tadesse and Sirgew Hable-Selassie (historians), Abraham Demoz (linguist), Getachew Haile (philologist), Makonnen Wolde-Amlak (physicist), Alemayehou Haile (mathematician), and Asrat Woldeyes (surgeon and head of the University's Medical School), and a good many others would become respected academics who would leave an indelible mark on the young university's evolution. Mesfin Wolde-Mariam, the perennial dissenter carried the mantle of political opposition but went about his teaching duties largely unscathed, except when someone thought that his rhetoric for development should be put to the test with an administrative appointment in a remote district.

In the defence area, a young generation of bright military officers was coming up the ranks. Among these were General Yohannes Wolde-Mariam of the Air Force who was briefly in command,[13] Colonel Workineh Gebeyehu of the Imperial Guard, the bright Major Tibebe Menkir of the Army, and Captain Mamo Gizzaw of the Navy, to name but a few. These held much leadership promise in a military establishment that was among the top three in Africa and that had proved its mettle in the UN's Korea and Congo Operations.

These men and many like them in law, medicine, engineering and the other professions who could not figure in this brief account were possibly among the finest collection of professionals in Africa and perhaps in the developing world. Their management capabilities were recognized more outside of the country than at home. Multilateral financial institutions like the World Bank and the African Development Bank would often speak favourably of the effectiveness with which development projects were managed and commitments honoured. Non-African World Bank staff often remarked Ethiopia was in but not of Africa. Ethiopians objected to this as an unhelpful remark at a time when the country and its leadership were strongly committed to many African causes. However, behind the remark was a testimony to the fact that of all World Bank projects in Africa those in Ethiopia were on average much better managed. It takes a competent civil service and a high level of work ethic to elicit such an appreciation. Much of this was the result of a long-standing government policy of expanding higher education at considerable public expense. And this in a poor country that had no oil, or gas, or diamonds as a major source of foreign exchange, but only coffee which was vulnerable to international price volatility.

Emperor Haile-Selassie on a foreign visit in the sixties

Emperor Haile-Selassie was the architect of this policy. From the very moment of his coming to power, he had set his sights on what was then regarded as a destabilizing modernization programme. And he had encountered stiff resistance from powerful conservative forces, which he had ultimately managed to overcome. He was, of course, not the first among Ethiopian monarchs to dream of bringing the fruits of science and technology to the country. Ethiopian Emperors going back to Dawit (1381-1410)[14],

Yisshaq (1414-29)[14] Zera Ya'icob (1434-68)[14], and Libne Dingel (1508-40)[15] had all been eager to introduce European techniques and know-how in construction, medicine, mining and manufacturing and, given their perennial conflicts with foreign powers, in arms, ammunition and port fortifications. Being Christian, they were inclined to see Europe's Christian kingdoms as models and on occasion as potential allies. In more recent times Emperors Tewodros (1855-1868), Menelik (1889-1913) and Yohannes (1872- 1889) had also been active reformers.[16]

Haile-Selassie (1931-1974) was the latest in this long line of reforming Emperors. Compared to his predecessors, he had done more. In comparison with monarchs in the developing world prior to the oil extravaganza (King Farouk of Egypt, King Idris of Libya, the Kings of Saudi Arabia, the rulers of Yemen, and the other Kings and Princes of the Middle East, developing Asia and Africa) he had been far more forward looking and had accomplished a great deal with the limited resources. Why was all this not recognized by his compatriots? For that was the clearest message of the tumultuous events of 1974. More importantly, why did his reform efforts fail in their objective to bring about sustainable change and prevent the violence triggered by the revolution of that year?

We would have to await the verdict of history for the final answer. In the meantime, it would be incumbent upon those who lived through these times and had the opportunity to take part in the management of public affairs to shed some light on this vital question. And to share with this generation of Ethiopians their dreams and forebodings, the challenges they faced and the different ways in which they tried to respond, and what they did or did not do as they were touched, briefly and in some instances not so briefly, by what has turned out to be a sea change in the history of their country. I shall try to do this in parts II and III.

PART II

Fin D'Époque

CHAPTER 7

The Monarchy on the Eve

The Gathering Storm

There was a five-fold tragedy which Emperor Haile-Selassie faced at the end of his reign. The first was the increasing challenge to his authority posed by the very modernization programme which he had so single-mindedly pursued from the very beginning of his rise to power. The second was the inadequacy of reform measures to meet that challenge. The third was fatalism and old age which impaired his capacity to manage events and situations. The fourth was the growing factor of ethnicity which generated strong centrifugal forces, especially in the province of Eritrea. The fifth and final tragedy was the fact that the Emperor and his government had become remote from their people.

The Increasing Challenge of Rising Expectations

Not long after he was designated Crown Prince in September 1916, Ras Tafari Makonnen (as the Emperor was called at the time) embarked upon an ambitious plan for the modernization of the country. As I have said on several occasions before, education was a key component of this plan. In 1908 Emperor Menelik had opened the first modern school in the country. In 1925 the Crown Prince added a second. In an effort to attract students from across the land, the Prince asked provincial Governors to send children to the two schools. Many young men soon came, the largest group being from Wollega in Western Ethiopia.

After a five-year setback caused by Fascist occupation, the reform plan was resumed. The two schools in the capital were reopened. New elementary and secondary schools were added. In the provinces, elementary schools were opened in each principal town and gradually in other urban centres. The same process was followed for spreading secondary and higher education. By the sixties, Addis Ababa had some twenty secondary and vocational schools as well as a University. A College of Agriculture was established in Alemaya (Harrar Province), a Public Health College in Gondar (the capital of Begemdir and Simien Province), a post-secondary Polytechnic Institute in Bahr Dar (Gojjam Province), and a University in Asmara (Eritrea Province). There were academies for the Army, the Air Force, the Navy, and the Police Force. The government had also launched a scholarship programme which enabled a large numbers of students to receive university education in Europe and North America.

With the spread of education, aspirations rose and the demand for radical reform grew steadily. This was obvious enough. What was not so obvious was that these aspirations would have a political impact far out of proportion to the relatively small number of citizens airing them. In the Emperor's old age, this small group of citizens started to clamour for a fundamental transformation of the political order. Most observers, including not a few among the radically inclined, did not think that the country's problems called for a bloody revolution. A tiny minority thought otherwise. It often takes only a handful of people to trigger events having far-reaching consequences for the fate of a nation. This would prove to be the case for Ethiopia.

Inadequacy of Reforms

In the early days of Emperor Haile-Selassie's reign, reforms were centrally driven. This was true of the Emperor's educational as well as administrative reforms. There was no pressure from below. Indeed such pressure as there was militated against change. Modern education was resisted by the aristocracy and the clergy for fear that it would undermine the country's established culture and way of life. A more practical cause of resistance was political. Given the reluctance of members of the ruling class to send their children to these modern schools, it was inevitable that the children of the lower classes would be the principal beneficiaries and acquire bureaucratic clout and influence. The big men of power were naturally apprehensive and tried hard to restrain the reforming Crown Prince. Contrary to their expectations, the heir to the throne would not be persuaded. When persuasion was replaced by threats and raw political pressure the prince and his loyal followers evaded them tactfully and, when necessary, confronted them frontally.

Following his coronation, the Emperor broadened his programme to include a consultative National Assembly as a first step towards an elected Parliament. The response of the country's leading aristocrats (according to what the Emperor himself told Haddis Alemayehu several years later) went something like this: Our people are innocent of politics. God put you on the throne to rule the country to the best of your abilities. Who are you going to consult? If you are uncomfortable wearing the crown, God could select someone else.

The Emperor persisted in his efforts, however, and the 1931 Constitution was ultimately adopted. It provided for a consultative parliament, leaving political power in the hands of the Emperor but granting some rights to citizens. Bejrond Tekle-Hawariat Tekle-Mariam, the Russian educated progressive individual who was Minister of Finance at the time, was largely responsible for its drafting. Tekle-Hawariat

Tsehafe-Te'ezaz Wolde-Giorgis Wolde-Yohannes (far right) with Ras Andargatchew Mesai (the Emperor's son-in-law) to his right, Prime Minister Aklilu Habte-Wold and Ras Hailu Belew of Gojjam

was assisted by Blatten Getta Hirouy Wolde-Selassie, a product of Ethiopia's traditional educational system who had been sent to Japan to observe that country's experience of modernization. It is believed that elements of Japan's Mejii Constitution had some influence on Tekle-Hawariat's drafting.

Resistance to reform diminished considerably after the Fascist occupation, thanks partly to a renewed sense of nationalism and partly to a decline in the influence of the aristocrats, a good number of whom had been compromised by collaboration with the enemy. A new trajectory of reform was embarked upon after the occupation years which focused on the executive branch. Here the Emperor worked, as initially feared by the aristocrats, with a young generation of close collaborators drawn from the lower classes. For practically the whole of his 33-year post occupation reign, the Emperor relied on a group of individuals who were of modest social origin and possessed a relatively liberal political orientation. Foremost among these was the person in charge of the politically powerful imperial secretariat (the Ministry of Pen), Tsehafe Te'ezaz Wolde-Giorgis Wolde-Yahannes.

Prior to the War, Wolde-Giorgis had been an Amharic-French interpreter at Menelik Hospital in Addis Ababa. He was spotted there by Makonnen Habte-Wold (a close associate of the Emperor) and was later presented to the monarch as an able young man worthy of imperial attention. Wolde-Giorgis was first brought to the Ministry of Foreign Affairs. Later he was moved to the imperial secretariat as a

Director General. During the Emperor's exile years in England, Wolde-Giorgis was at his side and became one of three or four close confidants.

Upon the Emperor's return, Wolde-Giorgis was appointed Minister of Pen. Not long afterwards, he reportedly asked the hand of Princess Tenagne Work, the Emperor's eldest daughter. Members of Wolde-Giorgis's immediate family say he himself never took the initiative. Whoever was behind the idea (and there was no shortage of self-serving matchmakers in those days), the Emperor was apparently agreeable. However, members of the aristocracy disapproved. Prime Minister Makonnen Endalkatchew, a leading aristocrat, took strong exception to the idea. How could someone of humble origin presume to marry a princess? A more personal reason for his objection was the fact that the Princess's former husband, Ras Desta Damtew who was killed by the Italians during the war of occupation, was a close relative. The thought of this upstart becoming a stepfather to the sons and daughters of a distinguished relative did not sit well with Makonnen. This was bound to strain Wolde-Giorgis's relationship with the aristocracy. Few Ethiopians easily forget an affront to their pride. Wolde-Giorgis was no exception.

Wolde-Giorgis worked closely with his pre-war mentor and fellow plebeian, Makonnen Habte-Wold, who successively held key Cabinet posts. Makonnen's younger brother, the French educated Aklilu Habte-Wold, was posted at the Ministry of Foreign Affairs after a brief stay in the Ministry of Pen. Another brother, Akale-Work Habte-Wold, was at various times Minister of Education, Agriculture, Health, and Justice. Indeed the Cabinet was for the most part made up of people who were, like Wolde-Giorgis, of humble social origin. Under his leadership, they vied for power with the aristocracy and came out on top much of the time. Folklore portrays Wolde-Giorgis as a man of reform who recruited like-minded persons into government service. By all accounts, he was a forward looking, industrious, and effective manager of government business.

An indication of Wolde-Girogis's early ideas on reform is given in a handwritten note dated Megabit 12, 1939 (March 20, 1947) which he drafted in response to a proposal submitted to the Emperor by certain unnamed officials. In his note, Wolde-Giorgis articulates his ideas on the legislature and on the constitution. Among them are the following three:[1]

a) Ethiopia's legislature should be a reflection of its political realities. Its members should be men of high social and political standing: members of the country's royal houses, the aristocracy, and traditional chiefs.

b) Ethiopia does not possess enough educated people and the few she has should be concentrated in the executive branch. Support by the legislature is essential; as it is only through such support that the executive branch can secure credibility. While it is evident that the views of the young in the executive branch and of their elders in the legislative branch might not always converge, the former need the support of the latter if they are to carry out their work effectively; and they should for that reason accord deference to their elders, the aristocrats. In time, mutual trust, respect, and a spirit of cooperation would be engendered. And the country would make progress, albeit only gradually.

c) Regarding the constitution, Wolde-Giorgis suggests that there is no need to make revisions of a substantive nature. The rights of the citizen which the constitution provides are adequate for the time being. Indeed, citizens are not yet aware of their constitutional rights. No significant revision is therefore required. Only changes in form are needed to render it more acceptable to outside observers.

The first impression one gets of Wolde-Giorgis's reformist ideas is not exactly that of a determined anti-aristocratic politician aggressively forging ahead with the government's modernization programme. It is rather of someone who is eager to accommodate the aristocracy. His views on parliamentary and constitutional reform look particularly timid. Why such timidity from a man widely regarded as an agent of modernization?

Realism appears to have been his most constraining reason. Wolde-Giorgis fully appreciated the powerful forces arrayed against him, especially in the mid 1940s when his note was drafted. He needed to package his reforms in language that rendered them attractive to the Emperor and the aristocracy. And he needed to buy time; time in particular to overcome the severe shortage of educated people. Another reason might have been the limited appeal libertarian ideas had for him. Temperamentally, Wolde-Giorgis was a man of authority very much given to setting in motion an accelerated programme of administrative reform for a country making belated efforts to emerge from medieval autocracy.

But none of this gained him the trust of his conservative adversaries. For in a brief response to his note, three members of the traditional class advised the Emperor not to leave the executive branch exclusively in the hands of Wolde-Giorgis and men of his class.[2] The three were Ras Kassa Hailu, the Emperor's cousin and *eminence grise*, Ras Abebe Aregai, the resistance leader and Minister of War, and Bitwoded Makonnen Endalkatchew, Prime Minister. Together with Wolde-Girogis and Makonnen Habte-Wold, the Bitwoded had been a member of a committee that had signed the note drafted by Wolde-Giorgis in the response to the original proposal. He now wears his hat as a member of the aristocracy sitting in judgment over the very note he had earlier endorsed. Was the Prime Minister duplicitous? Which politician is not? But more to the point is the Emperor's method of planting a reliable person in parallel committee's handling the same subject with the view to ascertaining who was saying what, when, and to whom.

One of the ideas advanced by the conservative group was to abolish the post of Prime Minister. Their view was that the functions of the office should be assumed by the Emperor himself, as in the U.S. where the President was chief executive. Another was that the portfolios of Defence and Interior should be reserved for members of the aristocracy, while Finance and Foreign affairs could safely be assigned to Wolde-Giorgis's men. The Emperor does not seem to have accepted the advice of the aristorcratic trio in its entirety; for Wolde-Giorgis continued as the *de facto* head of the executive branch while the aristocratic Bitwoded carried on with the empty title of Prime Minister.

We need to look beyond the ideas in the note to obtain a fuller understanding of Wolde-Giorgis's views on reform. The personal testimonies of individuals who worked with him are helpful in this respect. What these persons say is that Wolde-Giorgis was indeed a bold reformer of the executive branch within the boundaries set for him by imperial authority. He did this by packing the executive (and the judiciary) with persons who, like him, were mostly of humble social origin and with exposure to western ideas. He streamlined the administration of the central government and the provinces, transforming the country into a unitary state in sharp contrast to the situation before the war where a good number of feudal potentates held sway in their respective districts.

While there was justification for introducing uniform systems and procedures in a country which needed it, Wolde-Giorgis's centralized plan inevitably provoked local resistance. This was occasioned in part by taxes on land and in part by senior government appointees, both imposed by the central government. The Woyane rebellion in Tigrai in 1942 and a near rebellion in Gojjam some two decades later are cases in point. Wolde-Giorgis also played an active role in formulating foreign policy. Unlike many an aristocrat, he was a determined nationalist who understood and rebuffed external designs to compromise the country's sovereignty. A good illustration of this is his robust stand in 1941 (when others wavered) against an underhanded British plan to place the country under the protection of the British Crown.[3]

Wolde-Girogis exercised cautioun in his relations with influential members of the aristocracy, although privately he did not hide his disdain for those he judged ineffective. He was deferential to Ras Kassa Hailu and Ras Abebe Aregai; both men of considerable political insight whose views the Emperor respected. And he maintained his privileged rapport with the Emperor to the point where at the height of his power he was, as indicated earlier, Prime Minister in all but name. Under him, Ethiopia moved decisively towards a highly centralized state in which the influence of the aristocracy was effectively constrained. That is no mean achievement.

In the early fifties, Wolde-Giorgis was also involved in preparations for a revised constitution. New provisions were incorporated for an elected parliament with important powers of oversight and control over the executive (principally over the budget and international treaties). This gave added impetus to reforms, although the Emperor's authority remained unchallenged. Wolde-Giorgis's effective exercise of power (occasionally laced, as some allege, with vindictiveness), his growing assertiveness bordering on arrogance, and his dogged determination to sideline the power of the aristocracy inevitably earned him enemies. His foes grumbled that the man had not only become virtual Prime Minister but on occasion acted as if he himself were Emperor. Little by little doubts were raised in Emperor Haile-Selassie's mind about the loyalty and motives of his most trusted super minister.

Wolde-Giorgis was, of course, aware of all this. A short write up on his life cites an allegation in his unpublished memoirs that Minister Makonnen (his old mentor) had been plotting against him for some time.[4] That Makonnen was a key player in Wolde-Giorgos's removal has long been established, and I hope we shall learn more on this from Zauwde Retta's forthcoming book. The larger than life figure of an uncrowned ruler of Ethiopia stalking the length and breadth of the country disappeared from view in 1955. In that year Wolde-Giorgis was demoted to the humiliating post of Governor General of the smallest province in the Empire. The revised constitution in the crafting of which he had taken an active part was enacted a few months later.

Such was the power wielded by Wolde-Giorgis that just before his removal the Imperial Guard was reportedly instructed to take precautions to forestall possible trouble. There were a few anxious moments when, curiously, he seemed to linger in the capital for a few days prior to taking up his position as the new governor-general of Arussi. Nothing untoward happened, however. The anxiety and quiet commotion in the city was an understandable if not exactly fitting adieu to a man who had risen from humble beginnings to become the most formidable political personality in the Empire of Ethiopia second only to Emperor Haile-Selassie himslef.

For the fourteen-year period between 1941 and 1955, the Wolde-Giorgis/Makonnen/Aklilu band of 'Labourites' managed to sideline the 'Tories,' and power was to all intents and purposes in their hands, needless to say with the blessing of the Emperor.[5] Yet, these two groups could in no way be deemed to have played the role of organized political parties offering alternative programmes as to how the country should be governed. Neither the one nor the other group had a popular base or a political organization capable of facilitating a transition towards some form of participatory government. It was also obvious that neither faction could act as an effective counterweight to advocates of more violent change. Despite Wolde-Giorgis's considerable achievements in the administrative are, political reform was kept on the back burner.

With Wolde-Girogis gone and Makonnen Habte-Wold replacing him as the Emperor's right hand man, such reform as there was moved further back. In the meantime, a small but increasing class of dissidents started to demand a faster pace of change. An early indication was the attempted coup d'état of 1960 which failed but which served as a wakeup call of worse things to come. A feeble attempt at reforming Cabinet government was made in the spring of 1966 whose principal objective was to allow the Prime Minister to choose his cabinet colleagues (theretofore a prerogative of the Emperor) and make the Cabinet collectively responsible to the Emperor. Old habits resurfaced soon afterwards, however. Ministers resumed their visits to the Palace and the Emperor continued with his previous practice of dealing individually with them. At a later date, Prime Minister Aklilu toyed with the idea of fending off a possible conservative backlash and launching an effort to move towards a constitutional monarchy. However, little was done beyond trading ideas in secret with trusted collaborators.

There was another attempt at political reform from the Emperor's close associates. Towards the mid-sixties Ras Asrate Kassa, a cousin and high government official, defence Minister General Merid Mengesha, General Abiy Abebe, the Emperor's representative in Eritrea, Dejazmatch Girmatchew Tekle Hawariat, Information Minister, and Colonel Tamret Yigezu, provincial Governor General, submitted a hand-written eighteen-page memorandum to the Emperor outlining a number of reform proposals.[6]

The Emperor's reactions along the margins of the memo were on the whole dismissive. For instance, his rejoinder to the idea of creating an organization which would work towards strengthening unity among different ethnic groups was a simple "have we not done this already?" Regarding another reform proposal on page 17 (making the Prime Minister accountable to the Parliament), the Emperor noted that "this has been a long-standing feature of the constitution." In yet another dismissive remark on corruption, the Emperor remarked that the authors of the memo should "count the number of days which have elapsed since instructions were sent to the Cabinet to abolish corruption" (page 11). Evidently, the Emperor was of the view that he had taken the requisite steps to improve things in the very areas singled out for reform. The fault was with the officials responsible for implementation. The Emperor had done all he needed to do to move things forward.

The Emperor was particularly not receptive to the idea of a constitutional monarchy, a recurring theme throughout his regime though not specifically mentioned in this particular proposal. As much as he was a reformer, he was also a man deeply immersed in the venerable tradition of the *Kibre-Negest*, the great Ethiopian text which defines the role of monarchs in looking after the special flock of God: the people of Ethiopia. To have expected the Emperor to renounce his traditional role of supreme magistrate of the land anointed by God and answerable only to Him was to ask him to voluntarily excise the most distinctive part of his persona to the point where the remainder would be an unrecognizable residual of the original. That was in effect what a constitutional monarchy implied. It was hardly an easy thing to do for a leader who reigned under an age-old Mandate of Heaven. Vivid manifestations of this outlook are recorded in the autobiography of Fitawrari Tekle-Hawariat cited earlier in Chapter 4 and a little later in this chapter. Tekle-Hawariat was the principal drafter of the first constitution proclaimed in 1931 which the monarch pushed through against the resistance of the aristocracy. But he made sure that the deputies to the new parliament would be appointed by him and not elected (see page 410 of Tekle-Hawariat's autobiography). The 1955 constitution would allow deputies to be elected but the Emperor remained the source of ultimate political power.

Efforts continued after 1955 to persuade the Emperor to change his mind. During a state visit to the Soviet Union in the spring of 1959, the Emperor and his party were on a long train journey from Leningrad (St. Petersburg) to Moscow. Colonel Workineh Gebeyehu, a trusted aide and a passionate reformist, judged the atmosphere to be particularly conducive to raising the delicate issue of political reform. After briefly describing the disquieting signals about the country's future, he wondered whether the time had not come for the Emperor to step aside in favour of the Crown Prince to take over as a constitutional monarch. This would allow the country to move to a faster track of reform to prevent a bloodbath similar to the French Revolution. "Ah Workineh!" sighed the Emperor. "We thought that you were politically mature. It turns out you are not. You should know that for as long as we live, we shall continue to make use of the authority bestowed upon us by God. Afterwards, it is up to Him to look after the country."[7] Years later, he would speak in the same vein to his personal physician, Dr. Asrat Woldeyes, who inquired if he might not wish to initiate an orderly succession in his own lifetime.

To many who were not close to the Emperor and who were earnestly working to bring about a peaceful transformation of their country to a modern and democratic monarchy, 'Elect of God' was no more than one among a string of half a dozen lofty titles that could be dispensed with. To those like Workineh, the practical significance of that title would be plain every time they approached the Emperor with proposals for serious reform. The tragedy was that the Emperor had one way of introducing a constitutional monarchy without abandoning his Mandate of Heaven: stepping aside for his son to occupy the throne and providing advice and guidance for a brief initial period. All indications are that the Crown Prince would have gladly accepted the limitations on his authority that a constitutional monarchy imposed, and spared his father the painful act of political self emasculation. And quite possibly set in motion a self-sustaining process of political liberalization that might have forestalled a bloody revolution.

Another reason for the Emperor's reticence to undertake radical reforms was his own reading of the march of events. This was at variance with what was put forward by persons pressing him for more audacious reforms. He often said that, to be sustainable, change should be introduced gradually. Those advocating more rapid change overstated their case, or probably had their own motive.[8] In the event of some unexpected trouble he would, as on many occasions in the past, be quite capable of managing it. His self-confidence had reached a level barely distinguishable from benign neglect of his duties to govern. Also, he believed that he knew what was best for the country. The majority of his countrymen (and his army) would assuredly not let him down, even if a few overzealous young people might occasionally cause trouble.

His attitude to the young was often paternalistic, anchored in his belief that in the end they would come to their senses.

It should also be remembered that Ethiopia of the early seventies was in many ways very different from what it was in the late twenties when the Emperor embarked on his reforms. Major changes had taken place. It would not be surprising if the principal agent of those changes occasionally looked back and wondered whether the advocates of more radical change were really aware of the great transformation that had taken place already; and ascribed their overzealous demands to ignorance of their country's history. Indeed that is precisely what he told Haddis Almeyahuou when the latter got into an argument with him on the need to introduce more expeditious reform measures (see Chapter 5).

Above all, Haile-Selassie was an awesomely strong personality. The Emperor of Ethiopia was no bumbling Johnny-come-lately sovereign of some non-descript, recently concocted Empire in the heart of Africa who would lose nerve at the slightest sign of an impending threat. He saw himself as the proud flag-bearer of an ancient nation which had been contemporaneous with three of the most powerful empires in the Middle Eastern and Mediterranean region during the first millennium of the Christian era: Byzantium, Rome, and Persia. And he was an Emperor who, in the visionary universe of the *Kibre Negest*, was charged with a special mandate from the Almighty.

In the middle of the 1974 crisis when practically everyone in government lived in great anxiety and was wondering what would happen next, Prime Minister Endalkatchew Makonnen met with the Emperor on some urgent business and came back incredulous at the old man's quiet dignity and calm. "That man is made of steel," I remember him telling his Cabinet colleagues. The Man of Steel, who had also been a man of vision in his younger days and who had done so much to introduce a policy of modernization stretching over several decades, would now be tragically accused of holding back the country's progress by the very off-spring of that policy.

Under these circumstances, the initiative for political change was snatched by the young and by those charged to protect the nation from external adversaries. As we shall see later, the final act of the military was to surrender the country to extremist forces which had long prepared themselves to re-engineer the social, cultural, political, and economic life of the country to fit their ideological and sectarian agenda.

Fatalism and Old Age

At 82, Emperor Haile-Selassie had become visibly old and was gradually losing memory, concentration, and his usually quick grasp of issues. I myself occasionally noticed a bemused face trying to grasp what in earlier times would have been disposed of in the twinkle of an eye. In these moments of uncertainty, he tended to be manipulated by palace staff. At other times he would be his old self: perspicacious and decisive. When testifying before the Commission of Inquiry set up to establish accountability for the Wollo famine, Prime Minister Aklilu said how difficult it had been for him to carry on with his job. The Emperor would agree with him on some issue in the course of a discussion, only to come back the next day with an entirely different position. Someone had talked to him in the course of the previous evening and made him change his mind; something unthinkable in the days of imperial firmness and consistency.

Occasionally the Emperor's fatalism surfaced, giving a semblance of firmness to a mind often in a state of flux. His Orthodox faith was a principal driving force in his life. He firmly believed that no earthly power could prevent the occurrence of an event willed by God. Prior to a visit to two commercial farms in the province of Sidamo in 1970, he had a premonition that some difficulty was going to occur. Immediate members of his family advised a postponement, or at the very least that he and the Crown Prince should not make the journey in the same helicopter. An attempt was also made to involve Patriarch Tewoflos to prevail on the Emperor to change the travel plan. The Emperor was adamant and said nothing could be done to avert danger if it was the will of the Almighty.

The visit took place as planned. A convoy left Addis Ababa for Awasa, a town some 150 miles south of Addis. A helicopter was arranged for the onward trip to the two farms. Following the visit of the first farm, the helicopter carrying the Emperor, the Crown Prince, and other high officials tried to take off to proceed to the second farm. It immediately ran into trouble, failed to gain altitude and crashed to the ground with its underbelly facing up and fire spurting from its engines. The Emperor and his entourage were quickly rescued.[9]

In a second case illustrative of imperial fatalism, General Jagama Kello, commander of the Fourth Army Division, was called to the palace to be questioned about an intelligence report on his intention to overthrow the government. The General denied any such intention, although there was some truth to the report, as he recently confirmed to me. The Emperor's response was:" It really does not matter. If God wishes to take away the throne that He has given us, it is His will, not your scheming, that will prevail. If, on the other hand, it is God's will that we should carry on, neither you nor anyone one else could do any harm."

Not everything was left to fate, of course. The Emperor was often troubled about the fate of the country after his demise. He once asked two young officials close to the Palace what they thought would be the right kind of political system to bequeath to Ethiopia. Both independently told him that neither capitalism nor communism would do. What was most suitable for the country was a constitutional monarchy of the Scandinavian type with a social democratic system of government. He agreed (at least outwardly) and instructed them to put down their thoughts on paper. Other more urgent assignments got in the way and events soon moved fast towards the 1974 revolution.

Emperor Haile-Selassie might not have been fully cognizant of the far reaching implications of the advice. Parliamentary democracy is, of course, not a matter of imperial bequest. It is a system of government which evolves gradually and in which citizens freely choose their leaders through the ballot box: a notion totally at odds with the world view expounded by the *Kibre-Negest*. The Emperor never went that far in his reform efforts, and was consequently unable to prepare his country for an orderly transition.

During the hectic months of the summer of 1974 when senior government officials were being systematically detained by the military, a few of these officials approached the Emperor to seek his advice. He told them not to resist, and to give themselves up. Police and Imperial Guard Commanders said that the plotters could be easily ejected from their camp and order quickly reestablished. The Emperor was unwilling to authorize the planned assaults. The country's latter day leaders would rant and rave about storming the mighty citadel of power and accomplishing the unthinkable: the removal of a powerfully entrenched imperial regime. The truth was that Haile-Selassie was a fairly benign paternalistic monarch who had been grievously enfeebled by fatalism and old age.

The Emperor is Perceived as Shoan

The fourth tragedy facing Emperor Haile-Selassie was the latent but growing resentment of the country's various ethnic communities against what they perceived to be a Shoa-Amhara-Christian cultural and political domination, notwithstanding the fact that successive Emperors had directed their energies to pulling together the country's diverse communities into a cohesive modern nation.[10] In particular, Emperors Menelik and Haile-Selassie had been driven by a desire to accommodate the various cultural groups in order to refashion Ethiopia along more modern lines. Their nationalistic sentiments superseded whatever regional proclivities they might have harboured. All Ethiopian Emperors going back to Axumite times had been driven by a pan-Ethiopian rather than a parochial vision. Those of us who served under Emperor Haile-Selassie still recall credible anecdotes that occasionally circulated and in which the Emperor showed himself to be above the interests of a particular clan, community, or ethnic group.

One such anecdote told the story of certain Amhara officials who approached the Emperor with stories of a non-Amhara aristocrat believed to be a serious threat to his throne. The sovereign had to be on his guard, advised the officials. The Emperor's response was that the story was baseless and that people who gave it credence were narrow-minded Amharas like themselves who were envious of the man's persistence in pushing development programmes in his region. There were several other manifestations of inclusion. From the outset, the Emperor encouraged his children and grandchildren to marry into the country's different ethnic groups. He was also painstakingly even-handed in providing educational opportunities to all areas and sections of the population, and often reached out to those of modest origin. His own ethnic background was varied. His father was Shoa-Amhara and his great grandfather possibly an Oromo. His mother was the daughter Sheh Ali of Wore-Illu (Wollo). Credible sources also say that there was a Gurage forebear in the family tree.

In the long history of Ethiopia, Emperors and Queens from a variety of ethnic groups have occupied the throne or played key roles in the management of state affairs. Queen Elleni of the late 15th and early 16th centuries was from Hadiyya and acted as Regent after the death of her stepson Emperor Be'ede Mariam when young Emperor Libne Dingel, Be'ede Mariam's son, ascended the throne. In the Gondarine period Oromos rose to prominent government positions. The young son of Emperor Iyassu II, whose mother was Oromo, became Emperor Iyo'as, with his grandmother (Empress Mentiwab) acting as Regent. Ras Ali, another Oromo, was the *de facto* ruler of the Empire along with his mother, the Empress Menen, for an extended period during the *Zemene Mesafint*. Ras Sehul Michael of Tigrai was similarly the *de facto* ruler in Gondar during this time. Emperor Tekle-Giorgis of Lasta succeeded Emperor Tewodros and ruled for three years until he was captured in battle by Emperor Yohannes of Tigrai who in turn ruled between 1872 and 1889.

During the early reign of Emperor Menelik, there were two Rases who were first in rank among the nobility. One was the Emperor's own uncle Ras Darge Sahle-Selassie, an Amhara through his father and a Gurage through his mother. The other was the Oromo Ras Gobena Datche, whose son Dejazmatch Wodajo had a child from Menelik's daughter. Menelik was grooming the boy, Dejazmatch Wossen Seged, for the throne. Unfortunately the young man died at the age of 17. Afenegus Nessibu Meskello, Menelik's much respected and long serving Chief Justice, was a grandson of Meteko, the Abichu Oromo chief. Dejazmatch Balcha, Fitawrari Ibsa, Fitawrari Dechassa, and many other Oromos were influential officers of state under Menelik. The proverbially artful Fitawrari Habte Giorgis, part Oromo and part Gurage, was not only the power behind the throne during the last years of Emperor Menelik and in the years immediately following, but was the virtual head of government when Lij Iyassu, the heir apparent, found it difficult to manage the affairs of the nation. This comes out clearly in the days preceding the dismissal of Lij Iyassu. Habte-Giorgis was the one person to whom everyone looked to lead the way. In his autobiography, Fitawrari Tekle-Hawariat gives an eyewitness account of the crucial meeting chaired by Habte-Giorgis at which the decision was taken to bring in Zawditu Menelik as Empress and Tafari Makonnen as Crown Prince. "Every word enunciated by Fitawrari Habte-Giorgis is an instruction. What others say is purely advisory." says Tekle-Hawariat and notes that Habte-Giorgis acted like an executive president of a republic while his aides assumed the role of cabinet ministers.[11]

Ras Gobena's descendants, Ras Abebe Aregai and Lij Michael Imru (who was also related to the royal family), occupied key government posts during the reign of Emperor Haile-Selassie (Defence, Interior, and Justice in the case of Abebe Aregai, and Foreign Affairs and briefly Premier in the case of Michael Imru). Other prominent Oromo officials included Lij Yilma Deressa (Minister of Finance, Commerce and Industry and Foreign Affairs), Emmanuel Abraham (occupant of various cabinet and diplomatic posts), Dejazmatch Kassa Wolde-Mariam (in-law of the Emperor and Minister of Agriculture), provincial governor Dejazmatch Geressu Duki, Army Generals Mulugeta Buli (regarded by many as one of the ablest leaders of his time)[12], Jaggama Kello, Wakjira Serda, Abebe Gemeda and many other important personalities.

Eritreans included Foreign Minister Blattengetta Lorenzo Ta'ezaz (who was also Haile-Selassie's close aide in the period just before the Fascist occupation and the exile years), the diplomat Blatta Ephrem Tewolde Medhin, Chief of Staff Genereal Iyassu Mengesha, army General Issa'iyas Gebre-Selassie, Siyoum Harregot, a Minister without portfolio (not to say without influence) in the office of the Prime Minister, Deputy Speaker of the Ethiopian Senate Nibure Id Dimetros Gebre-Mariam, and Justice Minister Bitwoded Asfha Wolde-Michael. Tigreans were Ras Mengesha Seyoum (the Emperor's other in-law) who held a number of Cabinet posts, Ato Abebe Retta who headed key government departments such as Agriculture and Health, Justice Minister Lique Mekwas Tadesse Negash and Dejazmatch Zawde Gebre-Selasssie, Minister of Justice and briefly Deputy Prime Minister under Michael Imru. There were also officials like the central bank governor Menassie Lemma (a Wollaita), Police Commissioner General Yilma Shibeshi (a Gurage), and Pensions Minister Tadesse Yaicob (an Ethiopian Jew) who wielded considerable influence in their respective positions. In the minds of the aggrieved, none of this was enough to dispel the notion that Haile-Selassie stood for the interests of the Shoa-Amhara ruling class.

It must be said that many Shoa Amharas were indeed prominent figures in public service. There were two reasons for this. First, Shoa was the geographical and demographic epicentre of power. As the hub of Empire, Shoa's inhabitants (including Oromos) were the principal source of recruitment for the civil and military establishment. Judges, district governors, military commanders, officials of the clergy, and civil servants were largely from Shoa. Anyone seeking a career in government in an outlying province had to come to Shoa, while for Shoans the opportunity was on their doorstep.

Secondly, the modernization process was initiated and for a time largely stayed at the seat of Empire, Shoa. The first schools were opened in Addis Ababa. Much as Emperor Haile-Selassie tried to recruit students from the outlying provinces, Shoans predominated, followed closely by Eritreans and Wollega Oromos. Eritrea under the Italians offered only the rudiments of primary education and many young Eritreans consequently came to Addis Ababa in search of higher education. Among the provincial chieftains who had responded positively to the Emperor efforts at recruiting students for the modern schools in Addis was Dejazmatch Habte-Mariam of Wollega who sent some two dozen pupils. This explains the visibility of Eritreans and Oromos from Wollega in the higher echelons of government service.[13] But by and large, Amharas appeared to be numerically superior, though statistics were not kept on this sensitive subject and no figures could be cited to corroborate this perception. Apart from education, however, neither Shoa nor any of the Amhara provinces (Gondar, Gojjam, Wollo) obtained what might be deemed as their fair share of roads, clinics, agricultural or industrial projects. They were judged to be politically loyal constituencies in regard to which one did not have to be unduly concerned. For the most part, projects were located in the south and west which offered better economic returns.

Some of the Emperor's Muslim subjects resented the fact that he was an Orthodox Christian with a special relationship to the Church. Although there were strong historical reasons for this, sections of the Muslim population nurtured a degree of latent resentment towards a leader who, though born among Muslims and favourably disposed towards them, was still perceived as someone who promoted the interests of the established Church. Eritrea, which had become the soft underbelly of the Empire, should be seen in this general context. The secessionist sentiment in the province initially drew its early inspiration from a strong sense of resentment by the Muslim population. Christian Eritreans joined later.

The Eritrean story needs to be taken a step further. The proximate cause of the movement for secession was the dissolution of the federal status that the province enjoyed immediately after its reunion with Ethiopia in 1952. The Orthodox Christian community had struggled for full integration with Ethiopia, while most of the Muslims and other smaller groups (encouraged behind the scenes by Italy and Great Britain) were inclined towards independence, or merger with the Sudan. The United Nations Commission on Eritrea recommended an autonomously administered territory having its own flag, parliament, civil service, and political orientation. The responsibilities for national defence, foreign affairs, and trade were assigned to the federal government. This was intended as a compromise between those who wished full integration on the one hand and those who either wished independence or union with the Sudan.

Leaders of the Orthodox Christian community were unhappy with this arrangement and problems surfaced before long. They began to work in earnest on their long cherished unionist agenda. The Emperor (advised by unionists of the "people's" desire for full integration) was favourable to the idea of dissolving the federation and making Eritrea an integral part of Ethiopia. Foreign Minister Aklilu Habte-Wold argued against integration and was supported strongly by Tsehafe Te'ezaz Wolde-Giorgis Wolde-Yohannes, and a few other ministers. Aklilu pointed out that Ethiopia had solemnly committed herself to observe the federal arrangement amidst expressions of skepticism by influential members of the United Nations. Ethiopia needed to honour her commitment. Besides, a successful federal experiment might attract British Somaliland, Italian Somaliland, and French Somaliland (Djibouti) to contemplate association with Ethiopia. While it was true that these territories were being prepared for independence, they might be interested to join a well functioning Ethio-Eritrean federation. In any event, argued Aklilu, a proper dissolution of the federation could only be brought about through a referendum, not through short-cut arrangements conveniently packaged as expressions of the "people's" will.

After extensive consultations in the course of which the influential Defence Minster Ras Abebe Aregai supported Aklilu's position, the Emperor decided in favour of the unionists and the federal arrangement was terminated in November 1962, a little over ten years after its adoption in September 1952. In the minds of the general public the origins of the secessionist movement were traced back to this event. Key members of the unionist leadership (Bitwoded Asfeha Wolde-Michael in particular) later argued that it was a succession of events *after* the dissolution, and not the dissolution itself, that fueled the sentiment for secession.[14]

Had the Ethiopian government not worked with the Unionists to dissolve the federation, would the federal constitution of the province have endured, it might be asked? And would it have brought about (as many of its advocates contended at the time) a democratically governed polity in the Horn of Africa? It would be difficult to make a persuasive case of such an eventuality, given the fate of the many fine constitutions with which African countries celebrated their emergence from colonial rule in the fifties and sixties. Most were replaced by instruments of repression to suit the fancy of this or that group of power-seekers. In Eritrea itself, the Chief Executive had already started to sidestep some of the provisions of the federal constitution; as when he defied the constitution in annulling the election of a political opponent to the federal parliament. What we see in Eritrea today is, of course, further evidence of the fragility of the democratic experiment in Africa.

Whatever one's view of this issue, the secessionist movement was fueled by an underlying resentment against the dominance of Shoa/Amhara culture. By the early seventies, the movement had assumed a robust political profile. Its leaders, just as the extremist young Ethiopians in the rest of the country, were increasingly calling for the overthrow of the Emperor's regime as a step towards Eritrea's independence. They, too, were products of the modern educational system that Emperor Haile-Selassie had put in place over several decades.

A Government Out of Touch with the People

The fifth and final tragedy which confronted Emperor Haile-Selassie was the fact that, unlike Emperor Menelik, he and his government had become remote from the people. A benevolent monarch, Menelik maintained a close rapport with ordinary folk as with provincial chieftains. In his eagerness to institute a modern system of government Emperor Haile-Selassie lost Menelik's common touch. This would have mattered little had his modernization efforts gone far enough to allow citizens an opportunity to be politically involved in the government of their county. But they did not.

Emperor Haile-Selassie's policy of removing the provincial regional lords to make way for officials from the central government may have been initially justified as an attempt to consolidate the unity of the nation. Prior to the occupation, there had been strong resistance to the Emperor's programme of modernization from the conservative ruling classes of the provinces. The Emperor's energetic *de facto* Prime Minister, Wolde-Giorgis Wolde-Yohannes, was determined to use the favourable post-war political climate to push through reforms in provincial administration that centralized authority in Addis Ababa. It cannot be denied that the reforms brought a good measure of order and coherence to provincial administration. The downside, however, was that central government appointees were never able to secure the kind of local support an elected official or someone hailing from the particular place was likely to have. And there was, of course, no serious plan to move to a subsequent phase allowing devolution of central authority and political participation.

At the centre, Ministers were also appointees of the Emperor. Wolde-Giorgis Wolde-Yohannes did have a network of supporters and local officials who kept a close watch over the bureaucracy. But these were not representatives of local people. And whatever local network Wolde-Giorgis had put in place to advance his administrative reforms disintegrated when he left the scene. Unlike Wolde-Giorgis, his successor Aklilu had a foreign affairs background. He was perhaps the most westernized among the country's high officials. And he lived a private life, married as he was to a French lady and having a lifestyle little to do with that of his compatriots. Indeed many people believed that he was alien to his country's culture and tradition. His ministerial colleagues were also remote from the day-to-day lives of their compatriots. In summary, the Prime Minister and members of his Cabinet were for the most part unknown quantities to most ordinary people even in the capital city, to say nothing of those in the provinces. Two casual incidents vividly brought this home to me in 1972.

While driving my plumber home one day, I saw Prime Minister Aklilu Habte-Wold pass by. I asked if he recognized him. The plumber shook his head and said he did not know the man. I pointed out that he was the Prime Minister of Ethiopia. He shook his head more emphatically than before. Another incident which happened around this time sends a similar message. A young secondary school student in Addis Ababa taking part in a television quiz was shown a picture of the Minister of Interior, and asked to identify him. He took a few moments' pause and replied: "The Prime Minister of Ghana, I believe!"

The Ominous Famine

There was a palpable air of impending trouble in the late sixties and early seventies. No one could say for certain what was likely to happen, but the writing on the wall pointed to a bleak future. It was in this general atmosphere that rumours started to circulate in 1973 about a serious famine in Wollo province, intermittently at first but with increasing frequency as the days and weeks passed by. I myself had heard about it when one staff member of the Planning Commission telephoned to say that an expatriate staff of the Commission who had traveled back from Asmara by road had seen alarming scenes of starving people in Wollo. Not long afterwards, I was having dinner at the apartment of a friend who taught at Haile-Selassie University. Over coffee, he showed me shocking pictures of starving people in Wollo. It was obvious that he wanted to see what I could do in my capacity as a government official. We understood each other. I do not recall exactly what I said, but I do remember being careful not to say anything I might wish to do but would not be able to deliver.

Sometime later, I ran into the new governor in charge of Wollo, Dejazmatch Legesse Bezu, at the Palace grounds in Addis Ababa. I asked him how things were in the province. Very bad indeed, was his quick response: and this from a man who had appeared on national television only a few months before to say that the drought in Wollo province was not as serious as the rumours circulating in Addis had made it out to be. He was at the time a junior Minister at Interior and had probably been asked to make a reassuring statement about the problem. He now seemed to say that he had been wrong. He needed all the help he could get from the central government to respond to the catastrophe. I also heard him make an impassioned plea for support at a meeting of the Cabinet. I told him I was eager to visit Wollo and see for myself the gravity of the situation. Could he invite me when he got back, as I needed some such pretext to be absent from my office? He telephoned a week later to extend an invitation.

I left for Wollo by car subsequently with Mitiku Jembere and Kibret Mengistu, two colleagues from the office. The Governor immediately took us around the feeding centres in Dessie, the capital of the province. What I saw at the first feeding centre was incredible: famished men, women, and children spread out in the open, sitting or lying on their sides, some moaning, others struggling for breath; and children barely holding in their mouths the nipples of the flattened breasts of their mothers, or sitting up on the emaciated thighs of a mother or a father and struggling to steady their heavy, wobbling heads.

There was a spot in the feeding centre where food and blankets were being distributed. The impoverished peasants who had come from near and far were told to line up, keep order, be patient and await their turn to receive a blanket or piece of bread when they reached the head of the queue. These gentle people did as they were told. There were no scenes of clamouring for the handouts of the kind one often saw in the media of desperate men in many a developing country receiving food aid. Many did not have the energy, and those who did simply obeyed instructions. Some collapsed and died while waiting in line. I myself did not witness this, but was told by people who had.

I went to another feeding centre in town. Someone had foolishly announced that a minister from Addis Ababa had come to the centre. I had brought nothing and had come with no mandate to do anything. I had just come to inform myself. A barely audible clapping of listless hands was heard. I was overwhelmed by a sense of being unequal to the challenge; a sense of guilt, of deep sadness, and of embarrassment that

I had come to a heartbreaking scene dressed thoughtlessly as if I were going to some committee meeting.

A few hours later, we left in an army helicopter to visit the other feeding centres in the province: Mersa, Sekota, Bati, Kemissie, Kembolcha, and other places. The tragic scenes of the feeding centres that we saw in Dessie were repeated. Wollo was in the midst of a horrendous famine. The aid being distributed at the centres was a pittance. I discussed some of the things that needed to be done with the Governor and his deputy, Dejazmatch Kebede Ali Wolle, more from a desire to avoid irrelevant talk than with any confidence that people like me in Addis would be able to shake up things. And a shake up was precisely what was needed. I told the Governor that I would do whatever I could as Planning Commissioner, but that we were facing an enormous challenge and needed to keep in touch.

The rains had failed successively for the previous three years in Tigrai and Wollo. The government was aware of the situation and had taken some steps to respond to the shortage of food. It was soon clear that the magnitude of the problem went well beyond the government's capability. And so, outside support was mobilized. Shipments of grain started to arrive at Assab. But who was to move them? When private operators were requested to transport the grain to the famine areas, they complained that the poor state of the roads would ruin their vehicles. A government order to requisition them was never seriously contemplated; such was the pervasive lethargy in government departments. It was even rumoured that some highly placed officials harbouring latent opposition to the government were purposely folding their arms to allow the crisis to spread and finally bring it down.

There was s singular exception to this mood of lethargy and passive subversion. Ras Mengesha Seyoum, Governor General of Tigrai and a native of the province, was not a man to fold his arms as innocent peasants succumbed to the ravaging famine. The Ras mobilized Tigreans in Makalle as well as in Addis to secure transport vehicles. In this he succeeded and managed to move grain piled up at the port of Assab to the famine stricken areas of his province.

For Wollo, the story was tragically different. For reasons not altogether clear (although some alleged it was a case of deliberate sabotage), the Governor General who was not a native of the province, Dejazmatch Solomon Abraha, failed to act with any sense of urgency or responsibility. At the centre also, ministers were slow to move. In the meantime, people died in their tens of thousands.

Upon my return from Wollo, I called a meeting of senior staff in my department and briefed them about what we had seen and the actions we should take to respond to the tragedy. The first and obvious thing to do was to work towards increased awareness within the government as well as with our bilateral and multilateral partners. An early opportunity to do this came in a meeting I had with the Minister of Community Development and Social Affairs (Mulatu Debebe) who was in charge of coordinating short-term assistance to famine victims. He told me that he did not have qualified staff to prepare a needs assessment report requested by donor agencies.

I set up a small group of my staff to prepare a report at the earliest opportunity. It was perhaps one of the most difficult reports that we had to write at such short notice. Very little information, qualitative or quantitative, was available on the number of people affected, on the spread of the famine, on the size and type of food aid, clothing, shelter, medical assistance, or the equipment and personnel needed for the logistical arrangements. One could hardly give up the exercise for lack of data. None of us was satisfied with the quality of our report, but we submitted what we believed would be acceptable to anyone who knew the difficulties. Fortunately, the donor agencies were understanding and took what they were given in good faith. The report went some way to inform them of the gravity of the situation and the magnitude of support required. We also decided to include in the government's forthcoming capital budget a proposal to earmark U.S. $5,000,000 for Wollo.

I spoke of my visit to Wollo to a Cabinet colleague and how much of an eye-opener it had been for me. I suggested that he too should find an opportunity to go and see the problem for himself. The response was lukewarm. On another occasion, a senior Minister said that if he were to go, questions would be asked about his political motives. He did not say more but left the impression that he would be perceived as an ambitious busy body trying to make political capital out of the crisis.

The Emperor was no longer in full command and many ministers appeared negligent. Gone were the days when Haile-Selassie would take officials to task for acts of omission or commission. His watchful eyes were getting progressively dimmer. In the rare event of a royal question being posed, one only needed to be fast on one's feet to fend off imperial wrath. The most unfortunate reality of the day was that the system of governance kept public officials shockingly out of touch with the lives of ordinary people. For the few who knew what was going on, one is unfortunately led to ascribe their inaction to lethargy, incompetence, and a good measure of irresponsibility. It must be said that some ministers did go to Wollo, but nowhere near the number required. Alas, Ethiopia was not a democracy where politicians and bureaucrats were held accountable for their actions.[15]

In January 1973, a member of the Crown Council, Dejazmatch Girmachew Tekle-Hawariat and a friend, Worku Gobena, were surprised to find an unusually large crowd of peasants from Wollo milling around in a meadow in the neighbourhood of Holleta, some 20 miles west of Addis Ababa. When Girmatchew asked what the peasants were up to, they said they were from the drought stricken district of Berrera in Wollo. They were on their way to Wollega province to settle on government land. Worku Gobena rushed back to Addis Ababa and informed Crown Prince Asfa Wossen, the titular Governor General of Wollo province, of what he had witnessed in Holleta. The Crown Prince told his staff to collect all food items they could lay their hands on in his Palace and procure quantities of bread from the city bakeries.

With these he set out to Holleta. He was shocked by what he saw there. When he got back home, he consulted with his household staff about measures he should take. They informed him that 1,600 hectares of fertile farm land in his possession was available in the district of Limu, Kaffa province. This would be suitable for resettling the peasants. Dejazmatch Kassa Wolde-Mariam, Minister of Agriculture, agreed with this when approached by the Crown Prince, and said he would provide any support he could. The Crown Prince telephoned the Defence Minister to ask if he could arrange for a fleet of military transport vehicles to take the peasants to Limu. The Minister agreed, but immediately consulted Prime Minister Aklilu who said that a problem that serious had to be brought to the attention of the Emperor.

When informed, the Emperor immediately sent for Ras Mesfin Sileshi, the Governor General of Shoa province through which the peasants had to pass to reach Holleta. He asked Mesfin why he had failed to report the incident. Whatever he got for an answer, the Emperor decided to go to Holleta himself. He went. He saw the starving crowds. And promptly called a high level meeting of officials at which were present: the Crown Prince, the Prime Minister, the Governor-in-charge of Wollo Dejazmatch Solomon Abraha, the Minister of the Interior Getahun Tessema, the Governor General of Wollega Dejazmatch Wolde-Semait Gebre-Wold, the Police Commissioner General Yilma Shibeshi and others.[16]

The Emperor asked the Governor of Wollega if he was aware that people from Wollo were moving to his province in large numbers. The Governor replied affirmatively and added that he had written to the Minister of Interior requesting that other provinces be asked to help settle the starving farmers. The Minister of Interior confirmed this and said he had passed the matter to his deputy, Legesse Bezu. The latter said he had set up a committee to address the problem urgently. The buck had taken a pause there.

Emperor Haile Selassie then turned to the Crown Prince and reproached him over his failure to take action in his capacity as the overall Governor General of the province. In his own view, the Crown Prince had tried to offer his estate to accommodate the migrants and believed that he had been thwarted in his efforts. He probably felt he wasn't exactly being treated fairly. Father and son had not always been on the best of terms, especially since the attempted coup of 1960 which the Crown Prince had been coerced into leading, as some believed. The Emperor's view was different. He was convinced that the Crown Prince had been a willing participant. Father's harsh reproach to son in this new situation caused Crown Prince Asfa-Wossen much distress.[17]

To Dejazmatch Solomon Abraha, the governor in charge of the day-to-day management of the provinces affairs, the Emperor reportedly said: "and while the famine was decimating the people of the province, you were busy carpeting the road from Kombolcha to Desse with reeds in preparation for our arrival, uttering not one word about the victims."[18] Solomon was severely reprimanded and removed from his post. The tragic saga of the famine continued despite the ageing Emperor's attempts to shake things up. He visited the province and toured a number of shelters including Sekota, Alamata, Tehullederre, Kombolcha, and Bati.

Community Development Minister Mulatu Debebe was responsible for coordinating short-term assistance. For the longer-term problems, another committee was established under the chairmanship of the Minister of Agriculture, Dejazmatch Kassa Wolde-Mariam. He immediately embarked on a busy schedule of mobilizing international support, including a prolonged working mission to a number of donor courtiers. Regrettably, there was no time to show results. A matter of further regret for me was the rejection of the Planning Commission's proposal to set aside U.S. $5,000,000 for emergency assistance. The lethargy in government circles was debilitating. It was about this time that Lij Endalkatchew Makonnen, who would be named Prime Minister a few months later, said to me after a protracted but ineffectual Cabinet meeting that we had "come to the end of the road." At another meeting of the Cabinet some time earlier, I myself said in a moment of frustration that Ethiopian government Ministers on foreign visits were shunned like "lepers" by donor country officials; a most unusual use of language in a Cabinet where everyone was punctiliously well mannered.

These remarks were made at a time when a growing sense of *fin de regime* caused many to be lethargic. It was as if people, especially government officials, felt that the end of the regime was around the corner. What purpose would it serve to run around trying to get things fixed when one did not know what was going to happen or who was going to be in charge next? It wasn't perhaps a case of total inaction. But there was no doubt in anyone's mind that the actions taken were woefully inadequate. As always, however, efforts were made to appeal to foreign assistance.

With this in view, it was decided to secure the services of a recognized person to make a film and launch an international appeal. The well-known British television journalist, David Dimbleby, was invited to prepare the film. He was taken to Wollo and spent time taking dramatic pictures of the famine victims. When he completed his assignment, a group of junior Ministers were asked to go through the film and give their advice as to how it should be aired. The group was shocked beyond words, and advised that it would not be prudent to show it to the Cabinet, let alone air it on the national network. David Dimbleby left the country with a copy of the film which was later aired in the media. The world community was shocked and large amounts of aid started to flow in.

Many months later, I myself appeared before the Commission of Inquiry set up to probe into the Wollo famine. One of the questions I was asked was why the government had covered up news on the famine. I told Commission members that I did not believe there was a deliberate attempt to cover-up. To my surprise, an internal memo by the Minister of Information in which instructions were given to cover up news of the famine was read out to me. I was unaware of this letter, said so, and went into shocked silence.

Earlier, I had been busy at the Planning Commission working on the final phase of the preparation of the Fourth Five-Year Development Plan. An unusually large number of government officials had been involved in putting the draft together. We had also initiated a process of public consultation, following an internal discussion that this should be the new feature of the Plan. We held meetings with the officials of the Confederation of Ethiopian Trade Unions (represented by its president, Beyene Solomon, and an assistant) and with the employers federation. We briefed them on the principal objectives of the Plan and how we thought they might impact on their respective areas of concern. We were eager for their reaction. The representative of the employers' federation made some comments. The two persons from the trade union organization were extremely guarded in their views.

We went ahead with the exercise and were now ready with a zero draft of the Fourth Five-Year Development Plan, the most elaborately prepared document of its kind to that date. Out of the blue in early January 1974 (around the 10th), our attention was attracted by an event that would leave the zero draft of the Fourth Five Year Plan unattended for good.

An Army Mutiny, the Quadrupling of Oil Prices, and a Tottering Government

On that day in January, an army garrison in Negelle-Borana (a small town in Southern Ethiopia) mutinied over a severe shortage of drinking water. The well had dried and life was becoming unbearable. The garrison commander, Colonel Fikru, was in Addis to talk with his superior officers as to how this problem could be resolved. While there he received word that his men had revolted and told that his officers were being kept indoors. He rushed back to find the soldiers bitterly complaining about the water and about their condition in general. He talked to them and managed to calm down things temporarily.

The government dispatched the Commander of the Ground Forces, General Diresse Dubale, to look into the situation. When he arrived, he did not wish to talk to the soldiers, but only to the commander of the garrison and his officers. As he was about to fly back to Addis after his talks, he saw that the mutineers had posted guards on the road to the airport preventing anyone from leaving. The government sent the Commander of the Air Force, General Aberra Wolde-Mariam, to mediate and secure the release of General Diresse. Aberra communicated the Emperor's message to the soldiers that their grievances would be looked into. The soldiers took his word, allowed General Diresse to leave, and went back to their duties. The sensational stories which subsequently made the rounds in Addis about General Diresse being detained and forced to eat the soldiers' rations (the horrible food and unclean drinking water) were just that: sensational stories.

And yet, the short-lived mutiny was serious enough for the authorities to start worrying about what could follow next. Mutinies are scarcely welcome events in any military establishment. This one caused alarm; alarm which indicated that the incident might be a precursor of far more ominous trouble to come. As feared, events soon unfolded that made the small mutiny in a remote southern town look like a fairly well behaved class boycott in a girls' boarding school.

In the wake of the four-fold increase in the world price of petroleum towards the end of 1973 (from $3.00 to $12 per barrel), the government increased gasoline prices from Birr 0.50 to Birr 0. 75 per litre for the regular and from Birr 0.60 to Birr 0. 80 for the premium brand. Approximately a month later (on the 19th of February), taxi drivers protested against the increase and went on strike. People in the streets (many of them students) began throwing stones at passenger vehicles. When informed of these incidents, the Emperor sent for someone who had served him well in the past: Wolde-Giorgis Wolde-Yohannes. It was Thursday the 22nd of February 1974. The Emperor told him that he wanted him to take over as Prime Minister.[19]

Wolde-Giorgis was aghast. He had left government nearly two decades before, was now in his seventies, was in poor health, and was without his previous network of friends and allies. More importantly, this was a new ball game, with a younger generation of politicians and civil servants he was not familiar with. He informed the Emperor that he would find it difficult to find people to work with. He regretted he could not accept the offer and took leave. As he approached his residence, his car was pelted with stones. Wolde-Giorgis was deeply worried by the incident, suspecting a devious hand behind it. Stones were indeed being thrown at passenger cars. But these happened in the city's main streets and in broad daylight to get maximum publicity, not in neighbourhood alleys and certainly not at dusk. He sensed he was being targeted.

Unaware of this, his son Assefa called to say hello. The father took somewhat longer than usual to come to the phone and when he did the telephone went silent after only a few words were exchanged. In the evening of the following day, Wolde-Giorgis told Assefa over the phone that it was just as well that the telephone was temporarily out of order, as he was not in a position to talk to him at length. People had pelted his car with stones and he was worried. Assefa visited his father the following day. The old man did not look well. Guests came and Assefa went back home.

An hour later, his sister received a call saying that their father had become seriously ill. She immediately called Assefa and the two drove to their parent's home. When they arrived, Wolde-Giorgis appeared to have suffered a stroke. He had lost his speech. They rushed him to Menelik Hospital where he was placed under intensive care. Emperor Haile-Selassie heard the news and came to visit him the next day, Sunday. When the Emperor saw the patient lying in bed speechless, he remarked: *Aye yesew neger*, a phrase in Amharic which evokes the fragility of man.

Dejazmatch Tsehayu Enko-Selassie, a life-long friend and distinguished anti-Fascist resistance leader, was at Wolde-Giorgis's bedside. The Emperor asked what he could do to help. Tsehayu proposed that the patient be flown to London. Instructions were given for a medical evacuation, the Emperor paying the airfare for the patient and an accompanying doctor. Twenty-four hours later, Wolde-Giorgis was flown out to London accompanied by his wife, his son and a physician. Upon arrival at Heathrow, the party was met by a representative of the Home Office and the patient taken to hospital. He was discharged some four months later and started treatment as an outpatient.

Wolde-Giorgis recovered partially but never adequately to be able to return to the country to which he had devoted a lifetime of public service. The grand old man of Ethiopian politics passed away in London a couple of years later at the age of seventy-five. He had been a nationalist, often finding himself at loggerheads with Britain. Inscribed on his gravestone are these fitting words: "Destiny enshrines paradoxes. In lifetime I said nay to this soil where now I rest in peace."

The crisis continued. Teachers came out against the Education Sector Review, a report prepared by high level consultants and funded by the World Bank.[20] The Ethiopian Teachers' Association petitioned the Emperor for a salary increase. Students and workers also marched in protest. A small delegation of non-commissioned officers from the army in Eritrea came to Addis and demanded an increase in pay. The government was under intense pressure to do something.

On the 23rd of February, the Emperor responded to the pressure with four key decisions:[21]

(i) the implementation of the Education Sector Review would be delayed;

(ii) the increase in fuel prices would be reduced by half;

(iii) the request of the teachers' union for a salary increase would be given a decision within a short time; and

(iv) non-commissioned officers would receive an increase of Birr 18 ($9) in their monthly salary (raising it to Birr 100 a month). For officers, increments in pay shall be made in the context of an overall salary scale.

The army was not satisfied with the pay increases. On 24 February, the 2nd Division in Eritrea occupied strategic locations in Asmara and broadcast twenty-three grievances over the airwaves. All related to pay and conditions of service. The new list of grievances was presented to the cabinet by General Deresse Dubale, Commander of the Ground Forces. The cabinet discussed them and decided that a salary increase of the kind being demanded was not affordable, but improvements in conditions of service could be considered.

Pushing aside the decision of the Cabinet, the Emperor sent a mission to Eritrea to talk to the military. It was a little noticed but most unusual climb-down by the

Emperor. And the climb-down was not done away from the public eye. It was a first page news item in *Addis Zemen* which wrote: "Following the petition of the army in Eritrea that the recent salary increment was inadequate, a mission has reportedly been sent to Asmara to discuss the petition."[22] The wording may have maintained some semblance of respect for the monarch, but the fact that the soldiers had found the Emperor's earlier decision inadequate and the added fact that they had managed to get a mission sent from Addis to find out what more could be done was there for all to see. Much more unusual was the Emperor's subsequent decision to award salary increments that were far more generous than the previous one. The news was carried by the March 1 issue of *Addis Zemen* and was the first of a series of crucial incidents which indicated that the soldiers were beginning to dictate their terms.

In the meantime, Aklilu and his Cabinet had gone to the Palace to submit their resignation. This generated a debate about the language of the Palace communiqué. To say that the Cabinet had resigned would be an affront to the dignity of the Crown. It was the Emperor's prerogative to appoint and dismiss ministers. It could not be said that the Cabinet had *decided* to quit, only that the Emperor had *dismissed* his ministers. This fine point of protocol was reportedly made by Prince Ras Asrate Kassa, Chairman of the Crown Council. But it was not a matter of protocol for Prime Minister Aklilu and his colleagues. The language was perceived as an attempt to discredit them in the eyes of the public and Aklilu objected. In the end, it was agreed that the evening communiqué would say that the ministers had submitted their *request for resignation* and that the Emperor would give his decision shortly.

The following morning, I went to my office more to keep abreast of things than to attend to official business. In mid-morning, three of my friends arrived: Afenegus Tashoma Haile-Mariam, President of the Supreme Court, Getatchew Kebret, Deputy Minister in the Ministry of Foreign Affairs, and Negussie Fit'h-Awok, Deputy Minister of Land Reform. We were wondering about the precise reason for the resignation. Tashoma informed us that he had heard from a credible source that the military at the Air Force base in Debre Zeit (30 miles South of Addis Ababa) had demanded the resignation of Aklilu's Cabinet, failing which they would march on Addis.

We left my office and drove in the direction of the Old Airport area, curious as to what telltale signs we might witness along the way. We met with our friend Belatchew Asrat whose home was in the neighbourhood. Within a few moments of our arrival, we saw a helicopter showering down copies of a one-page leaflet. It was addressed to the Army, the Air Force, the Navy, and the Police Force. It did not say who it was from. But there were two clues. The first was that the leaflet was dropped by an Army Aviation helicopter. The second was the language of the leaflet which left the impression that the military themselves had drafted it.

Four demands were set down: first that the resignation request of the ministers be granted ; second that they should not be left unattended and should be made to

With friends at Addis Ababa Airport: Getachew Kibret (far right), Kifle Wodajo, Negussie Fit'h-Awok, Afenegus Tashoma Haile-Mariam, the author, and Assefa Eregnaw

reveal in which foreign land they had stashed away their plundered assets; third that their assets within the country be identified and repossessed by the government; and fourth that all former officials ("wolves we are now hunting") be assembled, the grain separated from the chaff and decisions taken with regard to the chaff."[23] Three points attracted our attention: the endorsement of the Cabinet's resignation, the charge of embezzled funds being stashed away in foreign lands, and the call for the chaff to be dealt with.

It all sounded ominous. We hoped that whatever change took place would be peaceful. Perhaps those suspected of wrong-doing would be tried by the courts. If so, no one, including the accused, would find it objectionable. Perhaps the army would take power, but peacefully. As we drove back to the centre of town, we saw military personnel guarding key buildings: the Army Ordinance Centre, the Commercial Bank of Ethiopia and the Telecommunications building near the defence ministry. Something must be brewing, we said to ourselves, and decided not to return to our offices. We each went to a grocery store, picked up food that we might need in the event of trouble, and drove home.

CHAPTER 8

The Interregnum: The Opening Four and a Half Months of Endalkatchew Makonnen's Premiership

A Hesitant Minister

In the evening of 28 February, Emperor Halile-Selassie appointed Lij Endalkatchew Makonnen to take the place of Prime Minister Aklilu Hable-Wold. General Abiy Abebe was simultaneously appointed Minister of Defence. Endalkatchew had been a member of Aklilu's Cabinet and General Abiy had served in several previous Cabinets. Both were from the traditional class. Many feared that the appointments might not go down well with the restive public.[1] The prevailing mood was for a relatively new and more acceptable face. There was unease in the air and everyone looked to the future with considerable foreboding.

I thought it would be prudent to stay home the following day. In the afternoon, I got a number of calls from friends that confirmed my decision. Soldiers were picking up senior government officials as they drove in the streets and detaining them at the headquarters of the Fourth Army Division. On television that evening, we saw a pre-recorded footage of the Emperor's announcement of the two appointments. The Prime Minister appeared next and read out a series of instructions: Deputy Ministers in each Ministry and the Governors General of provinces (and in their absence, their deputies) should be at their respective posts awaiting instructions; he himself would be in charge of the Ministry of the Interior; the Defence Minister would use the armed forces to maintain law and order; strict measures would be taken against trouble-makers. The Prime Minister finally said that the policy of the new Cabinet would be announced shortly.

There was something unreal about these announcements, especially the statement that the armed forces would maintain law and order. They themselves were in a state of indiscipline and were a principal source of unrest. A friend teaching at the University called the following morning to say that students carrying banners calling for the removal of the new Prime Minister and the establishment of a peoples' government were marching in the streets. Another called to inform me that the officials rounded up by the military the previous day had been released.

A junior Minister who was among the officials detained overnight recently told me that the soldiers were looking for Cabinet level Ministers and other high ranking officials, most of whom they were unable to identify or locate.[2] They detained officials who looked like ministers. All in all some twenty officials were detained. In the morning, the soldiers took them to the Palace and handed them over to the Emperor. "Do you realize who this thing is aimed at?" asked the Emperor of the released officials. Former Prime Minister Aklilu Habte-Wold, who was in the Palace at the time but who had not been among the officials detained, said he believed that he and his colleagues in the previous Cabinet were the targets. The Emperor responded that it is he, rather than they, that the soldiers were targeting. "And you are suffering on account of your services to us," he continued. "Do not lose heart. Nothing can happen without the will of God."

Sitting in my study that day, I started to think about my own future. I had weathered many a storm as Planning Commissioner and increasingly felt distressed about serving an enfeebled government that lacked a sense of purpose or direction. Admittedly, my six and half years had not been a waste of time. I had gained considerable experience on development issues. I had also had the good fortune of working under people whom I respected: Prime Minister Aklilu Habte-Wold to whom I reported directly as Planning Commissioner; Haddis Alemayehu, under whom I had worked when he was Minister of Planning and Chairman of the Development Bank of Ethiopia; and Abebe Retta, the Minister of Agriculture, who chaired the Bank's Board after Haddis Alemayehu left. These were people who had been in Government for decades and who were patriotic and knowledgeable of their country's problems. Besides, they projected a positive image of their country and culture on visits abroad. I had seen all three at various international meetings and had been favourably impressed.

I once accompanied Prime Minister Aklilu during an official visit to Yugoslavia. From the time he arrived at Belgrade Airport and delivered an impromptu press statement to the end of the visit, he carried himself with authority and confidence. I remember a particular incident in which he gave a first rate speech about the amicable relations between Ethiopia and Yugoslavia at a dinner given in his honour by Yugoslavia's Prime Minister. At the following dinner which he hosted for his Yugoslav counterpart, he delivered another excellent speech, unwritten as was the previous one but well thought out. His guest of honour had to speak in response. But there was no prepared statement like the one he had read at the previous evening's dinner. He was visibly ill at ease to get up and respond without notes. To his right and left were his deputies. Hushed conversations were conducted in Serbo-Croatian. Although we could not follow what was being said, the body language was clear: the Prime Minister moving this way and that as if to say 'leave me alone', and his deputies urging him to get up and say something. Eventually, he got up. He started apologetically and said he was still a young man when Aklilu as Foreign Minister and his Yugoslav opposite number, Popovic, discussed bilateral relations (something Aklilu had mentioned in his speech). He said a few words about his privilege to meet such a historic figure and sat down quickly after barely five minutes. Though a bit sorry for his embarrassment, I and the other Ethiopians were delighted with the distinctly positive impression left by Aklilu.

Aklilu had many other qualities: he had a keen intellect, broad experience in foreign affairs, a capacity to listen, and a distaste for the politician's proclivity for malice and vindictiveness. All that was memorable. But I had had enough. The time had come for me to move on. The thought of leaving government service had been recurring in my mind at different times over the previous couple of years. The new situation looked like a good opportunity to quit without raising too many questions. I did not wish to be the subject of speculation about the reasons for my departure. There was no risk of this in a situation where all ministers had resigned.

Even so, I could not help turning my thoughts to some of the core issues that were beginning to figure in discussions on the new political environment. Land tenure was an obvious concern. In my diary, I scribbled down a few ideas: setting a ceiling on individual holdings, reclaiming all grants of land previously made to officials and bureaucrats, and distributing land so acquired to landless peasants. Holdings in excess of the ceiling would not be confiscated but be purchased with long-term government bonds. The objective was to avoid the pains that would assuredly follow if measures of this nature were not taken quickly. To many like me, it was radical reform, not revolution that seemed the more promising avenue for peaceful and durable change.

My father and his brother Tadesse, both in retirement, drove from Gore to Addis Ababa immediately after they heard the news of the change in government. It was a 400-mile journey and I asked why they had taken the trouble to make the tiring daylong trip. "Trouble?" they both exclaimed. "What more serious reason could there be for us to come and see you?" They were alarmed by the wholesale resignation of ministers, something never experienced before. When I asked how things were in their locality, they said: "Things will be OK with us there as long as they are OK here in Addis Ababa."

Over lunch, I tried to address their concern about the Cabinet's resignation. They were not entirely reassured. In truth, I myself was not altogether certain. As we were pondering the issues of the day, the telephone rang. It was around 3:00 p.m. and the call was from the office of the new Prime Minister. His aide, Abeselom Zekie, said that the Prime Minister wished to see me. I told my father and uncle to await my return and left.

The Prime Minister was with Defence Minister Abiy when I entered his office. He said that he had asked me to work with him when he was appointed Ethiopia's

Permanent Representative at the United Nations in New York some nine years earlier, but that I had shown no interest. He had made another job offer a few years later which I had also not accepted. Turning to General Abiy, he remarked, "He is a difficult person." And to me he said, "I hope this time you will not say no. I would like you to be a member of the new Cabinet: either as Minister of Planning and Development or of Commerce and Industry." My response was that I had decided to leave government service and that this was a good occasion for me to do so.

"Didn't I tell you he is difficult? He refuses to join the Cabinet," he said to the General. A few minutes passed as each of us made his point. He told me he understood why many people would not be eager to join the Cabinet in these difficult times. But we were being called to serve the nation in its hour of need. "Is it only in good times that we serve? Do we turn our back on our country when the going gets rough?" he asked. I reiterated my position and told him that he faced what I believed would be insurmountable pressures in his new post. A man usually quick to understand his interlocutors missed my point and said that he was not the kind of person who was swayed by pressure. What I had in mind was, of course, the pressure of the major challenges facing him, not the kind coming from friends and acquaintances. I told him so, and went on to talk about the daunting political and economic questions facing the country.

When I first heard of his appointment I, like many friends, had been concerned that he might not have public opinion on his side, such was the clamour for change and for a new beginning. Besides being an aristocrat, he was a member of the previous Cabinet. Even if someone with previous ministerial experience were needed, there were others who had been on the sidelines for a long time and that might be more acceptable to the restive public: Haddis Alemayehu, Michael Imru, and perhaps the new Defence Minister who had not held a Cabinet position for a decade and a half. Indeed, it was the General who had been called first by the Emperor to be told that he would replace the outgoing Prime Minister; and he had gone home to prepare his acceptance speech. He was called back soon afterwards and told that it would be Endalkatchew and not he that would be the new Premier.

Different stories circulated in Addis about how this last minute change came about. One was that it was on account of a last minute intervention by the Emperor's *aide-de-camp*, General Assefa Demissie. In collusion with two young Army officers said to have connections to Endalkatchew (Colonel Alem Zaud Tessema and Yigezu Limeney), so goes this story, the General reportedly advised the Emperor that the military wanted a younger and more educated Prime Minister.[3] A degree of self interest was apparently at play here as the General was said to have cast his eyes on the Defence portfolio. The two young officers presumably had their own ambitions. All three were further alleged to be engaged in a plan to set up a cabal of junior officers to support Endalkatchew's new government from behind the scenes. Someone close to Prime Minister Endalkatchew dismisses the involvement of the officers.

This person's version is that a spokesman of the NCO's in the Ethiopian Army heard of the impending appointment of General Abiy and sought the advice of a senior Army officer whom he had previously served as chauffeur. The officer, General Girma Felleke, was in the Third Army Division in Harrar. This was a time when men in the armed forces were in a virtual state of mutiny and were pressuring the Palace for improved pay and conditions. General Girma purportedly advised his former driver that a younger and more educated person like Endalkatchew would be a better choice. Whether someone else was manipulating the driver is not clear. In any event, the NCO gathered a few of his colleagues around him and marched to the Palace. At the gate they got

Lij Endalkatchew Makonnen, Prime Minister in 1974

rowdy and caused a rumpus to attract attention. The *aide-de-camp* came out to enquire. They told him they knew General Abiy when he was Defence Minister and did not believe he was the right choice to be Prime Minister. They asked for Endalkatchew instead. The *aide-de –camp* conveyed the message to the Emperor. When consulted, Abiy said was willing to cede his place to Endalkatchew,

Abiy was a public servant of exceptional integrity. Moreover, he had written a short book seven years earlier entitled *Awken Enitarem* (Let Us Mend Our Ways On Our Own) in which he had made a plea for change. Although largely in the nature of a sermon, the 57-page booklet drew attention to the dangers facing the country if the leadership failed to take remedial measures. The public perception of the General was therefore favourable as an individual, but many were of the view that he did not possess the occasional ruthlessness that high stakes politics demanded.

To go back to my discussion with the new Prime Minister, I asked him to give me time when I realized that he was not going to give up his idea easily. Of all the things he said, his rhetorical question about turning our back on the country troubled me. But it was not enough to change my mind. My purpose in asking for time was to come up with instances of radical change that would be too onerous for him to accept. I told him that the changes that needed to be made were unusually demanding and asked for a day to reflect. That would be too long, he said. When he insisted for a quick decision I agreed to come back in a few hours.

As I entered his office a couple of hours later, I found him chatting with the Defence Minister. He asked if I had accepted the offer. I reminded him of what we had discussed earlier in the day and said that I had a few issues to raise. "If you don't want a regular Cabinet post, I can offer you the post of minister without portfolio in my own office." I insisted that we should talk for a few minutes. "If you persist in saying no," he continued, "I shall have to take your case to His Imperial Majesty." I replied that I would repeat to His Majesty what I had said to him earlier and what I was about to add.

Although pressed for time, he agreed to give me a few minutes. I started by addressing the difficult set of problems the country faced. They could not be resolved unless bold, decisive actions were taken. As I started enumerating the problems (with land reform as the opener), he interrupted to say that he would be prepared to accept any condition so long as I agreed to be a member of the Cabinet. "How could you, Prime Minister, without weighing the implications of this and the other reform measures I am going to mention?" I retorted. He turned to General Abiy and said: "You hear this? When I tell him that I am prepared to accept his conditions, he asks how and why?"

My hesitation to take his word at face value surprised him. He swore à l'Ethiopienne (*Makonnen yimut:* on my father's honour) that he was dead serious. On my part, I was surprised at his readiness to accept all the conditions that I had underlined, including the ones that he had not heard. I reflected briefly and said to him: "It would be more acceptable from my standpoint if you were to agree that, at the first meeting of the new Cabinet, I introduce a memo on the key questions requiring bold new directions in policy and have them thoroughly discussed. If a consensus emerges, I would be prepared to serve; if not, I would leave." That too was acceptable to him. I finally agreed that my name could go forward.

Behind his eagerness to go along with any condition was the desire to quickly put together a list of ministers he believed would be acceptable to the public. "What portfolio would you prefer," he asked. As I was not sure how things would work out, I thought of a post where the burdens of office were not too onerous. As a Planning Commissioner, I knew the relative burden of ministerial responsibility. The Ministries of Mines and Public Works had a fairly light load, so I asked to be posted in one or the other. The Prime Minister replied that both posts had already been assigned. He suggested the Ministry of Finance. That did not respond to what I had in mind. The Planning Commission, now transformed into a Ministry, appeared acceptable to both of us.

UNCERTAIN REFORMS

The first meeting of the new Cabinet was held on Tuesday 5 March. Only eight ministers were present. A number of positions had not yet been filled and a couple of appointees were still at their foreign posts. The Prime Minister asked me to handle the Finance, Agriculture, and Trade & Industry portfolios until ministers were appointed. I was a little suspicious that this might be a ploy to nudge me to posts I did not want and asked for his assurance that this was purely temporary. He said it was.

Two principal issues were presented for discussion at the first meeting of the new Cabinet: the security situation within the armed forces and the drafting of a revised, more liberal constitution. The Minister of Defence gave an optimistic report on the armed forces and said that things were returning to normal. He added that he had talked with the soldiers who had briefly detained government officials and persuaded them to refrain from such further action. They had indeed gone back to their barracks. But this had provoked taunts by the public that all the soldiers cared about was their pay and benefits. Now that their demands were met, they cared little about the problems of the country. How would the soldiers react to the taunts? One could not say, but it did not look as if things would turn to normal easily or quickly.

The Prime Minister spoke on the drafting of a revised constitution, an issue of great topical interest and one which was then believed to be the principal instrument of reform. All members of the Cabinet endorsed the Prime Minister's proposal that the Emperor would make a major statement to the nation and that a drafting committee representing a cross-section of society would be set up quickly. The aim was to craft a liberal constitution with a monarch who would no longer have an active role in politics.

At the end of the meeting the Prime Minister talked to me, Belatchew Asrat and one or two others and said he wanted us to put together a draft policy statement for the government. I took this as his response to my preoccupation with new policy directions to meet the challenge for fundamental reform. It is probable that others might have raised similar concerns. He, of course, had promised a policy statement in his first television address to the nation but had said nothing about its general direction or given a clue as to its contents. At the Cabinet meeting the following day, the 6th of March, he formally announced the establishment of a drafting committee. On the 7th, I finished a short note which listed the major elements of a new set of policy issues and the general direction in which we should move. I would use it as a check list for the work of the drafting committee.

At about this time, former Agriculture Minister Dejazmatch Kassa Wolde-Mariam returned from abroad where he had been mobilizing assistance for the victims of the drought. Over breakfast at the Hilton, he asked if it would not be appropriate for him to submit a report to the new Cabinet. He delivered his report after I secured the Prime Minister's consent. Kassa was one of the ablest ministers of the former Cabinet. He had brought a degree of dynamism and focus which had been lacking in the early stages of the emergency programme for the drought. When the new Prime Minister was looking for names to fill certain vacant posts in his Cabinet, I had suggested Kassa's name. The response I got was that the political climate was not favourable for an in-law of the Emperor to be included in the Cabinet. Dejazmatch Kassa was married to Princess Seble Desta, a granddaughter of the Emperor. He would not only have made an able minister, but had the leadership qualities and political base to lead the country in a moment of crisis. Regrettably, this was not to be.

The new Cabinet soon found itself in the midst of a well orchestrated series of protest marches, work stoppages, demands for salary increases by teachers, and threats by university students and faculty to close down if the Prime Minister did not resign.[4] Teachers came out against the Education Sector Review, a study commissioned by the government and paid for by the World Bank. It was a forward-looking exercise prepared by Ethiopian and overseas education specialists. It aimed at a major shakeup of the country's educational system with the view to transforming it into a more meaningful instrument of development. A key goal was to expand primary education significantly to a level where, in the words of the report, "some 90% of the children born in 1982/1983 will have access to educational opportunity... Not even in the most developed nations does school participation reach 100%, and it is considered that with a 90% participation rate *Ethiopia would have achieved effective universal education opportunity for those born in 1982/1983 and thereafter*" (italics added)[5].

Among the international experts who participated in the study were Dr. M.S. Adiseshah, the Deputy Director General of UNESCO and later the Director of the Madras Institute of Development Studies who acted as Chairman of the group. Others included Dr. Karl Bigelow of the School of Education of Columbia University, Professor Richard Niehoff of the University of Wisconsin whose special interest was mass education, and A. Calloway of the U.K.'s Institute of Commonwealth Studies. Ethiopian education specialists prepared extensive background papers. Although caution was aired by some that the Review would not in itself bring about the desired results unless corresponding reforms were made in other sectors, there was a remarkable professional consensus around the proposals.

But opposition spread. Teachers believed that their interests would suffer if the recommendations were implemented. Salaries might be negatively impacted and working hours prolonged. Parents were apprehensive that the goal of universal primary education might impact negatively on the quality of their children's education. Neither group aired their true concerns in public. The document's aim was after all to move Ethiopia's education forward. Other reasons had to be found to mask their real intent.[6]

The Confederation of Ethiopian Labour Unions was also up in arms. It presented a list of seventeen grievances to the Prime Minister. He accepted them in principle and said that he would work towards their early settlement. The issues must be settled immediately, insisted the Confederation, failing which it would call a general strike.

The Cabinet rejected the ultimatum and the union carried out its threat. Strikes and threats of strikes followed in quick succession. Rarely a week passed without some work stoppage or an ultimatum to strike unless exaggerated demands for salary increases and improved benefits were granted.

In the midst of this torrent of ultimatums and strikes, there appeared a short, unexpected, and urgent call for a strike by what looked like a new group of disgruntled workers. Four demands were presented which, if not met, would trigger a strike: the immediate lifting of the curfew imposed by the Prime Minister, an immediate increase in service charges to at least $10.00 per service rendered, drastic measures to reduce the rent on villa's used by members of the group to conduct their businesses, and immunity from investigation by the Commission of Inquiry regarding illicitly acquired fortunes.

The group took a particularly strong position on the last point, claiming that whatever assets its members had acquired resulted from years of "of toil and the sweat of our brows" in an occupation of acknowledged transparency, quite unlike the accumulated wealth belonging to feudal "looters." And who were these firebrands? The commercial sex workers of Addis Ababa!

Someone with a sense of humour had succeeded in providing a rare moment of relief in an otherwise mad rush towards chaos. A satirical leaflet also appeared at about the same time which portrayed an imaginary soccer match between the old and the new Cabinets. Despite the temporary sigh of relief offered by such attempts to present the lighter side of things, the crisis moved on relentlessly.

Over a period of several weeks, the government's Amharic daily, *Addis Zemen*, had been writing virulent pieces against former government officials. Given the obsequiousness of the paper to such officials in days gone by, the zeal with which its journalists expressed their new-found freedom was such that they often rode roughshod over the rudimentary rules of journalism. Persons vilified by their articles were denied the right of reply. One day, the Minister of Information was asked by his Cabinet colleagues to explain the behavior of his journalists. His reply was that there was a general air of freedom reigning in the country and that he would not sensor his journalists, or outsiders who contributed special articles.

No one was persuaded by his response. The Minister shrugged off the grievances of the persons attacked in the government press, mostly former government officials who were easy targets of individuals eager to settle old scores. Indeed, he increasingly gave the impression of being no less of a rabble rouser than the vociferous civil servants who were given a green light to contribute articles attacking their supervisors. Why had the Prime Minister picked such a man for a sensitive cabinet post? many of us asked. No one could tell. One guess was that he might have been looking for someone with a journalistic track record. Another was that he wanted someone with a reputation for defiance. The person had served as editor of an Amharic daily several years ago. He had also been known as someone who stood up to authority. A third guess was that the Prime Minister was probably trying reach out to an ethnic group which he felt was not represented in the cabinet.[7]

The strikes and demonstrations continued unabated, gleefully covered by the government press which increasingly assumed the role of a private opposition paper, non-existent at the time. The Prime Minister often said 'give us a break.' That was precisely what his opponents wanted to deprive him of. The intention was to frustrate and drive him out of office. Protestors clamoured for the immediate establishment of a people's government.

In the meantime, the draft Cabinet policy document was going through successive amendments. On April 3 it was finally adopted.[8] Only two ministers expressed dissent. One was the Minister of Foreign Affairs who said that the Cabinet was engaged in an exercise of deception. All along, he had appeared uncomfortable serving under the new Prime Minister. Some ascribed this to his suspicion that the Prime Minister was involved in the detention of his brother-in-law, General Assefa Ayene. The General was among a handful of the more enlightened members of Ethiopia's top brass who was intent on improving the quality of the officer class. Most of the seditious soldiers were of dubious professional competence and resented him. Besides, they were out to get the top brass and were not prepared to spare him, irrespective of what the Prime Minister thought of him.

Another dissenting member of the Cabinet was the Minister of the Imperial Court, Dejazmatch Kebede Tessema. Kebede was a remarkable individual who possessed close to six decades of experience at the highest echelons of imperial government and who had successfully weathered many a political storm, one reason why he was brought on board the new Cabinet. It was rumoured that he was the son of Emperor Menelik's illegitimate daughter and, as we shall see later, grandfather of Mengistu Haile-Mariam. When someone once mentioned this to him, the wily old politician shrugged off the remark with these words: "It is remarkable how favourably I am perceived by the people of Ethiopia who regard me as both offspring and father of the country's leaders." Kebede's principal objection was to the section of the policy document on land reform, which he believed went too far. Unbeknown to many of us at the time, this ever courteous and crafty member of the old guard was in close contact with an influential 'friend' among the young military officers plotting to take over power.[9]

The policy document was a serious attempt to come to grips with the vital issues of the day. Its two key features (land reform and fundamental freedoms) were long-standing problems around which practically all previous questions of reform had revolved. On land tenure, emphasis was given to the absolute priority of placing a cap on individual holdings and taking away the excess above the ceiling for distribution to landless peasants. This was desirable both on grounds of social equity and economic development. A limited number of privileged individuals owned huge tracts of land, while millions of peasants went landless. It was an intolerable situation.

The document did not specify a uniform ceiling. Three hectares of irrigated land in the rich alluvial Awash valley for growing a cash crop like cotton would be a pittance in the arid Tigrean or Menz highlands. The maximum limit would be determined by "climatic and soil conditions" of the specific locality, said the document. For rain-fed agricultural lands, many in the Cabinet thought that the upper limit should range from 40 to 120 hectares, although these ideas were not discussed in any detail; the predominant view being that a determination should be made only on the basis of empirical studies. As prudent as it might have been, this approach was quite out of tune with the extremist views being vociferously advocated by those determined to foment radical change in the country, with a bloody consequence if that were necessary.

The progressive Minister of Land Reform, Ato Belete Gebre Tsadik, was of the view that a general limit of 40 hectares should be the goal. Dr. Dagnatchew Yirgu, Minister of Agriculture and easily the most outstanding agricultural expert of his day, was inclined to think that 120 hectares would be the technically and economically more appropriate limit for rain fed agriculture.[10] Land would not be expropriated arbitrarily. Holdings beyond the maximum limit would be repossessed "on the basis of appropriate legislation," in the words of the document. No specific method was proposed for this, though some thought of purchasing the land in excess of the ceiling through long-term government bonds or imposing punitive taxes that would induce landlords to surrender the excess. Much government held forest land had been donated to individuals. There was little justification for this beyond what the supplicant indicated in his petition to the Emperor, the only authority to make such donations. All such land would be reclaimed by the state without compensation.

An issue scarcely less important than land tenure was political reform. Many years of dissent and periodic attempts at reform had finally created a fairly wide consensus among politically conscious citizens that the time had come for making a determined effort to go beyond rhetoric and introduce a system of government that would respect fundamental rights and freedoms: the right to free speech, to worship, to peaceful assembly, and to a free press. These were solemnly affirmed in the document. The obvious corollary to this was a participatory form of government in which citizens should have a say about who would or would not govern them. The new constitution would guarantee these and other rights.

Many of us believed that the spirit of the policy document was in tune with the popular mood for change, if not with the clandestine plans of extremist groups plotting a bloody revolution. There were some members of the Cabinet who struck a note of caution. In addition to the two Cabinet Ministers mentioned earlier, there were others who were uncomfortable. The reasons offered were not too persuasive, and one got the feeling that their reticence had more to do more with the fear of moving into uncharted waters than with anything else. In the end, the majority endorsed the document.

Regrettably but unsurprisingly, the document received little support from the left. Even among groups which envisioned strikingly similar policy orientations, neither the policy document nor the drafting of a new constitution was acceptable.[11] The overall message of change was unquestionably in the spirit of the times. But the messengers were politically not acceptable. Hopes began to recede for far-reaching reforms that would eschew a convulsive and bloody change.

An organized rebellion against authority was well under way, targeting the central and the provincial governments, the leadership in the armed forces, in the parastatal bodies, in schools and universities, in Churches, in factories, and practically everywhere. Law enforcement agencies were unwilling to intervene in timely fashion, in adequate numbers, or with anything approaching the requisite resolution. The enforcers of the law were themselves largely in a state of rebellion and confusion. It was clear that the younger members of the military and the police force were weighing their chances of taking over power. Officers below the rank of major were said to be holding meetings in the outskirts of Addis Ababa. No one needed to scrutinize the agenda of the meetings to know why.

Two months had passed since the new Cabinet was installed, and there was no let up in the spate of strikes, lockouts, protest marches, abusive leaflets, and brochures. Apart from the general sentiment that the Prime Minister was the wrong choice to lead the popular demand for major change, certain measures he took unsettled public opinion. One such was the appointment of governors general of the provinces. The new appointees were for the most part individuals who were in one way or another related to the aristocracy or the palace. This was widely perceived as a retrograde step. It also exposed the Prime Minister's own affinities to the traditional class. It did not do him any good.

On the 11th of April an ominous strike was called by staff in the Ministry of Finance asking for the removal of three senior officials. This was no ordinary strike. At stake was the collection of government revenue and the payment of salaries and wages. No government which did not pay its workforce could survive such a strike for long. A Cabinet Minister invoked the Amharic saying *ahunis bayne mettah.* [12] In a rare show of solidarity, the Cabinet decided to stand firm against the strike. Apart from being damaging, it was illegal. The decision was taken to call for an immediate return of the strikers to their posts, failing which the government would dismiss them and recruit new staff.

April 11 was the Thursday before Good Friday. It was agreed that the announcement would be aired on Good Friday, instructing the striking civil servants to get back to work on Saturday. The government should monitor the situation on that day and provide police protection to those willing to resume work. If staff failed to return to work on Saturday, a follow-up announcement should be made on Easter Monday giving Tuesday morning as the deadline, after which the government would recruit staff to take the place of those who failed to show up. The Cabinet adjourned in a spirit of resolve and decided to meet on Saturday at 10h00.

The following forty-eight hours were filled with suspense. The Saturday meeting took place as scheduled. Telephone calls were made to the various departments of the Ministry of Finance to find out if the striking civil servants had heeded the call to resume work. It was said that a few staff had attempted to come back to work on Saturday but that they had been prevented by strikers manning picket lines. The Prime Minster instructed the Police Commissioner to provide protection to staff willing to come to work.

A few hours passed. The Commissioner prevaricated and staff willing to work were not given police protection. A crack began to appear in what was a solid Cabinet forty-eight hours earlier. A senior minister led a pack of waverers. "We should ask ourselves," said this minister "whether the position we have adopted is the appropriate one for the situation. Are we not being too inflexible?" One, two, three, and a few more people supported him. Other ministers came in to say that there must be good reasons for going back on a solemn decision taken forty-two hours earlier. What were these reasons? they asked. No response was given. The threat to recruit new staff in place of the strikers was withdrawn. It was not a decision calculated to enhance the image of the Cabinet. A small group of ministers strongly protested, but the majority of their colleagues had lost nerve. The Cabinet went back on its decision. The humiliation was palpable.[13]

The topical issue of former Cabinet Ministers was raised at a meeting of the Cabinet some ten days later. The Prime Minister reported on an open-air gathering with members of the armed forces that had been arranged for him a few days earlier. A question that had been repeatedly raised by the soldiers was why former officials were not detained for their past wrong doings. "I get the impression that they have thought seriously about the issue and could take action," said the Prime Minister. "Our formal approach may not be satisfactory to them. The responsibility for the victims of the drought in Wollo was raised," he continued, "The soldiers said former officials had committed grave errors and asked what action had been taken." The Cabinet took no decision other than restating its position that the question was before the Inquiry Commission that had been recently established for precisely that purpose and that we had to await its findings and recommendations.

The strikes persisted and the general situation worsened. On the 23rd of April the government decided to call out the army to restore law and order. Soldiers were posted at strategic places. Four days later, the Prime Minister informed the Cabinet that the soldiers had insisted that former ministers be detained, as they were the cause of the ongoing disturbances. Speculation was rife that the Prime Minister himself was not altogether averse to the idea of restricting the movement of the former officials: keeping them under house arrest for a limited period of time, or even having them temporarily detained.

As I mentioned earlier, on 2 March 1974 a helicopter of the Army Aviation unit had dropped copies of a one-page declaration supporting the resignation of cabinet ministers and calling for a restriction on their movement. It had also stated that they should be questioned on the misuse of public funds. Phrases like "they should not be left free.... they should be assembled" in one place were employed.[14] It was clear therefore that their detention was a major objective of whoever was calling the shots from behind. The fact that an army aviation helicopter was dropping copies of the declaration does not in itself say that the military was behind the detention. But their collaboration was evident even if there was no direct evidence at the time that they took the initiative.

At the open-air gathering of soldiers which the Prime Minister addressed, he had said that the case of the former ministers would be taken up with the Emperor when he realized that the soldiers were not satisfied with his response that the case was in the hands of the Inquiry Commission. This might have led them into thinking that the Prime Minister was backpedalling on the issue. The case was not helped by actions some former ministers were said to be taking to make life difficult for him. They were reported to be inciting the soldiers not to pay heed to the Prime Minister's instructions and pleas. They and other colleagues were also visiting the Palace more frequently than was thought prudent. They were highly visible in other ways as well. When friends advised that their visibility might provoke the ire of a restive public, they replied that they were not culpable of any wrong doing and had no reason to hide from anybody.

It was unclear at what precise point and on whose orders or advice the military started detaining the former officials. When they did, there was alarm in government circles and especially in the Cabinet. At a meeting not long afterwards, the Prime Minster was asked point blank whether there was any basis for the allegation that he himself was behind the detentions. His response was unequivocal: he was incapable of such an act, as he too was a former minister. He could not possibly be immune to the charges the military were accusing them of. He then volunteered an interesting piece of information.

Following a long and difficult discussion at the Palace on this contentious issue, he started to explain, the former officials were persuaded to accept an arrangement whereby they would not be detained but would first spend an evening at a convenient location in Addis Ababa (Paulos Hospital was mentioned as a possibility) and be taken the following day to the resort hotel at Koka Dam, to be kept there for a limited period. Regrettably, they were subsequently put behind bars on the orders of the military. That, the Prime Minister seemed to say, should settle the question of who was responsible for the detentions. Indeed, a military officer did seem to admit as much at a subsequent Palace meeting which I shall describe in a moment.

The crisis deepened in the days that followed and it was decided to have a special meeting of the Cabinet. The purpose was to assess the general political situation, and in particular the position of the Cabinet, with the view to determining what action to take. At the meeting which was held on 27 April, it was agreed that the Cabinet faced serious difficulties. It did not have popular support. Nor did the military seem to pay much attention to it. After a lengthy discussion the decision was taken to resign.

There was only one dissenter: the Minister of the Imperial Court, Dejazmatch Kebede Tessema. His argument seemed to make sense. How could we resign at a perilous moment? "I am the oldest member of the Cabinet," he said, "and I should be the first to think of retirement or resignation. Yet I can't in good conscience endorse this proposal." He could not find anyone to agree with him, openly at any rate.

A carefully worded letter of resignation was prepared by a drafting committee. It made the following points: (i) the Cabinet was not being supported either by the population or by the armed forces; (ii) the Cabinet could not continue under these circumstances, and (iii) the Emperor should appoint a new Cabinet. Thoughts were not far from the minds of a few that a provisional military administration might provide a stop gap solution.

An audience with the Emperor was arranged through the Minister of the Imperial Court for 29 April at 5:00 p.m. When we arrived at Jubilee Palace we were ushered into the banquet hall and were surprised to find two rows of soldiers standing in front of the Emperor. The battle dress of the soldiers indicated that they were not there to receive us with military fanfare. It was a detachment of the army, with a certain Clolonel Mulugeta Negatu at its head who, immediately after we took our places, started to read out a formal message from a crumpled piece of paper which he took out of his breast pocket.

The principal points ran as follows:

(i) the armed forces shall henceforth *not detain anyone* (the first clear intimation of who was responsible for the detentions);

(ii) the allegation that six persons in detention have been killed is absolutely untrue;

(iii) the allegation that the armed forces are planning to usurp power is false;

(iv) the armed forces fully support the present Cabinet; and

(v) their loyalty to the Crown is beyond question.

Immediately after the Colonel had read his statement, we were politely but firmly ushered out. Our letter of resignation was neither delivered nor read. A nice little piece of political theatre, we all thought. The crafty hand of the Minister of the Imperial Court appeared to be in evidence. We also suspected that the Prime Minister was probably not altogether in the dark about the soldiers' pre-emptive initiative. As we later found out, however, it was the Minister of Finance who had unwittingly informed his brother, an army Colonel, of the Cabinet's intention to resign. It was the Minister himself who volunteered the information at a Cabinet meeting. The Colonel was apprehensive of the consequences of the Cabinet's decision and presumably informed his officer colleagues who then took the decision to dissuade members of the Cabinet from leaving office at a tense time for the country. But the sentiment lingered among some of us that the Minister of the Court might have had some role in the murky affair. The result was to give the scheming young officers more time to ready themselves for their ultimate objective.

A few days after this, an incident took place that precipitated my own personal resignation. In each department of government, a coordinated series of upheavals had been set in motion by forces that were working to bring down the government. These were being given wide coverage by the government press. My department's turn came within a day or two of the non-event at the Palace. A letter to the editor prepared by the professional staff of my Ministry appeared in the Amharic daily (*Addis Zemen*) taking their supervisors to task for their inadequate leadership and condescending attitude towards Ethiopian staff. The letter also said that staff were not being given enough opportunity to participate actively in the drafting of the country's development plan.

This was neither fair nor true. But the climate perpetrated by underground extremist groups was one of blind rebellion. Veracity or fairness had no place in judging senior officials. The climate also favoured those who wished to strike back in order to settle old scores. Bureaucrats unequal to their jobs and hence under the eye of supervisors were often at the forefront of the struggle for equality, for democracy, and land reform. In the armed forces in particular, they mobilized the lower ranks to rise against the senior officer corps. Personal gripes, the urge to get even, the desire to sweep away the perception of being a trouble maker or poor performer; these and similar purely personal motives played a not insignificant role in what otherwise appeared to be a laudable struggle to bring about a more just and democratic order to an ancient empire. Those who knew the would-be leader, Major Mengistu Haile-Mariam, would later say that he was a fine specimen of this phenomenon.

Although aware of this general situation, I found it difficult to disregard the unfair charges given ample space in the government's own press; for acquiescence might be interpreted as a validation of whatever was being hurled at us by the accusers. Increasingly, I was also feeling that there was no meaning to my continued stay in the Cabinet, whatever my initial reasons might have been for agreeing to be part of the new team. I decided to quit.

I prepared a letter of resignation addressed to the Prime Minister. To the editor of *Addis Zemen*, I also wrote a short letter in response to the charges against the leadership at my Ministry and personally delivered it to the senior official who had oversight responsibility for the paper.

The Travails of Resignation

I felt that the Cabinet had shown remarkable weakness in managing its own press. Far more disturbing was its unwillingness to stand firm on key issues. A desperate attempt to hang on to power invited increased humiliation and alienation from the public. I had for long believed that those called upon to render public service should at all times keep in mind the option to quit on issues of conscience or principle. Given my earlier misgivings about remaining in public service and the way events were drifting, I felt I could not continue any longer. I handed my letter of resignation to Endalkatchew Makonnen.

Agence France Press carried the news on May 5 saying, however, that it was only a threat to resign. I was surprised to see in the same report that the Minister of Information had dropped his intention to resign earlier in the week after a plea from his own staff as well as from the Prime Minister. As I handed my letter of resignation to the Prime Minister, I said that the Cabinet was doing little of significance. Besides, things were going from bad to worse. Even when our own colleagues are detained, like Air Force General Assefa Ayene who was widely known as a liberal and honest public servant, we could do precious little. I said I did not wish to continue as a member of the government. The Prime Minister looked unconcerned as I handed him the letter, saying only that I should, as a matter of courtesy, come to the following Cabinet meeting to inform my colleagues of my decision. I wasn't quite sure what he had in mind, but decided that I would say a few words and leave expeditiously.

I arrived a little after the meeting had commenced and took my seat. The Prime Minister read out my letter of resignation after which I gave a brief explanation of my reasons. A minister spoke saying that the reasons for my resignation were not sufficiently compelling. The situation of the country was very precarious. We should all exercise patience. A few more spoke similarly. All had agreed to resign collectively only a week earlier. I replied that I had come to the meeting as a matter of courtesy. I had made up my mind and would appreciate it if I were allowed to leave. Without waiting for a response, I got up, said good bye and left. It appeared that the Prime Minister had encouraged some ministers to dissuade me from leaving the Cabinet. He naturally did not wish anyone to leave for fear of rumours that his government was tottering. In truth, it was.

As I left the meeting, I was told that there was a message awaiting me at the office of the Prime Minister's aide, Abeselom Zekie. I went over and was told that His Holiness the Patriarch Tewophlos wished to see me. As Planning Minister, I was an *ex-officio* member of the Orthodox Church's Development Commission and thought that the Patriarch wished to discuss some related subject. It turned out to be something else, however. The Patriarch, a tall, ponderous, and pleasant man, started to talk in a leisurely manner about the general situation in the country. He went on in that vein for a while and finally said, "I feel sorry for the Prime Minister who is trying to do his best in a difficult situation. People like you should assist him."

"Your Holiness, I know that the Prime Minister's job is unenviable, but I have resigned," I responded. He did not show surprise. It appeared that Lij Endalkachew had requested him to discourage me from leaving the Cabinet. The Patriarch advised that I should not resign. I was not inclined to argue with the highest authority of the Ethiopian Orthodox Church, was deeply saddened that he should be used as an intermediary, and politely took my leave without saying yes or no. Immediately afterwards, I went straight to office of the Prime Minister to express my distress that the issue should reach His Holiness and that I suspected his office to be behind the idea. Calmly, he said that it was not the case.

I stayed home and awaited the Prime Minister's definitive response to my letter. Over the next few days, a few friends came to visit. They too advised that I should not resign. Most people were troubled by the way things were drifting. Lij Michael Imru, a senior member of the Cabinet, also talked to me and advised that I stay. Some friends mentioned the growing risk of war with Somalia. How could one abandon one's country at a time like this? they argued. I listened to everyone but persisted in my decision. To the best of my recollection, I do not remember any person saying that I had done the right thing to resign.

My decision was far from being precipitous. From the outset, I had harboured doubts about joining the new Cabinet. Later, the entire Cabinet had decided to resign but had been obliged to give up after its plan was foiled. Why was I being advised to change my mind? Perhaps there was something I did not adequately appreciate. I started to developed doubts about my position, and spent hours and days meditating, digging into the depths of my thoughts in the hope of finding some guiding light that would rescue me from anguish.

I held out for about a month, and finally succumbed to the fears and anxieties which continued to be expressed by friends and colleagues. The proverbial drip drop of the water had ultimately bored into the rock. Still reeling from self-doubt, I agreed to return to the Cabinet on the 28th of May, five days short of a month from my date of resignation. The thought of resignation was not put to rest, however. Rather it seeped into the inner recesses of my mind, not as a result of any conscious decision to put it away with the idea of retrieving it at a more appropriate time, but entirely on its own.

For obvious reasons, I did not want to go back to the Ministry of Planning. Finance and Agriculture were proposed, but I was reluctant to get involved in what were contentious departments of government at a time of political uncertainty. I simply wished to hang on for a while and observe how things evolved and chose the Ministry of Transport and Communications. The Ministry was was far from being a hyper-active department of government, or so I thought.

No sooner had I stepped into my office at the Ministry, however, than I was engulfed by strikes in the parastatal bodies under the ministry. Ethiopian Telecommunications was perhaps the worst in this respect. Civil servants in the central government and the corporations were not allowed to unionize or go on strike. But this was a formality that daily became irrelevant. Egged on by clandestine political groups working strenuously to destabilize the government, employees of Ethiopian Telecoms demanded exaggerated salaries and benefits. They threatened to sabotage the equipment and various facilities if their demands were not met. Staff in the Civil Aviation Administration (CAA), the Franco-Ethiopian Railways Corporation, and the Post Office were similarly vocal.

Crisis of the Congo Veterans

Into the simmering cauldron of chaos was added a new and more potent ingredient that brought the contents to boiling point. For a long time, the veterans of the U. N. military operations in the Congo had been expressing their grievances about unpaid benefits. As it later transpired, the root cause of this grievance was a mixture of bureaucratic muddle, misunderstandings, and greed. In a report made to the Council of Ministers on 12 August 1974 by Dejazmatch Zaude Gebre-Selassie, the new Minister of Foreign Affairs, the following sequence of events was outlined. In 1961, the Ministry of Defence submitted a request to the U.N. for the payment of its soldiers serving in the Congo. The amount submitted comprised the salary and allowances of soldiers and officers. The U.N. responded that it would pay only overseas allowances, not regular salaries. Morocco's initial submission had been turned down similarly, but a revised request had been approved later. Dr. Tesfaye Gebre-Igzi, Ethiopia's Chief of Mission in New York, suggested that his government submit a revised request based on the Moroccan proposal. Ethiopia resubmitted its request accordingly and payment to officers and men was made. There was, therefore, no unpaid amount.

Reference is made to this event in a recent book by Fantaye Wolde-Yohannes Zelibanos who at the time was a Deputy Minister in the Ministry of Defence, from which vantage point he could witness developments first hand.[15] I had the opportunity of discussing the issue with him in August 2009. Although different in some respects, his recollections corroborate the key aspects of the preceding stories and provide further context and detail. The first proposal for the conditions of service of officers and men which the Ethiopian Government submitted to the U.N. was judged too modest by Dr. Tesfaye Gebre Igzi. He proposed that a more robust budget be submitted. Fantaye's says an exaggerated request was prepared to which he objected. But a number of his colleagues criticized him for standing in the way of what promised to be generous payments by the U.N. from which the country and its defence personnel could benefit. The request was sent unchanged.

The U. N. turned down the submission as unreasonable. Dr. Tesfaye now advised that another request be sent along the lines of Morocco's proposal which was based on that of Sweden and which looked relatively satisfactory. The U. N. accepted this second submission. Fantaye's book says that men and soldiers were paid per diem, not salaries, on the basis of that submission. Indemnities were also paid to the injured and to dependents whose officers and men had been killed in action. In addition, payment was made to the government of Ethiopia to cover expenses on arms and equipment. Nothing was held back from the soldiers.

Fantaye's explanation of the soldiers' misunderstanding rests on two factors. First, the Imperial Guard had made initial payments to three or four of its medical personnel in the expectation that they would be reimbursed by the U.N. These were one time payments but were relatively generous. The soldiers made a mental note of that and its possible implications for their own payments. Secondly, the soldiers were aware that the Ethiopian government had submitted a request for large sums of money in support of its operations. Indeed it was much talked about and anxiously awaited. Most soldiers were unaware of exactly what had happened and persisted in the belief that large amounts of money had been received at some point.

After the return home of the Ethiopian contingent, even senior veteran officers who should have known better started to support the request of the soldiers. It was not lost on them that they too might benefit from monies that might be paid to the soldiers. Clandestinely, they advised their men to take their case to the Emperor. Veterans who had left the army several years earlier, many now in bad shape financially, marched to the Palace one day. The police blocked their way with batons and guns. "Blood was shed," in Fantaye's words. When the Emperor heard what had happened he set up a high level committee comprising the then Minister of the Interior, General Abiy Abebe, Dejazmatch Kebede Tessema, and a senior civil servant in charge of budget matters in the Ministry of Defence. A thorough investigation was undertaken. No unpaid funds were uncovered. Given what the unfortunate veterans had been through, it was decided that they should each be given farming land from the government's substantial holdings.[16]

It was obvious that a long standing grievance of this nature could not be easily resolved. In addition, the case had become charged politically. One story given wide circulation at the time alleged that a certain highly placed official who had his eye on the Prime Minister's job had promised the soldiers that he would help with their case if they in turn could work with their colleagues in active service to bring down Prime Minister Endalkatchew. What the Prime Minister did to counter this challenge is not clear. The issue was taken up by the Cabinet but could not be resolved, not because the facts were not known, but because it had become a political hot potato.[17]

According to reports circulating at the time, the high official arranged an audience for the soldiers. But when their representatives met the Emperor, they were told that there was no money to be paid. Incensed, the soldiers immediately walked over to the nearby Cabinet building and asked the Prime Minister to hand over ministers whom they believed had interfered with their case. One of these, Belatchew Asrat, had been seen walking out of the Emperor's office while they were waiting outside. Belatchew had met the Emperor in connection with an entirely different matter, but the soldiers suspected he had come to be consulted on their case. He had indeed previously served on a government committee charged with a review of their grievance. And the committee had concluded that there was no basis for their claim. The Prime Minister could obviously not accede to the veterans' demand to turn in Belatchew and Dejazmatch Kebede, who were members of his Cabinet, and other officials. The soldiers were furious and walked away menacingly, threatening that they would take action. Credible accounts say that they then went to the Headquarters of the Fourth Army Division in Addis Ababa and talked to officers on duty (among them Major Atnafu Abate) who took up their case and got down to work.

On precisely the same day (and by coincidence), a Parliamentary delegation of eight persons led by retired army major Admassie Zelleke visited the Division Headquarters. The delegation's aim was to obtain the release of senior military and civilian officials detained by a committee of officers headed by Colonel Alem Zewd Tessema.[18] Major Atnafu, who had been a member of the committee headed by Colonel Alem Zaud and whom the delegation met, was irate. He said it was a shame that representatives of the Ethiopian people should come to an army base not to inform themselves of the multitude of problems faced by the armed forces, but to ask for the release of former officials who had been detained for past wrongdoing.

Combined with the pressure from the Congo veterans, this pushed Atnafu into quickly drafting a note addressed to various units of the Army, the Air Force, the Navy, the Police Force, and the Territorial Army. In it he requested them to send representatives to the headquarters of the Fourth Army Division in Addis Ababa. Colonel Kale Kristos Abbai, Police Commissioner for the province of Harrar and other officers from the Third Army Division, met and selected representatives from the various units in the province. Major Mengistu Haile-Mariam was one of four selected from the Third Division. He was appointed leader of the group on account of his seniority.[19]

Birth of the Dergue and the Demise of Endalkatchew Makonnen

Major Atnafu had been studying business administration at Haile-Selassie University. He was known to have engaged in under-cover political activity with other military friends in the preceding few weeks. He now sensed he had found a golden opportunity to lead. Representatives of the various units of the Armed Forces started to arrive at the Headquarters of the Fourth Army Division. Soon there were 109. On 28 June they formed a coordinating committee of the armed forces.[20]

Soldiers were placed at strategic points in the city. More persons were rounded up gradually and detained: former Cabinet Ministers, senior officers of the armed forces, civilian officials, other prominent public figures and business persons. The number of detainees grew and grew, and the detentions spread to the provinces. The Coordinating Committee of the Army, the Air Force, the Navy, the Police Force, and the Territorial Army started to issue orders routinely on the public broadcasting system. Martial music was regularly played. And before long, the soldiers proclaimed their rallying cry: *Yaleminim Dem Ethiopia Tikdem!* (Ethiopia First, And Not a Drop of Blood!). To all intents and purposes, they became the government of the day. The civilian Cabinet was humiliated and its position became untenable. It was imperative to meet with the members of the Coordinating Committee, first to find out what precisely they were up to and, secondly, to find a solution to the confusion created by what clearly were two centres of authority. This was the least to do under the circumstances.

I should perhaps digress a little at this point to see exactly what transpired when the one hundred and nine men from the different units of the country's armed forces met at the Headquarters of the Fourth Army Division on that fateful day of 28 June 1974.[21] Before the meeting was convened, each delegate was carefully registered, Major Atnafu and his colleagues taking the responsibility for verifying the credentials of the newly arrived soldiers. When that was completed, Atnafu convened and chaired a meeting. He spoke of mismanagement, of corruption, and abuse of authority in the armed forces. There was a general discussion around this theme. He then ordered the detention of several military and civilian officials. "The fact that an ordinary major like Atnafu could do this," says an anonymous former member of the Dergue (comrade # 22) interviewed by Guenet, "shows the collapse of leadership within the armed forces at that time."

Major Mengistu was in attendance at the meeting the following morning. He spent the whole day listening intently, "not uttering a single word." It was at the next meeting that he raised his hand and was given the floor by Atnafu. He spoke clearly and persuasively on the need for determining "our goal" and for "a programme of work." The same comrade # 22 says: "All of us were surprised by his communication skills and by the weight of his ideas." Mengistu went to the blackboard, wrote 'Ethiopia Tikdem' (Ethiopia First), and proposed it as a motto. A number of ideas were bandied about regarding goals. Mengistu noted down alternative forms of government for the country: a constitutional monarchy, a democratic civilian government, or a military government. "Removing the Emperor was unthinkable at the time. Consequently, the first alternative was accepted," concludes comrade #22.

Mengistu left a positive impression on the meeting's participants. During the coffee break, committee members talked about the need for "a new leader for the new programme." When the meeting resumed Mengistu was elected chairman, and Atnafu vice-chairman. A proposal was made to elect a secretary, but Mengistu intervened to say that since members had reposed their confidence in him by naming him chairman, it was for him to choose his secretary. There was no objection when he selected his friend Major Gebreyes Wolde-Hana: a first sign that he would leave little to chance, or more accurately to the democratic process. Thirty odd years after these events, a large body of information has grown around his clever tactics, his deceptiveness, his capacity for scheming and his nationalism. I shall have occasion to come back to these in due course.

To go back to the main story, the Cabinet deliberated on the problems created by the new military body and decided to set up a five-man dialogue committee composed of Dejazmatch Zaude Gebre-Selassie, the Minister of the Interior, Ato Belete Gebre-Tsadik, the Minister of Land Reform, myself from the Ministry of Transport and Communications, Ato Mohammed Abdulrahman, the Minister of Commerce and Industry, and Fitawrari Demissie Taffara, the Minister without portfolio in the office of the Prime Minister. The Cabinet committee met with representatives of the Coordinating Committee on 30 June. All in all, 12 meetings were held between that date and July 24.

The Cabinet's principal preoccupation, apart from finding out what the soldiers were up to, was to resolve the confusion caused by two governments acting side by side, one illegal but *de facto* and the other legal but exercising little power. The soldiers were informed that this situation could not continue. In explaining their actions, they said that they had no interest in power, but only wished to support the new Cabinet with their various initiatives: imprisoning former officials, controlling travel, making sure that the nation's assets were protected from removal to safe havens abroad, etc. They were, of course, never asked to act in that or any other capacity.

Behind the scene, important developments were taking place which strengthened the hand of the Coordinating Committee and of which the committee of Ministers was totally unaware. Soon after it was established, the Coordinating Committee realized that it needed funds for its subversive work. It approached General Gizzaw Belayneh, Commander of Ground Forces, for help. The General could not provide the required funding. Mengistu Haile-Mariam sought the assistance of his relative (his grandfather as widely believed), the shrewd old politician and Minister of the Imperial Court, Dejazmatch Kebede Tessema.

Kebede introduced Mengistu to the Emperor, so goes a credible story which borders on the incredible. Kebede told the Emperor that the young army officer was head of the recently established Committee, that the body was loyal to the Emperor, and that it was working hard to bring an end to the confusion reigning in the country. Its objective was to assist the Emperor to run the country firmly. Funds were needed which the Defence Ministry could not provide. Only the Emperor was in a position to help. The Emperor agreed to provide Birr 80,000 (about $40,000). Was this a Machiavellian move to exercise control over a rebel group that the Emperor knew was working against him? Or did he fall victim to the even more Machiavellian ways of the devious Palace official who had a long standing grudge against him and who was ultimately trying to get even?[22] Or was the Emperor simply too old to handle the tricky case? Whatever the reasons, the money was a badly needed shot in the arm of the rag tag group of NCOs and junior officers intent on usurping power.

Another piece of good luck came its way when the Committee seized the radio station and started to imprison government officials. The Commander of the Imperial Guard, General Abebe Gemeda, had mobilized his men to eject the Military Committee from the headquarters of the Fourth Army Division. The Committee stood no chance to defend itself, such was Abebe's superiority in men and equipment. Some highly placed members of the traditional class feared that if Abebe succeeded in his efforts, he would place himself in a position to seize power. They poured cold water on his plan. The Emperor himself was disinclined to use force. And Abebe was removed from his post. Yet another danger was averted when the audacious commander of the paramilitary police, General Mulugeta Wolde-Yohannes, asked to be allowed to deal with the Coordinating Committee but was refused authorization. The Minister of Defence, General Abiy Abebe, said he did not wish to see bloodshed among compatriots. Things could scarcely have played out more favourably for the Coordinating Committee.

Over the next several weeks, the soldiers had an opportunity to assess the alignment of forces at play and to gradually prepare themselves to take over power at a moment of their choice.[23] The Cabinet committee, in its meeting with the soldiers' group, focused on their goals and on the unworkable dichotomy of power. It also used the occasion to explain the economic and political predicament of the country so that any steps taken would neither be hasty nor out of ignorance.

As I was perhaps the only member of the Cabinet Committee who had worked closely on the nation's economic problems over the previous few years, I took it upon myself to inform the military about the difficult economic situation we faced. I did not want any stone left unturned in informing them of the problems of the moment. Such was the intensity of my explanations that they were misunderstood as an attempt to educate 'ignorant soldiers.' My friend Haddis Alemayehu got wind of this and advised that I take care not to give the wrong impression. A Dergue officer had been to his residence on some unrelated business and had mentioned that I acted as if the soldiers were ignorant of the country's problems. The officer assured Haddis that they knew quite a bit.

The Cabinet authorized each agenda item that we took up with the members of the Coordinating Committee. When some of us suggested raising the issue of detained former officials, it showed reticence. But the Prime Minister finally agreed that one of us could raise it informally and on a personal basis. I consequently pointed out in a subsequent meeting that there were many innocent people who had been detained and that steps should be taken for the cases of all detained persons. A young army officer asked if I could give examples of persons I believed were innocent. I replied I could indeed, but my concern was not only about people whose innocence I could vouch for personally. There were many others. I suggested that the dossiers of all be re-examined thoroughly. If this were done, I said I had little doubt that the majority would be released. The officer, who probably wanted to say that I was only interested in cases involving my personal acquaintances, did not respond.

In the course of these discussions, it was announced over the radio that the Coordinating Committee wanted Rear Admiral Eskinder Desta (the Commander of the Imperial Navy and the Emperor's grandson) to hand himself in. The soldiers had been saying all along that they respected the authority of the Emperor. At a follow up meeting, I pointed out that they were going back on their word in asking the Admiral to give himself up. As usual they said nothing. But at a subsequent meeting, they informed us that they had rescinded the order to arrest the Admiral. There was hope that this would open the way to a review of the situation of other detained persons. Alas, it was not to be. The Admiral was detained within a day or two.

On 18 July the soldiers made their move. The Cabinet was in session when General Aman, appointed earlier as Chief of Staff upon the Coordinating Committee's request, walked in to inform the Prime Minister that he had an urgent message from the Emperor. The two stepped out. A few minutes later the Prime Minister returned to say that he had just been informed by the General that the Committee wished Haddis Alemayehu to be appointed Prime Minister as a matter of urgency and that he, the incumbent, should give himself up. The Emperor had not asked Aman to convey the message, as Palace circles later confirmed. It was the Committee which, in collusion with Aman, was calling the shots, the Emperor's name being used only as a ruse.

The Prime Minister had known all along that the military were after him. When the dreaded hour arrived, he did not betray any emotion. He quietly got up from his seat, went around the oblong Cabinet table, shook hands with everyone to say farewell, and stoically made his exit. His tenure of office had lasted exactly 109 days. It was a painful scene I recall to this day. A couple of days later he joined many of his former cabinet colleagues in detention, most of whom were now his adversaries.

The soldiers later accused him of moves to divide the military, of harbouring former officials they had wanted to detain, of efforts to thwart the payment of unpaid per diems to veterans of the Congo campaign, of being in league with the Governor General of Gojjam (a cousin) to undermine the military, and of using members of Parliament to secure the release of former officials who had been detained. A day or two later, the military announced that Haddis Alemayehu had turned down the 'call of the motherland'. The search was now underway for another candidate to be Prime Minister.

Haddis's response was more nuanced than the military announced, as I learned from him later. He had simply sought clarifications. Firstly, the constitution was being revised and would soon be completed, after which the Prime Minister was expected to be elected by popular vote. Was it really necessary to have a Prime Minister for what was bound to be a short spell? Secondly, even if a Prime Minister had to be appointed, what did the military expect him to do? More specifically, how was power going to be shared between the Coordinating Committee and the Prime Minister? Thirdly did the Coordinating Committee have plans for the future of the country?

Aman, who was acting as a go between and to whom these questions were directed, made an attempt to answer only one of them. He said the military's goal was "Ethiopia First". Haddis replied that this sounded well and good, but lacked specificity as a guide for policy. The Committee was dismantling the old order, but what was to take its place? If the Committee did not have a plan of its own, he (Haddis) was prepared to draft something as a basis for discussion. Only subsequently would it be possible for him to decide whether to take on the responsibilities of the post of Prime Minister. Aman listened and finally said: "Are you saying no to the call of the motherland?"

Haddis was dismayed and said that he was a man who had served his country in times of war and peace. He had fought against the Fascists in 1936, had been captured in battle, and had spent many years as a prisoner of war in Italy. "I don't usually talk about myself in this manner, General, but you leave me no option. You are of course too young to know all this," Haddis continued, "but you can find out from Ato Meles, your elder brother." The General, none too happy to be talked to in this manner, went to the Coordinating Committee and informed its members that Haddis had turned down the call of the motherland. The Committee announced that Haddis had refused the call of the motherland and quickly renewed its search for an alternative candidate. It now focused on Lij Michael Imru.

CHAPTER 9

The Interregnum:
The Closing Forty-Four Days of
Michael Imru's Premiership

Michael Imru was in Geneva while the events described at the end of the previous chapter were taking place. The Coordinating Committee approached his father, Ras Imru, to persuade Michael to be the next Prime Minister. Michael was reluctant. The soldiers brought the matter to the Emperor who personally telephoned Michael to return home. Michael said he was on medical treatment and wondered if his return could not be delayed. The Emperor agreed but the military were fidgety. Seeing the mood of the soldiers, Ras Imru suggested a more formal instruction by the Emperor, who called Michael again and told him that there was a serious reason for his early return. He agreed to return and was named Prime Minister on August 3, with Zaude Gebre-Selassie as his deputy. General Aman had earlier been made Chief of the General Staff. He now became Minister of Defence as well.

In my first meeting with Michael Imru, I was surprised to find a man who did not seem to show the heavy burdens of office thrust upon his shoulders. Instead, I found him talking about mundane matters regarding office supplies. He said that the desk of former Prime Minister Aklilu Habte-Wold which he now occupied was curiously bereft of essential office supplies such as clips and staplers. His predecessor was not, as Michael was, a person who spent too much time sorting out papers, drafting notes, assembling and disassembling dossiers for some project. He obviously had no need for clips, erasers, staplers, or staple removers. I wondered whether this was due to the differences in the backgrounds of the two persons or a reflection more of Michael's recognition that the soldiers had not let go of power and that he was in his post for only a limited period of time.

Confirming Michael's judgment, the soldiers started to flaunt their power openly and became increasingly assertive, oftentimes crudely. They did not know the new

Prime Minister well, although they were aware of his socialist inclinations and his reputation for integrity. Little did they know that he was also a man of determination. Two incidents would soon bring this home: the first involving the composition of his Cabinet and the second regarding the long saga in which he and the Congo veterans faced each other: the veterans confident of the support of their armed colleagues in active service while Michael had no one to turn to but his own firm convictions.

For his Cabinet, Michael Imru settled on a list of ministers who for the most part were members of the government immediately preceding. The soldiers objected to a few names and demanded that they be dropped from the list. They contended that the Prime Minister had gone back on his word to consult them in advance of the appointments. Michael responded that he would not dismiss in the afternoon people he had appointed only in the morning. He said that he had made it plain to both the Emperor and to them that he would not change horses in midstream.

In reality, the dispute was of little consequence. The soldiers not only knew that the days of the Cabinet were numbered, but were assiduously planning for the day and manner of their takeover. But they wanted everyone to recognize their power even before it was formally declared. In Michael Imru, they met a man who was determined to play by the rules. He had been named Prime Minister and he was going to play out his role until the final day of reckoning.

Soon, a familiar crisis resurfaced: the demand of the Congo veterans for payment of some $15 million. The previous Prime Minister had not been able to resolve the problem. The veterans renewed their demand with greater determination. As they were waiting outside Michael Imru's office one afternoon, they saw members of the Coordinating Committee of the Armed Forces coming out of a meeting with him and confronted them with a question: "What have you done with our case? The departing Prime Minister had promised to give us his final response by tomorrow." One member of the Committee replied that they had to allow the new Prime Minister time to settle down. The veterans were angered and said that they had asked for the appointment of a new Prime Minister to be deferred until after their case had been resolved. "You have disregarded our request. You forget that it was thanks to us that your Committee was established." A Committee member replied that the problems of the nation were also a matter of priority.

The veterans were enraged even more. "Fine," replied one. "We shall disband your Committee. If you want to fight, you will find us ready. Your motto of 'Ethiopia Tikdem' is plain humbug. We shall now alert our colleagues in the various units. You obviously want to usurp power and be appointed ministers. We shall see if you'll succeed." They then turned to the Palace guards (who were sympathetic to their cause) and said: "These people are plotting to overthrow the government. Kick them out of here if you wish to avoid bloodshed." Members of the Committee did not wait to be forced to leave.

Prime Minister Michael Imru brought the issue to the Cabinet immediately afterwards. Soon after we started our deliberation, we were informed that the veterans had assembled on the grounds of the Cabinet building and were threatening that no one would be allowed to leave or enter the building until their demands had been met. The Prime Minister was calm and led the Cabinet through an orderly discussion, notwithstanding the clamour from the veterans outside which was clearly audible in the Cabinet room. Ministers did not have the full facts regarding the claim of the veterans and were consequently not in a position to decide. What do we say when we go outside to meet the impatient veterans? we wondered. We decided to tell them exactly that and ask for time.

With Sudanese Mamoun Beheiry, centre, and Michael Imru, right, following discussions on future policy directions for the ADB; Mamoun was the first President of the Bank in 1964 and Michael had been Prime Minister in 1974

We came out to meet them, the Prime Minister leading the way. An unruly mob faced us: jeering, threatening, and in full commotion. The Prime Minister said that the Cabinet had to ascertain first if there were any unpaid funds, the question of payment coming only afterwards. He said he would set up a committee made up of representatives of the Ministry of Finance, Foreign Affairs, and Defence and suggested they nominate their representative to be the fourth member of the group. If necessary, one or two members (including their representative) could be sent to U.N. Headquarters in New York to collect information needed for a decision.

The mood of the soldiers was ugly. They flatly refused to designate a representative to join the proposed committee. Arguments went back and forth between the soldiers and the ministers which led nowhere. Eventually, the soldiers realized that Michael Imru would not budge from his position and grudgingly accepted the suggestion that the Cabinet needed a week to investigate the case in order to come to a decision. They were told to return the following week.

We entered the Cabinet room to allow the soldiers to disperse. But they showed no sign of moving out of the premises. We waited, waited, and waited; not entirely reassured by the messengers of the Cabinet office who periodically looked through the windows to check if the veterans were still there; and kept telling us that they saw no sign of their departure. At about 4:00 p.m. they left. We could now go home for lunch.

A week later, the committee appointed by the Cabinet submitted its findings: there were no unpaid funds. We had finally got to the bottom of this long saga, but there was little doubt how the soldiers would react. For years, they had believed that there were huge sums owed to them and had kept up their struggle. The passage of time and the emergence of a pushover government had transformed what must have initially been a quest for some remote and undefined treasure into a ready booty awaiting only the determined dash of an audacious gang of soldiers.

As the Cabinet deliberated on the committee's findings, ministers became increasingly apprehensive. We were aware that over the years the veterans had been imprisoned, beaten, and disciplined in other ways as they tried to get a fair hearing for their case. They had persisted in their struggle to get funds they believed they had been wrongly robbed of. How could they be expected to go home quietly when told that the new Cabinet had finally dug up the truth that there was not a penny to pay? A nice little problem in the handling of which only one man seemed to be quietly determined: Prime Minister Michael Imru. He was firm in his view that the soldiers be told the truth, irrespective of the consequences. Ministers were far less determined.

I took the floor and suggested that we should perhaps find a way of recognizing the fact that the soldiers saw another truth while holding firm to our well founded position that no money had been withheld by the government. We could do this by informing them that our investigation has turned up no evidence of any money owed to them but that we were nevertheless prepared to make some 'gesture' of compensation for their past troubles. This will not be in the form of cash. We should make arrangements to provide them with land from the government's holdings and grant them the wherewithal needed to establish themselves as farmers. I could observe nods of assent from some colleagues. But not from the Prime Minister.

He did not think that this was the right approach. His view was that we should simply tell the veterans precisely what the situation was. Any kind of 'gesture' would be perceived as a tacit admission that funds had indeed been held back but that we were constrained from saying so on account of the government's inability to pay the large sum of money claimed by the veterans. Seeing the strength with which he argued his case, I withdrew my proposal saying I was only trying to be helpful in finding a way out, but would certainly follow the Prime Minister's lead if he thought my proposal would complicate matters further.

Given its earlier involvement and the potential risk of a violent reaction by the veterans, we informed the Coordinating Committee of our findings and our intention to let them know of our decision. The Committee agreed and suggested that the decision should be read to the veterans in the presence of the Emperor. It should also be published in the press and broadcast on radio and television. The Cabinet should not be unduly worried about an adverse reaction from the veterans. Good news indeed, we said; although we were still not sure about what appeared to be a principled stand by the Committee, just weeks after it had accused the previous Prime Minister of thwarting efforts to meet the veterans' demand for back pay.

As agreed previously, the veterans came to hear the Cabinet's decision. Upon arrival, however, they were told to present themselves at the Palace at 4:00 o'clock in the afternoon. The decision would be communicated to them there in the presence of the Emperor. They were taken by surprise at the sudden change of venue. But they had to comply and go quietly as there was no person of authority at the Cabinet secretariat who could talk to them. In the afternoon, the Prime Minister and all but a few ministers proceeded to the Palace. The few were those who saw trouble coming and wished to avoid being involved. Soon after our arrival, the Prime Minister and his deputy were called to the Emperor's private quarters. They came back after a few minutes. A new situation had developed. "The Emperor's advisors have counseled that the Cabinet's decision should be read to the veterans in the presence of the Ministers themselves," said Michael Imru. Distress was written all over his face as he spoke these words.

Someone had belatedly realized that the issue was a political hot potato, too dangerous to handle even for the Emperor of Ethiopia. Without the slightest hesitation, Michael led the way to where the soldiers had assembled within the premises of the Palace. Not a few Ministers grumbled with what looked like a dangerous acquiescence by Michael Imru in the decision to change plans at the last minute. But what could he do? The veterans scarcely needed yet one more cause for fury. They were already reeling over the previous decision to change the venue of the meeting. Within hours they would be told of yet another change of plan. It was plain that they would not be amused by this flip-flop.

The anxious veterans were gathered in front of the Emperor's thatch-roofed bungalow which served as his weekend study. It was located on a slope facing the Palace. A few steps led to a marbled terrace leading to the principal entrance of the study. We climbed the flight of steps and stood on the terrace facing some 350 to 400 men spread out on the tarmac at the bottom of the steps. Michael Imru stepped forward to the edge of the terrace and started to address the crowd. "When you came to see us last week, we promised that we would examine your case carefully and give you our decision within a week. We have had the opportunity to examine your case, and have arrived at a decision," he said in a manner and tone that betrayed the-none-too welcome finding that no evidence had been uncovered to support their claim. He then turned to the Cabinet Secretary, Yoseph Ayalew, and said firmly: "Ato Yoseph, read our decision to them."

There was immediate uproar, people shouting, gesticulating, and expressing their fury in other ways. The rowdy scene continued for some three or four minutes. All of a sudden, two persons from the crowd moved up a few steps and gestured to the crowd to keep quiet. There was immediate silence. One of the two men then turned to the Prime Minister, raised his voice and said: "Honourable Prime Minister; as you were entering the Palace about half an hour ago, you saw us gathered just outside the gate and told us that the decision of the Cabinet would be read to us in the presence of His Imperial Majesty. That was also what we were told in the morning. Why this new situation now?"

The Prime Minister could obviously not go into the embarrassing details of the Palace decision. "Our decision is to be read to you upon the gracious wish and command of His Majesty," he replied. This provoked fresh uproar. After a while, the Prime Minister told the spokesman to restore order. The man raised his two arms, palms down as he faced the crowd, moving them up and down in unison and demanding silence. Again, there was total compliance. The Prime Minister could speak. "Our decision has been made and will not change whether it is read here or in the presence of His Majesty. Are you saying that, even so, it should be read only in his presence?" "YY E SS," came the deafening reply.

The door of the Emperor's study behind us was locked. And it was not possible to enter the study to telephone the Emperor's aides of the new situation and allow the veterans to move down in orderly fashion towards the main Palace building some three to four hundred yards downhill. In front of us stretched the crowd of four hundred souls covering the tarmac below the steps. I could not see a way out. We stood sandwiched, unsure how to make our way to the Emperor's quarters. Perhaps the Prime Minister would ask the veterans' spokesman to help find an exit, I speculated. Nothing of the kind happened.

Michael Imru started to walk down the steps with self-assurance, the crowd in front of him defiantly blocking his exit. There was not the faintest indication of a crack to suggest an exit. He came to the bottom of the steps, stared the first man in the eye and said, "Make way!" with his right arm stretched out pointing the way forward. The first man improbably moved to the side, the one immediately behind did the same, as did the third, the fourth, the fifth, and so on. And as with the biblical partition of the Eritrean Sea, the sea of veterans opened up and we were able to walk through the menacing crowd. It was an amazing act of determination by Michael Imru. Only minutes before, the man he confronted must have been among those angrily gesticulating at him. He was then in the warm bosom of the mob. But now he was face to face with a man whose determined stare left no doubt as to what he wanted him to do. He buckled under the stare and thought it prudent to give way.

The Emperor was informed that the veterans did not wish to hear the findings on their case from the ministers. They were told to come down to the entrance of the Palace building. After a few minutes, the monarch came out accompanied by palace staff, including the Minister of the Court. Following a short pause, the Cabinet Secretary took out the note he had been carrying all along and started to read it. After a few preliminary sentences tracing the history of the veteran's long-standing grievance, the note ended with the conclusion that there was no back pay owed by the government.

There was pandemonium among the men. Minutes passed and there was no let up in their angry comments, shouts, and defiant gestures. Who was to calm these wild men? The Prime Minister was now simply watching. One or two ministers tried to say something in order to have some semblance of control. By then the angry veterans were making unflattering remarks about the Emperor himself, not too loudly but audible enough to be heard by a few of us ministers. The Deputy Prime Minister attempted to calm down things, but was rebuffed. Another member of the Cabinet, confident that the new Cabinet was more favourably regarded by the soldiers, asked: "Don't you trust us when *we* tell you there is no money to be paid out. Do you think *we* are thieves? "YES!" came the resounding and insolent reply. The Emperor was advised to retire to his private quarters. The Minister of the Court informed the crowd that His Majesty had decided the issue would be reviewed upon the return of their much admired hero, General Aman, who was on a visit to Eritrea at the time.

As expected, the soldiers took their case to the Coordinating Committee of the Armed Forces. The Committee passed the hot potato to the Inquiry Commission, with the request that an extra effort be made to dig up the truth. The Commission spent a good deal of time examining all available evidence and finally concluded that there were no funds held back by the government. The Secretary to the Commission, Seifu Tekle-Mariam, hand-carried the Commission's decision to the offices of the Coordinating Committee but could at first find no one willing to take the envelope. He eventually managed to leave it in the hands of Major Gebre-Yesus Wolde-Hana, the Committee Secretary.

No more was heard of an issue that had been germane to the birth of the Coordinating Committee and that had caused so much anguish and confusion. Its anticlimactic demise raises questions as to how it was finally brought to closure. Were the veterans ultimately threatened by the Coordinating Committee to acquiesce? Or were they bribed? Those who know need to speak out.

The Coordinating Committee spread its net far and wide to detain more and more former officials and business persons. The threat of expropriation of personal property was enough to persuade the great majority of these persons to turn themselves in. Along with the detentions, government departments that the Committee believed were not necessary were shut down, including the Ministry of Pen (the Royal Secretariat), the Crown Council, and organs of the administration of justice that prepared cases for final review by the Emperor's court, the *chelot,* which was the summit of Ethiopia's judiciary.

The arrogance of the soldiers got progressively worse. They robbed homes (cash, handguns, jewelry, and vehicles), they intimidated, they arbitrarily threw people behind bars and they murdered. Soldiers also reveled in the delights offered by the wives, daughters, sisters, or other female relatives of people they had put behind bars. The women succumbed to their undisguised threats and occasionally to offers of petty bureaucratic favours. Executions and threats of execution against defenceless city dwellers, broadcast over the airwaves to the accompaniment of marshal music at the very moment when the nation's defences were being imperiled, hardly cut an image of valour or sacrifice. Nor could one find too many instances of idealism among the flag bearers of 'Ethiopia First'. Initially the soldiers had been given the benefit of the doubt as harbingers of a new dawn of hopeful change. They now revealed themselves to be no more respectable than a bunch of street thugs on the hunt. One bright young lawyer, Shiberu Seifu, foolhardy enough to speak out on how the nation's affairs were being mismanaged by childlike soldiers, was battered to death.

The soldiers, having sidelined the Emperor and his Cabinet, were now a power unto themselves. Though most members of the Coordinating Committee were unaware, a handful of their leaders were engaged in actions that would bring Ethiopia's imperial epoch to a violent end.

PART III

Transition to an Uncertain Republic

CHAPTER 10

The Contrived Revolution

Forces Behind the Upheavals of February/March 1974

In Chapter 7, I drew attention to the situation in Ethiopia on the eve of the 1974 revolution and attempted to show some of the more immediate reasons behind the six-month crisis that precipitated the soldiers' takeover of the government. The event brought to closure a long historical process in which Emperors had played a pivotal role in managing their nation's affairs. Any attempt to gain a fuller understanding of the crisis would consequently require a review of how, down the centuries, these monarchs had handled their mandate in governing the land and its peoples. Nothing like a full review is attempted here, nor is it necessary for the purpose at hand. It would suffice to provide a broad brush portrayal of imperial mandate and accountability as a backdrop for the crisis.

The dominant political rhetoric of leftist extremists which prevailed in the months leading up to the overthrow of Emperor Haile-Selassie casts him and his predecessors as the principal protagonists in the dialectical conflict between oppressor and oppressed. To be sure Ethiopian Emperors had their failings. And some of their more problematic legacies haunt us to this day, autocracy being perhaps among the most persistent. It would be a caricature of history, however, to portray these Emperors as mindless oppressors of their subjects, devoid of any sense of justice or of good governance. This is particularly true of the Emperors who came after 1320 A.D., the year in which the *Kibre Negest* was composed.

The mandate of the monarch in the Ethiopian universe depicted by the *Kibre Negest* was to assure the equal treatment of all citizens under God's law, from which all earthly laws were derived and for whose impartial administration the Emperors were responsible. They were accountable to Him for their actions; much as democratically chosen leaders are answerable to their electorate, but with sanctions that were far more unsettling. Culpable leaders in a democracy would be thrown out of office or at most suffer finite punitive measures prescribed by law; but Emperors would face their

Creator's sanctions on earth as well as eternal ones in the afterlife. That is not to say that Emperors could safely brush aside the existential concerns of their earthly subjects. They were, for instance, keenly aware that justice (and its ultimate provenance) was a central preoccupation of Ethiopians of all walks of life. Consequently, they kept their eyes and ears open to the peoples' grievances to guard against their reigns being stigmatized with oppression of the poor; aptly encapsulated in one of the more disparaging public strictures of the day: "Deha Tebedelle, Fird Tegwadelle" (the poor are mistreated and justice is deficient).

Regarding the impartial administration of justice, the injunctions of the *Kibre Negest* are arrestingly simple: "Do not be biased in your judgments. In whatever you say, refrain from unjust acts." Protecting the poor and the powerless was another aspect of this mandate. Here again the words of the *Kibre Negest* ring with clarity: "Do not allow ruptures in your judgments of the poor and the children of the dead."[1] It was not to demonstrate the supremacy of imperial will that Emperors Ze-Dingil and Tewodros attempted to restrain their soldiers or the much venerated church authorities from acts of plunder committed against the peasantry. It was, rather, to enforce the tenets of the *Kibre Negest*.

Upon ascending the throne, Emperors issued edicts proclaiming their solemn commitment to rule their peoples on the basis of these precepts. When Empress Zawditu was crowned in February 1916 she proclaimed that, like her Emperor father, she would rule the land such that the "poor are not oppressed and that justice is administered impartially." In announcing her death and his assumption of imperial authority in April 1929, Emperor Haile-Selassie assured the populace that he would rule "in accordance with the laws and rules I have inherited from my fathers."[2] These were far from being hollow mantras, but solemn undertakings to observe the role of sovereigns laid down in the *Kibre Negest*. There were doubtless many Emperors who too often deviated from this model. In their more sober moments, however, even they were in no doubt as to where their responsibilities lay.

It is against this background that we should view the reform efforts of Ethiopian Emperors over the last seven hundred years or so. The late Merid Wolde-Aregay of Addis Ababa University provides a helpful sketch of the reforms of past Emperors in an Amharic article contributed to a publication of the Institute of Ethiopian Studies in 1990.[3] Emperor Tewodros I (1412-14) who came almost a century after the appearance of the *Kibre Negest* was the first monarch to try to "protect the peasantry from plunder," writes Merid. Emperor Zer'a Ya'icob (1434-1468) also made several efforts in this direction. Emperor Ze-Dengil (1603-04) initiated "fundamental changes" in how the country was governed for which he paid with his life. Ze-Dingil enacted a law that the military would come under the direct command of the Emperor and that the peasantry would pay rent also directly to him. His intention was to protect the peasantry from the triple plunder of Church authorities, local chiefs, and the soldiery. Indeed, the author of a book on Ethiopian history goes so far as to suggests that Ze-Dingel's "edict attempted to abolish servility and serfdom."[4] He was frustrated in his efforts and was brought to a premature end. After his assassination, the *Abun* (the Orthodox Metropolitan) declared that Ze-Dingel was not to be given a Christian burial as he was suspected of harbouring Catholic sympathies.

In Chapter 6, I have made reference to the efforts of several Emperors to introduce the fruits of science and technology to their country. Among these were Emperors Dawit (1381-1410), Zera Ya'icob (1434-68), and Libne Dingel (1508-40). Other Emperors also tried their hand at social reform, including abolishing slavery. Emperor Susinyos (1607-32) was among the first to outlaw the practice. The Emperor also tried to "throw out the disorderly way in which the people were ruled and replace it with a modern system of administration," as Merid notes. Iyasu the Great (1682-1706) had strong reformist tendencies. In the third of his four-volume *History of Ethiopia*, Tekle-Tsadik Mekuria tells us that the Emperor issued orders to cut down the number of customs posts in order to promote trade. He reduced the overall level of taxes on merchandize and abolished those imposed on petty trade. Officials were appointed who had familiarity with overseas trade. Some were foreigners. Paul Henze, who calls Iyasu the greatest of the Gondarine Emperors, writes about his efforts to "revise the tax system" and about "his proclivity to regularize and codify administrative procedures."[5] The reformist role of monarchs is of course not unique to Ethiopia. Tsar Peter the Great (1682-1725), and Tsarina Catherine the Great (1762-1796) were great reformers. Closer home was Egypt's modernizer Mohammed Ali (1769-1849). Peter ascended the throne in the same year as Ethiopia's reformer Iyasu the Great. Catherine predated Emperor Tewodros II by about six decades and Mohammed by just under a decade. And one could site examples of similar monarchs in other countries.

Emperor Tewodros II followed this long tradition of innovation and reform. Merid points out that Tewodros called a great gathering in September 1863 in which the *Abun* and members of the clergy took part. At that gathering, he proclaimed that the peasantry should pay rent for land to the central government, not to the clergy or local officials. Tewodros also wanted to put an end to the practice of billeting soldiers with the peasantry, since they would be paid regular salaries by the government. All his plans were frustrated by the Church, the local chieftains, and the soldiery. On one occasion he was informed of the death of several peasants following fast on the heels of a raid. In a gesture resonating with the spirit of the *Kibre Negest* the Emperor, in the words of his chronicler, turned his face to God, expressed profound sorrow at what had happened and prayed that the Lord take his life and spare him of the great anguish that his undisciplined soldiers were causing him and his citizens.

Tewodros also had a passion for modern technology and know-how, and dispatched letters to Britain's Queen Victoria pleading for craftsmen to be sent to his homeland to train his people: an echo of Emperor Libne Dingil's letter to the Portuguese three centuries earlier. He said he would gladly meet their expenses. But he got into trouble with the British when he detained their Consul and other

Europeans. Matters were further complicated by his hostility to Ottoman Turks who were nibbling islands and territory on Ethiopia's Red Sea coast. The British were at the time eager to maintain an alliance with the Turks against Russia, which posed a threat to their Middle Eastern and Indian possessions. The Ottomans for their part were happy to side with Britain against their traditional Russian foe. Tewodros's plea for technical assistance and his dream of teaming up with Britain to rid the Holy Land of the infidels fell on deaf ears. Had Emperor Tewodros been aware of the perception prevailing then among British clerics of Russian (and doubtless of Ethiopian) Orthodoxy as a "semi-pagan creed" (*The Economist* October 10, 2010) and that they had fought the Russians in Crimea with the Turks on their side as allies, one can only imagine the horror and violent reactions of a monarch who was prone to drastic actions under less provocative circumstances.

But the imperial tradition of social and political reform persisted after a brief setback of two decades. Emperor Tekle Giorgis who succeeded Tewodros had a short four-year reign, much of it tumultuous. His successor Yohannes IV could not introduce significant reforms, given his preoccupation with the country's enemies for the greater part of his rule.[6] Schooled as he was at the court of Tewodros and exposed to new ideas thanks to his contacts with the contingent of foreign missionaries in Gafat (Waldmeier in particular), Emperor Menelik continued the tradition of imperial reform. He was fascinated with modern technology and eagerly introduced novel techniques, crafts, and institutions. It was he who started Ethiopia's modernization in earnest: his government was refashioned along European lines; modern means of transport and communications, agriculture, banking, public administration and finance were introduced. Concurrent with the extension of the country's borders, a policy of accommodation of the different cultural groups was also pursued.

Emperor Haile-Selassie, more formally educated than any of his predecessors, became Crown Prince in 1916 and quickly embarked upon fresh reforms, with education as his central objective. The Emperor's interest in the expansion of education in the two northernmost provinces, Tigrai and Eritrea, merits special mention at this point. Emperor Haile-Selassie's perception of the spread of modern education in Ethiopia rested not only on his goal of promoting development on a broad front, but also on his belief that education was an effective instrument for bringing together Ethiopia's different cultural communities. There was a particular historical reason for his keenness to promote education in Tigrai and Eritrea.

The Emperor's father, Ras Makonnen, was among the few of Emperor Menelik's immediate collaborators who understood the predicament of these Northern provinces. Tigrai had been devastated by the military campaigns during the reign of Emperor Yohannes. The Emperor's suzerainty over a sprawling empire had always been hobbled by a narrow demographic and economic base, as well as by the fact that Tigrai was located far in the northern edge of a much expanded country. When Yohannes confronted enemies on two fronts (the Italians to the East and the Dervishes to the

West), resources were stretched. He had to choose engaging what he felt was the more menacing of the two foes. He decided to contain the Islamist threat in the West after which he would deal with the Italians on the East. Regrettably he lost his life in the battle of Metemma in 1889.

The returning soldiers found a Tigrai devastated by famine, caused partly by fewer hands on the farms, but more importantly by cattle disease. The Italian occupiers of Eritrea had imported large numbers of draft animals (especially mules) from India for their own needs. This triggered an epidemic that decimated the livestock population in Eritrea and adjoining Tigrai. On his return from a visit to Italy during the subsequent reign of Emperor Menelik, the Italians requested Ras Makonnen to pass through Massawa and Tigrai on his way to Shoa. They were eager to see Ethiopian central authority fully reestablished in Tigrai to assure security on their southern flank and avoid a mass migration into Eritrea of a famished population.

Makonnen was shocked by the sight of countless emaciated Tigreans wondering around the towns and the countryside in search of sustenance. In Shoa, he drew Emperor Menelik's attention to the predicament of a people whose land had been the cradle of Ethiopian civilization. Menelik had been at loggerheads with Emperor Yohannes and was not willing to be tied down in a region where Yohannes's successors did not take kindly to his swift climb to the throne and were also quibbling among themselves. Although the Italians in Eritrea were favourably disposed to him for their own strategic reasons, he knew they were determined to block his country's access to the Red Sea. For all of these reasons, Menelik focused his attention on Zeila as an alternative route to the sea. Makonnen urged a more balanced approach and advised that the Emperor refocus his attention on Tigrai. He himself was subsequently appointed governor of the province and worked towards a policy of reconciliation and greater integration between the peoples of Tigrai and their compatriots to the south.

Makonnen's son, Emperor Haile-Selassie, was in all probability influenced by his father's thinking. For, in his programme to spread education, Tigreans and Eritreans occupied a special place. During the Italian administration of Eritrea, the Emperor financed the education of Eritreans in Ethiopia as well as overseas. Most of these joined the imperial civil and military administration immediately after their studies. When Eritrea was federated with Ethiopia in 1952, it became a leading beneficiary of the Emperor's programme of expanding elementary and secondary education.[7]

As I pointed out in Chapter 7, the fruits of his labours became gradually evident, first within the government bureaucracy and later in society at large. But with them emerged new ideas more potent than he had bargained for. These gradually coalesced around a few basic demands: a limit to the powers of the Emperor, an active participation of citizens in the management of their country's affairs, reform in the system of land tenure which would liberate the peasantry from years of exploitation by feudal and clerical officials, and more effective ways of managing the latent ethnic and cultural tensions which were a constant threat to political and social cohesion. Dissidents advocating a more rapid pace of reform grew in number; an early sign that the Emperor (a radical in his youth) was being overtaken by events.

When countrywide celebrations for the Emperor's eightieth birthday were held in 1972, there was an expectant air of *change du regime*, a good many observers expressing the view that the ageing Emperor should voluntarily abdicate his throne and allow the Crown Prince to take over. The Prince was a figure strikingly different from his father: more open in his general attitude to change and more willing to assume the role of a constitutional monarch, if only to drive home the point that he would make a different and better kind of monarch. That chance slipped when the hoped-for abdication did not happen. There was also the expectation that perhaps some reform-minded, dashing nationalist leader would emerge from among the increasingly enlightened young officer corps to save the nation from bloodshed. Gamal Abdel Nasser of Egypt had been such a leader. Japanese reformers responsible for the Meiji restoration were yet another model. These expectations did not materialize.

There are a number of reasons why events did not evolve in that direction and, more importantly, why centuries of reform by a long line of Emperors did not have a cumulative impact to preclude a bloody revolution. One is that the reforms lacked adequate depth and spread. Another is the centuries ;old turbulence in the political life of the country, caused in part by domestic conflicts but in good measure also by external adversaries. Isolation from the centres of learning and socio-economic change is another explanation. This was largely due to the rise of Islam in the Middle East and the domination by its adherents of a sea lane that had for centuries underpinned the country's external trade, its diplomatic and cultural contacts. Finally, European colonialism introduced a new geopolitical reality in which the country's border regions became outposts designed to bring the country under foreign domination. When that failed, colonialism left a legacy in the shape of a number of small nations which eventually crystallized around these outposts and became a source of permanent conflict. Indeed, at the time of the 1974 revolution, Ethiopia was being squeezed by the threat of Soviet-armed irredentist Somalia to the Southeast and by ethnically driven secessionist forces to the North; two powerful jaws closing in on a large and vulnerable prey whose viability seemed to be under threat.[8] There are doubtless other reasons.

In summary, the preceding historical sketch would seem to point to four key factors underlying the overthrow of the imperial regime in 1974 and its bloody sequel. The first was the inadequacy of internal reforms stretching over several centuries, despite efforts by successive Emperors to introduce an effective system of military and civil administration. The inability of reforming Emperors to shield the peasantry from the plunder of regional chiefs, the soldiery, and the church is significant in this regard. The second is the atavistic sentiment of ethnicity which persisted despite efforts by several Emperors (especially the more recent ones) to fashion a cohesive national body politic from a not-too-dissimilar yet distinct grouping of cultures and communities. The third is the potent desire for more fundamental change (the phenomenon of rising expectations) released by the educational reforms of the last of the nation's Emperors. And the forth is the hostile geopolitical environment in which the country had lived for centuries, especially after the fall of Axum in the tenth century and subsequent rise of Islam in the Arabian peninsula. This was followed by the expansion to the Red Sea of Ottoman rule in the sixteenth century, and finally by the rise of European colonialism in the nineteenth century. The environment became particularly pernicious in the sixties and seventies of the twentieth century when Ethiopia's viability as a nation state was put to the test yet again. In the first decade of the twenty-first century, the environment remains an abiding political preoccupation. This set of factors rather than the much touted process of dialectical materialism would seem to offer a more relevant backdrop to the crisis of February-September 1974.

An attempt to interpret the crisis in the context of some such non-Marxist and Ethiopia-specific historical background can be gleaned from the policy document which proclaimed *Hibrettesebawinet* (Ethiopian Socialism) in the first few months of military rule.[9] The document concluded that the "February movement is a reply to all this;" and proceeded to formulate what was perceived to be a historically relevant political response to this challenge: *Hibrettesebwinet.*

With the benefit of hindsight, we can now say that political approaches more relevant than Marxism could have provided an agenda that might have prevented the 17-year murder, mayhem, and social dislocation under the Dergue. In its formative years, the Dergue seemed to be groping for a non-Marxist path to reform, as is evident from some of the earlier statements of Mengistu Haile-Marima and the other leaders. It is tragic that this early outlook did not prevail. Even more tragic is the fact that Ethiopia's youth and intellectuals were so totally seduced by Marxism that hardly any intellectual effort was spared to search for an alternative political approach to resolve the nation's problems. And in the few instances where efforts were made towards a broadly socialist but non-dogmatic outlook, an approach that seemed to offer a sufficiently radical and non-viloent response to the challenges the country was facing, they were scorned as ideologically strange by professional politicians of the extreme left.

Behind these 'strange' attempts were individuals in government who were not entirely ignorant of Marxism, as I indicate in various sections of this book. Indeed, in their own youth these persons had themselves been seduced by the ideology. The difference between them and the new, younger flag bearers of the ideology was simply that they had outgrown their infatuation with the irrelevant ideology, had had the opportunity to familiarize themselves with the experience of disillusioned former ideologues, had been greatly dismayed by the untold misery brought upon millions of innocent citizens in communist countries, and were not willing to see these repeated in their country.[10] The tragedy was that there was not a large enough constituency of moderate reformers to counter the extremism of the inexperienced young radicals.

What is the upshot of all this? the reader might ask. Stated briefly it is this: in terms of dialectical materialism there was nothing inevitable about a proletarian revolution in 1974, and the horrendous human suffering that its proponents set in motion. Undoubtedly, there was a passionate desire by Ethiopia's young Marxist zealots (goaded occasionally by expatriate Marxists playing out their unconsummated revolutionary fantasies at the expense of Ethiopian blood) to replicate a Bolshevik-style takeover of power. Attempts at other types of radical but peaceful reforms could have succeeded if the military had been driven by nationalistic sentiments. The opportunity was available to push through far reaching peaceful reforms that might have brought about tangible and sustainable improvements in the daily lives of the citizen. The country would have been spared the destructive experimentation with an ideology which so weakened it that it became easy prey to Somalia and the northern guerillas. Mengistu and his colleagues in the Military Committee were in a position to prevent this danger. That they failed to do so is a serious indictment of those who gratuitously confer upon them the undeserved label of nationalist.

Though far from being historically inevitable, a bloody Marxist revolution was being advocated in the years immediately preceding the 1974 crisis. Militant groups were busy laying the ground for a violent regime change. In this they were partly assisted by an Emperor who was deeply conscious of his image as a respected father figure of a venerable old culture and of a new politically vibrant continent. There were officials who advocated strong measures to pre-empt the looming crisis. The views of these officials did not prevail. The Emperor was concerned that the resulting spilling of blood would tarnish his image; and that of the country.

Right from the outset of the February crisis, radical students and teachers openly advocated the overthrow of the new Cabinet and the establishment of a people's government, despite the absence of a properly organized political body that could exercise power even provisionally. There were also those among University professors who called for a bloody end to the Emperor's regime. One of the many pamphlets issued by this group asked why progressive forces were overly concerned with the blood of exploiters: the aristocracy. Much of the resistance to the Cabinet, especially to the Prime Minister, and much of the strike action was orchestrated by such groups. The February events had not been anticipated even by Marxists. When the groundswell of defiance suddenly broke out, the activists started scurrying around to push their chances of taking over power.[11] But they were unprepared. To the military who were weighing their opportunity to lead, this vacuum was an irresistible invitation to usurp power.

It might be useful to pause at this point and trace briefly the origins and development of radical ideas among the Ethiopian student body in the sixties and seventies, how this created a fervour for a 'Marxist' revolution, and how it impacted on the events unfolding in the months of February to September 1974.

In the early and middle fifties when I was an undergraduate at the University College of Addis Ababa, student radicalism was practically non-existent. Total enrollment at the College was less than 100 in 1952 and less than 200 when I graduated four years later in 1956. Being the first institution of higher learning, the College was of special interest to its founder, Emperor Haile-Selassie. Students were pampered, as described in Chapter 2. The Emperor visited the College regularly. He inspected the quality of food, and chatted with students on how they expected to serve their country after completing their studies. Service to the nation was eagerly awaited by all.

As enrollment of Ethiopians and of African students on government fellowships (the Emperor's initiative) expanded, political awareness grew correspondingly. The majority of African students came from Kenya, Uganda, Tanganyika, Malawi and Zambia where the first generation of political leaders were aggressively campaigning for freedom from colonial rule. The slumbering Ethiopian student body was awakened by these students. The annual poetry contests held on the occasion of College Day festivities were an early manifestation of this awakening.

One entry was tellingly entitled 'Milassen Tewulign' (Leave Alsone My Tongue) by Abebe Worke who would later become a well-regarded judge in the country's Supreme Court. Another was a poem by Eyesus-Work Zaffu (a prominent businessman today) which was critical of Emperor Haile-Selassie. So critical was it that the University authorities decided that while his name was announced on commencement day, he would not be allowed to line up with other graduates to receive his diploma from the hand of the Chancellor, Emperor Haile-Selassie. He was told to sit still during the ceremony. When his name was read out, it was greeted with applause far louder and more boisterous than for the others. He doubtless felt vindicated.

There was no let up in the political content of the poetry contests. The authorities attempted to censor the texts in advance of the event. The students would not cooperate. In 1962 the Emperor failed to turn up at the year's College Day celebrations. The next phase was the publication of a student journal called *News and Views*.[12] Its increasingly defiant stand on political issues was met with restrictions imposed by University authorities. When the paper's Ethiopian editor was detained for refusing to submit articles for advance clearance, a Tanzanian student promptly filled his shoes and kept the paper going.

With the establishment of the National Union of Students in 1963, Berhane-Meskel Redda was elected Secretary General and political activism scaled new heights: Ian Smith's racist regime in Southern Rhodesia was condemned, the civil rights movement in the U.S. lauded, and radical reform measures for Ethiopia openly advocated. In February 1965, a petition was submitted to the Parliament demanding 'land to the tiller'; adopted thenceforth as a shibboleth of the student movement. All colleges in the country (Addis Ababa, Gondar, Bahr Dar, and Alemaya) now acted in concert. The principal secondary schools in Addis Ababa were also brought in. Diplomats from East European Embassies started entering the University campus in Addis Ababa in official mini buses loaded with flyers and pamphlets critical of the government, and with duplicating machines to print additional copies as and when needed. In 1969 a radical political pamphlet came out with the redoubtable and irreverent title: *Haile-Selassie's Feudal Fascism: A Threat to the African Revolution*. In it, an outright overthrow of the regime was advocated.

Overseas, two student organizations emerged; one in the U.S. and the other in Western Europe. Berhane-Meskel Redda and a few colleagues high jacked an Ethiopian Airlines flight and landed in Algiers where they were given sanctuary and training in guerilla warfare. They soon opened a dialogue with the group in Western Europe led by Haile Fidda. The two groups could not see eye to eye on either tactical or strategic issues, however. Berhane-Meskel and his friends struck out on their own, later forming the Ethiopian People's Revolutionary Party (EPRP) which advocated immediate armed struggle as the only way to a Marxist revolution in Ethiopia. Haile Fidda and his group argued that this was premature, and that it was imperative to first prepare the ground. They later created a rival political party called the All Ethiopia Socialist Movement (AESM).

A key issue on which both parties found common ground was the question of the rights of ethnic groups that had been hotly debated over the years. The final position adopted was Lenin's dictum on the self-determination of nationalities. This was done in an article in *Struggle* by one of the student leaders, Wallelign Makonnen. The uncomfortable reality of Lenin's refusal to grant such a right to the various nationalities under the Soviet Union after the first 'error' was committed with Finland's exercise of self-determination was conveniently overlooked; as was of course Stalin's subsequent persecution of minority nationalities.

Both political groups transplanted their operations to Ethiopia immediately after the outbreak of the February upheavals in 1974. They offered organizational and ideological support to trade unions, professional associations, and civil servants; and were largely responsible for destabilizing the government of Endalkatchew Makonnen. The country was force marched towards proletarian revolution, notwithstanding the fact that the proletariat in Ethiopia, the presumed vanguard of the revolution, had scarcely gone beyond its infancy. It was in consequence a mad dash towards a contrived revolution. In no sense could it objectively be regarded as the end product of the historical process of dialectical materialism. Of course, the same had been true of Lenin's October Revolution and the many revolutions later perpetrated in the name of Marx that had brought untold suffering to Eastern European and Asian peoples.

Eritrean and Tigrean students were the principal flag bearers of the right for self-determination. The Tigrean People's Liberation Front (TPLF) created in February

1975 in the arid environment of Dedebit (Western Tigrai) was initially in favour of exercising this right within a united Ethiopia. But the extremists within the party (principally Meles Zenawi, Sebhat Nega, and Abai Tsehaye) worked assiduously and often deceptively for a policy of total independence for Tigrai and managed to have it adopted as a party goal in 1985. The Eritrean People's Liberation Front (EPLF) was established in 1970 by a group of left leaning radicals who split from the nationalist Eritrean Liberation Front but who continued with the earlier objective of fighting for Eritrea's independence. It is one of the ironies of Ethiopia's history that descendents of a people who had been responsible for the birth and development of the history and culture of a nation should set about working so strenuously towards its undoing. Even during periods of severe internal strife in the past, none of the country's constituent elements had contemplated to strike out on its own. As Paul Henze says in his recent book, "None [of the regional chiefs], however, aimed to separate from Ethiopia. The idea of the Ethiopian Empire remained intact...."[13] Historian Shiferaw Bekelle also argues that during the era of princes in the 19th century, central authority did not collapse as many currently seem to assume.[14]

In the summer of 1974, the armed forces looked around to find that they, and only they, were the organized group that could take over the country. Prime Minster Endalkatchew Makonnen had been forced out of office in the middle of July 1974. Michael Imru's Cabinet which came immediately afterwards was now tottering. It had been in power or, more accurately, had been desperately trying to exercise power for about a month and half. Its legitimacy had been derived from that of the Emperor. When the Emperor was overthrown on 12 September 1974, it ceased to exist.

The Emperor Deposed

As always in mid-September, it was a delightful day in Addis Ababa: bright sunshine, patches of cloud just enough to break the vast expanse of a clear blue sky, a dust-free fresh breeze of air gently swaying the eucalyptus trees, and well watered green grass everywhere after three months of bountiful rains. At 9 o'clock in the morning of 12 September 1974, I was driving from my home located about two kilometres East of Emperor Haile-Selassie's Jubilee Palace towards my office, an equal distance due West of the Palace. As I approached the Palace, I saw army tanks posted in front of its gates. Military vehicles, tanks, and jeeps mounted with machine guns had become commonplace sights in Addis Ababa. I was nevertheless a little surprised by the appearance of the tanks so close to the Palace. I continued to drive at a pace which allowed me to have a visual tour d' horizon of the neighbourhood. At a distance, I recognized a Cabinet colleague who was trying to catch my attention. We both slowed down. He rolled down his window and said there was something in the air. We drove to my office.

My colleague called his home and asked someone to switch on the radio and listen to the broadcast. As he suspected (or perhaps knew from his contacts with clandestine underground groups), an announcement was being aired. The person at the other end of the phone relayed to him what he was hearing on the transistor radio. My colleague's ear was glued to the telephone while my attention was transfixed on the words he in turn was relaying to me every fifteen seconds or so. What was being communicated to him on the phone phrase by phrase were the contents of Proclamation No. 1 of Meskerem 2, 1967 (September 12, 1974), issued by the Provisional Military Administrative Council [the Dergue].

Emperor Haile-Selassie was deposed, said the announcer, and would be succeeded by Crown Prince Merid Azmatch Asfa Wossen. The Prince (who was undergoing medical treatment overseas) would be crowned as soon as he returned. The 1948 (1955) Constitution was abrogated. The new draft constitution requested by the Military Council would take its place.[15] Parliament would be closed until elections were held under the new constitution. Pending its adoption and a general election for the formation of a new government, state power would be exercised by the Military Council. "Strikes, unauthorized peaceful demonstrations, opposition to the motto of 'Ethiopia Tikdem' and any act aimed at disrupting the country's peace and security are prohibited," concluded the announcement.

There were other pronouncements which gave the proclamation an air of legality and political legitimacy, though legitimacy would turn out to be an elusive goal for the military junta to the very end of its rule. It was clear to all that the country was in for a major transformation. Less clear was precisely what shape it would take, although there were faint hopes that it would be a bloodless fundamental reform rather than revolution. The country was, of course, ripe for such a reform.

Regarding the monarchy, there were strong doubts that a coronation ceremony for the Crown Prince would take place and that he would accept the invitation to return home. In all their earlier broadcasts, the military had been referring to his father as 'King', the first of many attempts to humble someone who had been known as King of Kings or Emperor. The simpler and more modest title of King was what they used in Proclamation No. 1 in referring to the would-be monarch. It was doubtful that the military who had denigrated the monarchy extensively for some two and half months would suddenly change heart and enthrone a new 'King'; especially someone about whom they had said precious little. Had they said something about the Crown Prince that set him apart from the alleged wrong doing of his father, they would have at least been given the benefit of the doubt. They pointedly had not. And it would have been naïve if the soldiers expected anyone to believe that Crown Prince Asfa Wossen would be crowned to succeed his father, given all they had said about the Emperor and his family.[16] They probably were not all that naïve, and were perhaps using a rather hollow promise to buy time.

One particular incident made that poignantly clear. An extensive television documentary was aired on the eve of the putsch in which heart-breaking scenes were shown from the Wollo famine, interspersed with footage of earlier state banquets in which members of the royal family and the aristocracy reveled. There was also one scene which showed the Emperor feeding morsels of beef to his pets, a none-too-subtle commentary on a lavish lifestyle in the midst of a raging famine. Whether the lions were photographed at the time of the famine or, as was most likely, at an earlier date, no one ever asked. Such scenes were hardly calculated to invite the Crown Prince to hurry back home for his coronation.

Early in the morning of September 12, a thirteen-man delegation from the Military Council went to the Emperor's Palace and read out to him a short statement which indicated that he had been deposed. The leader of the delegation who read the statement, Major Debella Dinsa, describes the scene in the following way. "The Emperor looked at me closely. He had a poker face and showed absolutely no sign of fear.... He kept looking at us. There was total silence. I did not know exactly how much time had elapsed in this way, but it looked to me like eternity...We all got nervous. I got close to Ras Imru and asked him to do something. Time was against us. I told him I could not tell the Emperor to hurry up. The Ras said to the Emperor respectfully: 'What they ask is what should be done. It is all over now. We have no alternative'. Finally, the Emperor spoke: 'We have carefully listened to what you have said. If you have been motivated by the nation's interests, it is impossible to place personal interests above those of the nation. We have so far served our country and people to the best of our abilities. If you are saying that your turn has now come, you should make sure that you look after Ethiopia."[17]

In another version of the event, the Emperor is reported to have spoken thus: "We have heard what you have said. Being 'Emperor of Ethiopia' is more than a name. [We have worked] for the nation and the people in peace time, and in preparing the country to defend itself against its enemies [in times of war]: we have no doubt that these are known by our armed forces. Yet, when changes take place that are in the interests of the nation, they should prevail. We have heard what you have just read. You should now stop."[18] In the previous version, the command to "now stop" does not figure. The Dergue member who was recalling the Emperor's words might have dropped the phrase to avoid the impression of portraying the Dergue delegation as subordinates receiving instructions from someone whom they had just deposed. By all accounts, however, the Emperor maintained his customary stoicism and air of authority. And he most probably ordered the soldiers to stop the painful humiliation he was being subjected to.

His Imperial Majesty, Haile-Selassie I, Conquering Lion of the Tribe of Judah, Elect of God, Defender of the Faith, and King of Kings of Ethiopia finally left the national stage which he had dominated for upwards of half a century. And he did so with unaccustomed modesty. The Emperor was driven away in the back seat of a Volkswagen beetle to a poorly maintained bungalow in the compound of the Fourth

Army Division: his place of detention for a few weeks, after which he would be moved to another modest building in the premises of Menelik's Grand Palace.

The preamble of the Proclamation broadcast by Radio Ethiopia gave the reasons for the Emperor's removal as follows: abuse of the trust placed upon him by the people of Ethiopia, illegitimate use of his authority to benefit members of his family and those serving under him; responsibility for placing the country in the difficult predicament which it was experiencing; and old age which was increasingly preventing him from exercising his authority effectively. It was a humiliation more poignant than what Fascist Italy had done to him in 1936.

CHAPTER 11

March Towards Bloody Saturday

Enter Aman: A Much Acclaimed but Tragically Inadequate Leader

On September 12, the Cabinet was called to a morning meeting. Michael Imru was in the chair. General Aman Andom was seated to his left, and next to him sat a row of middle level and junior officers. Ministers took their seats to the right of Michael Imru. Immediately to the General's left sat a police colonel, followed by a short, undistinguished looking army major whose name would become a household word before long.

Hours earlier, General Aman had been appointed Chairman of the Provisional Military Administrative Council (the Dergue). The army major introduced the General as a man of great integrity and unrivalled leadership qualities in the country's armed forces. Aman then took the floor and asked Air Force Captain Sisay Habte to explain the objectives of the Dergue. The captain read out the fifteen points that had been broadcast earlier in the morning. These included reform of land tenure, of the administration of justice, respect for human rights, improvements in education, health, industry, etc., etc. There was nothing new or ideological about the goals, nor could one detect an overarching vision.

Following the captain's intervention, Aman read out a further eleven points, most of which were on the working relationship between the Cabinet and the Dergue. The first of these was to clear the air, in case there were any lingering doubts, as to who was now in charge. The Council of Ministers would carry out its functions working *under* the Dergue. A comical working arrangement was indicated next: contacts between the Council and the Cabinet would be by telephone only! To make assurance double sure, another directive was added: The Council would *submit proposals* to the Dergue. The Military's intention to minimize the role of the Cabinet, if not to sideline it altogether, was evident. They had usurped power and they were going to use it as they pleased. There was no surprise in any of this.

It was now Michael Imru's turn to speak. His premiership had expired after exactly 44 days. He started by thanking the military group for the explanations, saying that political power and responsibility had finally been brought together; an obvious allusion to the two and half-month period during which the military was the *de facto* government, while the Cabinet was only nominally so. It will be recalled that the Cabinet had previously expressed its frustrations in this regard and had unsuccessfully tried to resign. The political situation was now clearer. Michael Imru ended his brief remarks with the request that the military should give an early indication of changes they might wish to make in the composition of the Cabinet, an understandable request for someone who had been Prime Minister until a few hours before but who did not know exactly where he and his Cabinet colleagues now stood.

A short recess was announced. The Prime Minister, the Minister of Foreign Affairs and the soldiers stayed behind. When the rest of us returned some fifteen minutes later we found out that Michael Imru's earlier question had been answered. Aman announced that he would serve as Minister of Information and that all ministers would remain in their respective posts. In addition to his Chairmanship of the Dergue, General Aman would chair the Cabinet, with the police colonel (Belatchew Jemaneh) acting for him in his absence. Aman would retain his position of Defence Minister and Chief of the General Staff. Those who knew his history regarded this unprecedented four-fold responsibility as a mark of confidence by the military. Colonel Belatchew's designation as acting Chairman of the Council of Ministers was obviously intended to secure the loyalty of the Police Force.

All in all, prospects appeared moderately encouraging. The choice of Aman was one reason for this optimism, at least to those of us who knew him only from afar. Unlike the other soldiers in the Dergure, Aman was a known quantity. He had served the army for years, and enjoyed a reputation with the rank and file. He was also someone who was very much in favour of *lewt* (change): that much used code word for a general liberalization of the country's political, social and economic life that had been uppermost in the minds of reformers, past and present. Aman had also been close to General Mulugeta Buli and Colonel Workineh Gebeyehu, both casualties of the coup d'état of 1960. In addition, he had overseas exposure: as Ethiopia's military attaché in a couple of countries and as a trainee in western military academies.

Above all, Aman was an Eritrean who was perceived as an Ethiopian nationalist. If there was any person to whom a resolution of the long festering political problem in Eritrea should be entrusted to, that person appeared to be Aman. Indeed, soon after his appointment, the guerrilla fighters in Eritrea were said to have been greatly alarmed. It was reported that young fighters were deserting the front and going back home. Their parents were also said to be sending messages to the guerilla leaders that they should now negotiate with an Ethiopian leader who was one of their own and try to resolve the conflict peacefully. The alarm of the guerilla leaders was such that they were rumoured to consider assassinating a man that posed a mortal threat to their plans.

By 1974, the Eritrean problem had grown into an insurgency costing money and precious lives. The military had tried but had found it difficult to bring the guerillas to heel. Here was a popular general of Eritrean origin with impeccable nationalist credentials who was well placed to bring a peaceful end to the strife. As everyone at the time knew, Aman had been closely consulted by members of the Dergue every step of the way as they gradually asserted their power. They had recommended him to be the new Chief of Staff and Minister of Defence. Making him Chairman of the Dergue was not only indicative of the confidence the military reposed in him but was also reckoned to secure the support of senior officers who had been deliberately excluded from membership of the body. Moreover, criticism that the Dergue was simply an inexperienced group of ambitious junior officers would be allayed with him as a leader. Hopes were high that this was the man of the moment.

To be sure, there were doubts. Among those who knew him well, there was concern that he was perhaps temperamentally not altogether the right choice for the daunting task.[1] General Iyassu Mengesha, Ethiopia's Ambassador to the U.K. in the early seventies, was said to be dismayed when told that Aman was to become head of state. In his view, Aman's leadership qualities did not go beyond that of a brigade commander. General Iyassu had served years in Ethiopia's military. He had seen action during the Italian invasion in 1936, had served in the military in various capacities eventually becoming Chief of Staff of the armed forces. He was also UN Chief of Military Operations in the Congo in the early sixties. He was well placed to judge Aman. Colonel Tesfa Desta, Aman's former friend and colleague living in Germany as a political dissident, came to Ethiopia soon after Aman became Chairman, met with him, and left the country after only a few days. It wasn't exactly a reassuring manifestation of the Colonel's confidence in the General's ability to weather the political storm.

Even as these misgivings started to circulate, the expectant mood for *lewt* was so strong that people were prepared to give Aman the benefit of the doubt. He was a man who felt that he had been aggrieved by the Emperor's government. This put him squarely on the side of change. He knew the old regime well and, unlike the soldiers in the Dergue, was best placed to judge realistically how a bloodless transformation could be brought about. There was therefore optimism in the air that the country was fortunate to have such a man at the helm. It would also be true to say that there was a certain degree of wishful thinking in all this, for nobody wanted to see things go wrong and the country miss a rare chance for a bloodless radical change. The transformative role of a man in his country's history looked tantalizingly within reach.

The first Cabinet meeting chaired by Aman (16 September 1974) got off reasonably well. It started with a review of the recent history of the military movement: its general goals, the soldiers' strong commitment to national unity, and the need for a plan of action. This was followed by a tour d'horizon of the new direction of polices, short- as well as long-term, although there was no vision underpinning what the military leadership had in mind. At one point police Colonel Belatchew Jemaneh ponderously pointed out that the Dergue was non-ideological.[2]

At the end of the meeting, Aman said that long-term policies would be prepared jointly by the Dergue and Michael Imru; while those for the short-term would be handled by another joint Dergue-Cabinet committee. At the next meeting (September 19), it was decided that Michael Imru would chair a Cabinet committee on long-term policies, which included me and two other ministers. As will be seen later, this committee prepared a political philosophy which initially secured the backing of the military, but which soon fell prey to extremist forces. After taking care of a few housekeeping chores, it was time to address Eritrea: the critical issue of the day.

Much was, of course, expected of Aman in this regard. At that meeting, General Aman circulated two draft bills regarding the province's future. Ministers were told to read both on the spot and offer comments. While the swiftness with which they were presented for discussion reflected the urgency of the question, it was nevertheless not entirely reasonable to plunge into a discussion of the two documents there and then; especially on a subject of such sensitivity and consequence. We were given little choice in the matter, however. Neither did we know which department of government was tabling it for Cabinet discussion. A related question was whether the bills had been reviewed by the Dergue. No information was given on that either.

The atmosphere did not allow posing procedural questions of this nature. We were given no more than five minutes to go through the two drafts, after which the Chairman invited comments. A few ministers spoke. My own comments were, first, that the moment appeared to be propitious for resolving the Eritrean problem. The fresh and widespread spirit of change favoured major initiatives of this kind. Secondly, the idea of decentralization which seemed to be a key point of the two draft bills was an essential condition for resolving the Eritrean problem. Restoring Eritrea's federal status appeared to be the unstated aim of the drafts. This or some form of devolution was obviously needed for the province. I suggested that we adopt, as a matter of principle, this approach for all fourteen provinces.

We should obviously start with Eritrea, but make it clear to the Ethiopian people and the outside world that decentralization would be applied step by step to the other thirteen provinces. If we did not make that clear, we would be sending the wrong message to these provinces: i.e. that they too should take up arms if they wished a decentralized administration of the kind being offered Eritrea. I added that excluding the thirteen provinces would create the wrong perception: that Eritrea was a special case with a unique set of problems. For years we have been saying that Eritrea is historically and culturally an integral part of Ethiopia. Treating it differently would negate this perception. From Aman's body language, I sensed that he was not entirely pleased with my intervention.

Aman's summing up at the end of the deliberations was somewhat of a misrepresentation. He stated that the consensus was to treat Eritrea as a special case. There had been no such consensus. The Army Major who had introduced General Aman to the Cabinet in such glowing terms at the first Cabinet meeting and who sat next to him raised his hand. His intervention was laconic and, more significantly, appeared to be somewhat discordant with Aman's. He stated that the subject was an important matter of policy. Though he did not say why, it was evident that an altogether different voice of the Dergue was speaking. The intervention was by Major Mengistu Haile-Mariam. Aman decided that the matter would be studied further by a Cabinet committee chaired by the Minister of the Interior.

Mengistu's brief intervention pointed to a problem lurking in the background. As would become clear subsequently, Mengistu and his colleagues in the Dergue were not in favour of restoring the federal arrangement to Eritrea. The military either believed (wrongly in my view and those of other ministers) that a federal arrangement would jeopardize national unity or that restoring the federal arrangement to Eritrea would be perceived as capitulation to the demand of the Eritrean separatists. And capitulation was anathema to soldiers who had only months before made the daring move of taking over the political leadership of the country.[3]

The soldiers were concerned that restoring Eritrea's former federal arrangement would be the first step towards secession. Here was an early indication that the General had not done the necessary groundwork with members of the Dergue on this highly charged political issue. He did not exhibit the skill required to steer this vital piece of legislation through the Cabinet or, as Mengistu's intervention implied, the Dergue. He seems to have underestimated the importance of advance consultation with key members of the Dergue; a surprising manifestation of poor judgment given that the Dergue was, to all intents and purposes, the one and only representative body of the armed forces and of the country at large.

The Eritrean question came up again at the third meeting of the Cabinet the following week (23 September). The Chairman announced that the matter had been submitted to the Dergue, that discussions were proceeding there, and that a joint ministerial-Dergue committee would study the two draft bills and present its recommendations. This was decided in the morning. The meeting continued in the afternoon during which the General announced that legislation was no longer necessary, and that an internal administrative circular would suffice to enable the Governor of Eritrea to have the necessary authority to administer the province. The issue would not come back to the Cabinet under Aman's chairmanship.

236 | TEKALIGN GEDAMU

What happened was not clear to me or my colleagues. But Aman was obviously facing difficulty with his plan. Hindsight suggests that he probably brought the issue to the Cabinet first in the expectation that the weak body would easily be intimidated into accepting his proposal. He would then take it to the Dergue and request a quick endorsement of a decision passed by a body made up of people more experienced than members of the Dergue. If so, his assumption of a compliant Cabinet did not hold.

Two other questions of policy came up before the Cabinet in subsequent meetings. The first (on October 3) was on land reform and the second (on October 17) on the national student campaign called *Edget Behibret* (Development Through Cooperation). The need to reform the country's land tenure system had been a long standing agenda. Limited attempts had been made during the regime of Emperor Haile-Selassie. The last land reform bill presented to the Ethiopian Parliament in the final days of the Emperor's rule aimed at improving tenant-landlord relationship with the view to maintaining the interests of the two parties in some reasonable balance. Everyone was aware that it had not gone far enogh.

As I mentioned in Chapter 8, the Minister of Land Reform had been working on a reform bill. On October 3, he presented a bill that had three key features. The first was a ceiling of 40 hectares placed on all privately owned land. This was a relatively drastic measure aimed at freeing up land for redistribution to landless peasants. No compensation was to be given for land repossessed in this way (a second drastic feature); although improvements would be eligible for compensation. The third feature was the granting of land averaging 5-10 hectares to landless peasants.

A number of questions were put to the Minister. Would not the drastic provisions of the bill (especially the cap on maximum holdings) give rise to resistance? The Minister responded that this was unlikely. Mengistu Haile-Mariam felt that the ceiling was perhaps too limiting: would 40 hectares not quickly dwindle into yet smaller plots through successive fragmentation? He had not yet been subjected to the *leb leb*[4] Marxist training that he would receive later from young ideologues.

There were others who felt that the bill did not go far enough. The left leaning member of the Dergue, Captain Mogus, said that private ownership appeared to be the guiding spirit of the bill. An alternative (and better) approach would be to make land the collective asset of the people of Ethiopia. I do not recall Aman saying much on the subject. The debate concluded with the recommendation that the bill be sent to the Economic and Social Committee of the Cabinet.

The other major issue to come before the Cabinet was the plan to send university and secondary school students to the countryside to educate the peasantry. But the more urgent reason had little to do with imparting knowledge to farmers. The school year was about to begin and the Dergue was concerned that the students would create trouble. Secondary school students had marched against the new civilian Cabinet in March 1974. Together with teachers and the Ethiopian Confederation of trade unions they had called for an immediate establishment of a peoples' government. The Dergue was apprehensive that such protest marches would resume. Something had to be done. Hence, the idea of closing the nation's secondary and higher education establishments for an entire academic year during which students would be conveniently dispersed in the countryside.

But what would they exactly do there? It was said that they would raise the awareness of the peasantry on subjects like land reform and revolution. A handful of left wing Dergue members had already set up an informal group of young civil servants in the Ministry of Land Reform to prepare a soviet-type land reform draft proclamation which sidelined the draft bill presented by Minister Bellette Gebre-Tsadik. The students would sell this to the rural population. They would also conduct classes in the three R's, in hygiene and basic health. The Somali government had apparently carried out something along these lines.

A Dergue member, Major Berhanu Bayih, presented the programme to the Cabinet in the form of a proclamation. A number of ministers immediately saw the far reaching implications of the draft proclamation: political, social, developmental, organizational and budgetary. There was little evidence that these had been worked out in any detail. Questions raised were not satisfactorily answered. Ministers were concerned that the programme would destabilize the countryside. Perhaps that was what was intended, the goal being to prepare the ground for revolutionary land reform. The idea of getting the students out of Addis Ababa to pre-empt a violent confrontation with the military had great appeal to the soldiers. But sending high school and college students to the countryside was bound to throw up fresh difficulties. Students had become a fiercely radical, independent, and a vocal political group in the country. It was difficult to see how the Dergue would control the programme and prevent problems that might be far worse than the troubles the students would foment through their marches if they were allowed to remain in school.

Some details of the draft bill were discussed four days later to get Cabinet approval for a budget of Birr 45 million (about U.S. $22 million). The plan was to dispatch 60,000 students, university professors, and teachers to the countryside for a period of one academic year.[5] Millions of peasant farmers would be educated in various fields; 5,000,000 in literacy alone. It was a gigantic programme. The Minister of Finance was cowed into agreeing that an initial Birr 10 million could be secured, with the rest following later. General Aman was not an active participant of these discussions.

A few meetings passed that dealt with issues of a routine nature but in which the Chairman's conduct took on an increasingly belligerent tone. He became irritable and complained that civilian officials did not seem to understand the discipline of the military. One day he threatened ministers with sanctions if they were found wanting in their performance. And he left no doubt as to what they would consist of. Ministers should not forget, said he, that their predecessors were behind bars. It was plain that he wished to intimidate and discourage serious discussion.

The Chairman also seemed to think that he was not being accorded the deference due to a head of state. Verbal and written warnings started to be addressed to ministers who did not show respect. One was summoned by the *aide-de-camp* to be told that he had been observed balancing himself on the hind legs of his chair, as people sometimes do when they are in a pensive frame of mind or wish to stretch while still in their chairs. Another minister was criticized for getting up to open a window to allow fresh air to come into a stuffy meeting room. Without the chairman's green light! On yet another occasion a minister made remarks not altogether to the liking of the Chairman, whereupon he ostentatiously reached into his pocket for a piece of paper and menacingly jotted down something. It was clear that the minister's unwelcome remarks had been noted and something nasty would follow.[6] I myself was able to assess the judgment and leadership style of the General in the course of two separate incidents in which I was personally involved.

One day, I was called to his office to respond to a startling question. "We have uncovered U.S. $16 billion dollars hidden away by the Emperor. How can we use it for the benefit of the Ethiopian people?" asked the General. Sixteen billion dollars in cash! Incredible, I said to myself, and proceeded to provide him with an illustration that I believed would demonstrate the implausibility of the figure. I informed him that Ethiopia's gross domestic product at the time was about $2 billion. How could the Emperor possess wealth that would take 26 million Ethiopians eight years to produce? I would be surprised if some of the well known billionaires in the U.S. were to claim *assets* worth $16 billion, leave alone cash.

The General was not pleased. His body language seemed to say that I was only being asked to advise how best the military government could use this money for the benefit of the Ethiopian people. I said that projects gathering dust on shelves for lack of funds were the first place to start. We should then initiate a vast programme of opening up the country with roads, railways, airports; and invest heavily in agriculture, energy, education, and public health. For good measure, we could declare that the people of Ethiopia would be free of all forms of taxation for the following 10 years. Tax revenues in those days brought in $100 million annually. That would mean that we would forego roughly two and a half billion dollars in uncollected revenue over the ten-year-period; about 16% of the $16 billion presumably stashed away somewhere in a Swiss bank. We should obviously refrain from building monuments, I added. From what I could judge, the last point struck the General as superfluous or even provocative.

No such money was ever uncovered, although a number of attempts were made to get information from the Swiss authorities. The view in Dergue circles at the time was that the Swiss were reluctant to divulge information, citing rules on banking confidentiality. Was this the real reason for the government's failure to obtain the alleged money? Years later, I was informed by someone who seemed to be in the know that the military, in searching through the Emperor's private quarters, had come across a figure which was 11 digits long It was the number of a modest bank account opened by Empress Menen for the children of her deceased son, Prince Makonnen, into which the Emperor himself had made a one-time deposit. Might this have been the origin of the $16 billion bonanza?

It was not clear if the military finally uncovered the precise balance of the account. If they did, it was never announced to the public, probably because it did not match the military's much publicized and astronomical sum. Revealing it would probably have been an embarrassment. Ethiopia was not a Middle Eastern country awash with oil; nor Emperor Haile-Selassie a General Abacha, a Mobutu, a Ferdinand Marcos, or a General Suharto. The Emperor naturally appreciated the value of wealth, but I never heard anyone credibly accusing him of cupidity or plunder, unlike many members of the Dergue, including Mengistu Haile-Mariam who allegedly stole an appreciable amount of money on his departure to Zimbabwe seventeen years later. I shall come back to this in Chapter 13.

In another incident illustrative of the General's style of leadership, a staff in his office was instructed to send me a warning letter for an unscheduled Cabinet meeting which I did not attend. I expressed surprise at the tone and content of the letter, said I had not seen the agenda of the unscheduled meeting, and was at the time tied up with the Cabinet's own official business. A second and far more threatening warning note was sent to me. Things had degenerated to the level of a school master and his pupil, but a school master who was no stranger to the loaded gun. I readied myself to resign, but thought it prudent to refrain from acting precipitously and decided to sleep over the matter for a day or so. As it turned out, the General was locked in a deadly power struggle with the Dergue at that very moment. To submit a letter of resignation in the midst of that crisis was plainly out of question. I decided to await the outcome of the tug-of-war instead.

The genesis of this power struggle went back to the time when Aman was appointed Chairman of the Dergue. A few days after the appointment, he raised an issue which put him on a collision course with the Dergue. One day, Aman came late to a meeting of the Dergue. When asked by Mengistu to take over the meeting, the General curtly told him to wind up "what you have started."[7] In due course, Aman assumed the chair and surprised the assembled soldiers with an unexpected question: "How far does your confidence in me go?" he asked. There was total silence, with everyone looking at each other in bewilderment. Mengistu replied that it was because the Dergue had full confidence in him that he had been appointed Chairman. A non-commissioned officer spoke in the same vein. Aman brushed aside the non-commissioned officer's support with the words: "I am awaiting the views of officers." Some half a dozen officers took the floor and expressed their confidence in him. Having secured their support, the General said, "You are aware that the post of Commander-in-Chief of the armed forces is vacant. As Head of State, I should assume that responsibility. What is your position on this question?"

Starting with Mengistu, the soldiers said that it would not be wise to place such a heavy responsibility on the shoulders of one man, sensing that if Aman assumed the post he would exercise power without their advice and consent. When Aman asked how the armed forces were to be commanded, Mengistu replied that this was the responsibility of the Dergue sitting in plenary and that General Gizzaw Belayneh, the Commander of Ground Forces, would provide the required assistance. Aman got annoyed and said that Gizzaw did not have the requisite capabilities.

His handling of the question left much to be desired and his ill advised remark in regard to a fellow general well regarded in the Army was a *faux pas* which spoke eloquently of his arrogance. Serious doubts emerged about his motives and his own leadership qualities. From then on his movements were closely watched, and his telephone tapped. Members of the Dergue began to say that there was too much concentration of power in his hands: Chairman of the Dergue, Chairman of the Council of Ministers, Defence Minister, and Chief of the General Staff. They now asked one of their colleagues, Dergue member Captain Mogus Wolde-Michael, to see how the General's powers could be brought into a more reasonable relationship with other centres of decision making. It was a question of time before something would erupt.

Insofar as the Eritrean question was concerned, Aman was no doubt aware that much was expected of him. Indeed a ceasefire had been announced after which he had toured Eritrea and held extensive consultations with elders. The ground for a peaceful resolution of the conflict appeared to be taking shape. Eye witnesses said that his tour was received well. Mengistu seemed to be worried about a well known General stealing the limelight and perhaps striking out on his own at some opportune time. Aman returned and rendered an optimistic report to the Dergue about his Eritrean visit. Immediately afterwards, the suspicious Mengistu dispatched his intelligence officer to check out things on the ground. The officer returned with a less encouraging report. Indeed, he warned that unless reinforcements were sent immediately, Eritrea would be a lost case. The guerrillas had apparently taken advantage of the ceasefire and brought up their forces to the gates of the capital. Government soldiers who had followed instructions to stay in their barracks felt gravely threatened. Talk soon started in Dergue circles about the size and composition reinforcements.

In the course of a Dergue meeting over the issue a few weeks later, Aman said sending reinforcements would be wrong at a time when negotiations for peace were taking place. As the discussion progressed, an Eritrean member of the Dergue remarked "when will the Eritrean people be free from the constant battering of the military?" This was bad enough for members of the Dergue. But making matters worse, Aman dropped his guard and added "if the Eritrean people wish the province's federal status to be restored, who is to stand in their way?"[8] That impolitic statement did much to undermine his credentials as an Ethiopian nationalist in the eyes of the military.

A little later in the discussion, he showed flexibility and supported a suggestion by someone to send a few tanks, not infantry. In the book by Tesfaye Ristie cited in endnote 11 later in this chapter, a young member of the Dergue (Captain Endale Tessema) is reported to have said that he was surprised someone who was familiar with Eritrea's terrain and who had the nation's interests at heart would advice that tanks be dispatched. This was an inappropriate and risky response; inappropriate because tanks were not suitable to the mostly rugged terrain occupied by the guerillas and risky because the tanks would be moved from the Somali front at a time of grave threat. This would only give the guerillas time to execute their plan: take over the city of Asmara and declare independence. The Dergue could not fold their arms and watch while this happened. Aman was infuriated with this impudent affront to what he said was his superior knowledge of military matters and his nationalist credentials. And he stormed out of the meeting.

Aman now decided to part company with the Dergue. He drafted a telegramme to all units of the armed forces saying that he was unable to work with the Dergue and was resigning with immediate effect. His secretary, Colonel Imbibel Ayele, was ordered to make arrangements for the telegramme to be sent to all units. The colonel immediately passed the contents of the message to the communications unit of the Ministry of Defence, with the General's instructions that it be dispatched right away. Conscious of the looming crisis and mindful of how he could get himself into trouble if he failed to play his cards well, Colonel Imbibel slipped a copy of the General's telegramme to Mengistu Haile-Mariam.

This caused alarm. The chief of the communications unit in the Ministry of Defense was quickly summoned by Mengistu and asked whether the telegramme had been sent. The chief replied that it was still with the staff of the Ministry who had been instructed to delay dispatch until further notice. Mengistu and his friends in the Dergue did not believe that the staff would keep such a piece of dramatic news to themselves. Discipline was very lax at the time and communications staff throughout the military were routinely sharing information on anything deemed newsworthy. What would be the reaction of the various units to the telegramme? It was a most unsettling thought. General Aman, not the Dergue, was held in high esteem and soldiers could side with the General over the row. At the very least, they could ask why the Dergue wasn't allowing the General to manage the country in the way he knew best. After all he, not the Dergue, had the experience. It was not hard to imagine that General Aman had all this in mind when he instructed that the telegramme be communicated to all units.[9]

Bloody Saturday: The Final Act of Fin D'Époque

Days before his final break with the Dergue, Aman was apparently preparing the ground for a showdown. He met General Gizzaw Belayneh at his residence and instructed him to move army units from the Eastern Front to Addis Ababa. Gizzaw asked why forces should be moved from a zone of high alert to Addis Ababa where there was no obvious need for them. He demurred, left Aman's residence and proceeded to his office in the Ministry of Defence. Aman reached Gizzaw on the phone a little later and enquired if his instruction had been carried out. Gizzaw not only replied that it had not been, but also advised against it. Sensing that Aman was positioning himself for a confrontation with the Dergue, Gizzaw suggested that accommodation rather than confrontation was the better course. Neither General was aware that the phone line was being tapped by Dergue agents.

The date of the conversation was Friday the 15th of November. It was probably after this that Aman decided to resign and had the telegramme sent to the Ministry of Defence. The following Saturday Aman failed to turn up in his office. The Dergue now made a hasty effort to take charge of the dangerous situation. They sent messages to Aman's residence that matters could be resolved through discussion. Ideas were exchanged through third parties and a brief cooling off period was secured. In the meantime, some middle ranking officers outside the Dergue approached Aman and told him that arrangements had been made to whisk him out of Addis Ababa discretely and take him to the Third Army Division in Harrar which he had once commanded. Aman fatefully turned down the offer with the dismissive remark that he was not a coward and wasn't running away from anybody. The young officers were heart-broken and were so worried about the turn of events that they fled the country post-haste.

The negotiations between Aman and the Dergue appeared to be leading to a compromise. And then something happened suddenly. The talks were broken off. The reason was Aman's displeasure at the publication of Mengistu Haile Mariam's profile in the government daily, *Addis Zemen*, in which the officer's leadership qualities were extalled.[10] The article came out on Tuesday, i.e. the third day of Aman's absence from his office and, more importantly, in the middle of the efforts to persuade him to go back to his office. The profile's opening words referred to Mengistu as "a young, decisive, and passionately patriotic officer who coined the motto 'Ethiopia Tikdem' around which the Ethiopian people and the armed forces have rallied." Speeches he made to various military units were also reported.

Nothing had been officially written on this officer before. Why this was done in the middle of the sensitive negotiations is not altogether clear. Was it to derail them? How could this be, given the eagerness of the Dergue to come to an amicable resolution of their differences with Aman? Were the soldiers trying to put pressure on Aman that it would be in his best interest to mend his ways, for if he did not the Dergue already had a tested leader to take his place? This is also plausible. Having been informed of

Mengistu's visit to the troops, Aman had objected strongly to an initiative that had been taken behind his back. He was reconciled only when he asked and was assured that the visit will not be reported in the press. Aman's reaction was predictable when the newspaper came out with a story of the visit and the profile. He broke off the talks, perhaps sensing that Mengistu was being groomed for leadership and that the talks were only a smokescreen. A man not known for his modesty, he might have also taken the article as an affront to his honour and reputation. Tesfaye Ristie writes that Aman also called Gizzaw on the phone and told him to lead his men against the immature people in the Dergue (far more offensive language was reportedly used) and save the nation. Gizzaw advised restraint. The conversation was once again tapped.

Mengistu now decided to arrest General Aman. He got the Dergue to issue instructions to a selected group of officers and men of the Imperial Guard to apprehend the General. According to Tesfaye Ristie's account, the men said they could not "raise their arms against a man like Aman." A second group of soldiers was assembled for the same purpose. Their response was the same. A third attempt with yet another group was made which also failed. At that point, Mengistu turned to the Dergue's own security chief, Colonel Daniel Asfaw, who put together a contingent composed of some members of the Dergue as well as men drawn from a commando unit brought from a military base outside the capital.

The Dergue was called into an emergency session the following Thursday (November 21) to discuss (it was said) the fate of detained government officials. Mengistu had apparently made up his mind to get rid of Aman but to do so as part of a larger massacre of senior officials in detention. As he chaired the meeting of the Dergue (re-enforced for the purpose by the attendance of soldiers belonging to a group called the Ne'ous or 'junior' Dergue), emissaries were sent to Aman to request him to give himself up peacefully. When he refused, Dergue officers were sent with a message that if he persisted in his refusal, the Dergue would be obliged to send armed men and heavy weapons. Aman allegedly responded that he was ready to fight. Colonel Daniel took his men and a tank to the General's residence late on Saturday afternoon. Through a loudspeaker, his soldiers called out on the General and asked him to surrender. He refused. Shots were exchanged and part of the front wall of Aman's residence was blown out by cannon fire from the tank. And Aman sadly perished. Whether he took his own life as his sympathizers claimed later or was a casualty of the cannon fire as his enemies (including Mengistu) alleged, it was not immediately evident. What was clear was that he had put himself in an inextricable situation.[11]

From the outset, Mengistu knew that getting rid of Aman would be a supremely risky undertaking. From his perspective, it was imperative that the murder be perceived as part of a wider security operation. And so he proceeded with a plan to implicate senior civil and military officials of the previous government with crimes against the nation. At the meeting of the Dergue that Saturday, charges were read against each detainee which said that he had abused his power while in office and was responsible for the loss of life during the Wollo famine. As each name was read out, participants raised their hands to vote yes or no to pass a death sentence.

A few voices were raised questioning the wisdom of such a precipitous act. Was it right to pass a death sentence without a proper trial? asked a participant. The Dergue had committed itself to bringing wrong doers to justice. A Commission of Inquiry was already examining the case of the detainees. What was the reason for the haste? Members airing these views were outvoted. Only a simple majority was required to pass the death sentence. Fifty two former officials of Emperor Haile-Selassie, three Dergue members presumed to be close to General Aman, and four military men of junior rank accused of an attempt to overthrow the Dergue, were sentenced to death. General Aman was the sixtieth victim who had been murdered earlier upon Mengistu's instructions. In the evening of the same day, the detainees were handcuffed in pairs and were driven by truck to Addis Ababa's central prison. There they were savagely mowed down by machine gun fire.

At 8:30 a.m. the following morning (Sunday 24 November), Radio Ethiopia carried the news of the massacre. Addis Ababa was stunned into silence. People walking the streets were subdued. If the military thought that those who had been clamouring for blood would come out in a show of support, they were badly mistaken. It was evident that there were people who felt that the soldiers had done the right thing. But it would have been imprudent for any of them to have come out in the open to say that the victims deserved what they got.

In a tortuous and transparently self-serving interview about his political experience that appeared in book form some twenty years later, Mengistu Haile-Mariam makes the following startling points in regard to this brutal act:[12]

"*First,* the meeting called on Thursday November 21 was convened to discuss the case of General Aman. "He was the sole agenda item. There was absolutely nothing about the former government officials of Haile-Selassie."

Second, the issue of the imprisoned officials was raised from the floor. "I remember the soldier who raised it. He was lieutenant Keddu from the medical corps of the Third Army Division. He was a fire spitting speaker.....'Today is a historic day,' he said. 'It is Ethiopia's resurrection....Let us make good use of this day. We should not disband without deciding on these murderers of Wollo and of Ethiopia; these people who are being fed on *dorro wott* [choice Ethiopian dish of spiced chicken stew]. Don't you smell it [the detained officials were kept in the basement beneath the hall where the meeting was taking place]? Even today these so called prisoners are sucking our blood,' he said. Applause and clamour rocked the meeting. Others asked why a meeting had been called to discuss the problem of just one general. 'He is nothing. We can dispose of him in an instant. After witnessing the famine in Wollo, the people are asking why these pigs are being fed and cared for. When are we going to decide on this question?'

Members of the *Ne'ous Dergue* were present. We were only one hundred and twenty. We were swallowed, we were submerged. The meeting turned into a shouting match and *fukkera* [war chants]. Individual cases were not properly weighed, nor the law observed... I was respected and loved by all [sic]. Never in my life had I experienced such a personal affront....[13] I was being accused of defending the detained officials........ *As far as I am concerned, I did not support the measure taken. Nor should other Dergue members be held accountable for the killing of the sixty officials."* (Italics added)

Third, when asked if he recalled individuals who supported the decision to execute the prisoners and others who did not, he gave the names of Atnafu, the second deputy chairman, and others in the Dergue who pushed for their execution. "Atnafu said they should be killed. For him it was not a question of principle, of revolution, or justice. He was not after ascertaining the guilt of the prisoners. He linked their case to the execution of Belai Zelleke.[14] 'It was only in a feudal court that the patriot Belai was found guilty and publicly hanged' was what Atnafu said." Mengistu also speaks of others "who spoke in support of me, in particular the Eritrean Michael Gebre-Negus. It was only in Aman's case that he showed bias. There were others who said: 'these people are under our control, under our feet. They are as good as dead. We have promised to bring them to justice. What will the public say about our decision? Those with legal training also raised questions."

Fourth, a few days before the incident "I was among a group of soldiers touring the city," continues Mengistu. "The turnout was immense. What were people saying to us?" he carries on. "'Give it to the pigs. What are you waiting for? See them off.' That was what they were shouting to us." Mengistu adds the names of two senior members of the Commission of Inquiry who pushed the Dergue to execute the officials, one of them openly telling the military to 'kill' them.

Fifth, the interviewer asks Mengistu point blank: "Do you recollect how you yourself voted? Was there anyone in regard to whom you raised your hand either to say that he should or should not be killed?" Mengistu's unedifying response is: "Listen, I am the chairman. My duty is to guide the discussions, as any chairman would. I present the agenda, facilitate the debates, and see that everyone is given a chance to have his say. When I feel everyone has had his say and is satisfied, I say, 'You have said such and such. Let us now wind up.' To proceed towards voting, I first ask: 'Are you prepared to vote?' Only when there is consent, does voting start. Nothing is done without the consent of the house. Votes are called. Those in favour of the death sentence raise their hands. This is recorded. The same procedure is followed for voting against, and for abstentions. We then follow our rules to verify that there is a simple majority for or against each individual's execution. Decisions are taken accordingly. *My voting or not voting does not make any difference* (italics added)"

The interviewer makes one last effort. "Participants say that the meeting was under your control, and place full responsibility on your shoulders." One thing is true," responds Mengistu. "All of us believe that the affair was not right. We *presided over the implementation of a wrong act.... But there was nothing regarding the imprisoned officials that I personally presented to the Dergue.*" Earlier in the interview he also tells the interviewer what is perhaps the whitest of his white lies when he says: "*On my part, I did not support the step taken*" [i.e. the killing of the officials]. (Italics added)

He, of course, was an active participant. In a recently published book, Mengistu Haile-Mariam's photograph figures prominently alongside that of other members of the Dergue with his left hand raised to vote yes to the decision to murder the officials.[15] But there is, of course, more to go by than a solitary photograph. Appendix 1 is an English translation of the official execution order in Amharic signed by none other than Mengistu Haile-Mariam himself. In it he gives detailed orders about who (54 senior civilian and military officials of Emperor Haule-Selassie) should be executed, how (by firing squad), when (at 20h00), and where the executions should be carried out (the central prison). A few issues of detail seem to have been recorded inaccurately. The first was the name of General Aman whom they had already shot and was included in the list only after the fact. The second was Michael Imru who was mercifully not killed, although he appears 30th on the list. Whether this was an oversight or a last minute change of mind, only history will tell; although I myself am inclined to think that it was a mistake. The military were favourably disposed to him and his father, both viewed as progressive individuals. Apart from these and a few other minor errors occasioned by the intense nervousness under which members of the Dergue must have carried out their plan, everything else was planned meticulously. Even the place and manner as to how the bodies should be disposed is indicated with chilling precision: a common grave large enough to accommodate 54 bodies should be excavated by bulldozer in the premises of the prison. Stripped of its glaring lies, inconsistencies, implausible statements, the repeated but unsuccessful attempts to dodge personal responsibility for the massacre, enough of what Mengistu says, comes near to saying, or does not say at all, clearly establishes his personal culpability. Scheming, mendacious, murderous, vindictive, and power hungry by nature, he was undoubtedly the chief architect and principal actor of the entire sordid affair.[16]

Some six years later, Patriarch Tewoflos, Dejazmatch Kassa Wolde-Mariam, Tsehafe Te'ezaz Teferra Worq (the old former Minister of the Imperial Court) and a few other former officials were marched out of prison, taken to a safe house, and were coldly murdered. The gruesome manner of their killing is still talked about in Addis. One by one, the unsuspecting victims were led to a dark room in the safe house. As they entered thugs jumped on them from behind with ropes (some say with barbed wire) and strangled them to death. Mengistu was of course the mastermind of this too. Telling white lies about his past is the only crutch that keeps him going. It should also be recalled that he and his colleagues were on trial in Addis Ababa at the time of the interview. He obviously had little interest in providing evidence to the public prosecutor.

Regarding Emperor Haile-Selassie's death, Mengistu says that the old man died of "a relapse of his prostate condition" following a successful surgery. The interviewer asks him if he denies the charge that he "had a hand in the death of Emperor." "I have no reason why I should have him killed" is his reply. Among the more compelling reasons to believe that the Emperor was murdered upon his instructions is the testimony of a valet who attended to him throughout the period of his detention. In the evening of 26 August 1975 the valet went to the Emperor's place of detention to spend the night. Colonel Daniel Asfaw, Mengistu's hatchet man and the chief of the Dergue's murder squad, told him not to bother spending that night with the Emperor. "It was around nine o'clock when I entered the Emperor's quarters to inform him of Daniel's decision," says the valet. The Emperor "got up from his bed and said, 'Do they find the room too crowded? You may leave.' Having said that, he knelt down, and wiping tears from his eyes, added: 'Oh Ethiopia; have we wronged you? Have we not toiled for you?'"; a rare and understandable moment of emotion for the usually phlegmatic monarch.

When the valet arrived the following morning, he saw the dead body of the Emperor on the bed. "I smelt the odour of a strange chemical in the room and saw a bandage near the neck of the Emperor."[17] It is believed that ether was used to put him to sleep permanently. The old method of inducing anesthesia on patients undergoing surgery was to cover their nose with bandage, sprinkle a measured amount of liquid ether on it, and allow the patient to breathe the chemical as it evaporated. A high dosage could cause the patient to breathe a lethal amount of the chemical to cause death. Besides, the manner and place of the Emperor's burial (some nine feet deep directly beneath Mengistu's own office) was intended to leave no trace behind. Given all this, few would be persuaded by Mengistu's mendacity.[18]

The quarrel with Aman undoubtedly precipitated the murder of the 60 officials. Had the quarrel not occurred, would the Dergue have refrained from killing the former officials? we might ask. It is difficult to say with certainty, but indications are that they would have executed some government officials at some stage. Betru Admassie, the former General Manager of Ethiopian Telecoms who spent some eight years in detention, once asked a detained ex-member of the Dergue, Major Teferra Tekle-Ab, whether the military had initially planned to kill government officials.[19] The reply was that they only wanted to get rid of a few senior generals. Air Force Lt. General Assefa Ayene was mentioned as an example. When asked why, Teferra responded that this was a General who was biased in favour of the better educated and younger members of the Ethiopian military. He was perceived to be divisive and had therefore to be removed.

There is little doubt that the deaths caused by the Wollo famine triggered the 1974 crisis and the eventual takeover of power by the military. The event was endlessly broadcast in the media as a crime which called for strong punitive measures against its perpetrators. 'The criminals should be dealt with' was the mood in the Dergue and among extremists. New legislation had also been initiated when Aman was still in power for trying those responsible for the famine. Article 27, Section 1 of the legislation specifically targeted the role of former officials in this regard. The maximum penalty was death.[20]

It was unclear whether the soldiers would implicate the Emperor in this regard. Some of us were apprehensive that they might, although he could not be accused of being aware but not taking action. I myself raised the issue one day with Captain Mogus, the left leaning member of the Dergue who was often inclined towards extreme measures. I told him that it would be politically disastrous to take precipitate action against the Emperor. He was a much revered figure internationally, especially in Africa and among those who remembered his struggle against Mussolini. His appearance before the League of Nations in 1937 in a dignified gesture of moral defiance to both the League and Fascist Italy had been indelibly etched in people's minds. You people should exercise great care, I said to him. I received no direct response.

This was a time when the military were insecure of their position. There had been talk by some senior military officers to forcibly eject members of the Coordinating Committee of the Armed Forces from their place of work, the headquarters of the Fourth Army Division. They were also concerned that they would not be accepted as legitimate leaders of an ancient monarchy unless they instilled fear among the people. The country's Emperors were of course feared and respected. But they had historical legitimacy. The junior soldiers had no legitimacy to rely on. They only had the gun. They believed they had to use the only weapon in their possession to instill fear and impose their rule. All this predisposed them to violent action.

To what extent would Aman have restrained the soldiers, had he not fallen out with them so early in the movement? If anyone was in a position to dissuade, it was of course Aman. He was regarded highly by the troops. But did he have the inclination to restrain members of the Dergue? And did he possess the leadership qualities required for bringing about a fundamental but peaceful transformation to the nation? After he passed away, a few of us who had briefly worked with him tried to find answers to these questions, especially the reasons for his popularity.

Several factors seemed to be at play regarding his standing with the troops. There was his bravado and his chumminess with the ordinary soldier. When the Ethiopian army was being re-established after the Fascist occupation, he was among the few relatively educated young officers in a largely undereducated officer corps drawn principally from the anti-Fascist resistance movement. His military good looks, his defiance of arrogant British training officers, defiance which sometimes manifested itself on the dance floor on Saturday nights at the Ras Hotel, and his endearing *faux pas* in his strenuous efforts to master the Amharic language which he had no opportunity to learn during his youth in the Sudan; all of these combined to create a persona admired by soldiers whose officer corps was known for its notorious haughtiness. Aman tended to be conceited, but not in his contacts with the ordinary soldier.

Were there other reasons for his popularity, we wondered. What was Aman's track record as a military leader? I sought out the views of former officers who knew and worked with him. Some, like General Jagamma Kello, spoke favourably of his leadership skills, but only in general terms. Others contested the claim. I talked to a senior officer who had worked with Aman closely about the General's accomplishments during his years in the defence establishment and in the few theatres of war where he was in command: in South Korea as part of the United Nations force defending the country against invasion by North Koreas in the early fifties, and in Ethiopia's Ogaden region. This officer was singularly unflattering.[21]

"Even the way he carried himself during the 20-day boat trip from Djibouti to South Korea was unbecoming of a commanding officer," recalled this officer. He said Aman had returned after only a short spell as deputy commander of the Kagnew Battalion and before seeing action. He did not know for sure the reason for his recall. Others said that Aman clashed with officers and had to be recalled. Whatever the reason, Aman failed to take advantage of a good opportunity to show his leadership qualities in a high profile conflict. Many others did precisely that and were rewarded for distinguished service.

I asked this officer about Aman's tour of duty as commander of the Third Division which was responsible for keeping the peace in the Ogaden. There was nothing of consequence to talk about, he replied. He would challenge anyone to come up with any evidence of Aman's military accomplishments in the Ogaden. He suggested that I interview a junior officer who was in the Ogaden at the time and who was much more familiar with the details. I asked if he could do this on my behalf, as I did not think that the officer would be forthcoming with someone he was seeing for the first time. He later talked with the officer and told me what he said: General Aman had done precious little in the Ogaden and was not even present there during the major operations.

The late Colonel Fikru Wolde-Tensai, who on the whole was favourably disposed to Aman, was more specific about the General's military record in the Ogaden. He told me that the only military engagement in which Aman took part involved an incident in 1960 at Danot. A few Somali's irregular soldiers dressed as civilians had infiltrated the area around this small settlement and had fired at an army patrol. A small contingent was assembled and dispatched. Aman was at the head and the chase and skirmish lasted for some five days. The infiltrators were overpowered and fled back. There were no casualties on the Ethiopian side. This was a modest operation, but the fighting men got close to Aman and liked what they saw: his simplicity, his willingness to mingle with ordinary soldiers, eat and sleep modestly. It was at this time, said Colonel Fikru, that the soldiers started to refer to Aman endearingly as 'kodda tirassu' (the man who uses a tin canteen for a pillow).

Aman was recalled to Addis soon afterwards and returned three years later to take command of the Third Division once more. The Somali threat was now grave. Unfortunately, Aman was ill and left his post to be replaced by General Wolde-Selassie Berekka. The Tog Wichalle incident, a far more serious affair than the incident at Danot three years before, took place not long afterwards. According to Colonel Fikru, it was General Wolde-Selassie Berekka, not Aman, who was in command of the successful Ethiopian counter offensive. But many would in later years erroneously talk of Aman's exploits during this encounter. In an officer corps whose probity was often the subject of considerable speculation, Aman was among the few who were known for their personal integrity.[22] This naturally gained him more respect. But there was precious little by way of proven performance that was anywhere near the kind of reputation he enjoyed,[23] which appears to have been more a matter of how he carried himself rather than what he actually accomplished.

Undoubtedly, Aman understood the country's general political situation on the eve of the 1974 revolution. Did he appreciate the desirability of radical but bloodless change? it might be asked. He probably did. He was familiar with the experience of Nasser's Egypt which had undergone a radical but bloodless revolution. His brother was Ethiopia's Ambassador there from whom he must have learned the basic facts. And he himself had briefly served as a military attaché in Cairo. Was he temperamentally equipped to restrain Mengistu and his colleagues? To those who observed him at close range, he did not seem to be. Indeed he was thought to have encouraged the young military officers to be more audacious in their plans, including the overthrow of the Emperor. It must also be noted that the special criminal code and military tribunal which came out soon after the military takeover were initiatives taken while he was Chairman of the Dergue. In answer to a minister's concern about strikes at Cabinet meeting one day, Aman told him to await a bill being prepared to handle situations like that effectively. He sounded menacing as he said that. And his brief Chairmanship of the Cabinet did not on the whole offer evidence of his moderation or other leadership capabilities.

In its issue of 30 November 1974, *The Economist* described General Aman as a leader inclined towards "gradualism and realism." The British weekly cited his membership of the Ethiopian Mekane Yesus Evangelical Church in support of that view. In the judgment of observers closer home, Aman did not give that impression. He was a man not particularly recognized for his insight or calm reflection. He was hasty in his actions and judgments and tended to underestimate forces arrayed against him, a telling illustration of which was his impulsive responses to the challenge he faced in his final relations with the Dergue. For a nation that looked to him for the kind of leadership that his long years in the army and his exposure to modern ideas seemed to suggest, his inadequacies turned out to be tragically disheartening.

The General's turbulent stewardship of the nation lasted no more than 65 days. One of the few potential leaders in Ethiopia's history to be given a unique set of favourable circumstances to lead the country to a promising future would bungle his brief tenure to a sad end.[24] His limited abilities and troubled personality had much to do with his failure. But he was also surrounded by advisors who, for a variety of reasons, were disinclined to offer ideas on how best he might resolve the challenges the nation was confronting. Some simply decided to play up to the man's hugely inflated ego as the best way of protecting themselves against potential charges that might be levelled against them in connection with their past services to the imperial regime. Others were intent on using their new positions of influence to settle old scores against officials the military had detained.

Aman's murder and that of fifty nine others was universally condemned by the world media. The *Times* of London called the incident "a lapse into savagery." The apartheid papers in South Africa were vindicated in their racist bigotry that one of the oldest nations in the world had still not learned to govern itself. The massacre of the sixty officials "puts Ethiopia on about the same moral plane as Uganda, whose General Amin has become a disgrace and an embarrassment to Africa," said the Nationalist Party newspaper *Die Burger*. Papers in friendly countries like Zambia, Tanzania, Nigeria, and others were unsparing in their condemnation. They were of course justified. It was painful for Ethiopians of my generation, brought up as we were on the notion of a mature country with a long, rich, and proud history, to witness such a universally expressed sentiment of opprobrium. The humiliation was overpowering. We drew scant comfort from the blood baths of the French, Russian, or Chinese revolutions. *The Economist* was right in remarking that the killings had taken place in a "nation unaccustomed to mass murder."

Bloody Saturday was a case of an unjust and mindless slaughter of the innocent. For the most part, members of the Dergue had not been selected for the purpose of leading the nation in those challenging times. Some were sent by their units to go and find out what the small group of plotters in Addis Ababa was up to. Others were habitual troublemakers whom their superiors wanted to get out of the way. Others still were handpicked for their capacity to hold their own in a verbal face to face with government ministers. In some cases, military posts were manned by a skeleton staff and if someone had to go, it was the person whose absence would cause least disruption. The most senior of Dergue officers were majors; the majority of its members being NCOs and junior officers.

The lower grades in the Ethiopian military greatly resented the senior officer corps who regarded them with an attitude barely distinguishable from that with which the old feudal masters regarded their lackeys. Resentment was not limited to the lower ranks. Even among the middle level officer corps (majors and captains) there were many that detested the top brass. In the Dergue, they all realized that if they banded together they had the power to right past wrongs. With this in mind they solemnly took a collective oath of loyalty. In the early days of power when things looked iffy, one of them said "we have seen it all, and we don't care what happens next." They had had their taste of fine cooking at the palace, had had access to money under various official pretexts, and had enjoyed the company of elegant women, choice meat and scotch. And they had murdered and humiliated top officials of state, including Generals and the sole Admiral. They didn't mind if all this were to come to an abrupt end.

There were, of course, Dergue members who were influenced by the widespread desire for change. These included graduates from the military academies who, like their civilian contemporaries, were idealistic, were conscious of the role the military had played in developing countries to bring change. But they were very few in number and were overwhelmed by the ignorant majority who were manipulated by the disagreeable thug at the top.

During the first few days following bloody Saturday, I went around the homes of victims to express my condolences. Families had been told that burial ceremonies, an important event in the Ethiopian cultural calendar, were unnecessary as the 60 officials had already been buried. The cathartic exercise of wailing was all that was left for the bereaved. I had been a holdover from the previous government of Emperor Haile-Selassie and had known almost all of the victims of the massacre. As I was performing the traditional act of expressing my condolences to the families of the deceased, the fact that this allowed me to distance myself from the heinous act of the junta was not lost on me. It was not enough, however, to attenuate my embarrassment of being part of a government that had committed the atrocity. I now began to think about a way out. The entry into my diary of Tuesday the 26th of November (three days after bloody Saturday), has the following words. "It is difficult for me to watch things with folded arms. I should find an early opportunity to resign. It should not take more than a month."

On Wednesday November 27, ministers were called to a meeting of the Cabinet. Major Mengistu, the First Deputy Chairman, entered the room followed by Major Atnafu, the Second Deputy Chairman, and three or four other young officers. There was a palpable silence in the room. The usual glances, nods, whispers, shuffling of papers, and repositioning of chairs to more comfortable positions preceding the opening of a regular Cabinet meetings were dispensed with. I kept looking at the gang of six, fresh from their bloody act. Their eyes were red shot and their hair uncombed. They looked uncomfortable as all twenty-six eyes of the thirteen ministers trained their collective gaze on them. This was not a routine meeting in which the Chairman quietly examined the day's agenda and made a quick visual check of members to ensure that the meeting could commence. The Cabinet's Chairman and 59 other people had been murdered 96 hours earlier. We awaited the opening words of the most senior of the officers.

Mengistu spoke: "Honorable Ministers. You are all aware of what has transpired. General Aman had started to manifest dictatorial tendencies, was adamant in his intention to resign and would not, despite our pleas, get back to his office to resume his duties. He was also engaged in a serious plot which would have allowed the imprisoned officials to gain their freedom and take up arms [a claim never heard before or after]. Much blood would have been shed. From the perspective of human rights, what has taken place is regrettable. However, a situation in which the blood of a few people is shed to save the nation is preferable to one which risks far more bloodshed. If the Dergue had crumbled, each of its members would have taken up arms and conducted an armed struggle with a large following. And the country would have been decimated."

The most senior of the civilian Ministers, former Prime Minister Michael Imru and at the time Minister of Information, took the floor after Mengistu. "Would the incident which has just transpired not put into question your goal of bloodless change?" He asked the very question that the soldiers dearly wished to avoid. "And would it not be advisable to take certain actions, like the release of detained persons for instance, to signal to both our people and foreign countries that future actions will follow the path of peace," concluded Michael with yet another unwelcome question.

Michael Imru showed courage in drawing attention to the murderous act. He also asked a review of the relationship between the Dergue and Council of Ministers; pointing out, in particular, the possibility of members of the Dergue assuming ministerial positions. That, too, was an important point which needed to be raised, for the civilian ministers did little more than watch the outrageous actions of a government of which they were part, but in which they had little say. In answer to the first question, Mengistu said with a bare face that the policy of bloodless change has not changed! No response was given to the idea of releasing detained persons. Regarding the suggestion that Dergue members take over Cabinet responsibilities, he said that it would be studied.

Michael had broken the ice with three vexing questions. And he had been fearless in doing so. Indeed he had come to the meeting wearing a black necktie. Six of the dead were close family members. Wearing a black tie could have been perceived as a sign of solidarity with the aristocracy as well as an overt disapproval of the murder. Another person in his position would have foregone the black necktie precisely to avoid giving that impression.

After Michael's questions, others took the floor. Three types of remarks were made all in all. There were, first, those made by a group of ministers who either directly expressed their support for the killings, or diverted attention to other inconsequential issues.[25] It was mostly fear, opportunism, and the reflex to duck the mortal flight of an oncoming lance. In short, the basic human instinct to survive, to prolong one's life for one more hour, one more day. There were also some (at least two) who did not like the previous regime. Another seemed to speak from an ideological perspective when he said openly that the "era of the princes has come to an end. I am a supporter of the current movement." He then added an insipid statement of the kind that a retired high school civics teacher would give to a Boy Scout gathering. "Those who are committed must be guided by three C's: Cooperation, Coordination, and Communication." He could not have sounded less trivial. In a shameful attempt to save the murderous soldiers from embarrassment, three other ministers spoke after him and urged that the meeting take up pending business. Another pointed to difficulties that might arise if the Cabinet did not act expeditiously to have the budget published on the statutory deadline. Yet another spoke of the need to expedite the dispatch of an economic mission to Saudi Arabia to discuss new projects to stimulate the sluggish economy. It was not exactly the most gratifying spectacle; this deplorable attempt to suggest to the murderers not to worry unduly about their crime.

The second group of remarks was on resignation. These were variously expressed. The respected Minister of Agriculture, Dr. Dagnatchew Yirgu, asked whether ministers could resign if they felt they could not work with the Chairman. Mengistu, now more confident on account of the supportive remarks, replied unequivocally. "Yes. And there are many young supporters of the Dergue who are ready to come on board." The Minister of Culture, the historian Ato Tekle-Tsadik Mekuria, raised the issue of ministers being kept in the dark about important issues which were routinely taken up by the Dergue, but which were only rarely brought to the Council of Ministers. Mengistu replied that only on questions of national security did the Dergue maintain confidentiality, a telling admission that the Cabinet was not trusted on these issues. In truth, practically all issues of consequence were decided by the Dergue. Some were not even referred to Cabinet. Those which were, simply served the Dergue's public relations objectives: to make it appear that it had consulted with the Cabinet, or to implicate a minister if something went wrong. No wonder there were a few ministers who did not wish to be part of this unedifying theatre.

The third group of comments revolved around the atmosphere of intimidation that had been created in the Council. Belatchew Asrat, the Minister of Justice, spoke on this and pointed out that it had become a major concern of ministers. They were inhibited from airing their frank views. A reign of terror seemed to be in the making. I myself intervened to say that the military should not assume that courage and patriotism were attributes possessed only by those in uniform. There were millions of Ethiopians not in uniform who were passionate about their country and who would act decisively in challenging situations. Intimidation will not work. I saw Atnafu, the Second Deputy Chairman, give a wry smile. Mengistu replied that it was unacceptable for ministers to work in this kind of intimidating atmosphere, an allusion to Aman as the source of the problem. This situation would not be allowed to continue in future, he concluded. The two-hour meeting ended at mid-day, with a pervasive sense of unease among many ministers.

The soldiers had crossed the Rubicon with their collective act of murder. Putting an end to bloodshed would not save them from answering for their crime at some future date. Killing more would not necessarily add to their culpability. And yet how fervently we all wished that the massacre we had witnessed would be the last. The soldiers had killed more than was necessary. If being feared was their motive, no more dead bodies were required. They should now settle down and attend to the countrywide desire for peaceful change, and secure acquiescence that way. Perhaps we were deluding ourselves in harbouring thoughts of a fresh opportunity to bring about peaceful change.

I remembered my vow not to linger in the Cabinet for more than one month. But what did that mean? Was I to sit it out for thirty days, avoiding all involvement in whatever was coming up before the Cabinet? How could I not take a position when major issues came up in a body which, though much enfeebled, still carried some responsibility? More specifically, there were policy issues awaiting cabinet action. An unfinished policy statement was still in a cabinet committee of which I was an active member and for which much of the groundwork

Guinea's Diallo Telli, the first Secretary General of OAU, and Prime Minister Aklilu Habte-Wold in 1966. Aklilu was murdered by the Dergue in 1974. Telli was jailed, tortured and murdered by Sekou Toure in 1977

had been completed. Reform was its overriding goal. It did not appear reasonable to boycott the deliberations of a committee handling such an issue. I could hardly sit and twiddle my thumbs at a time when the country was precariously poised on the edge of a precipice.

And so I decided to carry on with government business until at least the finalization of the policy document, fully take part in discussions on policy issues that would come up in Cabinet and in due course make up my mind about the exact moment of my resignation.

CHAPTER 12

The Initial Policy Orientations
of the Military

Ethiopian Socialism (*Hibrettesebawinet*)

On September 19, 1974 a Cabinet committee had been set up to formulate new policy directions. Former Prime Minister Michael Imru was chairman, with three ministers (including myself) as members. Work had been proceeding well. The shock caused by the massacre inevitably dampened enthusiasm, but the exercise had to be brought to closure; not least because there was still a lingering hope of peaceful reform. This thinking was shared by two members of the committee: Michael Imru and I. The other two were less concerned about the risk of violence. Unknown to us, one was a member of the All-Ethiopia Socialist Movement, a left-wing group that collaborated with the Dergue during the red terror campaign two years later. The other belonged to a disgruntled ethnic group. Both were more intent on pulling down the walls of the old order than on thinking soberly about non-violent ways of building a new one.

I had known Michael Imru in the past, though not very well. Our membership in Endalkatchew Makonnen's Cabinet gave us an opportunity to get to know each other better. We had worked together on the white paper of that Cabinet. We were now working on yet another policy document to respond to the new political situation. Michael Imru had always been regarded as a socialist. This was evident to anyone who knew him. A few believed, wrongly, that he was communist. In his discussions with friends, he often made a distinction between the democratic socialism of the West and the regimented and intellectually intolerant brand of socialism of the East. What he wished for Ethiopia was the former, adapted to the country's specific historical, cultural, and political situation.

I myself had earlier toyed with a brand of socialism which was more radical than democratic socialism: more authoritarian and more effective in introducing fundamental reforms without being unduly concerned with the 'democratic' element of social democracy, but not violent. This was no textbook version of the ideology, but the result of my immodest attempt to formulate something that would better respond to the country's specific situation. But I was now wary about it, having observed what a military junta without democratic scruples could do. After Bloody Saturday the shedding of blood was no longer an abstract concept. Even in days when I toyed with the radical socialism of my own definition, I had always felt that copying an alien ideology would be wrong. That inclination grew stronger, as young men close to the Dergue pushed for the Chinese, the Soviet, or the Albanian model. Some homegrown brand of social democracy appeared to be the best way forward. And this was what the policy committee had in mind when it recommended *hibrettesebawinet* (Ethiopian Socialism) in its draft to the Cabinet at the end of November 1974.[1]

After providing a non-Marxist historical background to the events of the previous ten months, the document analyzed the reasons why a new political philosophy was needed. Such a philosophy should "spring from the culture and soil of Ethiopia," not brought from abroad like "some decorative article of commerce." And so the document proposed "a political philosophy which emanates from our great religions which teach the equality of man and from our tradition of sharing and living together...."

Behind these ideas was an attempt to pre-empt a veering towards the extreme left, with its predictable consequences. It was still possible to hope that the more sober members of the Dergue would prefer a non-violent, more pragmatic transformation of the social order: an exercise in radical reform rather than a convulsive revolution which would wreak havoc and put to test the very viability of the nation.

The document traced the prevailing crisis to the constraints imposed by the country's traditions. Attention was also drawn to the more permissive aspects which could provide the basis for a new political order. The document was well received by the civilian members of the Cabinet. Everyone was curious to get the reaction of members of the Dergue. Major Atnafu spoke first and sounded skeptical. *Hibrettesebawinet,* he started, "can only be adopted as a long term goal. Our people are still largely ignorant, and considerable education is required to appreciate this philosophy. Besides, we should keep in mind the possibility of an adverse reaction by the U.S.A. which provides us with economic and military assistance. 'Do not provoke the crocodile before you clear the water,' goes an Ethiopian saying. We must exercise caution," he said in conclusion. Atnafu said it was more prudent to continue using the motto of 'Ethiopia First'. He was uncomfortable with socialism, even of a home-made variety. Major Mengistu's remark was limited to one question: how likely was this policy to be accepted by the people? Even at this early stage, it was evident that he had no personal vision for the country. He would accept anything that appeared likely to help him stay in power.

At the follow-up meeting of the Cabinet, the new Chairman, General Tafari Banti, surprisingly took exception to the private ownership of land indicated in the economic section of the document. This was consistent with the draft legislation proposed by the Minister of Land Reform, which at the time was being discussed by the Social and Economic Committee of the Cabinet. Tafari said that private ownership was a thing of the past. Land belongs to the people. This may sound surprising, he added, but who would have thought only a few months ago that "Ethiopia would be ruled by any person other than Emperor Haile-Selassie." It seemed as if Tafari was trying to reassure the young in the Dergue and left wing intellectuals outside it that he was a progressive individual who deserved their support.

A number of other comments were offered towards improving the text, the Chairman's views against the private ownership of land eliciting no support from anyone, and hence not requiring an amendment to the document. After four successive meetings stretching over a period of twelve days, the document was approved without major change. It went to the plenary meeting of the Dergue, was endorsed unchanged, and was published as official policy on 20 December.

New Relations with Soviet Russia

The Cabinet settled down to its routine business under the new chairman. A tiresome stream of supplementary budget requests for cost overruns, for transfers from one line item to another, for new expenditures not foreseen during budget preparation, etc. etc. vied for the attention of ministers; the more strategic questions being reserved for Dergue deliberation. Over the next three months or so, only a handful of questions of consequence came up, land reform being one. There were other important issues handled outside the Cabinet in which some ministers were involved. An example was the new government's policy on the Soviet Union and the related question of securing arms to defend the country against the growing threat of Somali aggression. Following the execution of the sixty officials, the Carter administration showed reluctance to release arms supplies on which agreement had already been made. It was essential to look for alternative sources.

From the outset, it was the military government's desire to have closer relations with the Soviet Union and Eastern Europe. For their part, these countries were not yet ready to welcome the military. Their relations with Somalia were close and they did not wish to take the risk of warming up to a country which was that country's principal adversary. Besides, the Dergue's espousal of socialism was still untested. Being insecure, however, the Dergue pressed for amicable relations.

Ratanov, a former KGB functionary now serving as Soviet Ambassador, was given a line of communication with Mengistu, and presumably a green light to drop in on government ministers to assess their stance on ideology and relations with the Soviet Union. He came to my office one morning with a curious proposal. Could I join him in sponsoring the unveiling of a Soviet made medium range civilian aircraft? he asked. He then opened a folder and pulled out an invitation card with my name and his printed on it as hosts of the event. I was somewhat surprised but did not respond immediately.

After some diversionary talk, I said that if the aircraft had been a joint Ethio-Soviet manufacture I would have gladly acceded to his request. Since it was not, I could only talk to the Civil Aviation Administration to arrange for a special area of the airport to display the aircraft. I expressed surprise that the card had been printed without prior consultation. He, of course, knew that what he had done was inappropriate. But his purpose was to see my reaction and judge where I stood on Ethiopia's relations with Soviet Russia.

Ratanov next asked whether I had a reply to his earlier request for permission to start regular Aeroflot flights between Moscow and Addis Ababa in tandem with Ethiopian Airlines. Soviet officials traveling to Addis on official business were obliged to fly to Khartoum and spend two days there for a connecting flight. Two days in the dust, heat, and humidity of Khartoum were unbearable for citizens of temperate climes. A direct link between Addis and Moscow was something his government wished to see early. I had put the question to the General Manger of Ethiopian Airlines and had secured his advice. It was a hectic time in my ministry and my time was largely taken up with a succession of strikes in the parastatal institutions under the ministry's oversight. As a result, I had not been able to send him a reply.

I informed the Ambassador that Ethiopian Airlines did not think the new route would be viable commercially. The volume of traffic between Addis Ababa and Moscow was limited and Ethiopian Airlines was concerned that the revenue would fall short of covering its costs. But if the management of Aeroflot thought differently, Ethiopian Airlines was ready to collaborate on condition that it was compensated for its losses in the event of inadequate traffic. If traffic was adequate, any profits would be split equally between the two airlines. The advice from Ethiopian Airlines was sensible and businesslike. And I informed Ratanov accordingly. He was not satisfied with my response, however. "I do not understand why it should take a whole month to come up with this answer," he said imperiously. Initially, I thought I might perhaps explain why. But his presumptuous attitude called for a different kind of response.

"Mr. Ambassador," I started, "you speak like a supervisor talking to an underling, not like a diplomat representing a country looking for improved relations with Ethiopia. First you suggest that I have a duty to shield Soviet citizens from the dreadful heat, humidity, and dust of Khartoum. Second, you query me for taking one month to respond to your request, and do not bother to say a word about the substance of the advice I have been given by the General Manger of our airline. Keep in mind that Ethiopia is a proud country with a long history and a strong spirit of independence. You will be committing a serious error if you think that Soviet Ambassadors could routinely dish out orders to Ethiopian politicians and civil servants."

My response probably got me branded as a sinner against the Holy Trinity of Marx, Engles, and Lenin. Ratanov left my office abruptly and never returned. Our meeting would have an interesting sequel, as I shall explain in a moment. Suffice it to say at this stage that subsequent Ethio-Soviet relations would prove me wrong and him right. In time, the tantalizing supply of Soviet arms would draw Ratanov closer to Mengistu. And Ratanov's minor complaints would send ripples of fear and insecurity through the Ethiopian bureaucracy. Ethiopia was on her way to becoming a client state of Russia.

The question of arms supplies continued to dominate discussion. The Dergue was desperate to shore up the country's defences against Somalia and to execute the war against the Eritrean guerrillas. A high level task force was appointed in the summer of 1975 to make preparations for a visit to the Soviet Union. A dossier of heavy arms, aircraft, equipment, and munitions was put together by the defence establishment. Michael Imru, Getachew Kibret, and I were asked to join the mission to Moscow. Everything had to be kept under wraps. The Soviet Embassy gave the three of us entry visa forms to complete. We did and they were duly checked and stamped. We were advised to keep these separately and place them inside our passports only when checking in for the last leg of our flight to Moscow. The pages of our passports would therefore never show evidence of our trip to Russia.

A pretext was found for Michael Imru, Getachew Kibret and I to visit Switzerland and Sweden. After a day in Geneva, we proceeded to Stockholm and met with officials of the Ministry of Foreign Affairs. Gunnar Jarring, a retired Swedish diplomat who had served in Addis Ababa in his early days and who was Sweden's Ambassador in Moscow a few years before, was present. Jarring was at the time special envoy of the U.N. Secretary General to the Middle East. His interests in Ethiopia were evident. He was curious about the new direction the country was taking and posed several questions. We left the Ministry after what turned out to be a political briefing on Ethiopia to a friendly country. We did not say anything about our closely guarded trip to Soviet Russia. The following day we flew to Moscow. The Swedes would doubtless find out as soon as we boarded our flight.

The military members of our mission had gone to Moscow via another route about which we were kept in the dark. There was confusion when the three of us arrived in Moscow. No one had come to meet us. We went to the information desk and asked if there were officials expecting us. The girl there made a couple of announcements but no one came forward. Could she call the Ministry of Defence, we asked. She was reluctant. As our own diplomatic representatives in Moscow had been purposely kept out, no one from the Embassy showed up. After a few idle minutes, I asked the girl at the information desk if she could give me a copy of Moscow's telephone directory. We ourselves would call the Defence or Foreign Affairs Ministry.

"What did you say?" she asked. "The Moscow telephone directory," I replied, enunciating each word distinctly to be understood. She shook her head. I was puzzled. Didn't she have a copy of the directory? Perhaps she did not understand my English, or perhaps she was suspicious and wished to keep her distance. A straightforward question had elicited a mystifying response. The question was, of course, far from being straightforward as I would learn later. Moscow telephone numbers (and street maps) were highly guarded secrets available only to members of the KGB (and no doubt to the CIA), not to official guests stranded at Moscow Airport.[2] After a long wait, a group of Soviet military officers arrived and rushed us to a hotel reserved for foreign officials. There we met the military members of our party. The hotel was noisy and crowded. Someone from our group complained of the rowdiness of the guests, all East Europeans. A few days later we were transferred to a large and quiet guest house.

Our meetings started with middle level officials to whom we explained the purpose of our mission. A day or so later we met Defence Minister Grechko, who made a few remarks on our request for arms. He must have been given a copy of our shopping list by Ratanov. He promised to be helpful, but said that we should not forget that his primary responsibility was to have enough military hardware for the defence of the Soviet Union. "Could you not disarm your civilian population and get some arms that way?" he asked, alluding to a situation where large numbers of non-combatant Ethiopians traditionally carried arms. At some point he also made a curious remark: "You have some people in senior positions in your government who seem to stand in the way of better relations between our two countries." Ratanov, the Soviet Ambassador to Ethiopia, was in the meeting. I remembered my last encounter with him in my office in Addis. It was obvious that Ratanov had briefed the Minister about that meeting. I tried to get a glimpse of him in the far corner of the room, but our seating arrangement did not allow this. Perhaps he had purposely placed himself in that position.

Our final meeting was with Prime Minister Aleksei Kosygin, to whom the leader of the delegation (Major Haddis Tedla) handed the official letter from General Tafari Benti soliciting the Soviet authorities' assistance for military hardware. Kosygin started the meeting with an air of contempt: "Are you a General, or what?" he asked Major Haddis curtly. While I was answering his question about the length of the railway from Addis to Djibouti, he asked peremptorily: "Are you an engineer?" I told him I was not. It was evident that his queries were intended more to humble his interlocutors than to elicit information.

Kosygin went on to make a few preliminary remarks about the recent changes in Ethiopia. He spoke disparagingly of the medal-bedecked Emperor, a curious observation from an official of a country where medals were shown off with tasteless ostentation. Leonid Brezhnev himself, the General Secretary of the Party, occasionally appeared in the uniform of a Soviet Marshall. The Emperor had been at the head of his troops during the Fascist invasion. And all monarchs occasionally appeared in uniform. But Kosygin had to say something to please the soldiers in our group. On the question of arms, he said he would talk to Brezhnev.

Over the next two or three days, we were taken around various sites in Moscow: a visit to an air force base where a flight demonstration of a MIG 19 was staged; another to an army base where we saw several armoured personnel carriers whose tires had been freshly painted with tar to make them look darker, cleaner, and brighter; a visit to the permanent agricultural exhibition where products of Soviet agriculture were on display; and the inevitable visit to the ornate Moscow metro. During lunch back at the guest house, our escort (an army colonel) proposed a toast in honour of our delegation. Someone from our group reciprocated. The rest of us were encouraged to make more toasts. I preferred to keep silent.

The escort looked at me and intimated that I too should say something. It was Soviet tradition for everyone to say a word, he said. Glasses had been raised for Ethio-Soviet friendship, for the great Union of Soviets, for their accomplishments, and so on and so forth. I scratched my head for a relevant subject. The colonel came to my rescue and said any subject would do. The sight of a huge sheep I had seen at the agricultural exhibition came to mind. "I raise my glass in honour of Soviet agriculture, which has produced the largest sheep I have ever seen," I said with an air of originality. The colonel was not amused. Was that really all I could say about the achievements of the Soviet Union, after everything that I had seen and heard? I had to get up again and say something that was more palatable to the humourless colonel.

After a few days, we were informed that a response would be sent to Addis Ababa in due course. Some three or four months after our return came a response which distressed the military. Some helicopters, engineering, transport and communications equipment would be provided. Ambassador Ratanov was called to the Chairman's office and asked whether the response related to a part of the list that had been presented or was meant as a final response. He was left in no doubt of the government's disappointment. A few days later, we heard that he had left for Moscow for 'medical treatment.' The Soviets were not sure where Ethiopia was heading. They did not see how they could maintain the confidence of Somalia, a small but longtime ally, as they made overtures to a country which, although bigger and potentially more important as an ally, was nonetheless its deadly adversary.

The Somalis for their part became suspicious of Soviet intentions and committed a grave error when they became friendly to a country they had long vilified: the U.S. Their initiative provoked Soviet ire. The Somalis went on to commit an even graver blunder by invading Ethiopia against Soviet advice and Cuba's efforts at mediation. Soviet doors were now open to massive military assistance for Ethiopia. Over a period of months, arms shipments arrived in sufficient quantities not only to repulse Somali aggression but also to punish the intransigent nomads for their expulsion of Soviet advisors. But Ethiopia also paid a hefty price for the assistance. For the first time in its history, it became a willing vassal of a foreign power.

Land Reform: Manipulating a Wrong-headed Policy

As I mentioned previously, a land reform bill had been submitted to the Cabinet by the responsible minister and was being examined in a Cabinet committee. It was strongly opposed by by the radical members of the Dergue: Captain Mogus Wolde-Michael and Major Demissie Deressa; the former an overzealous convert to the new ideology and the latter a rather dim-witted fellow traveler. The committee's majority report, with the Minister's draft bill as a basis, was finally presented to the Cabinet. It was evident that it would not be to the liking of the extremists.

When it came up for discussion in Cabinet, all members of the Dergue except one raised objections. It was their contention that land should not be owned privately. Mengistu Haile-Mariam who had previously taken the position that a ceiling of 40 hectares on private holdings might be too restrictive, now said firmly that no private ownership should be allowed. Tafari Banti had already been tutored to take the same line. Contrary to standard procedure, an alternative draft prepared clandestinely by staff of the Ministry of Land Reform behind the Minster's back was presented to the Cabinet. All rural lands were to be "the collective property of the Ethiopian people,"[3] it said. It was stated that "no person or business organization or any other organization shall hold rural land in private ownership." Land allotted to a farming family "shall at no time exceed 10 hectares." Peasant associations will be created. Their functions would consist of distributing land, administering and conserving "any public property within [their] area, especially the soil, water, and forest." They would establish "marketing and credit cooperatives and other associations," and launch "villagization programmes."

It was a most thoroughgoing overhaul of agrarian life, driven not so much by the tangible benefits that would accrue to the peasant farmer as by the romantic view of young ideologues that peasants would be liberated and that their energies would be mobilized to bring undreamed of results in short order. The Dergue also had its eyes on the opportunity the bill offered for the massive regimentation of the peasantry. Notwithstanding the deafening rhetoric about ending the exploitation of the peasantry, the new system was bound to bring the peasant under the yoke of a single, powerful, new landlord far more oppressive than the absentee landlords of the previous regime. And from whom there would be no escape.

To those who knew the agricultural sector well and who could not possibly be suspected of supporting the old order, such as Minister of Agriculture Dr. Dagnatchew Yirgu, the impractically of the bill was mind boggling. Dagnatchew said so during the bill's discussion. He was accused by Mengistu of adopting a negative predisposition to change. Dagnatchew had cautioned against bringing out the law prior to preparing the ground. He suggested its postponement until at least the next crop season. "Rather than being negative, why don't we say that the bill shall be proclaimed this year and work towards making that possible?" Mengistu remarked.

Michael Imru came in to say that *Hibrettesebawinet* (Ethiopian Socialism) which was still official policy implied that we should "move step by step," a characteristic Michael Imru understatement intimating that the bill's far reaching provisions did not appear feasible. He suggested that we should present the bill in phases. "We should also carefully ask whether this bill would not aggravate our internal security situation," he added. Major Atnafu also struck a note of caution. He said that he did not get the impression that the bill had been based on an adequate assessment of the different land tenure systems in the country. It was his view that local people knowledgeable about their particular tenure systems should be closely consulted. We should be "realistic" and not allow ourselves to "be guided by theory," he concluded. I myself had made my position clear when I supported the general thrust of the bill presented earlier by the Minister of Land Reform.

The Minister of Defence, Ayalew Mandefro, had earlier expressed concern that land owners among the military might create problems. Despite Mengistu's views to the contrary, he had been asked by the Cabinet to study the matter and report back. When he did, it was in a manner that strengthened his initial concerns. He reported that he had consulted with unit commanders in the army and had been told that men in uniform had interests in land too and that they might not support the proclamation in its present form. This is at variance with "what is being expressed here," he said in a thinly veiled allusion to Mengistu's view.

Mengistu had had enough of cautious talk. "For God's sake," he responded, "leave the worrying to us." It was clear beyond doubt now that the laborious work on the bill presented by the Minister of Land Reform in the preceding weeks was a protracted exercise in futility. The new bill was discussed extensively, but no amendments were made. The military only wanted to say that their bill had passed Cabinet scrutiny. It was a colossal waste of time for a publicity exercise of questionable value. The bill was published exactly as the ideologues had drafted it, with not a comma changed.

A great opportunity was missed to address meaningfully a centuries-old problem. In the bill proposed by the Minister of Land reform there was the distinct possibility of moving in a different direction: in a direction that would (i) institute a system of small-holder agriculture based on private ownership, (ii) notably improve the economic life of the farming population, (iii) endow peasants with a sense of independence and defiance against all perpetrators of oppression and injustice, and (iv) empower them to be the principal agents of a vibrant agricultural sector that would underpin the nation's economic fortunes. Ideological myopia sadly blocked this promising path. Mengistu and his immediate collaborators in the Dergue could now ride the wave of extremism sweeping the young off their feet and in the process secure a semblance of political legitimacy.

More Instances of Cabinet Manipulation

Even more manipulative was the discussion a few months later of the proclamation nationalizing privately owned urban land and property.[4] The Cabinet was called for an emergency session one Saturday morning. After we sat down, the draft bill was circulated. None of us had even had as much as a glance at this key piece of legislation. It was read out line by line by the Cabinet secretary, ministers offering their comments at the end of each paragraph. A range of detailed observations were made. By lunchtime we were only half way through. "We shall continue our deliberations in the afternoon, but please do not take away copies of the document. Leave them at your seats," said the Chairman. We complied and returned in the afternoon to complete our deliberations. The meeting ending at about 6:00 p.m., eight long hours after it started in the morning. We could now take home our copies of the bill.

At 8:00 o'clock in the evening, the proclamation was read out on radio and television. Given the usual tardiness of the bureaucracy, I was somewhat surprised at the swiftness with which a revised version was made ready for the 8:00 o'clock news. When it was published in the papers the following day, I took the trouble to compare it with the draft I had brought home and on which I had marked the amendments in pencil. Not one of these had been adopted.

Incidents such as these fortified my initial inclination to leave government service. As I shall explain in a moment, I had on several occasions told Mengistu Haile-Mariam that they should find a replacement for me. I received no response. There was little else to do but wait. The inevitable boredom would occasionally be relieved by some issue that the military had bungled or brought to the Cabinet for other reasons. A case in point was the decision to slash the prices of major consumer items. This had caused uproar among producers and merchants. Something had to be done.

Tamrat Feyye, an army sergeant-major and member of the Dergue, presented himself at the Ministry of Commerce and Industry one morning and demanded to see the Minister. He told him that consumers could not afford the high prices of teff (the staple grain), eggs, meat, etc., and that they should be slashed. This was to be treated as a 'political decision.' The ominous phrase had previously been used to announce the massacre of Emperor Haile-Selassie's officials. The Minister and his staff meekly accepted the order. A list of hurriedly revised prices was announced in the media.

At a Cabinet meeting a few days later, the Minister of Agriculture, Dr. Dagnatchew Yirgu, asked how a decision of such consequence could be taken without consulting the ministries concerned. "Were you not consulted?" asked the Chairman. Dagnatchew said no and the Chairman instructed that the matter be brought up at the Cabinet meeting the following week. He instructed that all staff involved in the decision should be invited.

Everyone was present at the following week's meeting, including the sergeant-major. The Minister of Commerce and Industry was not. He had conveniently traveled overseas on official business. He was represented by his deputy who had not taken part in the meeting at which the sergeant-major had made his 'political decision.'

The Minister of Agriculture started off the discussion by posing a series of searching questions. The response of the staff revealed that things had been done in haste. In their defence, they said that the decision was not the result of any study. It was a political decision. The Chairman appeared annoyed. "What do you mean by 'political decision' and who was behind that decision?" he asked. One of the staff pointed his index finger at the sergeant-major saying "it was he who told us that this was to be treated as a political decision."

The sergeant-major promptly denied. The Chairman and the other Dergue members came to his defence equally promptly. "How unfair to put the blame on this innocent soldier," said Mengistu. All in uniform agreed that it was the fault of the civilian officials. This was a bare-faced lie, as the minutes of the meeting held at the Ministry of Commerce and Industry (read out in Cabinet) clearly indicated. The sergeant-major was behind the whole affair from start to finish. He had said that this was an "important matter which had to be decided quickly." A man scarcely known for his firmness, the Minister had been intimidated into carrying out the sergeant-major's orders.

Dr. Dagnatchew felt guilty that he had unwittingly put the innocent staff in trouble and tried to defend them. "There was clear pressure on the civilian officials," he said at one point. "How could they be expected to stand up to someone who was a member of a body responsible for throwing behind bars powerful personalities like Ras Mesfin Selishi?"[5] "I cannot accept what Dr. Dagnatchew is saying," responded the Chairman. "If the Dergue decides to destroy the country, do we all chime in and say 'let us do it now'?" Mengistu added his voice and said: "We do not impose pressure. Our mission is the opposite: to free people from pressure!" Not to be outdone, Atnafu Abate declared: "I have been in the movement of the military from the outset. We started it in the interests of this beautiful country which has been rendered ugly. I am passionate about our nation," he said with his voice trembling. "This is sabotage. Anyone who tries to rack our brains will have his brain racked! The Chairman concluded the discussion with instructions that a revised set of prices should be prepared for the next meeting of the Cabinet.

Revisions were made, but fell short of being satisfactory. The Chairman went on a long lecture faulting the officials involved for not doing their jobs properly. They lacked commitment and did not deserve their salaries. Dr Dagnatchew was asked to offer his views. He gave a number of reasons which basically said that the decision to slash prices was arbitrary. Prices should not be regulated that way. The Chairman was annoyed and said that the comment "sounded scientific but was meant to make things appear difficult." The agenda item was deferred to yet another meeting, at which more statistical data were presented and discussed. No satisfactory conclusion seemed to be in sight.

The Chairman, ready as ever with interventions to please Dergue members said: "People [civil servants] have not changed their old ways, have they?" It was the day of reckoning for the officials and for Tadesse Mogese, the Deputy Minister of Trade sitting in for the Minister, Mohammed Abdulrahman. Tadesse had not participated in the meeting at which the sergeant-major had given his orders. Neither he nor the officials were responsible for the mess. The sergeant-major was. But who was to touch him? As we left the Cabinet room after an unsatisfactory decision, I sensed that something unpleasant was about to happen to the poor officials. I walked up to Dergue member Captain Mogus and told him how unfair it would be if the innocent officials were put in harm's way, leaving the principal culprit scot free. "I will try to do something about it," he replied worryingly.

Dr. Dagnatchew looked distressed as we walked to our cars. I asked him if he could come home for dinner. He agreed and we proceeded to my house. I switched the television set to listen to the eight o'clock news as we waited for dinner. The first item of news confirmed our apprehension. All the officials involved in the price fixing exercise, except the principal culprit, and the innocent deputy minister were accused of a major act of sabotage and were detained. Dagnatchew was incensed. "If these characters come to detain me, I assure you they will not find me," he said. He was deeply saddened by the outrageous disregard for justice. The sequel of this story needs to be told if only to illustrate the manner in which many an able and patriotic Ethiopian was disgusted by the murderous regime of the Dergue and vanished from sight.

In the evening of February 15, some twelve days after the Cabinet meeting at which the issue of consumer prices was last discussed, Michael Imru came to my house with a most disturbing piece of news. He said that earlier in the evening he had met Dr. Dagnatchew's friend, Hailu Mulatu, who showed him a note in Dagnatchew's handwriting indicating that he had disappeared. Michael asked if I knew Dagnatchew's residence. I knew more or less where it was. After a couple of enquiries addressed to neighbours, we finally spotted the house. We knocked at the gate and the watchman came out. When asked about Dr. Dagnatchew, he said that he had traveled to Wollega in the West. He was expected that very day but had not yet returned. Michael said we should discuss the matter further at his home.

Hailu took out from his pocket a pink routing slip with the markings of the Ministry of Agriculture. The note in Amharic read:

"Hailu, if I do not return by Yekatit 8 [February 15], please pass this letter [in a sealed envelope] to Befekadu Tadesse [a staff in the Chairman's office] in order that he may pass it on to Lt. Meles Maru [Dergue member and *aide-de-camp* to the Chairman] who in turn should deliver it to Col. Mengistu. If I do not return by Yekatit 8, it means I have disappeared. Please do me the favour of carrying out what we discussed. I am sorry to trouble you, and wish to thank you for the assistance. Thank you."

"Handle this letter in the [separate] envelope with prudence to protect yourself from being *implicated* [an English word in an otherwise Amharic text]. Deliver it to Lij Michael personally at his residence"

Dagnatchew's letter to Michael expressed thanks for appointing him Minister of Agriculture during his tenure as Prime Minister and went on to explain that he had found it difficult to work with the soldiers. We were obviously disturbed and at a loss. Michael suggested that Dagnatchew was probably on his way to the border, or that he might even have decided to take his own life. But there was a chance that he might change his mind. I too was inclined to think that he might attempt to take his life, for I had talked to him on the phone about scheduling a meeting a day before he left town. When he told me that he was about to leave for Wollega, I had said that we could hold the meeting soon after his return. "If I return," had been his puzzling reply. I also recalled what he said about soldiers who might come to his home to arrest him, but go away empty handed.

We contacted the Police Commissioner, General Berhane Teferra. He said he had been informed by the head of the provincial police in Wollega about a note that Dr. Dagnatchew had left at his hotel in Lekempt (the province's capital) in which he had written about the difficulties he faced in his work. He said in the note that he had disappeared and that no one should try to look for him. The Commissioner said that he had earlier instructed the provincial police to send out search teams. He then telephoned the provincial police officer and was told that despite a day long search, there was no sign of the Minister.

Dagnatchew, a graduate of Purdue in agricultural sciences and perhaps the foremost expert of his day on Ethiopia's agriculture, was never seen again. He would sadly join the ranks of the many committed, highly skilled and innocent sons and daughters of the country "devoured" by the revolution, to use the Dergue's macabre characterization of its victims.

Military Obduracy

Although the Cabinet was mostly engaged in bureaucratic minutiae, it frequently provided a convenient platform for the military to flex their political muscle. Their assertiveness was intended to browbeat civilian ministries into executing their decisions. This often succeeded. But it occasionally elicited principled responses from a few ministers who were holdovers from the previous regime. These officials tried to dissuade the soldiers from wrongheaded decisions. Sometimes they succeeded. But more often they failed.

The persistent attempt to moderate the rural land reform bill was the most heartbreaking instance of failure, as was the attempt to pursue a moderate socialist path more attuned to Ethiopia's realities and aspirations. But there were other instances as well. A case in point was the wrong-headed proclamation on the nationalization of urban land and property. The sufferings imposed on ordinary folk come out graphically in the distressing experience of a government chauffeur.

This chauffeur had built a modest home with money largely donated by friends on land similarly given by a benefactor. He had put up a simple rectangular bungalow with four rooms. Each room had a fenced-off private entrance as well as an outdoor privy at the back. The chauffeur rented all four units for about $5 per unit per month. He himself continued to live in a rented unit for which he paid $6.00 a month. An economist who had contributed money to help him put up the bungalow asked the chauffeur what the point of building a house was if he and his family did not move into it. The chauffeur's commonsense response was that he now had a fresh source of income of $20 a month with which he could cover his rent and clothe and feed his four children a little less stressfully.

While he could hold his own against the trained economist, contending against the new law turned out to be an intractable problem for the driver. The proclamation passed by the Dergue had instantaneously transformed him and untold numbers like him into 'landlords.' Anything beyond one 'residential unit' was nationalized. This chauffeur had to give up the three 'extra' units on his bungalow and retain only the fourth.[6] Poor single mothers whose only source of income was rent collected from ramshackle dwelling units had to surrender them.

A few of these mothers went to see the minister in charge one day, bitterly complaining that the government should now assume the care of their children, as they had absolutely no way of doing so themselves. The minister came up with a proposal to amend the proclamation in order to exempt anyone who collected rent of less than $75.00 a month. This was summarily dismissed by the military. Laws solemnly passed by the Dergue were not to be tampered with, they said. Muslim husbands with multiple wives living in separate homes were put in a difficult predicament. What were they to do? Divorce the extra wives enabling them to claim their respective residential units? Or squeeze them all under one roof to preserve the marriage but forego the other residential units? Such real life problems were of little concern to the military.

The obduracy and assertiveness of the military became more and more evident as they gained experience and garnered the support of opportunists and left wing extremists. The soldiers also began to feel that unless they showed their clout, ministers and civil servants would drag their feet in enforcing the torrent of new policies and directives. One afternoon, a special meeting of the Cabinet was called for precisely this purpose. The Chairman opened the meeting with a statement that for reasons not clear to him and his military colleagues, work in the various departments of government had slowed down. Ministers did not seem to be too keen to implement Dergue decisions. As a good instance of this, Major Atnafu gave the example of the Minister of Public Health who was accused of creating obstacles in the handing over of a government hospital to the Ministry of Defence. Chairs and benches bolted to the cement floor at the pediatric centre of the hospital had been removed and taken away; just as "the departing British had done at the end of the Italo-Ethiopian hostilities" in 1941, he said.

In an admirable display of mettle in the face of intimidation, the minister concerned (Dr. Jemal Abdulkadir) calmly explained that the clinic had been built with a grant obtained from the Swedish government. He left it to the soldiers to infer that he was accountable for the proper utilization of the grant and that it was his responsibility to make it clear to the donor government that he had salvaged as much of the assets as he could. At another meeting, the Minister of Public Works and Urban Development, Semret Medhane, was strongly attacked by Mengistu for the inadequate implementation of the law nationalizing urban real estate. A roving mission of the Dergue had come back from a province with a report that the law was not being implemented speedily enough in the province's capital. Mengistu claimed that 80% of what needed to be done was unattended to. Statistics was not exactly Mengistu's forte, while Semret, a graduate in aeronautical engineering from Imperial College (London), was not altogether unaware of its relevance to the task at hand.

Semret started his response methodically. He explained that perhaps 80% all nationalized urban land and property was located in three major cities: Addis Ababa, Asmara, and Dire Dawa. In these three cities, the law's implementation had almost been practically completed. Smaller provincial towns like Gondar (which was the subject of the roving mission's report) collectively represented the remaining 20% of the task at hand. Here the process of registering houses had been completed. This may not be visible to visitors but it was an essential first step before the government's takeover of "extra houses." Even if it were to be assumed that absolutely nothing had been done in these small towns, it would not warrant the assertion that 80% of the work was unattended to. The presumptuous soldier had learned a thing or two about statistics. Partly because of Semret's robust defence and partly because of his record at the ministry, Atnafu flatly (and improbably) contradicted Mengistu's criticism and strongly complimented Semret for the excellent work he was doing.

As I previously indicated, Semret had been managing Ethiopian Airlines. His removal from that post had been yet another instance of blind military assertiveness for which the airline would pay dearly. After my return from an official mission one Saturday evening, I was told by Abraham Workineh, my deputy, that I was wanted by the Dergue and was to be present at the Chairman's office at the National Palace at 8h00 the following morning, Sunday. There was something urgent to discuss, he said. The first thought that crossed my mind was that my own turn for detention had come. These were uncertain times and anybody could be picked up and be thrown behind bars any day or hour of the day for the flimsiest of pretexts. I braced myself for the worst and arrived at the Palace at the appointed hour.

The Chairman, his two deputies and a couple of Dergue members were waiting for me. It was a tense atmosphere in which the briefest of greetings were exchanged.

"What is going on at Ethiopian Airlines", asked the Chairman coldly. I was at the time Chairman of the airline board but was somewhat taken aback by the question. Nothing untoward had occurred at the airline before my departure. "There is nothing of significance I can recall, but perhaps you can tell me what you have in mind," I replied. He then raised the issue of British pilots who had been employed by the airline.

Ethiopian Airlines had secured a contract to lease aircraft to Iran Air with full crew. The lease agreement was lucrative. ETHIOPIAN had spare aircraft but not enough pilots. Semret had employed British Airways pilots who had recently been separated from the company with golden handshakes. He paid them less than what they would have demanded otherwise. It was a good deal for the airline. The Chairman's question was why pilots were recruited from a country that was hostile to "our revolution" while there were Ethiopian pilots willing to work "extra hours for their country. "We also hear persistent stories," continued the Chairman, "that the General Manager is arrogant and runs the airline as he pleases." The purpose of the meeting was clear: the removal of Semret.

Disgruntled staff at the airline had been using their personal contacts with members of the Dergue to smear Semret's name and have him replaced. A good pretext was now found. I explained to the soldiers that the case of British pilots had been adequately discussed and approved by the board. Ethiopian pilots might be willing to fly extra hours for patriotic reasons, but aviation regulations did not allow that. Passenger lives should not be exposed to the risk of pilots flying beyond the maximum permitted by industry standards. About the charge of arrogance leveled at Semret, I said that if there was one personal trait that he was known for, it was his gregariousness. No one should take the charge seriously. To my surprise, the Chairman quietly added that Semret was also from the "North", a loaded code word insinuating Semret's Eritrean origins (through his father). I told the Chairman, who was an Oromo, that Semret was also part Oromo (through his mother, who in turn had an Oromo father and an Amhara mother) making the man a full blooded Ethiopian.

Nothing further was said on this score, but the military were determined to have him removed from the airline. "You should find him a place in your ministry," said the Chairman. I responded that there was no position in my department which called for Semret's abilities and long years of experience. "He could quite easily head a Cabinet level post," I remarked and proposed the Ministry of Public Works as a suitable post for an engineer. The post was at the time occupied by Paulos Abraha, an economist who I suggested could be transferred to the more relevant Planning Ministry which was vacant. After an initial resistance, my proposal was accepted and Semret made head of what at that time was a fairly low-key department of government. At a later stage, he was charged with the onerous responsibility of implementing the law nationalizing urban land and property. It was on account of his professional stewardship of the ministry that many problems that would have risked lives were quietly resolved.

Regrettably, ETHIOPIAN would be without his management skills at a time when they were badly needed.

The Chairman's assertiveness showed no sign of restraint. The main reason for which he had been selected had been his unassuming and compliant personality. It is perhaps understandable for someone perceived to be compliant to try to dispel that notion by acting otherwise. The more the Chairman tried to demonstrate what was basically indemonstrable, the less he looked convincing. He once feigned extreme dismay at a minister's action and got into the amusing act of zipping and unzipping his military jacket. Mercifully it lasted only a few seconds. His purpose was to demonstrate his loyalty to the military. Regrettably this did not save him from the wrath of the man in whose good books he so desperately wished to stay. As we shall see shortly, an internal power struggles emerged at the beginning of 1976 in which he was caught up and paid dearly for choosing the wrong side.

CHAPTER 13

The Parting of Ways

My Delayed Exit

Background

The assertiveness of the military and their increasing radicalization made a good number of ministers think of an early exit from the Cabinet. In my own case, the desire to quit went back to the resignation of Prime Minister Aklilu's government in which I was a junior minister. When his successor invited me to join his team in February 1974, I had expressed reluctance. In chapters 8 and 11, I have given an account of my successive attempts to resign. The latter attempt was occasioned by my altercation with General Aman. As this coincided with the November massacre I had been obliged to shelve the idea temporarily.

Thoughts of resignation resurfaced when relations between the civilian Cabinet and the military deteriorated. Events also started to unfold which rendered my stay in the Cabinet increasingly meaningless. There was, for instance, the confrontation late one evening between the employees of Ethiopian Airlines and an armed detachment of the Dergue that had gone to the airline's head office to arrest a trade union leader. A phalanx of the man's co-workers blocked the way. The soldiers were furious and threatened to shoot their way into the company's premises unless the workers moved out of the way.

When I got back home from a late evening meeting I found a dozen or so telephone messages from the airline staff. I returned the call from Berhanu Endale, the acting General Manager, who informed me of the crisis. I telephoned Mengistu and volunteered to go to the scene and try to mediate. As there was a curfew in force, I requested a military escort to accompany me. Mengistu replied that he knew what was going on, that things were under control and that I should not be unduly concerned. I relayed the assurance to Berhanu.

The following morning, I heard that the soldiers had shot their way into the airline building. Half a dozen persons had been killed as a result. My attempt to be helpful appeared derisory. I could say that I had tried to do something to calm down the soldiers. But this was cold comfort to the families of the deceased. What was the point of being chairman of the airline if I was not allowed to help handle a dispute between employees of the company who came under my watch and agents of the military government in which I was a minister?

The airline union wrote a long petition to the board describing the sad event and requesting an inquiry. I convened a board meeting to discuss the petition and what actions might be taken. Some board members said that the airline staff knew very well where responsibility lay and did not see why the petition had been addressed to the board. I pointed out that we were duty bound to deal with the question and the least we could do was to forward the petition to the Dergue with a covering note requesting appropriate action. This alarmed those who thought that the Dergue might be provoked to act against board members themselves. I was distressed with what was plainly an attempt to duck the issue and said that I would forward the petition to the Dergue in my capacity as chairman if members thought they should not be involved. But in the end everyone was persuaded that something had to be done. A memorandum was sent to the Dergue requesting that the union's petition be responded to. No response came. I felt that staying in government under these circumstances would make me look like an accomplice.

A major source of concern, however, was the unstoppable process of extremism in Dergue policies. *Hibrettesebawinet* (Ethiopian Socialism) had been carefully crafted with the view to adopting a more moderate and Ethiopia-specific brand of socialism. Soon after its adoption by the Dergue, radical members of that body pressed for scientific socialism: a slogan they had picked up from underground extremists most of whom scarcely understood the meaning of the phrase. In one Cabinet meeting, Dergue member Captain Mogus said categorically that for him Ethiopian Socialism meant scientific socialism. Police Lieutenant Alemayehou, the other radical, added that Ethiopian Socialism lacked universality. A recently appointed progressive civilian minister chimed in with the thought that it was internationalism, not nationalism, that we should adopt as a guiding principle. My cabinet diary for the day said: "Our differences came out in the open today."

I countered the arguments head on. I cited the split between Stalin and Trotsky and how the romantic Trotsky (an internationalist) had lost the battle to the pragmatic and nationalist Stalin, who had gone on to build Soviet Russia. "Internationalism" was an impractical shibboleth of the left. We in Ethiopia would only be manifesting our naiveté if we were to sideline our national interests. Two members of the Dergue (Majors Birhanu Bayih and Asrat Desta) seemed to support my position. Mengistu took the middle ground, but was in reality moving steadily towards the extremists. At a subsequent meeting I spoke on the basic rationale of "Ethiopian Socialism": its relevance to the country's historical, cultural, and objective situation. The tide of extremism was gathering momentum, however, and soon seemed to engulf key leaders of the Dergue.

At the first anniversary of the revolution held on 12 September 1975, marchers from various departments of government and parastatal bodies carried placards denouncing "Bourgeois Socialism." The extremists were doing their best to discredit Ethiopian Socialism and those responsible for its drafting. Partly for political reasons and partly out of ignorance, they alleged that those responsible for drafting the document on Ethiopian Socialism did not understand the very term 'socialism'. The truth, however, was that the authors of the policy had been exposed to Marxist ideas for a far longer period than their critics, had taken the trouble to read a wide range of books on the subject, and had finally concluded that a copy cat approach to introducing a Marxist revolution in Ethiopia would ultimately do more harm than good.

Even the Chinese advised caution. This happened in the course of a visit to Beijing by an Ethiopian government delegation which included Dergue member Captain Mogus Wolde-Michael and Senai Likke (a rabid ideologue recruited to a newly established political bureau). During one of their meetings with Chinese Communist Party officials Senai spoke presumptuously on the purer brand of socialism which Ethiopia wished to follow. The Chinese were singularly unimpressed, and tried to disabuse him and his friends of their infantile infatuation with the ideology. They reportedly told the delegation that "ideology, unlike merchandise, cannot be imported or exported. We would not, even if you were to ask us, agree that you replicate our experience in your country. You have to have your own revolution." They also advised the delegation to be wary of "Social Imperialism," Chinese codeword for Soviet Russia's policy of laying down codes of conduct for socialist countries. The Chinese particularly underlined the need to handle the agricultural sector with considerable attentiveness and said that care should be exercised to avoid measures that might destabilize the sector.

The Chinese continued to emphasize prudence and the importance of an internally driven movement. When Mengistu met with Chinese strong man Deng Xiaoping some time later, the gentle advice had turned into a blunt rebuke. "What do you know about communism?" Deng asked Mengistu. As he pulled himself together to rehearse the little he knew of the ideology, Deng interrupted Mengistu with these words: "One does not have to go far to understand communism and its consequences. We in China have practiced it for 40 years. And poverty is the only thing we have reaped. People like you should learn from our mistakes. My Prime Minister will show you only the good side of things. Don't be taken in by what you see. Don't listen to him. For the most part, our experience has been one of poverty."[1]

At a meeting with Mengistu in late September 1975, I aired my concern about the drift towards extremist Marxist ideas. I told him that people who advocated scientific socialism had lifted it lock, stock, and barrel from communist propaganda booklets.

Not one person had taken the trouble to see what adjustments needed to be made to adapt the ideology to Ethiopia's social and economic reality. Many of us had been exposed to Marxism in our younger days but had outgrown it after an initial period of infatuation. In a language that I hoped would be intelligible to him, I said I did not wish our country to become a Soviet Russia or a Communist China. My fervent desire was for Ethiopia to evolve into the kind of social democracy which prevailed in the Scandinavian countries. These countries followed a political philosophy endorsed by the electorate which responded to the fundamental concerns of the individual citizen: health, education, employment, and the challenges of old age. "Every time I visit Sweden, I ask myself if we might ever grow into that kind of society. I don't ask the question when I visit Russia, or China; or the U.S.A. for that matter where the pursuit of private gain crowds out concerns for public welfare." In a further attempt to dissuade him from mimicking Stalin or Mao, I also said that a reformist leader like Gamal Abdel Nasser was a more relevant model for Ethiopia.

Mengistu's said that it was interesting that I had raised the issue. He gave me a brief rundown of the evolution of the Dergue. In the first few days, the soldiers' movement was about to fall into the hands of colleagues who wanted to raze the Palace to the ground, proclaim radical land reform, and raise the pay of soldiers. We had to restrain these people. Then we proclaimed 'Ethiopia First', a policy around which we believed the Ethiopian people could rally.[2] We later adopted Ethiopian Socialism," he continued with hardly a word about the civilian Cabinet's strenuous efforts to persuade the soldiers to move in that direction. "In doing all this, we were guided by one paramount policy: the national interest. This thing called scientific socialism cannot be applied in Ethiopia today. We are a feudal nation and cannot jump to communism. We have to do things step by step. There are differences of view within the Dergue itself. We are handling these with care. Captain Mogus had gone out on a limb, but we are restraining him." As usual, he was deceptive, but also clever in letting me know that he had a problem of managing wild characters like Mogus in the Dergue.[3] The obvious message was that I needed to understand his position. His response to my suggestion that Nasser was the kind of leader to emulate (he had eschewed communism but had managed to introduce extensive social and economic reforms) was that for his part the leader he admired most was De Gaule of France. In his eagerness to demonstrate the little knowledge he possessed of world leaders, he had regrettably missed my point. De Gaulle was of little relevance for Ethiopia.

Neither Aman nor Mengistu understood the dangers of a frontal attack on the culture and value systems of an old society. If, instead of a contrived revolution, they had had the wisdom of introducing fundamental reforms while maintaining a measurable degree of respect for the country's culture and value systems, both they and the country might have been spared of the pains that followed.

Working on my Resignation

The first time I mentioned my wish to resign to the Dergue had been in February 1975. It was triggered by the disappearance of Dr. Dagnatchew Yirgu. I met with Mengistu and told him how sad it was that one of the ablest and most forthright members of the Cabinet should be forced to flee. I myself felt that it had become difficult to work in an environment of intimidation. My inclination was to resign, and I wanted him and his colleagues to come to a determination on this after my return from an impending foreign trip. Mengistu deflected this with comments on Dr. Dagnatchew's disappearance. "It was true," he said, "that we did not see eye to eye with Dr. Dagnatchew. But there was nothing to lead him to the step he took." I pressed for a decision on several occasions afterwards: in the months of April, June, August, and November 1975.

On one of these occasions, I told Mengistu that I hoped they would find someone to replace me after my return from a planned trip to Eastern Europe. It was an attempt to drive home the point that I could decide not to return if I wanted to, but preferred not do so and wanted them to know that my reason for resigning had little to do with running away from the country. We spent some ten days on the trip during which Captain Sisay (the chairman of the Dergue's political committee which led the mission) explained the aims of the soldiers to government officials, while I dealt with issues on economic cooperation. I might digress here and give an account of the more interesting aspects of that mission.

Our visit to Yugoslavia included a courtesy call on President Tito. We met him one morning at 9 o'clock. Scotch whiskey was served, a premium brand (Chevas Regal) for him, and the regular brand for ordinary mortals, including his guests. The Yugoslav's followed their boss in sipping scotch and were surprised to see the weaklings from Ethiopia going for non-alcoholic beverages. After listening carefully to Sisay's presentation, Tito said that whatever criticisms might be made of Emperor Haile-Selassie's domestic policies, no one should doubt his contributions to international cooperation, especially among third world countries. There was silence from Sisay. Our discussions on economic cooperation did not break new ground, as Yugoslavia was a close development partner. We only presented a few projects for joint finance.

The visits to Bulgaria, Romania and Czechoslovakia were even less eventful in terms of broadening diplomatic relations, except for a series of amusing incidents. The Deputy Prime Minister of Bulgaria who looked and acted every bit as intimidating as a thug in a dark alley, hosted a dinner for our delegation in which he gave a long speech. Except for one incident, the speech was not memorable. At one point in his talk, he said that everything we saw on the table, the food and the wide variety of drinks was of Bulgarian origin. Superlative remarks were made about the quality of Bulgarian wine. Leading wine producers in Europe regularly "put Bulgarian wine in their bottles and sold them under their labels," he said.

As dinner was served, waiters saw to it that we did not miss any of the drinks displayed on the table. Casting a glance in the direction of our host, I saw a bottle fully wrapped in a large white napkin placed near his dinner plate. From time to time, the head waiter stepped forward and filled the host's glass with the contents of the concealed bottle. I thought it was a matter of Bulgarian protocol that the host's bottle should be protected from the evil eye. I got curious, however, and kept looking. All of a sudden the napkin wrap loosened and fell off. And there appeared, for a precious few seconds, the distinctive three-sided bottle of Grant's Dimple Scotch whisky! The waiter came to the host's rescue and quickly put back the wrap.[4]

In Romania, we were lectured on the country's oil production, with hugely exaggerated statistics on where Romania stood in the league table of major producers. It was ahead of everyone in the production of prospecting and production equipment! People used to telling grotesque lies to citizens deliberately kept in the dark continued with their habit even when interacting with foreigners who were better informed. At our early morning meeting with the country's stuttering boss (Ceausescu), scotch whiskey was served once again; with the boss's glass being accorded special attention as was the case with Tito.

The Czechs bragged less and did not seem to care much about our mission. I took the opportunity to look up a colleague from my days at the U.N. He was an economist named Vraney whose office was located right next to mine. He was ebullient with a perennial smile on his cherubic face. I asked our hosts if they could find out where he was and if I could meet him. The next day an official car took me to his office in Prague. The only thing familiar was his physical appearance. Gone was the happy smile and everything that made it fun to be with him. He looked at me and gave the barest of signs that he recognized me. His poker face and few words made conversation difficult. I said goodbye and left after only a few minutes.

In the evening, I was told that there was someone at the reception desk who wished to see me. I was pleasantly surprised to find another Czech colleague from my U.N. days waiting in the hotel lobby. He took me out to a wine cellar and said that he had read about our delegation in the daily paper. I told him about my meeting with Vraney and said that our good friend had changed a lot. "Well" he replied, "the poor guy was sent to a labour camp soon after his return from Addis Ababa and spent a long time with a crew fixing Prague's sewage system." Sewage system! I interjected. "Yes, sewage system" he confirmed. Couldn't they find him a job as an economist, I asked. "Let us not go into that," he said and asked if I could have another glass. As we parted after an hour of reminiscing about life in Addis, he said that I should not believe one word of what the officials told our delegation. Things in Prague were not as benign as they appeared, after all.

Our delegation returned after ten days. I heard nothing about my resignation. My repeated requests to quit had all been verbal. They were not getting me anywhere.

All I got in response was that the country needed experienced persons like me. At a meeting I had on one occasion in his office to discuss my resignation, Mengistu said that the military did not wish to stay in government. Their goal after the overthrow of the imperial regime was to set up political institutions, streamline the bureaucracy and go back to their barracks. And in what I can only describe as a breath taking departure from the truth, he went on to say that the soldiers had not originally intended to kill anyone.

I could not pass up this most inviting of opportunities to say something. "That was a mistake," I interjected. It was as if he had heard nothing while Atnafu, who was seated a little to the side, cocked his ears and asked, "What did you say?" He seemed to have missed what I said, or perhaps wanted a confirmation of what he had in fact heard. I repeated the four words. There was no reaction. Mengistu resumed his expose nonchalantly. Nothing I heard at the meeting nor what the soldiers did in their day to day management of government business made me change my mind about quitting. I now decided to put my resignation in writing.

And so on Saturday January the 3rd 1976, I addressed a short letter to the Chairman and copied it to the First and Second Deputy Chairmen, Mengistu and Atnafu, respectively. The delivery was, of course, not in that order. I knew who counted most and came first. After a Cabinet meeting in the afternoon that same day, I asked Mengistu if I could see him for a minute. He agreed and I followed him to his nearby office. I reminded him briefly of my repeated attempts to leave government service, took out of my pocket a white square envelope containing the letter of resignation, and handed it to him.[5] It was a short nine-line piece which said that I had felt obliged to stay in government service on account of the difficult times the country was going through. But I believed that the time had come for me to leave the Cabinet.

Mengistu dropped his head slightly in dismay and said: "If the need were to arise, Ato Tekalign, should we not be ready to sacrifice our lives in the interests of the nation. How can you do this? We are at war in Eritrea, face difficulties in Somalia, in Djibouti, and in Bale." I had thought long and hard about my wish to leave government and replied without much hesitation. "I have never served my country in the field of battle, but have put my life at risk at different times. I have crossed swords with as dangerous a man as Aman Andom. Had he stayed in power, I would definitely have faced grave risk. No one would have come to my defence in my confrontation with someone whom the military trusted and respected at the time.

"There was also a time," I continued, " when the Congo veterans surrounded ministers in the grounds of Jubilee Palace and would not leave unless they were given a firm commitment to be paid what they believed the government owed them. We told them that there was no evidence that the government owed them anything. This was a very risky thing to say. Among the threatening crowd were a few who had come with hand grenades in their pockets. If these had been thrown at us, nobody would have lifted a finger.

"My conscience is clear, Colonel Mengistu," I said in conclusion. "While I cannot point to any significant sacrifice I have made, I feel no sense of guilt that I have shirked from the call of duty. And as I just said I have twice faced a risk to my life." It was a short, tense meeting. At the end, I asked if I could leave behind a copy of the letter to his colleague and Second Deputy Chairman. "You may do so," he said unenthusiastically. I placed the envelope containing the letter on his desk and left.

The third and last person to whom the letter was delivered was the figurehead Chairman, General Tafari Banti. I met him two days after I spoke with Mengistu and handed him his copy of the letter. No more than five minutes were required to explain its brief contents. After a few remarks of a general nature, I drew his attention to the charge leveled against me by many in the Dergue that I was an obstacle to what the military wished to do. I told him that there might be some truth in this, although I did not mean to be an obstacle. I did often speak against extremist ideas and in particular against scientific socialism. I said it was evident that the Dergue was moving in that direction and I could no longer continue to serve.

I had come ready to defend my decision robustly, as I felt that the Chairman would be advised by his two deputies to dissuade me from quitting. To my surprise, I found General Tafari to be very understanding. "I can't say I know much about socialism," he remarked, "but to say that we should follow what Marx said a long time ago is tantamount to saying that time has stood still. There are some young officers who are against you, simply because you know their weak side. And the campaign against you has intensified in the last three months." He then said something revealing. "Some of us are holding office against our wish, but do so as a matter of national duty. Those in detention are better off than us. As to those who have been pensioned, who can be so lucky?" That was of course the face he carefully concealed in Cabinet meetings where he wished to impress his Dergue colleagues with his sympathy for their left wing policies. I felt sorry for his predicament. But I had my own case to sell and brought him back to the subject at hand by asking when I could get a response. In a manner which did not carry much conviction, he advised that I should be patient.

Colonel Atnafu was the next man to talk to. Following an appointment, I went to see him in his office. My first question was whether he had received the envelope I had left for him with Mengistu. He seemed unsure at first but soon recalled. "Oh, it is that thing on your resignation, isn't it? How could you do this to us, Ato Tekalign," he asked. "Your help is most needed and you are among those we consult on the most sensitive national issues," he said, having in mind the exercise a few civilian ministers were asked to undertake in connection with a request for Soviet military assistance. He said he was at a loss to understand why I wished to resign.

I informed him of my reasons and especially underlined the Dergue's recent drift towards scientific socialism. The ideology was not particularly appealing to me, nor did I think it was the right policy for our country. And have said so on a number of occasions. But the drift has continued. Under these circumstances, I did not see how I could continue to serve as minister. He replied that he himself did not support that ideology and had been called names. One needed to be patient.

What Atnafu said seemed to indicate an unsettled internal debate on ideology. This confirmed the thinking among some of us that there were moderate elements in the Dergrue who did not wish to impose an extremist ideology on the country. Besides Colonel Atnafu, Captain Sisay Habte, Air Force officer and Chairman of the important Political and Foreign Affairs Committee, was another Dergue member who did not believe in scientific socialism. There were others also. A power struggle seemed inevitable at some point, and it was by no means clear which side would win; another indication that there was nothing inevitable about Ethiopia's march towards a Marxist revolution.

I told Atnafu that it was a matter for the Dergue to resolve the problem, but as far as I was concerned I had come to the end of the road. He expressed concern about the "implications" of my resignation. "People would inevitably ask why," he said. He nonetheless promised to take up the matter with the Chairman and Mengistu. This is common practice in other countries, I assured him, and we should get used to it. No one should be surprised if occasionally people resigned on grounds of principle. After all, it was unrealistic to expect complete agreement on all issues in as diverse a group as the members of the Dergue and civilian ministers.

There were three persons with whom I shared my decision to resign. The first was Foreign Minister Kifle Wodajo. Kifle's reaction was one of bemused silence. I do not recall today exactly what he said; but I do not believe he said much. Next I informed Michael Imru, the former Prime Minister and subsequently advisor to the Chairman. He said he understood and that it had been a timely decision. To neither did I as much as hint that perhaps they too should contemplate the step I had taken. Decisions of that kind were personal on which advice should neither be sought nor given.

The third person to talk to was Colonel Molalign Belai, a close relative who had for many years been a member of the Imperial Guard. Being a senior officer, he had been kept out of the February military movement, but followed developments closely and seemed to know a good deal about the goings on in Dergue circles. I had asked him to come over to the house for drinks. After a few moments of light-hearted talk, I told him I had tendered my resignation.

He was stunned. "What is this? I thought you were an educated man. How could you possibly take such a risky decision? Don't you realize that these soldiers can imprison. And kill? Why in God's name did you not share your thoughts with me in advance?" I could not intervene; such was the spate of protest gushing out of an otherwise pleasant and courteous relative. He kept on talking for a few more minutes. When I noticed a slight pause, I replied to his last question: "I did not consult you in advance because I believe that it was a personal decision. Had I consulted you, your reaction would have been precisely what I am witnessing now, with less passion perhaps. I had already made up my mind and there was little you could do" "So what is the point of telling me now?" he shot back. I said that I just wanted those close to me to know. "Know and do what?" Just know, without being obliged to do anything, I replied. He got up, said that I had acted imprudently and should be prepared to face the consequences. He would not be in position to help, if help were required, he said as he walked away.

I, of course, understood this perfectly natural reaction of a relative. He was concerned about what might happen to me and felt let down that I did not share my thoughts ahead of time. Having made up my mind, I on my side felt that I only needed to inform those close to me. Strange things were happening in Addis. Dead bodies were found mysteriously resting on the steering wheels of parked cars. People were shot by unidentified persons in broad daylight. The police did not bother to follow up. If I were to be harmed, my friends and relatives would at least have a clue.

Late in the morning of Sunday 21 February, I was on my way home after visiting a friend. I switched the car radio for the news. Someone appeared to be reading a speech in which reference was made to "the new policies of our revolution, the urgency to implement them and the need to cut through the bureaucratic maze left behind by the feudal order." This went on for a few minutes. At the end, a list of new officials was read. One name struck me: that of my deputy. The announcer said that he was the new Minister of Transport and Communications and said nothing about the person he was replacing; me. When I reached home that Sunday afternoon, my friend Kifle Wodajo had heard the broadcast and said that I should now be a much relieved person. His body language betrayed a desire to be similarly relieved.

On Monday morning I went to my office, expressed my best wishes to my deputy Yussuf Ahmed. I phoned Mengistu to say that I was glad my request had been met. He said (deceptive as ever) that the announcement could have been done better, and there was a possibility to make up for it in the afternoon. I quickly collected my papers and left. In all seven ministers had been replaced. There were also deputy ministers and other government officials who were relieved of their posts. All of us were told to be in the Chairman's office at 3:00 p.m.

Upon arrival, we were ushered to the Chairman's office. Present also were his two deputies, Lt. Alemayehou Haile, the self-proclaimed Marxist-Leninst head of the Administration Committee of the Dergue, and others. Immediately, the lieutenant started to read a highly critical statement which at one point said that the removal of the officials had resulted from "the need to take decisive steps to replace the bloated maze of the old bureaucratic order with a new spirit of the revolution". The Chairman was more civil in his remarks. He said that the decision to relieve the ministers had been a response partly to their own requests and partly to the need to ensure that officials kept pace with the progress of the revolution. He thanked us for the service we had rendered the nation and concluded that we were free to work in our respective areas of expertise. Tafari was right to say that the move had been taken partly because of some ministers' wish to leave government service: for I later learned that in addition to me a few had asked to be relieved. Dr. Jemal Abdulkadir and Colonel Semret were among them.

We were given an abrupt adieu and left the Chairman's office. In the adjoining room Lt Alemayehou circulated a form in which we were asked to indicate our professional backgrounds and what we wished to do in future. Some people sat down to complete the form. After Alemayehu's nasty statement, it did not look likely that we would be posted anywhere. Alemayehou stood and looked at the persons completing the forms, assuming the posture of a grade school teacher in the course of invigilating a term exam. This last bit of humiliation was insufferable. I told him that we were public servants whose personal dossiers contained practically all the information requested in the form. In any event there did not seem to be any urgency to hand in the form then and there. I left saying I would send him the completed form in due course. I had spared myself the concluding scene of an insolent farewell. What the lieutenant had read out in the presence of the Chairman was humiliating enough. But I would soon find out soon that the drama was far from over.

A nice little media send-off was apparently in the works. Over the next few days all three government papers celebrated the event with scathing editorials. *The Ethiopian Herald,* the English daily, took its cue from the speech of Lieutenant Alemayehou. It opened its editorial pompously: "the removal of the seven cabinet ministers was a significant event pregnant with lessons of far reaching significance to people who conduct government affairs in today's Socialist Ethiopia." And what was the lesson? It was that government officials needed to serve the country "with revolutionary zeal, and without hesitation or fear"![6] *Addis Zemen,* its sister Amharic daily, also wrote along the same lines, heralding the good news that the edifice of the old bureaucracy had finally crumbled. The weekly *Yezareytu Ityopia* was not far behind in its castigation of the officials.

As if what was said in its editorial had not gone far enough, *The Ethiopian Herald* carried an unsigned article the following day in which it triumphantly proclaimed: "All said, it is gratifying that the sword of the Revolution has at last been drawn against the last bastion of the feudal order." We could do little but laugh off this amusing if awkward attempt to designate us as members of a new Club of the High, the Mighty, and the Ugly. Lieutenant Alemayehou was keen to cover up the fact that some of us had resigned of our own accord. His statement had said that we had all been dismissed and the newspapers gleefully reported this.

Fourteen Months in Anguished Furlough

Notwithstanding the hostile media send-off, I was glad to be free of the pressures of an office which offered little beyond a sense of guilt by association with members of a murderous regime. I now turned my attention to the mundane challenge of paying my bills. I was suddenly unemployed in a country with no unemployment benefits. My bank account showed a none-too-reassuring balance of two thousand Birr (roughly a thousand U.S. dollars). I owned a house on which I had been collecting rent. That was no longer allowed, as rents by private individuals had been proscribed. The government was now pocketing my rent. Either I had to move into my house or have a waiver of rent on the house I was occupying which was now also government property confiscated from my landlord. When I informed my tenants (a young German couple with a newly born baby) that I wished to move into my house, they said it would be difficult to find a suitable villa to rent and asked to stay if it was not too much of an inconvenience for me. I dropped the idea and decided to stay where I was. The rent I paid on my residence was waived. But I was short changed in the process. I was collecting a monthly rent of Birr 900.00 on my house which my tenants now paid to the government, compared to the Birr400.00 I was paying as a tenant to my previous landlord which was now waived. The Dergue made a cool Birr 500.00 a month in the process.

In the meantime, I got messages from friends that I should keep a low profile. One sent word saying that he had been informed by an acquaintance working for state security that instructions had been sent for my movements to be monitored. One day I saw a stranger standing outside my gate, idly turning a rolled copy of the local paper round and round in his hands and watching passersby. It appeared that the monitoring had started. No one from my house needed to ask the stranger what he was up to. Neither did he show any inclination to talk to us. We kept peeping through the gate to find out if he was still there. After several hours, he vanished. Whether he had moved to a more discreet location or felt there was nothing of interest to report, I never found out.

Next I was informed that my father, two uncles, and some of their friends had been detained and been brought to Addis Ababa. I started to visit them on weekends at the maximum security section of the principal prison. Each visit lasted two minutes. A bell rang as they came out and rang again after two minutes signaling that time was up. It was a depressing scene, but I did not brood over it. Many other families had fared worse. The weekly visits were something to look forward to, even if they did not go beyond the two-minute long eye contact.

Otherwise, the first few weeks after my resignation passed uneventfully. Gradually, I realized that I needed to follow a regular routine in order to keep my sanity. And so I struck on the idea of taking tennis lessons. There was a club not far from where I lived. I registered, began my training and soon started to play. One day, the owner of the club came up to me with a list of club members and asked if he could add my name. It was a petition addressed to the Dergue which had decided that the club's assets were to be nationalized. There was of course no compensation. The location was said to be too close to an arms depot. There was no legal basis for this act. But who was to say that to a bunch of bloody-minded soldiers. I agreed to the inclusion of my name, knowing that no one was likely to pay the least attention to his plea that the club was his livelihood and he would not know how to feed his family if it were to be nationalized. Predictably, he got nowhere with it. The club was taken over by the army and I joined another club. Apart from keeping me busy in those difficult days, tennis became a lifelong passion which continues to this day.

Roman had come back from the U. S. while I was still in government. When she first called to say hello, I had advised her not to call again, as "I was in the midst of a raging fire." Uppermost in my mind was the risk of resuming our former relationship. Imprisonment was a probability. Worse could happen. It did not make sense to expose her to these risks. Her response had been that it was precisely at times like this that friends should come together. I was adamant, however, and prevailed on her to stop calling. When she called after my resignation, I felt that the risk of something happening to me had abated somewhat and agreed that we could resume our relationship. It was indeed not a bad idea to have a close friend to weather the storm. Tennis and Roman kept me going.

I now embarked on a plan to find work. As I wanted to do something in my area of interest, I went to the Institute of Development Research at Addis Ababa University to find out if I could get involved in some area of economic research. The rules apparently did not allow this, as it was only those who were members of the teaching faculty that could engage in research. None of the responsible persons I met showed flexibility. Indeed some were distinctly nervous with the idea of an individual who was not on the best of terms with the government working for a University which got its entire funding from the state. There was no other organization in the public or private sector where I could work. Inevitably, I started looking for opportunities overseas.

James Pickett, a resourceful friend from my early days at the Economic Commission for Africa, arranged for me to be invited to a conference in Ghana on appropriate technology. Like many economists from the developing world, I was interested in the subject. But there was also the intention to take advantage of the occasion to explore possible avenues for my future. To add weight to the invitation, Pickett arranged for Professor Hans Singer to write me a formal letter of invitation. It was the advice of my friends in government that I should submit the letter to the Chairman of the Council of Ministers for permission to travel abroad. The Chairman's office passed the letter to the newly established Science and Technology Commission whose head I knew. A few days later the official response came. It said that such an invitation could only be extended to a government official, not to a private individual. Whether the head of the Commission arrived at this decision on his own or was instructed to respond in that fashion, I never bothered to find out.

I informed James Pickett of the government's decision. A month or so later, he managed to have me invited as a lecturer in economics at the University of Strathclyde. Surely, the government cannot ask for one of their officials to be offered that post, I said to myself and lodged an application for an exit visa. Like any ordinary citizen I presented myself at the visa section of the Ministry of Foreign Affairs. The new person in charge, a close friend of Mengistu named Major Birhanu Jembere, told me that my application had to go to the office of the Chairman as I was a minister and as my visa application had to be approved by the Council of Ministers. I reminded him that I *had been* a minister but no longer was one. I was now a private citizen and did not see why my old status had to be resuscitated for the purpose. One rarely won an argument with servants of the Dergue and I had little choice but to comply. My application for an exit visa was submitted to the Chairman's office once again.

After two weeks, I was informed that my visa request had been turned down. What could be the reason this time? I went to the immigration department of the Ministry of Interior to find out. The man in charge of the department (Colonel Tesfaye Wolde-Selassie) had been a long standing intelligence officer in the Ministry of Defence during the reign of Emperor Haile-Selassie. He too was close to Mengistu and was now a big wheel. I explained my case and asked why my application had been turned down. He promised to find out from the Chairman of the Dergue's Administration Committee. The chairman was none other than Lt. Alemayehou Haile, the young officer who had given me and six other ministers a nasty media farewell when we left government service. A few days later, I returned to see Colonel Tesfaye. He said that. Lt. Alemayehou had flatly rejected my application saying that people like me should not be allowed to travel.

Things were now getting to be more serious than I had initially thought. I was unable to work for a living, inside or outside of Ethiopia. The practical consequence of not earning a living became a stressful daily preoccupation. I now started to look for consultancy assignments and was able to obtain one from the ILO which kept me going for some time. But I was not totally free from anxiety. How is all this going to play out? I had never before been placed in a situation where my future hung so precariously in the balance.

An event occurred at this time which briefly took my mind off these daily anxieties, but which brought further distress in its train. At lunch one afternoon, my friend Kifle Wodajo who was still at his post as Minister of Foreign Affairs said that Major Sisay Habte, head of the Dergue's Political and Foreign Affairs Committee, wished to see me. When I asked why, he said he did not know. I told him he could come home any time in the afternoon, as my mornings were taken up with tennis.

Sisay arrived one afternoon at about 5:00 p.m. He was in a sports outfit, was wearing dark glasses, and drove a tiny, battered, non-descript car. I led him to my study and asked if he wished to have coffee or perhaps some drinks. "Lucky you," he started.

"Free of worries. And I can see that you are in the midst of these books," he said looking at my bookshelf. "You must be spending a good bit of your time reading, now that you are free of the burdens of office." What he said was more an indication of some problem preoccupying his mind than what he imagined to be a relaxed lifestyle. Coffee was served. And he started to pour out.

Although not popularly elected, the composition of the Dergue represented a good cross-section of the Ethiopian people, said Sisay. The soldiers came from different regions, family backgrounds, and varied in age from people who were in their early twenties to those who were in their forties and fifties. Their deliberations were democratic. Hours were spent on a decision to put (or not to put) someone behind bars. And I was happy, continued Sisay, that this democratic spirit would in time spread and move us forward. But things are changing and dictatorship is slowly emerging. Mengistu Haile-Mariam is now taking decisions by himself. "I represent the Air Force in the Dergue," said Sisay reflectively, "and when Mengistu visited the Air Force Headquarters a few days ago, I was neither informed nor invited. We are in bad shape in this country."

It was known that Sisay occasionally aired misgivings about the Dergue. It was also said that he longed for the day when he might be free from his Dergue responsibilities and set up an electronics repair shop for a living (he was trained as an electronics engineer). It was therefore not altogether surprising to hear him talk about his concerns regarding Dergue rule. But why in God's name should he take up this subject with me, I wondered? Members of the Dergue were extremely tight lipped about their internal affairs. I was not happy at all that he had come to discuss with me a hugely sensitive question.

My response to him was that this was a matter to be taken up at the Dergue's own meetings. "You must be joking Ato Tekalign," he shot back. "I am telling you that the man has become a dictator. No such discussion is possible today in the Dergue." What is this man getting at, I asked myself? In a minute he seemed to provide an answer to the question. "I would like you to think seriously about the economic problems of our country." Sensing the direction in which he was going, I had to distance myself from any discussion. "As you know, Sisay," I said, "I am no longer in government and do not monitor the country's economic situation. I think you should talk to people in government departments dealing with the issue." He said he had raised a very serious matter, but that I still did not seem to understand. Having delivered his message he got up to leave. As I accompanied him out of the house, he repeated his plea," please think seriously about our country's economic situation." His final unnerving words were: "You see, I came in this small car, but I am sure they are following me." He put on his dark glasses, got into the tiny car and drove away.

I was worried and momentarily thought to unburden myself to someone. But it appeared more prudent to exercise restraint. Curiosity mixed with anxiety prolonged the days and nights. Sisay had come to see me on a Tuesday. At lunch the following Saturday, I switched on the television set to listen to the news. It turned out that he was the main item of news. He had been detained by the Dergue for subversion! The news broadcast also said that General Getatchew Nadew, the Commander of Ethiopian Forces in Eritrea and military governor of the province who was on a visit to Addis Ababa, had been killed in an exchange of fire with security personnel while resisting arrest.

I spoke with Kifle about the incident. He did not seem to know much. Four days later it was announced that Major Sisay Habte had been executed.[7] What in God's name was going on? Had they tortured Sisay before killing him? And had he given information about his recent contacts? He had told me that he was being followed. Was someone shadowing him when he came to see me? Surely, I said to myself, someone must be preparing a list of people to interrogate. It would not be surprising if my name was on the list.

I readied myself for an interrogation, determined to state the facts as they occurred whatever the challenges. If worse were to follow, there was little to do but face it with as much serenity and integrity as I could muster. I recalled Sartre's short story on existentialism and decided to emulate Ibbeita's example. Every passing hour was a relief. Each hour that was yet to pass a mountain of anguish. Day followed day, but no one showed to pick me up. After a week, I started to think that I was perhaps unduly worried. And yet I was not altogether sure. Ethiopia's bureaucracy was never known for its efficiency. A piece of paper on which my name figured might perhaps be at the bottom of a pile of papers to be examined. It might take time, but the security people would ultimately get to it. I should not delude myself that something would not happen at some point. And so I waited and waited. Weeks passed but no one came.

It was rumoured that Major Sisay and General Getatchew Nadew had been plotting to get rid of Mengistu. Sisay had been visiting Eritrea at frequent intervals in connection with peace talks with the Eritrean guerillas. He had come to know General Getatchew rather well during these visits. The General had previously been the head of the elite commando unit of the army. He had kept in close touch with his former subordinates and had been upset by one incident. In an attempt to break down the distinction among units of the armed forces (which it said had been used by the previous regime to divide and rule), the Dergue had given instructions that the red beret, a proud symbol of the unit's special mission, should be dispensed with.

The decision caused resentment within the unit. General Getatchew shared the unit's sentiment. The General probably also had misgivings about the way the Dergue conducted the war with the guerillas.[8] It would not be far-fetched to speculate that Sisay wished to get rid of Mengistu and take his place. It is plausible to assume further that he might have rewarded General Getatchew with the Chairmanship of the Dergue in return for his support to oust Mengistu. Although no details are provided, a recent book in Amharic says that there was a well organized plot which was accidentally uncovered.[9]

Mengistu Becomes Top Dog

A Soldier with a Chip on His Shoulder

Colonel Mengistu Haile-Mariam had been the principal driving force from the early days of the Dergue. Several factors explain his rise to power. Like many of his rank, he was driven by intense animosity towards his superiors. Unlike most, however, he was an indefatigable schemer and was responsible for getting the Dergue out of tight spots time after testing time. A good number of his colleagues in the early days of the military movement genuinely looked to him to protect their newly acquired power and privilege. Also, he had a natural skill to dissemble and get away with it. He had a remarkable command of Amharic, which

Colonel Mengistu Haile-Mariam

served him well when he wished to assume a deceptive stance, to buy time, or to win over someone to his side. Though endowed with limited oratorical skills to move large crowds, he was articulate, persuasive, and effective in small gatherings.

Mengistu was also a calculating, ruthless thug to whom violence came naturally, almost routinely. Never confident of his acceptability as a national leader, he was constantly on the lookout for potential rivals and acted swiftly and murderously at the slightest sign of trouble; as we have already observed in the case of Aman and Sisay and in many other cases we shall see later.

Thugs are not exactly averse to money. Neither was Mengistu. Though it would be wrong to characterize him as a kleptomaniac, he was not above misusing public monies to further his political schemes and was not a man to lose sleep over embezzlement if that was needed to accomplish a private plan. The charge that he left for Zimbabwe with a tidy sum of money is consequently not implausible.[10]

Mengistu was perceived as a coward by those who observed him at close range.[11] The much cited Ethiopian saying that "a coward is the true son of his mother," is a particularly apt portrayal of him. Given the choice between a daring son predisposed to sacrifice himself for a cause as against a more reticent one who values dear life and constantly zigs and zags his way to negotiate fatal traps, most Ethiopian mothers would go for the latter. And true to the saying, this "son of his mother" survives to this day.

Mengistu also has a chip on his shoulder that seems to explain much of his attitude towards power and towards his countrymen. He came from a minority community (the Konso) which in years past had been a hunting ground for Ethiopian slave raiders. In his youth, in school, and during his career in the army, people made fun of his physical appearance and called him names. Few personss subjected to this kind of humiliation are likely to forget or forgive. Only persons of exceptional character are capable of transcending the emotional scars caused by bigotry. Mengistu was no Ghandi or Mandela.

I myself had occasion to observe this side of his character in a Cabinet meeting one day when he made the remark that people in Gondar traded in human beings as if they were ordinary articles of merchandise. He was trying to make the point that the spirit of the revolution had not yet penetrated provinces like Gondar, Gojjam, and Tigrai. He might have had reasons for his view, given the general perception that these provinces were the bastions of conservatism. But digging out of the grave an issue long entombed and practically forgotten to make that simple point could only be taken as a manifestation of a still festering psychological wound. Slavery had been banned in Ethiopia for centuries, and the practice had been completely eradicated by the third and fourth decades of the 20th century. We were now in the seventh decade. No one could make a credible case of the problem's gravity in Gondar or anywhere else in Ethiopia. As we left the meeting, I and a few members of the Cabinet expressed surprise at the man's sensitivity to a problem of interest only to historians. But we obviously underestimated his pain.

His antipathy towards superiors was well known in army circles. The most heinous manifestation of this was, of course, the massacre in 1974 of twenty-two senior officers (including eighteen Generals and a Rear Admiral) along with civilian officials of Emperor Haile-Selassie. All were alleged to have committed crimes while in authority. But it was clear from the beginning of the soldiers' movement that senior military officers were marked men that Mengistu would take care of sooner or later. He likewise showed hostility bordering on inferiority complex towards graduates of the Harar Military Academy, a college level institution modeled along the lines of Britain's Sandhurst. Mengistu himself graduated from a junior military training school which accepted primary school students. This powerful sentiment of inferiority would cause many of the Academy's graduates as well as potential rivals from the mainstream Amhara, Oromo, or Tigrai groups to be sidelined and murdered as he climbed the rungs of power.

Mengistu is frequently portrayed as a nationalist. As he assiduously worked for power, it was imperative for him to project that image. But given his deep resentment against the way he was treated when young, his readiness to ingratiate himself with left wing student groups for whom nationalism was a throwback to the feudal era, and given, moreover, the manner of his none-too-heroic dash to safety in Zimbabwe when national catastrophe stared him in the face, it is difficult to be persuaded that he had nationalist sentiments sufficiently strong to earn him that label. Any nationalist inclinations he might have had could only have been of the cartographic variety.

Borders of all kinds (demarcations delineating urban property, rural land, claims to grazing land and watering points, and above all the nation's frontiers) were matters of grave import to most Ethiopians, and particularly to those in uniform whose primary duty was to defend the frontiers of the motherland and prevent anyone, Eritrean or otherwise, to disfigure the nation's sacrosanct map.[12] He could identify with that perception of the country's borders by the military, rather than with the culture, traditions, sentiments, social values and history of the peoples living within them.

In a nutshell, one could say that the most powerful driving force in Mengistu's life was the psychological urge to get even with individuals and groups perceived to be the cause of years of his painful personal humiliation (which would consist of the majority of Ethiopians). Raw political power was the instrument that enabled him to get even with them, to subdue and mistreat them, as they had subdued and mistreated him. And that became the second most powerful driving force. Cartographic nationalism was needed as a cloak to conceal the preceding two motivations. It was also a useful rhetoric for the war effort. To the extent that it could be characterized as a driving force, it came far behind the preceding two. The fact that it failed to motivate the army or the public is evidence that everyone could see through the deceptive garb.

It is an irony of our times that among the reasons for Mengistu's election as Chairman of the Coordinating Committee of the Armed Forces in the summer of 1974 was precisely the fact that he came from an oppressed minority community. He did not come from the mainstream Amhara, Oromo, or Tigray ethnic groups: the principal rivals for power. He was perceived as a compromise candidate acceptable to all. In addition, he poignantly symbolized the new era of justice and social equality everyone longed for; which was another factor favouring his election. The fact that the Coordinating Committee was moved by these ideals to elect him as their leader and the additional fact that one of the early public statements issued by the Committee had strongly admonished past social attitudes which denigrated his ethnic group and similar others were not enough to erase the man's perception that the majority of his compatriots still carried residual sentiments of ethnic superiority towards him.

This complex man had been the principal protagonist in the successive internal power struggles of the Dergue. As he took out his adversaries one by one and as his confidence grew, his rivals began to look for ways to restrain him. Following the death of Sisay in July 1976, Mengistu's principal contenders were Captain Mogus Wolde-Michael and Lt. Alemayehou Haile. The All Ethiopia Socialist Movement, one of two clandestine left wing parties, supported Mengistu while the other, the Ethiopian People's Revolutionary Party, worked with Mogus and Alemayehou to rein him in. Mengistu had also organized *Seded*, a political group exclusively for the military. Mogus and Alemayehou were purposely kept out.

The Soldier Finally Reaches the Summit

Things came to a head in December 1976 when the two officers and their supporters succeeded in placing on the Dergue's agenda an item on internal re-organization. The purported aim was to strengthen collective leadership. In this they were able to get a majority to vote for a new Soviet-type organizational structure in which three principal centres of power were delineated: (i) the Congress of the Dergue: the highest plenary body in charge of legislation, major policies and programmes as well as the appointment of the Chairman, his deputies and the Secretary General; (ii) the Central Committee made up of 40 Dergue members which would act for the Congress in administering the country, implementing economic and social policies, overseeing internal security, monitoring external relations, and making appointments of high government officials; and (iii) a Standing Committee of 17: an executive body in charge of the day to day management of government business.[13]

The unstated objective was to clip Mengistu's wings. He was reduced to being Chairman of the Council of Ministers (the Cabinet), a body largely composed of technocrats and totally at the mercy of the Dergue. Tafari Banti became Chairman of all three Dergue bodies and commander-in-chief of the Armed Forces. Lt. Alemayou became Secretary General of the three organs with extensive responsibilities to organize and guide their day to day work. Mogus became Chairman of the powerful Political and Foreign Affairs sub-committee of the Standing Committee.

Everyone in Addis had been following the ongoing power struggle avidly. When the restructuring plan appeared in the press, most observers saw through the plot and said that it was like trying to put Mengistu in paper chains. He would break out before long. Gratuitous advice flowed into the ears of his adversaries: to put him behind bars, kick him out of the Grand Palace to which he had moved after an attempt on his life, get rid of him as he assuredly would get rid of them if he were in their position etc., etc. The public would turn out to be wiser than the man's adversaries.

On February 3, 1977, exactly 35 days after he was put in paper chains, Mengistu mounted a coup. General Tafari, Captain Mogus, Lt. Alemayehou, their closest collaborators and other members of the Standing were called to an early morning meeting. A few minutes into the meeting, a messenger came and whispered in Mengistu's ears that there was an urgent call for him in the adjoining room. Mengistu turned to the Chairman and requested permission to leave. The Chairman gave his consent. Within minutes of his departure, soldiers under the command of Mengistu's hatchet man (Colonel Daniel) stormed into the room and asked everyone to raise their hands. Those not wanted were told to leave. Mengistu's foes and their sympathizers, including the Chairman, were taken to the basement below and shot in cold blood.

A year and seven months after the meeting of the Coordinating Committee of the Armed Forces which elected him as chairman, Colonel Mengistu Haile-Mariam saw his dream come true. He was now top dog, succeeding Tafari Banti as Chairman of the Dergue, head of government, and Commander-in-Chief of the Armed Forces. Only one minor rival remained to be dealt with: Colonel Atnafu Abate.

Foreign Minister Kifle Wodajo had gone to Tanzania in advance of a planned state visit by General Tafari Banti. When he was informed that Mengistu had shot the General he decided not to return. I learnt this from a handwritten note he sent through a trusted friend. Kifle had worked closely with General Tafari, and it was said that he had helped draft a speech that the General had given at a public rally in Addis Ababa in which he called for a rapprochement with the EPRP, Mengistu's arch enemy. Would Mengistu eye this as a sign of political support by Kifle to the General? And would he dispatch plainclothes policemen to his residence to search for some incriminating evidence?

I started to go through Kifle's papers and set aside those that might be regarded as politically compromising: a letter from Secretary of State Henry Kissinger in which the Secretary had said that the U. S. was prepared to work with Ethiopia so long as its national security interests were not put into question. Although I did not detect anything that could be judged to be compromising, the U.S. was no longer viewed as a friendly country and the letter could easily be spinned out as evidence of secret links with the imperialists. There were also papers bearing the name of Mengistu's adversary, Sisay Habte. Among Kifle's papers were old Ethiopian Birr notes with the Emperor's image which he, in his customary casualness, had left inside a book. These were no longer legal tender and might give rise to questions. I decided to burn all these and others at a convenient time in the evening.

At 8:00 p.m. I started the fire place and went outside to see if anyone could notice smoke coming out of the chimney. And sure enough, it was visible. I thought it would be prudent to wait until everyone had gone to sleep. At 11:00 p.m. the papers went up in flames.

Once again, I expected people from the intelligence services to come and search Kifle's room. Days passed. And then weeks. Curious friends came to find out what had happened. I had little forewarning of what turned out to be the start of a long exile for Kifle. Neither did he have any inkling that the bloody event would take place and that he would not come back. More curious people came, but none from the intelligence department.

Looking for a Job and the Elusive Exit Visa

I was still searching for of a job while all this was happening. The Centre for Transnational Corporations at the U. N. had been newly established in 1976 and my name had been suggested to the new Finnish Executive Director who was looking for senior staff. While he was on a visit to Addis, I was able to establish contact through the ECA. Roman prepared lunch and we had what looked like a very promising conversation. He said that there was a senior post which fitted my qualifications and experience and that I would hear from him soon. I did all the required paper work and handed it to him. At about the same time, I got a call from the UNDP office in Addis saying that I was expected to present a study I had prepared for the ILO at a meeting in Nairobi. Would I attend? The troubling question of whether or not an exit visa would be granted surfaced once again.

Hailu Yimenu, who was one of my deputies in the Planning Commission, was now a senior minister in Chairman Mengistu's office. I decided to consult him. He said that he would first raise this with the Chairman to test the waters and get back to me. After two or three days, he did. "What is this person doing?" Mengistu had apparently asked. "He does not even bother to show concern about the state of the nation." I told Hailu what I had been doing since I left government (not too much). How, I asked him regarding Mengistu's second point, was I expected to manifest concern for the nation? Hailu did not want to get into the question. He advised that I write a letter explaining

Solomon Sebhatu signing the wedding papers at the Municipality of Addis Ababa in 1977 as the bride and groom and Ato Haddis Alemayhu conduct a lively chat

what I had been doing since I left government and why I needed an exit visa. I took the opportunity to inform Hailu about the prospective United Nations job and that, while I did not need the government's support, a no-objection response in the event the question was raised would be helpful. He did not see any problem in that regard.

As the U.N. had not yet made an offer, I used an unexpected job offer by the African Development Bank for the visa request. I quickly drafted a letter along the lines suggested by Hailu and sent it to his office. I informed Roman about all this and told her that my request for a visa was for 'me and my family' and that if we got a positive response, we should arrange a quick marriage ceremony and get out quickly. She informed her parents and started to prepare herself. I wasn't contemplating the usual kind of wedding, I told her. Neither the tense political environment nor my own personal disposition encouraged thoughts of a wedding. My folks were in detention and I did not have money to spare. I wasn't going to borrow money for a wedding that would be beyond my means. Roman conveyed these thoughts to her parents.

Her father's reaction was that some sort of wedding was necessary. "How am I to explain Roman's sudden disappearance from the house," he said. I agreed that her family could organize a modest reception limited to close family members and I would host a dinner for perhaps a dozen persons. Prior to that, we would go to the municipality and sign the necessary papers. There would also be a blessing at church in the middle of a quiet afternoon. One last formality remained: sending elders to Roman's parents to ask for the hand of their daughter.

The new couple outside Trinity Cathedral after the wedding. On far right is Roman's mother, Woizero Alemitu and on far left her father, Ato Sebhatu, and Amha Eshete is behind the groom

Ato Sebhatu Gebre-Yesus and his children. Lemma (far left) followed by Solomon, Mimi, Endalkatchew, Zellalem, Tesfaye and Tigist; Roman is missing

I chose Haddis Alemayehu to lead a delegation of three in which Amha Eshete, a very close friend, and my relative Colonel Molalign Belai were included. I was later told that Haddis was so glowing in portraying me as an ideal suitor that the girl's mother, Woizero Alemitu Habte-Mariam, felt it necessary to respond with a more formidable portrayal of her own daughter's talents and sterling character. Haddis retorted that nothing he said about Tekalign should take away from what the mother had said about her daughter. Tekalign would indeed be very fortunate to have their daughter as a partner for life. The little friendly skirmish was quickly brought to a conclusion in which each side felt it had made the best presentation of its case. The parents' consent was quickly secured.

Two weeks after submitting my application for an exit visa, I got a response. "An exit visa could be granted if evidence of a job is shown by the applicant," said a handwritten note along the margin of my application. My friend Getachew Kibret, who was at the time also in the Chairman's office, came to see me and said a bit more on Mengistu's reaction to my request. "Why are people like him not willing to serve the nation at a modest salary?" Hailu had explained my fruitless efforts at Addis Ababa University as a manifestation of my desire to work at home. And Mengistu had replied: "Tell him to make his request through the proper channels," as if to say 'I am no longer the approachable Mengistu he knew before. I am now the head of state and he has to go through the normal procedures like everyone else.'

Friends having a cocktail at the wedding in 1977; Getachew Kibret (left), the groom, Grazmatch Habte-Ab and Belatchew Asrat

The next step was to show the immigration department the permit written along the margin of my formal request for visas for me and my family. The head of the department, the same Colonel Tesfaye Wolde-Selassie who had informed me of the Dergue's negative response to my first request, pored over the note along the margin and said only one visa was allowed. When I asked why, he replied that the operative phrase in the note was "if evidence of a job is shown by the applicant…" That, said Colonel Tesfaye, referred to me and not to my wife. I tried to explain to him that the visa request had been for *both me and my family.* If the responsible officer who wrote down the note intended the visa to be granted only to me, he could have said so. "I cannot make that interpretation sir," said Tesfaye, "and I regret that you have to take this thing back to whoever made these remarks and ask him to clarify." It took a week to do that. The author of the note on the margin added a single word in Amharic (*kenebetesebatchew*): i.e. together with his family.

The job offer from the African Development Bank had come out of the blue. I had not applied. As the response from the U.N. did not come, I showed the ADB offer as proof that I was going to be engaged in a professional pursuit, not in a hostile political activity as the authorities might suspect. Both Roman and I now obtained our exit visas. We presented ourselves at the Municipality of Addis Ababa to have our marriage registered, had a brief ceremony at Trinity Cathedral followed by a very modest reception at Roman's home and an even more modest dinner at mine.

On the 26th of April 1977, we boarded Ethiopian Airlines on our way to Abidjan, the Headquarters of the African Development Bank. We spent a night in Accra, Ghana, and boarded an Air Afrique flight to Abidjan the following day. Such was the trauma of leaving our country after all we had been through that we feared we might never again be able to return. Roman was weeping and sobbing for a good part of the journey.

PART IV

Exile Years and the Birth of the Second Republic

CHAPTER 14

The African Development Bank

A Nice Little Challenge

April in Abidjan is unbearably muggy. One could easily imagine the first reaction of someone from a place like Addis Ababa where the air is dry and the shade is a ready refuge from the sun. "How could people live in this kind of climate?" I remember saying to Roman as we got off the plane. I quietly concluded that we should not stay in the place a day longer than it takes us to find another job. Little did I realize then that I would spend sixteen and half years in a climate to which I would adapt so well that I would complain about Addis weather being too dry for the skin and the nostrils upon my first homecoming.

Bank staff met us at the airport and took us to Hotel du Parc: an old, dark and claustrophobic structure near the Bank's Headquarters. We retired soon after dinner and went to bed hoping to recover from the fatigue of the transcontinental flight. But the constant hum of the air conditioner unit would not let us go to sleep. We turned it off. Half an hour or so later, we were woken up by the humidity which had built up in the meantime. We now switched on the unit once again to cool the room and tried to go to sleep. Again the noise from the unit prevented any sleep. And so the night turned out to be a fairly regular to and fro between the bed and the air conditioner unit. We were puzzled how such an obvious nuisance had escaped the attention of the hotel management. The puzzle was solved when we rented an apartment some time later. We got used to the hum. As we would find out later, children (including our own) would become so accustomed to the lullaby of the hum that they could not go to sleep without it even during the cool season when it was not needed.

The following day, a Bank driver came and took me to the office of the vice President, Goodall Gondwe. Gondwe was courteous and appeared sad that a former minister of His Imperial Majesty had fallen on bad times. I must confess that I did not cut an impressive figure, appearing in his office with sandals, a short sleeved open shirt, and a non-descript pair of pants; all of which I had hurriedly picked up from a store nearby as my first attempt to adapt to an inclement weather. Gondwe informed me that the Bank's president, Ghanaian Kwame Fordwor, was at the institution's Annual General Meeting in Mauritius. It would be a few days before he returned. In the meanwhile, I could relax and try to get acclimatized.

It was an opportunity for Roman and I to explore the city. We visited the two large open air markets, the commercial and residential areas, hotels, shops, and the wide variety of restaurants. Compared to Addis, Abidjan was much better planned. It had an impressive skyline, broad streets, and quality boutiques. The lagoons around which the city was built, the winding boulevards on their banks and the high rise buildings gave it a picturesque quality not too common in Africa. We asked if there were museums and were directed to one replete with masks, figurines, drums, and a variety of traditional sculptures.

Fordwor and I had never met. "Tenastilign" he greeted me in Amharic as I entered his office. He got down to business right away. Ten years after its establishment, the African Development Bank was at a stage where limited resources constrained further growth, he said. The Bank was established as an institution whose membership was purposely restricted to African states. A decade of experience showed that a collection of economically weak owners does not make a strong bank. We should think seriously about inviting developed countries to join the Bank as shareholders. Fordwor wanted me to examine the issue in depth and prepare a report for the following annual meeting of the Bank.

Being new to the organization and to the subject, I demurred. The Bank had been established following an ECA commissioned study carried out by Hans Singer. As a young professional working at the organization, I was familiar with the study and the discussions preceding the Bank's establishment by members of the Committee of Nine (among whom was Mamonu Beheiry of Sudan who would become the first President of the institution and Ethiopia's Yewondwossen Mengesha who would serve as a member of the first executive board). But that was a decade ago, and I had no clue how the Bank had evolved in the meantime and what its present challenges were. Besides, I was an economist, not a specialist in finance. I told Fordwor that I would be happy to work as a member of a task force to prepare the report, but did not see how I could do it on my own. He had apparently made up his mind, and persisted in his suggestion.

I had little choice in the matter. Fordwor asked me to jot down my thoughts as to how the report could be formulated. I was given some background documents. The resolution of the Bank's Board of Governors (passed only a few weeks earlier) was my starting point. It requested the president to examine how the shortage of resources could be resolved on "a permanent basis."[1] The language of the resolution did not make an explicit reference to the 'opening of capital' to industrial countries. Hans Singer had initially proposed the possibility of inviting these countries to join the new Bank, but the idea had been firmly turned down by African States. So soon after independence, few countries were prepared to invite back their former colonial masters. Ten years later, it was still a live issue and had to be handled with caution.

Other relevant documents were also put at my disposal. I took a couple of weeks in studying them and prepared a sixteen-page note as to how the report might be put together: the issues to be examined, the research effort required, and consultations with the multilateral development banks. Fordwor accepted its proposals and I subsequently prepared a detailed outline and a work schedule. I reckoned seven to eight months for its completion and soon got going on my own, with Fordwor providing advice and authorizing the necessary budget. Visits were scheduled to the World Bank and the Inter-American Development Bank in Washington, to investment banks in New York, to certain multilateral institutions in Paris, and to the Asian Development Bank in Manila, the Philippines.

My first study tour was to the U.S. I held extensive discussions with staff of the Inter-American Development Bank, the World Bank, and investment bankers in Wall Street. These went well. While in New York, I thought I should talk to the Finnish Executive Director of the Centre for Transnational Corporations whom I had met in Addis Ababa several months before. He had sounded positive about offering me a senior vacant post at the Centre. I was curious to find out what had happened.

I proceeded to the United Nations to see him. The Executive Director looked ill at ease. He told me that for reasons he was not at liberty to disclose, it had not been possible to offer me the post he had promised in our meeting in Addis Ababa. The meeting did not last long. Suspecting something fishy, I went to see Ethiopia's Permanent Representative to the United Nations, someone I had known for years and to whom I had previously talked about the U.N. job. Did he have a clue why the Executive Director was unable to offer the post? "Yes," he said. "As it was a senior position, the major powers had to be consulted. The Americans had opposed your appointment." My suspicion that there was something strange was confirmed. From my experience at the U.N. I knew that major powers were not involved in recruitment decisions regarding senior posts of the kind offered to me. And there was no reason whatsoever for the American to oppose my appointment. Most likely, it was the Permanent Representative himself who stood in the way. He was probably contacted by the Executive Director for information or took the initiative himself to talk to him unfavourably about me. I had left government. My friend Kifle Wodajo had also left. The representative presumably wished to play it safe with his bosses.

To get back to the main story, I completed my round of meetings in the U.S., travelled to Europe and returned to Abidjan after a month. Three months later the first draft of the report was completed.[2] It was discussed at a three-hour meeting one Saturday morning in the president's office. Fordwor's comments were the most detailed, reflecting in part his professional experience at the International Finance Corporation. He was also determined to leave an impact on the Bank's future.

A revised draft of my report was submitted to the Bank's Executive Board. Their discussion centered on the recommendation which all feared would be contentious: opening of the Bank's doors to former colonial countries. The resolution of the Bank's Board of Governors had requested the president to study the matter "with the view to examining the various possibilities for increasing the resources of the Bank on a permanent basis." An extensive analysis was made in report of different alternatives to resolve the Bank's financial problem once and for all conclusion was that none except opening the Bank's doors to membership by industrial countries would increase the Bank's resources on a "permanent basis."

The board debated the paper at length and finally endorsed the proposal that industrial countries should be invited to buy shares in the Bank. This would make it possible for the institution to borrow money in their capital markets (New York, London, Paris, Frankfurt, Tokyo, etc.,) to fund a meaningful level of operations. An illustrative projection of lending had been included in the report which showed loans increasing seven fold over a ten-year period. Some such lending programme would provide greater support to the efforts of borrowing countries. It was also argued that if the industrial countries joined the Bank, their commitment would be stronger to the African Development Fund (ADF), a soft window affiliate established in 1972 along the lines of the World Bank's International Development Association (IDA).

The report was finalized and circulated to member countries in February 1978. In May we proceeded to Libreville, Gabon, for the Annual Meeting.When the agenda item dealing with the report came up for discussion, the Board of Governors went into a closed session. I had up to that point not entered the plenary hall. When I was told that my report was coming up for discussion, I went to the entrance and, finding it locked, asked the Bank's protocol officer to let me in. Gatekeeper Bullock, a half-Egyptian half-British rotund chief of protocol well known for his laissez faire ways, put on the air of a no-nonsense sergeant-major and said he had been instructed not to allow anyone in. He of course knew that I was the report's author and that I should be allowed in to respond to questions that might be raised. I felt tempted to speak to him in that vein, but dropped the matter when I realized that his capacity to engage in conversation had temporarily been reduced to three words: "no entry please."

Bemused and not a little amused, I left pompous Bullock to his guarding duty and tried to follow developments from persons who occasionally came out of the meeting hall. I cannot now recall exactly how long the closed meeting lasted, but it was long enough to get some of us outside the hall worried. To most African countries, opening the Bank to non-African membership was an unwelcome reminder of the colonial era and an admission that Africans were still dependent on the industrial countries, despite their independence of ten years. To the Libyans, it was a scheme hatched to let Israel into the Bank. Was a crisis brewing, we wondered?

After a long wait, the large door of the conference hall opened. As participants came out one after another their poker faces gave no hint of what had been decided. I looked for a familiar face, but none showed up for the first two or three anxious minutes. I finally went up to gatekeeper Bullock and asked if he knew which way the vote had gone. He said that he had heard that the delegates had accepted the recommendations of the report. He could not say more.

The Ethiopian Minister of Finance, Tafarra Wolde-Semait, informed me later that there was a huge majority in favour of the recommendations. Only two countries, Mengistu's Ethiopia and Idi Amin's Uganda, had voted against. Ghadafi's Libya would definitely have joined the pair had his delegate not missed the meeting. Tafarra, an able official whom I had known for years, informed me that he had tried to persuade the Ethiopian Cabinet to endorse the report's proposals. Only one or two ministers supported him. He had consequently come with a mandate to vote nay. He was personally sorry that a report authored by an Ethiopian should be turned down by his own country. I understood his sentiments, but also those of Mengistu and his band of fresh converts to scientific socialism. They would not miss an opportunity to affirm their loyalty to the new creed.

Why had the meeting taken so long, I wondered? Much time was apparently taken up in defining the conditions of entry for prospective members. It was essential, so argued the ministers, to maintain the 'African character' of the Bank. A number of criteria were laid down for this, the most important of which was that two thirds of the voting power should remain in African hands. A few other stipulations were added: that only African members would borrow from the Bank, that the president of the Bank would always be the national of an African country, that the Bank's Headquarters would always be located in Africa, and that Annual General Meetings would be held only in African countries. While it was recognized that the report had made a strong case for admitting industrial countries as the Bank's members, there was apprehension that they might in time take over control of the institution unless preventive measures were put in place.

Three months prior to the Libreville meeting, Roman had given birth to our first child. When she was expecting, it had looked as if she was going to have twins. Her doctor said it was a fat healthy boy. Teshager was born on 24 February 1978. His birth coincided with the completion of the report on which I had been working since joining the Bank. I was relieved that my own nine-month ordeal was over. Roman and I joked that we had been blessed with twins.

A year and a few months into our stay in Abidjan, we had not yet fully adjusted to the climate. And the outrageous cost of living was a constant strain on our modest income. Above all, the ADB was not professionally stimulating, nor was it an estab-

Teshager with his grandmother, Woizero Alemitu Habte-Mariam in Abidjan, the Ivory Coast, in 1983

lished organization offering attractive career prospects. The president had one admirable quality: a dogged determination to accomplish what he set out to do. He was a good professional and possessed a high work ethic. And he had a good vision for the future of the institution. Yet, he acted like a small time village chief, manifesting his elevated status in the way he talked, walked, and behaved. At meetings, he talked down to staff and was often downright rude. He was abrasive, an attitude which rankled many board members who themselves acted like plenipotentiaries sent to monitor the actions of the chief executive. He was not the easiest person to work with even under the best of circumstances.

I had come from a somewhat different background. Self respect was a dearly held value in Ethiopia. You may be a high flying boss in the Ethiopian bureaucracy, but that did not give you the license to abuse staff. A staff in the lowest echelons of the bureaucracy was, perhaps for that very reason, particularly sensitive about his self respect. He would not accept a supervisor, be he minister or someone of lower rank, to humiliate him in public. Fordwor would sometimes do precisely that to everyone's embarrassment. He once berated staff for the complaints he received from single mothers who were not getting adequate child support for children fathered by them.

For all of these reasons, I had been using my contacts at the U. N. to move to a more agreeable and secure professional working environment. In Abidjan soon after the Libreville meeting, I got word from a friend at the UNDP that there was a vacancy for the post of economic advisor to a government in one of the smaller countries in Southern Africa. Would I be interested? I had heard about these countries: about their climate, culture and traditions having some similarity with those of Ethiopia. I accepted the offer. As a matter of courtesy, I felt I should inform the president of the Bank.

I told him that working on the report had been rewarding, but that I had never intended to settle in Abidjan, had been exploring other prospects, and had finally been offered a post by the UNDP. Unwisely as it would turn out, I mentioned the name of the person who had helped secure the post for me and what kind of post it was. He was disappointed, but in a restrained kind of way. He told me that major challenges lay ahead in bringing to closure the recommendation to allow non-African countries to join the Bank. When these countries became members, the Bank's prospects would improve and that it would be a professionally rewarding institution to work for. I was not persuaded.

I left his office feeling a little distressed that the *au revoir* was not going to be a smooth affair. A week later, I got a call from my contact at the UNDP headquarters in New York. Had I not said that I had agreed to take the post offered and was ready to travel? Of course I had, as I believed that my obligation to complete the paper had been met and that I was free to take other assignments. "The president of the Bank called to complain about our office," said my contact. "He accuses us of sabotaging his efforts to reform the ADB. He is unhappy that the offer of a job has been made to you. How should we move forward now? We certainly do not wish to be seen as an institution standing in the way of his reform efforts." I blamed myself for my naiveté, and sadly concluded that I should not be the cause of an acrimonious exchange of messages between two institutions sharing similar goals. I expressed my appreciation to my friend for his efforts, dropped the matter and reluctantly settled down to continue working at the Bank.

Negotiations with Prospective Member States

The next phase of the exercise was to negotiate with potential member countries in order to work out the details of the process of admitting two dozen or so of new members. The work commenced with a list of countries to be invited. The obvious first group consisted of 19 mostly Western industrial countries which were members of the ADF. We discussed whether countries in the Eastern bloc should be included. They themselves were, of course, developing countries. For political reasons, some had to be included in the list. Procurement was a further reason, as countries like India and China were increasingly able to supply capital equipment for Bank funded projects at competitive prices, a matter of obvious interest to African countries. The Soviet Union and China were consequently included. India figured on the list of 19 ADF state participants and would therefore be invited in that capacity. Letters of invitation were sent out to 25 countries in June. Practically all responded affirmatively. Russia and China did not.

Fordwor and I visited seven countries in Western Europe and North America and explained the spirit of the resolution, the conditions of entry, and the expectations of African countries from a reinvigorated bank. Other officials were sent to a further nine countries. These were followed by four multilateral discussions and negotiations in Washington D.C. (September 1978), Rabat (November), Abidjan (January 1979), and London (February). The negotiations were bumpy, lengthy, and on occasion embarrassing.

A report on the outcome was presented to the Board of Governors at the Bank's Annual Meeting in May 1979 in Abidjan. It was accepted and a resolution duly passed. The process of amending the statutes of the Bank to reflect this new reality would soon start. It was a happy ending in a long and adventurous journey. Sadly, something happened that dampened our spirits.

In July 1979 a crisis shook the Bank which seemed to put in jeopardy the hard-won achievements of the previous two years. An Extraordinary General Meeting of the Board of Governors called by Nigeria and some other countries took place in Abidjan at which the only agenda item was the president of the Bank. He had antagonized too many people in the course of his two-year stay. A recent memoir by Tadesse Gebre-Kidan, an Ethiopian official who took part in the meeting, offers an additional explanation. According to a story circulating at the time, Nigerian leader General Obasanjo was upset by the execution of fellow General Acheampong of Ghana by Flight Lieutenant Jerry Rawlings. He had strongly advised restraint but Rawlings had gone ahead with the General's execution. Tadesse leaves the impression that Fordwor, a Ghanaian, found himself caught up in a sudden deterioration of diplomatic relations between Nigeria and his country.

The Extraordinary General Meeting, spearheaded by the Nigerian Minister of Finance, resolved to put Fordwor on indefinite leave without pay (polite language for removal). It was a sad event, especially for those of us who had worked closely with Fordwor and who had tried to draw his attention to his needlessly abrasive style of management. Whatever his weaknesses, he had set out on an ambitious goal, had worked on it single-mindedly, and had succeeded. And the Bank would in time become a far stronger institution. Goodall Gondwe was appointed president ad-interim in place of Fordwar.

The Bank Goes Global

Following Fordwar's departure, the inevitable question on everyone's mind was who would succeed him. Before long I myself was preoccupied with a curious cable from Ethiopia. It was from Hailu Yimenu who occupied a post equivalent to that of a Prime Minister. The cable said that the government of Ethiopia was considering to forward my name as a candidate for the Bank's presidency and suggested that I come to Addis for discussions. The Minister of Finance, Tafarra Wolde-Semait, sent another cable confirming Hailu's message.

I had resigned from the government only three years earlier, giving as my reason my inability to support the government's policy directions. How could I accept in good conscience its endorsement of my candidacy? I did not feel comfortable at all. My wife Roman was uncomfortable for a different reason. She did not think that going back to Addis was a good idea, given my relations with the Dergue. My own view was that Hailu and Tafarra were persons I had known for several years. They would not be party to something that exposed me to danger. After reflecting on the cable, I decided that it would be nothing short of opportunistic to accept the proposal and decided to go to Addis to advise these two officials that I was not comfortable with the idea. And did so. Yewondwossen Mengesha, the former Deputy Governor of Ethiopia's central bank who had been close to the ADB in its formative years, was now living in London and was occasionally consulted by the Bank on various financial matters. When he later came to know that my name had been considered as a potential candidate, he said that had he known this earlier he would have offered assistance. He had good contacts in Africa and probably thought that he could be helpful in some lobbying effort. He was of course unaware of my position.

There was of course no shortage of contenders, not excluding the president ad–interm, Goodall Gondwe. Eventually Zambian Wila Mung'Omba was elected, thanks largely to Nigeria which went out of its way to mount a robust campaign on his behalf. Rumour had it that this was part of a deal with Nigeria in which Zambia would return the favour by lobbying African governments to allow Nigeria to have a permanent seat representing a constituency of eighteen African countries at the World Bank. While Nigeria fulfilled its part of the deal, the Zambians ran into difficulty. The prevailing practice was for the constituency to elect its representative to the Bank Board on a rotating basis, which gave every country an opportunity to occupy the seat for a term of four years. When Nigeria's turn came up, the Zambian delegate proposed that the Nigerian candidate be elected as a permanent representative of the constituency and not, as was customary, for a four-year term. The Ethiopia's Minister Tafarra asked the obvious question: what is wrong with the current practice. No plausible answer could be offered. Zimbabwe, a newly independent country still enjoying the diplomatic limelight, protested strongly. And the idea was scuttled

The process of amending the ADB's statutes proceeded slowly. Countries having parliaments had to secure the approval of their legislatures, which naturally took time. Those that had done away with that democratic nuisance took time on an issue that did not appear all that urgent. States numbering two-thirds of the Bank's total membership exercising at least seventy-five per cent of the voting power were required for the ratification to take effect. This was achieved three years later at the Annual Meeting in Zambia in 1982 when Nigeria, a country which often goes out of its way to make a point of its political weight, announced that it had completed the ratification process. Surprisingly, Mengistu's Ethiopia also ratified the agreement; and much earlier than expected. Idi Amin, who had fled Uganda in April 1979, was not given Mengitu's opportunity to flip flop.

The non-African countries had ratified the statutes earlier. By 1982 an initial group of 18 countries had met the legal requirements to join the Bank. The combined effect of non-African and African subscriptions to the Bank's capital was to increase it by almost eight-fold (from roughly U.S. $800 million to U.S. $6.3 billion). The African states had to increase their subscriptions substantially in order to maintain the 2/3 voting ratio. The Bank was now ready to accept board members from the non-African states and begin the process of accessing capital markets in Europe, Asia, and North America. There was hardly an eye catching event to mark the occasion, the only exception being the decision by the U. S. government to have a fifteen- minute ceremony at the White House to which were invited Bank officials as well as a number of African diplomats in Washington.

The Reagan administration had been under some criticism for cutting aid, especially to African countries. Here was a photo opportunity to make things look good. The president and staff of the Bank, African diplomats, and U.S. Treasury officials were assembled in the East Room of the White House one winter morning in 1982. President Reagan walked in, shook hands with Mong'Omba, the Bank president, and gave a short welcoming address, drawing our attention to the significance of the event and the important place Africa occupied in U.S. foreign policy. The great communicator made an impressive short speech on a subject we all knew he was hardly aware of. The only thing noteworthy was the ease with which Reagan pronounced a name that poses a challenge even to African tongues. He took a quick look at Mung'Omaba and started his speech with the words: President Munyei. Sitting in the front row, that was how it sounded to me. Others heard variations on the theme that came nowhere near Mung'Omba.

Preparations were now underway to enter the capital markets. The first step was to get a rating. Finance vice president Babacar N'Diaye, working closely with staff from Kidder Peabody & Co. of Wall Street as well as the Bank's own staff, arranged for a rating review by the three New York rating agencies: Standard and Poor's, Moody's, and Fitch. The initial ratings were not too high but were good enough to enter the markets. This happened in 1985 when the Bank issued five bonds in New York, London, Tokyo, Frankfurt, and Zurich totaling some U.S. $770 million; a landmark in the history of the Bank.

From the backwaters of West Africa, the Bank had scaled the heights of international finance and was now at par with its sister banks: the Inter-American Development Bank and the Asian Development Bank. It would confound observers in 1992 by being voted, against all expectations, the best borrower among the multilateral sovereign borrowers (i.e. the above two, the World Bank, and the European Investment Bank among others) by *Euromoney* Magazine: a reflection of the favourable terms and conditions negotiated on its bonds that year. This achievement was largely due to those who had worked hard for several years to make it possible for the ADB to be a player in international finance. Bank staff who worked on the borrowings of that year, particularly Ghanaian Koffi Bucknor, played perhaps the key role. Koffi had been with the Chase Manhattan Bank for some ten years before joining the ADB. He did much to raise the Bank's profile among investment bankers in the U.S., Europe and Asia.

The Years of Growth

Access to the capital markets was essential for a significant expansion in lending. Simultaneous with the exercise of opening the Bank's capital to non-African countries, the practice of corporate planning was also launched and borrowing operations were now driven by a lending programme formulated within a ten-year perspective. Leaders of the Bank in later years would ignore this in an attempt to give credence to their contention that little was done before they took over. This was hardly surprising, given the well entrenched pattern of behaviour among African officials of sprucing up their image by denigrating those from whom they inherit leadership responsibilities. Opportunists and adventurers from the developed countries often lend a hand to such small minded officials, as was the case at the African Development Bank in the middle and late nineties.

It was thanks to the corporate planning initiative introduced in the late seventies that a robust lending programme changed the face of the African Development Bank. From a level of $154 million in 1977, annual lending increased steadily until it reached $1,034 million at the end of the ten-year planning period in 1986; a seven-fold increase.[3] The rapid growth in lending volume would inevitably throw up problems of loan quality. It must be said that the senior leadership of the Bank, though fully aware of the risks involved, occasionally pushed loans on countries which were far from being creditworthy; due partly to political pressures and due also to a general desire to raise the profile of the Bank. These difficulties should nevertheless not mask the badly needed dynamism injected into Bank operations.

The growth in lending was accompanied by developments in other areas as well. Staff numbers grew two and half times during the period: from 405 in 1977 to 966, 40% of whom were professionals. With its growing profile and stronger financial position, the Bank was now beginning to attract high calibre professionals, a good number from the World Bank. Two professional journals were a new feature of an increasingly confident Bank. Seminars on development issues began to figure prominently at its annual meetings. A trading room was set up in Abidjan in the late eighties and liquid funds were managed with an increasingly active volume of transactions in the financial markets. Presentations of the Bank's financial performance on the occasion of its annual meetings became more and more sophisticated and attracted the attention of a growing number of investment bankers. Net income grew from $13 million in 1977 to $60 million in 1986, and well beyond that in later years.

Behind these developments were years of challenge and forward movement: of teething problems at the birth of the institution, of modest accomplishments during the first decade, of dynamism brought in the second decade, and of a promising injection of professionalism into senior management positions in the eighties and nineties. A succession of chief executives had made all this possible.

First in line was Mamoun Beheiry, the Bank's first no-nonsense Sudanese president who laid the foundations for the institution. His Tunisian successor, Abdelwahab Labidi, did much to consolidate its early operations and helped establish the African Development Fund in 1972. The third chief executive, Ghanaian Kwame Fordwor, focused on broadening the capital base of the bank by opening its doors to non-regional membership, a strategic decision that laid the foundations for future growth. Zambia's Wila Mung'Omba succeeded Fordwor. His country's leader was instrumental in bringing the ever troublesome Nigerians to finally come on board in ratifying the Bank Agreement. Mung'Omba did much to improve staff welfare. Senegal's Babaccar N'Diaye started promisingly in 1985 with a plan to secure Bank entry into the financial markets and its subsequent acquisition of a triple A rating.

On a personal level and contrary to my initial misgivings, life in West Africa's leading metropolis became increasingly enjoyable, I travelled extensively on official business, visited many interesting places and made friends. Roman enjoyed cooking and entertained a lot. Both of us were keen to demonstrate Ethiopian cuisine which. most of our guests found delicious and nutritious, especially the vegetarian dishes served during lent. An urbane elderly French gentleman wrote a letter to say how pleasantly surprised he was to see Ethiopia's culture so admirably manifested in its cuisine. ADB Executive Director from Libya and a friend, Muftah Sheriff was another admirer. We had dinner for a few friends one evening where continental food was served. "What is all this?" asked Muftah pointing to the buffet table. "Where is *injera*? I am not going to have any of this." Roman went to the kitchen and got him *injera* and *wot*. We also en-

Alitash Kebede Abozen cautioning Itagegnehou as twin sister Beshowamyellesh wonders what it is all about

tertained Ethiopians who came to the Bank on official business. Some sent us spices when they got back home to help us restock our supply.

My family was also growing. After giving birth to Teshager in 1978, Roman was expecting a second child in 1983. As in the case of Teshager when both she and I thought she was going to have twins, she had put on considerable weight. Another big child seemed to be on the way. In September of that year, I left to attend the World Bank's Annual Meeting in Washington with a long list of things to buy for the new baby. At the end of the meeting, I spent two unseasonably hot days shopping when Roman telephoned

The author with Roman and the children, Abidjan 1989

to ask if I had succeeded in getting all the items on the list. I told her that the shopping was mercifully over and that I would get back home in a day or two. "Could you get one more set?" she asked. She must be pulling my leg, I thought, and asked why. "Your niece in Addis has just delivered and is wondering whether you could include her baby's needs in the list." she replied. Who could this presumptuous niece be to whom I was expected to send a replica of what has taken me two grueling days to buy, I wondered? Noticing my annoyance, Roman said: "It is for our second baby. The doctor tells me I am expecting twins!"

The shopping had to be done all over again. Roman told the doctor she did not wish to know in advance what sex the twins were. When they came into the world, it was in the shape of fraternal twin sisters; Itagegnehou and Beshowamyellesh. Our son Teshager, who was five and a half at the time, looked at them in the delivery room and remarked that they would grow up to be close friends. He had probably looked forward to a brother to play with, but guessed that the two would prefer to play with each other. Though all three were close in the earlier years when Teshager enjoyed playing the role of elder brother at every opportunity, his prediction held; for the two girls grew up to be inseparable.

Members of the African Business Roundtable (a group sponsored by the ADB) with President Bush at the White House in 1988. ADB chief N'Diaye is to left of the President Bush and the author is immediately behind

nother surprise came some three years later. One Sunday afternoon in February 1987, Roman and I were having lunch at the home of Fiammetta and Yohannes Kaypaghian, two friends from Ethiopia who had set up a successful insurance business in Abidjan. Yohannes had in years past part owner and lead executive of the Lion Insurance Company in Addis Ababa before it was nationalized by the Dergue. As we were relaxing over coffee, I received a telephone call from the president of the Bank, Babacar N'Ddiaye. He wanted to see me early the following morning.

We met in his office at 8:00 a.m. as he was preparing for a board meeting. He said we had worked closely over the previous two years of his tenure. Now, he wanted us to work even more closely. The post of vice president had fallen vacant and he had decided that I should fill the vacancy. This reminded me of the cable from Ethiopia some six years earlier indicating that my name was being considered as a possible successor to Kwame Fordwar. I had been reluctant. I was once again disinclined to accept N'Diaye's offer, but for a different set of reasons.

My candidature could be the cause of a contentious argument in the Bank's board which had the mandate to elect vice presidents. There were two members of the board whom I and most staff found singularly disagreeable: a boorish Nigerian and a Chadian of malodoreous ethics with close ties to Mobutu. They were the embodiments of the mendacity, vile, obsequiousness, corruption, and incompetence some of the lower echelons of African civil servants are notorious for. It was one of Africa's bitter mockeries that such people should sit on the Bank board to preside over projects and policies whose ultimate purpose was to improve the lot of millions upon millions of African citizens living in misery and despair. Their reprehensible professional and ethical conduct reeked egregiously. Their daily pre-occupations were light years away from the predicament of poor folk, but only a telephone call away from the wishes and caprices of the Mobutus and the Abachas. I had often clashed with these individuals in the course of my professional duties. They knew my distaste for them, and I was fairly aware that I was not in their good books, which I obviously regarded as a badge of honour but which meant that they would be sitting in judgment over my suitability for the post. The thought that they would now have the opportunity to vet my credentials was not altogether agreeable.

There was another reason for my reluctance. In my ten years at the Bank, I had observed only two types of vice presidents: the majority who were yes men to the president and a few who were inclined to pick up a quarrel with him. I told N'Diaye that I did not fit the mold: I did not want to be sweetly compliant nor did I have the temperament of being cantankerous. My inclination was to be professional, independent and give my best advice. In the annals of the Bank, I had not come across a vice president who behaved in that manner. If I were to accept his offer, the opportunists at the Bank who wished to manifest their loyalties to him in order to protect their jobs would pounce on the first opportunity to drive a wedge between us. Sooner or later friction would develop. Continuing with my professional career was more preferable.

N'Diaye was not persuaded. Indeed he had already circulated my name to the board and had secured the consent of its members including, he said, the disagreeable duo. I was surprised. How could he do that without talking to me first and finding out if I were interested in the post? For a moment I toyed with the idea of declining the offer, but was concerned by the unintended negative impression that it might create. Ethiopians are regarded by many other Africans as being aloof and perhaps even haughty. Might rejection of the offer run the risk of fortifying this insistence and creating practical difficulties in my work? This as well as N'Diaye's persistence made me accept the offer, but with considerable misgivings. Having given my response, I told him that we should sit down in a day or two in order that I could explain my approach as to how the Bank might best be managed and what his own thoughts might be in this regard.

Two or three days after my name was approved, we discussed some of the more fundamental factors involved in managing a complex multicultural institution such as the African Development Bank. I emphasized the more pressing of these. There was a crying need for reform which would transform the Bank into a more professional institution, especially in the human resources area. The Bank had more than its fair share of deadwood. It needed an intake of fresh high calibre staff. A few had been recruited over the previous months, but nowhere near what was required. A significant recruitment of able staff working with the few on board, would determine the Bank's future. He as president should give early signals of this to all Bank employees. I advised that the next batch of staff considered for promotion should be made up predominantly of those who were of above average performance. A few other points were also discussed.

N'Diaye seemed to have no difficulty in agreeing with these ideas. Our meeting ended fairly quickly. Before long, he requested my recommendations of staff for promotion. Using professional performance as the criterion, I drew up a list of deserving staff in various departments of the Bank and handed it over to him. The great majority of these did not work under me and I had no direct experience of their professional performance. I had to use various methods to identity staff with talent and skills. Board meetings were a good forum to judge staff. The views of peers were another guide. Reports and papers authored yet another. I used all of these measures in making my selection. When the promotions were finally announced, I found out that my views had been taken into account to a degree I deemed satisfactory. I got indications that the promotions were well received by most staff. We were off to what looked like a promising start.

A Short Honeymoon

This initial mood of optimism created a climate in which much useful work was accomplished. My first major responsibility soon after I was elected vice president was to conclude the negotiations for the fourth replenishment of the ADF, the Bank's soft window affiliate, which had been going on for the previous six months. An interesting incident took place in the course of the negotiations in Cairo, Egypt, which initially created concern but which in the end paved the way to a better rapport between the Bank and its negotiating partners, the donor countries. For me, however, it would signal an early manifestation of the problems I had earlier discussed with N'Diaye.

Progress had been made in the previous two negotiating sessions (in Rome and Paris) when most of the technical issues were resolved. The Cairo meeting was expected to address the vital issue of the size of the Fund's replenishment: i.e. how much money donors were willing to contribute to the following three-year cycle. At that meeting, the U. S. delegate, Assistant Secretary of the Treasury Jim Conrow, asked a question which took me by surprise. The African Development Bank which managed the ADF was not an efficient organization, said Conrow. Could I explain why the U. S. should channel its aid to Africa through the Bank? It had other channels available to it: the World Bank, a more efficient manager of aid funds, and USAID, its own donor agency.

I was puzzled. At the two previous meetings, another vice president had been the leader of the Bank delegation, although I had participated at the technical level. This was my first meeting at which I was leader of the Bank team. Was the questioner's intention to probe the new team leader? Was the Reagan Administration sending a signal that its contribution to the current replenishment exercise would be modest? We were getting close to a coffee break, and I needed time to collect my thoughts for an appropriate response. I informed the Chairperson (a senior French official from the Elysée Palace) that I would offer a response after the break.

I took the floor after the recess and responded briefly along the following lines. The U.S. delegate was expressing an outsider's view of the Bank. I would offer the views of someone from the inside. First, inefficiency was a problem at the Bank as it was in other development finance organizations; although we would admit that we had more than our fare share of the problem. The situation was not static, however. A number of measures had recently been taken to address the problem. (And here I gave half a dozen illustrations). In time, these would make the Bank a more efficient organization. Secondly, these measures were being introduced not to persuade donors to provide increased aid. To be sure, we needed additional resources. But the efficiency measures were being introduced because it was imperative that we make the Bank a more efficient and credible instrument of development. The U. S. was sovereign in its decision of whether or how much to contribute. The Bank would not be affected one way or another and would proceed with its reform agenda. I ended my intervention with a few additional points. No questions were asked. I got the impression that intervention had gone down well.

In the evening of that day, a reception was given by the U. S. Embassy in honour of participants. Jim Conrow and the Ambassador were on the receiving line. I shook hands with the Ambassador and next turned to Conrow. "You shake hands with me after what I have done to you this morning?" remarked Conrow. It is your duty to ask and mine to respond, I replied. He said he was pleased with the response and informed the Ambassador of the details of the morning's exchange. I was encouraged about U.S. support for our efforts. Most donor countries were equally encouraging. In the end, almost twice as much money was raised for the three-year cycle beginning in 1987 as for the previous three years ($1.95 billion compared with $1.05 billion).

The earlier exercise on the opening of capital had secured a significant expansion of the Bank's resource base. We were therefore making good progress on the financial front. Action had to be taken in terms of building a core of able staff. N'Diaye had earlier recruited staff such as Koffi Bucknor of Ghana, Cheik Fall of Senegal, Stokes of the U.K., and Morcos of Egypt. I myself initiated an effort to attract African staff from the World Bank and the financial markets: the Algerian Belhadj Merghoub, the Camerounian Ted Nkodo, both from the World Bank, and Nigerians Ogundipe and Ali from Wall Street and the City, respectively. The able and amiable Delphin Rwegasira of Tanzania had joined the Bank earlier. Ethiopia's quietly competent economist, Henock Kifle, soon came on board. Among the more talented of the older staff were Susungi from Cameroon, Rukerebuka from Tanzania, Oketokun from Benin, Bouabdalli

With Yohannes Kaypaghian, middle, and Beshowamyellesh in Abidjan in 1987

fromMorocco, Mbaye from Senegal, Mwamufiya from Congo, Bouzaher from Algeria, Shongwe from Swaziland, to name but a few. They all made an impact and gave impetus to the dynamism of the institution.

This was also a time when the Bank's presence in Africa was becoming increasingly visible. The network of regional offices expanded and covered East, North, Central, and Southern Africa. A branch had been operating in London for a number of years. A modest office in Washington was now added. A major transformation seemed to be in the making.

After a three-year stint at Central Operations (the Bank's policy and resource mobilization arm), I was made vice president for Finance in 1990. Koffi Bucknor was Deputy Treasurer at the time and was the most skilled in that area of the Bank's operations. I was an economist with no particular expertise in finance, but I had always been interested in what I thought was a sub-specialty of economics. I was greatly helped by Bucknor (who was soon promoted Treasurer) and others in getting a hang of the key aspects of the Bank's finances. The Bank's president had passed his career in this field and took close interest in day to day developments.

ADB's borrowings attracted increasing interest among investment banks. It was through them that the Bank floated its bonds. A lead manager would line up investment banks to underwrite the Bank's bonds, which meant that in the event that the bonds did not sell well, the underwriters purchased the unsold bonds. In the normal course of events, the Bank did not face problems selling its bonds. All the underwriters did was essentially to lend comfort to the markets that ADB bonds were a

good buy. The other key function of the lead manager was to
keep borrowing costs low using
different approaches: choosing
the most opportune time to float
bonds, offering affordable fees
and charges, and generally doing
public relations work to raise confidence in the Bank. Lead managers
were paid a commission for their
services. No wonder investment
banks followed ADB's borrowings
with a keen eye.

By the time I became finance
vice president, borrowing operations had become fairly routine.
Prior to that, I had heard that
investment banks regularly offered
gifts to Bank staff in the Treasury
Department, and of course to the

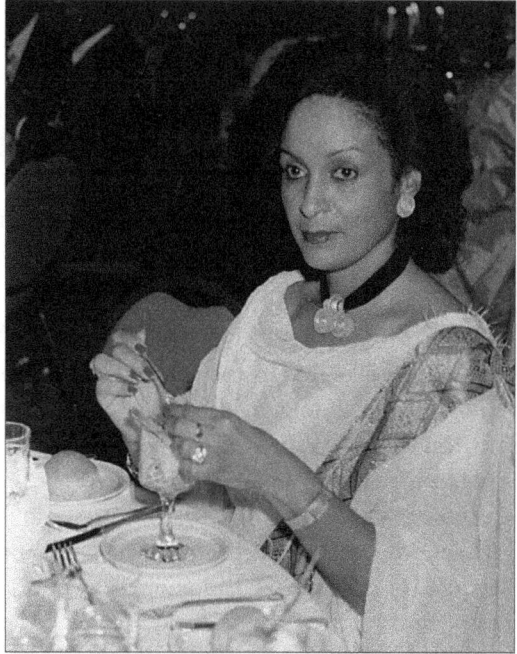

Roman during a break at an ADB Annual Meeting

vice president. I was especially uncomfortable with the practice in Japan, where gifts
(so I was told) tended to be more than symbolic. I told the Treasurer (Bucknor) that
I was ill at ease with the gifts and wondered if he might inform the banks, especially
those in Japan, about my sentiments. Bucknor's reaction was that this would be an
impolitic thing to do, as gifts in Japan were normal practice and were for the most part
symbolic. If they were not I would have a problem, I said to him. The first batch of gifts
(always given on the occasion of signing ceremonies for bonds) was indeed symbolic.
The one for me consisted of a set of a miniature Samurai sword, head gear, and bow
and arrow. The Japanese felt that an Ethiopian with a feudal cultural background might
appreciate mementos of Japan's own feudal past. They were not wrong.

A year or so later, I led a Bank delegation to Tokyo for a signing ceremony. Such
occasions lasted a couple of days and were tightly programmed. The lead manager was
responsible for determining the hospitality programme. Its own dinner (or lunch)
was a high point of the round of receptions, breakfasts, lunches, and dinners. All
investment banks associated with the bond issue were given slots in the programme. It
was an ordeal which had to be endured: the Geisha girls who seemed to compete for a
most hollow exhibition of what was supposed to be a venerable tradition of Japanese
hospitality, the immoderate drinking (which Japanese men seemed to relish), the
noise, loud music, and the excessive smoking at night clubs.[4]

We had accessed the Japanese market about four times since I came to Finance.
Lead managers were selected on the basis of rigorous criteria worked out by the

Treasury Department. An investment bank which had not been selected as lead manager in the Bank's half a dozen or so appearances in Tokyo suspected things were being passed under the table that kept it out; and tried to find a way to get selected for the next bond issue. As I entered the restaurant at which this bank offered lunch, I was greeted by the host who said he wanted to have a word with me. He took me to a side room, pulled out an unmarked white envelope from his pocket and handed it to me. Instinctively I took it. Realizing that it was unmarked I asked what it was. "Oh it is just a small gift for your wife." I said my wife was away in Abidjan and immediately gave the envelope back to him. It was not clear what its contents were. But I noticed that it did not bulge or weigh noticeably. I guessed that it was a cheque and was upset.

Nothing like that had ever happened to me during my entire professional life. I wanted the lunch to come to an end quickly, but had to observe minimum courtesy and decided to be patient. We were taken to another room for coffee and liqueur after lunch. When the host's deputy came to sit next to me, I told him what had happened and how disappointed I was with the mysterious gift. If his bank wished to be treated the same way as its competitors, it should offer a modest gift. Most of the banks offered inexpensive cuff links. I had enough of these to open a kiosque upon retirement. His company was welcome to add to my collection. He responded that he had no knowledge of what I was talking about. "Perhaps" I said, with a body language that made it clear that I did not believe him. Early the next morning, there was a knock on my hotel door. It was someone from the front desk with a gift box which contained a pair of inexpensive cuff links.

Vice President: A Post More Vicious than Presidential

A few more months into my tenure as vice president, I was facing some trying moments in my personal and professional life. First, my uncle Tadesse Gizzaw died. I had learned so much about our county's past from him and he had been an unfailing source of wise counsel. My father's death followed after a long illness and not much after Tadesse's. And finally Endale Biressaw, the person who had done so much to shape my life, passed away subsequently. All three had spent two and half years of detention under Dergue rule. At the Bank, things were also getting to be more and more problematic for me. One of my reasons for showing reticence when the Bank's president first asked me to be vice president was that staff presuming to protect his interests would not hesitate to drive a wedge between the two of us at the slightest perception of disagreement. My fears were borne out by the events which started to take place some four months after my appointment. The president's men began to tell him that I was an ambitious person bent on unseating him. The first I heard of this was soon after the Cairo meeting on ADF's replenishment. My robust defence of the Bank at that meeting was cited as exhibit one. It was alleged that I had launched my campaign to become president at that forum. The rumour mills got going.

One of the vice presidents advised that I should talk to the president and quash the rumour before it spread too far. My inclination was not to be bothered. The president and I knew that sooner or later self-serving staff would start creating problems. The rumour had come sooner than I had expected. But the best thing to do was not to do anything at all for the moment. I thanked the vice president for his concerns and said that I would not be taking up the matter with the president.

The rumour kept spreading, however, to the point where I felt I had to act on my friend's advice. I asked the president one day if he was aware of what was being said about me. He replied he was but that he did not give it much credence as I had anticipated some such thing happening when he first asked me to be vice president. With a sense of relief, I went about my work in the way I knew best: professionally. Apparently, it was precisely this approach which was part of the problem. It was perceived as a threat to the president by some non-performing senior staff. In reality, it was they themselves who were beginning to feel threatened. They had to move fast to protect their jobs. It was also alleged that I was not sufficiently respectful and loyal to the president. In the context of the ADB, loyalty included exaggerated deference to the president and unquestioning acceptance of anything he decided. There was not much I could do in this regard.

The problem was coming not only from staff but also from some board members who wanted to hang on to their cushy jobs and who for that reason courted the president's favour. They were elected for terms of three years. The president's views carried much weight among countries. A few favourable words from the president about a board member at the end of his mandate could easily pave the way for a reelection. The president's own turn for reelection would come and he too would need their support. Mutual interests drew them together and it was inevitable that gratuitous advice would be regularly exchanged.

Not every board member behaved in this fashion. There were a good many who refrained being entangled in petty bureaucratic politics and who played their roles commendably. And yet, it was the self-serving few who got the president's ears. While their conduct was deplored by their more responsible colleagues, a sense of cozy collegiality prevented them from acts of dissuasion or open criticism. The result was that an unscrupulous minority of board members (all Africans insofar as I could tell) was given the liberty to exert disproportionate influence on the president's conduct of the Bank's business.

Everyone knew that these board members were principally motivated to prolong their stay at their well paying jobs. But their posture was calculated to give the impression that they stood for the interests of the Bank. A tiresome claim often made was their alleged struggle to protect the Bank from being dominated by European and North American member countries: a bogus claim which most people could easily see through. This often translated into rearguard action against policy and organizational reforms aimed at improving the institution's efficiency and the quality of its loan portfolio. If the Bank needed any protection, it was against the irresponsible and corrupt behaviour of these very people. In the absence of countervailing influence or advice, they persisted in their actions, assisted in good measure by the president's reluctance to stand up to them. As he exercised less and less of his responsibility, these characters flexed their muscles more and more. In the end he was enfeebled and become a helpless victim.

It was in this general context that my relations with the president steadily deteriorated. Following a honeymoon period of just a few months, my advice became less and less actionable. Decisions I took were rolled back. It was now clear that the president was made to believe that I was a threat to his position. While I had to some extent anticipated this, I never imagined that the situation could get that bad. The post of vice president had turned out to be more vicious than presidential. The only option open to me was to carry on as professionally as I could. First because this had always been my principle and secondly because I had expressly said so at the time of my election. It was also something I felt the Bank needed badly.

The president had been re-elected once. The time for his second re-election was now fast approaching. I was of course doing nothing to stand in his way. Could I have offered help? As he seemed to be conducting his campaign with the help of a few trusted lieutenants and as I was not asked to play any role, there was nothing I could add. His campaign for a second re-election rolled on smoothly, and he was reelected without a hitch. I was relieved and thought he too would finally realize that I was far from being a threat to his position. It was not without reason that I looked forward to a better working relationship. Unfortunately, things worked out differently.

A Reluctant Vice-President and the Predictable Adieu

While the first few months of the president's new five-year term appeared to create an atmosphere relatively free of tension, and while my own three-year term was renewed for a third time, the underlying problems persisted. I started to feel that the best thing for me to do was to move on, and said so to the president on one occasion. My idea was to make a smooth exit. Also, Roman and I were thinking to move our children to an environment that would offer better opportunities for an early preparation for college education.

It was the summer of 1993 and I had come to Ethiopia for an extended holiday: something I had not done since I left the country in 1977. A couple of weeks into my holiday, I was surprised by a telephone call from Muftah Sheriff (the Libyan member of the board who was among those I respected and had a good rapport with). He suggested that I rush back to Abidjan for an urgent matter. I did and when I arrived I was faced with a full-blown crisis.

To go into the details of the saga of the crisis would be tedious. Briefly, an ugly incident took place which aggravated my relationship with the president. Prior to my departure on holiday, malicious pamphlets had been circulated by unnamed individuals against the president and his spouse (who was a staff in the Treasury department). I was deeply saddened that people could descend that low to malign a man and his family. There is no way anyone could protect himself against attacks by guttersnipes on one's honour and integrity. As I was president-ad-interim, I ordered an internal inquiry and left on a holiday that I had previously planned. N'Diaye was away on business when he heard of the incident. An emotional man under less trying circumstances, he went berserk and accused me, a deadly rival, of masterminding the affair.

Certain board members advised him to withdraw his accusation, as it would reflect badly on him. They told him they did not believe I was the type of person who would stoop to such disreputable tactics. N'Diaye would not listen, however. His reelection for a third term was coming up in two years and he thought the incident was intended to undermine that. Regrettably, he fell victim to the familiar malady in the developing world, especially in Africa, of officials who, in their eagerness to prolong their stay in office, go to extraordinary lengths to clear the field of potential adversaries. It was also said that he had consulted a *marabout* (soothsayer) in his native country and was acting on his advice. I neither had the time nor the appetite to verify this noxious practice.

N'Diaye wrote me a strange letter replete with trumped up accusations of past wrong doings, all pointing to the conclusion that we could no longer work together. It was not difficult to respond to the charges, which I did promptly. Some board members approached me with suggestions for a possible reconciliation. There was no likelihood of patching up differences easily. Others said that they had received instructions from their governments to support any position I took and that I should hold my ground and fight. Fighting false accusations was not difficult, but I was worried about the impact on staff morale and on the institution's image. There were already reports in the print media. *Jeune Afrique* had featured a cover story labeled the 'Battle of the Chiefs.' My instinct was not to engage in a damaging in-fighting simply to stay in my job. For the greater part of my professional life I had been fortunate to have supervisors whom I respected and from whom I had learned a great deal. Regrettably, that was not the case now. I decided that the honourable thing to do was to resign after receiving an appropriate response to my letter.

N'Diaye replied in a manner that I considered acceptable. In mid-September I submitted my letter of resignation. After my departure the board set up a committee to look into the matter and came to the conclusion that "no evidence was put before the board linking this highly respected officer of the bank with the tracts, or in any way impugning his universally acknowledged integrity or loyalty." The crisis deepened, with N'Diaye increasingly at loggerheads with the majority of the board. His proposal for a vice president to succeed me was rejected, and this was followed by a prolonged

Elizabetta F. Prizzi and Gedeon Demetros (with cane) at Addis Airport to meet the author Legesse Tikeher, a government official is on the far right

period of recrimination that seriously impaired the Bank's image and operations. Inevitably the institution's triple A rating was downgraded.

Because of our children's education, Roman and I decided to move to the U.S. I also wanted to have some time to reflect as to what I should do next. In the meantime I decided to engage in consultancy work. My first opportunity was an assignment with the South African Development Bank. The Bank sent me a ticket conveniently routed from Washington, D. C. through Abidjan, Addis Ababa, and back to Washington. A short visit to Abidjan appeared convenient. We owned a house which we wished to sell. We also wanted to touch base with friends and acquaintances. A number of people inside and outside the Bank had started to speculate about the possibility of my running for the post of ADB president for the next election, which would come up in just under two years; the very idea which was haunting N'diaye.

The suggestion had first been put to me by Mamoun Beheiry of the Sudan, the first president of the Bank. The occasion was the Annual Meeting of the Bank in Abidjan in May 1992. I thanked Beheiry for his kind thoughts but replied that I was not interested in a post which had become unacceptably political. My difficult experience as the Bank's vice president scarcely motivated me to serve it much longer. Besides, I had lived in Abidjan for the previous sixteen years. The time had come for me to move on. I finally said to Beheiry that there was a government in Ethiopia to which I was an

The author with Teshager and Roman on holiday at Tisissat (Blue Nile) Falls; Colonel Molalign Belai is to Roman's left and his daughter to her right

unknown quantity (so I thought at the time) and that I did not want (did not need) to court their favour to become president of the Bank. Beheiry said: 'Oh! You Ethiopians are so conceited and stubborn, aren't you?'

As more and more people talked to me about the subject after I left the Bank, I discussed it with my wife. She knew my reluctance for the post very well, but said that it might nevertheless be a good idea to "shake him up a little." The "him" was the president of the Bank whom she thought had not behaved honourably towards me. Her advice did not put to rest my reluctance to the idea. I nevertheless felt that I should perhaps touch base with people in Abidjan and test the mood of staff and some board members.

The day after my arrival in Abidjan, the new Ethiopian Ambassador came to my hotel to say that in the course of his courtesy calls on his diplomatic colleagues, many had mentioned my name as a possible candidate for the upcoming election of the president of the ADB. On that basis, he had sent a message to the Ethiopian Foreign Ministry to support my possible candidature. He gave the names of two persons in the Ministry whom I should try to talk to during my stopover in Addis Ababa after my South African trip. He also suggested that I should contact the Minister of Finance, for he was the person that would submit the name of Ethiopia's candidate.

My reaction was that it would have been preferable had he consulted me in advance. He responded that he had taken the initiative as a matter of duty to his country. Soon

Mulugeta Wodajo (right), Afework Zelleke and his wife, Tirsit Demberu on the beach in Abidjan, Roman is at the far left

afterwards, I talked to a few board members. They were all favourably disposed to the idea. The French board member expressed the strong support of his government if I were to be interested. I replied that I did not know the new government in Ethiopia, but was prepared to explore their reaction, now that their Ambassador in Abidjan had sent a message to Addis Ababa requesting government endorsement. Although it was too early to say, it seemed that there was a group of important countries that would come forward if the Ethiopian government were prepared to submit my name.

I left for South Africa, spent about a month there, and flew to Addis. Upon arrival, I called the offices of the two officials in the Ministry of Foreign Affairs whom the Ambassador had suggested and left a message. They did not call back. I did not make a follow up call nor bothered to approach the Minister of Finance. It soon became clear that officials at different levels in government departments were averse to the idea. And that the senior members of the ruling party were against it. The reasons given were varied. But they seemed to focus on a report by the young Minister of Finance that I had been reluctant to see him when he was in Abidjan for the May 1992 Bank's Annual Meeting.

In the course of that meeting, my secretary had informed me that the Ethiopian delegation wanted to see me on a particular date. As vice president for Finance, I had given several appointments to bankers in Europe, North America, and Japan. There was no way of canceling these. As acting vice president for administration, I was also busy with the administrative arrangements for the meeting. It was therefore not possible to see the Ethiopian delegation on the date they had indicated. I told my secretary to look for an alternative opening. She came back to say that the Ethiopian Minister insisted on his initial request. I dropped the matter, as no compelling reason was offered for turning down alternative arrangements.

Earlier in the year I had met with another Ethiopian delegation which wanted to pay a courtesy call on me. There was no reason why I would not meet with another delegation, had I not been in the midst of a tight schedule and had its leader been open to an alternative time. I had to treat the Ethiopian delegation in the same manner as I would any other, and could not accommodate them by cancelling appointments given earlier to other delegations. Regrettably, my response was taken as a pretext to avoid meeting the Ethiopian officials.

Cousins and childhood friends, Roman and Seble-Wongel

Later on, I was told that I had also not entertained this particular delegation during their Abidjan stay. As the months went by, an increasing number of stories gushed out of the government mill: that I had been against the secession of Eritrea (one of the new government's central objectives),[5] that I had used insulting language in speaking of the new rulers, that I did not believe that the EPRDF was a legitimate government, that if I ever became ADB president Ethiopia would not get a loan, that I had an unstated political agenda, that the government would not support an Ethiopian citizen for an international post who did not in turn support it, etc.

In the midst of all this, a particularly offensive incident took place which made me decide to stop all direct and indirect contact with government officials. Someone called my wife in Washington D.C. to say that a government functionary in the Prime Minister's office had given his word to assist my candidature. He would see to it that the letter proposing my name for the presidency of the Bank would be submitted by the Prime Minister (Tamrat Layne) to the headquarters in Abidjan within days of payment of U.S. $100,000! I had been in the government of Ethiopia before and was deeply shocked that the country had sunk to this level of corruption. I naturally turned down the offer.

Rumours had circulated previously about ADB's incumbent president (N'Diaye) making a shady deal with the Prime Minister's office to secure support for his third re-election. I did not make an effort to establish the veracity of the story. I simply decided to put an end to the sordid affair insofar as I was concerned and I told Kifle Wodajo (who had started to make his own enquiries on my behalf) to drop the idea altogether. Kifle later told me that Dawit Yohannes, the party functionary who was asked to meet with me and report back, had submitted a favourable recommendation to the then President, Meles Zenawi. The reply Dawit got from Meles was that this was a matter for the Prime Minister to decide, not for the President.

No one was convinced by this. What was becoming increasingly clear was that the new rulers were not interested in supporting non-Tigrean Ethiopians for posts in international organizations. They had previously blocked the candidatures of two other Ethiopians outside the tribe: that of Terefe Raswork for the International Telecommunications Union and Yilma Tadesse for the Organization of African Unity. My case fit the pattern. Even within their own tribe, there were instances when they seemed to give preference to members of the Adwa cabal, Meles's paternal home base. A credible story told to me in this regard involves the case of a well qualified Tigrean who was approached by party agents for some important post. In the course of their enquiries they discovered that he was not from Adwa, but from another town in the region (Adigrat if I remember correctly). The person got wind that his precise origins were being probed and promptly told them he was not interested to work with them. That is an illustration of how far the politics of ethnicity would carry its adherents.

CHAPTER 15

Mengistu Falls and a Second Republic Takes Shape

The Cartographic Nationalist Flees and the Guerrillas Take Over

Mengistu Haile-Mariam had single-mindedly manipulated his ascent to power. At almost every crucial rung of the power ladder, he had ruthlessly killed his potential rivals. Dergue Chairman Aman Andom was the first to go. Major Sisay Habte and General Getachew Nadew were taken out while scheming to get rid of him. Tafari Benti, the second Chairman, Captain Mogus and Lt. Alemayehou were silenced soon after they succeeded in temporarily restraining him. Colonel Atnafu was taken out next. The last to be swept away were the generals who attempted to unseat him towards the end of his regime. In between he had routinely mowed down large numbers of people suspected of being adversaries.

Outside the military, many rivals for power were also put to the sword. Prominent among these were members of the Marxist Ethiopian Peoples' Revolutionary Party and the All-Ethiopia Socialist Movement. The latter were initially Mengistu's allies but turned into enemies when they were suspected of overthrowing the government. Only the guerilla movements in the north eluded a final solution, though large numbers of their supporters had been murdered as routinely as his other foes. In 1984 Mengistu felt secure enough to celebrate the tenth anniversary of the revolution. As the military wallowed in the lavish events of the anniversary celebrations, the country was being ravaged by one of the worst famines in living memory. A decade earlier, Mengistu and his cabal of junior officers had used another famine as the battering ram to bring down Emperor Haile-Selassie's regime. Ten years of tyranny, murder and mayhem had pushed that event beyond the pale of their collective memory.

The problems of husbanding the nation's affairs could not, however, be shut out that easily. Managing the national economy turned out to be more daunting than the Dergue and its supporters could ever imagine in the heady days of 1974. On the political front, the insurgents in the north grew ever more intransigent and destabilizing, despite the huge cost paid in lives and materiel. And ominously, the Dergue's principal military benefactor and ideological godfather, the Soviet Union, was now entering a period of historic decline calling for a reassessment of the very purpose and structure of the state. Aid to Ethiopia and other friendly countries was no longer a priority. Its own survival was.

The Economy in Decline

Hearing Dergue officials and their young supporters talk about the prospects of the country's economy in the early days of wholesale nationalization, one was left with the impression that the country was on the brink of a huge economic bonanza. One of the regime's Minister of Agriculture seemed to be losing sleep over the shortage of storage space for grain. He expected a huge harvest after the nationalization of land. The peasants now knew who the beneficiaries of their toil were: themselves. Other officials spoke in a similar vein about nationalized industries. Of the Coca Cola plant in Addis Ababa, it was said that factory hands turned out bottles of the stuff in record quantities, now that the employees knew the plant belonged to them.

All such naive talk soon evaporated. Concern for a shortage of storage space for grain turned into apprehension of a serious shortfall in a harvest that had been expected to outdo all previous harvests. Prices of consumer goods shot in response to supply shortages. It wasn't in vain that people would whisper the familiar anti-communist adage that if Mengistu were to take over the Sahara Desert, there would be a shortage of sand in short order. Some of the young officials (including the Ministers of Agriculture and Industry) who spoke so glowingly of a surge in production soon found themselves behind bars.

Though huge sums were spent on the war effort, an appreciable volume of investment did go into development projects. Yet the returns were meagre. Project preparation was often hurried and the management of a hugely expanded public sector programme became a perennial headache. Despite this, figures were routinely churned out in an attempt to show that the economy was doing well. It was not just government agencies which published growth data, but donor agencies as well, not excluding the World Bank.

Even the shock of the 1984 famine did not seem to raise more than a temporary doubt among those who believed that growth was proceeding at a comfortable pace. And yet this was a famine far graver than the one that had brought down the government ten years before. In the words of someone familiar with Ethiopia's rural economy, it was "three or four times the level it had been in 1973, [and] was the worst famine in Ethiopia in over ninety years."[1] Eager not to allow anything to spoil the spectacle and banqueting of the celebrations, the Dergue covered up the devastation of the peasantry, blissfully oblivious of their massacre of government officials whom they had accused of covering up the previous famine. In its view and in the minds of its apologists, the economy clanked forward vigorously. In time, however, the truth would come out. According to a recent account, output per person during the seventeen-year period of the Dergue (1974-1991) *declined* by a yearly average of 1.22%, in contrast to a rise of 1.51% per person per year in the preceding years of the monarchy as well as in the years after.[2]

The Ruinous War

Over and above its direct cost, the war in the north was ruinous in other ways. Mismanagement, indiscipline, corruption, lack of training, and communist command and control military protocol wreaked havoc in the largest military establishment south of the Sahara. Conducting the war became a well nigh impossible task. Former Dergue officials have recently published graphic accounts on this theme. Below are some of the highlights.[3]

First, and as a direct consequence of the soldiers' uprising in 1974, military discipline collapsed. During the early mutinies, plotters removed their insignias to guard against possible sanctions for undisciplined conduct. No one could tell who was officer and who was not. As the mutiny spread and this practice continued, the chain of command broke down. The idea of passing down orders to subordinate officers was thrown out of the window. Everyone's view was given equal weight; something perhaps necessary for cementing relations among fellow conspirators, but a suicidal practice for any military establishment.

Second, the rebellion was in part a revolt against the top brass, many of whom were trained and battle tested. To further underline that senior officers were unwanted, Atnafu and Mengistu restricted membership of the Coordinating Committee of the Armed Forces to soldiers and officers of the rank of Major and below. After the massacre of high ranking officers in November, the Dergue systematically got rid of senior and middle level officers, among whom were many graduates of military academies and other institutions of higher learning. In their place were appointed people who were believed to be loyal to Mengistu and the soldiers' movement. Experience, professionalism, and personal leadership qualities were completely disregarded.

Thirdly, the elite Harrar Army Academy was closed at the very moment when well trained officers were required to lead the tens of thousands of men being mobilized for the war front. Mengistu and those like him who graduated from the junior military training school in Holetta were envious of academy graduates who had been given preferential treatment by the top brass. They were now marginalized. These and other well trained middle and high level officers in the army, the navy, and the air force were dismissed or forcibly retired. Closing the academy in Harrar was a sure way of drying up the supply at the source. The junior officers who instigated the military uprising, Mengistu in particular, were fully aware of the major risk their country was facing. That they subordinated national security concerns to purely personal preoccupations is a puzzle to be solved by those who credit Mengistu and his cronies with nationalistic sentiments.

In time the shortage of officers would hobble the unwieldy army. So serious was the problem that Mengistu embarked on a harebrained scheme to train 6,000 officers in three months in hurriedly organized military camps. This time frame was woefully inadequate to prepare even foot soldiers for battle, let alone officers. Predictably, it failed miserably. In *Misikirnet,* author Tesfaye Riste tells the story of a young lieutenant, a fresh graduate of one of the new training camps who appears before a visiting senior officer to report on men under his command. Asked how he had deployed them, the young officer keeps silent. The visiting officer persists in his question. The embarrassed young officer pulls himself together and says, "I myself am ready to fight. But I have no clue as to what to do [with my men]. Since I am unable to assume command, I have asked my sergeant-major to take over. He is now in command."[4]

Morale and discipline were abysmal and corruption rampant. Wrist watches, gold rings, and other valuable possessions of soldiers killed in battle were stripped and shamelessly stashed away by their comrades. Payrolls continued to show the names of the dead and missing long enough for their salaries to fill many pockets. Rations and other supplies sent to the field were sold openly on the black market by the officer corps and the proceeds passed around. Merchandise confiscated from contraband traders was routinely shared, as were assets occasionally captured during combat. Promotions were given not on merit but on the basis of illicit common interests. Anyone suspected of reporting these to higher authorities was subjected to retaliation. Family allowances took months to arrive, and spouses of men at the front sometimes engaged in prostitution to make ends meet.

The battlefield commander, pursuant to communist protocol, could not act without consulting the political commissar and the inspector (intelligence officer). Political commissars were for the most part selected from the ranks of non-commissioned officers or those slightly above. They were trusted party apparatchiks with scant knowledge or experience of even the basic tenets of warfare. Their mandate was to keep war commanders on a short political leash. Commanding generals had to make sure that they enjoyed their support for any major undertaking. Inspectors who had comparable political clout were similarly regarded. The commander, hobbled by his two minders, was often frustrated in his efforts to bring meaningful results in any given campaign.[5]

In one of the more strategic military operations, politics went as far as puting a bottom-ranked soldier at the head of an entire army corps. This was the case of Sergeant-turned-Captain Legesse Asfaw who was appointed Commander in Chief of the Third Revolutionary Army and supremo for the Administration of the province of Tigray in 1989. The fact that he had previously been kicked up to the rank of captain did not endow him with battlefield experience or fresh leadership insights. In the face of a catastrophic defeat at the hands of the TPLF, Legesse turned tail and ran. "It was an unprecedented reverse and a turning point in the military operation of the government," says Teferra Haile-Selassie, a former official of the Dergue. "The massive weapons, armoured vehicles, tanks, ammunition, etc., which were captured at the headquarters of the Army in Enda Selassie, Shire," continues Teferra, "completely changed the balance of power in favour of the TPLF. The disintegration of the Army was due to lack of able leadership."[6]

In Eritrea, the turning point of the war came in 1988 when Mengistu was on a tour of the province's military establishment. During a visit to the headquarters of the Nadew Corps, Mengistu reviewed allegations of negligence and insubordination against its commander, General Tariku Ayne. The General who, like Mengistu, was a graduate of the military school in Guenet and knew him well but who was not particularly sympathetic to the prevailing ideology, put up a robust defence and denied all charges. His denial went as far as being 'insolent' to Mengistu, as a recent book contends.[7] Tariku probably did not think highly of Mengistu's limited abilities as commander-in-chief. In his career, Mengistu had rarely been in any major military engagement, spending most of his working life in various undemanding tasks. His last job before his rise to power had been in the quartermaster's office for military supplies in Harrar. As commander-in-chief he was now dealing with a daunting task he had never even contemplated in his wildest of dreams. He had little alternative beyond flying by the seat of his pants. Mengistu could not stomach the criticism of the General, and personally ordered his insignia to be removed in front of his men and to be shot right there and then. There was no court-martial. Men under the General's command and fellow generals were shocked. Morale plummeted. Learning of the incident and its impact on the troop morale, the EPLF launched an attack a month later at Afabet, defeated the Nadew Corps and forced the troops to abandon their headquarters.

The decline in morale within the Ethiopian military impelled the insurgents into increasingly audacious attacks. Captured tanks, rocket launchers, artillery pieces, anti-tank and anti-aircraft weapons and tons of ammunition transformed their operations from hit and run guerilla tactics to conventional set piece engagements. The guerillas won again and again. In unpardonable acts of treachery, demoralized and corrupt senior military officers sold them intelligence.

Someday, historians will hopefully get to the bottom of this sad story of the loss of the proverbial spirit of bravery of a hardy people. But it was evident that Mengistu's troops saw no reason to fight a war led by soldier politicians who undermined military professionalism and who were grossly incompetent in handling the political and military challenges facing the nation. Besides, they had eroded the sentiment of pride and confidence of yesterday's men of war. The bond to the land of one's birth (in Ethiopian parlance to the place where one's 'umbilical cord is interred'), the ownership of a precious piece of real estate in that land, the valued assets inherited from one's forebears and the one's acquired through the sweat of one's brow, the vision of a closely knit parish community, the uplifting folk songs, the glorious folklores, the myths and exploits of past generations: these were the enduring inspirations which roused the patriots of yesteryear to march valiantly to war. Instead, Mengistu's soldiers were being asked to draw inspiration from scientific socialism: the very system that had severed their bond to the land of their ancestors, confiscated their hard earned assets, demeaned their religion and culture, and turned them into serfs of an omnipotent military landlord that was busy harvesting their offspring as cannon fodder for a war without end.

Mengistu was now more unpopular than ever, especially among the general staff who were constantly badgered, insulted, and on occasion murdered. He was feared but also passionately despised. He had failed as a political leader and as commander-in-chief. In the country at large, people dearly wished his downfall. A coup d'état was staged in May 1989 while he was on a state visit to East Germany. The plotters (the Chief of General Staff, the former Commander of the Air Force, his successor and a handful of other generals) met in the premises of the Ministry of Defence. Loyalist officials quickly gathered at the National Palace and decided to send emissaries to find out. They also took several preemptive initiatives as the plotters awaited the arrival of troops from the northern front. The air force, initially sympathetic to the coup attempt, hesitated when ordered to strike a few selected targets. When the troops from the north arrived by air, they fell into loyalist hands.

The poorly coordinated coup was foiled within hours and the principal instigators committed suicide. Twelve long serving generals implicated in the attempted coup were mowed down after a show trial. Together with those who were killed in hot pursuit, who committed suicide, or were murdered at their posts, some 25 high ranking officers were wiped out at the very moment the country needed them most. They were hurriedly replaced by mediocre junior officers. Of the eight most senior appointments, five were catapulted to positions that would normally take years of experience and proven leadership to reach. The new Chief of Staff was a Colonel who overnight became a Lt. General. Three Majors had a second qualifying word added to their title. They became Major Generals. The morale in the armed forces sank deeper.

From here on, the Ethiopian military entered an almost irreversible process of implosion. In a desperate search for military assistance, Mengistu visited Soviet leader Gorbachev on what was to be his last trip to Russia. Gorbachev was in the midst of a major reorientation of the country's direction and was in no mood to oblige. He advised Mengistu to negotiate with the guerillas. In the course of their discussion Mengistu is reported to have expressed concern about the future of communism. Amused, Gorbachev said that the soldier was speaking like the leader of a great power. The presumptuous soldier-politician flew home empty handed.

The U.S. Acts as Midwife and Power Changes Hands

The Reagan administration had for years been supporting groups opposed to the Dergue. Given Mengistu's espousal of communism, his close military and political relations with the Soviet bloc and his gross human rights violations, this was to be expected. As the TPLF's march on Addis progressed, the State Department and the CIA began to work on a plan to facilitate Mengistu's departure. Mengistu himself was already making preparations for an eventual flight. A year earlier, he had appointed his uncle Asrat Wolde as Ethiopia's Ambassador to Zimbabwe. In April 1991, Mugabe had sent an emissary to Addis on an ostensibly diplomatic mission but in reality to discuss details about Mengistu's plan to flee to Zimbabwe. The CIA prepared the ground for the tyrant's escape to the country of a fellow tyrant who was willing to pay back favours received during Zimbabwe's independence struggle.[8]

As the insurgents advanced to the heartland of Ethiopia, government soldiers threw down their weapons and surrendered, or just ran away. Eritrea, Tigrai, Wollo, Gondar, Gojjam, and Northern Shoa fell. The noose tightened around the dictator's neck as TPLF forces came to within 100 miles of Addis Ababa. The cartographic nationalist had been saying that he would fight to the last bullet. When the moment of truth came, he threw his bullets to the wind. Early in the morning of 9 May 1991, Mengistu boarded a small aircraft to pay a visit, so he said, to a military training camp in the south of the country. On the way, he ordered the pilot to fly to Nairobi instead. Upon landing, he asked to see Arap Moi, the Kenyan President. A meeting was hurriedly arranged. Over lunch Mengistu informed Moi that he was en route to Zimbabwe and requested if he could arrange his flight there and also inform Zimbabwe's Mugabe. Moi obliged and Mengistu was put aboard a Kenya Airways flight late in the day on 9 May and arrived in Harari around midnight. His wife had been flown there earlier in the day by a chartered aircraft in the company of Asrat Wolde. Addis Ababa was now safely behind him. What was to happen to the city and the nation was no business of the cartographic nationalist.

Disintegration of civil and military authority accelerated. Military leaders abandoned their posts and carried out their much touted vow to "March Forward with the Comrade Chairman;" The march was not exactly "forward" but there was little doubt they were following in the direction blazed by their Comrade leader. The State Department's Assistant Secretary for Africa, Hermann Cohen, organized peace talks to take place in London between the representatives of the Ethiopian Government and its adversaries: the TPLF, the EPLF, and the OLF. The talks failed before they could even start. Against the vociferous protests of the government delegation, Cohen arranged for TPLF forces to move quickly into Addis to set up a provisional government. The EPLF took over the administration of Eritrea where a 100, 000 strong Ethiopian army had been abandoned by its leaders. Ethiopia lay prostrate.

The New Rulers and Their Political Vision

In the course of their march to Addis Ababa to take over the country, senior TPLF officials declared their plan to introduce Marxism of the Albanian pedigree, notwithstanding the fact that much of the country had turned its back on the ideology and was longing for a respite. In some ways the declaration was understandable. The insurgents had been in the bush for several years, totally immersed in a movement driven by Marxist ideology. The ideology had been crucial to mobilizing the young, to conducting the war effort, and to indoctrinating TPLF members about a new Marxist-Leninist administration in liberated Tigrai. What else could they say about how they would govern the nation which had fallen into their lap so swiftly? And how, it should perhaps be asked at this point, did such a group find itself on the brink of governing, not an independent republic of Tigrai which some of its key leaders had been working towards, but a far larger and far more complex country whose people it had shown little concern for?

The story is told in a recent book written by one of the founders of the TPLF.[9] When the party was established in February 1975 in Western Tigrai, the goal was to struggle for the right of self-determination of the people of Tigrai within a united Ethiopia. Sometime later, three extremist party members calling themselves 'the communist core' (Sebhat Nega, Meles Zenawi, and Abai Tsehaye) embarked upon a plan to change party policy and work towards the establishment of a Tigrai republic. They contended that the people of Tigrai could no longer live in peace and freedom with their oppressors, the Amharas. In particular, Sebhat Nega believed that Tigrai was a colony of an Amhara dominated regime and that it was essential for its people to strike out on their own. In 1976 the three issued an unauthorized document (Manifesto 68) propagating the goal of creating an independent Tigrai state, though careful not to attach their names to it. Their consistent advocacy of the objective during party discussions made it plain, however, that they were responsible for its drafting.

The party leadership rejected this policy, as did the EPLF and the EPRP which, for different reasons, preferred a united Ethiopia. EPRP's policy was for the unity of Ethiopia, including Tigrai but not Eritrea whose secession it supported. The EPLF was against the independence of Tigrai and the other ethnic groups in Ethiopia. The front advanced a variety of reasons for this; it felt first that Tigreans did not have as strong a historic or economic case for independence as Eritreans. The antagonisms against them were also less acute. But the real reason was the concern that EPLF's struggle might be robbed of the lion's share of the limelight it was enjoying at the time. Its condescending attitude towards the TPLF (and by extension towards the others as well) was another hidden reason. Notwithstanding this, the EPLF encouraged the Oromos and others in their struggle for secession whenever it suited its purposes. But on Tigrai it held firmly to its position. This created enough pressure on the three TPLF extremists to withdraw their separatist project and refrain from propagating it in public, at least in the short-run.

The group continued, however, to undermine TPLF's official attempts to broaden its political and military strategies to include collaboration with other groups opposing the Dergue. As intimated by Aregawi, an anti-Amhara campaign was launched through "theatrical performances as well as jokes and derogatory remarks" with the view to discouraging the idea of living side by side with the Amharas in a unified state, and hence pouring cold water on plans to cooperate with Amhara opposition groups during the years of struggle (page 162). A 1983 resolution by the TPLF Congress urging party officials to reach out to Ethiopian opposition groups with the view to creating a common front was opposed by the group when the issue was raised at a the Central Committee meeting.

Meles Zenawi

The communist core ultimately gained prominence when it was decided to create a political party under the TPLF (which was viewed only as a front) to provide direction in ideological and military matters. Meles was selected to spearhead this important undertaking. Aregawi remembers that "Meles Zenawi was delighted more than anyone else when the Central Committee delegated him the responsibility of making preparations to form the party. He found suitable space within the Front to cultivate his own power base without involving himself in the frequent armed clashes." Aregawi also quotes one party official as saying that "Meles Zenawi got the golden opportunity to avoid his [worst] nightmare: i.e. the danger of physical participation in the civil war" (page 174). Meles worked assiduously on the task he was assigned and recommended the establishment of a Marxist Leninist League of Tigrai to the TPLF Congress held in July 1985. The Congress endorsed the recommendation and elected a 21-member Central Committee for the new party, the Marxist Leninist League of Tigrai (the MLLT), which in turn elected a politburo composed of 11 members. Tsehaye became the Secretary General and Meles the department head for ideology and propaganda.

Aregawi and others have given heartbreaking accounts of the lavish celebrations for the founding of MLLT held in the midst of a devastating famine in which tens of thousands of Tigreans (and other Ethiopians) were perishing. Huge sums of money were spent on food, drinks, and a "congress hall that would accommodate well over 500 delegates...carved out [of] the Gorge of the River Worie under Meles's supervision" (page 177). Of the $100 million received by aid agencies for famine relief (which other sources say came from the proceeds of Bob Geldorf's Live Aid concerts) Meles proposed the following allocation: "50% for MLLT consolidation, 45% for TPLF activities, and 5% for famine victims" (page 184).

When Aregawi spoke against the ludicrously low figure allocated to the raging famine and the need to raise it substantially, he was booed by Mele's supporters one of whom said: "you should understand that if MLLT is strengthened, everything would be solved scientifically." This was a time when hungry Tigreans were marching to the Sudan in huge numbers and in searing heat to receive food aid. In one such march 13,000 people perished. Incredibly, Meles's proposal was accepted by the party's Central Committee. In similar fashion, Mengistu Haile-Mariam was willfully oblivious of the dire needs of his famished countrymen during the tenth anniversary celebrations of the Ethiopian Revolution which took place within months of MLLT's formation. Both incidents speak volumes about the callous insensitivity of tyrants to the interests of the needy and the oppressed, which they tiressomely rant about to legitimize their rule.

On the strength of a journal article sent him by the Union of Tigrean Students in North America, Meles (who would ultimately become leader of the TPLF) had moved MLLT's ideological orientation from a pro-Chinese stance to Albania's interpretation of Marxism-Leninism. While the internal ideological bickering had thus been resolved in favour of the communist core, the situation on the ground posed new uncomfortable realities. Meles and his group could not realistically go back to resurrect their cherished dream of an independent Tigrai and transform it into an uncontested goal of the TPLF. Nor could they persist in their policy of not collaborating with non-Tigrai groups to bring Mengistu down. The guerrilla war had to be extended into the heartland of Ethiopia if the Dergue army were to be opposed effectively. And collaboration with other opposition groups was essential for this.

Among the principal non-Tigrean groups whose collaboration was sought was of course the EPLF: an early supporter of the TPLF with which differences regarding ideology and military strategy had emerged over the years, especially between 1985 and 1988. These were put aside in 1988 when the Dergue army looked as if it might not hold together for much longer if adequate pressure were applied. Other non-Tigrai opposition groups were created by the TPLF from defectors of the EPRP and from captive soldiers of Mengistu's army. These became malleable junior partners and were helpful in forming the Ethiopian Peoples' Revolutionary Democratic Front (EPRDF): a TPLF dominated façade giving the impression that the party was now working in close cooperation with a multiethnic front drawn from different parts of a country. The goal of a Tigrean republic was put on the back burner as Ethiopia became the new theatre of military and ideological struggle.

When the TPLF assumed power in Addis Ababa in early 1991, the new men of power were faced with yet another reality. The Soviet Union had collapsed, as had its

East European and Central Asian client states including Albania. The United States and Western European countries were now the dominant actors on the world political scene. The TPLF could not merrily go about preaching and practicing Enver Hoxha's gospel without risking the support of Western governments which it was eager to cultivate. The party had to revise its plans.

Marxist excesses in human rights violations were pushed to aside. Sustained mass killings did not, therefore, take place. There were haunting moments of what appeared to be acts of ethnic cleansing against Amhara communities in the south of the country. For reasons not entirely clear to observers, the authorities did not intervene. Woizero Almaz Haile-Mariam and other leading Amharas quickly formed an advocacy group to protest the killings and defend the interests of the Amhara communities. They prevailed upon the well known and respected surgeon, Doctor Asrat Woldeyes, to head the group.[10] Amhara communities from neighbouring regions also dispatched armed men to fight off the killers. Thankfully, the troubles did not spread or last long. They were, however, a vivid illustration of what happens when ethnic passions are given free reign.

Freedom of the press was also introduced, but within narrow limits and with periodic acts of harassment whenever authorities felt that journalists went too far. Within limits also, freedom of assembly and speech were allowed. Citizens were generally left free to practice their faith, although religious authorities were kept under close watch. Market oriented economic policies were also introduced, but the government would act arbitrarily and precipitously whenever it was inclined to do so. A wide range of party investment ventures (dubbed 'endowments') became a new feature of Ethiopia's economic landscape. These not only had the effect of crowding out private investors but emerged as privileged ventures with which bona fide entrepreneurs could not easily compete, given their proximity to the men of power. Marxism Mark II (TPLF's) appeared to be generally more liberal in its economic dirigisme and less brutal in its human rights violations than Marxism Mark I (the Dergue's as well as TPLF's while still in the bush).

Despite the accommodation to global political and economic realities, there is little sign that the party leadership has had a change of heart. This is borne out by a party document entitled Revolutionary Democracy which was published in Amharic in the summer of 2000. The document was hurriedly put together during an internal party feud as an ideological whip with which to castigate Siyye Abraha and a few members who had accused the leader, Meles Zenawi, of treasonable conduct during the Ethio-Eritrean war. A document prepared in the heat of the moment and motivated almost exclusively by a consuming desire to destroy lethal adversaries might perhaps at first sight not be the best indicator of the party's true ideological stance. But that is indeed the way the party looks at the document.

The term 'revolutionary democracy' is not new, having made what seems to be its debut on the eve of the 1917 takeover of power by the Bolsheviks. Lenin made use of the term in a speech he deliverd in St. Petersburg in April 1917 (often referred to as his April thesis) in which he argued in favour of a true democracy: a democracy not of the petit bourgeois such as that of the Provisional Government of Prince Lvov, but of true revolutionaries. Around that time, a more theoretical definition was offered by Iulli Osipovich Martov, a leading Marxist thinker.[11] Martov held the view that a non-bourgeois revolution should be launched in Russia by a government representing workers and peasants (which he termed 'Revolutionary Democracy'), not just by the proletariat alone as had been previously held by followers of classical Marxism.

A throwback to times and circumstances of a bye gone age is scarcely relevant to the Ethiopia of the 21st century. The pains that its practitioners have inflicted upon millions of innocent people throughout the world (including, of course, Ethiopia) are among the enduring tragedies of the twentieth century. Suffice it to say for our purposes that the ideology has turned out to be triply fraudulent. Its pretense, firstly, to possess the sole key to understanding the movement of history; its promise, secondly, of ushering in an enduring epoch of genuine democracy; and its claim, thirdly, of supplanting the evil system of the exploitation of man by man by an economic order which provides citizens with their needs but requires of them only what they are able to offer: all of these have turned out to be as hauntingly empty as abandoned prehistoric caves. And yet, its Ethiopian adherents continue to struggle (and straggle) for the cause; in declining numbers to be sure, but singularly unrepentant.

Ethiopians who long for genuine democracy and fundamental freedoms can hardly find solace in Marxism. Marxist thinking is inherently anti-democratic, since Marx claimed that only his theory had a scientific, and hence infallible, intellectual foundation. Lenin added a further element of intolerance when he contended that only proletarian dictatorship can bring about socialism and ultimately an ideal democracy. It is consequently difficult for Marxists, especially those in the third world, to have an open mind on issues of politics. That mindset has to change among the ideology's present adherents if democracy is to take root in Ethiopia.

Closely wedded to ideology, perhaps even its principal *raison d'être*, is TPLF's commitment to the politics of ethnic identity. Much has happened over the last nineteen years or so during which the TPLF and its coalition partners have been at the helm of an undivided country save, of course, for the secession of Eritrea for which the TPLF acted as mid-wife. And yet the Tigrean party continues its commitment to the 'liberation of the Tigrean' people, if the words in its appellation are to have any meaning. The implication is evident that it still nurtures the desire to exercise the Tigrean people's right to secede from the rest of the country when favourable circumstances emerge.

Neither Marxism nor identity politics is likely to respond to the fundamental challenges facing Ethiopians today: autocracy, poverty, and communal antagonisms. Are there alternative avenues for a democratic, reasonably prosperous, and peaceful social order? Where do we go from here? Or, more accurately, where *could* we go from here? In Part Five, I shall attempt to address this existential question. Needless to say that I do not suffer the illusion of coming up with the right answer. I offer my thoughts in the hope that those better qualified and more politically engaged than I will take the responsibility to lead the way in a rational, sustained, and grand national dialogue on the future of one of the better known historic peoples of the world. But let me first wind up the story of my life with a narrative of my years at the Bank of Abyssinia and my subsequent and not altogether trouble free retirement.

CHAPTER 16

The Bank of Abyssinia

A Homecoming with Misgivings

Having spent two years in Washington D.C. in the early nineties, I began to think of going back to Ethiopia. The consultancy business turned out to be much more competitive than I had thought. Besides, the pace and lifestyle of the city was stressful after sixteen and half years in languid but agreeable Abidjan. I shared the thought with my wife. Given what was being said about me in government circles, she demurred. I had never bothered to acquire a residence permit in the U.S. or any other country. Ethiopia was my country. I had deep roots there and had always wished to return. Our son was now in college in Virginia and we decided, Roman very reluctantly, to return with our two twin daughters who were now twelve years old. They had never lived in their country. It was a good age to reconnect to their culture.

While agreeable in many ways, living in exile had distanced us from our country and culture. This was most visible on the children. We had brought domestic help from Ethiopia to enable them to learn the language. In the end, they managed to speak it. More distressingly, they were deprived of the warmth and support provided by aunts, uncles, grandparents, nephews, nieces, and childhood friends. They were by and large strangers to their written language, their history, and the tales and folklore which children imbibe as they grow up. They could distinguish their country's music but they had far stronger inclinations to the music of the West. Attachment to their Orthodox culture was even weaker. It was all painful for parents.

The revolution not only forced many into exile, but also split families. A mother would move with her children to a country which offered better educational opportunities, or would be transferred overseas if she happened to work with an international organization. In many cases, husbands stayed behind to lessen the financial burden on the working mother, or for other reasons. Strains inevitably developed and feelings would never be restored. This added to the complications of bringing up children in a stable and stress free environment. Roman and I had stayed together after leaving Ethiopia in 1977. We now decided to move back home with our children, leaving behind our eldest son Teshager who was in college.

Besides my wife, friends were skeptical about my decision to return home. The guerilla group that assumed power had taken some unsettling measures. It was autocratic and had declared its unabashed intent to introduce ethnic identity as the critical factor in the political restructuring of the country. At that time, a draft constitution of ethnic federalism was being debated for the Second Republic. I was opposed to the policy and had made my views known. My friends saw the pitfalls of someone like me living in that kind of political environment. How could I live in a poltical system that did not tolerate dissent? Temperamentally inclined to take risks, I was disinclined to pull back from my decision to return.

Roman and the children left Washington for Addis Ababa in September 1995 in time for the new school year. I followed three months later. An incident indicative of the political mood of the time took place at the French Lycée as one of our daughters, Beshowamyellesh, was being registered. Poring over a name she found somewhat out of tune, the secretary of the Deputy Director asked whether the girl had come from Mars or another planet. My daughter is named after my maternal grandmother whom I had never met but whose name had always held a fascination for me. It is not common and denotes a woman of exceptional beauty rare even for Shoa, my grandmother's birthplace. Shoa was Ethiopia's political and cultural epicentre in days past. Names were given with Shoan suffixes or prefixes to signify not only one's place of origin but also the seat of monarchy, of culture, and whatever fashion the country could take pride in. Hence Beshowamhellesh, Mulushewa, Showarkabish, Tekezeshoa, Shoandagn, and so on. Occasionally, even individuals not born in Shoa would be given such names, as was the case with Showanesh Abraha, the aristocratic lady from Tigrai who was married to resistance leader Dejazmatch Hailu Kebede of Sekota.

The Deputy Director's secretary was a fresh new citizen of Eritrea for whom the name was anachronistic and objectionable. A good many Eritrean residents of Addis in the early days of the TPLF regime were a supremely triumphant bunch eager to show Shoans that their days had gone. The Eritrean lady was surprised that there were young people carrying names reminiscent of the place, the symbol of Empire and all that was politically objectionable about Ethiopia of yesteryear. No wonder she queried whether Beshowamyellesh had just descended from Mars.

I was amused when the story was narrated to me after my arrival and toyed with the idea of raising the subject with the secretary at some point. My wife did not agree. What was there to talk about, she said? She, of course, wanted to avoid a potential confrontation. Some four years later, we noticed that the secretary was no more to be seen in the precincts of the Lycée. We guessed that she must be one of the Eritreans expelled from Ethiopia as an undesirable alien when the two countries improbably found themselves at war. Did she go back to Eritrea? No one knew. Someone later remarked that the secretary might have ascended to Mars.

A few weeks after my return home, I sought the advice of friends about a plan to set up a modest think tank. Kifle Wodajo was one of those I talked to. He did not say much about the idea but proceeded instead to ask for my comments on a paper he had put together to establish a centre for the study of conflict in the Horn of Africa. In the course of discussing his draft, he dropped the suggestion that maybe we could work together at the centre. I did not see how. Although the subject was doubtless topical and of particular relevance to Ethiopia, it was far from what I intended to do. Besides, it was not something in which I, unlike Kifle, could say I had experience.

Launching a New Private Bank

Hailu Shawul, a person I knew from my high school days, was another person I spoke to about the think tank. The idea was interesting but the environment did not seem favourable for such an initiative, he told me. Instead, he drew my attention to a group of people who were establishing a private bank. Debebe Habte-Yohannes, the former banker was the initiator. The new government had introduced legislation allowing private banks to operate once again in the country, following the Dergue's seventeen-year ban. The group was looking for someone to lead the new private bank. Would I be interested?

Hailu said that he had mentioned this to me in Washington two years earlier, but that I had been unresponsive. I did recall the conversation, but it had been my impression that I was being asked to provide advice, and I had given the name of a good Ghanaian private banker who had worked with me in the African Development Bank. Hailu had taken this to mean that I personally was not interested, which was of course the case; although it did not occur to me that I was being asked to join the group and manage the Bank.

As to his renewed request, I told him that this was not the purpose of my return home, but that I would think about it. When I got to my hotel I informed my wife. She was of the view that my own project was bound to take some time to launch and that, in the meantime, I could help with the establishment of the new bank. It might take me six months, or at a most a year. She sounded persuasive enough for me to give a positive response to Hailu Shawul a week later.

Aside from the consultancy work in which I had briefly engaged previously, this was the first time in my professional life that I would be working in the private sector. I was an offspring of the public sector in more senses than one. My education had been a public sector affair from start to finish, and I had been employed by the public sector (at both the national and international levels) all my professional life up to that point in time. This would be a whole new experience. In many ways I was also new to the country.

A new generation was now active in business, the government, and the professions. There were only three persons that I knew on the board of directors of the new bank.

My previous experience had been largely in development banking where lending was managed conservatively. But I had been exposed to commercial and investment banking when I was vice president of Finance at ADB. The Bank's Treasury operations were conducted with commercial banks, investment banks, and the equity and bond markets. I had also been on the board of the Commercial Bank of Ethiopia for a number of years during Emperor Haile-Selassie's reign. Notwithstandng all this, I felt I was entering a sector which was relatively new to my professional life.

The more daunting challenges were of a different order, however: the new policy environment and the inexperience of the regulators being among the more important. The regulators knew little about banking supervision. Moreover, the new government was in the hands of people who had professed Albanian communism prior to taking over the country and had only reluctantly committed themselves to promote the private sector. Many naturally had doubts about their new commitment.

Of no less concern was the fact that the private sector had been wrecked by long years of Dergue rule. Many experienced private investors had left the country. The new economic order had spawned entrepreneurs whose success grew out of their close contact with the current and previous rulers. A few had made millions from illicit trade deals in tandem with corrupt members of the Dergue. It was widely rumoured that some of these continued their corrupt practices with members of the TPLF/EPRDF regime. Moreover, the banking sector had been insulated from the world of global finance and had consequently been left far behind. All these posed challenges. I had my doubts about the way forward, but being a risk taker by inclination, I decided to give it a try.

After an extended period of internal consultation, I was invited to join the Bank of Abyssinia (BOA) as its General Manger. Though many months had gone into the idea of opening a bank, much precious time had been lost through internal bickering. Indeed, a good number of the founders had withdrawn. As I would soon learn, there was also a residual degree of wrangling among the reconstituted board members. One reason why they had delayed my takeover of the Bank was the objection of a young board member who at the time had close business interests with the party and who probably believed that my appointment would not go down well with the government. He of course did not give that as his reason. Rather, he said I was new to the country, that I had held a high profile job previously and that I might not have my heart in the modest job. No one talked to me about any of this at the time.

The Bank was indeed a small institution. Its capital was about $3 million, an infinitesimal fraction of the $23 billion of the capital of the African Development Bank from which I had resigned two years earlier. Many people were skeptical that I would agree to join the Bank. But my perspective was different. In addition to the challenges working at the new Bank presented, I had the nostalgic urge to work with my compatriots once again after an absence of some twenty years. I had never suffered the vanity of considering myself too big for a challenging professional task, an attitude I would not describe as typically Ethiopian. There was the further attraction of working in the private sector for the first time. That said, I did not plan to stay long in the job. In my own mind I gave myself six months, at most a year, to put things in place and move on.

From my first day in office, I went about the task of managing the embryonic Bank as zealously as if I were leading a multi-billion dollar institution. Six weeks or so after I joined what was quaintly termed as the 'Bank of Abyssinia in Formation', it got a license from the National Bank of Ethiopia, the country's central bank; ninety years to the day after the establishment by Emperor Menelik of the original Bank of Abyssinia on February 15, 1906. Owned by a group of Ethiopian officials and foreign investors, the Bank was ultimately bought out by Emperor Haile-Selassie's government in the early thirties, only to be taken over by the Fascists in 1936. There was initial controversy around the name, as 'Abyssinia' was presumed to apply to Christian, highland Ethiopia by some of the country's ethnic communities. A number of founders were concerned that the name was politically incorrect. Others argued that they were attracted by its historic resonance and said they would quit if the name were changed. A lively debate was sparked off at a shareholders meeting. The majority view was to retain the name. Partly for this reason and partly on account of personality differences, those who found themselves in the minority withdrew from the venture.

As the central bank moved ponderously on the question of a licence, opening the bank's doors to business at the earliest opportunity became our principal preoccupation. This meant four things: first, recruiting and training a full complement of staff for the head office and the first branch; second, transforming a large empty hall into office space for the first branch and furnishing it with the requisite banking paraphernalia (checkbooks, computers with the necessary software, safes, etc., etc.,); third, launching an publicity campaign to attract depositors and borrowers; and finally making sure the new regulatory guidelines were observed. Daily meetings were held to monitor the progress of work on all fronts. Everything was in place to start operations. The National Bank of Ethiopia was invited to send their representative to the opening ceremony scheduled for 3 August 1996. Much to my surprise, no one showed up. And no one bothered to say why.

Initial Objectives

Following the Dergue's wide-ranging nationalization of physical and financial assets in the private sector, no private bank was allowed to operate and Ethiopia was sealed off from the world of private banking and finance for upwards of two decades. At the BOA, we believed that the new private banks should be the principal vehicles for introducing the practices and procedures in international finance that had evolved over the previous twenty years while Ethiopia stood still and in many ways regressed. That became a key objective for the Bank of Abyssinia.

Paying interest on current accounts, minimizing delay in the deposit and withdrawal of funds, scrapping the Dergue era's curious requirement of asking any and all clients for business licenses simply to open a checking account, a more realistic and less restrictive requirement of collateral on loans, and a host of innovative practices (for Ethiopia) were introduced.[1] Customer satisfaction was such a major preoccupation at the Bank that staff who were recruited from the fifty-year old Commercial Bank of Ethiopia said that at the BOA clients were spoiled. The CBE had itself been a customer friendly institution before the revolution but had regrettably been transformed into a bureaucratic arm of the state, insensitive to client concerns and interests.

A second objective was to increase capital substantially. The Bank had been licensed with a prescribed capital of less than U.S. $3 million and an authorized amount of U.S. $8 million. Given the uncertain environment in which the new private bank would be operating, I sensed that $3 million fell short of providing adequate cover in the event of trouble. But board members with substantial shareholdings stood in the way. They feared that issuing new shares would dilute their power. And there was lack of understanding of modern banking. After a frustrating and long drawn out debate, agreement was eventually secured.

Side by side with these objectives was the need to assemble the right number and quality of staff. It was essential to quickly bring on board persons with a good track record in banking and management. The Commercial Bank of Ethiopia was the obvious raiding ground for all the new private banks and the Bank of Abyssinia was not far behind its competitors in this respect. Asselefetch Mulugeta, Alatchew Admassu, Woube Kinfe, Eshetu Yessuf, Sewnet Beshah, Tekle Alemneh ,and other veterans of the CBE were among those who had previously worked at CBE and who helped the BOA get started. The able lawyer Amsalu Baye joined the institution at a later stage and provided much valued legal guidance for its operations. Among the young I remember as being promising were Lea Mengistu and Gerawork Getachew who unfortunately left the Bank for more promising career prospects. At the Board of Directors level individuals who provided valued professional counsel and guidance included Ermyas Amelga, Getachew Tessema, Tamru Wondimagegnehu, Abraham Workineh, and Worku Megra.

The fourth objective was profitability, an obvious goal for any commercial bank. But there was a nuance to this at BOA. Profits could be made in any number of ways. Given, however, the prevailing environment of poverty, massive unemployment and underemployment, it would be incumbent upon both managers and shareholders to find ways of making the Bank profitable as well as socially responsible. Borrowers who were forward looking and whose businesses offered promising employment opportunities would be among those encouraged. New projects into which commercial banks normally did not go but which created jobs or significantly improved the level of living of low income families would be equally encouraged. Risks naturally had to be weighed and projects monitored.

Though not a priority objective, there was also my view that the Bank had to encourage promising young business persons who showed dynamism, commitment, and independence of spirit in pursuing business objectives. They might in time be role models for others and help build a vibrant private sector. Some were business school graduates from overseas universities who had come back to their country to invest. But most were persons who had not even finished grade school. Many were of modest origins (village tailors, merchants, truck drivers, etc), but manifested a remarkably keen sense for emerging business opportunities, for competition, and a single-minded drive to go out and make money. It was people like these who created jobs and made a dent on the huge problem of unemployment.

Agricultural credit was plainly not an area where the BOA could build a meaningful loan portfolio. But even here, we felt that we could initiate pilot schemes which would bring benefits to the farming population. It was on this basis that the Bank, in close cooperation with a U.S. credit guarantee scheme (managed by an organization called VOCA), initiated a loan programme for agricultural marketing cooperatives. The Bank was the first to embark on the scheme, but its example was soon followed by others. A similar French government scheme was on offer for small-scale industrial entrepreneurs, but was dropped when donor officials saw the arbitrary arrests of bankers and businessmen in 2001.

Driven by the objective to inject a degree of social purpose to its operations, the Bank introduced a savings programme for a group of farmers on the outskirts of Addis Ababa who had sold land to a real estate developer. Overnight they were handed cash they had never imagined. The Bank's interest was naturally to increase deposits. But the farmers were made conscious, even if only in a modest way, of the virtues of savings. Many would have faced the pains of profligate spending (and said so themselves) had the Bank not approached them with its plan. The Bank's principal aim was of course to build deposits.

Operations and profits grew year after year. Pre-tax profits were a modest $250,000 in the first full year of operation. In the fifth year they increased to about $6 million. The private banks were beginning to be active in other ways.[2] They created a Bankers Association and initiated a study to establish a stock market. Funds were secured from the International Finance Corporation and a consultant hired to prepare the study. On that basis, a decision was made to initiate a pilot project. The government poured cold water over the idea.

Hurdles Along the Way

Some of the steps we had taken at BOA with the view to making it a forward looking, efficient, professional, and independent financial institution were beginning to raise eyebrows with the managers of the central bank many of whom had not been able to shake off their Dergue era habits of command and control. This came out clearly in their first audit of our Bank's operations. A number of straightforward decisions were faulted. It was alleged, for instance, that the Bank had violated the provisions of the commercial code in making salary advances to its staff to purchase shares. A provision in the long standing statute did indeed proscribe this practice but for third parties only. We contended that our staff were an integral part of the first party: the Bank. They could not be regarded as third party. As was their wont, the managers of the central bank neither contended nor affirmed our stand. Central bank staff also had difficulty understanding their own guidelines which they had drafted in a language (English) they apparently did not fully grasp. We were following their directives to the letter, but they kept dropping hints that our interpretation was wrong, but never explicitly in writing or even over the phone. In a further instance of ineptitude, the Deputy Governor (who later became Governor) objected to a name we had chosen for one of our branches. He felt that the name was politically not correct from the perspective of the new order! We responded that this was no business of a central bank. Our firm position on each of these was taken as insolence. And they were determined to show us who was boss.

To add to our problems, and opening the way to the central bank's vindictive intentions, our exposure to some of our major shareholders was becoming a cause for concern. There were a number of reasons behind this. The first was our strategy in the formative years of the Bank to rely on our principal shareholders in order to generate. One of these, the Star Business Group, was a firm which was a major borrower of the government owned Commercial Bank of Ethiopia and was paying annual interest of approximately U.S. $5 million. And according to information shared among private banks, it was a client in good standing. Although we had not yet built up enough deposits to be this shareholder's main source of borrowing, we did adopt the strategy of gradually weaning it over to our side. The fact that the firm was owned and run by two dynamic young men, Minwiyelet Atnafu and Abebaw Desta, who rose from modest origins (one a village tailor the other a truck driver) to major business figures in the country's capital was an additional attraction. They had a feel for business, mobilized able managers like Worku Megra, and were well on their way to creating a large business establishment providing employment opportunities to thousands in a country desperately in need.

Secondly, long haul transport was in dire straits soon after the war with Eritrea. A minister informed me on one occasion that Eritrean citizens had cornered this sector of the economy and that their sudden expulsion had triggered a major disruption in the service. What had happened to their transport trucks he did not say, but I assumed that they had been immobilized. Some of our major clients wanted to take the opportunity to fill the gap. In this they were strongly encouraged by the government. Our Bank was favourably disposed to the idea both because there was a manifest demand and because we were lending to our own shareholders. This increased our exposure, but we were fairly confident that it was a good risk.

Thirdly, one of our staff had, without the knowledge of senior management, advanced unauthorized short term credits to these very clients. The sums involved were not modest. We were always aware that there was the risk of staff doing some such thing, occasionally even committing acts involving embezzlement. The staff member in question was suspended, an investigation launched, and measures taken to reduce our exposure. We were fairly certain that these efforts and the close monitoring we were beginning to make would gradually reduce our exposure.

It was in the context of these developments that a political crisis occurred which caused considerable collateral damage to the Bank of Abyssinia. Immediately following the Ethio-Eritrean war in May/June 2000, rumblings were heard about a split within the TPLF. Much has been written about the real causes and consequences of this split. The latest is by one of the principal protagonists, Siyye Abraha, former TPLF party official and one of the seven members of the Central Command, the highest organ conducting the war effort.

In his book *Netsanetina Dagninet Be-Ityopia* (Freedom and Justice in Ethiopia)[3] Siyye explains the origins and circumstances of the split that occurred over the objectives and strategy of the war. Siyye and his colleagues argued that the overriding objective of the war should be to annihilate completely the military machine of the Eritrean regime. This would not only enable Ethiopia to repossess territories taken by force, but would prevent the recurrence of similar Eritrean adventures in the future. It would simultaneously make it impossible for Eritrea to act as a proxy of outside powers which are known to have long term geo-political designs in the Horn of Africa. Ethiopia's sovereign interests whould be well served in the process. Siyye and his group managed to secure endorsement of these objectives.

According to Siyyee, Prime Minister Meles and a few supporters started to create impediments in the execution of these guidelines. Various pretexts were used to prevent the procurement of military hardware. War plans were prevented from running their full course. Although the war was eventually won, the disagreements persisted and progressively grew bitter. The result was to tear the TPLF asunder.

Those who believed that Meles was not acting in the national interest, had stood up to him and had managed to keep him on a short leash during the war, were ultimately expelled from the party. Included in the group were Siyye, Tewolde, Alemseged, Gebru, and the Chief of Staff General Tsadkan. Siyye and members of his family were detained on trumped up charges. The country's high court released Siyye on bail. As he was leaving the court in the midst of celebrations by friends and supporters, he was immediately rearrested. In a flagrant breach of the hallowed principles of modern jurisprudence, a retroactive bill was passed promptly by the rubber stamp parliament disallowing the right of bail to anyone accused of corruption.

On May 29, 2001 a number of businessmen as well as officials and staff from the government owned Commercial Bank of Ethiopia were detained. The Bank officials were suspected of having been influenced by the detained politicians into granting loans to their family members. Businessmen who were major borrowers and shareholders of the Bank of Abyssinia were also jailed. They were suspected of close ties with the detained politicians. When no evidence could be adduced, they too were charged with undue influence on CBE officials to obtain loans. Three senior Bank of Abyssinia staff who had previously worked for the Commercial Bank of Ethiopia were similarly detained. One of these had been a staff representative on the board. He had gone along with other board members in approving loans to the businessmen now charged of corruption. High government officials who sat on the board and were party to the decision were untouched.

After almost five years in detention, the businessmen were cleared of all charges by the High Court and released. But their businesses had been ruined in the meantime, which was perhaps one reason for their long imprisonment. In addition, these businessmen were such energetic competitors of party owned businesses that they were winning government tenders most of the time. The laid back bureaucrats managing party ventures, instead of rolling up their sleeves and working harder, often took their problems to party bosses who pulled strings to penalize their competitors for their audacity. Inevitably, our Bank was affected by the political fallout. Firstly, a certain category of short-term advances had been made to them based on their good standing with the Bank. The Bank was now vulnerable. Secondly, and to make matters worse, assets held as collateral by the Bank were arbitrarily brought under the management of a shadowy inter-ministerial group of civil servants. Thirdly, directives were issued preventing banks from selling assets held as collateral without the consent of the public authorities. Fourthly and outrageously, a Federal High Court injunction was secured by the public prosecutor that repayments should not be made to the Bank of Abyssinia on loans granted to the detained business persons.[4]

These measures inevitably undermined the Bank's operations. I contacted relevant officials and proposed actions that might go some way to respond to the difficulties. Upon the advice of friends I also did something which I had been reluctant to do until then: explain the predicament of the Bank to influential members of the TPLF. I underlined the damage caused to the Bank, to the business establishments, to the livelihood of innocent employees and to the public interest at large. I urged them to use their influence to help bring the problem under control. Nothing came out of these contacts. One of them told me that the Bank had been at fault, notwithstanding the fact that for the most part our troubles emanated from the government's own actions. I was reminded of the saying that politics determines who has the power, not who has the truth. Fortunately, the Bank's capital base and reserves were large enough to absorb the unexpected political shock.[5]

In the meantime, some politically connected shareholders who had been spared the arbitrary detentions began to panic and advised me to mend my ways with the central bank. One (a Tigrean) made the curious suggestion that I should designate someone from my Bank to look after its interests at the central bank. He proposed that this person should go there at frequent intervals and offer the traditional bow to the authorities there. It would have been amusing had it related to a less serious problem. I told him that even in the days of the Emperor when such courtesies might have seemed appropriate, persons in the central bank never ever expected commercial bank officials to render demeaning homage of this nature. He was of course reflecting a gathering view among like-minded shareholders that the Bank of Abyssinia should caste away all semblance of professionalism and meekly submit to the dictates of the ignorant regulators at central bank.

At the Bank of Abyssinia, events took a turn not exactly calculated to help the Bank out of its difficulties. At the end of March 2002, the National Bank of Ethiopia hurriedly introduced stringent directives regarding provisions for non-performing loans. In principle this did not appear objectionable. But in practice we faced two difficulties: the first was their timing and the second the very short deadline allowed for putting them into effect. There had been a slowdown in business activity at the time and even the best of clients were finding it increasingly difficult to service their loans. Besides, the period allowed to reduce the level of arrears was unrealistic. The precipitous manner with which the directives were introduced manifested bureaucratic insensitivity at best and petty vindictiveness at worst. The central bank issued the directives on March 29 and said they would come into effect on April fool's day. To the commercial banks it was far from being a matter of jest.

The Bankers Association addressed a letter to the Governor of the central bank raising the concerns of its members and asking for a dialogue. Neither the central bank officials nor their political masters were inclined to listen. Within weeks, the Bank of Abyssinia was asked by the central bank to present a plan as to how it expected to get out of its difficulties. The central bank had now unveiled its plan of bringing the Bank to heel. Being holdovers from the Mengistu regime many senior staff of the central bank (including the Governor) were more eager to attune themselves to the prevailing political climate than to learn their new and professionally more demanding mandate of banking supervision.

The travails of the Bank of Abyssinia came to their climax when a handful of major shareholders started to work hand in glove with the central bank on a scheme to elect new board members who would be more amenable to them and to the bank. A couple of these had been hiding overseas when the detention of the businessmen, some of them close friends, took place soon after the political crisis of the TPLF. According to reports circulating at the time, they had negotiated their way back to the country and been allowed to resume their businesses. They now felt they owed a debt of gratitude to the government for not being thrown behind bars. They started to volunteer information on the detained persons, their erstwhile friends. And to collaborate with staff of the central bank on a plan to have a new more compliant board at the Bank of Abyssinia. By the time of the Bank's Annual General Meeting in December 2002, they had done their homework. They clandestinely prepared a list of candidates to replace the incumbents. Except for two members who were close to them and an able third director who had been thrown in as a red herring, the list excluded all incumbent board members, including of course myself.

As the names were read out for a reconstituted board, a shareholder rose and proposed my name. I said I was not interested, but the clerks taking down names went ahead and included my name in the list against my objection, for reasons I did not (and do not today) understand. Only a shouting match would have stopped the inclusion of my name, which I was obviously not inclined to do. Besides, I had already made up my mind to terminate my association with the Bank whatever the decision of the meeting. From the clandestine list, names were read out by different people to make it appear as if the proposals were coming from a wide range of stockholders. A campaign had been conducted on their behalf for the previous few weeks. All the major shareholders who were manipulating the conspiracy voted for the proposed candidates who were duly elected. I parted company with the Bank and was relieved. What started out as a short stint had lasted for six long and contentious years.

Much of what happened afterwards is of no particular significance except for the fact that the Bank of Abyssinia weathered the political storm into which it had been plunged purposely. It was able to bounce back principally because it had accumulated relatively large reserves in a short space of time. Its capital had also been substantially increased to fend against possible risks. Finally, the Bank enjoyed strong client, shareholder and popular support, although it was not clear how long this would last if the central bank persisted in its ways: led and staffed as it is by persons whose livelihood is entirely dependent upon the whims and caprices of their political masters. In that kind of environment, it is not altogether surprising if few are motivated to practice the little they know of their profession.

The Bank and its sister private banks face significant challenges in the future. The most daunting of all is the control the government exercises over the economy and the banking sector. In my address to the Ethiopian Chamber of Commerce in September 2001, I had indicated this as the most potent of all the risks when I said, "Therein lies the new risk private banks face. And it is essentially a political risk against which banks here or anywhere else could not protect themselves." Regrettably this has turned out to be true, although I must admit I had no clear idea about when it would come or how it might strike. In the mind of Ethiopia's central bank, the current global financial crisis might appear to give a semblance of credibility to its intrusiveness. Fundamentally, however, the motives of the central bank's coercive measures against Ethiopia's private banks are light years away from the remedial measures currently being undertaken in Europe and the U.S. to better regulate financial markets. Only Ethiopia's central bank officials and their masters could mistake the cheese of global financial turmoil for the chalk of Ethiopia's banking pains which are a direct outcome of a command and control mentality.

Another challenge is the excessive control exercised by a handful of shareholders. This arises from weaknesses in banking legislation. Currently, a person or institution can own up to 20% of a bank's stock. A thousand or more shareholders could be effectively disenfranchised by three or four major shareholders who can muster a voting power of over 50% to get any decision passed against the wishes of the majority. That is bad enough. Worse is when these shareholders adopt rival postures, each having enough power to frustrate the position of the other but failing to muster the voting power required for a majority decision. Naturally the work of banks is disrupted and public confidence impaired. Amending the legislation to prevent a shareholder or any member of his family from owning more than, say, 2-3% of a bank's capital will enfranchise small shareholders and introduce a large measure of economic democracy and good governance in banking.

There is thirdly the challenge of poor business ethics among borrowers and bankers alike. Getting loans through dissembling and outright deceit is common enough to cause concern. Corruption is reported to be spreading among senior and junior staff of the private banks, having apparently entrenched itself in the older government banks. Allegations are easier made than substantiated, and are sometimes driven by personal motives. When I dismissed an alleged incident of bribe taking by a senior manager I thought I knew well, the person who made the allegation volunteered to bring to my home the client who had offered the bribe. My curiosity did not go that far, but I was saddened to realize that new institutions I thought would be role models appeared to play host to a debilitating evil.

At the time of writing, the government and the central bank continue to pursue their vindictive designs against the Bank of Abyssinia and a few targeted shareholders.[6] Looking back at my Bank of Abyssinia experience, I sometimes regret my decision to get involved. Much as I had misgivings about TPLF's ideology and governance, I believed that its recognition of the important role that private banks play in promoting economic development should be put to the test, and not be rejected out of hand as the deceptive gambit of unreconstructed ideologues. My commitment to creating a modern, innovative, and independent bank with a mandate not simply to provide a decent return to investors but also to make a meaningful contribution to the alleviation of poverty was in large measure due to this spirit of pragmatism. I must say that I did not pay enough attention to the intrusive political environment which in the end became a redoubtable impediment.

All my life, I have entertained the belief that if one keeps one's integrity and maintains high professional standards, one would eventually get things done; except perhaps in the worst of tyrannies and kleptocratic regimes. In this regard, I had managed to keep my head above the water during the regime of Emperor Haile-Selassie and when working briefly with the Dergue. I could speak similarly about my long years at the African Development Bank. Under the TPLF/EPRDF regime, I was doing little more than knocking my head against a stone wall. Those who come after me would hopefully fare better, for in the end all walls tend to be breached under persistent pressure.

The author soon after his return to Ethiopia (1995)
from a stay abroad lasting almost two decades

CHAPTER 17

Retirement: Working with Charities

It did not take time to decide what to do with life in retirement. Being an eyewitness, I had always wanted to write a monograph of the revolution of 1974. Following suggestions from friends, I decided to incorporate it in a much broader story of my life. Partly because of the kind of work in which I was engaged towards the end of my career and partly because of my own professional interest, I also started to be active in charity work. Little by little, my involvement grew to the point where I served on the boards of half a dozen or so non-governmental organizations. In many ways it was an exciting and fulfilling experience.

A Johnny-Come-Lately Rotarian

Rotary was one such organization. My first contact with Rotary was when a friend of mine invited me to a luncheon at the Rotary Club of Addis Ababa soon after I had been appointed Planning Commissioner in 1971. There were about one hundred Rotarians in attendance, all prominent figures from the business establishment, the public sector, and the professions. After the lunch, my host explained the objectives of Rotary and wondered whether I might join. I told him I would think about it.

When told that Rotary was a network of international clubs, I took it for granted that there must be similar clubs in a country like South Africa. What did I have in common with the bigots in that land who had devised a system to keep Africans in bondage? Why should I subject myself to the painful hypocrisy of seeming to share the sentiment of fellowship, a key Rotary goal, with these people? I told my friend a few days later that I did not wish to be a Rotarian, without telling him why.

When I took over the management of the Bank of Abyssinia twenty-five years later in 1996, meeting with businessmen and talking about the new bank was one of my first duties. Rotary was a good place for that. And so I asked a Rotarian on our board to sponsor my membership. The fact that Nelson Mandela was now President of a democratic South Africa had put my earlier reticence to rest. While my main reason for wishing to join Rotary was to promote the bank's business, I also wished to take part in the kind of charity work for which Rotary International (RI) had become recognized. And so belatedly I became a Rotarian.

The Rotary Club of Addis Ababa had been established in the mid-fifties and had carried out considerable humanitarian work during the reign of Emperor Haile-Selassie. The Addis Ababa Fistula Hospital, the School for the Blind, and the Ethiopian Association for the Disabled were among the Club's early beneficiaries. During Dergue rule, a cloud of suspicion hovered over its activiies. It was perceived as an imperialist outpost and had to raise substantial funds in support of the relief programme for the 1973 famine to earn the government's benign neglect. When I joined, veteran members were struggling to instill new life into a Club whose vitality had been sapped by falling membership. Yet, the challenges had greatly expanded: homelessness, squalor in the cities, the explosion in the number of urban mendicants, the great demand for water supply, health and sanitation services, and above all the new menace of HIV/AIDS.

In 1998, RI President Glen Kinross of Australia visited Addis Ababa. As he toured project sites that badly needed funding, he came accros a particular location crowded with filthy shelters made of discarded plastic sheeting, rusted corrugated iron sheets, card board, and wood debris in which displaced persons were accommodated. There was no potable water, and sanitary conditions were deplorable. He was shocked and quietly remarked that human beings should not live like this. Rotary had never funded housing projects. Kinross was so moved by what he saw that a new policy of supporting low cost housing was introduced by RI. A modest project to accommodate 100 families was later submitted and approved. This set the precedent for projects in India and other countries.

In the spring of 2000, Leon Wilson, then President of the Rotary Club of Columbia/Patuxent in Maryland, U. S.A., visited the Addis Ababa Rotary Club where I had just been elected President and wondered whether our two Clubs could not join hands to develop a project for HIV/AIDS victims in the Addis Ababa area. I told him our Club would be delighted to cooperate. Leon subsequently got the support of his Club and obtained RI funding for preparing a project document. Leon and Lon Chestnut from the Club, Dr. John Sever, a noted physician from the area, Rotarian Phillip Bradbury from the Rotary Club of Washington D.C., and Arlene Fonaroff visited Addis and put together a project for voluntary counseling and testing (VCT).[1] A grant of just under $300,000 was subsequently secured from the Rotary Foundation, the funding arm of RI. The funds were channeled through six municipal clinics in Addis Ababa to support VCT and raise awareness in surrounding communities. A charity called the Foundation Against HIV/AIDS (FAHA) was set up in the U. S. to ensure the project's continuity and to assist in the replication of similar projects in other parts of Ethiopia and, eventually, in Africa.

This modest project has had an impact which its supporters could have scarcely imagined at launch. Access to testing prior to the project was about $10.00. Under the project it was provided free. Over a period of five years, the six VCT centres reached some 125,000 beneficiaries. Awareness of the HIV/AIDS menace expanded to the point where going to a clinic to be tested was no longer a stigma. In addition, the project spurred the Municipality of Addis Ababa to expand its own VCT programme to the remaining 21 clinics in the city. The incidence of the virus was contained and, in places, reduced. Finally, the project facilitated the introduction of antiretroviral drugs to better control the pandemic throughout the city.

Working for Rotary has been gratifying and instructive. Many are those who readily respond to the Rotary motto of *Service Above Self* and give generously of their time, effort, and money to assist the less privileged.[2] The feeling of relief that a project brings to a community whose womenfolk walk miles to fetch water on their back; the born again sentiment of a fistula patient after a successful procedure; the immeasurable joy of someone finding a modest new home after enduring the elements in the depths of the rainy season; the happy smile and warm embrace an orphan offers a housewife who, in the midst of her many conjugal duties, has found it possible to provide food, shelter, clothing, and schooling: all these are sources of a great sense of fulfillment which only institutions like Rotary offer those who volunteer to serve.

The Hamlin Fistula Hospital

Gynaecologists Reg and Catherine Hamlin's story is a unique saga of a Christian couple whose work has achieved international acclaim. The Hamlin's left Australia for Ethiopia in 1959. Being devout Christians, they did not wish to spend the rest of their lives "living in a suburban house in Adelaide when we had so much to offer people in a less privileged part of the world."[3] And they started looking for job offers in medical journals. One day, they saw an advertisement in the British Medical journal, *The Lancet*. It was for a midwifery teaching post at the Princess Tsehai Hospital in Ethiopia. Reg applied and was offered the job. Catherine too was granted a post at the Hospital.

The couple arrived in Addis Ababa in May 1959 and started practicing at the Princess Tsehai. A week or so later, they encountered their first case of obstetric fistula; a young girl who was incontinent of urine. Obstetric fistula (fistula is a Latin word for 'hole') is a childbirth injury following prolonged labour which results in lacerations to the birth passage, bladder, and sometimes the rectum. The victim ends up being incontinent of urine and occasionally of faeces. She is rejected by her husband, by her community, and ultimately by her loved ones. As the unceasing stench drives away all and sundry, the woman becomes a social outcast roaming from church premise to church premise in search of alms and shelter. If she has parents, she might be thrown into a backyard shed where she would spend her days and nights on a straw mat spread over a dirt floor.

This is the world in which fistula victims live. And it is from this world of spiritual darkness and despair that many are extricated to live healthy, dignified, and productive

Addis Ababa Fistula Hospital Board member Dr Tim Tuesink (far left), Dr. Schaeffer of the U.S. Fistula Foundation, Catherine Hamlin, the author and, in the back, CEO Mark Bennett and Legal Advisor Nardos Lemma

lives; thanks to the Hamlins' indefatigable work over the last five decades. Obstetric fistula happens in situations where public health facilities are unavailable. That was the situation in rural Ethiopia when Catherine and Reg started fistula care. By and large, it still is. Patients from far and near came to the Hamlins in Addis Ababa. Friends and family paid for their transport expenses, but they were in no position to meet their medical expenses. The Hamlins offered their services free.

The Tsehai Hospital provided half a dozen beds, but not for free. At first the Hamlins covered all expenses themselves. They started looking for support when they could no longer handle the increased flow of patients. An early donor was the Rotary Club of Addis Ababa, which agreed to pay the monthly expenses for one hospital bed. The American Women's Club, a local group, pledged US$60 a month for transport to send patients back to their villages. They also agreed to provide ten dresses a month which patients could wear on their journey home; a practice followed to this day. More funding was obtained from overseas.

The number of fistula patients flocking into Addis Ababa (the 'fistula pilgrims' as the Hamlins called them) expanded. A special hospital was needed. Reg and Catherine mentioned the idea to Princess Tenagne-Work, the eldest daughter of Emperor Haile-Selassie. The Princess was sympathetic and offered land on which a hospital could be built. The Hamlins next created a trust under Ethiopian law, the Hamlin Fistula Welfare and Research Trust, with their own savings and the Princess's grant of land as the initial contribution.[4] A series of fund raising initiatives was undertaken in New Zealand, Australia, the United Kingdom and the United States. In time the couple built a forty-bed hospital (the Addis Ababa Fistula Hospital) which opened its doors in May 1975.

Ninety percent of fistula patients can recover fully, allowing the girls to re-marry and deliver healthy babies under professional care. For the remaining ten percent, injuries are too severe to allow complete recovery. Patients continue to be incontinent and require regular care. They are otherwise capable to lead normal productive lives. A remarkable illustration of this is the case of Mamitu Gashaw, a former fistula patient who has been with the Hamlin family for the last four decades and who now performs surgery at the Hospital; an improbable story anywhere else in the world for someone who has never finished primary school.

In 1989 Reg Hamlin was awarded a Gold Medal by Britain's Royal College of Surgeons for his fistula work. Sir Ian Todd, the society's President, came to Ethiopia to deliver the award. When Sir Ian wished to see a fistula operation, Mamitu was asked to do a "big case, with Reg assisting...There she was with this eminent surgeon looking over her shoulder," writes Catherine about Mamitu, "and he was amazed that she could do it perfectly." Mamitu's record of successful surgery is now well over a thousand.

The Addis Ababa Fistula Hospital is growing into a global centre of excellence for fistula cases, with an outreach programme in Ethiopia and beyond. The Hospital also provides training to doctors coming from countries in Africa, Asia, and Europe; an implausible story in a country often associated with heart breaking accounts poverty and misery.

In 2002, Catherine invited me to join the Hospital board as a Trustee. I have been privileged to see the Hospital's remarkable work and growth over the years. Currently the Hospital has 132 beds and a network of five outreach centres in different parts of the country, each equipped with 20-30 beds. The work of the organization is supported by a global network of charities. In 2006 the Hamlin Fistula International Foundation was established under Swiss law to underpin the financial sustainability of the Hospital. So far, AUSAID (the Australian government's donor agency) has been the sole (and generous) contributor to the Foundation. The Australian Hamlin Fistula Foundation, an NGO, is also a major contributor.

Beyond surgery, the Hospital is engaged in prevention and research work; two activities which, in addition to the training programme mentioned earlier, are bound to grow in importance in coming years. A new school for midwives has recently been opened on government donated land. The graduates will be the principal instrument for the Hospital's awareness and prevention programme.

Rotary International's financial support, though relatively modest, continues. In 1998 Catherine Hamlin received the organization's prestigious Award for World Understanding and Peace, joining the ranks of distinguished personalities like Nelson

Mandela, Dr. Albert B. Sabin, developer of the polio oral vaccine, Dr. Norman E. Borlaug, father of the Green Revolution, and Dr. Pramod Karn Sethi, orthopaedic surgeon and inventor of the artificial limb known as Jaipur foot. She and her husband Reg had earlier received the Emperor Haile-Selassie Prize for Humanitarian Services.

Catherine Hamlin and her late husband are humbling examples of Christian charity and a powerful inspiration for all who contemplate to bring new life and fulfillment to people in physical and mental anguish. It is also an abiding moral rebuke to all 'Christians' that descend upon the developing world for reasons little to do with charity (a friend calls them CRINOs: Christians in name only). And, I should add, to others who put their narrow political and personal interests ahead of the welfare of the voiceless fistula victims.

The challenge for the Addis Ababa Fistula Hospital is to keep CRINOs and other detractors at bay and protect the Hamlin legacy in the coming years. In this regard, the Hospital is blessed to have partners in a number of donor countries (especially in Australia) who strongly support its mission of bringing the benefits of care and prevention to yet more of Ethiopia's fistula victims whose hopes have been kindled by the Hamlin promise.

The Gondar Development Association

In describing my family background in the first Chapter, I indicated how I was brought up by my maternal grandparents and the special bond between me and my grandmother, Itagegnehou Lemma, who was for all practical purposes a mother to me. As I said earlier, she was from the parish of Beyyeda Iyesus in the Semien region of Gondar. Our relatives had maintained contact with us in Gore down the years. From Semien in Northern Ethiopia to Gore in the West was a long way (roughly 1000 miles), particularly at a time when there was no surface or air transport. It was a journey on foot or mules which took some two and a half to three months. Family bonds must have been exceptionally strong to justify the arduous and costly journey. Upon my grandmother's insistence, I had contacted relatives in Addis when I went there for my secondary school education, and had managed to meet Colonel Molalign Belai of the Imperial Guard. From there on, the number of relatives with whom I made acquaintances steadily grew.

The Gondar Development Association, a grassroots self-help organization with a mission to promote development in the Gondar region, had been established during the reign of Emperor Haile-Selassie, but had been moribund during the period of the Dergue. A successor body (the Gondar Reconstruction, Rehabilitation, and Development Association: GRRDA) took its place under the TPLF regime in 1992. While overseas, I had been informed of this initiative and had expressed my support. Its beginnings were somewhat problematic. Initially, the regime seemed to be in favour of the new organization. The Prime Minister at the time, Tamrat Layne, was someone who claimed to be from the area and sounded supportive. He sent out feelers to

Members of the Gondar Development Cooperation Organization in Washington D.C.; seated in front row are: Alemante Gebre-Sellasie (2nd from left), Colonel Imru Wonde (3rd), Ayalew Bezabih (4th), the author (5th) and Colonel Asnake Shiferaw (6th); behind Colonel Asnake is Wondayehou Kassa and behind Ayalew is General Webetu Yimer

GRRDA founding members that they could work closely with the government and might indeed join the party affiliated broader body called the Amhara Development Association. It was a move intended to bring GRRDA and others like it under control. The founders were not interested.

At about this time, the President of GRRDA, Dagnew Wolde-Selassie, and a senior member of the Association, Fit'h-Aye Assegu, wrote an open letter bitterly criticizing the new Tigrai dominated government's unilateral decision to remove fairly sizeable districts of land in the Gondar Region (the Telemt, Tegede, Wolkait, and Setit Humera districts) to their contiguous Tigrai Region. This added fuel to the none-too-amicable sentiment that the government was beginning to harbour towards the Association. Pretexts were conveniently created to detain members of the organization in the Gondar area. It was evident that the government was not altogether in favour of GRRDA. I was familiar with all these developments.

When I was approached by the outgoing Board of the GRRDA in 2005 to be the organization's chairman, I expressed reluctance. I was, I told them, already serving in seven charities in Ethiopia and in North America. Moreover, aware of the organization's rocky relationship with the government, I was concerned that joining the board could make that relationship even more problematic, as I myself was not regarded in a favourable light by party officials. The reasons for my reluctance were not sufficiently persuasive to dissuade those who had been designated to talk to me about the matter. Very reluctantly and unsure how the all intrusive government might take this, I gave in to the pressure of friends and relatives. My name was presented at the following Annual Meeting and I was elected chairman of the Board of Directors.

The new Board mapped out a medium-term plan to put to the Annual General Meeting. This was a time when the government had proclaimed a virtual state of emergency following the 2005 elections. Public meetings and demonstrations were prohibited and it was not thought prudent to go ahead with our meeting. There was little to do except to follow the progress of work on ongoing projects. One of these was the Association's plan to construct, in cooperation with Gondar University and a sister organization in North America, a new hospital building to replace the dilapidated facilities which could not cope with the growing demand for treatment and care.

The hospital is the only one in the region. The buildings it occupies were used as a military camp during the Fascist occupation in the thirties. Today they are in a poor state of disrepair. Such is the shortage of space that corridors and toilets have been transformed into wards. The shade provided by trees in the hospital's premises serves as a temporary holding areas for patients awaiting admission. It is not uncommon to see an intravenus feeding or treatment pouch dangling from nails driven into a tree trunk and the syringe going into the artery of a moaning mother or child.

Thanks to the initiative of Dr. Edemariam Tsega, a former Hospital Director, an initiative was launched in the nineties to build a modern new referral hospital. The GRRDA in Ethiopia, its sister organization in North America (the Gondar Development and Cooperation Organization), and Gondar University Hospital accordingly undertook to construct a 300-400 bed hospital to serve as a referral centre for the Gondar region and its adjoining areas. During a fundraising event for the project which was organized in the city of Gondar in 2006, more than $5 million was raised, the bulk of it from an individual contributor. At the time of writing, preparations are well under way to commence the construction of a new hospital using the funds raised so far as well as resources provided by the University of Gondar.

Here, too, I ran into difficulty with party stalwarts. Bereket Simon is a senior party member who was born in Gondar. His parents are Eritrean. The ruling party has conveniently rechristened him as an Amhara and has accorded him a leadership post in the Amhara wing of the ruling coalition. This is a common practice by the TPLF which has transmogrified many a Tigrean or Eritrean into an Oromo or Amhara to exercise better control. In the course of the fundraising event mentioned above which he attended, Bereket took the liberty to inform a couple of my board members that the government would not be happy working with me as Chairman of GRRDA. Rather than create problems for the organization, I informed my colleagues that I should move aside. I had indeed anticipated some such government reaction from the very beginning. I consequently left the board. But more trouble was on the way, as I shall explain later.

The Institute of Ethiopian Studies

While working at the Bank of Abyssinia in the late nineties, I was approached by Richard Pankhurst concerning fundraising for the Institute of Ethiopian Studies

Members of the Society of Friends of the Institute of Ethiopian Studies (SOFIES) and IES officials; front row (right to left) Demeke, Debebe Habte-Yohannes, David Shin (former U.S. Ambassador Ethiopia), his wife Judy, Yewoinshet Beshahwured, and Ahmed Zakaria. Others are: Ian Campell (with baby), Rita Pankhurst (to Ian's right), Richard Pankhurst (Northeast of Ian), Abdussamad Ahmad (below Richard), Birhanu Gizzaw (furthest back with glasses, author (to Birhanu's left), and Fikre-Mariam (to his right)

(IES). Richard is the son of the well-known Sylvia Pankhurst, the English suffragette of the early twentieth century whose anti-fascist inclinations eventually transformed her into a life-long advocate of Ethiopian causes, first as a campaigner against Italy's occupation of Ethiopia and subsequently as an ardent supporter of the modernization efforts of Emperor Haile-Selassie. Sylvia and Richard settled in Ethiopia in 1956. Richard taught economic history first at the University College of Addis Ababa and later at Haile-Selassie University. At the University he was appointed Director of the newly created IES, much of whose library and museum collections had been acquired earlier by Stanislaw Chojnacki. Stanislaw had been Librarian of University College, the precursor of the University.[5] Richard's wife Rita replaced Chojnacki as University Librarian when he was appointed Head of the IES Library and Curator of its Museum.

Like most government supported institutions, the IES did not have an adequate budget, especially for Museum acquisitions. This led to the establishment in 1964 of an advocacy group, the Society of Friends of the Institute of Ethiopian Studies (SOFIES). In the early years the Society was administered by a group of committed members who were also its initiators. A among these were Richard and Rita Pankhurst, Stanislaw Chojnacki who acted as Secretary, Amde Akalework the honouray treasurer and Princess Hirut Desta the patron. Early supporters included Madame Colette Aklilu, the Prime Minister's wife and Professor Charles Longmuir and Betsy

With Stanislaw Chojnacki in Addis around 2002

Longmuir. Important work was done in the formative ten-year period leading up to the 1974 revolution. Substantial funds were raised which made it possible to acquire important objects of artistic and historical value for the Museum. SOFIES also offered a programme of lectures which helped increase membership. The widespread disruption following the revolution led to the departure of most of the Institute's principal officers and supporters and the Society practically ceased to function. The Institute itself faced a bleak future under a regime which had little sympathy for its mission. It survived thanks to the efforts of academics like Professor Tadesee Tamrat. Tadesse served as Institute Director during the troubled years of Dergue rule.

With the return of the Pankhursts in the 80s, SOFIES was brought back to life. I myself had just returned home after almost two decades. After a while, I became a life member of SOFIES and was finally invited to be a member of its Steering Committee in which capacity I served for about five years. SOFIES's latest initiative is the construction of new premises for IES. After several disappointing years of fundraising, a benefactor finally came up with enough money for a three-story building which is named after Richard Pankhurst, the Museum being simultaneously named in honour of Stanislaw Chojnacki. Professor Andreas Eshete, the University President, played a crucial role in securing the consent of the benefactor. Construction worked started in 2009 and is expected to be completed soon.

Thanks largely to the efforts of the pioneers and others who came later, the Institute is currently among the most well regarded centres of research and learning on Ethiopia's history and culture. There is, however, an inadequate awareness among average Ethiopians of the important place the Institute occupies in preserving the heritage of the nation: a key challenge for SOFIES and the University authorities over the coming years. The new building project should help in raising the Institute's profile in the public mind. It might also encourage the University authorities to inject greater dynamism in the organization and management of the Institute.

Jember Teffera's Urban Renewal Project

Dr. Jember Teferra is a remarkable lady who spent long years in prison under Dergue rule along with her husband, Dr. Haile-Giorgis Workineh; the last Mayor of Addis Ababa under Emperor Haile-Selassie. Prison conditions were primitive (still are), treatment by wardens inconsiderate, and oftentimes abusive. Jember and her husband were ultimately 'pardoned' for no longer posing a threat to the revolution. She lost her husband a few years after prison. Her son, who was attending school in England, plunged to his death from a 10th floor window when told about his father's death. Her mother's death followed.

This chain of tragic events would have broken the will of many a brave man. Jember's spirits stood up. In the midst of these tragic events, she decided to dedicate her life to the struggle against her country's most formidable foe: poverty. With assistance from foreign donors, she established an urban renewal project whose goal is to address the major causes of poverty in a holistic and integrated manner. She has been doing this community by community in the worst slums of Addis Ababa for some eighteen years. What has she achieved?

It is in the stories told by the beneficiaries of her project that we begin to understand the meaning of her work, like the story of two unskilled non-literate labourers (women) who came to Jember's office one day to break the exciting news that their two sons under the care of the project had passed their college entrance exams. Or the old lady who had been blind for several years but who had been successfully operated for a cataract condition. She not only was able to regain her vision but was also gainfully employed, free at last from the humiliating dependence on family, friends, and strangers. Former residents of makeshift shelters through which raw sewage had been flowing freely tell happy stories of how they could now cook, eat, rest, and sleep free of the sight and stench of the dreadful stuff. Communities assisted by the project would talk proudly of 100% protection of their children against communicable diseases. And of their new self esteem in being able to afford adequate meals, send their children to school, participate in community activities and even elect managers for their project.

I came across Jember's project in 2000 when serving as President of the Rotary Club of Addis Ababa. We had approached Jember to find out if her project could take part in an evening programme the Club had organized around the theme of poverty alleviation. She readily agreed and suggested that her youth group stage a play illustrating the programme's theme. The Amharic play turned out to be a powerful narrative which drew praise from even the non-Amharic speakers who had been provided with only a brief summary of each act in English. Our Club made a modest contribution to the project and subsequently cited Sister Jember's project as one of the more meaningful it had been privileged to support in its programme of community service.

Sister Jember has improved the lives of some 53,000 inhabitants in Addis Ababa over the past eighteen years. And these are the poorest of the poor living in some of the worst slum conditions on the continent.

Alemnesh Mogesse's Children's Support Project

Over Rotary lunch one day, I was asked by one of our members to attend the opening ceremony of a small elementary school. At 10h00 hours the following Saturday, I arrived at the school site where I was met by the project director, Alemnesh Mogesse, and was taken to where about 50-60 empty chairs were awaiting invited guests. A group of about 80 boys and girls aged four to nine years were noisily milling around the premises of the new school. Guests were slow in coming, which gave me time to learn a little about the project. I asked Alemnesh if she could explain how she had got into the project. It was a fascinating story.

She was in her neighbourhood Church one Sunday morning attending Mass when she saw a mother struggling with three children: one of whom she was breastfeeding while the two others made a nuisance of themselves amongst the Orthodox faithful. The children's mother had come to church to solicit alms, an age-old practice in Ethiopia. She was too busy restraining the kids and wasn't making much headway with her collection. Alemnesh proposed that she leave all three kids at her home in the morning, spend the day begging, and come back for them in the evening. The mother was delighted.

She took in more and more children until a friend remarked that she was exposing herself to accusations of exploiting the children for an ulterior motive. Alemnesh was incredulous and did not understand how anyone could entertain such a thought. But the family budget was also being stretched. She asked the friend for advice. He suggested that she should have her activity registered as a charitable undertaking, approach a donor agency, explain that she was feeding and looking after the children on her own, and that she could no longer afford the expense. She did that and was now above suspicion. She also obtained a modest grant from a religious charity.

In the meantime, the number of children grew and she ran out of space. She approached another donor to help her acquire rental space and succeeded. She now wanted the children to be able to read and write. She did that too. But what was she to do with the growing number of mothers? Some of the more able-bodied ones could be gainfully employed. And so she started a side activity: weaving and handicrafts work for them. Her project expanded.

For the children, reading and writing was just a beginning. Their need for formal education was evident. Setting up the first few grades of a modest school became her next preoccupation. She looked around for space and was shown an abandoned schoolhouse not far from her project site. She was advised to apply to the municipality. When she did, the response was typically bureaucratic: she should sign a formal agreement to open a full-fledged elementary school. The Ministry of Education would have to approve the curriculum and governance. She had not even started a kindergarten; only a group of ill organized kids learning to read and write.

I had up to that point silently listened to her with considerable suspense. When the narrative came up against the bureaucratic stonewall, I interrupted her. "And what did you tell the bureaucrats? You couldn't possibly do what they asked you to. Their intention was perhaps to get rid of you." She looked at me and said calmly, "I agreed to sign the document." "But how could you do such a thing. You had no plan, no money, and no committed donor for the school." "I put my faith in the good Lord" she said quietly. I had been in the fundraising business most of my professional life. Rather than explaining to the good Christian lady the niceties of how she should have gone about preparing a project document for a donor, I thought it would make more sense to let her finish her story.

After she duly signed the document with nothing in hand except her trust in God, she was taken to the abandoned school by city officials. When they arrived, they encountered a fierce looking gang of teenagers. They put themselves between the gate of the schoolhouse and the visitors and asked why they had come. The visitors replied that they had been authorized by the municipality to take possession of the building and its premises. "You can't enter. This is our place. Leave right away." Alemnesh and the officials left in bewilderment. They were later told by people in the neighbourhood that the gang had been using the building to store stolen property. It took some time for law enforcement agents to evict the gangsters and allow Alemnesh to take possession.

When I visited the project, she had opened the first three grades of an elementary school, had persuaded one of the local hospitals to provide free medical inspection and first aid services, and had obtained funding for a set of school uniforms. The Rotary Club of Addis Ababa had contributed $15, 000 towards the school, which is why I was invited to the ceremony. The remarkable story of a modest housewife's efforts to alleviate the misfortunes of poor mothers was humbling. Nothing in my professional career as a licensed practitioner of anti-poverty plans and programmes (which is one way of describing economists working in the developing world) could match her work.

Much as charity work in Ethiopia is fulfilling, it can on also be disheartening. Among the more distressing factors is the unfavourable political climate for Non-Governmental Organizations (NGOs). The ruling party regards NGOs as safe havens of its political opponents. In an undated party document entitled *Democracy and Democratic Unity in Ethiopia* published in Amharic and circulated in 2006, the following statement is made: "These are times when NGOs spawn like ants. They provide opportunities for lucrative jobs to intellectuals and serve as their safe haven and breeding ground. Intellectuals in the pay of NGOs, together with business persons who rely on the illicit support they obtain from government establishments (*tigegnaw balehabt*) are impediments to the democratic process. Indeed the employees of NGOs are the *prominent flag bearers of the fight against democracy*."[6] (Italics added).

Only the party faithful have the special insight to see how someone employed in an NGO is instantaneously transformed into a foe of democracy. For the rest of us, it is enough to know that NGOs in Ethiopia lead a precarious existence so long as this policy remains. A recent illustration of this is the imprisonment of employees of a number of NGOs during the aftermath of the 2005 elections. More recently legislation has been passed which constrains their activities and promises punitive measures for awareness programmes on democracy and fundamental human rights.

CHAPTER 18

Retirement: A Disagreeable but Not Unexpected Episode

A Visit by the Federal Police

One December day in 2008, something happened which disrupted my daily routine. I was informed that the federal police wanted me for questioning. The constant threat of personal insecurity bedeviling the lives of citizens in countries ruled by tyrants materialized in the shape of plainclothes police officers who presented themselves at my gate.

Detention of persons perceived to be adversaries is often a ready answer for regimes in the developing world that live in perpetual fear of opponents. Guerilla fighters who spend years in the bush are conditioned to see the world as a two-dimensional space inhabited by either friend or foe. They cannot easily shake off this mindset when they assume power. Their reaction to anyone regarded as an enemy borders on the Pavlovian. Almost invariably their inclination is to stalk and detain when conditions are right. Military governments behave similarly. The vocation of the soldier predisposes him to be constantly on guard against potential adversaries.

The date was Thursday December 18, 2008. The time was 11:30 a.m. and I was on my computer working on this book. For the previous three days, plainclothes policemen had been circling my residence. I had been told that on one or two occasions they had come to the gate, peeped through the keyhole and gone. On Wednesday, they knocked at the gate and asked the gatekeeper if I was in. When told that I had stepped out, they left without a word.

The following day they returned. I was now in the house. Two persons entered my study and said that the Federal Police wanted me for questioning. Did they have identity papers and a police warrant, I asked as I was certain that finally my turn had come to be an involuntary guest of the government. They showed their identity papers, but said that the warrant was in their car parked outside. They asked me to follow them. I said that I had to change my slippers for regular shoes and take along things I might need. The slippers were suitable for the place I was about to be taken to, they replied, and that the blankets, bed sheets, mattresses, and reading materials could follow later. They did not try to hide that I was to be detained.

My son Teshager, who was born abroad and had lived there most of his life, asked a laconic question: "Why did you come to this country, dad?" When I thought of returning to Ethiopia in 1995, family and friends had said that I was perceived as an adversary, faced risks and should not return. Some had said I was unwittingly giving legitimacy to a government bent on sowing the seeds of social strife and national disintegration. My response was that I had deep roots in Ethiopia and had resolved to return to my country after almost twenty years of self-imposed exile.

I asked Teshager to pull up his car to the front of the house and suggested to the two men that they should tell us precisely where we were going and escort us as we drove there. They preferred to get into my son's car, instead. Their car would follow us. I agreed and proceeded to the front seat next to my son who was already in the driver's seat. The more senior of the two men said that he would be sitting next to the driver and lead the way. I should be in the back seat with the other officer. I was already losing my freedom to move as I pleased.

Never in my life had I been arrested, and the thought of being under watch twenty-four hours a day was naturally unsettling. But I quickly decided not to be overwhelmed. My familiarity with the prison experience of family and friends who had spent years behind bars during the regime of the Dergue and subsequently during TPLF rule shored up my spirits. From my readings over the years I was also familiar with the detention and torture of persons under the Soviet, East European, Nazi, Fascist, and Falangist regimes. As I was not favourably regarded by the ruling party, I had always lived in anticipation of a visit by the police. All this helped.

Our destination was the Central Federal Police Station in the middle of town. In the prison courtyard, I was introduced to a certain Teklai who was to be my principal investigating officer. Instinctively, I offered my hand in greeting. Somewhat taken aback, he stretched out his right arm but pulled it back after an indifferent handshake. He then led me to his office on the first floor of one of the old buildings, registered my name, address, occupation and other particulars, and informed me that I was being questioned for the transgression of a federal law.

While I served as Chairman of the Nile Insurance Company nine years earlier, I had allowed two board members to obtain the firm's financial guarantee for a loan from the government-owned Commercial Bank of Ethiopia. This was a breach of Federal legislation regarding officials of insurance companies. I told Teklai that I had no recollection of the issue ever coming up for board decision, and asked him if there was any evidence in the company's records. He did not respond. According to the company's statutes, board members were collectively responsible for their decisions. I did not see other board members upon my arrival. One had been interrogated briefly and released on bail two days earlier. He was known to have close links to the central bank. Some even alleged that he was working hand in glove with the bank to exercise control over the Bank of Abyssinia where he was also a board member. I asked Teklai that I should be granted bail. His brusque reply was that I could make a formal request at a later stage.

He then led me to two officers: one who again asked for my name, address, etc, and another who searched me, took my belt, wallet, shoe laces, driving license, identity card, medicine, and suspicious looking objects like scented tissues. As he was busy doing that, I noticed what looked like the image of Meles Zenawi dangling from his key chain. It was an enamel encased colour likeness of the Prime Minister. There were also desk calendars bearing the Prime Minister's photograph. I wondered if this was how personality cults make their early appearance. Another officer was summoned to escort me to my cell. All in all, there were six officers who handled my case that day. All but one were Tigreans. I would see more of this phenomenon both at the police detention centre and later in Kallitty Prisons.

I was taken to cell number 2, a sixteen square-metre (160 feet square) room in a concrete building which accommodated 12 persons, I being the thirteenth. This meant that there was 1.2 square metres (12 square feet) of space available for each detainee. I spent the afternoon hours exchanging views with former Nile Insurance staff who had been detained earlier on the same charge. They said I was not involved at all. The case had not been brought to the board while I was chairman. It was the management who had offered the financial guarantee for the loans the clients were given by the Commercial Bank of Ethiopia. These loans had been arranged by none other than the government itself. There was a reason for this.

As I mentioned previously, the government had expelled Eritrean citizens soon after the opening of hostilities in 2000. It said that they had become a national security threat. This immediately triggered a crisis, for a great many Eritreans had become dominant players in freight transport to and from the ports of Djibouti and Assab. Their expulsion resulted in a serious disruption of foreign trade. The government had to do something. What it did was to call on prominent businessmen in Addis, explain the critical situation and request their collaboration in responding to a national emergency.

The business persons were told to replace the Eritrean operators. The government owned Commercial Bank of Ethiopia was ready to provide the required loans for the purchase of new trucks. For the businessmen, it was an excellent investment opportunity, with the added attraction of something sanctioned by the government to respond to a national emergency. They obliged. Approximately $60 million was made available by the Commercial Bank. Given the shortage of privately owned tangible assets to serve as collateral, the businessmen went to different insurance companies and obtained financial guarantees. All in all, some four hundred freight trucks were ordered. Not only did the government initiate the transaction, but it was also fully aware that insurance companies were providing the required collateral to members of their board of directors. It kept silent. The regulatory agency, the National Bank of Ethiopia, was also silent. And continued to be silent for nine long years.[1] It was as near as anyone could get to being complicit.

At my first appearance in court, my attorney requested the judge for my immediate release on bail. She told the police that they should hurry up with the case. I appeared before this judge three more times. Each time, the request for bail was deferred. In the case of two of the accused whose detention preceded mine by two weeks, the judge ordered their release on bail. Instead of being released, however, the accused were promptly transferred to a high security section of the detention centre. This was an unambiguous signal from the government to the judge and to the defendants. We were not to be released on bail.

On the day when I and those detained with me were to appear before the judge to get a ruling, our case was suddenly removed from her hands and taken to the Sixth Bench of the High Court. There, we were all formally charged with a breach of the insurance law. The evidence provided by the prosecutor against me consisted of two board minutes which bore my signature but which had otherwise nothing to do with the charge that I had allowed two board members to obtain financial guarantees for their loans from the Commercial Bank of Ethiopia. The minutes did not have a single word on the two board members or on their financial guarantees. It became plain to me that my detention was politically motivated. At the High Court, our attorneys lodged another request for bail. It was rejected, whereupon we appealed to the Supreme Court.

Later, we were transferred to Kallitty, the city's main prison: a maze of primitive barns, fences, dirt roads and foot-tracks on the outskirts of Addis Ababa. Corrugated iron sheets were used for roofs and walls, with branches of eucalyptus trees for trusses and wall frames. The floors were made of rough concrete which had over time developed a layer of dirt. I was placed in a cavernous barnlike hall without a ceiling. It measured thirteen-metre square in which 175 detainees were accommodated. Outside the space taken by bunker beds, there was free floor space where prisoners without beds slept. My rough calculation showed there was 0.55 square metres (5.5 square feet) of space per detainee, less than half of the space available at the police detention centre. Imagine being cramped into an area one metre (3.3 feet) long and 55 centimetres (1.8 feet) wide. Incredibly, there were rooms far worse than this. In one of these, the number of inmates sometimes reached 700. When night fell, some prisoners slept on top of each other.

A couple of weeks or so after our transfer to Kalllitty, we made our first appearance before the Supreme Court. There, we found judges who, though under apparent pressure from the government agent in their midst, appeared to be open to our appeal for bail. After listening to our attorneys and to the public prosecutor, they adjourned their ruling for a fortnight. In the meantime, we received information that a number of people were interceding on our behalf, and on their own initiative. When a senior party official was approached regarding the business persons detained with me, he reportedly said: "these people should be made to understand that there is a government in this country." The remark reminded me of the comment made by another party bigwig several years previously that I did not appear to believe that Ethiopia had a government. Another senior party functionary who was similarly approached remarked that we had misbehaved and needed to be pinched a little. Pinching on the thighs was a physical penalty inflicted on naughty children in days gone by.

We appeared before the Supreme Court for a second time to be informed of yet another adjournment. In preparation for our third appearance, the judges had apparently examined our case to their satisfaction and were about to give a favourable ruling. Rumours circulated in town that all eleven of us were to be released on bail. Although I myself was skeptical (given the sensational propaganda in the print and electronic media following our detention), a good number in our group were optimistic. When we appeared in court, the senior judge made a statement in a low almost inaudible voice that a further adjournment of nine days was needed to look into the case further. Most detainees were dejected. One among us was so certain of his release that he fell ill immediately.

Why had the Court adjourned once again? Had we been wrongly informed that the judges had made up their minds? Did something stand in their way? We soon learned from visitors that the judges had indeed decided to grant bail but that the party agent in their midst had raised objections. He is reported to have complained about the leak of their impending ruling, and was not altogether happy that their decision should be seen to confirm the rumours. A judge who disregards the concerns of a party agent would do so at his own peril. The three judges agreed to defer their ruling.

At the fourth hearing on March 6, the Court ruled to release seven of the eleven accused on bail, in which I was included. The four who were kept behind had long been regarded with hostility by senior members of the party. Their release was prolonged on the ground that all witnesses should first testify, in order that they might not fall under their influence. It appeared the judges had found a way to accommodate the party agent without capitulating completely. And the government agent had done something to satisfy his masters. The 6th of March being a Friday, the release papers could not negotiate the bureaucratic hurdles for us to be freed on Saturday. One more working day was needed. We were released in the afternoon of Monday, the 9th of March.

I spent much of my time in detention reading and talking to inmates, some of whom I could never have met in the normal course of events: fourteen, fifteen-year olds imprisoned on charges of theft or 'intended' theft; highjackers of aircraft; a South

The author with his family in Philadelphia, January 2010; from left is Itagegnehu, Roman, Teshager, the author, and Beshowamyellesh

Korean businessman; a Syrian IT investor, two Egyptian cooks who had crossed the border from the Sudan to work in a hotel, etc. etc. It was fascinating to hear their stories. To my surprise, I found most Ethiopian inmates to be strong adherents of their country's values: showing deference to the elderly when going to the toilet, or entering a room, or queuing up, sharing food, praying at regular intervals, and a general willingness to observe discipline without which prison life would be impossible.

I had lost 22 pounds in detention. When I came out, family and friends said I did not look well and needed to go overseas for medical treatment. I was also advised that the authorities would not leave me in peace. It was said that senior officials overseeing the case were furious with the baseless charges that the police had put up against me. They were now working on fresh pretexts for another detention.[2] Yet another problem was my book project which had been interrupted and which now looked increasingly unlikely to be published in Ethiopia, given the critical comments it contained. I had to leave the country.

I obtained a U.S. visa, bought a ticket, and boarded an Ethiopian Airlines flight to Washington D.C. on the 19th of March. I went through the immigration and customs formalities without incident. Soon after my arrival in Philadelphia where my family was, I took an appointment with my family doctor, John Butler. He made a preliminary examination and wrote a report saying that my state of health was a cause for concern. I had to be under medical treatment and surveillance until my condition stabilized. I sent the report with a covering note to the High Court judge where my case was being heard and asked for a deferment.

In the meantime, I had missed a court appearance at which my attorneys informed the court that I had left the country for medical treatment on account of the deterioration of my health and that a medical report would soon be submitted. It would be recalled that this judge had initially rejected our request for bail and was not altogether pleased that he had been overruled by a superior court. He now felt vindicated. He said that he had refused bail for precisely this kind of eventuality and ordered the police to make every effort to look for me and see to it that I would appear at the following hearing.

When my attorneys submitted my physician's medical report on the day of the hearing, the judge arbitrarily rejected both my note and the physician's report, saying that anyone could easily obtain such a report. In a similar case a month before, he had accepted a doctor's report regarding one of the eleven defendants in our group. The same court had allowed an accused person to go overseas, not for medical treatment, but to attend the graduation ceremony of a son. The judge's conduct was plainly not fair and appeared to be politically motivated. But there were stronger pointers that my case had political undertones.

Five instances of the breach of the country's insurance law were cited in the charge sheets against the accused. I was charged in regard to only one of these. To start with, the case involving me never came before any board meeting I chaired. The prosecutor could not provide evidence by way of board minutes or other internal documents. Secondly, by the prosecutor's own admission, I had served as Chairman of Nile Insurance for only seven months. And that was nine years previously. Besides the obvious surprise that it had taken that long to bring up a charge against an alleged transgression of the law which the regulatory agency was fully aware of, I was the only Chairman of the board who was charged. The other Chairmen during whose tenure four of the five financial guarantees were granted were not charged. Yet one more surprise was the fact that no regular board member who served with me was charged. According to the statues of the Nile Insurance Company, oversight responsibility for the firm was not exclusively vested in the Chairman. It was a collective responsibility of all board members. The government apparently had no political reason to bring charges against other board members or chairmen. The focus was on me. Finally, there were businessmen other than the three detained with me who had seats on the board of Nile Insurance Company and who had obtained similar insurance guarantees. They were not charged either.

It was plain that the charge against me was politically motivated. One reason was my troubled relations with senior officials of the National Bank of Ethiopia during my tenure at the Bank of Abyssinia. They often complained that I was insolent and willfully disregarded their instructions. Their knowledge of banking supervision was limited, as I explained before, and they resented anything that looked like a reminder of their weakness. I had also made two well publicized speeches: the first to the Addis Ababa Chamber of Commerce in September 2001 on the problems facing the banking sector, and the second at the fifteenth annual meeting of the Ethiopian Human Rights Council in May 2006.

In the first speech I had said that government arbitrariness was a major risk for banking business in Ethiopia and had also criticized the government for the arbitrary detention of businessmen. More importantly, I had been critical of Revolutionary Democracy (the party ideology) and suggested that it was not favourable to private business. In the second speech, I had stated that the human rights situation in the country was a cause for concern and had said that ideology was the main reason for this. All this was naturally perceived as a deliberate attack on the government. Three of the business persons who owned major shares in Nile Insurance (and the Bank of Abyssinia) had been on the black books of the government, and two had spent several years in detention. The party was continually on the lookout for a suitable pretext to put them back in detention. When it was found, they were promptly thrown behind bars along with persons perceived to be their accomplices. It must finally be added that the prevailing mindset among Ethiopian officials in matters of governance is totalitarian. Intrusiveness in the affairs of private entities and civil society organizations is the inevitable consequence. Laws are passed by the rubber stamp Parliament (often retroactively) to intimidate and to assist the political police to keep institutions and individuals in check. Corruption, national security, sovereignty are, in line with the practice of all tyrants, the pretexts for all such repressive measures. The prosecutor's (and the High Court's) handling of my case should be seen in this general context.

I would not wish to overstate my arbitrary and distressing detention, the deplorable conduct of the High Court judge, the police, or the public prosecutor. Many of my compatriots have been subjected to far harsher treatment by the current and the previous government: they have been imprisoned for much longer periods and have been vilified more stridently in the media. A good many have been murdered by the monstrous regime of the Dergue. To show bitterness about my detention would be to trivialize the pains and privations of these unfortunate victims. Mercifully, my detention was not too long; being nine days short of three months. But it was long enough to enrich my experience and deepen my understanding of life in Ethiopia today. And, I should add, to be able to see through the Machiavellian ways of the regime.

Detention and its Compensations: The Many Faces of Prison

My stay at the police detention centre lasted for about three weeks. At Kallitty it covered some two months. Both places were human laboratories where Ethiopians and expatriates of different ages, backgrounds, and temperaments intermingled. The foreigners I came across included a Syrian, a Chinese, two Egyptians, three or four Cameroonians, a Congolese, a Yemeni, a few Liberians, a South Korean, a Sudanese, a

Nigerian, a Tanzanian, Eritreans and a good number of non-Ethiopian Somalis. Most of the foreigners were detained on immigration charges at airports or other entry points and could have been repatriated on the spot without much fanfare. Talking to these detainees was an agreeable experience in an otherwise disagreeable environment.

Fahdy: A Syrian Investor's Painful Three Months

After spending a few days at the police detention centre my attention was attracted by Fahdy, who was wearing a wrap-around in the fashion of Muslim males in Ethiopia. I asked Fahdy why he had come to Ethiopia and what had got him into the prison. "I came to this country because I was stupid," he said emphatically, resting his forefinger on his forehead. He had been told that the IT sector in Ethiopia was virgin territory for investors. A compatriot was in the country already. He decided to come and try his luck.

Upon arrival, he was met by his friend and was offered a room until he found a place to stay. Fahdy applied for an investment license, was given one, and started to work. A few weeks later, his friend went to Dubai on a business trip. Fahdy himself needed to travel there subsequently, bought a ticket and proceeded to the airport. After checking in, he walked to the immigration booth. A few questions were posed, following which he was taken aside. What was the purpose of his residence in Ethiopia, he was asked. He said he was an investor, had obtained a license, and was now working on his project. The officials informed him that he could not leave. The friend with whom he was staying had left the country without paying rent on his residence. He would have to answer questions.

Fahdy protested that he had nothing to do with the rent. The lease on the house was between the landlord and his friend, not him. As more and more questions were asked, Fahdy realized that he was suspected of providing illicit long distance telephone call services to clients. All telephone services are a monopoly of the government owned Telecommunications Corporation. The interrogators did not accept Fahdy's repudiation of the false charge. Nor did they seem to pay attention to his business license or his residence permit. He was handed over to the police who arrested him. A criminal charge was filed against him, with no evidence to back it up: a standard procedure in TPLF-ruled Ethiopia, where the police arrest first and look for evidence later. After a couple of court appearances he was found innocent. The police were ordered to release him.

Fahdy felt vindicated. He packed his personal effects, got his release papers and stepped outside as a free man. Within seconds, he was rearrested, or "kidnapped" as he put it. This time was not allowed to see a judge. Intelligence officials visited him on several occasions and questioned him closely. They could uncover nothing incrementing. What they discovered was a man who had a good knowledge of the IT business. Would he kindly organize training sessions for them, they asked one day. Fahdy gladly accepted, hoping that this might pave the way for his release. He spent many hours training. He was commended for his efforts. Unfortunately, the trainees could not intercede on his behalf as he had hoped and as they had promised. "Here I am ninety days later, still in illegal detention," he lamented.

Fahdy and I compared notes about freedom and democracy in Syria and Ethiopia. He did not hide that Syria was ruled by a dictator. But the situation was better. He had been detained for two months in his student days, and been told by security officials that he had a big mouth. He downsized it and was thenceforth left alone. In time, he built up a successful IT business and was doing rather well prior to his Ethiopian adventure. When he regains his freedom, Fahdy will have a thing or two to say about how the Ethiopian government treats foreign investors it so eagerly courts.

Triple H: Bin Laden's Soulmate

Another man I came across was Hammar Hawash Harrar: a name which appeared to have been concocted to make a political point rather than one given at birth. Triple H was born in Fedis, a small town in Harrar province. He was 50% Oromo (through his mother), 50% ethnic Somali, and one thousand percent Islamic extremist. At the age of twelve, his father had taken him to Somalia, where he joined Siad Bare's army and took part in the invasion of Ethiopia. After Bare's defeat, he lived in the Sudan and Kenya. The Kenyans arrested him as a terrorist and passed him on to Ethiopia. He was badly tortured in both countries, one consequence of which was his difficulty to pass urine normally. I was informed on my first night that the man was the most colourful character at the detention centre.

Tripple H was easy to talk to and enjoyed exchanging jokes. Despite his limited Amharic, conversation was possible. Whenever the going got rough, a young man who spoke Amharic (half Oromo half Somali like himself but with a strong sense of Ethiopian identity) acted as an interpreter. Triple H disdainfully referred to him (and all Oromos) as OPDOs, the Oromo party affiliated with the TPLF, which he loathed wholeheartedly. Triple H did not like Amharas either. All OPDOs and Amharas must be wiped out, he declared from time to time. "OK" I said to him one day. "That might take care of a large portion of Ethiopia's population, but what about the Tigreans, Gurages, Wolaitas, Sidamas, Gambellans, etc.?" "As far as I am concerned," retorted Triple H, "Tigreans are Amharas; as are Gurages, Wolaitas, Sidamas, and Oromos. In my eyes, anyone who is Christian is an Amhara. There will be no peace in this country until all Christians are wiped out and an Islamic government is installed." He smiled broadly as he uttered these menacing words.

In the course of the following days, I and the other persons in the cell talked to him about alternative ways of bringing peace and harmony to the country. When someone said that he would one day help convert Triple H to the more peaceful Orthodox Christian faith, the man was beside himself. I myself was a little taken aback by the ill-advised remark, and came up with what I thought was a better approach. I asked Triple H whether he would go to Fedis, his birthplace, if he is released one of these days. He shook his head. He had no relatives there. Mengistu and Meles had massacred them all. Why would he go there? I told him it was unlikely that all of his kin were killed; but I singularly failed to convince him. He said he would go back to Mogadiscio and resume the fight against Ethiopia. He was a Somali, not an Ethiopian. I said I and my friends regarded him as a compatriot and felt that he should stay in Ethiopia, a far more peaceful and better place. He disagreed.

I thought of another approach. Has he ever been told of a region in Ethiopia called Wollo, I asked. Tripple H said he had. Christians and Muslims there lived in peace. More than that, they intermarried. And their offspring were Christian or Muslim, depending on their choice. That, I concluded confidently, could someday be the situation in Ethiopia as a whole. A peaceful Ethiopia. I said that he should visit Wollo when he was released from prison. Triple H said: No, No, No; he would not go to Wollo. How could there be peace in a place with multiple religions. "One country, one religion! That is what I believe in." he said. He concluded with an unconvincing metaphor: "One cannot split an arm into several bits and pretend that it is still an arm, can one?" It was worse than talking to a brick wall.

But you could not resist talking to Tripple H. He had no relatives in Addis to bring him food. He was happy to forego the prison ration and share food with those getting it from home. I gave him an apple whereupon he took off on his favourite theme: Islam and Ethiopia. I reminded him of the previous day's conversation and his idea that all Christians should be massacred if peace is to come to Ethiopia. "I am, as you know, a Christian. What would you do if you were to find yourself in a position to kill Christians and I happened to be among them? "Tekelle" said Tripple, as always mispronouncing my name. "You, too, would be killed." There was no need to seek further enlightenment.

Triple H had heard that I had once worked for Emperor Haile-Selassie. Out of the blue one day he said that Haile-Selassie was a good leader. I wasn't sure that I had heard him right. When I appeared puzzled, he repeated what he said. During his reign Muslims in Fedis were well treated. He had opened Koranic schools for them. And Somalis could travel freely, unlike today, to Mogadiscio, Hargessa, Djibouti, Assab, and come back home without being harassed. His own relatives used to do that frequently. "Tell me Tekelle," he continued. "Does Haile-Selassie have children?" I told him he had grandchildren. He asked whether any were living in Addis. When I responded that a few did indeed live in the city, he got surprised. "What are they doing in Addis?" he asked. He was astonished to hear that they were making a living like everyone else, and asked, "Is that all they do?" What else did he expect them to do, I inquired "Kill those that murdered their grandfather. That is what they should do. Mengistu in Zimbabwe and all the rest of them. If I were in their position, I would not sit still. I would avenge the death of my grandfather."

Every now and then, Tripple H said or did something that attracted attention. He was standing in line one morning waiting to have his cup filled with tea. There was a bit of space between him and the man in front. The prison officer watching the queue put his hand on Triple H's shoulder and told him to move forward a little closer. When Triple H said he did not like being touched, the prison guard pushed him forward forcefully. Triple H picked up a broom and started beating the guard on the head. Caught by surprise, the guard could only put up his arms to fend off the blows. Other armed guards quickly overpowered Triple H, beat him repeatedly, twisted his arms behind his back, put handcuffs around his wrists, and threw him on the floor where he was left lying. He could not go to the toilet nor feed himself.

There was a big gash on his head. He suffered from chest pains, suggesting that some ribs had been bruised or broken. In the afternoon his wrists were badly swollen. At dusk, an inmate approached a prison officer and said: "In Christ's name, remove the handcuffs from the wrists of this mad Muslim." The officer unlocked the handcuffs with the words, "Mad indeed is he who tries to subdue his armed guards with a broomstick." All in the cell were relieved. There was not a word of appreciation from Triple H for the person that had interceded on his behalf. Freed from his handcuffs, he got up and went to the toilet swearing and cursing his attackers. Vituperation and violence were never too far from Triple H's lips.

Dawit: My First Encounter with an OLF Guerilla Fighter

Dawit, an Oromo from Wollega, was an undergraduate student at Jimma University. While many of his friends had fun, Dawit focused on his studies. Often he sat under the shade of a tree and spent hours working on his papers. Suspicious, the local police kept an eye on him. One afternoon they detained him. What exactly was he doing under the shade of the tree? Dawit said he was studying, away from the noise and fun of friends. The police did not believe him. Torture and beatings followed to make him confess his sympathies for the Oromo Liberation Front and its goal of seceding from the country. He denied any sympathies or links. His professors came to the police to speak on his behalf. Dawit was released for lack of evidence after serving time in jail.

The police beatings and their crude attempt to incriminate him incensed Dawit. Though free, he believed they would not leave him alone. In their eyes he was identified as an OLF supporter. They would henceforth pursue him. He might as well join the OLF, he said to himslef. And so he did. After serving time in the bush he was sent to Mogadiscio as an OLF communications officer. While there, he saw an attractive Somali girl and thought of marriage. Dawit had been told that the Oromos and Somalis had much in common culturally. Language was one. There were other affinities. Marriage to a comely Somali girl did not look like a wild adventure. Was he not indeed reaching out to a distant kinswoman? With that in mind, he decided to make his first move.

He shared his idea with a Somali friend. In Somalia, much like the situation in many Islamic countries, males did not mix freely with females. He had to express his interests indirectly, through intermediaries. The friend volunteered to help him start the process. He would be his first intermediary. But since he did not know the girl's family, he would have to find someone who did. A second willing intermediary was found. Then a third, a fourth, a fifth, and so on until the ninth. It was at that point that contact was established. The contact was not with the girl, however. It was with her brother.

The brother asked who Dawit was, what he was doing in Somalia, whether he was a Muslim, and what his future plans were. Dawit said he was an Oromo from Ethiopia. He said that he, Daoud by name, professed the Muslim faith. This was, of course, not true. But he was not about to be robbed of a beautiful girl by agonizing over one of Moses's Ten Commandments. It did not take long for him to stumble over a question, however. How do Muslims pray, asked the brother. Dawit/Daoud floundered nervously. His ignorance was transparent. The brother took him to task for telling a lie. Daoud took cover under yet another deception: he had thought long about the question and was ready for a conversion. As to his plans, he said he was going abroad for higher studies, and would take the girl with him. Going abroad was a Godsend for any Somali. Daoud seemed to be making headway. The brother agreed to arrange a meeting with his sister. Daoud would not, however, be allowed to lay his hands on her until the day of marriage. In the meantime, he should accede to all her wishes.

Daoud was delighted. He asked what the girl wished to have. Perfume, she said. He went to a shop, bought a bottle of perfume and went to meet her. The girl took one quick look at the perfume bottle and smashed it on the concrete floor. She was not about to degrade herself by accepting some nondescript perfume. He consulted friends and bought a far more expensive bottle for the next encounter. This was grudgingly accepted. But more gifts were demanded: more perfume, colourful material for dresses, more of them, yet more perfume and sundry other gifts. Daoud was unsure when the shower of gifts would cease.

The end came after his finances were badly dented. On the day when the terms of the marriage were negotiated, Daoud was told to come up with $30,000.00 and 1,000 camels. He protested strenuously and managed to bring down the dollar amount to 10,000. Dawit did not tell me how the issue of the camels was resolved. Perhaps he promised a hundred and never managed to deliver them, or perhaps the matter was deferred to an indefinite period. At any rate, he was allowed to marry the girl largely on the basis of his undertaking to take her abroad.

During the gift scouring exercise that had lasted several days, Daoud's contact with the bride to be had been at a distance. Naturally, he looked forward to the big day (or rather the big night) when he could get much closer. The big night arrived, but the wedding ceremony looked needlessly drawn out. Daoud had to be patient, suppressing his erotic imagination as best he could. When night fell, he was relieved. He slipped into his modest bedroom, his bride now confidently following in his footsteps. When he placed himself next to his brand new wife now resting on her back and ready for his embrace, he encountered an unexpected snag. He tried to make headway, once, twice, and several more times. He was not getting anywhere.

The bride broke down in laughter as Daoud continued in his strenuous efforts. "What in Allah's name are you trying to do?" Daoud groped for words to respond to a question best answered in deed. The girl continued to be hugely amused as he struggled. Every so often she would burst out in laughter. Daoud persisted in his labours until his organ (rather than hers as is customarily the case) was bruised. It dawned on him ultimately that the attractive, profusely perfumed bride was wearing chastity stitches.

Early the following morning, Daoud recounted the embarrassing incident to a friend. The man expressed surprise at his ignorance. Why had he not arranged for a knowledgeable old lady to remove the stitches, another question he was in no mood to answer? He started making preparations to move to Kenya and soon left with his new wife. There he found a doctor who was conversant with Somali culture and who removed the stitches for a fee. He advised Dawit to desist for a fortnight. Keen to avoid further embarrassment, Dawit waited a whole month before he decided to consummate the marriage. What a far cry all this was, he thought, from the more relaxed approach of the Oromo to sexuality. One had to look elsewhere for instances of Oromo/Somali cultural affinity.

While in Kenya, Dawit quit the OLF and started working for an international organization (the UNHCR I believe he told me). After a few years, life became dreary. His Somali wife was in the meantime taking him to task for his liberal ways with women: his female boss in the office, his friends' wives, his neighbours, or anyone wearing a skirt. In the apartment they shared with another couple, Dawit was careful not to look in the direction of the other half of the apartment. The co-tenant was also married. Dawit's wife kept an eye on every inch of his movements. One morning Dawit had to leave early for work and woke up before everyone in the apartment. He got dressed and walked quietly, very quietly, in the direction of the common kitchen to make tea. In a matter of seconds, he heard a loud shriek behind him followed by the smashing of the teapot on the tile of the kitchen floor. It was his wife who was incesensed by an unusually early morning tip toe to the kitchen.

He wondered how he could get away from it all when he saw an advertisement in a Nairobi newspaper urging Ethiopian refugees to return home. It was from the Embassy. Dawit and a few of his friends discussed the matter and decided to talk to Embassy staff. They were well received when they arrived. The government would do all it could to reintegrate them into their respective communities, said the men of the Embassy. The President of Oromia, Aba Dula Gemeda, would welcome them at the border town of Moyale and would facilitate everything.

Dawit and his friend accepted the offer and proceeded to Moyale. His wife would join him once he got settled. When the OLF veterans reached Moyale, they asked to be taken to Aba Dula. After the routine debriefing, Dawit and his friends were met with the *dula* (truncheon) of the police, rather than with Aba Dula. They were taken to Addis Ababa and were subjected to repeated beatings and torture (which included the removal of their toe nails). They finally appeared before a magistrate who judged them innocent. The police disregarded the verdict and kept them in jail. They were in illegal detention at the central police station when I met them.

In the course of his years of struggle, Dawit's views regarding Oromo self-determination and independence had mellowed considerably. He said that Ethiopians should join hands to build a country where all ethnic groups and cultures would be treated equally and where democracy reigned. Secession was not a practical option. If Oromia were to be independent, wars would break out all along its borders with the different ethnic groups: with the Benishangul, the Gambela, the Amhara, the Somali, the Afars, and the peoples of the Southern Region. Many of the other OLF veterans I met were similarly disparaging of Oromia's secession. The war of independence, so they said, was an agenda of the OLF leadership. No good was ever likely to result from an interminable war.

Jemal Negash: The Innocent Teenager Labelled Criminal

Jemal was a seventeen-year old from Armatchiho in North Gondar, a region where the Ethiopian Peoples Patriotic Front (EPPF) is said to be conducting guerilla activity. After a year's unsuccessful hunt for a job in Azezo in South Gondar, Jemal had come to Addis. He wore tattered clothes and hand-made crude leather sandals. As he roamed the town looking for a job one day, he was stopped by police and asked for his identity card. He replied he had not yet reached the legal age to be issued a card. Suspected of spying for the EPPF, he was arrested, beaten, and told to confess that he was a spy. Jemal appeared before a magistrate and denied the charge. He was found innocent and ordered released. The police ignored the court order. The young man did not know what awaited him and sank into depression.

As I talked to him in the miniscule courtyard of the detention centre one afternoon, I noticed the purple coloured inside of his left arm. I asked what it was. Young Jemal had heard stories about persons who committed suicide by cutting the blood veins on the inside of their arms. One day he borrowed a razor blade and started cutting the veins on his left arm, but haphazardly and without much conviction. He was restrained by onlookers and taken to the detention centre's makeshift clinic. There, the nurse put some iodine on the cuts (the reason for the purple colour) and sent him to the superintendent of the prison. "If you were man enough, you would have cut your throat instead of messing around with your veins" said the superintendent and ordered him back to his cell.

Sentayehou Haile: A Fourteen-Year Old Forced into Petty Crime

Over the public address system one morning at Kallitty, I heard a high-pitched voice reading out instructions to inmates. I knew that the announcer was from our part of the prison, but I had not seen a woman detainee before. I asked whether they had brought a girl from another part of the prison. No. it was a young male inmate, I was informed. Curious, I proceeded to where the announcement was being made and saw a young boy with a microphone in his hand.

I took him aside when he was done with his announcement and asked how old he was. Fourteen, he said. How could a fourteen-year old find himself in jail? I asked again to make sure. He said he was only a few months past fourteen. Is there not a minimum age for inmates I wondered? Sentayehou told me that the police who detained him had sworn before the magistrate that he was seventeen. And the magistrate had taken his word. Why was he in jail? He was from a poor family, he told me. His father, Haile Tola, was a security guard in a modest establishment and his mother was bedridden. They lived in a battered down government shack whose rent was low. But when it was due each month it was a family headache. There were six in the family.

Sentayehou was often in need of clothes to wear to school, but did not dare ask his father to buy him clothes. When threads appeared on the seat of his pants or the elbows of his jacket, neighbours would notice and give him their children's used clothes. This was how he managed to keep up appearances in school. Sentayehou got tired of showing up at the neighbours every time his clothes wore out. Together with a couple of like-minded friends, he decided to steal in order to buy second-hand clothing. Easily removable car parts were their target: hub caps, rear view mirrors, windshield wipers, brand labels, etc. One day Sentayehou and two friends ventured to where a number of cars were parked and managed to detach enough parts to sell for fifty birr (five dollars). They did this successfully three times, and had enough money to buy used clothing in the flea market nearby. Senatayehou was happy that he no longer had to make embarrassed appearances in front of neighbours' homes.

A few months passed and holes re-appeared on his pants and jacket. Sentayehou organized another car raid. This time his luck ran out. He was caught by police and was arrested. At the police station, an officer told him to admit his theft. Sentayehou responded that he was not a thief, and had never been one. His interrogator started slapping him in the face and beating him all over the body. When blood came out through the nose, the boy admitted that he had been caught removing car parts. The beating stopped. Along with his two friends, Senatayehou appeared before a magistrate. The boys complained they had been beaten. The police denied. When they protested, the magistrate asked the officer to put his hands on a bible and swear that he had not beaten them. Unflinchingly, the police carried out the magistrate's instructions. And that settled the matter for the judge.

The boys were asked for their age. Sentayehou said he was only fourteen. The police countered that he was seventeen. The magistrate asked the boy whether he had a birth certificate. That precious piece of paper had gone up in flames when his parents' shack was burned to the ground a few years back. In the absence of the certificate,

Sentayehou was declared seventeen; the word of the policeman prevailing one more time. The boy and his friends were found guilty and sentenced to six months in jail. As there are no detention centres for juvenile delinquents in Addis Ababa, they were brought to the central prison in Kallitty.

After listening to his story, I asked Sentayehou how he was going to address the problem of clothing after he leaves jail. You are not going to go back to removing car parts again, are you? I asked. "No," he said. "I have thought it over and have decided to go to school only in the evenings. During the day, I shall do odd jobs to save money to buy clothes. And pass on any spare coins to my father."

The Aircraft Highjacker

He was relatively young and his head was shaven. Short but well built, he walked the dusty prison grounds briskly for his daily exercise. Someone who noticed that I liked talking to people said that the young man had an interesting story to tell. High profile prisoners like him were usually taciturn, as they felt they were being watched. I asked my interlocutor if he could convey my wish to talk to the young man. He replied that he had done so already. It did not take time for Gattew to open up when I greeted him and asked a few questions. He too was eager to talk, as he had been informed of my desire to have a conversation. I quickly got down to the business of asking questions about his highjacking of a military transport aircraft of the Ethiopian Air Force. Why had he taken the risk to do that? And how did he do it?

"Haven't you ever seen TV footage on aircraft highjackings?" he said in response to my second question. He and his colleagues went over these films repeatedly. Four young men and a girl made up the group. The boys were armed with handguns, grenades, and knives. The girl was unarmed. I wondered how they could possibly board a military aircraft with all that in their possession. "It can be done if you are determined," was Gattew's guarded response. As to their reason for the highjacking, he said it followed a student demonstration during which police severely beat the marchers. A handful of young people were also killed. This enraged Gattew and his friends. They decided to avenge the death of their colleagues and set an example to others.

The five passed the security checks without incident and boarded the aircraft. They proceeded to the second class section where soldiers sat, the first class being reserved for officers. A few minutes into the flight the girl was instructed to execute her mission. She gulped down three bottles of Coca Cola in quick succession, induced herself to vomit and fell flat on the floor of the aircraft feigning a sudden illness. Her four colleagues threw up their arms in despair, crying that their friend was about to die. The other passengers instinctively joined in and shouted for help. In the officers' section, which was separated from the soldiers' compartment by a metal door, the aircraft attendant looked at the scene through a peephole. He yelled to the crowd to tell the sick girl to get up and come to where he was. "She can barely move. How can she get up and walk to you?" shouted one of the highjackers. "Pick her up and bring her," shouted back the attendant.

In an instant, a colleague carried the girl to the metal door, her legs and arms dangling on his sides. When the attendant opened the door, the girl suddenly came to life and threw her arms around his body, momentarily immobilizing him. At that split second the four highjackers instantaneously went into action and took control of the aircraft. Gattew, the chief highjacker, immediately ran to the cockpit, took charge and instructed the pilot to announce that the aircraft was now under the control of gunmen. The second in command placed himself in the officers' cabin. The third highjacker stayed behind in the second class area where the soldiers were seated and took immediate control there. The fourth moved around monitoring the general situation.

Gattew kept close watch over the pilot, co-pilot and a non-commissioned officer (NCO) seated just behind the co-pilot. At one point he noticed through the corner of his eye the NCO moving gingerly towards him. He turned to him and yelled he had noticed his movement. If he moved a millimetre one way or the other, he would be as good as dead, warned Gattew. As he was discretely monitoring the situation, the foolish man moved slightly towards him again, thinking that he was not being watched. Gattew struck instantaneously and lopped off the man's left ear with his sharp knife. The man fell to the floor and started nursing his ear, which had not been detached completely. That, said Gattew, enabled him to concentrate on the pilot and copilot. I gasped when he reached that point in the story. "You literally cut off his ear?" I asked in astonishment. "You forget that I was on a dangerous mission involving death and destruction. I could have killed him, but it was too early in our plan and I did not want to create a crisis needlessly."

The pilot pleaded with Gattew to spare the aircraft and its passengers. And himself. He was the father of five kids and did not want to die. The highjacker told him to follow instructions and not to worry about the rest. Gattew got a little suspicious as the pilot lingered on the instrument panel at one point. He knew next to nothing about aviation. But the pilot's handling of the instruments and his general attitude worried him. Highjacker number two who was monitoring the general situation in the aircraft was now standing in the cockpit. Gattew said he was not sure of the pilot's movements and wished to give him a jolt. "I am going to prick his thigh with my knife. What do you think?"asked Gattew. His colleague nodded, and Gattew thrust the tip of his knife into the pilot's thigh. The man shrieked and pleaded for mercy. For a few moments he put his palm on the fresh wound to stop the bleeding. The instrument panel was left in peace.

The highjackers' plan was to fly to Saudi Arabia. As the aircraft was low on fuel, they agreed with the pilot to refuel in Khartoum. Just before landing there, the communications officer who was seated in the tail section of the aircraft parachuted to the ground. He feared that the aircraft might be blown up once on the ground. The plane landed safely and Gattew instructed his number two to descend and arrange the refueling; and keep him posted every two minutes over the mobile phone. If that did not happen, Gattew would conclude there was trouble, begin killing one officer at a time and dump bodies on the tarmac.

Highjacker number two descended and asked if there were any government officials around. It took some time before contact was established. The Sudanese were extremely reluctant to allow the refueling, which they said would be a breach of their law. Negotiations continued until the local official of the United Nations High Commission for Refugees arrived. He, too, pleaded with the highjackers to surrender. Sanctions against aircraft highjackings under Sudanese law were lenient, the maximum sentence being a three-year imprisonment. The UNHCR representative gave assurances that the young men would not be ill treated and that he would do everything in his power to see to it that their rights were respected. After 11 hours of inconclusive negotiations the highjackers decided that they had secured adequate media attention. They handed over their weapons to the UNHCR official and gave themselves up to law enforcement agents.

In prison, Gattew found himself sharing a villa with Hassan al-Turabi, the Sudanese Islamist ideologue who had been a mentor to his country's President but who had eventually fallen out with him. What were al-Turabi's views on Ethiopia, I asked Gattew. On the whole positive, he replied. I was somewhat surprised, given the man's extremist Islamist inclinations. I had heard that in his early years he had set up a camp in the Sudan to train agents to destabilize Ethiopia. Gattew said that he shared an air-conditioned, well-furnished and comfortable villa with al-Turabi; a far cry from his unhygienic and overcrowded cell at Kallitty.

The group appeared before a Sudanese court, were found guilty, and sentenced to three years in prison. "If you have money in the Sudan, you can get away with murder," said Gattew who told me that he and his friends bribed their way out of jail in a year. The girl highjacker left for Europe to pursue her studies. Gattew and his three male colleagues stayed behind. Before long he was arrested by Sudanese police at the instigation of the Ethiopian Ambassador and handed over to Ethiopian authorities.

In Addis Ababa, he was interrogated. Witnesses came to the detention centre to help identify him. One supposed eyewitness was asked who among the persons lined up was the highjacker. He pointed his finger at Gattew without the slightest hesitation. Gattew could not recall ever seeing this man before. "Can you put your hand on this Bible and swear that you have ever seen me?" he asked. The witness hesitated and said he was not sure. The interrogator was furious and removed the Bible promptly. He warned Gattew not to ask questions. Another witness appeared later who confidently pointed to Gattew as the highjacker. The man's left ear showed a long thin scar suggesting restorative surgery.

The interrogations were completed and Gattew was charged, tried and found guilty. Prior to the sentencing, he appeared before the three judges of the High Court and was asked if he could cite extenuating circumstances for his crime. Gattew said that when young he had seen too many movies of aircraft highjackings and had been influenced by them. One of the judges got furious. "Films! How dare you regard your crime so frivolously? Do you think you were found guilty of highjacking a bicycle?" The case was adjourned. I left Kallitty before the sentence was delivered.

There were a good number of other interesting individuals whose stories would take too much space to narrate. I met a South Korean businessman who had been arrested on a charge I never had time to find out. He was unable to live on the prison's rations which in the main consisted of Ethiopian food. The prison administration allowed him to cook his own food at the prison kitchen. He told me that he had become an accomplished chef. Improbably, I also encountered a gay person from one of the minority groups in the west or south of the country whom everyone called Almaz, despite his strenuous objections at being given a girl's name. He was derided every time he proceeded to the toilet.

A couple of young Orthodox priests officiated at Sunday Mass in a makeshift chapel. One had been charged with physical assault causing bodily harm. No evidence was found and he was released. His replacement was another priest who was alleged to have stolen a *Tabot*: the revered wood block on which the Ten Commandments are inscribed and which is kept in a specially designated holy place in each Orthodox Church. I was told that it was a trumped up charge. The trial had not concluded when I left prison. I should finally mention the young burglar who deeply regretted his unfortunate experience and who now wanted to become a film director. When he knew I was about to be released, he asked if I could get him a handbook on filmmaking. Soon after arriving in the U.S. I purchased a copy of *Filmmaking For Dummies* and sent it to him.

Prison experience has made me a little wiser about the predicaments of life in today's Ethiopia. No less instructive has been the opportunity to see at close range the reality behind the rhetoric on the rule of law. Kallitty and the other detention centres are excellent vantage points for observing the Ethiopian government's methods of fighting corruption, enforcing the law, and administering the judiciary. I shall conclude this section with a few observations on this theme.

Detention: Further Compensations

The frequency with which the police ignore magistrates' rulings to free detainees is such as to raise serious questions on the executive branch's much touted commitment to the role of an independent judiciary. More often than one imagines, magistrates themselves allow the police to prolong the period of detention well beyond the statutory limit. They appear to be apprehensive that a tendency to follow the letter and spirit of the law could be perceived as creating a hurdle to the work of law enforcement officials. One told a friend that her few rulings to free prisoners on bail in compliance with the law had lately attracted the attention of the authorities and that she would have to ease up.

Judges in higher courts often play it safe when handling politically sensitive cases. They find pretexts to deny release on bail to persons they believe the government is unfavourably disposed to. I have cited instances of this in the foregoing sections. An overzealous judge does not have to be approached directly or indirectly by a government agent. He could act on his own initiative if he contemplates (and who among them doesn't) promising career prospects. Our defence lawyers had raised well-reasoned technical objections to the prosecutor's charges (including the generally accepted legal doctrine that legislation cannot have retroactive effect). The judge summarily dismissed the totality of their objections. One would have thought that at least one or two might be admitted, if only to save face. No. All eight objections were dismissed. It was plain that the judge had more weighty concerns in his mind than his obligation to the law. Where judges are party members which is increasingly the case, there is of course much more reason to side with the public prosecutor

The Federal Anti-Corruption Commission is known to intimidate judges who do not tow the party line on fighting corruption, or who ignore intercessions by the Commission's high officials on behalf of friends and acquaintances. A judge was once threatened by the Commissioner himself for obstructing the Commission's work when he refused to meet a client who tried to reach him through a high official. Members of the executive branch have been known to openly complain about the intransigence of courts. None of this is calculated to inspire a sense of independence among members of the judiciary. That a neo-Marxist ruling party should pressure the judiciary to further its political objectives is, of course, not surprising. It is equally unsurprising that the political rhetoric should be totally at variance with this bitter reality.

Corruption is obviously a not insignificant preoccupation in today's Ethiopia, although the country cannot be considered to be among the major league players in Africa. The government makes much noise about the iniquities of corrupt officials and their private sector collaborators. It understandably does not talk much about its habit of employing the resources of the Anti-Corruption Commission to falsely incriminate civil servants who refuse to support its agenda. Indeed that appears to be the overriding preoccupation of the Federal Anti-Corruption Commission.

Twenty-four senior and middle level managers of the Ethiopian Telecommunications Corporation were imprisoned a couple of years ago on corruption charges. I had the opportunity to talk to some of them at Kallitty. Corruption usually involves offers of gifts in return for official favours, or the willful embezzlement of public funds. It appeared that there was no such case against these managers. A charge I read accused a manager of discarding the equipment of an old billing system in favour of a more advanced one without ascertaining the proper functioning of the newly acquired hardware and its software. Even if one were to disregard the responsibilities of the equipment supplier in this respect, it would be a wild exaggeration to accuse the manager of corruption. Wrong judgment, poor oversight, and negligence are the kinds of things he could be held accountable for. Jailing civil servants accused of such indiscretions has little to do with fighting corruption.

All those charged in the above case said the main reason for their being locked up was their reluctance to cooperate with the government's wish to have a Chinese firm selected for a major bid. The civil servants followed standard bidding procedures and awarded the contract to two Nordic firms. The Ethiopian government's interest in a Chinese award was apparently in response to the offer of a supplier's credit by the government of China totaling some $U.S. 1.5 billion. Staff who evaluate bids usually keep away from supplier's credits as these stand in the way of international competitive bidding. I had no way of independently confirming what I was told, but the flimsiness of the charges and the firm view of the victims did suggest strong political reasons at play. It should be mentioned that Chinese personnel and equipment are intimately involved in the current plan to upgrade telecommunications services in Ethiopia. The government was keen to secure the huge credit and, one suspects, Chinese know-how for monitoring and censoring electronic communications. No bidder is likely to beat the Chinese in these matters.

Two civil servants of the Municipality of Addis Ababa were charged for breach of procedures governing the award of land to investors. Their alleged corruption involved the presumed violation of a guideline that had come into force *after* they had taken decisions on the basis of the prevailing guideline. Several witnesses testified in support of the two officials, but they were found guilty of corruption by two of the three overzealous judges and sentenced to five years in prison. The third judge persisted in his view that the two were innocent in the eyes of the law, but his minority view did not save the unfortunate civil servants. The purpose is to intimidate civil servants into being loyal servants of the ruling party.

Whenever pressure is brought to bear on the government regarding the unjustified imprisonment of dissidents, its frequent response is that everyone is equal before the law. And if dissidents are put behind bars, it is not for their political views but because of the rigours of the law. Nobody should presume to be above the law. While in detention, I learned of at least one high profile case of fraud in which senior government officials were involved but were not held accountable, while junior civil servants were detained. This relates to the celebrated case of car springs painted in gold that were then sold as solid gold bars to the National Bank of Ethiopia.

In Ethiopia today, anyone wishing to sell gold to the central bank has to have it certified by an authorized laboratory. One such laboratory is at the Ministry of Mines. Gold is tested there, certified, sealed, and is handed over to the owner to be taken to the central bank. The inevitable happened one day when some unscrupulous merchants, instead of proceeding to the bank, took home the sealed crate of authentic gold, removed the paper seal after carefully scanning it, opened the wooden crate, and exchanged the contents for gold painted steel bars cut from car springs. They then resealed the crate with the scanned facsimile of the original. To the naked eye the scanned copy is indistinguishable from the original. The real gold bars were kept at home and the fake ones in the crate were taken to the National Bank of Ethiopia (NEB). It took some time before this was discovered.

Employees from NBE and the Ministry of Mines were arrested. High officials who were responsible for the general oversight of these two departments were not. These officials had failed to act on a recommendation by civil servants that the gold crates should be given police escort en route to the NBE, rather than being handed over to merchants. The recommendation had been made by civil servants in the Ministry of Mines, had been addressed to the Minister of State for Mines with copies to the Minister and the Governor of the National Bank. None of the three senior officials took the trouble to react to the recommendation. The three high officials (all members of the ruling party) were above the law, and were hence not bothered by law enforcement officials. The junior civil servants, including those who had made the recommendation, were not. They were charged and imprisoned. Three years into their imprisonment, they had not obtained a court ruling.

My short stint at Kallitty was instructive in other ways. As an economist, I was attracted by the multitude of activities at Kallitty which formed a bustling mini-economy. The activities ranged from the modest businesses of enterprising individuals (like a young man who rented strings to serve as laundry lines) to the prison-wide economic organization initiated and run by the inmates themselves. Substantial revenue was generated from a wide range of fees. Fees were charged for barber shops, coffee shops, and stalls for handicraft items such as belts, woolen caps, metal chairs, shoe laces, and a variety of *objects d'arts*. Revenue was also obtained from space rented for volleyball and games as well as for improvised billiard tables. The young man renting strings had netted $300 in three months and was aiming to make another $600 in the remaining six months of his term; a substantial amount by Ethiopian standards. The prison-wide self-help organization had $50,000 in reserves and expected to see a steady increase.

Going into the details of how the mini-economy functioned would needlessly take up space. Suffice it to say that it sustains itself on the unending paradoxes of prison life. Strings, belts, and shoelaces are forbidden by the prison administration. That is why new inmates are obliged to give them up when they are strip searched. After parting with my belt and shoe laces, I was taken to my cell where I saw several individuals sporting impressive looking belts. Are they not forbidden, I asked someone? "Yes they are, but you can get them for $6 a piece right here in prison. The same with shoe laces" he said indifferently. Needles, razor blades, strings, and other forbidden items can also be obtained. The space that is rented for volleyball games, barber shops, kiosques, etc, obviously belonged to the state which has a monopoly of leasing all land in the country.

In prison, land is rented not by the state but by the voluntary prison wide organization: a grave crime outside the walls of prison.

All these keep the Kallitty economy humming under the watchful eyes of the prison administration. At critical moments, these eyes conveniently look the other way, which is when strings, needles, razor blades, and other forbidden items are smuggled in.

PART V

Whither Ethiopia?

CHAPTER 19

Footprints of History

A Bird's Eyeview of the Recent Past

A good many Ethiopians today are anxious about their country's future. On the eve of their graduation, college students agonize over job prospects. Secondary school students often think of crossing the country's frontiers in search of better prospects. Peasant farmers in the central highlands faced with mounting fertilizer prices and ever diminishing plots look far and wide for off-farm employment. The urban unemployed and underemployed skip meagre meals to make ends meet and wonder if they will ever have the luxury of a square meal. Parents with children in the U.S. anxiously await news of their precious green cards. Young Orthodox priests daydream of going to a newly opened Church in some corner of the globe to serve a Diaspora community. Countless Ethiopians spend days in anguish as the time approaches when names of lucky winners of the much-prized U, S. diversity visas are disclosed. Many are also without hope. Writing from Addis Ababa in May 2010 a reporter of *The Economist,* the British weekly, remarked that Ethiopians believe "only God can change their government" and their prospects for a better life.

To be sure, there are those upon whom fortune smiles. But they are the lucky few who, barring a tiny minority of hardworking bona fide business persons in their midst, make it a point to cultivate and maintain illicit relations with those in power. Or they are unscrupulous hustlers and influence peddlers who have managed to accumulate cash and assets. Practically all regimes in the developing world (and not a few in the industrialized countries) shelter such shadey beneficiaries. But that is small comfort to the millions of citizens who live in despair and wonder what the futue holds for their children.

The widespread feeling of anxiety and despondency is a relatively recent phenomenon. In the fifties and sixties, Ethiopians were by and large a fairly optimistic bunch and kept their sights firmly within their country's borders. Emigration scarcely entered anyone's mind. Young students overseas counted the days of their jubilant return home at the end their studies. Some did not bother to wait until graduation day. Their diplomas followed by mail. Those who lingered longer or stayed behind for good were the negligible few who were often derided by their homebound compatriots.

At the end of World War II Ethiopia had a population of no more than 10-12 million inhabiting a large and rich land mass. It was at peace. Although hugely underdeveloped, the agricultural sector produced enough to feed the country. In the urban sector, there was no lack of jobs for the small number of school leavers. The Ethiopian civil and military services were badly in need of skilled manpower, as was the private sector. Graduates and dropouts of educational institutions were eagerly snapped. Since the motivation to serve one's country was strong, there was more than a ready response for the demand. The country had been humiliated by the Fascist occupation in the thirties; the principal reasons being the backward state of the country's economy, its civil service and, needless to say, its military establishment. Educated young men and women were powerfully motivated to offer their skills to the lofty cause of ending the country's backwardness.

During much of the post-war period, the economy performed well enough for income per head to grow consistently over a number of years. The rains came regularly and harvests were generally good. Prices for the country's principal exports were relatively high, caused in good measure by the rise in raw material prices following the Korean War. Gradually, foreign investors became active in a number of sectors: in the sugar industry (the Dutch group HVA), in textiles (the Indians, the Japanese, Greek residents and Coptic expatriates from Egypt), and in agriculture (the Italians exporting bananas and producing dairy products for local consumption, the British growing cotton, and a Swiss entrepreneur exporting winter vegetables to Europe). In the sixties, economic opportunities in agriculture began to attract young Ethiopian investors, primarily disgruntled civil servants and graduates of the College of Agriculture at Alemaya. The early success of these pioneers captured the imagination of yet more young Ethiopians who sought government land in the Awash Valley and elsewhere. The future looked promising. Obviously, the problems of the peasantry were an abiding concern, but there was still hope that reforms could prevent the situation from getting out of hand.

Slowly the mood began to change. As educational opportunities expanded, they fueled the demand for more and more change. Awareness spread about political developments in the world, especially in the third world and more particularly in Africa. The struggle for freedom from colonial rule and for a more rapid pace of economic and social change brought forth a growing number of independent countries. The early euphoria of these new countries attracted the attention of politically conscious Ethiopians. Emperor Haile-Selassie's reforms gradually began to be perceived as inadequate by an increasing number of disgruntled young citizens.

Columbia University graduate Germame Neway and Colonel Workineh Gebeyehu, graduate of the Imperial Guard academy, were among the leading malcontents; the former openly so, the latter in a far more guarded manner as he was a close aide of the Emperor. Both applied themselves energetically to initiate reforms from their respective positions. Germame was involved in land tenure and local administration. Workineh was active in reforming the functioning of the central government. He also wished to introduce a greater degree of political liberalization. But neither believed he was making much progress. It was in this context that the failed coup d'état of 1960 in which both took part was hastily mounted. Although the economy continued to grow in the aftermath of the coup, political disaffection spread. And many began to sense an impending political crisis. No one quite knew just when it might strike or what shape it might assume. But there was a palpable feeling in the air that it would be severely destabilizing.

Fourteen years after the attempted coup of 1960, a more carefully prepared putsch succeeded, thanks to the 1973 oil crisis and a devastating famine which had been building up over a three-year period. Emperor Haile-Selassie was deposed in September 1974 and a military junta took over. Seventeen years of bloody revolution, tyranny, civil war, worse famine, and social dislocation ensued. In 1991 Tigrean and Eritrean insurgents together with a sprinkling of guerilla fighters from other areas of the country toppled the much hated military government. Everyone felt a sigh of relief, but not for long.

A grand design of socio-political engineering resting on the double pillars of Marxist ideology and ethnic identity was put in place which paved the way for the secession of Eritrea. The rest of the country was re-configured in line with the new policies. In some respects, the current regime is an improvement over the murderous ways of its predecessor. However, the improvements are one of degree. Marxism continues to be the dominant ideology. And as long as it does, democracy and fundamental human liberties are bound to be elusive goals. But there is also a sense in which things have become worse. The retrograde politics of tribalism has exacerbated social harmony and national cohesion. The result is a country which is intrinsically unstable and increasingly autocratic; an autocracy whose instruments of coercion are reaching practically every corner of society.

Ethiopia today is a country of more than eighty million inhabitants possessing a much higher level of political consciousness than their placid predecessors of five or six decades ago who numbered far less. How are they to address their anxieties about the future? An appreciation of the country's history is essential for a consideration of this vital question. We need to have some understanding of the long journey we have traversed over the last several centuries and where we find ourselves today. It is primarily the responsibility of Ethiopian historians to maintain a lively public discourse on this crucial subject. For our present purposes, it would suffice to offer a brief exposition of the more significant elements of our heritage in order, first, to better understand the predicament in which we find ourselves today and, secondly, to explore possible avenues for a more promising future.

The Heritage of a Multicultural Polity

A key feature of our heritage is the multi-cultural character of Ethiopia. Conflict between our different cultural communities has been a recurring theme down the centuries. The origins go back to Axumite kings and their successors who greatly extended the frontiers of the kingdom. Not surprisingly, local communities resisted. By the fourteenth and fifteenth centuries bloody wars were waged between Christian highlanders and the Muslim inhabitants of the eastern and southeastern regions of the country (Yifat, the land of the Afars, Haddiya, and Harar). Military garrisons were posted in places like Harrar and Gurage to contain the conflicts. Also, Christian monarchs married women from the ruling families defeated in battle. Neither effort worked satisfactorily. Early in the sixteenth century a major counter movement was launched by Ahmad ibn Ibrahim (Mohammed Gragn). Eventually, Ahmad was killed near Lake Tana in 1543, but not before he had wreaked massive destruction in lives and assets during a twelve-year civil war. Subsequently, successive waves of Oromo migration from the south fanned out into the eastern and south eastern reaches of the country and ultimately into its northern heartland.[1]

Views have surfaced recently from certain Oromos which attempt to show the origin of the Oromo migrants to be further inland: in the neigbourhood of the lakes district in what is today the Southern Peoples' Region. Whatever their precise geographical origin, Oromo migrations spread progressively into the various parts of the country over the following five centuries; often in the shape of sustained wars against eastern Afars and Somalis, the indigenous Sidama populations of the south and west, and northern Christian highlanders. The end result is a settlement pattern that took its current shape towards the close of the nineteenth and the beginning of the twentieth centuries. Side by side with the prolonged conflict, however, is a synergetic development which is often overlooked; for a people who have co-habited an ancestral homeland have also given rise to many commonly shared values. It is essential to keep this in mind as we explore future avenues for communal peace and lasting national accord.

The Legacy of a Nation State

A second legacy is a nation state which has evolved from this diverse but interrelated set of cultural communities and which endures to this day. There is a current tendency in certain political circles that overstates past divisions, disparages any notion of constructive give and take, and denigrates the enduring vision of a pan-Ethiopian polity. Yet, in the midst of these conflicts a nation state which originally took root in Axum has steadily expanded, absorbing in the process certain features of the cultures with which it came into contact while imparting, in turn, equally important aspects of its own culture.

The Kingdom of Axum reached the zenith of its glory in the early centuries of the Christian era. Its decline and demise in the seventh century came when it lost control of the Red Sea route that had underpinned its maritime trade. A rebellion by one of the subject peoples spearheaded by an unusually energetic and fierce queen is believed to have been another reason for the Kingdom's collapse. The Zagwe dynasty of the neighbouring Agaws succeeded the Axumites and ruled the kingdom from their capital in Lalibella for about a century and a half: from 1137 to 1270. In the latter year, Yekuno Amlak ascended the throne and set in motion seven centuries of governance headed largely by Amharas, but in which Tigreans and in later stages Oromos took active part. In the words of one historian, "the 'Ethiopian golden era,' it is conveniently assumed, began when the Amhara-speaking rulers replaced the Agaw-speaking Zagwe as leaders of the Christian state. The new rulers established a dynasty in 1270 that would bring Ethiopia to a historic prime. During this era – beginning more significantly in 1314 with the region of Emperor Amda Zion – the rulers gradually expanded the kingdom's boundaries until it included what is present-day Ethiopia's heartland, creating a vast Empire. They assumed the title of Emperor and established Ethiopia's set of classical political and cultural institutions. Much of their legacy was to last until the 1974 revolution and beyond."[2]

And so a nation has come down to us which is made up of multiple cultural communities that have developed, in the course of several centuries, many shared values; a nation which, as some claim, is neither a recent invention nor an imitation of the European model of the nation state. Donald Levine observes that,"..... the profound differentiation of regions, peoples, and traditions [has] meant that conflict and competition among the diverse components of the Greater Ethiopian culture area comprised the dominant feature of her civilization. Nevertheless, the sovereignty of a powerful 'King of Kings' and a hegemonic religion organized to support a multi-ethnic nation provided a continuous basis for overcoming those centrifugal tendencies. From early times, the symbolism of Ethiopian statehood could mobilize members of diverse ethnic groups and regions on behalf of their national homeland."[3]

Throughout their reign, many of the sovereigns were preoccupied with instituting a system of government that would allow their citizens to go about their businesses in relative peace and security. An impartial system for the administration of justice was of central concern. The sovereigns were keenly interested to insulate vulnerable groups, the peasantry in particular, from rapacious warlords and their own soldiery, as described in some detail in Chapter 10. Down the centuries Ethiopian rulers have consequently devoted a non-negligible part of their energies to building a nation possessing its own system of civil, military, and judicial administration. They have also made notable attempts at introducing reforms in that system.

Regarding the administration of justice it is worth mentioning that the concept of the rule of law is deeply imbedded in Ethiopia's culture. As I pointed out earlier, the *Kibre Negest* lays down that all laws emanate from God and that the King is His principal magistrate on earth. Ethiopia's perception of the rule of law is a derivative of this outlook. In their daily lives, Ethiopians manifested their deep faith that all litigants will in the end find God's true justice. Hence their unending quest for it; and the respect they manifested for all laws promulgated by their sovereigns. The sovereigns had no illusion about where they themselves stood in relation to the country's laws. They, like the ordinary citizen, were governed by God's law and had the duty to obey and administer it impartially. The guilty verdict and death sentences which Emperor Zer'a-Ya'iqob (1434-68) passed on his seven children is a vivid illustration that no one, not even the king's own sons and daughters, stood above the law.[4]

In my analysis of the upheavals of February/ March 1974, I suggested that placing them in the context of the country's history rather than interpreting them in the light of an irrelevant and outdated ideology would have provided a more meaningful backdrop and might have opened an avenue for far reaching peaceful reforms in place of the contrived and bloody revolution that ultimately took place. Why, it might be asked parenthetically, did the prevailing intellectual climate in 1974 not favour this alternative approach?

Perhaps a key explanation is the limited awareness by the general population of the country's history and culture. Traditionally, history has been the preserve of a tiny minority of Ethiopia's literati, especially those near the centre of political power. Even persons actively engaged in the country's political life were largely ignorant of the extent and diversity of their past. The process of modernization in the nineteenth and early twentieth centuries offered a unique opportunity to take remedial measures in this regard. The modern system of education could have served as a powerful tool for disseminating historical knowledge through the schools, the media, publishing houses, public libraries, and other means. Yet, such was the eagerness of the agents of modernization for novel ways and lifestyles that Ethiopia's history was sidelined. The learning of history was consequently left to individual initiative. And such self teaching as occasionally took place was bound to be fragmentary. To the extent that the young men of the sixties and seventies (who are in power today in Ethiopia and in Eritrea) were aware of their heritage, their sentiment was more of antipathy than of empathy. An urge to rewrite the past to fit their political vision was the effortless next step,

To be sure, there were a tiny minority of Ethiopians who had always been enamoured with their country's long history and distinctive culture as an object of national pride. This was based less on historical knowledge than on the general notion that the country had more recorded history to its credit in comparison with many a nation in the vastness of Africa. A sense of perspective seems to have been lost in the process, to the point where observers were increasingly turned off by talk that Ethiopia had a unique culture, a history with few parallels in the developing world and, the tale topping all tales, a people that the Almighty had taken time to create with just the right kind of skin colour (neither too dark nor too light). It wasn't just foreign observers but the bulk of the young generation of the sixties and seventies that was turned off by this embarrassingly immodest portrayal of the country's history and culture. That generation gradually came to the view that among the factors holding back progress was precisely this false perception of the country's history. It was in some ways for this reason that Marxism got a foothold among young intellectuals.

Times seem to have changed. Three and half decades after the 1974 revolution during which Ethiopia's history was demonized and deconstructed, a favourable environment seems to be emerging for a more balanced appreciation of the past among an important segment of the current generation of Ethiopians. And this is to be welcomed; for a nation cut off from its history is like a rudderless boat. It moves without a sense of direction or purpose. History is both rudder and ballast. It also serves as a foundation on which to build. A resurgent interest to reconnect with their history should consequently go some way towards mitigating the current anxieties Ethiopians have about their nation's future.

It must also be added that there are growing signs of mellowing among the generation of the young Marxist extremists of the sixties and seventies. As always, there is a minority for whom the ideology will continue to be a creed rather than a hypothesis to make sense of the real world. But for the more open minded, the violent storms of the world of reality have exposed the vulnerability of an intellectual edifice that once looked impregnable. And more and more of the young ideologues of yesteryear are speaking out, as we shall have occasion to mention briefly in the next chapter. They, too, are showing increasing signs of a desire to learn about their country's past.

A 'Minimum Cultural Base': Yet Another Legacy

The third legacy of our past is a set of cultural assets which not only gives us our distinctiveness but which also provides us with 'a minimum cultural base' for meeting the modern challenges of development, as John Kenneth Galbraith believed. One such asset is our long experience of public service. The survival of Ethiopia as a nation state is not an accident of history. It is the outcome of a political system which enabled rulers to mobilize citizens in defence of the country in times of war and to hold together a far flung nation fragmented by long mountain ranges, precipitous gorges, torrential rivers, and scorching deserts. It was a system which succeeded in implanting the sentiment among citizens that service to the nation in war and peace was an honourable calling; in sharp contrast to the attitude of many colonized peoples where the nation state was often perceived as alien, and hence as fair game for plunder and subterfuge. A strong sense of purpose and of responsibility prevailed among the country's administrators, soldiery, courtiers, and peasants, coupled with a willingness to discharge one's public duty in earnest when called upon. This legacy of public service has a practical bearing on the management of public and private institutions in today's world.

A relatively high work ethic is another feature of this heritage.[5] The Ethiopian peasant is noted for his grueling labours. He can ill afford to disregard the discipline imposed on him by the exigencies of the seasons, the nature of the soil, and the rigours of plant and animal life. The generally temperate climate of the highlands enables the peasant to spend long hours on his farm, while his counterparts in the tropical climes are often debilitated by intense heat and humidity. Obliged to adapt to a more disciplined work environment when he relocates to the urban economy, the peasant brings with him a work ethic that facilitates integration into his new life.

There are other facets of our culture which are conducive to development. Although tradition plays an important role in our lives, we as a people are not averse to change. The willingness to accept new ideas is a valuable asset for the competitive world of business, industry, and politics. Moreover, the status of women is superior to that of many a country in the Middle East, Central and South Asia. Bad as it is today, corruption is not to be compared with the deplorable situation in many African, Asian, or Latin American countries. Traditionally, dishonesty has been frowned upon as deviant behavior. As the following anecdote demonstrates, it was often the cause of public disgrace to the culprit and his family.

As a young schoolboy, I recall the case of a low level civil servant in the provincial branch of the Ministry of Finance. The man had come under suspicion for misappropriating funds. As my school friends and I were walking home for lunch one day, we saw a long line of people veering towards the side of a nearby hill. Out of curiosity, we followed and soon came upon a scene that has been etched in my mind ever since: that of a man with a tight rope around his neck dangling from the branch of a sycamore tree. The civil servant had heard that he was about to be charged for embezzlement. Such was his sense of shame that he decided to take his life in the wee hours of that morning.

Another development friendly feature of our culture is the tradition that recognizes the worth of the individual. This derives in part from the Christian notion that man is created in the image of God. I am made to understand that Islam's conception of the individual is similar, as the nature of man is believed to have been fashioned after that of the Creator. Both doctrines have molded behaviour in Ethiopia for millennia. At a more pragmatic level, the individual is recognized for his skills, his character, and standing in the community. The judge adept in resolving knotty litigations, the cleric who excels in his mastery and interpretation of religious texts, the warrior who distinguishes himself in battle, the traditional *gadda* leader who dispenses justice wisely, the man of integrity who is often sought for the custody of valued assets: all elicit society's admiration and esteem. Development flourishes in this kind of context where the individual is both the central purpose and active agent of social interaction.

There are also elements in our culture that could support today's struggle for democracy. Democracy is in part about equality and about open criticism of public figures. The *gadda* system could pride itself for the right of self-expression, and of the equality of all before the scheme of things. In his forebodings of perilous times, the Orthodox hermit (*bahtawi*) is as scathing in his condemnation of the mighty as he is of simple folk when their conduct deviates from accepted norms of moral comportment. The artful minstrel (*azmari*) evokes acclaim for the barely disguised gibes at king and commoner alike that he occasionally weaves into his verse.[6] Equality of all in the eyes of the law has of course been a fundamental precept of the *Kibre Negest* and the *Fit'ha Negest*.

Donald Levine takes up this theme in a recent address given at a conference in Addis Ababa. He analyzes the tradition of public communication and consensus building among several of Ethiopia's cultural groups (the Qemant, the Sidama, the Tigrai, the Oromo, and the Amhara) and concludes thus: "Nearly all local traditions in the Greater Ethiopian culture area exhibit some form of public action, through which persons express mutual respect, effective conflict resolution, and public problem-solving." And usefully reminds us that: "Their levels of public responsibility and civility might put to shame many modernized Ethiopians, at home and in the Diaspora......"[7]

In public gatherings, modernized Ethiopians do indeed tend to manifest a disinclination to act in concert in seeking common ground and in moving forward with ideas and actions bearing the stamp of a collaborative effort. Witness, for instance, the distressing tug of war that has taken place in 2007, 2008, 2009, and 2010 among and within the major opposition parties and their support groups. Or the unseemly power struggle within the Ethiopian Patriarchate which has characterized the greater portion of the tenure of the current Patriarch; a struggle which became so serious in the summer of 2009 that the government had to intervene. Or yet the observation Ethiopians make of their preference to come together to dine and wine rather than to toil for a common goal.

To a considerable degree, the underlying explanation is our limited exposure to modern democracy. While it is true that there are elements in our culture which allow the airing of diverse views leading to consensus and compromise, these have yet to translate into the kind of adversarial political discourse that characterize contemporary democracy. Time is needed for the culture of modern democracy to take root in a new but not altogether unfriendly soil. The same is true of the skills for governance required in institutions as diverse as the Ethiopian Patriarchate, the Ethiopian Football Federation, and political party organizations save, of course, the ruling party whose leadership has little interest in nurturing democracy.

The core values of our culture are currently under threat. The country's work ethic has been eroded. The *gadda* system, the *Kibre Negest*, and the *Fit'ha-Negest* are not exactly vibrant current realities. The same is true of the cultivator's care for *his* plot of land and for *his* trees, and the other elements of our heritage that have been under siege during Dergue rule. While the current regime's attitude to culture might not be as openly hostile, it cannot be said to be altogether favourable.

What sense does it make then to talk about a cultural heritage when so much of what we see seems to point to its decline? There is no denying that our culture has been enfeebled by an unfavourable political environment, by new legal and social systems, and generally by the passage of time. But cultures do not crumble and disappear without trace, especially if each new generation makes a determined effort to reconnect to its past. A special responsibility rests in this regard on the shoulders of present day politicians, especially those in opposition parties. One's hope must be that in time passions will subside and minds freed, allowing everyone to unite around a common heritage to build a better future.

I cannot conclude this section without mentioning two debilitating elements in our culture with which we will continue to grapple for some time to come. The first is our heritage of autocracy. As I have indicated previously, a positive feature of our imperial tradition is the constant if inadequate process of reform and innovation. That very tradition is also responsible for the autocratic frame of mind of leaders that have come after the monarchy. Barring the consensual political systems of the Oromo *gadda* system and others similar to it, our dominant political experience has been one of authoritarianism. It should not be surprising if residual elements of the tradition of autocracy were to be found deeply embedded in the minds of our political and clerical leaders.

I do not know if there are empirical studies that lend credence to this view. But it is not difficult for Ethiopians to detect the heritage of autocracy whenever their leaders conduct themselves like petty kings or regional potentates of old. There is an Ethiopian anecdote, apocryphal perhaps but no less telling for that, which underpins the ingrained propensity among many Ethiopians to dominate. What is the most comfortable seat you could possibly think of, someone asks a friend? The saddle of a horse, the *berchuma* (the three-legged Ethiopian stool), the *mekeda* (a cushion), the *medeb* (a small bed-like structure built on the floor where people could recline), or something else? The friend ponders for a while and gives his considered response: "It may not be easy to come by," he says, "but nothing beats the comforts provided by the shoulders of a human being."

Closely linked to autocracy is the second element of our tradition which debilitates the struggle for democracy; namely, our tradition of timidity. Obey the king (and hence the government) is a biblical injunction which has molded social behavior for centuries. That is also what the *Kibre Negest* prescribes. As we have seen, there is also a tradition of defiance by men of religion and by artists when kings and commoners deviate from acceptable norms of conduct. But the general rule is to conform and to abide by the dictates of rulers. Throwing off the shackles of timidity will take education, experience, and freedom from abject poverty. All this is bound to take time, but the innate human urge to be free will in the end prevail.

CHAPTER 20

The Shape of Things to Come

In the foregoing chapter, I have attempted to show that much as we Ethiopians are anxious about our current predicament, we possess a political and cultural legacy that could serve as a foundation for building a promising future. I have not addressed all the major challenges we face internally and have said little regarding those beyond our borders. Nor have I considered the natural resources we could mobilize to build an economically less troubled country. I should now turn my attention to these; not altogether unmindful of the analytical pitfalls involved but in the conviction that an open dialogue would enhance our collective understanding of a problem that weighs so heavily in the minds of most Ethiopians. I shall first deal with the external challenges and take up those on the domestic side subsequently.

The External Environment

At critical junctures in her history, external factors have played a significant role in Ethiopia's political life, positive as well as negative. Control of the Red Sea littoral by adversaries deprived the Kingdom of Axum of its maritime trade and ultimately led to its decline and fall. In succeeding centuries, Ottoman expansionism further isolated the country and cut off the flow of trade and knowledge. On the positive side, Portugal's intervention in the sixteenth century rescued the monarchy from imminent demise while Emperor Yohannes's victory over Egypt at Gura in 1876 and Menelik's over Italy at Adowa in 1896 assured the nation's continued viability. Similarly, Italy's declaration of war against the United Kingdom in 1940 resulted in Britain's change of policy from diplomatic recognition of Fascist rule in Ethiopia to active support of Emperor Haile-Selassie's campaign to liberate the country. Soviet military assistance in the latter part of the 1970s was instrumental in defending Ethiopia against a Somali aggression which the Soviets themselves had initially encouraged. The collapse of Ethio-Soviet relations following Gorbachev's glasnost and perestroika was a factor contributing to the demise of the Mengistu regime and the emergence of a new political order which has greatly weakened national cohesion. Any attempt to assess future political trends is rendered difficult by the probable occurrence of such unforeseen events. Even as these lines are being written, the forces of Saudi Wahabism and Al-Qaeda are casting a disquieting shadow over East Africa's political horizon. While keeping such imponderables in mind, we could focus on a number of the more tangible geopolitical realities facing the country today and try to see how they might affect the country's political evolution.

The Nile

Ethiopia contributes 86% of the Nile's flow to the Sudan and Egypt, two countries which currently account for 80% of the river's exploitation (Egypt alone taking up 66%). Countries upstream, i.e. Ethiopia, Uganda, Tanzania, Kenya, Rwanda, Burundi, and the Democratic Republic of the Congo are understandably eager to enhance their own exploitation of the river's resources. They need to increase agricultural production to feed their expanding populations and to generate electric power for their economic growth. Sudan and Egypt are apprehensive that this might put an end to the generous use of the river which they have enjoyed historically. And this has given rise to concern that conflict might flare up.

Past treaties for the exploitation of the river's resources were largely crafted by the United Kingdom, the dominant power in the region during the colonial era. In a 1929 treaty, the U. K. assigned the lion's share of the water's resources to the two downstream nations which it administered (Sudan and Egypt). Countries upstream, a good many of which it also ruled and others like Ethiopia which it did not but which were more or less kept in the dark, were judged to need the water less. There might have been some justification for this at the time, but priorities have changed significantly over the years. Today, these upstream riparian states strongly feel the need for a more equitable exploitation of the river's waters. Their increased demand could be met in a manner that would not seriously compromise the interests of the two dominant downstream states. That is the spirit of a draft agreement (the Common Framework Agreement) which Ethiopia, Kenya, Tanzania, Uganda, and Rwanda proposed in May 2009. The five countries gave the other riparian states one year to come on board. Owing, however, to the political problems Egypt is currently facing, Ethiopia has taken the initiative to defer the one year deadline until after° the parliamentary elections.

The agreement was prepared, negotiated and initialled within the context of the Nile Basin Initiative, an organization to which all of these countries belong. The body was established ten years ago with the view to "achieve sustainable socioeconomic development through the equitable utilization of and benefits from the common Nile Basin water resources." Simultaneously, the organization is mandated to "promote regional peace and security." That the riparian states have come together to establish such an organization is not accidental. It is preceded by years of research and dialogue as to how best the river's resources could be best managed and exploited.

In 1904, the British conducted a study that proposed the construction of two dams: one at Lake Tana in Ethiopia where the Blue Nile originates and a second on the outlet of the While Nile in Lake Victoria. The goal was to provide reservoirs for long-term storage in locations of minimum evaporation. In 1958, a study commissioned by the Sudan (an Anglo-Egyptian dependency) recommended dams on the Blue Nile and the Baro rivers. A 1964 study by the Ethiopian government concluded that four dams could be built in the Blue Nile basin, turning Lake Tana and the Nile gorge into a primary reservoir with minimal evaporation that would significantly enlarge and help regulate the amount of water flowing to the Sudan and Egypt.[1]

It is also widely recognized that better conservation practices could bring about significant savings in water. This is particularly the case for countries downstream where flood irrigation through muddy canals, an age-old and inefficient method, is still prevalent. These canals could be replaced by pipes or concrete structures to reduce current levels of waste. Additionally, modern irrigation techniques like sprinkler systems or drip irrigation could save water that would otherwise be lost through evaporation. Translating these into workable schemes would obviously call for high levels of investment as well as changes in cultural practices. But if conflict is to be avoided, these and other measures would be needed for a more equitable and efficient exploitation of the river's potential. Whether the political will exists to move in this direction remains to be seen.

Much depends on the degree to which Sudan and Egypt understand and accommodate the genuine needs of the populations of states upstream for greater access to the waters of a river which is becoming increasingly crucial to their livelihoods. There are moderate voices in the Sudan which indicate that the country's interests are not best served by aligning itself totally with the hard-line position of the Egyptian government. Egypt itself, while totally dependent on the Nile, might begin to appreciate the long-term need to accommodate the development needs of the countries upstream and doing so would not necessarily stand in the way of its own national interests. Prospects for an amicable solution are therefore not all that bleak, if the political will could be mustered to look for a solution that responds to the interests of all riparian states.

Eritrea

Eritrea and Ethiopia will continue to be difficult neighbours unless a new class of leaders emerges on both sides of the border that is prepared to restructure bilateral relations on the basis of a pragmatic set of economic policies and the shared identity binding the two historic peoples. There are signs that the people of Eritrea are increasingly disenchanted with a tyrannical political cabal whose claim to leadership seems to rest largely on ethnic affinity. Tyranny does not become less disagreeable simply because its perpetrators happen to be one's kith and kin. It is to be hoped that a new class of leaders will emerge which represents the true long-term interests of Eritrea and works towards better relations with a sister state sharing strong cultural and historical bonds.

An issue of primary concern for Ethiopians today is the antipathy the current leadership of Eritrea's ruling party harbours towards an Ethiopian polity whose different cultural groups act in concert to pursue their long-term goals of socio-economic development and preserving the unity of their ancestral homeland. Eritrea's current leaders believe that in order to secure their country's independence it would be essential to guard against the re-emergence of a united, dynamic and peaceful Ethiopia. They have consequently adopted the strategy of pitting one Ethiopian ethnic group against another to enfeeble the country to the point where Eritrea and other adversaries could manipulate her at will.

While this is generally well known, the length to which the Eritrean leadership is prepared to go in pursuing its strategy is perhaps less well known. An astonishing account of several incidents stretching over several years is given in a recent book by Asgede Gebre-Selassie Wolde-Michael, a former TPLF guerilla fighter who describes in chilling detail the thuggish and brutal machinations of EPLF leaders not only against the people of Ethiopia, but also against those of Tigrai and the TPLF, their supposed ally.[2] Among the incidents cited is the betrayal by the EPLF, during the years of struggle, of the whereabouts of 10, 000 TPLF fighters to Dergue intelligence. The aim was to trigger a devastating air and ground attack, which was duly executed. Another was the refusal by EPLF fighters to allow some 70,000 drought stricken Tigrean civilians who wished to cross over to the Sudan in search of shelter and sustenance and their exposure on their forced journey back to scorching desert heat and punishing thirst. As if this were not punishment enough, intelligence was once more provided to the Ethiopian military about their location. This resulted in the predictable massacre of women (some of them pregnant), children, and hundreds of adults by Mig bombers and helicopter gunships. Soon after the TPLF takeover of the country in 1991, EPLF fighters carried out a most brazen plunder of Ethiopia's assets in both the public and private sectors that was barely distinguishable from the Fascist ransacking of the country immediately following the 1936 occupation. Other astonishing acts of money laundering, widespread illegal currency dealings, kidnappings, and murder were also perpetrated by Eritrean fighters and civilian personnel under the very nose of the TPLF leadership.

During the years of struggle, EPLF envoys actively spread the damaging information in Arab capitals that the TPLF were a bunch of communists with a mission to destroy Islam and that it would be ill-advised to provide them with material and other assistance. In Saudi Arabia, Kuwait, Sudan and other Middle Eastern capitals TPLF agents were exposed, thrown behind bars, and tortured. That the bosses of the TPLF bent over backwards to allow the EPLF to get away with all this is yet another astonishing aspect of the account for which Asgede unfortunately does not provide adequate explanation. Over and over again, he emphasizes the submissiveness of TPLF to the EPLF, without explaining why, remarking only tangentially that one reason for this is the fact that leading TPLF members had Eritrean "blood' running through their veins, an allusion to Meles, among many others, who are partly of Eritrean descent (His mother, to whom he is said to have been strongly attached, is from Eritrea). Perhaps there were other reasons.

But Asgede is a man who was determined to inform himself about what was going on around him. He kept copious notes of the vindictive and criminal conduct of the EPLF as well as of the TPLF. Much of this he observed first hand, and assiduously gathered credible information about important events which he did not personally witness. One should obviously not take all that is said at face value, be it in regard to the somewhat secondary role ascribed to the EPLF in conducting the guerilla struggle or in respect of TPLF's alleged achievements. On the latter, Asgege makes the implausible claim that the party has succeeded in forging unity among Ethiopia's nationalities and has put the country on a fast track to progress. On the whole, however, this is an instructive book, not least because of one significant message which pervades the overall narrative: i.e. that there are stout-hearted patriots among mainstream Tigreans whose political outlook and aspirations might someday displace the ideological and ethnic myopia of the TPLF leadership; a point which I shall take up again in the concluding chapter when I attempt to explore the possible avenues leading us out of our present difficulties.

The Ethio-Eritrean war of 2000 and the subsequent tensions between the two countries are enough to dispel any notion that these incidents are only a matter of historical interest. The Eritrean leadership continues with its anti-Ethiopian strategy described in rich detail by Asgede's book. Today, there are a number of armed resistance fighters based in Asmara which the government funds and which it keeps on a short leash to carry out its own agenda, not theirs. And recent reports indicate that in an effort to assure total control, some of their leaders are being held in undisclosed detention centres while others have even been disposed of brutally. The airwaves are also replete with Eritrean charges against the TPLF 's machinations to undermine the country's unity, as if the Eritrean leadership has a soft spot for Ethiopia's unity in some remote corner of its heart. This duplicitous strategy is unlikely to work to Eritrea's advantage. Only a long term strategy focusing on bringing together peoples with multiple commonalities pursuing the goal of liberating their peoples from centuries of backwardness and poverty is likely to succeed.

Another issue of concern to Ethiopians is access to the waters of the Red Sea which was lost when the TPLF engineered the secession of Eritrea from Ethiopia. Even if one were to downplay the ties of culture and blood between Eritrea and Ethiopia, there are firm legal and geopolitical grounds for Ethiopia's right to harbour facilities on the Red Sea coast, especially in regard to the port of Assab and the surrounding region inhabited by the Afar people. Without going into the details of the case, two brief points might usefully be made.

The first is the fact that socially and culturally the Assab Afars are an integral part of the far larger community of Afars on the Ethiopian side of the border. The second is that a country of over 80 million inhabitants (and growing) could not be indefinitely bottled up in a large land mass deprived of its own maritime facilities, however strenuously Ethiopia's current leadership might try to mask a plain economic and geopolitical reality. Any improvement in bilateral relations would very much depend on how this thorny question is resolved.

Being landlocked is a daunting development challenge. Oxford economist Paul Collier includes it among his four development traps that ensnare the majority of African economies. He notes that one reason why most African economies stagnated in the forty-year period after 1960 was because being landlocked "was a fundamental impediment to prosperity."[3] A number of UN studies on the problems of landlocked countries have similarly underlined the enduring vulnerabilities of these countries. In contrast, access to the high seas has been a crucial factor for the export-driven economies of several countries, especially India, China, and the countries of South and South-East Asia. In view of this, it is disingenuous for Ethiopian authorities to make light of this handicap by arguing that possessing harbour facilities is not indispensable, as access to other country's facilities could be easily secured for a fee. It is also shortsighted politically. After losing her ports, Ethiopia is today little more than an impotent observer of the havoc caused by Somali terrorists to maritime trade in her immediate neighbourhood. An outlet to the sea is essential to protect Ethiopia's maritime and long term national security interests. It is far from fanciful under these circumstances to contemplate the role that a future Ethiopian navy could play in bringing about greater security to the area.

On the matter of acquiring port facilities for a fee (the Ethiopian government's current policy), it should be kept in mind that agreements governing access to foreign harbours are far from being dependable, especially in the Ethiopian context. The Horn of Africa is a region notorious for its political instability. Ethiopia would always be at the mercy of efforts to disrupt peace and stability in neighbouring countries, to say little of hostile acts aimed directly at her. There is the added burden of relying on someone else's harbour facilities. Fees could be costly and subject to arbitrary hikes. A country exercising sovereignty over a harbour would naturally give priority to its own needs, be it in the normal course of managing port traffic or in the maintenance of infrastructural facilities. This could expose a neigbouring lessee to periodic disruptions in services. Further disruptions could occur on account of inefficient management over which the lessee has no control. The same set of problems is likely to affect access to undersea fibre optic cables with terminals in neighbouring harbours. The cumulative cost of all these factors could be onerous. What economic sense does it make to be the tenant of an expensive, inefficient, unreliable, arbitrary, or hostile landlord when one has the option of being a homeowner?

An effective resolution of this and the other problems between Ethiopia and Eritrea could in principle be brought about by a political integration freely entered into by the peoples of the two countries. It can be reasonably assumed that Eritreans and Ethiopians are today wiser about the pains and presumed benefits of secession. It can be similarly assumed that they have both learned a great deal about the slippery road to democracy and fundamental freedoms. Any future movement towards closer ties between the two peoples, if ever the opportunity presents itself, would need to be anchored to a rigorous assessment of all relevant factors and in response to the genuine wishes of citizens expressed in a transparent and credible ballot.

How realistic is it today to contemplate the possibility of a political integration? Notwithstanding the cultural, strategic, and economic factors that argue in favour of close ties between the two countries, the current environment does not seem to be favourable for such an association. Citizens of a country which has broken off from a previous union develop strong vested interests that stand in the way of a more than symbolic restoration of former relationships. Moreover, it would not be easy to go back on an emotive a sentiment as ethnic identity over which deadly battles have been fought and the blood of thousands shed. Economic misery and tyranny do not necessarily create the dynamics for the re-emergence of historic ties or for a larger, more viable economic unit. The unexpected could always happen, of course. Issa'iyas and his associates could evolve into a level-headed, non-ideological, accommodative, and a truly citizen-focused group of democratic leaders stretching their hands to an Ethiopian leadership similarly inspired. Alternatively and as intimated earlier, a new leadership might emerge in both countries capable of rekindling the brotherly sentiments of the two peoples and leading them towards closer, mutually beneficial ties; both economically and politically. Nothing today suggests the imminence of such an eventuality. And the recent discovery in Eritrea of sizeable deposits of gold can only embolden the country's leaders to persist in their hard-line policies both domestically and externally

One should obviously not exclude the possibility of improved bilateral relations at some point in time in the distant future. The practical thing to do in that event would be to focus on some form of *economic* association that addresses the principal concerns of the two countries and their citizens. Eritrea has a narrow resource base and a small internal market. A close economic association with Ethiopia would open up significant investment and employment opportunities for her citizens. Arrangements could be worked out under which the citizens of the two countries would enjoy the same reciprocal rights to trade, invest, own, and transfer assets. The principal beneficiaries of such an economic arrangement would be Eritrea. For Ethiopia, the attraction would be to secure access to the Red Sea unfettered by considerations of Eritrean sovereignty.

Practical arrangements might conceivably be made whereby a designated harbour(s) under Ethiopia's control would handle Ethiopia's large volume of foreign trade. Investments in infrastructure facilities would of course be Ethiopia's responsibility. These Ethiopia-controlled harbours might be a quid pro quo for access by Eritrean citizens to Ethiopia's substantial resources and huge market in which they would have a stake as investors, employees, and owners with rights to transfer and/ or repatriate assets or income. Ethiopians would be accorded similar privileges in Eritrea. This comes close to being an *economic* as distinct from a *political* federation or confederation.

It would be presumptuous to present this as anything other than a possible point of departure for a dialogue among concerned citizens of the two countries. The challenge would lie in working out the details and formulating a vision that would secure widespread consent among the citizens of the two countries. The more demanding and ultimate challenge would be to mobilize political forces to translate the vision into an enduring reality such that the two historic peoples could enjoy the economic benefits of their substantial human and natural resources and live side by side in peace and relative prosperity. Needless to belabor the point that neither the current leaders of Eritrea nor of Ethiopia would be willing or capable to embark upon such a plan. The task falls squarely on the shoulders of the peoples of the two countries and a new group of authentically democratic and pragmatic leaders.

One should of course not exclude the possibility of a situation in which the desire for economic and cultural convergence is so limited as to discourage initiatives towards bringing the two countries into this kind of collaborative relationship. In that event the rational thing to do would be to respect the dictates of political reality and refrain from engaging in what could only be a sentimental but fruitless venture of pushing the two states to an unwanted economic collaboration.. And hope that an adversarial relationship of the kind that has plagued India and Pakistand for upwards of half a century could be avoided.

Somalia

Somalia has been undergoing a process of fragmentation for more than a quarter of a century. This does not bode well for Ethiopia, much as some might take comfort in the predicament of an adversary state reduced to bickering fragments. The prospects for peace will not improve with a collection of three or more mini-states perennially at each other's throats or at Ethiopia's. Nor with extremist Islamist movements aided and abetted by foreign forces that wish to install a theocratic state in Somalia perennially needling Ethiopia with threats of jihad. There would be fierce resistance by Ethiopians to any such agenda. And the consequences for Somalia and the other peoples of the horn would be tragic.

A more rational and pacific vision would be for the Somalis and Ethiopians to set their sights on a mutually advantageous economic collaboration. The advantage for Somalia would be the benefits it would reap from cooperating with a country endowed with sizeable and varied natural resources. Bilateral trade and investment would be the obvious initial vehicles for promoting development on both sides of the border. In addition, Ethiopia's and Somalia's trade with the outside world could grow significantly if the two countries were to jointly develop ports on the Indian Ocean littoral, with Ethiopia using her political and diplomatic clout to mobilize the required resources internationally. New ports could emerge that would grow into significant hubs of commerce and investment. Manufacturing, building and construction, catering and tourism, trade and financial services could grow around busy harbours. Somalia's peoples (not far away Ethiopians) would be the primary beneficiaries of such an enhanced economic activity, be it in regard to employment, investment in trade and services, and ownership of assets. Ethiopia's principal interest would be an entry into the world of globalization that an unimpeded and free access to the high seas would facilitate. Two peoples who have so much in common should in the process find it possible to create a much-improved climate for cultural and political cooperation.

It would take time for some such arrangement to materialize. In the short term, Ethiopia's hope must be for the peoples of Somalia to be at peace with themselves first and foremost, and spare their neighbours the pains of being sucked into their internecine conflicts. If Ethiopia's hopes do not materialize, she would have no alternative but to hold herself in readiness for all possible contingencies.

Somaliland

Prospects for cooperation appear more promising with Somaliland, the peaceful (at least so far) *de facto* state to the east that might better appreciate the economic benefits of maritime collaboration with Ethiopia. Once again, trade and investment would be the main vehicles for economic collaboration. Ethiopia could assist in port development, in facilitating the growth of manufacturing plants for exports, and in encouraging tourism on Somaliland's coasts. All this could take place in the context of an agreement which would allow Ethiopia to develop her own sovereign port at Zeila or some other convenient location to handle her large volume of trade. Somaliland would obviously need to be compensated (possibly through territorial adjustments on the Ethiopian side of the border). The more ambitious alternative would be to forge a political association with a country which has waited twenty years to gain acceptance by the community of African nations and by the global community at large.

There is a credible story that immediately prior to independence, the territory's elders (under British trusteeship at the time) approached Emperor Haile-Selassie for integrating their homeland with Ethiopia, professing closer ties with people across their border with Ethiopia than with the inhabitants of the Somali territory to the south, then under Italian trusteeship. The UN plan was to bring the two territories into a united Somali nation. Reportedly, the Emperor's response was that union under the umbrella of a future United States of Africa would be the more preferable route for bringing together Ethiopia and British Somaliland as well as other countries.

There are pointers that even today Somaliland's people are much more favourably disposed to Ethiopia than their neighbours to the south. That is why it would not be idle to contemplate some kind of loose political association which Somaliland might forge with Ethiopia following a properly organized plebiscite in which the country's citizens exercise their basic right of determining their future. Ethiopia has paid dearly for the principle of self-determination. She would have the political credibility, if she is so inclined, to be an advocate of a Somaliland that wishes to exercise that right and perhaps assist the country to secure political recognition within the halls of the African Union in the first instance and further afield subsequently. Besides the mutual benefits that would accrue, this might well also serve as a practical example for others to follow, both inside as well as outside the Horn. The dream of Africa's political and economic integration is more likely to be achieved, if it is ever going to be achieved, in modest and incremental steps of this nature, rather than through the sweeping schemes interminably talked about at meetings of the African Union.

Sudan and Other Neighbours

After almost half a century of conflict in which two million inhabitants perished and a further four million were displaced, the Sudan has entered a period of fragile peace following the agreement signed in 2005 between the central government and the Sudan People's Liberation Movement, an umbrella organization which has been fighting for the liberation of the people of Southern Sudan. And in accordance with the provisions of the agreement, a referendum was recently held in Southern Sudan to determine whether the region's inhabitants wish to opt for an independent state or remain an autonomous entitiy in a united Sudan. In a plebiscite which stretched from January 9 to 16, 2011 an overwhelming majority of citizens voted in favour of independence. The vote took effect in July and Southern Sudan joined 53 independent African countries as a sovereign state recognized by the United Nations and the African Union. The vote was not held in the small but oil-rich area of Abyei, inhabited by the Messiria tribe of Northen Sudan and the South-Sudan oriented Ngok Dinka tribe: a potential source of trouble unless it is amicably resolved.

Apart from Abyei, the new nation will face many of the challenges bedevilling the great majority of African countries. There are internal ethnic and cultural fissures which could fuel rivalries for power and resources, especially revenues from oil. The environment of corruption and poor governance which is already in evidence is unlikely to get any better with oil and aid money flowing in at higher levels. The question for Ethiopia is how the emergence of a new nation on her western flank might affect her external relations. Ethnic tensions might possibly spill over to the Gambela region of Western Ethiopia. Other problems might also emerge. In general, however, prospects for diplomatic relations look encouraging at this point in time; and it is not altogether unreasonable to expect bilateral relations between the two countries to evolve along the Ethio-Kenya model, an amicable relationship that has endured for more than half a century.

Northern Sudan would in all likelihood continue to pose sporadic difficulties for Ethiopia: be it in regard to contentious issues involving Eritrea, border disputes along the Sudan/Gondar line, Sudan's stance on Islamic fundamentalism, or issues arising out of the country's cultural ties with its wider Arab-Islamic constituency. These are not new challenges. As in the past, Ethiopia should use diplomatic measures to safeguard her national security interests.

In regard to the remaining two neighbouring states, little of significance could be said at this time. Relations with Kenya have been consistently amicable since independence and are most likely to remain so. The same could be said about Djibouti, unless the country allows itself to become a proxy to a regional geopolitical power game aimed at Ethiopia.

Africa and the Middle East

Africa and the Middle East, two important segments of Ethiopia's broader diplomatic space, will always figure prominently in her foreign policy priorities. For the most part, the strategy of forging and maintaining friendly relations with Ethiopia's partners in Sub-Saharan Africa has generally succeeded. Relations with neighbouring Muslim and Arab countries are affected by Islam's ambivalent perception of Ethiopia: on the one hand, a hospitable land which gave refuge to the early followers of the Prophet Mohammed and, on the other hand, a land accused of discriminating against its Muslim subjects.

There have been moments in Ethiopia's history where she has had to contend with the hostile perception. Today, there are signs of its resurgence in Somalia and beyond. Ethiopia cannot be indifferent to challenges that threaten her social and political fabric. She must, however, make every effort to resuscitate the more positive view of Ethiopia as an old Christian country which predates Islam and which was a safe haven to the followers of the Prophet at the very moment he and his flock were being hunted down in their own homeland. Moreover, Ethiopia is a country whose Christian and Muslim citizens have learned the benefits of moderation and accommodation the hard way. As I shall explain in the following chapter, Wollo in central Ethiopia provides a striking instance of peaceful co-existence between followers of the two faiths. That, rather than war and confrontation, holds the key to Ethiopia's relations with her Islamic nieghbours; a strategy Ethiopia should try to formulate jointly with them.

Our relations with the broader community of nations beyond our proximate geopolitical region are not of particular relevance for the present discussion. But there are three specific aspects which need to be mentioned, even if only briefly. The first involves our present struggle for a more democratic political order. The point to underline in this regard is that the international environment for that struggle is currently favourable and justifies a certain degree of optimism about the future. It goes without saying that when all is said and done it is each society that has to make the commitment and sacrifice to bring about democracy. A good deal of the discussion in the following section revolves around this theme.

The second aspect concerns our relations with major regional powers and multilateral institutions, financial as well as political. Ethiopia's long tradition of diplomacy should stand her in good stead as she navigates the multiplicity of global challenges facing her. There have been occasions in the past when her leaders have faltered, a major instance being the domination of the country by Soviet Russia in the seventies and eighties. It is to be hoped that today's excessive reliance on Chinese technical and financial assistance (and political influence) would not turn out to be yet one more instance of a short-sighted policy that is detrimental to the nation's long term interests.

There is thirdly the question of globalization. I have briefly alluded to this question in the context of Ethiopia's need for seaports. I shall have more to say in the section on economic prospects at the end of this chapter.

The Domestic Front

A book on Ethiopia written in the early fifties by British author Spencer Trimmingham offered the following grim view of the future of the country. "After the anarchic situation which prevailed in Ethiopia for so many centuries, it is impossible for any truly democratic and constitutional government to materialize even in our time; nor could such a government hope to fulfill either the immediate or deeper spiritual needs of its peoples. The overwhelming need of the country is primarily for social justice, for such constructive material achievements as will not upset social foundations, and for that unity *which only an autocratic government could impose upon a land whose every characteristic leads to disunion.* So only can habits of confidence in rulers, good-neighbourliness, and lawful behaviour be engendered which, without change from the organic to the organized type of life characteristic of Western society, might in time lead to a new form of political structure"(italics added).[4]

There is no need to belabor the point that unity cannot be imposed from above by an autocratic government. It can only be built on the common bonds and values of Ethiopia's different cultural groups. I have drawn attention to the strong commonalities among these groups which Trimmingham himself recognizes but which he in the end rejects in favour of the notion of "a land whose every characteristic leads to disunion." Solutions to our present problems should be sought outside Trimmingham's jaundiced vision and at three different levels: political, social and economic.

Our political heritage is one of autocracy. That is one legacy we should put to rest. We need to seek solutions within the framework of genuine democracy; not the kind of democracy imposed on citizens by self-serving republican autocrats. At the social level, we need to fall back on the more enabling aspects of our cultural heritage as we build the foundations for development, social harmony, and national cohesion. Economically, we need to take cognizance of the magnitude and diversity of our resources and pursue the kind of growth promoting policies that will liberate our people from the scourge of poverty. Aspects of this three-part narrative have been broached earlier. But it is essential to probe deeper, address fresh issues, and attempt to offer a more coherent and fuller picture.

The Political Level

Identity politics and ideology are the immediate challenges to building a new, genuinely democratic order. This dual challenge needs to be considered at some length as we look for ways to try to extricate ourselves from our present predicament.

Identity Politics

About eighty per cent of Ethiopia's cultural communities are from the same Hammitic/Kushitic stock: the Northern Kushites (the Beja, the Bilen, the Amharas and the Tigreans); the Southern Kushites (the South-Western Sidama communities); and those referred to as the 'Low Kushite' (the Afar, the Somali, and the Oromo). Whatever linguistic, religious and other dissimilarities they have developed over time, they retain strong commonalities.[5] Today, this polity faces a major challenge. Identity politics is being employed as a battering ram to enfeeble the bonds of culture and blood. A powerful political agenda has been forged which underplays their shared values and accentuates their differences.

The secession of Eritrea is in some measure an outcome of this mindset. Article 39 of the Ethiopian Constitution bestows the right of secession upon the remaining communities of the Ethiopian nation. But secession might not necessarily be the end of our troubles. The last logical step of the process of political disintegration that identity politics brings in its train is reached only when the forces driving that process arrive at their final resting place: the clan or the cultural group where there is no further room for political fragmentation. Somalia's breakup into irreducible clans is an illustration. The stories we occasionally hear of the Adwa cabal within the TPLF group might also be an instance of this disquieting process.

Allegiance to cultural identity need not always have sinister motivations, nor should it necessarily set in motion disruptive political forces. There is a sense in which an individual's allegiance to an ethnic or religious community, or to a locale with particularistic characteristics, could provide the basis for constructive action. Voluntary associations are currently operating in Ethiopia whose goals are to support the development of disadvantaged districts or localities. Even during the regime of Emperor Haile-Selassie when parochial tendencies were frowned upon, such self-help associations did exist; the most prominent example being the Gurage Peoples Self-Help Association whose primary goal was to promote development projects in the district of Gurage. Similar voluntary associations existed then and exist today: Gondar, Metcha/Tulema, Gojjam, Illubabor, Harrar, etc.

Amartya Sen describes this type of allegiance persuasively when he says: "The sense of identity can make an important contribution to the strength and the warmth of our relations with others, such as neighbors, or members of the same community, or fellow citizens, or followers of the same religion. Our focus on particular identities can enrich our bonds and make us do many things for each other and can help to take us beyond our self-centered lives."[6]

Many of us in Ethiopia often experience the warm sentiments evoked by the music, the poetry, the folklore, the mannerisms, the idioms, the quaint language accents, the land where the umbilical cords of our ancestors are interred, the family history, and the many other cultural characteristics of communities we hail from. At a wedding party, we are carried away by the music, by the thumping of the drums, the clapping of the hands in unison with the gentle movement of the head and shoulders, by the rhyming couplets which extol the beauty of the bride, the graceful *iskista* of the comely girls, and by the harvest dance of stick-wielding men folk. We sway and snap our fingers to the tune and the crafty encomiums of the *azmari* as he dishes out clever couplets flattering now this and now that lady or gentleman, and to the responses of his poetically inclined listeners who take turns in offering their own couplets that the *azmari* obligingly weaves into his music.

We struggle to sit still as we are moved by the electrifying *shilela* of the warrior, challenging all men of stout heart to rise and smite the nation's cowardly foe and send him home swearing never again to set foot on the country of the brave. At an Ethiopian Orthodox Mass, the initiated often experience moments of ecstasy as they inaudibly hum along with the priest and deacon Yared's highly ornamented *zema* gracefully flowing from their melodious voices; or as they audibly respond to the hymnal call of the priest or deacon. And, of course, those of us who belong to cultures other than the one described here doubtless experience similar moments of sublime joy in our respective cultural milieu.

There is nothing wrong with any of this. On the contrary, such sentiments are precious social assets that could be harnessed for good causes. Sen underlines this in the following manner: "The recent literature on 'social capital', powerfully explored by Robert Putnam and others, has brought out clearly enough how an identity with others in the same social community can make the lives of all go much better in that community; a sense of belonging to a community is thus seen as a resource — like capital."[7]

The problem with this kind of sentiment is that it does not tell the whole story of an individual's allegiance to identity, even less of the perils of identity politics. One need only recall the Jewish holocaust, the mindless massacres in India and Pakistan during partition, or the more recent atrocities in Rwanda, Bosnia-Herzegovina, or Sadam's Iraq in order to appreciate the menace that lurks beneath the surface of passionate identity. Social harmony is corroded when politicians unashamedly build an entire edifice of governance resting on the throwback of ethnic identity, and equally unashamedly place the key levers of political power in the hands of members of their ethnic cohorts or political lackeys to promote narrow sectarian interests. This is precisely what the TPLF government in Ethiopia is doing today, with Tigreans and their stooges dominating the executive, judicial, and legislative branches and, needles to say, the security forces. In situations where non-Tigreans occupy positions of prominence, Tegrean minders are placed under them.

It is of course an abiding political fact that ethnic identity has been, is, and will continue to be a feature of Ethiopia's social fabric. Competition over political power and resources is inevitable. Conflict is bound to arise when old grievances drive the instinct to get even with those presumed to be past perpetrators of injustice. The problem is unlikely to be resolved either by chastising those who harbour exaggerated sentiments of ethnic identity or by consciously nurturing ethnic distinctiveness. Nor can it be expected to peter out in time through indulgence. And whipping up passions is the surest way to empower fanatics to wreak havoc and bloodshed.

The starting point for managing the problem is a better understanding of how ethnic identity manifests itself through individual conduct. Once understood, avenues could be explored to manage it. There is a spate of recent literature on identity politics and self-determination, a relatively new phenomenon, though identity itself is as old as the mountains. The global surge in self-determination appears to be an outcome of the worldwide spread of the aspiration for democracy which Samuel Huntington ascribes to the "third wave" of democratization; i.e. the third stage in the evolution of modern democracy.[8]

In the developing world, this has often engendered hostility among ethnic groups who wish to right past wrongs. The perception of identity such parties profess is essentially one- dimensional: one is a Hutu, a Tamil, a Tigrean, a Kurd, an Oromo, an Ibo and not much else. Yet an individual's identity is rarely one-dimensional. Amin Maalouf, a Lebanese author, an Arab, a Christian, and a man who has lived in France for some three decades, who writes in French and feels French, explores the multidimensional nature of identity in a recent book.

"Of course, of course -- but what do you really feel, deep inside?" Amin says he is sometimes asked.[9] "As if deep down inside everyone," he continues, "there is just one affiliation that really matters, a kind of 'fundamental truth' about each individual, an 'essence' determined once and for all at birth, never to change thereafter. As if the rest, all the rest -- a person's whole journey through time as a free agent; the beliefs he acquires in the course of that journey; his own individual tastes, sensibilities and affinities; in short his life -- counted for nothing." And what is Maalouf's response to his interlocutors? "Each individual's identity is made up of a number of elements.... A person may feel a more or less strong attachment to a province, a village, a neighborhood, a clan, a professional team or one connected with sports, a group of friends, a union, a company, a parish, a community of people with the same passions, the same sexual preferences, the same physical handicaps, or who have to deal with the same kind of pollution or nuisance."

An understanding of this crucial aspect of identity is an initial step towards exploring ways in which multi-ethnic communities could begin to address the challenge of living together in harmony. Nurturing a one-dimensional perception of identity will breed suspicion, misunderstanding, hatred, and ultimately violence. As Sen warns: "With suitable instigation, a fostered sense of identity with one group of people can be made into a powerful weapon to brutalize another.... Indeed, many of the conflicts and barbarities in the world are sustained through the illusion of a unique identity. The art of constructing hatred takes the form of invoking the magical power of some allegedly predominant identity that drowns other affiliations and in a conveniently bellicose form can also overpower any human sympathy or natural kindness that we may normally have. The result can be a homespun elemental violence or globally artful violence or terrorism."[10]

A one-dimensional perception of identity puts greater emphasis on the rights of groups and correspondingly less on the rights of the *individuals* that make up these groups; and lesser still on those outside the group. That inevitably leads to a situation where new injustices take the place of former injustices that aggrieved parties attempt to correct. In the words of Amy Gutman: "Subordinating individual [rights] to group [rights] is another name for tyranny."[11]

Maalouf likens identity to a panther. Why? Because, he says, "A panther kills if you leave it alone, and the worst thing you can do is to leave it alone after you have wounded it. But also because a panther can be tamed." And the taming process requires that the animal "be observed, studied calmly, understood, and then conquered and tamed if we don't want the world to become a jungle, or the future to resemble the worst images of the past, or our sons to look on as helplessly in 50 years time as we now do at massacres, expulsions and other 'cleansings' -- to look on at them, and perhaps even to be their victims." Untamed, the panther leaves us with a situation in which "*the sense of belonging to different 'tribes' grows stronger while the sense of belonging to the national community weakens until it disappears, or almost.* Always amid bitterness; sometimes in a bloodbath.... In the matter of 'ethnic' problems this is the scenario you head for as soon as community allegiances are allowed to turn into substitutes for individual identity *instead of being incorporated into a single wider, redefined national identity*" (italics added).[12]

These are thoughts well worth pondering in multi-ethnic societies like Ethiopia. Ethiopians are not a collection of compartmentalized ethnic groups consisting of one-dimensional Tigreans, Oromos, Gurages, Agaws, Amharas, or Sidamas. Each of these is internally varied and shares common values across the ethnic divide, thanks to a long history of cohabiting a common ancestral land, possessing a not uncommon outlook on life, a not dissimilar culture or set of cultures, ties of blood, faith, and a defining common experience of holding external adversaries at bay. And it goes without saying that each is made up of individuals who, as individuals, could find common ground with members of other ethnic groups or even expatriates in a wide range of professional, intellectual, artistic, religious, or other pursuits.

The ethnic policy followed by Ethiopia's current rulers is a prescription for social discord. For a leading TPLF official to openly ask: "What could the Axum obelisks possibly mean to the people of Wollaita?" is divisive. For the same official to publicly declare his pride in being a Tigrean, besides undermining his credibility as the leader of a country in which the overwhelming majority of citizens are non-Tigreans, is to caste the aspersion that individuals belonging to other ethnic communities are somehow deficient by comparison. That hardly promotes social harmony. Behind such atavistic remarks lurks a one-dimensional perception of identity. It will not do for Ethiopia.[13]

Ethiopians should resist giving in to the temptation of living in ethnically circumscribed geographical kraals. (This is clearly implied by a recent statement of an extremist politician who bemoans the encroachment of his ethnic group's territory on several fronts).[14] Or lend sympathetic ears to the prodding of opportunistic politicians who describe in graphic detail past injustices purportedly inflicted upon their group; often with no historical evidence to back up their allegations. An instance of this is the accusation that Emperor Menelik was responsible for chopping off the breasts of Oromo women; a horrific act which belies the personality of one of the least violent and most accommodative Emperors in recent memory. The story is said to be the fabrication of mischievous TPLF/ EPLF operatives carrying out their party's policy of sowing discord between Amhara and Oromo. Ethiopia's history suffers no shortage of injustices. Those whose forebears are accused today of having committed injustice could delve into the past and unearth even worse atrocities committed by the forebears of their present day accusers. Rehearsing past wrongs, actual or imagined, can only incite future ones. When incitement provokes violence, no one can tell how it would end or what the cost would be in lives lost or opportunities foregone. And in the Ethiopian context, no cultural or ethnic group would be the winner, so many are the threads of commonality among the protagonists.

Sanity requires that we look at past wrongs with perspective. After all, we are not a nation trying to find our feet after throwing off an iniquitous system of apartheid or the indignities of a caste system. Sanity also requires us to occasionally turn our attention to the experience of countries manifesting similarities with ours and to their more inspiring leaders. I shall come back to this later in this chapter.

Let me make one final point before I move on to the next crucial issue. Much as men exercising political power can cause great harm to community relations through policies which pit once social group against another, we should not underestimate the countervailing power of the silent majority of citizens. A case in point is the desperate attempt by the Dergue during its last years of its rule to incite Amharas,

Oromos and others against Eritrean and Tigrean secessionists; an attempt which failed miserably. It would not be unreasonable to assume in this respect that the majority of mainstream Tigreans are probably not persuaded by the false claim of ethnic and cultural distinctiveness advocated by the TPLF.

Ideology

Revolutionary Democracy is the guiding ideology of Ethiopia's ruling party today. Some suggest that this is no more than a formal declaration intended to keep the party faithful in line, rather than a practical guide for conducting day-to-day government business. There could indeed be persons in leadership positions within the party who, left to their best judgments, might be capable of seeing the ideology's irrelevance to today's Ethiopia. The key question for public policy in Ethiopia today, however, is not so much whether some senior party members could see the anachronism of the ideology in their more reflective moments. Rather, it is the extent to which they are prepared to free their minds from the fetters of ideology in their management of public affairs. Though a few instances have recently surfaced of diehards who have experienced a change of heart, we do not as yet see enough of these among members of the ruling party to suggest imminent change in the way the country is run.

Old habits and reflexes die hard, even if one were to persuade oneself of the obsolescence of the ideas they spring from. We observe evidence of these subconscious reflexes when the government decides, for instance, to pass retroactive legislation to nullify the right of bail of persons who are perceived to be threats to the regime; or when repressive legislation is brought out to keep the press and civil society organizations on a tight leash. The Marxist-Leninist reflex that turns its adherents into control freaks is not easy to shake off.

But Revolutionary Democracy goes beyond being a reflex or a public relations tool aimed at shoring up the confidence of the party faithful. It is the party's guiding light for the new Ethiopia its members say they wish to build and is the basis for the whole spectrum of policies regulating the country's political, economic, and social life. Often, it is also the yardstick against which the performance of party members is judged. One instance of this is the remark by a senior party official a few years ago regarding the Acting Mayor of Addis Ababa who was upbraided for his failure to turn Addis Ababa into a *menaheria* (a bustling centre) of Revolutionary Democracy. This was an unwarranted criticism of one of the few party members who, in the public eye, had done far better than his predecessor: a much talked about paradigm of self-confessed incompetence.

More regrettably, the party has been transformed into a deity revered by members. In the minds of the faithful, it ranks higher than the interests of the nation and its peoples. A party purportedly set up to serve as a means to the objective of liberating millions from oppression has transformed itself into a mighty machine of political repression, and in the process has metamorphosed from being a means to an end into a much sanctified end. It is in this ideological environment that the democratic and human rights experiment in Ethiopia is taking place today. If the democratic process is kept under tight leash, it is because of Revolutionary Democracy which, being a variant of Marxism, is inherently anti-democratic. If the press is muzzled and civil liberties are curtailed, it is also because of Revolutionary Democracy.

A by-product of the politics of ideology is the tendency for acrimony in political discourse. Since the 1974 revolution, Ethiopia's political dialogue has been marked by extremism and animosity. It is rare for ideas to be discussed on their merit. Political dialogue is employed as a vehicle for exchanging sentiments of intolerance, of distrust, of vindictiveness and hostility. Our very language has been debased by these sordid attitudes and by the growing vocabulary of insult and vituperation.

Nothing in the world is constant, however. Sooner or later the party leadership will be obliged to alter their policies in response to economic and political challenges; or be pushed out of the way if they do not. Notwithstanding occasional statements by party bigwigs that such a change would only come to pass 'over the party's grave', new directions in policy cannot be ruled out. Indeed, many of the economic policies currently followed by the party are a far cry from the centrally planned *dirigiste* model of Soviet Russia or Maoist China. They manifest a degree of resemblance to the post-Mao tolerance of private sector growth allowed in trade, housing, manufacturing, and agriculture.

More importantly, there are growing instances of former party members who appear to have turned their backs on the ideas and attitudes they grew up with. An instructive illustration of self-liberation from the fetters of ideology (and ethnicity) are the observations recently made by Siyye Abraha, a founding member of the TPLF who was obliged to spend six years behind bars for his political views.

Siyye fell out with the inner circle of TPLF's leadership during the Ethio-Eritrean conflict, to be detained subsequently on bogus charges. Though released on bail by the judge, he was promptly rearrested and retroactive legislation brought out to deny him and others the right of bail. He was found guilty on a number of charges by a politically compliant judiciary and given a long prison sentence. Six years behind bars appear to have given him the opportunity to reflect on his political outlook. In an interview given to a local paper a few months after his release, he made statements on ideology and ethnicity which stand in sharp contrast to the party line and, of course, to his own earlier convictions.

On ethnicity he had this to say: "We Ethiopians are a multi-ethnic country, which is not to say that we are a mere *collection* of ethnic groupings. We are one nation... Being Ethiopian is not something I have invented. *It is an identity that I have inherited from my parents and from our history*....It would be wrong to accentuate our (ethnic) differences for short-term political advantage" (italics added).[15]

Regarding ideology, he said the following: "Ethiopian politicians are still beholden to the leftist inspired, confrontational, divisive and acrimonious politics of class struggle of the sixties and seventies. Ours is the politics of mutual recrimination and of overblown differences; not of tolerance, of mutual respect, or of constructive give and take." Siyye says many other things in the interview which put him squarely on the side of free speech, the rule of law, ethnic tolerance, an independent judiciary, and a democratic political order; not the 'democratic' political order of the Marxist lexicon, but the kind which the ordinary man in the street readily identifies with. No trace of ideological dogmatism or ethnic divisiveness can be detected in his long interview.

Former TPLF members Gebru Asrat and Aregash Adane have also recently made statements that show them embracing authentically democratic ideals. In a statement to a gathering of Ethiopians held in Washington D.C. on 20 September 2008, Gebru dwelt at length on the problems facing Ethiopia under TPLF rule. A major point of his criticism was Revolutionary Democracy's undemocratic (or, in his word, hegemonistic) character and the ruling party's strenuous efforts to create a monolithic power structure aimed at depriving dissenters of political space. In a report filed from Ethiopia by VOA's Peter Heinlein on 18 March 2010, Aregash is also quoted as characterizing Revolutionary Democracy as "an outmoded ideology" and takes the Prime Minister to task for his obstinate views. All these are encouraging illustrations of men and women who seem to have unlearned what has been drummed into their heads during the impressionable years of youth.

Or is all this an elaborate hoax, as some observers suggest, intended to mask a sinister plan that these former TPLF members still share with their adversaries in the ruling party. That is the contention of a recent book in Amharic by Tesfaye Gebreab.[16] Tesfaye, a former TPLF party member whose credibility is not altogether above suspicion, contends that both Siyye and Meles are committed to the objective of ensuring that political power stays firmly in the hands of their ethnic group. If power falls into other hands, it means that "TPLF's sacrifices will have been made in vain."

Tesfaye says that the difference between the two protagonists for power, Siyye and Meles, differ only as to how best this objective should be carried out. Meles and his group believe that the Tigray region could exercise supreme political power for a long time to come provided that the electoral process and the ethnically based federal structure of the country are firmly under their control. Siyye and his group, on the other hand, are of the view that this strategy is inherently vulnerable and will not serve for the long term. Their preferred alternative would be to use, as the Amharas in the past, "Ethiopian nationalism as a cover while creating economic and educational opportunities for Tigreans to prosper and accumulate political power. In time, they will become the foundation of the nation's economy. Tigray nationalism will also be fortified in the process." The issue was apparently discussed in closed meetings over a long period of time and that the rank and file of the party are fully aware of the two approaches.

There is little doubt that Meles Zenawi has been carrying out this strategy for the last two decades. As for Siyye, is he dissembling; or has he finally recognized the ultimate failure of a strategy advanced by an ethnic group which makes up only 6% of Ethiopia's population and which whishes to dominate the economic and political life of the remaining 94%. To say time will tell betrays an attitude of inexcusable indifference, especially on the part of those who are actively engaged in the struggle for a more democratic order. All concerned citizens need to encourage Siyye, former guerillas like Asgede Gebre-Selassie (whose work I cited earlier), and others like them to persevere in their vision of a fraternal and historic community of peoples whose future lies in mobilizing their common bonds to build a more prosperous, democratic, and peaceful nation.

The Social Level

The discussion in Chapter 18 on the minimum cultural base for development and part of the analysis on identity politics in the preceding section are instances of the second of the three-part narrative on the solutions to our current problems that I cited earlier in this section. My contention in Chapter 18 was that, contrary to the view of many pessimists/realists, we have on the whole a favourable set of social and cultural factors that could constitute a strong basis for national cohesion and progress. Examination of the role of civil society is needed to complete this facet of the narrative.

Civil society groups (opposition parties first and foremost, human rights organizations, religious institutions, professional associations, and other civic groups) are important actors in Ethiopia's struggle for democracy and political stability. Opposition parties do not presently have adequate political space to advance their programmes. And the novelty of adversarial politics has at times exposed them to fractious debates. The situation has been aggravated by the calculated efforts of the ruling party to sow dissent and rivalry within and between opposition groups. The party has in addition used its extensive political clout to throw roadblocks on the day-to-day work of its adversaries. Yet there are encouraging signs of groups that have learned from their past errors and that are making strenuous efforts to use the limited political space to good effect. This will be a positive factor in the evolution of a democratic culture.

Religious institutions are another potential contributor to the democratic process. Regrettably, they have by and large refrained from playing that role. Reticent of exercising their traditional if spasmodic role of standing up to leaders who commit gross acts of social injustice, leaders of the Ethiopian Orthodox Church seem to be regressing to their none-too-laudable role of siding with the ruler even as he acts 'in defiance of God's justice'; or of being silent when that has meant condoning injustice. At times, they have engaged in inordinate flattery of party leaders when speaking truth to power would have been the more responsible thing to do.

In a meeting between church leaders and senior party officials on the eve of the May 2005 elections, an Orthodox priest drew biblical parallels on leadership in his eagerness to flatter the leader of the ruling party present at the meeting. The priest is reported to have compared him with the wise King Solomon and with the 'future Tewodros' of popular imagination: a King who "would bring a period of peace and plenty to his people."[17] One clergyman's overzealous assertions should obviously not be taken as a reflection of the Church's position. Yet nothing different was subsequently said by Church authorities on this unfortunate clerical episode. Given what appears to be the favourable disposition of Church leaders towards the ruling party, the silence was perhaps inevitable.

It should perhaps be mentioned in this context that the Ethiopian Orthodox Church is undergoing a serious internal crisis which it needs to address with resolve. Besides the demands of its critics that it play a more active role in Ethiopia's search for democracy, it faces pressure for change from both within and outside. Among its more liberally minded adherents who value their attachment to the Church, there is a growing disenchantment with the Patriarchate's inadequate efforts for internal reform. Thanks to Emperor Haile-Selassie, several initiatives were taken to breathe new life into the Church during his reign: translation of holy books from the Geez to Amharic, holding mass in the vernacular, allowing the faithful to view the seat of the *tabot*, simplifying the multiple remembrance services to the dead, etc. It was of course the Emperor who made it possible for the Ethiopian Church to have its first native Patriarch after the subterfuge of the Egyptian Coptic Church lasting several centuries. Church administration and religious education were also improved.

Far more needs to be done today. The priesthood is poorly trained and does precious little social work. High Mass continues to be excessively time consuming. In the Ethiopian Orthodox Church, time is presumed to be as plentiful as the air we breathe. Bishops and priests exercise the liberty to subject their captive congregations to punishing rites which they impose during weddings, requiem masses, choral group performances, and other similar events. The rigours of fasting are needlessly debilitating and completely at odds with the exigencies of modern life. Holy Communion is administered only after Mass which starts at six in the morning. Mothers are forever battling with their children who are reluctant to interrupt their Sunday morning dozes for Holy Communion. Why doesn't our Church have multiple Communions during the day like the Catholic Church, they ask?

An increasing number of the faithful are giving up the demanding rigours and anachronisms of the Church in favour of the simpler and more practical ways of other churches. Sermons are a case on point. The great majority of Ethiopian clerics offer sermons that are uninformed and annoyingly boring. No wonder the Orthodox faithful are drawn to sermons of other churches which better respond to their emotional and spiritual anguish. Significant defections are taking place, the protestant sects (especially the Pentecostalists) being the most favoured destinations. The politically motivated proselytizing activities of Saudi Wahabists among the economically vulnerable sections of the population is another challenge.

It is not for the first time that the Ethiopian Church is facing such a formidable challenge. The Muslim insurgency led by Mohammed Gragn in the first half of the sixteenth century saw large numbers of Orthodox faithful involuntarily embracing the Muslim faith. Immediately afterwards, the Jesuits succeeded in converting Emperor Susineyos to the Catholic faith and were well on their way to disestablishing the Ethiopian Orthodox Church in favour of the Church of Rome. In the nineteenth and twentieth centuries, Catholic and Protestant missions spread throughout the land with the consent of Church and state and often ended up attracting Orthodox Christians, a far simpler proposition than converting Muslims.

But it is perhaps for the first time that the Church is confronting the challenge of large-scale voluntary defections to Pentecostal churches and to the Saudi driven Wahabist campaign. The objective of the Wahabists is to produce large numbers of converts that profess an intolerant brand of Islam. It is not hard to imagine how this could undermine the spirit of tolerance between Ethiopian Christians and Muslims which has taken years to build. Obviously, both the Orthodox Church and the National Islamic Council should be concerned with what in time could engender social strife.

Insofar as the Orthodox Church is concerned, the degree to which it can meet the many challenges it currently faces largely depends on how soon it can put together measures for internal reform and renewal. When Martin Luther challenged the Catholic Church in the sixteenth century, the response was to launch the Reformation. The landmark Council of Trent (1545-1545) initiated several forward looking reforms which revitalized the Church. The Council's decree on the education of priests is particularly relevant to the serious challenge the Orthodox Church faces today. It might well be that some such council is needed. The present Synod is deeply divided, however, and does not appear to possess the moral authority to initiate meaningful reforms. But delay will only worsen the crisis and speed up migration to other faiths.

While necessary, reforms need not stand in the way of measures which could be taken to respond to a number of challenges. The Church could, for instance, take initiatives to assist the faithful in their yearning for a less repressive and more liberal political environment. The Ethiopian Church has a long and commendable tradition of standing up to unjust politicians and of telling them to mend their sinful ways. It would not be idle to hope for a resurgence of this tantalizing tradition?[18] Leaders of Ethiopia's Muslims should also be sensitive to the aspirations of their followers in regard to democratic and human rights. They should in addition counter the subversive influence of Saudi Wahabists and Somali extremists through a better appreciation and advocacy of the 'Wollo paradigm' (see next chapter). The current policy of excessive timidity manifested by the leadership of both religious establishments only helps those in power to persist in their repressive ways and is a regrettable renunciation of one of the few avenues available to Ethiopian citizens for peaceful change.

A heartening exception to the timidity of the Orthodox and Islamic leadership is the independent stance of the minority Ethiopian Catholic establishment. Following the violent suppression of the demonstration in November 2005 against the general elections held earlier in the year, the Church's Bishops issued a statement openly deploring the killings and appealing for tolerance: an object lesson for other religious leaders.[19]

Among civil society groups working towards the country's political transformation is the Ethiopian Human Rights Council, the nineteen-year old pioneer in the struggle to advance the cause of human rights. Over the years, the Council has conducted a sustained programme of exposing violations of human rights by public authorities. It has, in the process, sown the seeds of a spirit of independence and audacity, so essential for an active role by citizens in the defence of their rights. The Council has also set a fine example of what citizens are capable of doing on their own in a country much accustomed to the helping hand of donor agencies.

Professional associations (trade unions, teachers, lawyers groups, youth and women's groups, and others) are at present either weak or serve as loyal regiments of the ruling party, showing little sign of independence or vitality. Are they going to stay that way? In the short-term, perhaps. Gradually, however, they are bound to find their true calling and an increased willingness to participate in the exciting experiment of democracy.

The Economic Level

Scattered throughout the preceding narrative are ideas which justify a certain degree of optimism as we explore the prospects for improvement in the country's social and political climate. Given this general setting, what natural resources does Ethiopia possess that could make the daily life of the average citizen materially less and less miserable with the passage of years, leading ultimately to a level of living which could meet the minimal standards of nutrition, health, education, and economic well being?

Land

The point of departure for any discussion of the country's economic prospects is an assessment of its principal resource: land. Historically, land tenure has been a major roadblock to development. All indications are that it continues to be so. The predicament of Ethiopia's agricultural sector today has few parallels in the nation's history. The most notable aspect of that predicament is the dramatic decline in the carrying capacity of the land in the traditional crop growing areas. When I was an undergraduate student in the opening years of the fifties, the country's population was about 15 million. Expatriate agricultural experts often remarked that, given improvements in farming methods and agricultural technology, the land could support four times as many inhabitants. Over the last fifty years, farming methods and agricultural technology have not made much headway. But the country's population has mushroomed more than five-fold.

The result has been a progressive fragmentation of individual holdings, to the point where average family plots in grain producing regions have dwindled to about one hectare. Persistent soil erosion has further reduced the productive capacity of the land. Little more than 20% of the farming population has access to fertilizers or improved seeds. Yields have consequently stayed low in most areas. To add to these constraints, the peasant is forced to live under a tenure system where the government has the last word. Periodic redistributions of farm plots are made, purportedly with the objective of providing land to the landless. As redistributions are carried out by party agents whose decisions are not infrequently based on political and personal grounds, the objective is often undermined. Redistribution also leads to further fragmentation and insecurity.

The challenges for the future of Ethiopia's smallholder agriculture, the determinant factor in the sector's growth, are thus varied and formidable; the most formidable of all being the system of tenure. Not only should the peasant be assured of a degree of security of tenure over the short term (the government's apparent policy) but of outright ownership as well, since only in this way could full security for him and his inheritors be assured. Private ownership is also critical for soil and water conservation as well as for the protection of forests, pastures, plant, animal and wild life in general. The role of government should be regulatory, not proprietary.

Outside Ethiopia, there are not too many countries where the primitive ox-drawn plow stands out as a defining logo. That should say something about our chronic dependence on food aid and the potential for much higher levels of output. It also evokes the crying need for a land tenure policy which responds simultaneously to the twin goals of social justice and high productivity. These are not new ideas. They have been aired for several decades, but have singularly failed to impress the country's successive leaders. Given a fast changing world, one wonders if there might not be quicker strategies to get Ethiopia's agriculture moving: a sector that has been bypassed by major advances in technology, animal husbandry, and natural resources management. Is the recent rush to lease huge tracts of land in Ethiopia by Middle Eastern and Asian investors for the production of large amounts of food crops suggestive of a possible way out in this respect? After several centuries of virtual stagnation, is Ethiopia's agriculture finally on the threshold of a major transformation?

Ethiopia possesses substantial amounts of water for irrigaton. But only 5% of the land suitable for irrigation has been brought under cultivation. World Bank data suggest that as much as three-quarters of the country's arable land of 175 million acres is uncultivated. It is this combination of abundant land and water which, together with cheap labour, has attracted foreign investors to the country. On 23 November 2009

The *Washington Post* reported that the country "is rapidly becoming one of the world's leading destinations for the booming business of land leasing" and "few countries have embraced the trend as zealously as Ethiopia." In its issue of 22 November 2009, *The New York Times Magazine* wrote that more than 7 million acres of land (5% of the total of 131 million acres of uncultivated land) have been identified for leasing, half of which is to be contracted out before the next harvest "at the dirt cheap annual rate of 50 cents per acre." India alone has invested $4.2 billion, with more to come from the Middle East. Huge industrial farms churning out massive quantities of wheat, rice, barley, fruits, and vegetables will soon dot the countryside. In the fifties and sixties Ethiopia was often talked about as a potential breadbasket for her food deficit, oil rich Middle Eastern neighbours. At long last, are the visionaries about to be proved right?

The potential economic benefits would be considerable for a country which has for decades failed to produce enough crops from rain fed agriculture even to feed its population, let alone supply foreign demand. With a large inflow of capital to raise production to significant levels, the picture could change. Employment opportunities for the rural population are another potential benefit if fair wages are paid. While the object of the exercise is to produce food for export, the government might conceivably negotiate that a certain proportion of the food grains produced should be earmarked to the Ethiopian market to cushion periodic supply shortages or to facilitate a gradual build up in food stocks to respond to drought situations. Additionally, the inflow of foreign exchange would strengthen the country's balance of payments position. Leases could also be negotiated at levels which are high enough to generate substantial revenues but not so high as to deter potential investors.

Outside of these immediate gains, are there longer term benefits to the economy? Exports are a principal source of foreign exchange. To what extent would this be true of the crops exported by the concessionaires? There is a lack of transparency on this key issue. It is not evident if the country will stand to benefit from the foreign exchange which could be generated by the export of the food crops, or if the investors have been given a carte blanche to evacuate products at will. Could the investments have a positive impact on the rural economy? If these operate along the lines of mineral and oil extracting industries which are well known for their weak linkages with host country economies, the multi-billion industrial farms could leave the vast rural economy virtually untouched. But that need not be the case. Policies could be formulated to encourage investors to forge links with the rural economy. Out-growers could be promoted and investments encouraged in economic and social infrastructure in order to provide a strong impetus to long-term development. There is little information on this.

And what are the possible drawbacks? Leases have reportedly been offered at nominal prices and with minimal conditions. The article in *The New York Times Magazine* quoted an official of the FAO who said that "contracts are pretty thin; no safeguards are being introduced" and that everything is promised "with no controls [and] no conditions." According to the most recent reports, African countries which have offered huge tracts of land to international investors have not seen significant increases in employment opportunites and other related benefits. Only time will tell if the situation is to improve. There is also the more serious challenge of environmental degradation: soil erosion, salinity, a decline in the water table, damage to fisheries, plant and wildlife, displacement of farmers, and disruption of water supply to consumers downstream. It is not certain if the rush to lease land and the eagerness to show a quick turnaround in the country's agricultural fortunes has sidelined these long term concerns. Many concerned citizens are deeply troubled that a government which seems to be primarily motivated by the short term prospects of significant cash flows and by the thinly disguised desire to empower its own ethnic constituency might not be adequately sensitive to the direct and indirect long term costs that its current policies are bound to impose on future generations.

A related question is the reaction of the rural population to these mega projects. Whether it is in Afar or Arsi, Tigrai or Gambela, Gojjam or Benishangul, the farming population's relationship to land has historical, cultural, and patrimonial dimensions; factors which the country's present rulers would be ill advised to ignore. The government has the last word on how land is to be allocated and for what purpose, while millions who are most intimately affected appear to stand on the sidelines and watch. What this might bring in its train in future years cannot be foreseen, but it would not be surprising if the seeds of discontent are currently falling on fertile ground. There is lastly the possibility, remote perhaps but nonetheless real, of this whole exercise being one more cause of tension between Ethiopia and its Arab neighbours unless contracts are designed with a special eye for this.

Summing up, this new opportunity to exploit the nation's land, water, and human resources could generate a significant stream of benefits for the longer term provided: (i) leases are prudently negotiated, (ii) export crops are managed in such a way that they generate significant amounts of foreign exchange, (iii) projects are designed with a view to forging strong links with the rural economy, (iv) farming communities are meaningfully involved, and (v) environmental concerns are addressed effectively.

Even if these conditions were to be fully met, it must be remembered that the greater portion of the country's farming communities, the key players for the future of agriculture, will not be materially affected one way or the other. As I have suggested earlier, visible improvements in their daily lives and the prospects of a dynamic agricultural sector would depend on the degree to which radical changes in land tenure policy are to be introduced in tandem with pragmatic and development friendly policies.

Water

A bird's eye view of water resources throws up the following picture. Official estimates indicate that the nation's water resources are substantial. Surface water is reckoned to be 123 billion cubic metres a year. Underground fresh water is another 2.6 billion. Water for household consumption and sanitation is, of course, vital. In terms of the economy as a whole, however, it is energy, agriculture, and industry that account for the greatest portion of demand. In a country like the U.S. where per capita water consumption is very high, only 7% of water resources goes to household use, as pointed out by the Washington-based World Watch Institute in one of its brochures in the 1980s. The rest is for electric power, irrigation, and industrial use. Water use for these purposes in Ethiopia is currently very limited and the potential enormous.

Take electric energy, for instance. It is estimated that Ethiopia's hydroelectric potential is in the region of 30,000-45,000 Megawatts. At present, the country generates 450 Megawatts of hydropower, 1.5% to 2.0% of the potential. In Africa, only the Democratic Republic of the Congo exceeds Ethiopia's hydropower resources. This enormous source of energy augurs well for industrial growth. It could also be an important new source of foreign exchange, assuming political hurdles do not stand in the way. Ethiopia's utility corporation contemplates exporting electric power to the country's immediate neighbours and to others further afield. Solar energy (5 KW per square metre per day) and wind power (with an average speed of 6 metres per second) are untapped. The same is true of the nation's geothermal resource, only 1% of which is being exploited.

Much as water is a critical resource for energy and irrigation, it causes massive soil loss in the Ethiopian highlands. Recent estimates by the Ethiopian government indicate that the sediment yields of the different rivers range from 180 to 900 tons per year per square kilometre. The great bulk of this soil leaves the country. The amount of sediment that the Nile and its tributaries carry to the Sudan and Egypt every year is *1.3 billion tons*. This results from poor water management, imprudent farming practices, and the loss of grass and forest cover. There are areas in the country where prudent soil conservation methods have been practiced for centuries. Konso is reputed to have done so for five hundred years. Modern soil conservation measures are beginning to get a foothold in a number of localities. For some years now, reforestation projects have also been introduced in selected regions. Given social peace and a political leadership inspired by an all-Ethiopian vision in which all communities have a stake, environmental degradation can be arrested and reversed.

Minerals and Fossil Fuels

Minerals and fossil fuels are another asset. Gold, platinum, and silver have been exploited in modest quantities for a long time. This is likely to continue. New mineral deposits of coal (230 million metric tons) and iron ore have been discovered in quantities to justify commercial exploitation. Apart from being an important source of energy, coal is a raw material for the manufacture of urea, a chemical fertilizer. In addition, there are promising prospects for oil and natural gas (the latter estimated at 2.7 trillion cubic feet). Diammonium phosphate (DAP), another fertilizer, could be extracted from the country's rich potash deposits in the east.

A batch of precious metals (opal, sapphire, emeralds, and garnet) promises to be a new source of foreign exchange. Tantalite has also been discovered and is being produced on a modest scale. This is a crystalline material that is an essential component for the manufacture of cellular phones. Tantalum powder can be compacted to produce very small-sized capacitators: the key to reducing the size of cell phones. Besides, it has remarkable qualities for super-conductivity and is an essential component of military hardware and scientific equipment for space exploration.

Limestone, kaolin, graphite, feldspar, sandstone, marble, and granite are plentiful. The country's current dependence on imported cement speaks volumes of its inability to invest, produce, and market this key ingredient of the construction industry. While it is unlikely that Ethiopia would ever be as important a mining nation as South Africa or the Democratic Republic of the Congo, the economy's mineral sector is likely to play an increasingly important role in generating wealth. As in agriculture, however, the removal of policy and administrative constraints is pivotal to future growth.

Under the present climate of ethnic rivalry, it is not inconceivable for communities to regard natural resources within their geographical boundaries as communal patrimony to be protected against the encroachments of neighbours. In a situation where internal security is weak, it is also possible for conflict to arise. This is what has happened in Nigeria's oil delta and the Congo. Nothing can be ruled out, of course. But in the case of Ethiopia, there are reasons to believe that things might play out differently.

The first is what appears to be the generally well balanced geographical distribution of these resources. Natural gas is located in the Ogaden: oil in Gambella,Wollo (Worre-Ilu), Gojjam (the Nile Basin), and south Gondar; coal in Chilga, Mush Valley, Illubabor (Yayo), Dilbi-Moye (Jimma), and generally in the western and southern coal belt; gold in Wollega and southern Ethiopia; precious metals (emeralds, ruby, sapphire, opal, aquamarine, garnet, tourmaline) in northern Shoa; industrial minerals (vast quantities of limestone, marble, and granite) in Amhara, Tigrai and in the Rift Valley; iron ore in Wollega and Bale; potash deposits and geothermal energy in the Afar homelands; water resources in the north, south, west, and south east of the country; and rich agricultural land in all but a handful of regions (principally the torrid zones of the Danakil Depression). The risk that some regions might make haste towards secession with a monopolistically held resource is mercifully not a major threat.

The second reason is political. The heritage of a pan-Ethiopian nation state is still alive, as I have argued previously. The current government's fierce resistance to the secessionist movements in Oromiya and the Ogaden, its rhetoric of self determination notwithstanding, is a case in point. The kind of conflict in Nigeria's oil rich Delta State and in the mining areas of the Congo is unlikely to occur on any significant level in a country where the heritage of a nation state capable of maintaining law and order is very much in evidence; a mixed blessing, it must be admitted, in the context of the struggle for democracy and human rights.

Demography: Good News at Last?

I have said enough about the quality of the country's human resources in the preceding pages. Little more needs to be added at this stage than to point out that it is time to harness this inestimable asset to give greater impetus to the country's growth. Ethiopia's human resources potential (the entrepreneurial talent of her citizens, their drive towards self improvement, their enduring sense of individual responsibility, and their creative energies) can significantly transform the country's economic landscape. And it goes without saying that an appropriately designed policy of promoting private initiative supplemented by development friendly public sector policies, rather than the *dirigiste* policies of control freaks, would be an effective weapon against the assault on poverty.

On the general demographic situation, the following could be said. Ethiopia's population has been growing steadily over the last seven decades or so. The growth was particularly sharp after the decade of the sixties and seems to have peaked at 3% by the mid-nineties, if we are to go by official data. The rapid growth during the last four decades of the previous century reflects the situation of countries in the early stages of development where the death rate sharply declines well before the birth rate. The result is the familiar phenomenon of population explosion. Improved public health services are the principal reason for an earlier decline in the death rate. A decline in the birth rate takes far longer, and usually results from the spread of education giving rise to late marriages and smaller sized families and policies to reduce fertility.

Though by no means conclusive, there are indications that Ethiopia might be entering a phase where its rate of population expansion is on the decline, which suggests that the birth rate has started to go down. According to official data, population growth has dropped from 3% to 2.6% over the last decade and a half. This is a significant development and appears to be a response to new policy initiatives aimed at reducing the birth rate. In 1993 the government introduced a population policy focusing on a significant reduction of the fertility rate: a much increased availability of contraceptives, improved mother and child health, increased access of women to education, and the introduction of a country-wide awareness about the benefits of small family size. Reports indicate that key government departments and many NGOs have been actively involved. Two surveys carried out recently and discussions with government officials suggest that the policy is beginning to show results.

Further reductions are expected over the next three decades. Officials project that by about 2030 the rate will come down to 1.8%. If that materializes, it would mean that a major constraint to Ethiopia's development will have been significantly eased: yet one more piece of good news on the economic landscape. While future developments need to be closely watched, there seems to be little doubt about the government's intention to curb fertility.

There is another reason why a high growth rate is a cause for concern in a country like Ethiopia: the pressure it creates on cultivable land. In regions like Western Europe, advances in farming methods and technology have dramatically increased agricultural productivity and, together with emigration to the new world, have offset the effects of demographic expansion. The carrying capacity of land in a country like Ethiopia could be put to severe test (as we are currently beginning to observe in the highland areas) if technological improvements are not introduced on a significant scale throughout the country. Holdings could be fragmented further and environmental degradation would not be easily checked. At its extreme, the problem could fuel social conflict, as in Rwanda where it became a powerful contributory factor to the dreadful genocide of the nineties. A slowdown in demographic expansion is consequently a most welcome news.

Globalization

And how, it needs to be asked finally in this context, can Ethiopia take advantage of globalization? Globalization (a freer movement of goods, services, capital, people, and knowledge around the globe) has brought enormous economic benefits to countries in South, East, and South East Asia. Ethiopia has to overcome a number of major hurdles before she can position herself to benefit from this relatively new economic opportunity.

In his book *The Bottom Billion*, Collier observes that the least developing African countries have lost the first round of the globalization opportunity to Asian countries, China in particular, and it will be some time before Asian wages rise to a level which would make Africa's wages more attractive to foreign investors seeking low cost manufacturing locations.[20] Already Chinese wages have grown to a point where garment manufacturers are turning to low wage countries like Bangladesh, Vietnam, and Cambodia.[21] In time, wages in these countries would rise to a level which could drive manufacturers to countries like Ethiopia, provided that other enabling factors like good infrastructure and the spread of elementary and secondary education among the labour force play their part. There are additional hurdles to overcome, however.

Most African countries, says Collier, are constrained by four traps: the conflict trap, the natural resources trap (large oil or minerals exports inviting corruption and bad policies), the poor governance trap in a small country, and the trap "of being landlocked with bad neighbours." These have to be negotiated first before countries could begin to take advantage of the opportunities offered by globalization.

Thankfully, Ethiopia does not fall under the group of countries hobbled by the natural resources trap. Nor can it be classified as a small country with poor governance. While its governance is problematic, it is not a small country. The more serious hurdles are its being landlocked (with bad neighbours) and its discredited ideology and identity politics which create the conditions for conflict. Although, there is currently no country-wide major conflict as in the days of the Dergue, there are localities where the government occasionally faces problems: the Ogaden, Armatchiho, and parts of Wollega. Far more worrying is the possibility at some point in time of a more generalized rebellion against the repressive policies of the TPLF regime, a subject which I shall take up in the chapter that follows.

I have earlier indicated how the problem of being landlocked might be addressed and how this albatross around Ethiopia's neck might be removed. Going forward, we should also take into account factors that place the country in a comparably more advantageous position than the typical African country: a large internal market, a fairly varied and geographically balanced resource base, a long tradition of self-governance and public service, a relatively high work ethic and a creative and enterprising population. Provided access to the high seas is secured and provided an enabling environment for a dynamic modern economy is created, this is not a bad starting point for globalization.

It would be pertinent at this stage to look at India, a country I will discuss further in the next chapter, and consider for a moment how it has succeeded in exploiting the tremendous benefits globalization offers. Consider the following graphic illustration of how powerfully transformative globalization has been for her economy. "Zippies are the huge cohort of Indian youth who are the first to come of age since India shifted away from socialism and dived headfirst into global trade and the information revolution by turning itself into the world's service center. *Outlook* [an Indian weekly magazine] called Indian zippies 'Liberalization's Children' and defined a zippie as a 'young city or suburban resident between 15 and 25 years of age, with a zip in the stride. Belongs to generation Z. Can be male or female, studying or working. Oozes attitude, ambition and aspiration. Cool, confident and creative. Seeks challenges, loves risks and shuns fear.' Indian zippies feel no guilt about making money or spending it. They are … … 'destination driven, not destiny driven, outward looking, not inward, upwardly mobile, not stuck-in-my-station-in-life.' With 54% of India under the age of twenty-five, six out of ten households have at least one potential zippie."[22]

This dynamism did not come out of the blue one beautiful morning. Besides liberalizing its economy, India invested heavily to spread education at all levels and, more particularly, on technical education. A network of high-level institutes of technology was created. The Ethiopian government needs to break the shackles of ideology and liberalize the economy, support first rate technical education throughout the land (not just in some favoured areas) and do away with its stranglehold on information technology which only serves to keep the country at the tail end of Africa. A recent article by *The Economist* notes that "Entreprise, skills, and connectivity are years behind neighbouring Kenya"[23] and, it should be added, Uganda, Tunisia, Egypt, Sudan, and probably Senegal.

There is no magic factor which is capable of bringing about the realization of the many promising prospects I have sketched out in this chapter. But there is little doubt that leadership is among the few of the critical factors that could ultimately enable the country to make a turnaround in its fortunes. This is also an issue which I shall examine in the concluding chapter.

CHAPTER 21

Conclusion

Thoughts on National Cohesion

A range of challenges facing Ethiopia were discussed in the previous chapter. In a nutshell, they consist of two which arise from the country's geopolitical location and four that are internal. The two are: (i) the strategic factors that are the cause of Ethiopia's troubled relationship with her neighbours in the horn of Africa and with those in the Middle East and (ii) the formidable impediment to her development that being landlocked poses, especially in a situation where the neighbouring states are weak, unstable, and not better off economically. The four on the domestic side are: (i) identity politics and the formidable threat it poses to social harmony and national cohesion, (ii) the ruling party's Marxist-Leninist ideology, (iii) the struggle for democracy, and (iv) the challenge of endemic poverty.

National cohesion, one of the more daunting problems, might justify a few additional comments. The importance I have given to the multiple commonalities binding the Ethiopian peoples might appear overstated. After all, communities having more in common have defied efforts to bring them together into a unified polity. A case in point is the multiplicity of Arab nations which continues to stand in the way of forging a single "Arab Nation." The same can be said of Somalia's different clans which have so much in common and yet appear unable to establish a functioning state. In Ethiopia's case, however, there are potent factors that underpin the expectation that one of the oldest nation states in the globe will in all likelihood continue to weather threats to its survival. I have cited a number of reasons in support of this view in previous chapters. The following could be added.

One factor that might discourage communities from opting out of the pan-Ethiopian polity is the grim prospect awaiting them once the thumping of drums, the waving of a million flags and the razzmatazz of Independence Day are relegated to modest annual commemorations. If the Eritrean experience is anything to go by, secession in a developing country context would throw the ordinary citizen into a maze of existential challenges. This is unlikely to happen in advanced countries. When Norway broke off from Sweden in 1905 nothing untoward happened. The same was true when Slovakia seceded from Czechoslovakia. If Flanders and Wallonia in Belgium were to go their separate ways, the event would go little beyond dominating the news media until the public begins to tire. In poor countries, conflict is easily provoked by improperly marked borders, rivalry over resources, rivers crossing national frontiers, migration, sectarian interests and other factors. Dawit, the OLF guerilla veteran I met in 2009, said that if Oromia were to be independent wars would flare up along its frontiers with Benishangul, Gambella, Amhara, Somalia and the Southern Peoples' Region.

Another deterrent is the threat that mini-states are likely to face from powerful neighbours and all pretenders to regional or global hegemony. The threat has multiplied in today's world as nations use petro-dollars to undermine the way of life of others in order to impose their own and as aspiring regional hegemons engage in a show of muscle flexing.[1] A mini state is less able to stand up to such challenges than a large country like Ethiopia. We should perhaps point out in this regard that even the TPLF leadership probably appreciates this and probably also relishes the international limelight that comes with representing a country of some demographic and historical gravitas, at least for the time being.

One should also take note of the fact that contrary to party rhetoric and much to the surprise of its leaders, the sentiment for national unity occasionally surfaces in unexpected quarters. In 1993, party chairman Meles (then President of the country) was in the midst of a meeting of representatives of minority groups where he was holding forth on the repressive ways of Emperor Menelik. At the end of his exposition, a representative of the people of Wollaita in the Southern Region made the following response. "Mr President," he started "we the people of Wollaita are much indebted to Emperor Menelik. Why? Because it was he who took us out of our small overcrowded homeland and gave us a vast country called Ethiopia where we could go forth, work, and earn a living." An eyewitness at the meeting says that the President was so stunned that he was lost for words in response to the man's wholly unexpected riposte. There are several anecdotal pointers that this sentiment is shared by other ethnic communities in Southern Ethiopia.

Yet another optimistic pointer to the future of a pan Ethiopian entity is what might be termed the Wollo paradigm. As we all know, Ethiopia's Wollo region has been the melting pot of different cultures for centuries: Amhara, Oromo, Tigrai, Agaw, Afar and, above all, Christian and Muslim. The result is a multicultural community whose live and let live outlook is an example not only for the rest of Ethiopia but perhaps also for other multicultural nations. Children of mixed marriages carrying names like Haile-Selassie Hussein, Abdul Rahman Wolde-Michael and Gebre-Giorgis Mohammed are every day reminders of peaceful cohabitation between Christians and Muslims.[2]

It should further be noted that the ruling party's early fervour for secession has subsided somewhat. This is partly because of the economic benefits offered by a large country with a relatively broad resource base. That the party, its subsidiary organs, and its individual members have reaped substantial financial benefits over the last two decades is a widely observed fact. The zealotry of secession seems to have momentarily given way to the lures of wealth accumulation. Occasionally, the urge to get rich goes to extremes, as the following anecdotes illustrate.

As an Oromo military officer now in exile contends, Tigreans in Jimma cut down trees in pristine forests to fill their pockets. "Tigrean businessmen," he says, "load twenty to thirty trucks of timber a day for shipment to Saudi Arabia… I and others have seen this with our own eyes." In a further example of greed he goes on to say: "No one can rival [Tigrean] army generals when it comes to grabbing urban land and turning it into cash. They have snatched prime real estate in Dukem, Nazareth, Debre-Zeit and Addis Ababa."[3] He also gives a graphic account of the culture of embezzlement, drinking and fornication among senior TPLF military officicers reminiscent of the conduct of Dergue officers at the height of the civil war. What emerges is a picture of a political party and its supporters so insecure of their hold on power that they are frantically accumulating wealth before time runs out. The objective is to transfer much of it to Tigrai and decamp there (or perhaps overseas) in the event of trouble.

In the book cited in the preceding note the observation is made that TPLF members often say they would secede if chauvinists (presumably Amharas and Oromos) come to power (page 320). All this is a manifestation of the deep-seated antipathy that extremist TPLF members harbour against these two rivals for power: an antipathy which blinds them from appreciating the tragic backlash that is bound to ensue if they persist in their policies. An independent Tigrai built on assets plundered from Ethiopia is the surest prescription for a potent reprisal that would be an unending source of conflict for the new state. More menacingly, Tigreans living in Ethiopia would be exposed to vengeful acts of violence too fearful to contemplate. The silent majority of Tigreans is doubtless conscious of this and will hopefully prevail upon the party fanatics to pursue a policy of multiethnic collaboration and accommodation.

There was a time, according to some reports, when the threat of Tigrai secession came close to being credible. On the eve of the fall of the Mengistu regime when the EPLF and the TPLF had worked out a rapprochement following years of an uneasy relationship, there was talk of a plan to liberate the Tigrigna speaking peoples of Eritrea and Tigrai from what was perceived to be a long period of repression by the Amhara ruling class. The purported goal was to declare independence for both Tigrai and Eritrea and to create of Tigrai-Tigrign industrial state in full control of the Red Sea coast. Underpinning the plan was the idea of securing a resource rich but agrarian hinterland as a source of raw materials and a convenient market for manufactured goods. The homelands of the Amhara, Oromo, Afar, Wollaita, Gurage, etc., were to be held in perpetual economic and political subjugation.

Following the quarrel between the TPLF and EPLF, the idea went up in smoke. There have also been reports of an alternative plan for a Tigrai state with a much expanded area incorporating parts of Gondar, Wollo, and the Afar lands bordering on the Red Sea which would declare independence at the right moment. As we all know, lands have be taken away from all three regions (i.e. Gondar, Wollo, and Afar), although the expansion into the Afar homeland has fallen short of the Red Sea littoral. While one cannot rule out a possible resurgence of the dream of an independent Tigrai state installed on the Red Sea coast, the hurdles have become formidable for any realistic attempt to embark upon such a hair-brained adventure.

An encouraging development countering this grim scenario is the recent establishment of a new multi-ethnic political coalition (*Medrek* or Forum) which seems to understand the value of preserving national unity. Siyye Abraha, Negasso Giddada, Gebru Asrat, and Gizatchew Shifferaw toured the U.S. in the spring of 2010 in the course of which they explained the coalition's aims and objectives. Its political orientation is liberal democracy. And in sharp contrast to the TPLF vision, it stands for inclusion, national cohesion, economic pragmatism, and Ethiopia's historic right of access to the waters of the Red Sea. It is too early to say what impact *Medrek* will have on future developments, although efforts by the ruling party to destabilize and wreck its plans are inevitable. But two observations are worth making. First, the coalition seems to signal an important stage in the evolution of political parties. Here is a party whose leadership includes politicians who appear to have drawn valuable practical lessons from their previous errors, jettisoned their sectarian agendas in favour of the broader and common interests of Ethiopia's peoples, and affirmed the need for political compromise. Secondly, these brave men and women have put together a pan-Ethiopian vision incomparably more appealing than that of the ruling party and capable of mobilizing the majority of their countrymen.

Lessons From India and China

A willingness by our politicians to reassess their past experience is obviously to be welcomed. But it is also important that they occasionally examine the roads traversed by other multicultural societies? Like Ethiopia, practically all the countries in the African continent are a mosaic of ethnic and cultural communities. Unlike Ethiopia, however, none of them has used ethnic identity to be the basis for party or governmental stuctures. Indeed they often take measures to discourage citizens from forming political groups along ethnic lines. Tanzania, a country where tribalism seems to have been effectively defanged, is an inspiring example in this regard.

Apart from this, there is not much that we could learn from our African sister nations. One cannot say, for instance, that Nigeria is secure in her democracy, has achieved enduring social peace, is pulling her people out of poverty and therefore offers lessons in these areas. Given the tragedy of Darfour and the most recent developments in the southern region, Sudan is no better placed to offer pointers. Post-apartheid South Africa is in many ways a special case, as are Mauritius and Botswana which have been doing relatively well economically and politically. Ghana, Morocco, Senegal, and Mauritious are interesting instances of relative stability. On the whole, however, the jury is still out on the track record of African countries as functioning democracies successfully battling poverty.

Further afield we observe the experiences of China, India, and to a lesser degree Japan which might merit closer attention. Historically, there have been intermittent contacts between India and Ethiopia. The country has been a subject of curiosity if not sustained interest among Ethiopian Emperors going back to Emperor Libne Dingel in the sixteenth century and the Gondarine monarchs in the seventeenth to the early nineteenth centuries. More recently, Emperor Haile-Selassie appears to have toyed with the idea of using India and Japan as object lessons for his country's development. A mission was sent early in his reign to explore what could be learnt from the Japanese experience in modernization. As part of his attempt to cultivate amicable relations, the Emperor also floated the idea of a relative (Lij Araya Abebe) as a postential spouse for a Japanese princess. With Ethiopia and Japan swept into the vortex of World War II, the idea was botched in its infancy.

In respect of India, post-war diplomatic relations were established with India and tentative approaches made to emulate India's experience. At one point the Emperor even contemplated a plan to bring Indian settlers to the country, but was dissuaded by advisors (prominent among whom was Ethiopia's Ambassador to India, Emmanuel Abraham). Their fear was that this could in time give rise to political and social friction. Instead, limited cooperation was pursued in manufacturing, trade, and education. A few Indians had been active in commerce ever since the Emperor ascended the throne. At a later stage, a major Indian investor was invited to set up a large textile mill, and a good number of Indian teachers and headmasters were brought over to run elementary and secondary schools during the fifties, sixties, and seventies. Indians also helped establish the Military Academy in Harrar.

Interest in China is more recent and could be traced to the Emperor's state visit in 1972. Young Ethiopian radicals have of course been fascinated with Mao's thinking and revolutionary struggle. At present, it is the country's phenomenal growth that appears to draw attention. Ethiopia's ruling party relies heavily on Chinese financial and technical assistance, particularly in the transport and telecommunications sectors. Looking further back, one could point to certain aspects of China's experience that might have some relevance to the kinds of development challenges Ethiopia faces today. But one should also recognize that there are signficant historical or social dissimilarities that would limit the usefulness of China's experience to Ethiopia's development efforts.

Two points quickly come to mind in pondering where China and Ethiopia differ. The first is the fact that about 92% of mainland China's population is made up of one ethnic group with a pervasive common culture: the Han Chinese. Though sharing a common history and manifesting similar cultural predispositions, Ethiopia's cultural groups do not quite reach the level of cultural homogeneity of the Han Chinese. The second is the political experience of China over the last six and half decades. The country's transformation into a multi-party democracy is not yet in sight. The Communist Party is still largely in control, despite occasional signs of tolerance of citizens critical of the ruling party.

China's political evolution over the last three decades or so offers little by way of replicable lessons for Ethiopia. Even less relevant is China's earlier experience under the much celebrated but brutal leader, Mao Tse-tung. Directly or indirectly, Mao was responsible for the deaths of over 70 million Chinese. Hundreds of millions more were obliged to feed on inedible plants while Mao wallowed in a life of obscene debauchery.[4] No measure of good he did for his country could possibility justify the loss of millions of lives, of the profound pain and despair in which people lived, or of the abject poverty endured for decades by a proud people. We have had our own brand of murderous leaders and have little need to look to Mao's experience.

But China holds out important lessons in the domain of economic policy. In post-Mao China. Deng Xiaoping dramatically departed from Communist orthodoxy and advocated a policy of liberalizing the Chinese economy. The experiment started in the agricultural sector where peasant farmers were allowed a certain degree of freedom in producing and marketing their crops. When criticized for abandoning the hallowed principles of the party, Deng's ringing response was that it did not matter whether the cat was yellow or black so long as it caught mice. This reverberated throughout the country in the years that followed and unshackled China's economy.

China's economic performance today is even more striking, and it might be suggested that there are lessons to learn here as well. While that might have a element of truth, Ethiopia's challenge is not simply economic. It is also political. And politically China offers little besides artful repression. No country practicing repression, artful or otherwise, can be said to be stable. Ethiopia possesses enough repression and political instability to export to other countries which are foolish enough to take it. She should not expect to be commended for importing repressive systems and practices which she is adequately supplied with.

India's experience holds promise in both the political and economic domains. Here too we need to exercise caution. Our ability to draw the right lessons depends on the extent to which we understand our similarities as well as our differences. Ethiopia's experience over the last three and a half decades is a painful reminder of the folly of the blind replication of other countries' policies and practices. What we need to do is to draw broad lessons within which specific policies and actions could be crafted to suit our particular situation.

A major difference between the two countries is that India has been ahead of Ethiopia in the modernization process. As noted by Vincent Smith: "The British period in India came to an end after nearly three and a half centuries of trading, two centuries of political power, and a hundred and thirty years of general supremacy."[5] During this long period, science and technology, commerce, the administration of justice, the civil service, the private press, and civil society organizations developed. In Ethiopia, the process of modernization started in earnest a few years into Emperor Menelik's reign; which is to say, only one hundred and twenty years ago.

India also has a longer history of participatory politics such that by the time the Indian Constitution was being discussed in 1947, Nehru and his colleagues were among its principal and articulate crafters. Their political maturity is encapsulated in the following quotation from a recent book. "These ideas," says Peter Robb about the exchange of views on the draft Constitution, "were debated with a high degree of sophistication among India's already experienced leaders and public. They implied continuity in many respects with the colonial state rather than with the anti-colonial movement."[6] The contrast with the stage managed debate of Ethiopia's draft constitution in 1993 in which political novices predominated (some literally dancing on the floor of conference hall at the conclusion of the deliberations in what seemed to be a party planned act of 'spontaneous joy') requires little elaboration.

The first political party in India was a comparatively later development, but it did not come later than 1885. Outside the fledgling parties that operated in Eritrea before the federation and the nationalist movements that emerged after the breakup of the federal arrangement, the first politically active parties in Ethiopia were the clandestine, student-led, and Marxist inspired All-Ethiopia Socialist Movement which was established in July 1968 and the Ethiopian Peoples' Revolutionary Party which emerged in April 1972.[7] The government's Workers Party of Ethiopia was inaugurated in 1984, amid much fanfare and, it should not be forgotten, in the middle of one of the worst famines on record. All three elitist parties consequently appeared on the scene 80 to 100 years after the grass-roots-based Indian National Congress.

None of this is to suggest that we have to retrace India's long process of economic and political evolution in all its details, but to point out that we need a degree of experience in modern political systems before we can begin to see the signs of a sustainable and truly democratic order. In the meantime, we should resist the temptation to succumb to debilitating thoughts we sometimes hear that our people are not made for democracy, that our leaders have an autocratic heritage which will permanently incapacitate them from working for democracy in earnest, or that opposition parties are a bunch of power hungry and bickering individuals unlikely to be any better than those they wish to replace.

There are other differences as well, some of which work to Ethiopia's advantage. In many ways Indian society is much more fractured than Ethiopia's. Nothing approaching the wicked caste system can be found in Ethiopia's history. In addition, both the level and frequency of communal tension in India today are more pronounced. Traditionally also, the great bulk of Ethiopian women have had far more rights than those of India, be it in matters of divorce, property rights, inheritance, or social standing. India is, of course, a country where spirituality is a much more pervasive human experience than the hermetic life pursued by a tiny minority of the followers of the Ethiopian Orthodox Church.

India and Ethiopia have similarities too. India has a tempestuous past: prolonged wars among communities, violent transitions from one monarch to another involving killings, the blinding of eyes, bloody conflicts between parents and their offspring, among siblings and close relatives as well among other rivals for power. Any Ethiopian who thinks that our history is embarrassingly unique in its medieval brutalities should take time to read the history of India (and of medieval Europe). Of course both countries have for centuries been populated by communities of diverse faiths and cultures.

A more significant similarity for our purpose is the distinctive historical thread of centralized administration that goes back to early times. Chapter 19 has examined the Ethiopian story at some length. Insofar as India is concerned, the following quotations from Robb provide an analogy. "What has made India distinct," says Robb, "is not the vitality of the regional states (many at least the size of European nations), but the trajectory of greater consolidation....from ancient to early modern times." Robb continues: "Thus the present states of the Indian subcontinent may be said to mark a stage in time, in the project of political consolidation and incorporation that began with Chandragupta Maurya and Ashoka, and ebbed and flowed until it produced its current definition and borders, under Mughal and then British rulers."[8]

There are similarities in the cultural area as well, although we should take care not to overstate them. Family connections are strong. In both countries, it is not uncommon to find three generations of a family living under the same roof, sharing food and working in close proximity. The interests of the family take precedence over that of its individual members. Decisions on the most intimate matters affecting individuals, like marriage, are often taken by those who are deemed to be best qualified. Parents choose spouses for their children, a practice fast disappearing in Ethiopia but surprisingly vibrant in India. I recently asked a young Indian engineer whose wife had been chosen for him by his father how he, an educated person, felt about it. "Not only is my father as educated as I," he replied, "but he also has something I do not have: experience. His judgment is bound to be better than mine. And the evidence of that is that I am happily married with three children." As in Ethiopia, the practice will in time probably fade.

The rationale behind this preoccupation with India should be evident. A country as multicultural as Ethiopia and offering striking historical and cultural parallels, India has evolved into a functioning democracy over a period of six decades. Slow at the beginning, its economy has entered a period of rapid growth. This is particularly true of the post-reform years going back to the mid-nineties. Growth rates in the latter part of that period have averaged 8.5% a year. According to a recent World Bank report (*India: Sustaining Rapid Economic Growth*), India is among the world's best performing economies. Although poverty is far from being a thing of the past, there is little doubt that it will be dented significantly if growth rates of this order are sustained.

What is the upshot of all this? Stated briefly, it is that India's combination of democracy and economic development in a relatively stable multicultural setting holds promise for the future of Ethiopia. A vision inspired by India's relatively long experience of democracy and socio-economic development would be immeasurably more reassuring than the TPLF vision of a country built on the double pillars of Marxist ideology and identity politics imposed on 80 million reluctant inhabitants.

What is behind India's story of success as a functioning democracy and a society enjoying a reasonable degree of social peace? Political leadership of an exceptionally high order is without doubt among the more potent explanatory factors. India has been very fortunate in having visionary leaders of the caliber of Mohandas Gandhi and Jawahalaral Nehru to lead the way at a time of momentous change. The same was true of Japan in the latter half of the nineteenth century when Okubo Toshimichi, Ito Hirobumi, Kido Takayoshi and other nationalists of the Meiji restoration introduced policies that were to transform Japan into a modern industrial state. Mustafa Kemal laid the foundations for a secular and resurgent Turkey. Gamal Abdel Nasser was instrumental in mobilizing Arab nationalism to usher an era of considerable social and economic change, although democracy remains a daunting challenge. Nelson Mandela has also been a transformational figure for South Africa. Ethiopia could perhaps do with leaders who might be less luminary, but not less inclusive or visionary. A key component of their vision should be a desire to jettison the current attitude of fractiousness and ethnocentrism in favour of a new vision of transcendent nationalism and social cohesion.

Regrettably, the country's present-day leaders operate within the narrow confines of a one-dimensional ethnic constituency. Their visions, sentiments, and aspirations are largely limited to their ethnic constituencies. Collaboration across the ethnic divide is at best regarded as an economic and political opportunity to be exploited, having little regard to do with a sentiment for commonly shared values. A telling instance of this comes out in an interview the Prime Minister recently gave to an Ethiopian journalist based overseas. In that interview, the journalist expresses his concern about Ethiopia's identity politics. "I am an Oromo," he says. "If I were to assert my identity as an Oromo, would I not run the risk of enfeebling my identity as an Ethiopian?" The Prime Minister says no, and points to the economic and strategic reasons that keep Ethiopia's different ethnic groups together. And in the end concludes thus: "Being Ethiopian *is not a matter of sentiment,* but of objective economic, political, security, and other considerations" (italics added).[9] The Prime Minister is, of course, not

452 | TEKALIGN GEDAMU

altogether without political sentiments, if his rhetoric is to be believed. His sentiments are reserved for the ethnic group from which he hails, as he made clear in another interview a few years ago in which he expressed his pride in being a Tigrean.

But claims by politicians are not always credible. In his recent book, Asegede Gebre-Selassie provides much evidence that Prime Minister Meles has manifested precisous little sentiment for the people of Tigray during the years of struggle, and especially in his dealings with the EPLF when time after time he gave precedence to the interests of Eritrea's leadership over those of 'his own people': the people of Tigray. Former party operatives like Aregawi Berehe and Gebre-Medhin Ar'aya make a similar point in their graphic accounts of how Meles and his close associates in the party hierarchy squandered millions of Birr of aid money on lavish party meetings while the unfortunate people of Tigray were being ravaged by famine. But the point to keep in mind is the Prime Minister's recognition, even if at the level of political rhetoric, that sentiment is among the defining elements for identity. He of course has ethnic identity in mind, but the logic applies equally to national identity.

Being Ethiopian *is*, of course, a matter of sentiment and not simply a question of economic or political convenience. It is the pride in and the joy of sharing a common history and culture. It is the strong feeling of attachment to a common ancestral homeland which is held in custody for one's children, grandchildren and succeeding generations. It is the obligation to manage the nation's resources prudently and responsibly, shield them from the ravages of environmental degradation and from the mindless plunder of parochial groups and unscrupulous foreign investors. It is the uplifting sentiment of a common destiny, and a common identity. Consider, for a moment, the following manifestations of sentiment for one's nation.

Major Belihou had gone to the Sudan soon after the Fascist occupation of Ethiopia in 1936. He was restless there and returned to his homeland, saying: "I was not happy living in Khartoum though I was leading a comfortable life. I chose to return and die in my country. If I get killed, is my body not returning to my soil? And if perchance vultures feast on my body, are they not Ethiopian vultures?"[10]

When marathon runner Abebe Bikila conquered Rome and Tokyo in the summer Olympics of the sixties and the Ethiopian flag was raised to the tune of the national anthem, were not his compatriots elated, as they were years later when Mamo Wolde, Mirutz Yifter, Derartu Tulu, and Haile Gebre-Selassie won their races? Doesn't Emperor Tewodros's vision of a strong united Ethiopia and his decision to take his own life rather than surrender to the enemy evoke pride in the hearts of Ethiopians, in the same way as Emperor Yohannes's victories over the soldiers of Egypt's Khedive Isma'il Pasha, or his supreme sacrifice in Metemma. Did Emperor Menelik's triumph over Italy not rekindle Europe's memories of a historic people that will not tolerate an affront to their independence and national identity? And what Ethiopian is he who does not derive pride from that? Do we not celebrate the memory of the sons and daughters of this land who stood in valiant defiance of a Fascist enemy incomparably better armed: of Abebe Aregai of Shoa, Belai Zelleke of Gojjam, Hailu Kebede of Wag, Gerusu Duki of Maru, Hailu Wonde of Tigray, Amoraw Woubneh of Gondar, Jagamma Kello of Metcha, Omar Semeter of Harrar, lady Shewareged Gedle of Shoa and many others.

Few Ethiopians who have seen film footage or read the prophetic address of Emperor Haile-Selassie at the League of Nations in 1936 could resist a sentiment of pride in a leader who stood so morally tall among a gathering of the high and the mighty who had lost their moral compass. Indeed, that sentiment went far beyond Ethiopia and moved the hearts of large sections of the world community, especially those in the developing world. Ethiopians are, of course, proud of their written language and of their heritage of Axum, Lalibella, Gondar and Harrar.

All these *are sentiments* that transcend the barriers of ethnicity and ideology. They are also potent agents of national cohesion, far more potent than the economic and political rewards which come with being big geographically. It is the absence of such sentiments that explains why former Yugoslavia and the Soviet Union disintegrated; and why China and Japan, or Thailand and Vietnam, or Iraq and Iran do not merge to form even larger and more advantageous economic and political entities. And it is the abiding sentiment of a common identity that has driven European nations to come together in a union of over 490 million people. Ethiopia badly needs leaders who appreciate the importance of this cardinal political imperative and who embrace the challenge of building a rejuvenated nation of fraternal communities on the foundations of a heritage at once rich and inspiring.

Nationalism could be taken to excesses, of course. In the Ethiopian context, however, the risks are less pernicious than those emanating from ethnic and religious extremism. And in the fullness of time, the weight of nationalism as an agent of social and political cohesion is bound to make way for more durable values like democracy, individual liberty, culture, and an ever expanding vista of artistic and intellectual pursuits which not only create further bonds among a nation's citizens but also serve as bridges to outside cultures and communities. And to humanity at large.

Final Words

The challenges confronting the present generation of Ethiopians are no less daunting than those of preceding generations in their most trying of times. Much has been said in the foregoing chapters about the prospects for meeting these challenges. They are not altogether discouraging. But it will take time for things to take a turn for the better, unless of course there is a precipitous change occasioned by an internal crisis, which is always a possibility. As I indicated before, there is little sign today that the TPLF is about to re-examine its dual doctrines of revolutionary democracy and identity politics. On the contrary, its leaders are employing every means at their disposal to persist in their ways and to prolong their hold on power. Their security apparatus, military establishment, and bureaucracy are all primed to that objective. Torture and intimidation are often employed by security personnel to extract confessions of alleged crimes. An appalling manifestation of this is given in a recent and what appears to be authentic report of severe maltreatment of political detainees at the central investigation branch of the Federal Police in Addis Ababa.

The account is put together by persons in the internal security, criminal investigation, and prisons administration departments of the government. It is based on eyewitness reports of staff working in close proximity with those who carry out acts of physical and psychological torture. The narrative focuses on the alleged plot by the opposition Geunbot Seven Party to murder senior officials of the government and take over power. In an extensive thirty-two page report which gives chapter and verse of: who did what to whom; the complicity of judges; the hierarchy of responsible officers, all Tigreans including the head of the central investigation department (Tadesse Messeret), the overall chief of internal security (Getachew Assefa), and the Prime Minister (Meles Zenawi); the final confessions of the victims following unbearable beatings (some with the intent to castrate male victims); the beating of females on their breasts (Sister Emawayish Alemu); subjecting victims to electric shocks administrered to the teeth; mock summary executions; and hateful ethnic insults towards Amhara detainees; the authors of the report conclude that the courts passed guilty verdicts on the accused for what were essentially a series of bogus charges.[11] All were sentenced to death or life imprisonment

TPLF's strategy is to be in full control of the levers of economic and political power for the long run. A statement ascribed to Meles Zenawi by a former collaborator reports him as having once said: "To gain power, we had to endure being whipped on our backs with red hot steel chains."[12] The inference is plain that the party will not give up power for which it has paid a heavy price.

Another statement of Meles is unambiguous about the party's ultimate objective: "When Revolutionary Democracy permeates the entire society," he says in a party document, "individuals will start to think alike and all persons will cease having their own independent outlook. In this order, individual thinking becomes simply part of collective thinking because *the individual will not be in a position to reflect on concepts that have not been prescribed by Revolutionary Democracy.*"[13] (Italics added). How someone who is doubtless aware of the incalculable sufferings that this kind of thinking has brought to countless lives in Eastern Europe and the developing world could start afresh to chart a similar course for his own countrymen is mind boggling. To try to uncover the psychological reasons driving him in this direction would be a distraction from the central concern of the present exercise. Whatever they are, the vision of human beings looking, behaving, and acting as if they were inanimate entities coming off an assembly line will ultimately come to ruin, in the same way as the insane fantasies of tyrants like Lenin, Stalin, Hitler, and Mussolini.

No one could seriously contend that such a disquieting vision is on the wish list of the people of Ethiopia.

The wind of change that has swept away decades of tyranny in Tunisia and Egypt in January 2011 and that has sent shock waves to Morocco, Algeria, Libya, Syria, Bahrain, Yemen, and others in the Middle should serve as a potent warning for the regime that its own turn is only a matter of when and not if. Yet, it is unlikely that the right lessons are being drawn. In all probability the security apparatus of the regime is currently racking its brains as to how that storm could be averted and continuity assured.

But the more strenuously the ruling party tries to prolong its tenure of power, the closer it gets to the day of its violent ejection. It can hardly be said that that is something to look forward to. Throughout her history, Ethiopia has had more than her fair share of bloody successions. It would be tragic if yet more blood were to be shed to bring down the present regime. It is essential that all avenues for peaceful change must first be exhausted, however unappealing, time consuming, and inefficacious they might appear.

In this regard, it would not be entirely unreasonable to contemplate a situation in which the silent majority of mainstream Tigreans find it in their long-term interest to work with their Ethiopian compatriots in facilitating the emergence of a more pragmatic and inclusive leadership. For centuries, the people of Tigrai have cohabited a common ancestral land with Amharas, Oromos, Gurages, Afars and other communities; have intermarried, have quarreled and made peace, and possess a history and culture they share. There is no reason why they should acquiesce in TPLF's ludicrous misrepresentation of their identity as a people apart; as a community singled out for egregious acts of injustice by past regimes. Or acquiesce in the party's campaign of political repression, ethnic animosity, ideological dogmatism, and disdain for the nation's cultural heritage; all carried out in their name.

They have the responsibility of being in the forefront of the struggle for peaceful change; a responsibility to expose the fraudulent claim of the party that it speaks and acts on their behalf. For they have never granted it their mandate in anything resembling a free and fair plebiscite. Not to do so would give credence to the widely held but unproven allegation that the majority of them stand behind the party; a party whose agenda has no appeal for the people of Ethiopia. The 2010 election results plainly showed that the party's level of support is as impressive as that of the failed regimes of Soviet Russia and Eastern Europe which had to routinely fabricate bogus poll numbers to persuade themselves, and no one else, that they have near total support among the electorate. Failure by mainstream Tigreans to act now would be to turn a blind eye to the potential of a haunting backlash in subsequent years: a risk party fanatics have willfully ignored. And to confirm the growing sentiment among Ethiopians that violence is the only way left to get rid of the regime.

To say Tigreans have a special responsibility to help us get rid of TPLF tyrants does not exonerate non-Tigreans. Indeed, the ultimate responsibility rests squarely on the shoulders of *all Ethiopians*. It is they who should assume leadership in securing the vitality of their nation. If they as a people fail to rise above their debilitating ethnic antagonisms, if they fail to mobilize their multiple bonds to undo the damage wreaked by those who sow discord in their midst, if their thoughts and dreams fail to rise above the adversities of their daily lives, it will not do to look for scapegoats, or to say that Ethiopia's God has finally forsaken his people. "Anyone who marries my mother I consider my father," goes an unedifying Ethiopian saying. "When hard times and flying lances approach," goes another, "the prudent thing to do is to duck and let them pass;" as if to say that it would be pointless to try to understand the force that propels the lances and the hard times, and do something about them.

The people of Ethiopia have a choice, however. "When threads of yarn unite," goes another saying, "they make a rope to immobilize a lion." That is the more instructive and inspirational maxim. There are many instances in Ethiopia's history when the people have risen as one to overcome forces bent on destroying their viability as a nation. It would be a grave error to underestimate their resilience, as it would to preclude the emergence of a new breed of leaders climbing out of their ethnic foxholes and standing on the mountain tops of their glorious history to offer their countrymen a vigorous, new, pan-Ethiopian vision of a fraternal people free of the claws of a primordial ethnic animosity, of autocracy, and a humiliating poverty that has become the defining stigma of a once proud people.

Appendix 1

Provisional Military Government of Ethiopia (Translated from the Amharic original)

Hidar 13, 1967 (23 November 1974)
Operations and Security Officer of the Dergue
Addis Ababa

VERY URGENT

Subject: Implementation of a High Level Political Decision
Regarding Former Government Officials

Having accepted the responsibility to lead the people's uprising against the cruelties of the feudal order, members of the Dergue who have been selected from the ranks of the oppressed in the military have assumed the authority to manage the nation's affairs.

Following its establishment, the revolutionary Dergue not only succeeded in liberating the country from the autocratic rule of the monarchs but also undertook to round up senior civilian and military officials of Emperor Haile-Selassie. After taking time to review their cases, it has finally arrived at a high level political decision in regard to those senior officials who, over a forty-year period, have been plundering and oppressing the downtrodden people of Ethiopia.

The decision was taken in a recent high level meeting of the Dergue at which it was determined unanimously to impose a revolutionary measure on the first batch of former officials whose names are attached to this order.

Order:

1. Lieutenant General Aman Andom to be apprehended at his residence and to be brought to the Palace to be with the other detainees.[1]

2. A pit large enough to accommodate 54 bodies to be excavated by a bulldozer in the premises of the central prison. At 8:00 p.m. senior civilian and military officials numbered 1 to 54 to be separated from the rest of the detainees, and;

3. These officials to be driven to the premises of the central prison at 8:00 p.m. and be subsequently shot.

Seal Signed
Provisional Military Government of Ethiopia
Mengistu Haile-Mariam, Major
First Deputy Chairman
Provisional Military Adminstrative Council

Lt. General Aman Amdom Michael	Chairman of the Dergue Chairman of the Council of Ministers
Lt. General Abiy Abebe	Minister of Defence
Lt. General Issa'iyas Gebre Selassie	Member of Parliament (Upper House)
Lt. General Assefa Ayene	Minister of Transport & Communications
Admiral Iskinder Desta	Commander of the Navy
Lt. General Diresse Dubale	Commander of the Ground Forces,Army
Lt. General Debebe Haile-Mariam	Emperor's Resident Representative, Eritrea
Lt. General Assefa Demissie	Aide-de-Camp to the former Emperor
Lt. General Abebe Gemeda	Commander, Imperial Guard
Lt. General Yilma Shibeshi	Commander, the Police Force
Lt. General Haile Baykedagn	Chief of the Staff, the Armed Force
Lt. General Belette Abebe	Chief of Staff, the Territorial Army
Maj. General Gashaw Kebede	High Government Official
Maj. General Siyoum Gedle-Giorgis	High Government Official
Maj. General Tafesse Lemma	High Government Official
Brig. General Wondimu Abebe	High Government Official
Brig. General Girma Yohannes	Commander of the Police, Wollo Province
Brig. General Mulugeta W. Yohannes	Commander of the Para-military Police
Colonel Solomon Kedir	Chief of Intelligence
Colonel Yigezu Yimeney[2]	High Government Official
Colonel Alem Zaud Tessema	Command of the Air Borne Regiment
Colonel Tassew Mojo	Armed Escort, the Imperial Palace
Lt. Colonel Tamrat Yigezu	Emperor's Resident Representative, Gondar
Maj. Berhane Mecha	Police Officer
Capt. Belai Tsegaye[3]	

Lt. Tesfaye Tekle	
Corporal Tekle Haile	
Aklilu Habte-Wold	Prime Minister
Lij Endalkatchew Makonnen	Prime Minister
Lij Michael Imru[4]	Prime Minister
Ras Asrate Kassa	Chairman, Crown Council
Ras Mesfin Sileshi	Emperor's Resident Representative, Shoa
Dr. Tesfaye Gebre-Egziabher	Minister of Information
Afenegus Abeje Debalk	President, His Majesty's Court
Ato Abebe Retta	Member, Crown Council
Ato Akale-Work Habte-Wold	Minister of Justice
Ato Mulatu Debebe	Minister of Community Development and Social Affairs
Ato Nebiye-Leul Kifle	Vice Minister, Imperial Cabinet
Ato Solomon Gebre-Mariam	Vice Minister, Ministry of Pen
Ato Tegegn Yeteshawork	Vice Minister, Ministry of Information
Lij Hailu Desta	Assistant Minister, Ministry of Defence
Dejazmatch A'emro-Selassie Abebe	Emperor's Res. Rep., Gamu Goffa
Dejazmatch Workineh Wolde-Amanuel	Emperor's Res. Rep., Harrar
Dejazmatch Solomon Abraham	High Official in retirement
Dejazmatch Sahlu Defaye	Emperor's Res. Rep., Arussi
Dejazmatch Worku Enko-Selassie	Emperor's Res. Rep., Illubabor
Dejazmatch Legesse Bezu	Emperor's Res. Rep., Wollo
Fitawrari Tadesse Enko	Governor, Limmu District
Dejazmatch Kifle Ergetu	High Official in retirement
Fitawrari Amede Aberra	Farmer
Dejazmatch Kebede Ali Wolle	Emperor's Deputy Res. Rep., Wollo
Fitawrari Demiss Alamirrew	Governor, Gore District
Dejazmatch Yilma Aboye[5]	Official, Palace Protocol
Ato Hailu Teklu	Official, Imperial Palace

Appendix 2

Author's Letter of Resignation (Translated from the Amharic original)

3 January 1976
General Tafari Banti
Chairman
Provisional Administrative Military Council

Though not politically inclined, I have been obliged to serve in various political capacities on account of the political problems that were triggered since February 1974. It now seems to me that the time has come for many of us to pursue our respective professional interests and inclinations.

I accordingly request the Provisional Administrative Military Council to allow me to relinquish my membership of the Council of Ministers.

Signed
Tekalign Gedamu

cc Major Mengistu Haile-Mariam
First Deputy Chairman
The Provisional Administrative Military Council

Lt. Colonel Atnafu Abate
Second Deputy Chairman
The Provisional Administrative Military Council

Notes

CHAPTER 1

1. *With Ethiopian Rulers: A Biography of Hasib Ydlibi by May Ydlibi*, Addis Ababa University Press, 2006.

2. At that time, the colonial powers (Britain, France, and Italy) were busy pushing into Ethiopian territory from all directions. The Egyptians, though themselves subjects of the Ottoman Empire, had their own territorial ambitions and had dispatched two military expeditions against Emperor Yohannes. Both were decisively beaten back.

3. *Kayehut Kemastawisew*, the Amharic Memoires of Ras Imru published by Addis Ababa University Press, 2009 (2001 in the Julian calendar), pages 280 ff.

4. Memhir Abozen was the father of the much-admired Kebede Abozen, at various times Deputy Chief Justice of the Province of Illubabor, Assistant Minister of Public Works, Deputy Mayor of Addis Ababa, Mayor of Gondar and finally Senator in the Upper Chamber of Parliament. His defiant manner and progressive political views often got him into trouble with the authorities.

5. *Kibre Negest*, Chapter 44, sections 10-12.

6. Aleqa's Amharic response was: "Abune Michael deg neberu; enantem deg gedelachihu." This could be interpreted in one of two ways: (i)Abune Michael was a good man, and you killed a good man, which Aleqa meant. Or (ii) Abune Michael was a good man, and your killing was good," the superficial meaning picked up by the interpreter.

7. Ato Emmanuel Abraham recently explained to me that the object of this tradition was simply to release the passions of youth within circumscribed limits. Mothers would caution their daughters not to succumb to the temptations of sexual intercourse; for a girl would seriously compromise her chances of marriage if she were to become pregnant. He also informed me that the boys would refer to their steady girlfriends as 'Quebdo'.

8. The manuscript consists of court records on the trial and execution of Belai and is found among the collection of the personal papers of Blatta Mersie Hazzan Wolde-Kirkos.

9. It was generally believed that Belai had been requested by Ras Hailu Tekle-Haimanot not to stand in the way of the Fascist troops, a request with which he complied. He was eager to be in the good books of Ras Hailu Tekle-Haimanot who, though a Fascist collaborator, was the son of King Tekle-Haimanot of Gojjam and commanded respect among the population of Gojjam. It was said that Belai, a Gojjamei commoner, was hoping to marry the daughter of the Ras and thus elevate himself to the pinnacle of the social ladder of his native region.

10. Anthony Mockler who gives a detailed account of this incident does not say that Wingate asked for any disciplinary measures; only that "there was nothing Wingate could do, except fume." Mockler is also the source for parts of the preceding and subsequent narratives. See Mockler, *Haile Selassie's War*, Random House, New York, page 359.

11. A credible source says that Emperor Haile-Selassie had been ill at ease with the sentence, had tried to stop the execution at the very last minute, but that he had acted too late. Another source holds the view that the Emperor was remorseful about Belai's execution. Soon after arranging an agreement between Morocco and Algeria regarding a border dispute, Foreign Minister Ketema Yifru took the opportunity of the happy occasion to pose an interesting question: "You have done great things for this continent and for your country, your majesty. But I am curious to know if there is anything which you might look back at with regret in the course of your long reign?" Yes, replied the Emperor: the execution of Belai Zelleke. (I am grateful to Zewde Retta who kindly provided this information.)

CHAPTER 2

1. From an unpublished monograph entitled, "Brief Narrative of Our Voyage From Djibuti to Haifa With the Abyssinian Royal Family and Staff on Board," by Captain C. E. Morgan, H. M. S. Enterprise, April 1936.

2. Edward Said, the Palestinian-born author and academic, speaks of a similar experience with a milk machine on his first visit to the U.S. in 1948. "I made repeated trips to the milk spigot," he says, "twice forgot to place a glass underneath (making a spectacle of myself as I watched the milk pour itself into the trough), twice mistook "buttermilk" for ordinary milk, and twice left the glass I had paid for sitting rather pointlessly on the counter." *Out of Place: A Memoir*, by Edward W. Said, Vintage Books, New York, 2000, page 134.

CHAPTER 3

1. At about that time, Alex Quaison-Sackey, the Ghanaian diplomat who served as his country's Permanent Representative at the U.N., wrote a book entitled *Africa Unbound* (reminiscent of *Ethiopia Unbound*, authored by another Ghanaian, Casely Hayford) in which he expounded a euphoric vision of a resurgent Africa. We were captivated by the title and vision of the book.

2. Huberman and Sweezy, *Cuba: Anatomy of a Revolution*, Monthly Review Press, July-August 1960. Half a century later, I still keep in my study a much thumbed copy of the special issue.

3. As I expected, she was shocked that I had decided to marry a white girl. When I was growing up with her she had told me that in the course of her long life two incidents had scared her so badly that she had gone without sleep for days. One of these was when she first saw a white person. She could not get over the impression that the man had been skinned alive and was walking around merrily regardless. In his book on Ethiopia, John Spencer tells the story of a Christian village woman who, it seems, was similarly shocked by his white face and cried "Christos, Christos" in astonishment. He, however, was puzzled that the woman should mistake a beardless white man like himself for Jesus Christ. See Spencer, John H., *The Lion at Bay*, Reference Publications, Algonac, Michigan, 1987, page 120.

4. According to one account, Workineh requested Ras Imru Haile-Selassie, whom the coup leaders had named Prime Minister but who was communicating with the American Ambassador, to explore a peaceful resolution to the crisis: with himself as emissary to the Ambassador. Workineh said that once he was out, he would take measures to undo the coup which he knew would not succeed. The Ras was reluctant to get involved in this risky venture. The Police Commissioner who was also drawn to the coup unwittingly said to the Ras: "Are you also with these boys?" It was Ras Imru himself who communicated this to Dejazmatch Wolde-Semait who was kind enough to pass it on to me. In his account of these events, Richard Greenfield cites General Mengistu's testimony at his trial in which he says Ras Imru considered using Workineh as the carrier of his message, but eventually chose Germame to talk to the Ambassador. The plan did not succeed. See Greenfield, R., *Ethiopia: A New Political History*, Frederick A. Praeger, New York, 1965, page 426.

5. *Gizzie* in Amharic literally translates into 'time'. In saying this, Mengistu was conveying the notion that the high officials who were executed had been the victims of a measure whose time had come; a remarkable thing to say for someone who had been widely perceived as a womanizing and carefree bon-vivant.

6. The interplay between culture and economic development has a long history in development economics. Culture can strongly influence the prospects for a country's political and economic progress, but is in turn influenced by economic and political forces. See Harrison, Lawrence E. and Huntington, Samuel P. (editors) *Culture Matters: How Values Shape Human Progress*, Basic Books, New York, 2000.

7. On April 30, 2006 I was on the computer putting these notes together. I took a lunch break and subsequently turned on the news channel on BBC television. It was announced that John Kenneth Galbraith had passed away at the age of 97. The announcer said that unlike other economists of his day, his main instrument for driving a point home was not some fancy econometric model, but his formidable wit, one instance of which I have given.

CHAPTER 4

1. *Autobiography: Takele Wolde-Hawariat*, written in Amharic and published by the Addis Ababa University Press, in 2005 (1998 in the Julian Calendar), page 155.

2. See Birhanu Dinke's short Amharic piece on Emperor Haile -Selassie entitled *Keissarina Abyot* (Caesar and Revolution) June 1981. Publisher and place of publication not indicated. The Amharic equivalent of the phrase 'remained behind' (izziaw bekeru neber) could also be taken to mean 'would have died.' Birhanu himself was a dissenter of some repute who had left his post as Ethiopia's Ambassador to the U.S. in opposition to the Emperor. But in this booklet, he shows a remarkable degree of detachment in assessing Emperor Haile-Selaassie's rule and personal traits.

3. See for instance *Yachi Ken Teressach* (The Day No Longer Remembered), a personal account in Amharic of the war years by Hiywot Hiddaru, Berhanina Selam Press, Addis Ababa, 1975, pages 139-141.

4. I met Afenegus Gebre-Medhin for the first (and last) time in 1991 through a common friend. The Afenegus was one of a handful of political dissidents who held considerable propaganda value for the Dergue. This was cleverly exploited in one or two cases. But not with the independent minded Gebre-Medhin who had never been anybody's tool.

5. Information obtained from Dejazmatch Wode-Semait Gebre-Wold who succeeded Germame as Governor of the district and stayed on that job for over ten years. He was no less progressive than Germame but was relatively more purposeful. He transformed his district into a model development region which attracted the attention of the World Bank and which led to a Bank funded research and development programme named the Wollamo Agricultural Development Unit (WADU).

CHAPTER 5

1. The Prime Minister had not only been Foreign Minister, but had also been an active participant in the debate on the drafting of the U.N. charter. He was also a signatory.

2. Haddis is best known for his novel *Fikir Eske Mekabir* (Love Unto The Grave) in which he portrays feudal Ethiopia in a manner which I thought might not exactly please Emperor Haile-Selassie. When I asked him if he ever ran into trouble with him on that account, he replied, "You forget that the Emperor regards himself as someone who did away with feudalism in Ethiopia."

3. The manuscript, which is in the possession of the writer, is entitled Memorandum (Mastawesha in Amharic) and is dated January 31, 1960 (Tirr 23, 1953 in the Julian Calendar). A copy is also available at the Library of the Institute of Ethiopian Studies in Addis Ababa.

4. The Prime Minister gave the 57-page narrative to the Chairman of the Inquiry Commission on September 22, 1974. The Commission was established by the government of Endalkatchew Makonnen to investigate the circumstances of the famine which devastated Wollo in 1973/1974 with the view to establishing the accountability of public officials.

5. I knew Haddis's father, Memhir Alemayehou. He was an Orthodox priest who would perhaps not be best described as poor. In the context of Haddis' discussion, however, one can understand him being put in that category. And, of course, Haddis's proximity with the common man was much closer than the Emperor's and he surely encountered instances of poverty much more frequently than the monarch.

CHPATER 6

1. See Brecher, Michael, *Nehru: A Political Biography*, Beacon Press, Boston, 1959, pages 76 and 201.

2. Among those who rose to cabinet position during Dergue rule were Hailu Yimenu, Mersie Ejigu, Aklilu Afework, Tekola Dejene, Wole Chekol, Yusuf Ahmed, Tesfaye Maru and Shifferaw Jammo, although Shifferaw was averse to assuming the chores of office and served for a brief period only. Philipos Wolde-Mariam and Yusuf Abdullahi were appointed to cabinet and sub-cabinet positions, respectively, by the EPRDF/TPLF regime.

3. I am indebted to the late Ato Menassie Lemma and to Colonel Semret Medhane for much of the material in this section: to Menassie on the story of how the Airline was created and to Semret, the first Ethiopian General Manager of Ethiopian Air Lines, on how TWA management was gradually phased out. Semret is also responsible for putting together the details of the two projects I describe in this narrative later on. John Spencer claims that it was he who "entirely on my own initiative" contacted a U.S. State Department official during the San Francisco meeting to find out if one of the American airlines might be interested to establish an Ethiopian national carrier and that everything followed from there. The idea of establishing a national carrier was, however, one of the Emperor's more pressing priorities for which he had requested British assistance in the early forties but which had been denied. Prior to the war, a couple of light aircraft were used to fly messages and passengers on government business between Addis Ababa and provincial capitals. The idea of a national carrier was therefore not new to government officials. Spencer was doubtless aware of all this and might have raised the subject with U.S. officials, but it is doubtful that his intervention was as crucial as he suggests.

4. Captain Alemayehou tells his story in a recently published book entitled *Hiywote Bemidrna Be'ayyer* (My Life on Earth and in the Air), February 2005, Addis Ababa.

5. General Assefa Ayene gave me a copy of the feasibility study in 1973 when I was Planning Commissioner. My first reaction to the feasibility of producing the aircraft locally was one of hesitation, as I had at that time no firm idea of the airline's capability in this regard.

6. The first address was delivered on 22 Nehassie 1951 (28 August 1959) and the second on 7 Meskerem 1952 (19 September 1959). See the government daily Addis Zemen , Nehassie 23, 1951 and Meskerem 8, 1952.

7. Unbeknown to us at the time, Chou en Lai was suffering from cancer of the bladder and Mao Tse-tung had turned down his request for surgery. This and Mao's cruel treatment of other party colleagues, the Chinese people and members of his own family is exposed in rich detail in *Mao: The Unknown Story* by Jung Chang and Jon Halliday, Anchor Books, New York, 2005. Chou En-Lai's more disagreeable traits also come out in this remarkable book, which removes

any lingering doubts young people in the third world might have about the total bankruptcy of Maoism as a model for developing countries. I come back to this theme in the concluding chapter of the book.

8. The friendship stadium, the likes of which the Chinese had put up in a number of African countries, was never built. The project came up for official government approval in the course of the 1975 budget discussions. I was then the Chairman of the Economic and Social Committee of the Cabinet which reviewed the budget before Cabinet consideration. Despite my attempts, the Committee failed to endorse the project. I am inclined to think that, had it been endorsed, the Dergue might not have approved it; as its primary focus at the time was Soviet Russia, not China.

9. Ministry of Finance officials should know whether the Chinese ultimately kept their word.

10. In his autobiography Emmanuel Abraham gives a detailed account of his amicable relations with Emperor Haile-Selassie. See *Reminiscences of My Life*, Lunde Forlag, Oslo, Norway, 1995. At this point in time, however, his relations with the Emperor were somewhat strained and occasionally gave rise to acrimonious encounters of the kind described here.

11. 1 See Strategy Outline of the Fourth Five-Year Plan: 1974/75 to 1978/79, Planning Commission Office, Addis Ababa , 1974, page I.1

12. These figures compare favourably with those of other developing countries, as in the case of India whose per capita income was growing by about 2% in the early fifties. See Brecher, Michael, op. cit., page 202.

13. In the mid-sixties, Yohannes was ranked first in a competition organized by the United States Air Force (labeled Top Guns) to test the shooting skills of fighter pilots. Yohannes's competitors were air force officers from the U.S., Europe, and other regions with fairly well advanced military establishments.

14. See Tadesse Tamrat, *Church and State in Ethiopia: 1270-1527*, Oxford University Press, London, 1972, pages 258-265.

15. See Beckingham, C.F., and Huntingford, G.W. B., (editors), *The Prester John of the Indies*, Cambridge University Press, Cambridge, 1961. The book is a narrative of the travels of Francisco Alvarez in Ethiopia in the years 1520-1526. It might be of interest to cite letters dispatched by Emperor Libna Dingel to two of his Portuguese counterparts and to the colonial administrator in Goa. The first was to King Dom Manoel in which the Emperor, having introduced himself in the high flying style of the period ("beloved of God, prop of the faith, descendent of the lineage of Judah, son of David, of Solomon, son of the Pillar of Tsion [i.e. Amde Tsion], Emperor of the high and vast Ethiopia", etc.) requests the King to send him different types of artisans whose expenses he would fully cover. "Send me craftsmen ," reads the letter, "who can make figures of gold and silver, copper, iron, tin, and lead ... for the churches; and craftsmen in type-founding to make books in our characters...; and craftsmen in gilding with gold leaf to make the gold leaf." (page 501). A second letter was addressed to King Dom Joam, successor to Dom Manoel, in which he asks for "artificers to make images, and swords and arms for all sorts of fighting, and also masons and carpenters, and men who make medicines, and physicians and surgeons to cure illnesses;..... and men who also know how to extract gold and silver and copper from the veins .. and make sheet lead and earthenware" (page 505) . A third letter was sent to Diego Lopez de Sequeira, Captain Major of the Indies: "Your kindness will now be fulfilled in that which I desire, and so send me craftsmen to work gold and silver, to make swords, and weapons of iron and helmets, and masons to build houses, and skilled men to make vineyards and gardens, and all other craftsmen that are necessary, and in better crafts that are named, and to make lead to cover churches, and to make clay tiles in our country, so that we may not cover our houses with grass: of this we have great need, and we are

very distressed at not having them." page 478. Interestingly, Henri Troyat's biography of Tsar Ivan the Terrible of Russia (1530-1584) indicates (page 90) that in 1555 the Tsar instructed his envoy to England to "hire craftsmen, miners, and doctors to take back to Moscow...... so as to steal some scraps of knowledge from them" [the English]. This first attempt by a Russian sovereign to import technology came some three decades after the letter of Emperor Libne Dingel. Similar messages were sent later by Emperors Sertse-Dingel (1563-1597), Ze-Dingel (1603-1604), Susinyos (1607-1632) and others. It is remarkable how these early Emperors would articulate their needs in a manner which several centuries later would become a key facet in relations between developed and developing countries: i.e. the phenomenon of technical assistance.

16. Emperor Tewodros's vision and lofty ambitions were scarcely matched by the little he was able to accomplish, thanks to resistance by the established church and the landed gentry. Blessed by a long and relatively peaceful reign Menelik accomplished more. He manifested a strong predisposition for new ideas and techniques, acquired in part from his association with European prisoners during his days of captivity in the court of Emperor Tewodros. He was deft, so it was said, in dismantling watches and putting the pieces back together again. He was eager to get the modern camera and X-ray machines and, naturally, the motor vehicle. The mulberry tree for the propagation of silk worms and the eucalyptus tree were imported during his reign.

CHPATER 7

1. The six-page note is untitled, except for a word at the top left hand corner which reads "copy" and a phrase at the right hand corner which reads "copied later." It was reviewed by Prime Minister Makonnen Endalkatchew and Minister of Finance Makonnen Habte-Wold who, together with Wolde-Giorgis, had been requested by the Emperor to go through the memo of the unnamed officials. Wolde-Giorgis's draft response was accepted without amendment by the two Makonnens.

2. The response is a three-page note entitled "Memorandum." On the left hand corner is the date of the memo (April 1947) below which is written "lejanhoy yekerebe" (presented to the His Majesty). The note looks like a hand written copy of the original apparently made by Wolde-Giorgis himself for his own file.

3. Mosley, Leonard; *Haile Selassie: The Conquering Lion*, Prentice-Hall, U.S.A., 1965, pages 247 and 257; and Makonnen Tegegn, Walda-Giyorgis Walda Yohannes and the Haile Selassie Government, North East African Studies, Vol. 4, No. 2, (New Series) 1997, page 113.

4. Makonnen Tegegn, *Walda-Giyorgis Walda-Yohannes and the Haile Selassie Govenmenet* p 123. It is not clear what the author has in mind when he writes about Wolde-Giorgis's unpublished memoirs. Assefa Wolde-Giorgis says that his father had indeed written some notes for the record but that these were removed from his summer home in Debre-Zeit by a neighbour (an Air Force officer) during the early days of the 1974 revolution.

5. Was there a possibility, one is tempted to ask, for the two groups to evolve into modern political parties? Had parties been allowed, it is conceivable that political discourse might have revolved around class interests, and the pains of identity politics from which we currently suffer might have been constrained. In time, the situation might have paved the way to a culture of non-violent political give and take. Regrettably, political parties were discouraged for fear that their establishment would be along ethnic lines and that this would undermine national unity, an apprehension borne out by TPLF's political program.

6. From a copy of the original kindly made available by Zauwde Retta.

7. From an unpublished monograph by Berhanu Asresse to whom Workineh disclosed the account.

8. Like leaders in his position, the Emperor was suspicious of the advice of subordinates on issues of consequence. Early in the soldiers' movement, Prime Minster Endalkatchew Makonnen advised that the consequences would be grave for the country unless he did something about it. The Emperor's reply was:"Both the armed forces and the people are with us. You are simply expressing your personal ambition for political power." The quotation is from an interview given by Ato Gebre-Tsadik Haile-Mariam who was a Dergue detainee along with Endalkatchew Makonnen and from whom he got the story. See the Amharic monthly magazine *Ityop*, vol. 4. no. 039, Pagumen 1994 (September 2001).

9. The incident was related to me by Dejazmatch Wolde-Semait Gebre-Wold who was responsible for organizing the trip and was among the passengers on the helicopter.

10. During the Gondarine period and the subsequent Era of Princes (17th and 18th centuries), Shoa (one of the homelands of the Amhara peoples) emerged as an autonomous kingdom in middle Ethiopia. Following the death of Emperor Yohannes, a descendant of the royal house of Shoa (Menelik II) ascended the throne. Emperor Haile-Selassie was the successor of that royal line and was occasionally perceived as a Shoan Amhara monarch even by Amharas from Gondar, Gojjam, and Wollo.

11. Tekle-Hawariat *Autobiography*, op.cit., page 302

12. An Imperial Guard officer (Major Angagaw) who worked with General Mulugeta Buli for a number of years and who later wrote a short undated monograph on the 1960 coup d'état speaks of the General's strong leadership qualities: his capacity for organization and management, for military planning, and his probity and personal discipline. See *Yetahsas Yemefenkile Mengist Mukera Mastawesha* (Note on the December Attepted Coup D'État), page 2. Dejazmatch Kebede Tessema, a principal actor/observer of Ethiopian politics for more than half a century (and putative grandfather of Mengistu Haile-Mariam) also had a high regard for the General's leadership. In a conversation one day about the high officials killed in the attempted coup of 1960, he said Ethiopia lost "a reserve leader who had the ability to extricate the country out of political mire at a time like this." He was referring to the tumultuous crisis Ethiopia was going through in Februay-September 1974.

13. For a brief treatment of this subject see Clapham, Christopher, *Haile-Selassie's Government*, Praeger, 1969; pages 76 and 77.

14. For a detailed account of this story and the long struggle to reunite Eritrea with Ethiopia, see Zaude Retta's book in Amharic entitled *Ye Ertra Guday* (The Eritrean Affair), Central Printing Press, Addis Ababa, 1999.

15. In his book *Development As Freedom* (Anchor Books, 2000) Amartya Sen underlines this point when he writes: "It would not be unreasonable to conclude that democracy can be a very positive influence in the prevention of famine in the contemporary world" (page 184).

16. The bulk of the information in this section was kindly made available by Dejazmatch Wolde-Semait Gebre-Wold who attended the meeting. Another source is Ato Eshetu Worku who was on the household staff of the Crown Prince.

17. It is now widely believed that the Crown Prince was so saddened by the unfair rebuke that he subsequently suffered a stroke from which he never fully recovered.

18. Covering the floor in one's home with reeds during holidays is customary. Doing this on a twenty-mile stretch of a highway as a mark of welcome to the Emperor is somewhat of an exaggeration.

19. I am grateful to Assefa Wolde-Giorgis who kindly supplied the details of this incident.

20. "Report of the Education Sector Review, Education: A Challenge to Development," Addis Ababa, August 1972. For further details see Chapter 8, Section 1.

21. *Addis Zemen*; 17, 19 Yekatit 1966 (24, 26 February 1974).

22. Addis *Zemen Yekatit* 20, 1966 (Februay 27, 1974).

23. From a copy of the leaflet saved by the author.

CHAPTER 8

1. Indeed rumours soon began to circulate that it was the aristocracy which had instigated the resignation of Prime Minister Aklilu's government in an attempt to seize power before the death of the ageing Emperor. In this connection, the name of Prince Asrate Kassa was frequently mentioned.

2. Ato Tedla Teshome who at the time was a junior Minister at Finance and was himself a detainee recalls an officer in disguise telling him not to worry, as the soldiers were only after high ranking officials, including the new Prime Minister and Defence Minister.

3. See Fantaye W. Zelibanos, *Yaba Tekil Atse Haile-Selassie Zemene Mengist* (The Reign of Aba Tekil Emperor Haile-Selassie), Berhanina Selam, Megabit 1999 (March 2007). page 374.

4. Reports also circulated that among the former ministers there were a vociferous few who argued that the new Prime Minister, a member of the former Cabinet, should not, for that precise reason, be given the responsibility of heading what was presumed to be a brand new Cabinet. There were other highly placed politicians outside as well as within the Cabinet who were also engaged in undermining the Prime Minister. At a time when the country's fate hanged in the balance, the rest of us could only watch in amazement as inordinate rivalry robbed its captives of all sense of perspective and responsibility.

5. See Education Sector Review, op. cit., page V-2.

6. In a one-page open letter to the Emperor released in the opening days of March, the Ethiopian Association of Teachers set down the reasons why there was so much disaffection amongst its ranks. Nothing specific was said about the Education Sector Review or other grievances having a direct bearing to the teaching profession. All the reasons given (six in all) were political in nature: (i) the need for land reform, (ii) for an overhaul of the administrative system, (iii) for large scale publicly owned development projects, (iv) for the protection of the rights of ethnic minorities, (v) for the reduction of the price of consumer items, and (vi) the replacement of the new Prime Minister.

7. The Minister (Ahadou Sabourin), who apparently entertained an amusingly false notion of himself as a progressive individual with an important role to play in the unfolding drama for change, was later hobnobbing with the new military rulers who appointed him as the administrator of an important province. This did not last too long, however, as he soon fell foul of his new masters and was detained along with the very people he and his overzealous journalists had been harassing.

8. The title of the English version of the official Amharic document was: "Policy Statement of the New Council of Ministers," Ministry of Information.

9. There are many who claimed (and claim to this day) that the 'friend', none other than Major Mengistu Haile Mariam, was more of a close relative, even a grandson, who had been brought up in the Minister's household.

10. An abstemious man of great knowledge and integrity who could not work with the Military Government mysteriously disappeared in 1975, never to be seen again. The revolution would

rob Ethiopia of many like him, who were not only innocent but who were also great assets to her future development (see Chapter 12 for more on Dr. Dagnatchew).

11.	In a twelve-page political statement issued on 5 March 1974, the Association of Ethiopian University Professors called for a land tenure system which was similar to that spelt out in the policy document. "A ceiling on agricultural holdings must be determined," said the statement on page 8, "in a manner which takes into account the general interests of all concerned." This was being said by a group which was in the vanguard of the movement for radical change, not some feeble-minded liberal democrat. In an interview given to *Africa Magazine* (3 May 1974) the President of the Confederation of Ethiopian Labour Unions had a similar view on land reform and put the ceiling at 40 hectares.

12.	Literally "you are now posing a threat to my very eyes;" the eyes being among the more vital organs on which there could be little bargain or compromise.

13.	It must be said that there was not a very good chance of the Cabinet's decision being enforced by a vacillating Police Commissioner. But it was the minority view that the chance needed to be taken with a threat to resign as a sign of our firmness. Such a determined sense of dealing with the strike could have persuaded the army to inject some sense of purpose into the vacillating leadership of the police force. In the event of that not happening, resignation was the next logical step, leaving the door open to the Emperor to appoint a new Cabinet. The Prime Minister and his close associates evidently did not wish to go that far.

14.	See footnote 23 of Chapter 7.

15.	See Fantaye W. Zelibanos, op. cit.

16.	Unaware of this, I would make a similar proposal when the issue came before the Cabinet many years later. (See following chapter).

17.	In a moment of frustration one day, the Prime Minister told me that some of his own relatives were working against him. He did not mention names, but given the rumours widely circulating at the time about a senior government official and relative of the Prime Minister, I was inclined to believe that the unnamed person was probably Prince Asrate Kassa.

18.	Some suspected that the Colonel had undertaken the action in collusion with Prime Minister Endalkatchew Makonnen. It was said that the Prime Minister's motive was to rid himself of the interference of the former Prime Minister and some of his Ministers who were now making themselves available for regular consultations at the office of the Emperor. As I indicated earlier, the Prime Minister was asked about his role in the Ministers' detention in Cabinet one day but denied that he had anything to do with it.

19.	*Ye 1953tu Yemengist Gilbetta Mukerana Ke 1908-1966 A.M: Ye Itiopia Tarikawina Politikawi Hidet* (The Attempted Coup D'État of 1953 and Ethiopia's Historical and Political Evolution From 1908 to 1966), by Colonel Kale-Kristos Abbai, Berhanina Selam Press, 1977, Addis Ababa, page 407. The dates are all in the Julian calendar. Colonel Kale-Kristos was a participant in the attempted coup of 1960 and tends to see the 1974 military takeover in a somewhat favourable light.

20.	The Committee later became known as the Dergue. Its membership was widely believed to number 120. This was apparently a wrong figure given by a member, Major Asrat Desta, in the course of a hurried interview soon after its creation. When asked by an interviewer, he was reluctant to give the correct number, and threw the arbitrary figure of 120, for which he was later criticized by his colleagues. See *Yeletena Colonell Mengistu Haile-Mariam Tizittawotch* (Recollections of Lt. Colonel Mengistu Haile-Mariam) by Guenet Ayele Anbessie, Mega Publishers, Addis Ababa, 1994 in the Julian calendar; 2002 in the Gregorian, pages 6 and 7. On page 125, however, we see Mengistu's ex-cathedra statement that the "correct number was

120", contradicting the list of 109 members which appears on pages 99-105 of this book as well as in another one [see *Neber* (And So It Was) by Zenebe Zelleke pages 17-26] published later. A little over seventy per cent of Recollections is devoted to an interview given by Mengistu to Ms Guenet Ayele, an Ethiopian journalist. As is to be expected, Mengistu studiously avoids taking personal responsibility for the tragic events of his regime, particularly the massacre of the sixty officials and the collapse of the Ethiopian military in the face of the Eritrean and Tigrean insurgency. I shall take this up in later chapters.

21. *Recollections*, op. cit., pages 4, 8,9,10 and 11.

22. Kebede Tessema had carried the honorific title of Dejazmatch for a quarter century. He had been considered for promotion to the rank of Ras. While a handful of his friends were raised to that level, he was not. Kebede, so it was widely said, never forgave the Emperor for the snub.

23. One Minister had started to meet in private with some members of the Coordinating Committee. He was not only passing information about the Cabinet but was apparently encouraging the soldiers to be more audacious in their actions. He himself once told me that he was meeting with them clandestinely. I did not pay much attention at the time. One day, the Prime Minister saw this man and I waiting outside for a Cabinet meeting and called us in. He said there was a mole in the Cabinet who regularly passed information to the Committee. I naively said I did not believe there was anyone amongst our group who would do such a thing. Wagging his index figure and looking at me the Prime Minister said, "Don't make that mistake, Tekalign." In Recollections, op. cit., page 11, one of the persons interviewed by author Guenet Ayele says that a member of the Cabinet (whose name he was not willing to disclose) passed information to the Dergue about "Endalkatchew's secret plan to break up the Dergue and kill some of its members. It was for this reason that Endalkatchew and his friends were detained." I cannot say, however, whether it was this or another mole who informed the soldiers of this particular "secret plan."

CHAPTER 10

1. *Kibre Negest*, chapter 90, sections 13 and 16. Though written in 1320, the origins of the document can be traced to at least the 9th century. See Tadesse Tamrat, op. cit,. page 249.

2. Mersie Hazen Wolde-Kirkos, *Yezemen Tarik Tizitaye Kayehutina Kesemahut, 1896-1922*, (My Recollections: Based on What I Have Seen and Heard) Addis Ababa University Press, pages 192 and 409.

3. Merid Wolde-Aregay, "The Origin's of Emperor Tewodros's Goals," in *Kassa and Kassa*, Tadesee Beyene, Richard Pankhurst, and Shiferaw Bekele (editors), Institute of Ethiopian Studies, Addis Ababa, 1990.

4. Crummey, Donald; *Land and Society in the Christian Kingdom of Ethiopia: From The Thirteenth To The Twentieth Century*, University of Illinois Press, Urbana and Chicago, 1999, page 65.

5. Henze, Paul, *Layers of Time: A History of Ethiopia*, Hurst & Company, London, 2000, page 103.

6. Of Emperor Yohannes's reign Trimmingham says: "John had little opportunity for internal reform, for throughout most of his reign he was distracted by the encroachments of external powers, Egyptians, Mahdists, and Western nations, over all of whom he won a remarkable series of victories." See, Trimingham, J. Spencer, *Islam in Ethiopia*, Frank Cass, London, 1952, page 120.

7. I am grateful to the late Professor Merid Wolde-Aregay for much of the preceding information on Ras Makonnen and Empeor Haile-Selassie's policies for greater cohesion with Tigrai and Eritrea.

8. John Spencer deals extensively with this theme in his book *Ethiopia at Bay* op. cit. See especially pages 357-360.

9. Declaration of the Provisional Military Government of Ethiopia, 20 December 1974.

10. The 1973 atrocities in Cambodia, covered extensively by the world media, were particularly frightening. Arthur Koestler's *Darkness at Noon*, George Orwell's *Animal Farm*, and *The God That Failed* by a number of Western intellectuals disillusioned by Marxism (and many more books and articles in a similar vein) had taken the fire out of the early enthusiasm for Marxim that these persons had been infected with.

11. For a detailed account of the role played by the students, civil servants, and the trade unions see Andargachew Assegid's book (in Amharic) entitled *Bachir Yeteketche Regim Guzo* (A Long Journey Cut Short), Addis Ababa, Central Printing Press, 2000. The book's principal focus is the history of the All Ethiopia Socialist Movement, one of the two frontline Marxist parties active during the period. The history of the other, the Ethiopian People's Revolutionary Party, is covered in a two-volume book in English entitled, *The Generation*, by Kiflu Tadesse, and published by Independent Publishers, Silver Spring, Md, U.S.A. 1993.

12. *The Generation*, by Kiflu Tadesse, op. cit

13. Henze, Paul; op cit, page 119.

14. Sheferaw Bekele, "The State in the Zamana Mesafint (1736-1853)" in Kassa and Kassa; pp. 25-68, Institute of Ethiopian Studies, Addis Ababa, June 1990.

15. The military had of course not asked for a revised constitution. The initiative had been taken by the short-lived government of Endalkachew Makonnen. Not that it was something that anyone would try to claim credit for, as practically every politically conscious Ethiopian going back to the post war years (including some members of the military) had appreciated the need for a more liberal constitution in which the monarch would be a symbolic head of state. Once in power, the soldiers realized that it would constrain their power. Their preference was to rule by decree until a Soviet style 'democratic' constitution, together with a rubber stamp people's parliament, was introduced several years later.

16. The story of requesting the Crown Prince to come home for the coronation ceremony is dealt with in some detail in a recently published Amharic book written by someone who was close to the Dergue. It had been the intention of Mengistu and the more radical members of the Dergue to abolish the monarchy altogether. There was therefore no plan to replace the Emperor with the Crown Prince. The proclamation's provision of holding a coronation ceremony was only intended to mollify Dergue members who were favourably disposed to the preservation of the monarchy. See Zenebe Zelleke, op. cit., pages 15, 31, 46, 77 ff.

17. *Recollections of Lt. Colonel Mengistu Haile-Mariam*, op. cit., page 23.

18. Kale-Kristos Abbai, op.,cit.

CHAPATER 11

1. Aman was said to be a mercurial personality. He was a Luthern who tried to find remedy for his personality disorder in the Holy Springs of an Ethiopian Orthodox Church. At one point, he also approached Abune Tewoflos, the Patriarch of the Church, to baptize him in accordance with the rites of the Church. Abune Tewoflos obliged, but the affair remained a closely guarded secret until the Patriarch revealed it during his detention by the Dergue. Aman's family life was also said to be turbulent.

2. Belatchew said that this was no time to search for a political philosophy. The country was in poor health and what it needed was treatment, not philosophy. Before long, he would find out how out of step he was with his military colleagues.

3. According to Zenebe Zelleke, op.cit., the Eritrean issue was abruptly tabled for Dergue discussion by Aman some 20 days after it had first been presented to Cabinet, a date at variance with Aman's assertion to the Cabinet only a week later that the issue had been tabled before the Dergue. Whatever the precise date, four members of the Dergue (all Eritreans) supported Aman's proposal to grant federal status to Eritrea. This only added to the Dergue's suspicion that the General was preparing the ground for Eritrea to secede. Mengistu took the floor after the General and said that this was an issue that needed an in-depth study and should only be considered along with other provinces which may need a similar internal administrative arrangement (an echo of the argument at the Cabinet meeting of 19 September, which the author of Neber is apparently not aware of). Mengistu was supported by Atnafu, the Second Deputy Chairman of the Dergue. Their position was endorsed by a "general applause of members of the Dergure" and the matter was dropped. See Neber, page 94. See also page 143 where Mengistu says that it was only later that they [the Dergue] clearly understood that Aman's goal had been to "partition Eritrea."

4. *Leb leb* is an Amharic term signifying a hurriedly barbequed piece of meat; and hence anything executed in haste.

5. At their meeting of 18 September 1974, the Association of University Students of Addis Ababa issued a statement which condemned actions taken by the Dergue among which was this particular programme. The statement said that the programme's objective was to disperse the student population to avoid trouble in the cities.

6. These insignificant incidents were significant to the General perhaps because he felt that they would not have happened to his predecessor, Emperor Haile-Selassie. Both of Aman's successors, Tafari Benti and Mengistu Haile-Mairam, occasionally made remarks that they were not being given the respect accorded the Emperor. None of the three soldiers could sense the irony of leaders who were ostensibly republican but who were loathe to do away with imperial protocol. Soon after my return from an official trip overseas one day, General Tafari Banti (Aman's immediate successor) casually asked:" Doesn't someone back from an official mission report that he has returned?" I equally casually replied: "I thought those days were gone." His surprised reaction was a gentle dip of the head and a restrained smile as if to say 'I did not expect such a disrespectful response from you.'

7. Zenene Zelleke, op. cit., pages 79, 83, 84 and 85 for this and the following quotations.

8. Dergue member Captain Sisay Habte who was present at this meeting revealed this in a rare confidential private conservation with one of the civilian Ministers.

9. A friend who was working in Asmara at the time (the late Getachew Medhane) wrote me a letter that the units of the armed forces in the province had asked the reasons as to why General Aman had resigned. They wanted him to come and explain his side of the story. It is quite possible other units were thinking along similar lines.

10. *Addis Zemen* Heddar 10, 1967 (November 19, 1974).

11. A recently published book states that Mengistu's hatchet man (Colonel Daniel Asfaw) approached him while he was chairing the Dergue meeting which was in the process of passing death sentences on the detained officials. Daniel whispered something into his ears. Mengistu raised his voice so that all participants could hear, and instructed Daniel to use a loudspeaker to tell Aman to give himself up. All necessary force must be used to arrest him in the event he refuses. If he tries to cause harm, he should be eliminated. Aman had already been killed.

Mengistu was simply engaged in act of deception to make it appear that the instruction was being given with the knowledge and tacit approval of the meeting's participants. See Tesfaye Ristei *Misikirinet: Bebalesiltanatu Andebet* (Testimonials as Voiced by Dergue Officials), Addis Ababa, May 2001 (2009) page 58. Publisher not indicated. Also see pages 64 and 65 for a complete list of the sixty persons executed by the Dergue.

12. *Recollections*, op. cit., pages 140-150.

13. This must surely figure among Mengistu's more grotesque exaggerations. Throughout his life he had been the butt of derisive remarks about his looks and modest background. Only after he took over the Chairmanship of the Dergue in March 1976 did he become a murderous and much loathed dictator. He was neither loved nor respected outside his small coterie of thugs and shady characters.

14. Belai Zelleke was the resistance hero from Gojjam (from which Atnafu hailed) who, as I indicated in Chapter 1, was found guilty at two separate trials. His first death sentence was commuted to life, but he was executed after the second.

15. See *Ye-Anabist Midir* (Land of Lions), by Tadesse Telle, Rom Publishers, page facing 120, Addis Ababa, 2007 (1999 in the Julian Calendar).

16. A former colleague of mine in the Cabinet of Endalkatchew Makonnen recently informed me that a relative of his who was a member of the Dergue told him that Mengistu Haile-Mariam had said to his colleagues that all detained former officials should be killed. After Aman's murder, it was again Mengistu who proposed that the detained officials should also be killed. According to this story, Major Sisay said to Mengistu that there should be a proper procedure and adequate grounds for taking people's lives. It was essential for the Dergue to examine the case of each detainee to establish the reason for each death sentence. That of course did not happen. The massacre could have been far greater if Mengistu's initial proposal had been carried out, according to my informant.

17. This and the preceding quotations are from *Recollections*, op. cit., pages 28 and 168. The Emperor used the royal "we" in speaking of himself. In *Misikirinet*, Tesfaye Ristei writes that following the sprinkling of the chemical intended to murder the Emperor a soldier was instructed to smother him with a pillow, presumably with the view to speed up his death. When the soldier lost nerve Daniel Asfaw himself came into the room and asphyxiated the Emperor. See Tesfaye Riste Misikirinet, page 47.

18. Another mendacity, too detailed to report here, is the premeditated murder of the Ethiopian Patriarch along with some half a dozen of the Emperor's officials and the young left wing ideologue Haile Fida. In the interview Mengistu flatly denies he had anything to do with their execution. Ibid, pages 207, 208, and 209.

19. Major Teferra Tekle-Ab was a close friend of Mengistu and an active participant in the early days of the military movement. He was detained for what were said to be extremist views and an impulsive temperament. It should be noted that Teferra was also leader of the team which was sent to Harrar with the view to arranging a proper election of representatives from the units of the province. Mengistu had been selected by General Tilahun Bishane and others, not elected by his unit. Teferra was in the end not able to carry out his mission. One might speculate that Mengistu probably did not take kindly to the Major's assignment and wonder whether this might have been one more reason for Teferra's detention. See *Misikirinet*, Tesfaye Ristei, op. cit., pages VI and 20.

20. "Whosoever intentionally by commission or omission directly or indirectly or with culpable negligence commits any prejudicial act leading to .....a grave state of misery, want or famine.... [and] fails to do whatever [is] within his power to control it, is punishable ... where the offence

was intentional and where death has occurred ...[by] death." Proclamation no. 8/1967, Section 1, Hiddar 12, 1967 (November 21, 1974.

21. The person is a senior officer of the army, now retired, who knew Aman well and who was himself well regarded while in active service.

22. Like many of his officer colleagues, however, Aman was a grateful beneficiary of the occasional gestures of imperial benevolence, whether it was cash to meet his medical expenses, a car, or a residence to accommodate his family. It was common knowledge that the Emperor was fond of him.

23. *Ye-Anabist Midir*, the recently published history of Ethiopia's armed forces hardly says anything in support of Aman's reputation. It simply makes a passing note that the General crossed the Somali border "with a large contingent which caused great concern to the Mogadiscio regime." Tadesse Telle, op. cit., page 130.

24. Kifle Worku, a civilian who had worked with the Ethiopian army for decades and who knew Aman well, spoke of him as a leader who had suddenly appeared on the national stage like lightning and had equally suddenly disappeared. Kifle confirmed that Aman's popularity did not arise from any proven leadership skills in matters military. It was style rather than substance that drew many an ordinary soldier. A self assured figure who spoke his mind freely but sometimes unwisely, Kifle was later found murdered in mysterious circumstances.

25. On Monday November 25 (i.e. 48 hours after the massacre of the 60 officials) one of the ministers in this group called me to check the time of a previously scheduled meeting. When I expressed surprise that he should call on "such a day", his nonchalant reply was, "What do you mean by 'such a day'? This is a day like any other." I had to cut the conversation short. The Committee which I chaired did not meet that day. The man was the first who tried to divert attention at the Cabinet meeting.

CHAPTER 12

1. Members of the policy committee initially faced difficulty to get a proper Amharic term for Ethiopian Socialism. *Hibretteseb* (Amharic for society) was the logical starting point. I added the suffix awinet (the English equivalent of ness or ism) and proposed *hibbresabiwinet*, dropping the syllable 'tte' for easier pronunciation. A Ge'ez scholar, Memhir Yiheyis Worke, was consulted by Michael Imru about the newly coined word. Memhir Yiheyes suggested that the syllable 'tte' be reintroduced, as the term might otherwise give a different connotation: 'hibre-' denoting a mix of colours rather than the coming together of individuals to form a social group. Hibbrettesebawinet was consequently adopted, although the shorter form *hibresebawinet* would occasionally appear in official documents.

2. Telephone directories would soon disappear from the face of Addis Ababa, thanks to Ethiopia's imitation of communist practice.

3. This and the following quotations are from the Proclamation on Land Reform which was imposed on the cabinet. Publication was considerably delayed. Presumably, the Dergue was working hard to adopt a united front on this vital issue. See Proclamation no.31 of 1975; Addis Ababa, 29 April 1975.

4. See Proclamation No. 47 of 1975: A Proclamation To Provide For Government Ownership of Urban Lands And Extra Urban Houses, Addis Ababa, 26 July 1975.

5. Ras Mesfin Sileshi, a leading political figure during the Emperor's regime, was among the sixty senior officials killed in November 1974.

6. The sequel of this story is that though the chauffeur was never able to persuade the bureaucracy that, in truth, he only had one unit and should be allowed to move into it. He was perceived as a 'landlord' during the entire 17-year period of Dergue rule and the period following.

CHAPTER 13

1. This is an account given by one of Mengistu's aide's who was present at the meeting. See *Recollections*, op. cit., page 61.

2. As indicated in Chapter 8, the slogan 'Ethiopia First' had been proposed by Mengistu himself. When Mengistu spoke of some 'colleagues who wanted to raze the Palace to the ground' he seemed to be referring to the impulsive officer, Major Tefera Tekle-Ab, who was a close friend but who later fell out with him and was jailed. (See Section Chapter 10).

3. In *Reflections* op. cit., Mengistu says that the idea of Ethiopian Socialism had been presented to certain "experienced" intellectuals who had been active participants in the student movement and that he had been advised to cast away this "strange" philosophy. "We need to march side by side with progressive forces in the world and you have to remove this camouflage and come out clean," they had said. See pages 184-185.

4. Dinners and banquets in Communist regimes tended to be lavish affairs in which invitees indulged with gusto. Given the general shortage of consumer goods, especially of foreign make, invitees helped themselves to the food and drinks liberally. Eating and drinking freely on such occasions was also one of the few liberties they could enjoy in their lives.

5. See Appendix 2.

6. *The Ethiopian Herald*, 25 February 1976.

7. Sisay's detention took place on 9 July and his execution on 13 July, 1976.

8. For a more detailed account of this affair, see Zenebe Zelleke, op. cit., pages 183-191.

9. Andargatchew Assegid writes about an organized plot by Sisay and Getachew aimed at the overthrow of the Dergue regime, and asserts that the plot was supported by the U.S. and the Sudan. Andargatche Assegid. op. cit., pages 357-358.

10. When asked about this in an interview in Zimbabwe, Mengistu flatly denied that he stole any money. Both he and his close associates have revealed, however, that there were three separate accounts in Ethiopia under his control at about the time he left the country: an account into which the proceeds of the sale from chat (Ethiopia's mildly narcotic plant) were regularly deposited, an account with a twenty million dollar balance which was a donation by Kuwait for Ethiopia's diplomatic support during the first Gulf war, and a Birr 7 million ($3.5 million dollars) fund kept by his personal secretary. It is hard to imagine that he did not help himself to some of these funds. Mengistu never gave evidence of being a person of conscience or probity. There is also the murky issue of a large sum of money (alleged to be $30 million) that the Israeli's paid to Mengistu to get planeloads of Ethiopia's Jews out of the country in time before the collapse of the Dergue. I am unaware of any information in the public domain that provides an accurate account of how this money was disposed of. It would be stretching the credibility of ordinary mortals to exclude the possibility that Mengistu or his close associates did not help themselves to this tantalizing treasure. See *Recollections*, op. cit. page 52.

11. See, for instance, Tesfaye Ristei, op. cit., pages 123 ff.

12. In an early address to different units of the Armed Forces in Addis Ababa, Mengistu Haile-Mariam is reported to have said: "From now on, Ethiopia's borders will not be like the doors of

a husbandless whore (sic) which anyone can open or close at will." See *Addis Zemen*, 10 Hidar, 1967 (19 November 1974).

13. *The Ethiopian Herald*, 30 December 1976.

CHAPTER 14

1. Resolution 07-77 on the Mobilization of Resources for the African Development Bank, Port Luis, Mauritius, May 5, 1977.

2. "Resource Mobilization for the African Development Bank: (1977-1986)," ADB, Abidjan, Cote d'Ivoire, 1978.

3. These and the other figures are drawn from the Bank's various Annual Reports, in particular those for 1978, 1986, and 1993.

4. I must confess that I did occasionally enjoy the hospitably, as in the case of an opera evening at the New York Met in the winter of 1990 or 1991 where the celebrated tenor, Luciano Pavarotti, performed. I had been to a number of performances at the old Met in the early sixties when I was a young U.N. employee. Coming back again after a long spell was particularly enjoyable.

5. Like most non-Eritrean Ethiopians and a few Eritreans, I had regretted the partition of the country. Indeed I had told someone who was working at the ADB (who, unbeknown to me, was of Eritrean origin although I thought he was a Tigrean) that a new political arrangement under which Eritrea remained part of Ethiopia with perhaps Issa'iiyas Afework as the President of such a re-structured country was a distinct possibility and would, in my judgment, be a welcome one. The person expressed incredulity at the suggestion, and apparently informed agents of the new government that I was opposed to its policy of granting independence to Eritrea. I was informed that he also told them that I was insolent and contemptuous of the regime, fortifying the regime's perception that I was an opponent. I had of course candidly expressed my views about the party's politics to one of the regime's ministers during an encounter in Abidjan. They therefore did not have to go far to know that I was not sympathetic with their political or economic orientation.

CHAPTER 15

1. Crummy, Donald; op. cit., page 250.

2. Easterly, William; "Growth in Ethiopia: Retrospect and Prospect," Institute of International Economics, Washington D.C., April 2002, page 4.

3. Tadesse Tele, *Qissim Yesseberw Ermija* (The Confidence Shattering Initiative), Addis Ababa 1992 (1985 in the Julian calendar). See also *Misikirinet* (Testimonials) by Tesfay Ristie, pages 232-300.

4. Tesfaye Ristei, op. cit., page 269.

5. Two additional factors accounted for the quandary debilitated the military effort. The first was the difficulty of absorbing the huge and poorly trained militia forces into the regular army. The second was the sharp contrast in military strategy and tactics between Ethiopian and Soviet officers, a factor which led some of the more able Ethiopian officers to act in defiance of their arrogant Soviet counterparts, further aggravating an already contentious relationship. See Neber op. cit., pages 312-318.

6. Teferra Haile-Selassie; *The Ethiopian Revolution: 1974-1991*, Kegan Paul International, U.K., 1997 page 284.

7. *Jeneralotchu* (The Generals) by Captain Iyob Abate Endale, page 65. This is a short account of the attempted coup of 1989 against the Mengistu regime which led to the execution of more

than a dozen generals. No publisher is indicalted for the book in Amharic which was issued in Addis Ababa in 2008.

8. See Teferra Haile-Selassie, op. cit., page 312.

9. Aregawi Berhe. *A Political Histroy of the Tigray People's Liberation Front (1975-1991): Revolt, Ideology, and Mobilization in Ethiopia*; Tsehai Publishers and Distributors, Los Angeles, USA, July 2009; pages 119, 162, 163, 174, 177, and 184.

10. The group subsequently evolved into a political party, the All-Amhara Peoples Organization, and soon ran into trouble with the authorities. Dr. Asrat was imprisoned on politically motivated charges. In poor health already and deprived of proper medical care in prison, his family requested the government to allow him go overseas for medical treatment. The request was denied for almost two years. In the end, his doctors advised that his life was gravely in danger. It was at that point that the government gave him an exit visa. Dr. Asrat travelled to the U.S. and was admitted to a hospital. He lost his life not long afterwards.

11. Jane Burbank, *Intelligentsia and Revolution: Russian Views of Bolshevism, 1917-1922*, Oxford University Press, New York, 1986, page 17.

CHAPTER 16

1. Many studies of banking practices in the third world (including those of the World Bank) had indicated the excessive reliance on collateral and how this was inhibiting development. The case of Ethiopia was particularly constraining, as the Dergue's policy of nationalization had robbed the private sector of practically all assets that would normally be offered as collateral for loans. Our thinking at the Bank of Abyssinia was that it would be unreasonable under those circumstances to insist on physical collateral and that we had to make judgments based on business prospects and client credibility.

2. The new environment of free speech and openness to private initiative offered, so I believed at the time, the private banks an opportunity for dialogue and debate of policies that might help the country in its efforts at economic reform. With this in mind, the Bank of Abyssinia played host to a series of three lectures in what it hoped would ultimately evolve into a Bankers Forum. There was regretfully no follow-up by the other private banks; such was their aversion to new initiatives that might raise eyebrows in party circles.

3. Siyye Abraha, *Netsanetina Dagninet Be-Ityopia* (Freedom and Justice in Ethiopia), Signature Book Printing, USA, 2002 (2010), pages 15-25.

4. See letter of the Federal Ethics and Anti-Corruption Commission to the Federal High Court dated 14 Tikimt 1995 (25 October 2002).

5. In September 2001 I gave an address to the Addis Ababa Chamber of Commerce regarding this and related problems facing banks. Some of the present material is drawn from that address which provides a comprehensive picture of the risks and challenges facing the sector at that time. I was informed that the government was none too happy about this address. Some officials from European Embassies who had read the paper and felt it contained a number of useful ideas asked me if I had received any positive reaction to the proposals made in my address. They were surprised that there had been none.

6. In early August 2011, I was informed by friends in Ethiopia that the ludicrous changes levelled against the staff, Board members and shareholders of the of the Bank Abyssinia in 2009 had been withdrawn by the Public Prosecutors.

CHAPTER 17

1.   The other Americans who participated in the project were Peter Kunz, and Sandy Timmins. On the Ethiopian side the active participants were Getachew Tessema, Tadesse Alemu, Yemane Bisrat, and Berhanu Tadesse.

2.   It would not be possible to recognize all those deserving mention even in my own club. I hope I will not be taken to task if I take the liberty to mention the outstanding commitment of veterans like Habte-Selassie Tafesse, the late Shifferaw Bizuneh, Yohannes Vayonakis, Nahu-Senai Araya, Charalambos Tsimas, Lotfi Bibawi, Bekele Nedi, Girma Beshah, Abebayehou Yilma, Hirut Workalemahu, and more recent Rotarians like Rolf Gautschi, Wisdom Lopa, Salahadin Khalifa, and Melbana Seifu.

3.   This and the following quotations as well as much of the information for the story come from Catherine's absorbing book: *The Hospital by the River: A Story of Hope*, by Catherine Hamlin, with John Little; Macmillan, Australia Pty Limited, 2001.

4.   The grant of land on the outskirts of Addis Ababa was later nationalized by the Dergue. Husband and wife had to buy another plot of land on which the Hospital was eventually built.

5.   Chojnacki recently published a short memoir of his twenty-five year stay in Ethiopia in which he traces the history of the Institute in some detail. See Chojnacki, S.; *Twenty-Five Years of Service at the University College and the Institute of Ethiopian Studies, Addis Ababa, Between 1950 and 1975*; Toronto, Canada, 2010. Stanislaw Chojnacki is well known for his publications on Ethiopian art and culture, chief among which are *Ethiopian Icons* (2001) and *Ethiopian Crosses* (2006). Stanislaw sadly passed away in July 2010 in his home in Sudbury, Canada. He had spent six decades of study and research on Ethiopia's culture and had become a leading authority of the history of her art. He had a large circle of friends, Ethiopian as well as others interested in Ethiopia's history and culture. He will be greatly missed. Just before he passed away, Addis Ababa University named the new IES building after him in recognition of his services to the Institute.

6.   The English translation of the quotations only captures the substance of the statements made. No indication is given in the document of exactly who or which body in the party was responsible for its publication. Nor is the publishing house among the handful of the familiar government (Berhanina Selam) or private establishments (Commercial, Central, or Artistic Printers). But the language and content of the document are unmistakably those of TPLF/EPRDF.

CHAPTER 18

1.   The ruling party is well known for its tactic of waiting for the right moment to trap its foes. In a case in which it was the principal instigator, it would naturally not make sense to bring charges against the accused without allowing a decent interval. But why did the interval last nine years? There appear to be two reasons for this. The first was the need to revise the criminal code in order to have appropriate provisions which could be used by the public prosecutor retroactively against the targeted individuals. This took some time. Secondly and just before the detentions occurred, an event took place which provided the pretext to go ahead with the long intended plan. At the Annual Meeting of the Bank of Abyssinia in early December 2008, the outgoing board informed shareholders that arrears on loans taken by the Star Business Group were causing a major problem. A shareholder subsequently asked why a committee should not be set up to advise on measures that could be taken against the company. One of the major owners of the Group got up to explain that the reason for the unpaid loans was the arbitrary arrest of their leading officials for five long years during which their businesses had been irreparably damaged. His intervention implied that it was the government which was responsible for the problem.

He was applauded by the shareholders present. The representative of the National Bank of Ethiopia who was in attendance did not like the government being exposed in this manner and informed his bosses accordingly. The Bank got down to business and, working closely with the police, initiated the detention of the Group's principal shareholders and managers. The net was widened to implicate their presumed collaborators.

2. And these friends were proved right. For a few months later, fresh charges were brought against officials and staff of the Bank of Abyssinia, including myself. As in the case of the Nile Insurance Company the charges were principally motivated by vengeance against two Amhara business persons who were suspected of being close to a faction of the TPLF that was fiercely opposed to Meles during the Ethio-Eritrean war. They had been charged with alleged breaches of the law, had been imprisoned for five years but had been found not guilty on all charges and released. Their latest sin had to do with their alleged influence on the officials of the Bank of Abyssinia to obtain large loans some ten years previously. The authorities apparently had their reasons to wake up from their sleep after a full decade. Once again, new statutes were used which had been passed retroactively to go after the businessmen and the Bank's officials. As pointed out in endnote #6, Chapter 16, the charges have now been dropped.

CHAPTER 19

1. Sources for much of the historical material are: Alvares's *The Prester John of the Indies*, op. cit.; Almeda's *Some Records of Ethiopia*, The Hakluyt Society, 1954 (especially page lxxi); Trimingham's *Islam in Ethiopia*, op. cit.; Tadesse Tamrat's *Church And State in Ethiopia: 1270-1527*, Oxford, 1972; and Tekle-Tsadik Mekuria's Amharic *History of Ethiopia: From Emperor Yekuno Amlak to Emperor Libne Dingel*, Tesfa Press, Addis Ababa, 1959.

2. Erlich, Haggai; *The Cross and the River: Ethiopia, Egypt, and the Nile*; Lynne Rienner, Boulder, Colorado, p 40, 2002.

3. See Donald Levine's essay "Reconfiguring the Ethiopian Nation in a Global Era" in the International Journal of Ethiopian Studies, Vol. I, No. II; Winter/ Spring 2004, Hollywood, CA, U.S.A. See also Peter Robb's similar observation for India, a country that offers interesting comparisons with Ethiopia (footnote 8 in Chapter 21).

4. A more extensive treatment of this theme is given in the statement I made to the 15th Annual Meeting of the Ethiopian Human Rights Council in Addis Ababa in May 2006.

5. Writing on the industrial transformation of developing societies, economist David Landes says that the key factor for this is a country's cultural endowment: in particular the degree to which it has internalized the value of hard work, honesty, thrift, patience, tenacity, openness to change, and equality for women. Cited in Freeman, Thomas: *The World is Flat: A Brief History of the Twenty-First Century*; Farrar, Straus and Giroux; New York, 2005, page 324.

6. In a similar vein, author and Economics Nobel Laureate Amartya Sen says that India's tradition of dissent and argument has influenced the country's current politics and "is particularly relevant, I would argue, to the development of democracy in India..." Sen, Amartya *The Argumentative Indian*, Farrar, Straus and Giroux, 2005, New York, page 12. The relevance of India in this narrative shall become evident shortly.

7. Levine, Donald N., The Promise of Ethiopia: Public Action, Civic Forgiveness, and Creative Power; Addis Ababa, Ethiopia, January 15, 2008, page 4.

CHAPTER 20

1. Erlich, Haggai's *The Cross and The River* and Tekle-Hawariat's *Autobiography*.

2. *Gahdi 1*, a book in Amharic by Asgede Gebre-Selassie Wolde-Michael, Signature Book Printing, 2007; pages 83, 139, 193, and 194.

3. See Collier, P., *Wars, Guns, And Votes*, HarperCollins, New York, 2009, page 64.

4. J. Spencer Trimmingham, op. cit., page 138.

5. A major treatment of this theme is presented in Donald Levine's book, *Greater Ethiopia: the Evolution of a Multiethnic Society*, The University of Chicago Press, Chicago, USA, 1974.

6. Sen, Amartya, *Identity and Violence: The Illusion of Destiny*; Allen Lane, London, 2006; page 2.

7. Sen, Amartya, *Identity and Violence*, pages xii, xiii.

8. The 'first wave' started with the American and French Revolutions, the second with World War II, and the third in the early seventies with the Portuguese revolution. See, Huntington, Samuel P., *The Third Wave*, University of Oklahoma Press, Norman, Oklahoma, 1991.

9. Maaluf, Amin; *In the Name of Identity: Violence And The Need To Belong*; Penguin Books, New York, 2001, pages 2, 10, and 11.

10. Sen, op. cit., page xv.

11. Gutman, Amy; *Identity in Democracy*, Princeton University Press, Princeton, New Jersey, 2003; page 192.

12. Maaluf, A., op. cit., pages 143, 149.

13. There are various ways of responding to ethnic assertiveness, heal the wounds that it creates, and lay the groundwork for a more harmonious social order. Schools would be a good place to start where the young need to get a proper understanding of their common heritage, of the disruptive nature of identity politics and how it should be handled. It might also be useful to set up centres for research and dialogue to promote social harmony. These and other initiatives should help to gradually liberate the current political environment from the constraints of one-dimensional politics of identity.

14. See the Amharic weekly *Addis Neger*, 12 Hamle 2000 (19 July 2008), Addis Ababa.

15. *Addis Neger*, Yekatit 8, 2000 (16 February 2008).

16. Tesfaye Gebre-Ab *Yederaseew Mastawesha* (Recollections of An Author).

17. *The Reporter*, Miazza 2, 1998 (April 10 2005).

18. In my address to the 15th Annual Meeting of the Ethiopian Human Rights Council, I take up on this tradition of the Ethiopian clergy.

19. *The Reporter*, Heddar 18 1988 (28 November 2005).

20. Collier, Paul; *The Bottom Billion*, Oxford University Press, pages 53-63, New York, 2007.

21. See, for instance, the article "As Labor Costs Rise in China, Textile Jobs Shift Elsewhere" in the July 17, 2010 issue of *The New York Times*.

22. Friedman, Thomas; *The World is Flat: A Brief History of the Twenty-First Century*; Farrar, Strauss and Giroux, New York, 2005, page 184.

23. *The Economist* October 23rd 2010.

CHAPTER 21

1. See, for instance, the following statement by a Saudi journalist (Raid Qusti) in the English daily *Arab News* of May 5 2004: "Our education system, which does not stress tolerance of other faiths - let alone tolerance of followers of other Islamic schools of thought- is one thing that needs to be reevaluated from top to bottom. Saudi culture itself and the fact that the majority of us do not accept other life styles and impose our own on other people is another." (Emphasis added). As quoted in Friedman, op. cit.; page 327.

2. In his book Saudi Arabia & Ethiopia Haggai Erlich mentions the research work conducted by Jon Abbink and Eloi Ficquet on Wollo culture who confirm the moderation of the region's inhabitants. It is pointed out that Wollo Muslims have by and large rejected the fundamentalist tenets of Wahabism in favour of their own co-existential interpretation of Islam. See page 227 and the note 4 on page 230.

3. Tesfaye Gebre-Ab, op. cit., pages 235-238.

4. Haliday, Jon and Chang, Jung; op. cit.

5. Smith, Vincent A.; *The Oxford History of India*, Oxford University Press, Oxford, 1967, page 833.

6. Robb, Peter; *A History of India*, Palgrave Press, 2002, United Kingdom, page 9. By comparison, the managed discussions of the draft constitutions displayed at meetings of the constituent assemblies of the Dergue and of the EPRDF regimes (I had been invited to observe the latter) were make believe exercises whose crudeness was often repelling.

7. Andargatchew Assegid, op. cit., pages 65 and 99.

8. Robb, P., op. cit., page 5 and 9. Maurya and Ashoka ruled in the third century B.C. The beginnings of Axum go back to the fifth century B.C.

9. The interview, given on 26 November 2009, was posted on www.ethiopiafirst.com

10. Translated from the Amharic original quoted in Berhanu Tessema's note on the anti-Fascist resistance posted on www.ethiopianreview.com/content/2599

11. Tesfaye Gebre-Ab op cit, page 24.

12. Meles Zenawi, "Perspectives and 'Bonapartisme'" in The Gimgema Papers, Addis Ababa, 2001; cited in "Development Without Freedom: How Aid Underwrites Repression in Ethiopia," Human Rights Watch, October 2010.

APPENDIX 1

1. As mentioned in Chapter 11, General Aman had already been killed when this order was given. His inclusion is intended to convey the message to the rank and file among whom the General enjoyed considerable popularity that he had not been singled out but was only one of many against whom the "high political decision" had to be taken.

2. This victim's second name is variously given as Yimeney and Limeney. I have used the latter in the text, a name I frequently heard while the officer was in service.

3. This officer and the following two appear to be the members of the Dergue mentioned in Chapter 11.

4. Lij Michael Imru is wrongly included in the list, while the name of another high official who was murdered along with the others, former Defence Minister Kebede Gebre, is not.

5. The title of the person is Kegnazmatch, not Dejazmatch.

Glossary of Amharic Terms

Aleqa	Head of a major Church in the Ethiopian Orthodox clerical hierarchy
Like-Tebebt	A clerical title denoting erudition
Merigeta	The principal clergyman in a Church who leads the cantors during prayers
Debtera	A cantor of the Ethiopian Church.
Emahoy	Term used to address an Orthodox nun
Abba	Term used to address a monk, priest, or Bishop
Ge'ez	The old Ethiopian written language from which, Amharic, Tigrigna, and Tigre are derived. All old religious texts are in Geez. It is currently used only in Church services.
Quine	Geez poetry with a distinctive reliance on metaphors. For the most part, *quine* relies on religious themes.
Shamma	A white, finely woven cotton cloth in the shape of an over-sized shawl with embroidered edges. It is the top piece of the traditional Ethiopian dress for both men and women
Injera	The thin, flat, and pancake-like bread baked on clay and usually eaten with vegetable or meat stew.
Wot	Vegetable, meat, or chicken stew.
Teff	The grain from which injera is made.
Tej	Meade, or wine made from honey
Mesob	A circular basket with an attached stand and cover used as a table for *injera* and *wot*
Archumie	A twig used to punish (hit) children on the legs .
Neguse-Negest	King of Kings or Emperor
Negus	King
Le'ul	Prince

Ras-Bitwoded	Rank immediately below Le'ul and followed in descending order by those shown below.
Ras	Title originally conferred upon someone of the aristocratic class, a regional lord, or a military officer of the highest rank. This as well as those ranging from *Dejazmatch* to and including *Balambaras* (below) in time became honorific titles given to individuals who were neither from the aristocracy nor the military class but who had rendered long years of service to the state.
Bitwoded	"The Favoured One." Title conferred upon someone well regarded by the Emperor. On occasion, it was also the title carried by the principal officer of state, as during the reign of Emperor Libne-Dingel (1508-1540). One of Emperor Haile-Selassie's three Prime Ministers was also a *Bitwoded*.
Dejazmatch	Commander of the military contingent placed immediately in front of the Emperor's quarters during a war campaign.
Fitawrari	Commander of the advance guard. A title also given to the Minister of War, in which case it was equivalent to Ras.
Kegnazmatch	Commander of the right guard.
Grazmatch	Commander of the left guard
Balambaras	Commander of a fort
Ato	Mr.
Woizero	Mrs.
Mesenqo	A single stringed musical instrument played with a bow
Krar	A small guitar-like instrument.
Azmari	A minstrel who plays a *mesenqo* or *krar*. For the most part each Azmari relies on a repertoire of well rehearsed lyrics. But he often also composes couplets extemporaneously as he sings. Listeners occasionally contribute their own which he weaves into his music and sometimes embellishes.
Shifta	An outlaw of the great outdoors living on plunder.
Araqui	A home-made spirit usually distilled from selected herbs and food grains.

Note on the Ethiopian Calendar

Ethiopia still follows the Julian Calendar, which was replaced in the West by the current Gregorian calendar in 1582. If dates are given in the Julian calendar, the Gregorian equivalent is indicated in parenthesis. Unless otherwise specified, all dates in the book are in the Gregorian calendar.

Index